A Companion to
Literature, Film, and Adaptation

Blackwell Companions to Literature and Culture

This series offers comprehensive, newly written surveys of key periods and movements and certain major authors, in English literary culture and history. Extensive volumes provide new perspectives and positions on contexts and on canonical and post-canonical texts, orientating the beginning student in new fields of study and providing the experienced undergraduate and new graduate with current and new directions, as pioneered and developed by leading scholars in the field.

Published Recently

A COMPANION TO

LITERATURE, FILM, AND ADAPTATION

EDITED BY

DEBORAH CARTMELL

WILEY-BLACKWELL

A John Wiley & Sons, Ltd., Publication

This edition first published 2012
© 2012 Blackwell Publishing Ltd

Blackwell Publishing was acquired by John Wiley & Sons in February 2007. Blackwell's publishing program has been merged with Wiley's global Scientific, Technical, and Medical business to form Wiley-Blackwell.

Registered Office
John Wiley & Sons Ltd, The Atrium, Southern Gate, Chichester, West Sussex, PO19 8SQ, UK

Editorial Offices
350 Main Street, Malden, MA 02148-5020, USA
9600 Garsington Road, Oxford, OX4 2DQ, UK
The Atrium, Southern Gate, Chichester, West Sussex, PO19 8SQ, UK

For details of our global editorial offices, for customer services, and for information about how to apply for permission to reuse the copyright material in this book please see our website at www.wiley.com/wiley-blackwell.

The right of Deborah Cartmell to be identified as the author of the editorial material in this work has been asserted in accordance with the UK Copyright, Designs and Patents Act 1988.

Wiley also publishes its books in a variety of electronic formats. Some content that appears in print may not be available in electronic books.

Designations used by companies to distinguish their products are often claimed as trademarks. All brand names and product names used in this book are trade names, service marks, trademarks or registered trademarks of their respective owners. The publisher is not associated with any product or vendor mentioned in this book. This publication is designed to provide accurate and authoritative information in regard to the subject matter covered. It is sold on the understanding that the publisher is not engaged in rendering professional services. If professional advice or other expert assistance is required, the services of a competent professional should be sought.

Library of Congress Cataloging-in-Publication Data

A companion to literature, film, and adaptation / edited by Deborah Cartmell.
    p. cm.
  Includes bibliographical references.
  ISBN 978-1-4443-3497-5 (cloth)
  1. Film adaptations–History and criticism.   2. Television adaptations–History and criticism.   3. English literature–Adaptations.   4. American literature–Adaptations.   5. Motion pictures and literature.   6. Television and literature.   I. Cartmell, Deborah.
   PN1997.85.C64 2012
   791.43'6–dc23
                              2012008957

A catalogue record for this book is available from the British Library.

Cover image: James McAvoy and Keira Knightley in *Atonement*, directed by Joe Wright, 2007. Image courtesy of Focus Features / The Kobal Collection, Alex Bailey.
Cover design by Richard Boxall Design Associates

Set in 11/13 pt Garamond Three by Toppan Best-set Premedia Limited
Printed and bound in Malaysia by Vivar Printing Sdn Bhd

1   2012

Contents

Contributors

Judith Buchanan is author of *Shakespeare on Silent Film* (2009), *Shakespeare on Film* (2005), editor of *The Writer on Film: Screening Literary Authorship* (forthcoming) and runs the Film and Literature program at the University of York.

Richard Burt is Professor of English and Film and Media Studies at the University of Florida. His most recent book is entitled *Medieval and Early Modern Film and Media* (2008; paperback 2010).

Richard Butt is Head of Media, Communication and Performing Arts at Queen Margaret University, Edinburgh. His publications include essays in *Critical Studies in Television* and *From Tartan to Tartanry: Scottish Culture, History and Myth* (2010).

Deborah Cartmell is Professor of English at De Montfort University and co-editor of two international journals, *Adaptation* (Oxford University Press) and *Shakespeare* (Routledge). She is currently working on a history of screen adaptations.

Shelley Cobb is a Lecturer at the University of Southampton. She has published on adaptation, Jane Campion, chick flicks, and celebrity; and is writing a monograph entitled *Women, Adaptation and Post-feminist Filmmaking*.

Kamilla Elliott is a Senior Lecturer in English at Lancaster University. She is author of *Rethinking the Novel/Film Debate* (2003) and *Portraiture and British Gothic Fiction: The Rise of Picture Identification, 1764–1835* (2012).

Christine Geraghty is an Honorary Research Fellow (Glasgow University and Goldsmiths, University of London). Publications include *Now a Major Motion Picture* (2008) and a study of *Bleak House* (BBC, 2005) in 2012.

Pamela Church Gibson is Reader in Cultural & Historical Studies at the London College of Fashion, editor of the journal of *Film, Fashion & Consumption* and author of *Fashion & Celebrity Culture* (2011).

Yvonne Griggs is a Lecturer at De Montfort University and has published articles in a number of leading adaptations journals. Her study of *King Lear* on screen was published by Methuen in 2009.

Lisa Hopkins is Professor of English at Sheffield Hallam University. Her publications include *Relocating Shakespeare and Austen on Screen* (2009) and *Shakespeare's* The Tempest*: The Relationship between Text and Film* (2008).

Richard J. Hand is Professor of Theatre and Media Drama at the University of Glamorgan. He is the founding co-editor of the *Journal of Adaptation in Film and Performance*.

Ariane Hudelet is Assistant Professor at Paris Diderot University. Her books include *Pride and Prejudice: Jane Austen et Joe Wright* (2006) and *The Cinematic Jane Austen* (with co-authors David Monaghan and John Wiltshire, 2009).

Ian Inglis is Visiting Fellow at Northumbria University, with research interests in music, film, and television. His books include *Popular Music and Film* (2003), *Performance and Popular Music* (2006), and *Popular Music and Television in Britain* (2010).

Diane Lake, a screenwriting Professor at Emerson College in Boston, has written films for Columbia, Disney, Miramax, and Paramount. Diane's film, *Frida*, opened the Venice Film Festival in 2002 and was nominated for six Academy Awards.

Douglas M. Lanier is Professor of English at the University of New Hampshire where he teaches and writes on Shakespeare, performance, and modern media. He is working on a book about *Othello* on screen.

Thomas Leitch teaches English and directs the Film Studies program at the University of Delaware. His most recent books are *Film Adaptation and Its Discontents* and *A Companion to Alfred Hitchcock,* co-edited with Leland Poague.

Tamar Jeffers McDonald is Senior Lecturer in Film at the University of Kent. Her recent publications include *Hollywood Catwalk: Costume and Transformation in Contemporary Hollywood Cinema* (2010) and the forthcoming *Doris Day Confidential* (2012).

Simone Murray is Senior Lecturer at Monash University and author of *Mixed Media: Feminist Presses and Publishing Politics* (2004) and *The Adaptation Industry: The Cultural Economy of Contemporary Literary Adaptation* (2011).

Gregory Robinson is an Assistant Professor of English at Nevada State College in Henderson, Nevada.

James Russell is Senior Lecturer in Film Studies at De Montfort University and author of *The Historical Epic and Contemporary Hollywood* (2007).

Jamie Sherry is a Lecturer in Screenwriting at Bangor University. He is a Trustee for the Association of Adaptation Studies and serves on the steering group for the Screenwriting Research Network.

Jeremy Strong is Head of Higher Education at Writtle College and Chair of the Association of Adaptation Studies. Widely published on adaptation, his most recent book is *Educated Tastes: Food, Drink and Connoisseur Culture* (2011).

Imelda Whelehan is Research Professor at the University of Tasmania, Australia and Visiting Professor at De Montfort University, UK. Her most recent publication is *Screen Adaptation: Impure Cinema* (with D. Cartmell, 2010).

Martin Zeller-Jacques is a Teaching Fellow in the Department of Theatre, Film and Television at the University of York. He has contributed chapters to several edited collections.

Acknowledgments

Many thanks to Hester, Ian, and Jake Bradey for their patience; to Ashley Polasek for much needed editorial help; and to Kamilla Elliott for reading an early draft of the introduction.

Foreword

Adaptation studies today owes a great deal to Deborah Cartmell for its constitution as a recognizable field. Prior to the annotated bibliographies compiled by Jeffrey Egan Welch and Harris Ross, it was difficult to trace writing on adaptations to their disparate roots in literary, film, art, and media studies. These bibliographies, however, only span the years 1909–1988 and deal only with literature and film. In the absence of subsequent annotated bibliographies, scholars of adaptations have relied heavily on edited collections of essays to keep up to date with the field. Since 1996, Deborah Cartmell has co-edited ten collections of essays addressing intermedial relations among literature, film, and other media, bringing together scholarship from many nations and critical perspectives. Cartmell also co-edits the Oxford journal, *Adaptation*, founded in 2008, another forum that gathers together disparate aspects of the field. She was further instrumental in establishing the Association of Adaptation Studies (formerly the Association of Literature on Screen), which has, since 2006, brought together scholars from around the world to share research.

Adaptation studies also owes a great deal to Cartmell and her co-editors, Imelda Whelehan, Ian Q. Hunter, and Heidi Kaye, for bringing cultural studies to bear on intermedial adaptations. Prior to 1996, the vast majority of studies on adaptation were aesthetic, formalist, narratological, canonical, humanist, and practitioner-based. While these were valuable studies, Cartmell, her co-editors, and contributors brought other perspectives to bear upon adaptations.

While for Robert B. Ray and others, the preponderance of edited collections in the field can result in a lack of "cumulative knowledge," a sense of conceptual scatter, and repetitive argumentation, they can also showcase the amazing range and diversity of our field. The essays in this companion go beyond local analyses to make larger arguments about the definition, genre, and parameters of adaptations.

They engage with broader issues of authorship and *auteurism* in adaptation, word and image relations, the adaptation of history, and industrial, economic, legal, and commercial aspects of adaptations. Some return to the "classics" that have been and still are a staple of adaptation studies, but do so in the context of new media, recent theories, and fresh interpretations. Others develop scholarship in understudied areas, such as words in film, costumes, editing, filmed theater, DVD extras, comic-book adaptations, adaptations of songs, and adaptations that never quite got made.

In this era of globalization, an international collection of essays such as this one can be said to think globally while illuminating locally. It should prove invaluable to students and scholars of adaptation and intermediality.

Kamilla Elliott

100+ Years of Adaptations, or, Adaptation as the Art Form of Democracy

Deborah Cartmell

It has always been the case that new technologies are greeted with suspicion. Plato, for instance, expressed horror over the invention of writing in the fear that it would destroy the art of memory: the invention "will produce forgetfulness in the souls of those who have learned it, through lack of practice at using their memory, as through reliance on writing they are reminded from outside by alien marks, not from within, themselves by themselves" (Plato, 2005: 275a–b 62). Today the words "memory" and "writing" could be replaced with "literature" and "film" insofar as writers and literary critics, from the very beginning of film history, were deeply suspicious of cinema, especially adaptations of literary works. While Plato is probably right that the art of memory was on the decline due to the rise of writing, most would agree that it was a price worth paying. Whether writing and reading are threatened by the presence of film, in particular film adaptation, which like Plato's "writing" has been condemned as only a reminder or "an appearance of wisdom, not the reality of it" (275a–b 62), has been a topic of debate for over 100 years, indeed since the beginning of cinema. And whether film fails to show its full potential due to its reliance on the written word is the flip side of the same coin. After over 100 years, the jury is still out as to whether film adaptation, which arguably inflicts some costs on both literary and film studies, insofar as its inclusion usually results in the exclusion of something else, is, in fact, a price worth paying.

Skepticism often follows innovation: photography could be the ruination of painting; the car of the horse; and the film of the book. In a remarkably similar manner to the fear of people in societies without technology that photography

A Companion to Literature, Film, and Adaptation, First Edition. Edited by Deborah Cartmell.
© 2012 Blackwell Publishing Ltd. Published 2012 by Blackwell Publishing Ltd.

would kill the soul, film was initially regarded by some as sucking the life out of a literary text, a view forcefully articulated by Theodore Dreiser in 1932:

> [Film adaptation of novels] is not so much a belittling as a debauching process, which works harm to the mind of the entire world. For the debauching of any good piece of literature is – well, what? Criminal? Ignorant? Or both? I leave it to the reader (Dreiser, 1972: 211).

Since the beginning of cinema, adaptations have been a staple of the business of film. Among the earliest films were adaptations of literary works. If we take the year, 1900, for instance, we find titles such as *Romeo and Juliet, Aladdin and the Wonderful Lamp, The Stocking Scene from "Naughty Anthony,"* and a series of films entitled *Living Pictures* (1900), described on the Internet Movie Database (IMDb) as "faithfully representing well-known art masterpieces," summing up the perceived function of an adaptation to re-create art in order to vicariously achieve the elusive status of "artistic" itself. While other reasons can be found for why filmmakers in the silent period turned to literature for their plot lines, such as the stories were well known and were not dependent on dialogue to explain them, or adaptations were a way of bringing the great works of literature to the masses, some filmmakers were of the view that a dependency on literature or "great art" would also elevate the status of the film.

Such was the evangelical mission behind many of the films of the Vitagraph Film Company that included *Uncle Tom's Cabin* (1910), *The Life of Moses* (1910), and *Vanity Fair* (1911) as well as a number of Shakespeare adaptations. While these films drew in the crowds they were normally despised by serious film enthusiasts and literary critics alike, the former for wanting film to stand on its own feet without a reliance on literature, the latter for regarding film as cheapening, contaminating, and potentially threatening the literary text (Corrigan, 2007). Famously Virginia Woolf expressed the concern of many in her circle in her essay, "The Cinema," in which she laments how *Anna Karenina* translated to screen is barely recognizable. Indeed film's attempt to "re-create" literature, according to Woolf, not only is a disservice to literature but also to film. Woolf's comments on a predatory and significantly male cinema's rape and pillaging of the literary text prophetically reflect a number of the concerns both film and literary critics had with film adaptations that "try vainly to work in couples," a marriage characterized by jealousy, deceit, and an obsession with who owns what:

> So many arts seemed to stand by ready to offer their help. For example, there was literature. All the famous novels of the world, with their well-known characters, and their famous scenes, only asked, it seemed, to be put on the films. What could be easier and simpler? The cinema fell upon its prey with immense rapacity, and to this moment largely subsists upon the body of its unfortunate victim. But the results are disastrous to both. The alliance is unnatural. Eye and brain are torn asunder ruthlessly as they try vainly to work in couples (Woolf, 1950: 168).

A further anxiety regarding film as "the art form of democracy" in its leveling of audiences (and classes) intrudes into the criticism of adaptations and held sway for much of the twentieth century. The first issue of the groundbreaking literary journal, *Scrutiny*, included an essay by William Hunter on film. Entitled "The Art Form of Democracy?" – and enlarged into a book in the same year – the essay decries the "talking" narrative film, exposing the incompatibility of the terms "art" and "democracy" (1932a). It is worth pausing on this, seemingly un-interrogated assertion, as the root of the problem dogging the appreciation and the academic study of film adaptations for most of the twentieth century: an assumption that art cannot be aimed at the masses and that art cannot be mass produced. In other words, art cannot be democratic.

Significantly Hunter's essay's position in the first volume of *Scrutiny* strikes a warning to literature students, issuing an exclusion order to film and, in particular, film adaptation, in literary studies for much of the twentieth century. The fact that an article warning of the addictive and nullifying effects of film was included in the first issue is evidence of the concerns surrounding cinema and especially "the talkies," which threatened to invade the literary terrain through the introduction of words into a new media. Hunter cannot disguise abhorrence for the popular talking narrative film (a.k.a. adaptation) in words echoing those of Plato: "The extent to which second-hand experience of such a gross kind is replacing ordinary life is a danger which does not seem to have yet been realised, and against which certainly no steps have been taken. But *can* steps be taken?" (1932b: 10). According to Colin MacCabe steps were taken in what he describes as "a valorization of literature against popular culture in general and film in particular" (2011: 7) and an effective moratorium on any serious study of adaptations in the English literary curriculum. MacCabe observes, literary criticism "was largely designed by Eliot and Richards in the late 1920s to render the elephant [in the room: film] invisible" (2007: x). Even now there seems to be a remnant of this literary anxiety about film in the tendency for academics to apologize for declaring their enjoyment of a literary adaptation, and for critics of adaptation, particularly in terrains that have yet to be established, to begin their analysis with an apology, implicitly confessing to being a fan before a critic, with the study itself regarded as something of a guilty pleasure. Adaptation, in particular, is damned with praise in its "democratizing" effect: it brings literature to the masses but it also brings the masses to literature, diluting, simplifying, and therefore appealing to the many rather than the few. Attitudes change but as Timothy Corrigan has noted, while new film courses emerged in the later twentieth century, initially largely populated by English academics, adaptations, for the most part, were off the menu (Corrigan, 2012: 39).

Up until recently, the field has been dominated by case studies in classic adaptations, possibly a remnant of the class-ridden debates between literature and film in the first half of the twentieth century. The retention of the word "literature" in adaptation studies causes certain theorists to wince as it seems to bring elitist associations back to the field. Thomas Leitch in his groundbreaking essay, "Adaptation

Studies at a Crossroads" (2008), objects to an inelegant referencing to "literature on screen" in my own and others' works: "It is as if adaptation studies, by borrowing the cultural cachet of literature, sought to claim its institutional respectability and gravitas even while insuring adaptation's enduring aesthetic and methodological subordination to literature proper" (64). It is my contention that the word "literature" is not restricted to so-called classic texts, but includes popular fiction, cartoons, newspapers, advertisements, instruction manuals, anything that appears on paper. The trajectory can be reversed – adaptations can be, possibly should be, conceptualized as film on literature rather than literature on film (Cartmell and Whelehan, 2010). A certain privileging of "prestige film" and the discomfiture in uniting what are problematically regarded as binary opposites – popular and classic, money and art, high and low culture – are gradually fading away and literary and film scholars are uncovering a wealth of material in the previously unchartered territories of what has normally been dismissed as merely "entertainment," "the art form of democracy." Video games, comic books, and popular cinema are all deserving objects of consideration and they can be approached from a variety of perspectives, including consideration of economic, historical, commercial, and industrial conditions. Adaptation studies have finally begun to celebrate rather than conceal its early identification with "the art form of democracy."

There were a few – most notably André Bazin, who had a good word to say about film adaptation in the middle part of the twentieth century (1948) – academics on both the literature and film fence who were entrenched in turf wars, or purity debates, regarding adaptation studies as intruding negatively and unproductively into someone else's territory. Returning to Virginia Woolf's essay, "The Cinema," however, a clear admiration of cinematic narrative techniques and effects can be detected, and it is impossible not to note the influence that this new art form had on literature, in particular Woolf's own fiction. The cinematographic form of *Orlando*, for instance, is virtually impossible to miss. To take one of many examples of readings of Woolf's fictions, the vista from Orlando's oak tree is read by Sharon Ouditt as a series of shots, "a panning shot which takes in the southern view and zooms in on pleasure boats and puffs of smoke . . . [a] sharp cut to the west then brings the Welsh mountains into view [and] the changes in focus and the range ('thirty or forty counties')" (1999: 150). Artistic influences run two ways and Woolf's translation of cinematic devices into fiction is mirrored by D. W. Griffith's famous translations of Dickens' stylistics into cinema (Eisenstein, 1963). Peculiarly, the cinematic or modernist novel, as typified by Virginia Woolf's writing, does not translate so well to cinema as does its predecessors of the nineteenth century, as in the case of Dickens. A list of "unfilmable" novels, compiled in 2007, places at the top of the list Joyce, Proust, and Kafka, paradoxically novelists who have been observed to explicitly replicate cinematic devices in their writing ("Screenhead," n.d.).

While some modernist writers were staunchly "anti-adaptation," one by one they seem to be seduced by the lure of Hollywood. Aldous Huxley, for instance, was transformed from someone who could barely live with himself after sitting through a "talkie" (which he fictionalizes in *Brave New World* in the reaction to the "feely" adaptation of *Othello*) to becoming a Hollywood screenwriter (Huxley, 1972). Cinema inspired not just new techniques in writing and genre but also provided the context for novels and plays, among them Moss Hart and George S. Kaufman's *Once in a Lifetime* (1930), Horace McCoy's *They Shoot Horses, Don't They?* (1935), Nathanael West's *The Day of the Locusts* (1939), and F. Scott Fitzgerald's *The Last Tycoon* (1941).

Since the beginning of the twentieth century, it is clear that literature adapts film techniques and cinematic genres creating new types of fiction but, for some, the influence of film has a damaging effect on the quality of the novel. Alan Spiegel concludes *Fiction and the Camera Eye: Visual Consciousness in Film and the Modern Novel* (1976) speculating on the future of the novel in the age of film: "the contemporary novel at its most advanced now consorts with the coldness and passivity of the photographic plate. Just as photography seemed to release painting from its representational functions, so perhaps the film was always meant to appropriate the mimetic tradition in literature and thus leave literature itself free to – well, to do what? Self-destruct?" (197). It has been lamented that some novels are written not *just* as novels, but as future films. Take the case of Harry Potter. It has been argued that the experience of reading the books is akin to watching a film (Cartmell and Whelehan, 2010: 73–83); Harry's control of the gaze through the emphasis on his glasses, the influence of the blockbuster, especially the obligatory action sequences, and the intertextual references to *Star Wars,* in particular, in the first volume, call attention to the ways in which Hollywood has shaped popular fiction. While the first film, albeit successful, disappointed its audience due to its excess and lack of fidelity, the last two films seem more independent of the books while reinforcing the books' cinematic qualities. For instance, the influence of the road movie genre, implicit in the novel, is made explicit on screen in the penultimate installment, *Harry Potter and the Deathly Hallows*, Part 1 (dir. David Yates, 2010). Rowling's translation of Hollywood genre to fiction may be part of her recipe for popular and financial success and it has been observed that cinema's financial lure is too much for some novelists to resist, with the contemporary novel reduced to a first draft of a screenplay. Writing in *The Guardian* in 2008, John Patterson, following in the footsteps of Alan Spiegel, suggests Virginia Woolf's worst nightmare has now come true: films have destroyed the art of novel writing and novels are destroying movies: "film-makers – especially the literate ones, the ones who really need their English Lit thought-patterns beaten out of them – might delve more deeply into the possibilities unique to film once they realise, finally, that cinema is not a branch of literature, and that the opposite is now true" (Patterson, 2008).

An anxiety about the potential death of writing posed by film adaptation in the early twentieth century, still prevalent today, is perhaps as much about a fear concerning the death of the author, a concept that André Bazin notes is at the core of hostilities to adaptation. In his essay, "Adaptation, or the Cinema as Digest," Bazin's remarkably astute observation on the roots of the disapproval of film adaptation anticipates Barthes' "Death of the Author" (first published in 1967) and possibly explains the rise of the concept of the auteur in film theory, the undeniable, potentially illogical need for a single artist as qualification for the appellation of "art." Bazin's observation on the author's irrelevance, or to quote *Shakespeare in Love*'s (1998) ironic definition of Shakespeare as "only the author," in film adaptation is defiantly addressed in the biopic genre, arguably a genre, with some exceptions, held in the lowest estimation by film and literary critics alike, in which the author becomes increasingly fictionalized; witness *Shakespeare in Love*, *Becoming Jane* (2007), or *Bright Star* (2009), in which the greatness of the writings of Shakespeare, Austen, and Keats is ultimately explained and reduced as inspired by passionate love affairs. The author, whether overtly (as in the biopic) or covertly present, is a persistent feature in "classic" film adaptation and simultaneously functions to both announce and denounce the film's "authority." A good example of this is adaptations of *Pride and Prejudice* in which Austen's voice is transferred to Elizabeth Bennet, culminating in the biopic of 2007, *Becoming Jane*, in which *Pride and Prejudice* is "explained" as concealed autobiography. It goes without saying that such a reading would fail an English literature exam, with many an English and history teacher in agreement with G. K. Chesterton who, in 1936, points to the dangers of "historical falsehood being popularized through film": "A false film might be refuted in a hundred books, without much affecting the million dupes who had never read the books but only seen the film" (Chesterton, 1972: 116).

The screen fictionalization of historical authors continues to be met with outrage as is evident in the furore caused by Roland Emmerich's *Anonymous* (2011), a film that claims that Shakespeare was a fraud. Shakespeare academic associations, Shakespeare critics, and those involved in the Shakespeare heritage industry have publically denounced, protested against, and boycotted the film, engaging in what can be regarded as the most extreme form of "fidelity criticism." Film critics, while for the most part, dutifully rejecting the allegations that the Earl of Oxford was the true author of Shakespeare's plays, ultimately overcome such qualms about the need for historical fidelity, as in the *New York Times* review (albeit a review which inspires a long thread of readers' comments arguing for and against the authorship question): "*Anonymous*, a costume spectacle directed by Roland Emmerich, from a script by John Orloff, is a vulgar prank on the English literary tradition, a travesty of British history and a brutal insult to the human imagination. Apart from that, it's not bad" (Scott, 2011). The early twentieth-century concern that film adaptation can contaminate the public and the moral imperative to protect the author from screen vulgarization are still very much alive and kicking.

In spite of a hostile intellectual climate in which film adaptations of literary texts were effectively banned from literary studies (accused of diluting and usurping literary texts) and film studies (which sought value for itself rather than dependence on another art form), film adaptations themselves continued to thrive, receiving accolades from the viewing public and, since its inception, the Oscars have routinely chosen adaptations as best pictures; *All Quiet on the Western Front* (1930), *Mutiny on the Bounty* (1935), *The Life of Emile Zola* (1937), *Gone with the Wind* (1939), and *Rebecca* (1940) are among the Oscar winners of the Academy's early years. Regardless of their success in Hollywood, adaptations received little attention in film and literary studies. The first full-length study of film adaptation by George Bluestone in 1957 was slowly followed by monographs in the 1960s, 1970s, and 1980s. Thanks to the work of, among others, John Collick, Anthony Davies, Peter Donaldson, and Graham Holderness in the 1980s and 1990s,[1] "Shakespeare on Film" has emerged as a major academic discipline and is now followed by the increasing work on Jane Austen on film and television. Scholars of adaptations tend to forget the contribution made by the "Shakespeare on Screen" industry in achieving respectability by bravely venturing into what was previously forbidden territory. By the twenty-first century the field begins to expand with an extensive list of work that begins to move beyond the one-way trajectory from literature to film and canonical authors (which, on the whole, tends to applaud the author's superior literary knowledge to that of the filmmakers), embracing other forms of adaptations, such as popular adaptations, film to novel adaptations (novelizations), television, video games, the economics of adaptation, interrogations of the role of the author and the author on screen, novel to film to musical adaptations. Following from the often groundbreaking work of *Literature/Film Quarterly,* two international journals have emerged in the twenty-first century, *Adaptation in Film and Performance* (Intellect) and *Adaptation* (Oxford University Press). The work of Sarah Cardwell, Kamilla Elliott, Christine Geraghty, Linda Hutcheon, Thomas Leitch, Brian McFarlane, Julie Sanders, and Robert Stam has stretched the field beyond the single case study that offered little more than a comparative analysis, restricted to adaptations of canonical writers, in particular Shakespeare and Austen.[2] Linda Hutcheon and Thomas Leitch have undoubtedly played their part in the democratization of the subject, extending the remit of adaptations to a seemingly limitless number of forms, from popular fiction to video games, while Robert Stam has provided an invaluable summary of the state of the discipline in 2005, especially through his influential approach to the subject through his own adaptation of Gérard Gennette's *Palimpsests* (1982). Dogged by its sense of inferiority, as reflected in its problematical self-definition, "impure," adaptation studies has come a long way; but alas the field is still dominated by Anglo-American texts, the adaptations of which tend to fetishize their nationalistic features. To take one example, the shared views of the couple in the adaptation of David Nicholls' *One Day* (dir. Lone Scherfig, 2011), what can be regarded as an adaptation *qua* adaption in its reconstruction of the same day for over twenty years,[3] is obsessively visualized in their seeking out and sharing panoramic and touristy views of Edinburgh, London and Paris, hallmarks of Western European tourism so familiar, and possibly in its insularity, reassuring, to audiences of classic adaptations.

This volume celebrates the establishment of adaptation studies with the aim of identifying where the field is now and in what direction it is going. The "only the author" syndrome attached to screenwriters is undergoing something of a sea change, thanks to the success of Andrew Davies who has achieved "fame" in his capacity as adaptor, possibly because Davies "sums up" what audiences look for in a good adaptation: this can be defined simply as what is *added* to the hypotext (to borrow Gérard Genette's term for the source) rather than what is left out. In anticipation of his adaptation of *South Riding* (2011) Davies has identified ten "secrets" to becoming a successful adaptor:

1   Read the book.
2   Ask yourself: why this book, and why now?
3   Ask yourself: whose story is this, really?
4   Don't be afraid to change things, especially openings.
5   Don't start without a plan.
6   Never use a line of dialogue if you can achieve the effect with a look.
7   Crystallize dialogue to its essence.
8   Write scenes that aren't in the book.
9   Avoid voice-over, flashbacks, and characters talking directly to camera.
10 Break your own rules when it feels like the right thing to do (*The Telegraph*, 2011).

Davies' "secrets" are governed by democratic values, or the rules of commonality: the adaptor need not be a servant of the adapted author but free to change the text to appeal to a mass contemporary rather than elite audience – adaptation is the art of democratization, a "freeing" of a text from the confined territory of its author and of its readers. Significantly, his advice seems to be to liberate the text from what has been identified as the death knell of the adaptation: the devotion to an author's words. Adaptation is, indeed, the art form of democracy.

This collection is concerned with the democratizing effect of adaptations from the very beginnings of cinema to the current day, covering historical, ideological, economical, and different theoretical approaches, ranging from canonical to popular literary and film texts within the ever-expanding mediasphere. At the end of the twentieth and beginning of the twenty-first century, this so-called "democratizing effect" has finally lost its derogatory connotations. It is the case, however, that literature and film are still the dominant areas of debate and this collection, while branching into new territories, unashamedly reflects this majority position in adaptation studies (in true democratic fashion). Undoubtedly, this edited volume is a far cry from the types of collections which Robert B. Ray decried in 2001 in which "Literature and film scholars could only persist in asking about individual movies the same unproductive layman's question (How does the film compare to the book?), getting the same unproductive answer (The book is better)" with each article "isolated from all the others, its insights apparently stopped at the borders of the specific film or novel selected for analysis" (126). On the whole, as the chapters in this volume testify, adaptation studies is no longer haunted by the "heresy of paraphrase" (so entrenched in the mindsets of mid to late twentieth-century literary critics in which repetition or plot replication is regarded as a disservice to the literary text).

Judith Buchanan, in the opening chapter, considers early cinema's impulse to tell stories, the need for narrative material and the birth of film adaptation through the pictorializing of literature, the simplification of literary texts, and the "uplift movement" in which literature was seen to enhance the cultural value of film. The second chapter continues with the visual representation of words on a screen, so commencing not with the word, but with the seemingly blasphemous or, at least, paradoxical, *image* of the word, literalizing the metaphors, "reading a film" and "literature on screen" associated with film and adaptation studies. Gregory Robinson offers an early history of writing on screen, and the progress and mixed quality of the intertitle in silent cinema, initiating the beginning of the longstanding adaptation image/word war, but one in which, right from the beginning of cinema, the words were added after the visuals. The historical pre-eminence of the image to the word has dogged our appreciation of adaptations, but as Judith Buchanan demonstrates these "picturizations" (another name for "adaptation"), through their reliance on images to tell stories, produced films in the latter half of the silent era of considerable imagination and influence. And then came sound. Film adaptations' negative reception in the Modernist period is the subject of Richard J. Hand's and Deborah Cartmell's chapters. Taking the example of the first talking adaptation of Shakespeare, Sam Taylor's *The Taming of the Shrew* (1929), the coming of sound and the introduction of words into adaptation is seen to reduce critical responses to screen adaptations to two responses: too wordy or not wordy enough. The obsession with words, it is argued, is responsible for stagnating the field in fruitless debates over fidelity. Richard J. Hand's chapter considers how adaptation was considered hackwork by writers such as Thomas Hardy and Henry James resulting in critical failures of adaptations of their works. His chapter, covering various forms of adaptation in the Modernist period, including drama, film and radio, reveals the vast extent of unchartered territory in adaptation studies and how the different media cross over and influence each other.

Shelley Cobb considers a gendered notion of film authorship in her analysis of the rise of the auteur and the consequent demotion of adaptations to an inferior status in "Film Authorship and Adaptation." In this chapter Cobb considers the lowly status of adaptations in relation to Alfred Hitchcock's avoidance of adapting "great literature" in order to safeguard the director's own authority and ponders why Jane Campion's adaptation of *The Portrait of a Lady* (1996) jeopardizes her "auteur" status while Martin Scorsese's adaptation of *The Age of Innocence* (1993) does his auteur reputation no harm. In "Adaptation and Intertextuality, or, What isn't an Adaptation, and What Does it Matter?" Thomas Leitch flamboyantly critiques nine definitions of adaptations, from those that are essentially dualistic (literature to screen) to those that focus on the process rather than the product itself (intermediality), to those that see adaptation as self-consciously positioning itself as adaptation. Just how to define and approach adaptation has been the major preoccupation of adaptation studies in the new millennium and Simone Murray asks for more open-ended contextual approaches that move beyond the parameters of humanities subjects, in particular, literature and film models, considering how industrial, economic, legal, and commercial forces both facilitate and mould adaptations. Indeed, venturing outside the usual literature/film fora, Murray considers events such as the Cinema and Literature International Forum convened annually in Monaco, whose mission to "extend the range and reach of literature" recalls the democratizing mission of early adaptors while at long last no longer sworn to secrecy about mentioning the economic and legal dimensions governing adaptation choices.

The dominance of classic adaptations to adaptation studies and the elitism and sense of inferiority that this has perpetuated (good book = bad film, bad book = good film) is challenged here in the inclusion of what have historically been considered inferior source texts. Martin Zeller-Jacques contextualizes comic book adaptations within the field of adaptation studies, expanding on Harold Bloom's *Anxiety of Influence* (1973) and Geoff Klock's engagingly entitled *How to Read Superhero Comics and Why* (1999). Comic book adaptations are seen retroactively to revise what has come before and influence what is to come and rather than examining them as adaptations, the films are seen to be more akin to sequels and prequels, expanding on rather than compressing or rearranging "original" narratives.

The astonishing number of adaptations of songs, or the "the film of the song" is the subject of Ian Inglis' chapter in which he accounts for how "Yellow Submarine," "Alice's Restaurant," "Ode to Billy Joe," "Convoy," "Harper Valley PTA," and "Big Bad John" are expanded into films. Why the song to film adaptation has flourished for so long without receiving sustained critical attention is a question we could ask of many of the forms that adaptations take. Jeremy Strong looks at the phenomena of bad book = good film in the demotion of David Morrell from author to novelizer of the Rambo films. This virtually undiscovered country for adaptation scholars raises the issue of the elitism of the field that until the end of the twentieth century tended to privilege adaptations of canonical literary texts. A wealth of material remains largely unexplored: among them, video games, advertising adaptations, book to film, and film to theater.

Yvonne Griggs and Christine Geraghty offer two readings of Joe Wright's 2007 adaptation of Ian McEwan's *Atonement* (2001), a book and film that are receiving widespread attention in both literary and film studies. Geraghty convincingly reads the film as a reworking of the novel into what has become identified as the "adaptation genre," while Griggs sees the film as a systematic cinematic translation of the novel's postmodern features. Moving from "classic film" to "classic television," Richard Butt's chapter surveys the classic novel on British television noting how fidelity, heritage, and nostalgia have been stalwart terms in academic critique; if this can be termed a "genre," then it's in this form in which cries for fidelity, even mediated by the self-consciousness – or self-deprecation – of the form as an adaptation, have persisted longest.

In an exceptionally challenging and provocative chapter, Richard Burt, through the lens of Jacques Derrida, glances at similarities between adapting and editing by taking the example of *Hamlet* adaptations and reflecting on how the power of the dead over the living in Shakespeare's play is mirrored in the process of adaptation, what he refers to as "hauntographology." In his own words, Burt puts "text and film into dialogue without returning to unproductive comparisons between original and adaptation" along the way raising "philosophical, philological, and technological questions about the limits of a 'textual forensics' of print editions and film adaptations with respect to their ontology, media specificity, and legibility". In the chapter entitled "Screened Writers", Kamilla Elliott notes the development of the representation of the author in cinema, and the ways in which film can be seen to keep "the ink wet" through the perpetual return of the authorial body in films that adapt their writings, constituting narrator, character and audience, very much against the grain of the literary texts and the literary critical insistence that the author is either dead or has been converted into a "function." The rift between how the author is perceived by literary critic and film director is a subject area that continues to bewilder and fascinate and the two authors whose works are most discussed by enthusiasts of adaptation are undoubtedly Shakespeare and Austen.

It is impossible to avoid the dominance of critical work on screen readings of Shakespeare and Austen in this field. But adaptations of these authors are far from straightforward. Douglas M. Lanier surveys the murdering Othello motif in films from 1911 to 1947, reflecting on the vexed place of filmed theater and Shakespeare in American cinema where what was then uncommercial Shakespeare film is both celebrated and condemned. These films have their cake and eat it too, reflecting both the complementary and competitive relationship of film and theater, both reproving a class-ridden and decadent theater while presenting it at the same time. Lisa Hopkins looks at the rise of the Shakespeare and Austen adaptation industries and the screen dialogue between adaptations of these authors. Ariane Hudelet compares adaptations of Austen to Stern through *A Cock and Bull Story* (2005) and *Lost in Austen* (2008), in particular, as very loose adaptations, relishing in the freedom of the adaptor to interact with the novels and related to the rising attraction of the "making of" the film, as included in DVD special features. In the spirit of work such as Philip Pullman's *His Dark Materials* (1995, 1997, 2000), Hudelet argues that these adaptations flaunt fidelity in order to recreate an alternative world to that presented in the hypotext. Continuing with aspects of adapting history, Imelda Whelehan considers how recent neo-Victorian adaptations, "write the novel that Victorians could not" while reflecting on how neo-Victorian criticism displays a very old-fashioned hostility to screen adaptation. Adaptation of canonical authors, especially within their own historical periods, is often identified as "costume drama," implying the significance of costume to film adaptation. The important, often unsung, contribution of costumes to adaptation is stunningly revealed in Pamela Church Gibson and Tamar Jeffers McDonald's analysis of *The Heiress* (1949), *Washington Square* (1997), and the 1968 and 1996 adaptations of *Romeo and Juliet*. Both Shakespeare's and Henry James's use of costume to articulate what is unspoken is extended to the sophisticated employment of costume in film adaptations to tell the story on its own. This chapter foregrounds how what is often taken for granted as on the fringe of a film – costumes, light, set, soundtrack, color, casting – is skillfully constructed as something like an alternative to an authorial presence. In "Authorship, Commerce, and *Harry Potter*", James Russell looks at how the Harry Potter films "write the book" on the potential of adaptations by, on one hand, seeming to valorize authorship, while on the other, increasingly and radically departing from the novels; and in spite of corporate and commercial demands, creating a product which Russell describes as "far better than it needed to be." The seemingly "unfilmable" nature of *Heart of Darkness* is the subject of Jamie Sherry's account of the light shed onto Orson Welles' aborted project and Francis Ford Coppola's *Apocalypse Now* (1979) through both films' paratexts. Rounding off the collection, Diane Lake speaks from direct experience as a screenwriter of an unfulfilled and finished project and like Sherry, and many of the contributors in this volume, sees the need to discuss adaptations from perspectives (economic, industrial, circumstantial) that remained virtually unmentionable for most of the twentieth century.

Acknowledgments

Many thanks to Kamilla Elliott for her comments on a draft of this introduction.

Notes

1 See Collick (1989); Davies (1988); Donaldson (1990); and Holderness (1988).
2 See Cardwell (2002); Elliott (2003); Geraghty (2007); Hutcheon (2006); Leitch (2007); McFarlane (1996); Sanders (2006); and Stam (2005).
3 See Chapter 20 for an analysis of the "adaptation genre."

References

Bazin, André. "Adaptation, or the Cinema as Digest (1948)." In *Film Adaptation*. Ed. James Naremore. London: Athlone, 2000, 17–19.

Cardwell, Sarah. *Adaptation Revisited: Television and the Classic Novel*. Manchester: Manchester University Press, 2002.

Cartmell, Deborah and Imelda Whelehan. *Screen Adaptation: Impure Cinema*. Basingstoke: Palgrave, 2010.

Chesterton, G. K. "About the Films (1936)." In *Authors on Film*. Ed. Harry Geduld. Bloomington: Indiana University Press, 1972, 112–17.

Collick, John. *Shakespeare Cinema and Society*. Manchester: Manchester University Press, 1989.

Corrigan, Timothy. "Literature on Screen, a History: In the Gap." In *The Cambridge Companion to Literature on Screen*. Eds. Deborah Cartmell and Imelda Whelehan. Cambridge: Cambridge University Press, 2007, 29–44.

Corrigan, Timothy. Ed. *Film and Literature: An Introduction and Reader*. London: Routledge, 2012.

Davies, Anthony. *Filming Shakespeare's Plays*. Cambridge: Cambridge University Press, 1988.

Donaldson, Peter. *Shakespearean Films/Shakespearean Directors*, New York: Unwin Hyman, 1990.

Dreiser, Theodore. "The Real Sins of Hollywood (1932)." In *Authors on Film*. Ed. Harry Geduld. Bloomington: Indiana University Press, 1972, 206–22.

Eisenstein, Sergei. "Dickens, Griffiths and the Film Today (1944)." In *Film Form*. Ed. Jay Leyda. London: Dennis Dobson, 1963, 195–256.

Elliott, Kamilla. *Rethinking the Novel/Film Debate*. Cambridge: Cambridge University Press, 2003.

Geraghty, Christine. *Now A Major Motion Picture: Film Adaptations of Literature and Drama*. Lanham, MD: Rowman and Littlefield, 2007.

Holderness, Graham. *The Shakespeare Myth*. Manchester: Manchester University Press, 1988.

Hunter, William. "The Art Form of Democracy?" *Scrutiny*, 1:1, 1932a, 61–5.

Hunter, William. *Scrutiny of Cinema*. London: Wishart & Co., 1932b.

Hutcheon, Linda. A *Theory of Adaptation*. New York: Taylor and Francis, 2006.

Huxley, Aldous. "Silence is Golden (1929)." In *Authors on Film*. Ed. Harry Geduld. Bloomington: Indiana University Press, 1972, 68–76.

Leitch, Thomas. *Film Adaptation and its Discontents: From* Gone with the Wind *to* The Passion of the Christ. Baltimore: Johns Hopkins University Press, 2007.

Leitch, Thomas. "Adaptation Studies at a Crossroads." *Adaptation*, 1:1, 2008, 63–77.

MacCabe, Colin. "Foreword." In *Cinema and Modernism*. David Trotter. Oxford: Blackwell, 2007, viii–xii.

MacCabe, Colin. "Introduction: Bazinian Adaptation: *The Butcher Boy* as Example." In *True to the Spirit: Film Adaptation and the Question of Fidelity*. Eds. Colin MacCabe, Kathleen Murray, and Rick Warner. Oxford: Oxford University Press, 2011, 3–26.

McFarlane, Brian. *Novel to Film: An Introduction to the Theory of Adaptation*. Oxford: Clarendon, 1996.

Ouditt, Sharon. "*Orlando*: Coming Across the Divide." In *Adaptations: From Text to Screen, Screen to Text*. Eds. Deborah Cartmell and Imelda Whelehan. London: Routledge, 1999, 146–55.

Patterson, John. *The Guardian*, March 15, 2008. www.guardian.co.uk/film/2008/mar/15/fiction. Accessed August 23, 2010.

Plato. *Phaedrus*. Trans. and Ed. Christopher Rowe. London: Penguin, 2005.

Ray, Robert B. *How a Film Theory Got Lost and Other Mysteries in Cultural Studies*. Bloomington: Indiana University Press, 2001.

Sanders, Julie. *Adaptation and Appropriation*. London: Routledge, 2006.

Scott, A. O. "How Could a Commoner Write Such Great Plays?" *New York Times*, October 27, 2011. http://movies.nytimes.com/2011/10/28/movies/anonymous-by-roland-emmerich-review.html?src=dayp. Accessed October 31, 2011.

"Screenhead." www.screenhead.com/reviews/the-unfilmables-a-list-of-the-hardest-novels-to-film/. Accessed August 22, 2010.

Spiegel, Alan. *Fiction and the Camera Eye: Visual Consciousness in Film and the Modern Novel*. Charlottesville: University of Virginia Press, 1976.

Stam, Robert. "Introduction: The Theory and Practice of Adaptation." In *Literature and Film: A Guide to the Theory and Practice of Film Adaptation*. Eds. Robert Stam and Alessandra Raengo. Oxford: Blackwell, 2005, 1–52.

The Telegraph. "How to Adapt Classic Books for Television – By a Master." February 18, 2011, 32.

Woolf, Virginia. "The Cinema." In *The Captain's Death Bed and Other Essays*. London: Hogarth Press, 1950, 160–71.

Part I
History and Contexts: From Image to Sound

1
Literary Adaptation in the Silent Era

Judith Buchanan

When the nascent moving picture industry emerged in the 1890s, its significance in technological, social, and economic terms quickly became apparent. Less clear, however, was the dominant use to which moving pictures should be put. What did they do best? Through what sort of subjects could they most effectively broadcast their technological wizardry, showcase their artistry, and maximize their returns? Was this a medium for recording the world with previously untapped verisimilitude, or a medium in which the fantastical imaginary could be given rein as never before? A vehicle for exploring life as it was, or life as it might be? A medium of description or creation? A mechanism or an art form? Film offered what James Monaco has termed a "neutral template" (2009: 45) to be appropriated differently by producers according to their priorities, interests, and broader thinking about the medium's strengths and potential. And surveying the uses to which this "neutral template" was put in cinema's pioneering years (1896–c.1906) reveals no immediate consensus about where the industry thought it should principally channel its energies. This sustained equivocation about what sort of films it should be producing is graphically reflected in the diverse nature both of production company output and of exhibitors' film programs across this period.

An 1896 Edison catalogue advertising its films to exhibitors, for example, reveals much about the company's breadth of production. Each film subject that Edison had for sale is, as the catalogue introduction announces, "tabulate[d] and concisely describe[d] . . . in a manner which will enable our patrons to select intelligently from our list, those pictures which are best suited to the tastes of their audiences"

A Companion to Literature, Film, and Adaptation, First Edition. Edited by Deborah Cartmell.
© 2012 Blackwell Publishing Ltd. Published 2012 by Blackwell Publishing Ltd.

(Herbert et al., 1996: 19). At a cost of £4 for each fifty-foot film subject, the catalogue lists films by genre: "Dances" (stick dances, Sioux Indian dances, Japanese
dances, London Gaiety Girl dances, buck dances, and a dancing dog); "Combats"
(a Mexican knife duel, a broadsword fight in full armor, a Graeco-Roman wres-
tling match, female fencers, and a pair of boxing cats); "Military Scenes" (a dress
parade, a mess call, a skirmish drill); "Acrobatic Performances" (trapeze acts, head
balancing, an Arabian knife tumbler, and a "marvelous lady contortionist"); and
"Descriptive Scenes" (a fire rescue scene, a scalping, 'Chinese Laundry' scene, Joan
of Arc, and two different scenes adapted from David Henderson's stage burlesque of George du Maurier's popular 1894 novel *Trilby*). Some exhibitors may
have favored one film genre over another in deciding what was "best suited to the
tastes of their audiences." Surviving exhibitors' programs, however, suggest that
what was most frequently valued in exhibition venues of the period was variety.

Let us consider one London film program from 1899 to sample the flavor of a
picture-going audience's viewing experience from the very early days of the industry.
The program of "The American Biograph" exhibited at the Palace Theatre of Varie-
ties in London on September 20, 1899 featured shots of Queen Victoria in her
carriage inspecting the Honorary Artillery Company, of "Madame Dreyfus Leaving
the Prison" (capitalizing on the popularity of the ongoing Dreyfus affair), of the
Henley regatta, of a panoramic view of Conway Castle, of the Meadowbrook Hunt,
of a sketch entitled "Man Overboard," and of an international hurdles race at the
Queen's Club. And, on the same program, sandwiched directly between "Polo at
Hurlingham" and some actuality footage of American naval hero "Admiral Dewey,"
was the first public exhibition of the first Shakespeare film ever made (some brief
action recorded from Herbert Beerbohm Tree's contemporaneous London stage
production of Shakespeare's *King John*).[1] Moreover, as part of a broader program of
music-hall acts, the films projected were also jostling for position alongside live
variety acts of various sorts (comedians, acrobats, musicians, actors performing brief
"scenes," jugglers). What might a brief encounter with a Shakespearean dramatic
fragment on screen such as that on offer here have been expected to achieve in the
midst of such varied fare? Or, similarly, how might audiences have responded to
the comparably fleeting encounter with a re-textualized work provided by Edison's
scenes from *Trilby* (parodically mediated through Henderson's stage burlesque),
or by American Biograph's contemporaneous releases dramatizing scenes from the
same novel?

Exhibited at a standard projection speed, each of the Edison films from the 1896
catalogue represented approximately a minute's runtime. The short films on the
1899 London Biograph program would have had a projection time of between
one and four minutes. Each film therefore gave merely a sample snapshot, isolated
episode or temporal slice of the subject being showcased. It was the task of the
accompanying musicians in the exhibition venue to attempt to make sense of the
transitions of pace and tone between actualities and brief sketches, the skittish and
the serious, that bumped up against each other so percussively on picture programs

of the period. The joy to be had in any one performance, or in any one projected film short from such a program, was, therefore, dependent in no small measure on its contribution to the cumulative variety line-up.

The adaptive life of early cinema was certainly not limited to an exclusive relationship with literary texts. In the fluid intermedial traffic of subjects and ideas that characterized the freewheeling cultural momentum of the period, material and styles from vaudeville skits, music-hall acts, magic lantern shows, topical, satirical and saucy cartoons, works of art, *tableaux vivants,* opera, illustrations, popular songs, and other forms of cultural expression (performed and printed) were variously appropriated, referenced, and re-couched by filmmakers. In the interests of delimitation for this volume, however, it is those films (more than plentiful in themselves) that had a discernible relationship with prior literary and theatrical texts that will absorb my attention. This being the case, what particular value might a film trailing literary and theatrical associations have brought to the giddy and fast-moving mélange of other spectating pleasures that made up the early film programs? To consider this question, I return to the 1896 scenes from *Trilby* released by two separate (competitor) American production companies and to the Biograph's *King John* scenes. Firstly, both *Trilby* and *King John* were on offer as the vehicle for heightened dramatic performances – and both featured the hyperbolized drama of a death scene (of Svengali and King John respectively). Secondly, drawing upon the invaluable early cinema commodity of "audience foreknowledge" (Musser, 1990a: 257–9), for some in the audience both films would have triggered a bank of broader familiarity with the novel or play synecdochically summoned by the brief scenes projected. Thirdly, in the person of Herbert Beerbohm Tree, the *King John* film gave international audiences access to one of the "great" Shakespearean actors of the moment as was explicitly acknowledged in the film's altered title for its U.S. release, "Beerbohm Tree, The Great English Actor" (Brown and Anthony, 1999: 228), thereby self-consciously adding cultural ballast to an exhibition program. Fourthly, the Edison *Trilby* scenes, being an 1896 satirical quotation from a recent stage burlesque of an 1894 serialized novel, signaled both the contemporaneity of the new moving picture industry's pool of reference and its will to insert itself directly into the cross-referencing networks of other expressive media, as both commentator upon and contributor to their cultural operations. Fifthly, and relatedly, as the Biograph *Trilby* scenes were played on London programs in 1897 (Buchanan, 2009: 60–1), these would have evoked Herbert Beerbohm Tree's own famously successful London stage adaptation of *Trilby* from the 1895–6 season – a production in which he had himself played a memorably creepy Svengali. Lastly, as played at London's Palace Theatre in autumn 1899, the *King John* short film cannot but have served, in an innovatively transmedial marketing ruse and further indication of the industry's up-to-the-minute topicality, as, in effect, a teaser-trailer for Tree's full-length stage production of *King John* then playing at Her Majesty's Theatre down the road (Buchanan, 2009: 68; McKernan, 2000).

The networks of intermedial reference to, and association with, the world beyond the exhibition hall that these adapted films courted made them some of the most allusively intricate of any of the 1890s films. Tom Gunning's influential argument (1989) that pioneering cinema created "an aesthetic of astonishment" as part of a "cinema of attractions" has now passed into the received wisdom about what early cinema *was*. In the process, Gunning's paradigm has, in the way of things, sometimes been reduced to a cruder and misleading summary of itself in which a stupefied audience for early cinema is posited, watching in awed astonishment as the wondrous moving images unspool before their eyes. Many of the generously allusive signals within early films such as *Trilby* and *King John*, pointing knowingly (and multiply) beyond their own borders, provide an antidote to that critically reductive tendency by reminding us that the "astonishment" provoked by early cinema was not one that deactivated participative discernment or associative think-ing, or that equated in any way to stupefaction. From the first, in fact, the moving picture industry offered a product whose viewing pleasures were partly to be found specifically in active and judicious comparison – comparison with the extra-cinematic world of lived experience and, crucially, comparison with other, known cultural works and styles of artistic address.

For all the stimulating associative reach of these films, catalogues and programs from the 1890s and the early years of the twentieth century reveal that titles with literary and/or theatrical connections were far from dominant in terms of industry output and market exposure. Nevertheless, in the fast-moving early cinema period, all production and exhibition conventions were subject to ongoing adjustment as they responded relatively nimbly to evolving market demands. And, as other things in the industry changed (camera and projection technology, film stock, exhibition venues, distribution channels, the commercial relationship of production companies to distributors and exhibitors, the authorial branding of films, ticket pricing, star power, the legislation that governed the industry), so too, through the early years of the twentieth century, was the balance of type of production company output significantly adjusted. Audiences, now accustomed to the wonders of the no-longer-new technology, became less satisfied by films simply celebrating the pure kinetics of graceful, powerful or startling movement, and, alongside this, correspondingly more ambitious in their own viewing tastes and narrative aspirations. In relative market terms, therefore, in a move traceable from c.1903 onwards, the brief actuali-ties, scenic views, sporting snapshots, whirling dancers, and fight films that had dominated early film exhibition, were losing out to cinema's impulse to tell stories (Musser, 1990b: 337–69). And with the enthusiasm for stories came the need for narrative material. Original scripts were not forthcoming fast enough to meet industry needs, nor to provide the tonal variety required to please all corners of the house. Given the dizzying production rate and voracious appetite of the market, where should the industry turn for material? Unsurprisingly, it reached gratefully for the library shelf and from c.1907 onwards, adapting the work of existing authors became one in a range of standard story-telling production practices for most of the leading film companies. In his published catalogue of *Books and Plays in Film, 1896–1915,* Denis Gifford lists 861 authors (alphabetically organized, Adams to Zola) whose work was adapted to film in the first twenty years of the industry. But what "adapted" meant in practice, of course, changed significantly across exactly this period.

In the pioneering years, making a film of a novel or play would rarely require an interest in the totality of the work, or even in its overall structural shape. The brevity of each exhibited film in this period did not allow for such comprehensive ambition. Rather the project was, in effect, to produce cinematically animated, brief, visual quotations from a work. Where possible, the cameos were attractively designed and entertainingly played but rarely under an obligation to generate narrative coherence across the ellipses between scenes.[2] Gunning has termed the privileging of isolated cameo references over a consistent narrative drive in such films a "peak moment" approach to a source (2004: 128). Choosing key moments from the inherited story – whenever possible those that already had some heightened recognition-value in the public consciousness – gave the advantage of speedy intelligibility for a picture-going audience independently able to contextualize the unplaced moment playing out before them. This text-allusive/audience-collusive approach produced a slew of short films that "quoted" selectively from literary sources in cinema's first decade. Even post-1907, when the desire to tell a coherent story had become the usual aspiration for a film, film stories were still typically structured as a medley of strung-together "moments" rather than as a fluently progressive narrative. For this reason, they continued to depend upon an audience's familiarity with the original, or upon its access to other sources of information beyond the film, to become meaningful in narrative terms.

Well into early cinema's transitional period (c.1907–c.1913), therefore, literary films were frequently composed of an unapologetically bumpy sequence of the best-known dramatic and iconic scenes from their literary sources. These were familiar to many not only through direct access to the literary works themselves but also from exposure to artistic representations, edition illustrations, vaudeville sketches, satirical cartoons, and a wide variety of other forms in which many literary sources were culturally disseminated through the nineteenth and into the early twentieth century. Thus it was, for example, that the Vitagraph Company of America's 1909 *Oliver Twist* (dir. J. Stuart Blackton)[3] could move apparently seamlessly from Oliver Twist's mother dying to Oliver asking for "more" in the workhouse orphanage that needed, and received, no introduction, and from there straight to Oliver's introduction to the Artful Dodger and Fagin. The story, and a fairly stable bank of related imagery, was sufficiently well known for an audience to be trusted to keep up across the narrative leaps. Understanding the savviness of its market in this way, Vitagraph did not need to invest in supernumerary plot-clarifying transitions between the "peak" moments that were, by implicit accord, most cherished in the popular consciousness and therefore most vital to include.

Vitagraph were, in fact, famously proficient at producing, marketing, and globally distributing popular, visually attractive but partial versions of literary classics (Uricchio and Pearson, 1993). In the five-year period between 1907 and 1912 alone, for example, they produced two films adapted from Dickens, three from Victor Hugo, two from Greek mythology, five from the Bible, twelve from Shakespeare, three from classic fairytales, and one each from William Thackeray, Oscar Wilde, Ellen Wood, Arthur Conan Doyle and Arthurian legend. This impressive legacy of literary adaptations, in fact, formed part of the company's campaign to be considered purveyors of quality cinema with artistic aspirations (Buchanan 2009: 105–46). In response to the release of their 1908 one-reel (c. twelve-minute) *Julius Caesar*, they were specifically commended by the *New York Dramatic Mirror* for having omitted all but "the vital scenes" (1908: 6). The action of such vigorously truncated versions of novels or plays necessarily moved swiftly from one dramatic highlight to another, offering a sequence of consolingly familiar, or near-familiar, scenes and thereby implicitly establishing and confirming an analogue version of these cultural works (in effect a "best of" abridgement) in which they could circulate manageably and more or less intelligibly to a broad market.

"Like a Cruikshank brought to life": Literature "pictorialized"

Edison's catalogue entry for the "Trilby Death Scene" back in 1896 had included the descriptive sell: "The dramatis personae of this act are made up in exact imitation of the illustrations given in Du Maurier's book" (Herbert et al., 1996: 21). Identifying the costuming and look of the film characters as precise evocations of the illustrations published in *Trilby*[4] was evidently considered a promotional boost for the film. It certainly signaled a desire to authenticate the film not only in relationship to the theatrical burlesque that was its most immediate, and declared, source, but also with the literary publication whose prior popularity had inspired that burlesque. From these early beginnings of layered adaptive referencing, the will specifically to "pictorialize" literature for the cinema then became part of the most prevalent early cinema terminology used in both trade press and popular review to describe what would now more typically be called the adaptation process. And sometimes, within the general project to "pictorialize," specific illustrations or illustrators surfaced to give recognizable focus to the particular character of the "pictorializing" being undertaken.

British filmmaker Thomas Bentley adapted the work of several authors across the course of his filmmaking career, but it was Dickens who claimed his passion. In total he made eight Dickens films for four different production companies: *Oliver Twist* (Hepworth, 1912), *David Copperfield* (Hepworth, 1913), *The Old Curiosity Shop* (Hepworth, 1913), *The Chimes* (Hepworth, 1914), *Barnaby Rudge* (Hepworth, 1915), *Hard Times* (Transatlantic Pictures, 1915), another *The Old Curiosity Shop* (Welsh-Pearson, 1921), and *The Adventures of Mr Pickwick* (Ideal, 1921).[5] Bentley's four-reel

Oliver Twist came out in 1912, amidst a rash of other Dickens tributes of various sorts in honor of the centenary of his birth. Upon its release, the reviewer for *Bioscope* expressed his appreciation for many aspects of this production, including set, costume, story-telling, and the cast. However, his special commendation was reserved for Willie West's "quite inimitable" performance as the Artful Dodger:

> He whisks through the film with his tremendous tail coat draped about his body and trailing around his legs, with his shy, impish cock of the eye, and his immortal top hat wobbling in ancient but perilous state on his head, like a Cruikshank brought to life ("Oliver Twist," 1912: 281).

Part of the evident pleasure the reviewer takes in the film's aesthetics and performances derives from the way he sees the film connecting precisely and reassuringly with imported properties deemed "immortal" and with the precarious angle of hat placement declared "ancient." As the reviewer saw it, both the detail and the flavor of illustrator George Cruikshank's pictorial account of the Artful Dodger were discernibly retained, but simply now with the added virtue of an injection of movement (character "whisk[ing]", tail coat "drap[ing]", hat "wobbling", and so on). Or, in the analogous words of a subsequent review of Bentley's *The Old Curiosity Shop* (1913), Bentley the filmmaker was, at root, "an illustrator" who had "the additional advantage of working in a living medium instead of in pen, pencil and paints" (*Bioscope*, 1914: 217).

Given the levels of public investment in, and sense of cultural ownership over, these novels, discussing the films as Dickensian (where the label was generously able to incorporate the Cruikshankian) but *with additional value*, as opposed to couching them apologetically as a reduced, diluted or highly compromised allusion to Dickens, probably revealed as much about the promotional needs of the market as it did about the specific character of the films themselves. The perceived levels of public investment were explicitly acknowledged in the praise lavished upon *Oliver Twist*. Not only was this film on offer as "one of the most accurately correct 'animated novels' yet done", but the *Bioscope* reviewer declared himself relieved that Bentley had not been tempted either to omit any key scenes ("Everything essential in or notable to the story has been included") or to interpolate any invented ones ("a particularly material consideration in the present instance where the original is well-known to practically everyone") ("Oliver Twist," 1912: 279). If "practically everyone" was a cultural stake-holder in how *Oliver Twist* was rendered on the screen, those amassed stake-holders, having handed over the price of their ticket, were then, it seems, owed the *Oliver Twist* they had previously imbibed from the Dickens/Cruikshank literary double act. In reality, many picture-goers might actually have encountered that literary double act through its subsequent diffused dissemination across other cultural forms – including, for example, in Thomas Bentley's own appearances impersonating Dickensian characters on the music-hall stage (MacFarlane, 2003: 59). At the turn of the century there was, as Russell Merritt reports, "a considerable vogue for one-act versions of famous plays and literary works" for performance at fairgrounds and in vaudeville – a vogue to which D. W. Griffith had been amply exposed in his days as an actor in a touring company in ways that had a considerable influence upon his subsequent filmmaking:

> Later, such sketches became Griffith's principal source for his Biograph literary adaptations, the vital crib sheets that enabled him to film all those Great Works – the leviathan novels, Victorian poems, and short stories – without actually having to wade through them (Merritt, 1981: 6).

Griffith was, of course, far from alone in knowing his "leviathan novels" and other literary works chiefly through familiarity with popular performed abridgments. Nevertheless, the myth of unimpeded access to uncontaminated originals was strategically adhered to in promoting the cultural value of the work. From such a starting position, anything that unduly advertised the processes of transmediation in Dickensian filmmaking (plot restructurings or interpolations, innovative approaches to mise-en-scène, interventionist cinematography) was to be suppressed and the temptation to make interpretive expansions upon an original "well-known to practically everyone" eschewed. Meanwhile anything that contributed to persuading spectators they were being given renewed and undistorted access to the "immortal" and "ancient" qualities of the original, only now not just as novel but as "*animated* novel," was to be commended – even if the undistorted access allegedly on offer was to an original that audiences might not, in fact, have encountered directly.

Some films worked harder than others on this unacknowledged agenda to suppress the signs of interpretive engagement for fear of being thought to be playing fast and loose with the specific character of their respected sources. In 1915, the American poet and early film theorist, Vachel Lindsay, argued that inherited literary and dramatic values were stifling cinema's uninhibited engagements with its own "language." He made the case that cinema should distance itself decisively from a trammeling theatrical heritage:

> . . . the further [the motion picture] gets from Euripides, Ibsen, Shakespeare, or Molière – the more it becomes like a mural painting from which flashes of lightning come – the more it realizes its genius (Lindsay, 1970: 194).

Nevertheless, in adapting theatrical material, films of the transitional era were sometimes caught by a counter-impulse to signal a sustained allegiance to the medium of derivation of their source material, the stage. This was particularly true of Shakespearean filmmaking. While it sometimes broke free into freshly conceived ways of seeing and narrating, equally its blocking, cinematography, and performance codes sometimes timidly courted the look and feel of theatrical productions in an attempt, perhaps, to legitimize its own presumptuous project in adapting

Shakespeare for film at all. The intermittent adherence to a set of conventions more usually associated with stage practice was partly an unthinkingly atavistic approach to medium-appropriate codes, and partly a strategic move to telegraph an alignment with the theatrical conventions to which filmmakers of adapted theatrical material felt, or thought they should feel, a cultural allegiance.

The years 1908/1909 proved to be key years of vacillation for Shakespearean cinema in deciding whether to embrace a set of cinematic codes or to reassert a stubborn theatricality in styles of presentation. As this tussle was played out, sometimes both impulses – to produce an innovative and fluid piece of cinema on the one hand and to contain the will to innovate on the other – were illuminatingly co-present within a single film, as if in graphic and fraught testimony to some of the broader debates being conducted in the industry of the time. The Clarendon Film Company's *The Tempest* (dir. Percy Stow, 1908), for example, exhibits a medium-savvy delight in its capacity to evoke beautifully choreographed, tense drama through its own simple but effective arsenal of special effects for the storm and shipwreck scenes (layers of evocative superimposition, oddly angled shots, impressionist and dynamic edited sequences for the storm, savage lacerations made directly on to the film print to create suggestive streaks of lightning). And yet every expression of cinematic adventurousness in this film is countered by another of cinematic conservatism (shallow sets, theatrically blocked entrances and exits, cluttered frame composition, stage-bound performance trickery in the "magical" conjuration of doves, and so on). For all its undeniable charm, therefore, the film emerges as a document in stylistic indecision, poised between embracing and rejecting the cinematic resources it finds at its disposal in ways that, from the perspective of Shakespearean filmmaking of just a few years later, would seem notably coy (Buchanan, 2009: 78–88).[6]

However, the most striking and high profile example of strategically self-limiting filmmaking is to be found in Kalem's big-budget, five-reel *From the Manger to the Cross* (dir. Sidney Olcott, 1912) starring Robert Henderson-Bland as a gesturally graceful and neo-painterly Jesus.[7] This production actively refuses the raft of cinematic story-telling devices potentially available to the medium of its moment out of conspicuous deference to its biblical subject matter. In "pictorializing" the Gospel account, Olcott (who proved a more technically adventurous director in other productions of a similar moment) eschewed even a modest use of cut-ins, mobile camera work, variable focal lengths, cross-cutting between planes of action and any suggestion of a psychologically investigative approach to character. In fact, *From the Manger to the Cross* is a film that almost gives the impression of having made self-conscious efforts to try and deny the fact that it was a film at all. It used extensive biblical quotation on its title cards, each in an antiquated and biblically evocative font and each conscientiously referenced by Bible chapter and verse. It superimposed its chapter titles (for example, "The Flight into Egypt," "The Last Supper," "The Crucifixion and Death") over known paintings of the life of Christ. And its only minimally animated "action" was structured as a sequence of largely static vignettes, many of which were recognizable as visual quotations from known religious paint-ings. The effect (and perhaps the purpose) of minimizing the animation of the action, reducing the camera work to static and distanced observation in scene-length takes (already stylistically retrograde by 1912) and alternating between the frequent use of direct biblical quotation and a series of close painterly references, is to simu-late the appearance of an illustrated Bible whose illustrations happen, in this cinematic instantiation, to have been lightly (but only lightly) animated. Despite the film's title (whose *from* and *to* formulation misleadingly suggests that central to the film's interests will be dramatic pulse and narrative trajectory), the film therefore courted the feel of a conservatively illustrated, cinematic Gospel (Bucha-nan, 2007: 52–54; Keil, 1992: 112–20).

The conception of cinema implicitly (and unskeptically) peddled by those advo-cating, or working on, the production of "animated novels," cinematic Gospels, and the "pictorializing" of literature in this way was one that celebrated cinema not as a vehicle of interpretive intervention and potential re-imagining, but as, in effect, itself a continuation and heightened version *of* literature – simply one now with the decorative embellishment of movement. Even the word "pictorialize" suggests that a process of direct lifting and relocation of a stable and knowable meaning from linguistic expression to pictorial form is possible. Or, to borrow Dudley Andrew's later terms, it "presume[s] the global signified of the original to be separable from its text if one believes it can be approximated by other sign clusters" (Andrew, 1984: 101). The more anxious, and consequently the more insistent end of the public discourse about literary filmmaking in the early cinema period, is, in effect, predi-cated upon just such a presumption of a text's meaning residing in something beyond, or separate from, the specificity of its medium of expression. To follow the logic of such a presumption, meaning may then be amenable to extraction from the particular mode of expression through which it was previously delivered (novel, play, biblical account) to be parceled up and more or less equally deliverable through an adjusted mode of expression (in this case, a film). According to such a premise, the uninterrupted transmission of signification from word to (animated) image was, therefore, a perfectly feasible ambition.

It is understandable that such an upbeat, if uninterrogated, position should have been rhetorically seductive for filmmakers working with literary source material in which the community felt some significant investment. In the main, however, it may have guided their own filmmaking practice rather less than it did the justifica-tory discussions of the films in the trade press (though the deliberate "stylistic retardation" (Keil, 1992: 112) of Olcott's *From the Manger to the Cross* makes this film a notable exception in this respect). Indeed, for the marketing men and trade reviewers tasked with reassuring the public about the worth of the adaptive enter-prise, the rhetoric of transcriptive "fidelity" as evidenced in "animated novels," cinematic Gospels, and "pictorialized" literature must sometimes have seemed not just seductive but imperative. The "global signified of the original" was, however, at no point in this process a stable entity, and the appropriative intervention of other "sign clusters" (in this case through the communicative medium of film) inevitably worked its work to recast and remake the material in defiance of attempts to deny its interpretive involvement.

As the transitional era segued into that of the feature film (post c.1913), filmmakers and reviewers became braver about broadcasting the nature of the contemporary interventions that were in any case being made as an integral and inevitable part of the adaptation process. A comparison between *Oliver Twist* releases across this period is illuminating in this respect. Whereas the 1912 Bentley release had been described in terms of (a) its recognizable rendering of the detail of the Dickens novel that "practically everyone" already knew, and (b) its faithful engagements with Cruikshank's illustrations, the 1916 *Oliver Twist* from U.S. production company Famous Players-Lasky was promotionally reviewed for its British release in the following terms:

> [T]he Lasky "Oliver Twist" . . . was, of course, intended primarily, and will be appraised ultimately as an ornate and finished work of art. . . . The plot has been slightly adapted, it is true, to meet the demands of the screen, but such alterations are entirely justifiable and indeed inevitable. Although it will appeal strongly by its self-contained dramatic interest, even to those who have not read the novel, Lasky's "Oliver Twist" impresses us mainly as a notable, beautiful, and comprehensive illustrated version *de luxe* of the original. From a purely pictorial point of view, it is perhaps the most striking Lasky film we remember. It is a series of noble studies in black-and-white, worthy of Brangwyn, but etched in living material. Almost every scene is a notable piece of composition, and in its examples of the bold, strong use of light and shade it is a work of pictorial art of which no painter would need to be ashamed ("The Lasky 'Oliver Twist'," 1917).

This film, in line with the earlier Dickens releases, is still being configured as an "illustrated version *de luxe* of the original".[8] However, the Bentley film's appeal to a public armed with narrative foreknowledge has given way here to a film which is declared autonomously intelligible "even to those who have not read the novel"; and an audience imagined as caring deeply about the levels of fidelity to the original has been replaced by a film in which the plot has "been slightly adapted" in ways that are "entirely justifiable and indeed inevitable." Moreover the conservative nostalgia of the Cruickshank reference that the earlier *Oliver Twist* had inspired has ceded to the suggestion that the use of "light and shade" in this film specifically calls to mind the work of the progressive, contemporary Anglo-Welsh multimedia artist Frank Brangwyn (1867–1956), known more for his contemporary and visually challenging approach to his subjects than for a respectful or sentimental interest in nineteenth-century pathos or a draughtsman-like interest in nineteenth-century realism. The adjustment of artistic allegiance as perceived across these reviews signals a shift in the interpretive priorities of the adaptive approach of the period more generally – from a process of detailed reconstructive homage to one of more freely licensed, creative engagement.

"The Great Art of the Lecturer": Literary Films "Explained"

Above I discussed how adapted narratives for film in the pioneering and transitional years of early cinema were often constructed by a series of strung-together "moments" that might or might not follow on fluently from each other, and might or might not add up to a story that was autonomously intelligible. Through into the transitional era, I argued, films adapted from literary sources "continued to depend upon an audience's familiarity with the original, or upon its access to other sources of information beyond the film, to become meaningful in narrative terms." One of those supplementary "sources of information" upon which audiences could sometimes rely in order to make sense of films was the presence of a live film lecturer in the exhibition venue. Where present, it was the lecturer's job to explain and enliven the moving pictures by means of a running commentary (see Altman, 2004: 133–55).

The "craze" (Musser, 1990a: 264) for employing a "narrator," "lecturer," or "explainer" in those picture house venues that could afford such a thing was at its height between 1907 and 1912 – that is, as story films were getting longer (two- and then three-reelers) and more complicated, but not necessarily yet always autonomously intelligible. In those cases where the triangulated relationship between players on the screen, lecturer, and picture-goers worked well, the lecturer's mediating presence could provide a more intimate conduit into the subject viewed, helping to set the scene, sketch the history, voice the parts, and make the drama *live* in ways sensitively attuned to the artistry of the production, the twists and turns of the developing story and the interpretive needs of the particular assembled audience. Most of all, he could smooth over narrative ellipses and the stop–start progress of successive *tableaux* by weaving a series of on-screen "moments" into a continuous narrative and so the succession of scenes into a cohesive fictional *world*. About the 1909 release of *Oliver Twist*, I claimed above that "Vitagraph did not need to invest in supernumerary plot-clarifying transitions between the 'peak' moments" because they could trade explicitly on their audiences' existing knowledge of the plot to make sense of the film. This was true, but it was also the case that production companies, Vitagraph included, specifically came to trade additionally upon the anticipated presence of a lecturer in many of their exhibition venues in the way in which they constructed their film narratives. That is, they could depend upon a supplementary source of explication being available to provide the links across their own narrative gaps – negotiating the transitions between Oliver in the workhouse and Oliver meeting the Artful Dodger in the 1909 Vitagraph *Oliver Twist*, for example, with an improvised or scripted "filler" narration. Some companies even published scripts to accompany their more culturally aspirational film releases for the use of local lecturers.

Where, however, the triangulated relationship between players on the screen, lecturer, and picture-goers worked less well, or the lecturer was less proficient, his mediating presence could sometimes prove an active impediment to an appreciation of the production, an obtrusive obstacle to an audience's enjoyment of the pictures or simply a diversionary side-show (Buchanan, 2009: 12). Since a lecturer's manner of delivery could decisively affect an audience's experience of the films viewed, commentators were keen to establish a set of performance benchmarks to which lecturers should aspire. In August 1908, with characteristic clarity and emphasis, W. Stephen Bush – the prominent American commentator on the movies and himself a lecturer available for hire on the East Coast – laid out the ground rules as he saw them:

> [A] good, descriptive and well-delivered lecture is . . . much appreciated by the people. . . . What, then, are the requirements of such a lecture? What are the requisite qualifications of the lecturer? An easy and perfect command of the English language is the first essential requirement. A clear, resonant voice, trained in public speaking, is the next. Some skill in elocution, rising, when occasion offers, to the heights of eloquence, is likewise indispensable. . . . The great art of the lecturer consists in making the picture plain and at the same time attractive. To achieve this, his language, while absolutely correct and free from the slightest blemish of slang or vulgarity, should be plain and simple. There are points of power and beauty in very many pictures, which appeal strongly to any artistic temperament, and to bring these out forcefully and effectively is the business of the lecturer (Bush, 1908: 136–7).

The ideal lecturer for Bush was both articulate and erudite and this vision of the refinement of the ideal lecturer was in tune with the industry's burgeoning "uplift movement" which was to find increasingly insistent expression over the next few years on both sides of the Atlantic. The uplift movement was designed to counter the charges of scurrility and degeneracy so often thrown at the industry in response to its history (salacious mutoscope reels), choice of subjects (sex and violence remaining popular sells), and suspect exhibition venues (whose darkened auditoria were thought to encourage vice of every sort). In the face of considerable negative publicity from influential quarters, prestige literary sources were vigorously harnessed and promoted by the film industry as key players in the campaign to overhaul its reputation and respectabilize its social standing. The lecturer's identity, dignity, and the air of cultured sophistication his presence could bring to the moving picture show, in collaboration with the elevated and allegedly elevating character of the films themselves, could help to assert the educative and edifying tone of the industry more generally. In effect, therefore, the lecturer was invited to fulfill a double role, combining the functional requirement to clarify a particular film with the symbolic requirement to legitimize the event of its exhibition.

As a potentially useful resource for other lecturers (and a small money-spinner for himself), Bush published some of his own independently produced lecture scripts – including for films on biblical subjects and for an adaptation of Balzac's novel *La Grande Bretèche* (Bush, 1910: 19). He also expressed his active disapproval of those less-than-generous exhibitors, as he saw them, who left picture-goers "bewildered"

by showing them a Shakespeare film, for example, *without* live simultaneous commentary (Bush, 1908: 136). While some audiences for Shakespeare films were denied
the additional boon of a good lecture, however, others hit the jackpot in this respect.
Through early 1913, for example, audiences for some screenings of the Shakespeare
Film Company's early feature-length *Richard III* (dir. James Keane, 1912)[9] in some
exhibition venues on the East Coast of the United States were made privy to an
accompanying lecture and recitation given by Frederick Warde, the famous stage
classical actor who himself starred in the film (Buchanan, 2009: 10–14). Warde was
known for his mellifluous voice as well as his strong physical presence and, given
his own distinguished stage background, it must have been a pleasure for him, as
well as for his audiences, to witness the intermedial reuniting of famous body with
famous voice in the exhibition space for his screen performance as Richard III.

Warde – a rare celebrity high point on the film lecture circuit – was employed to
give an unrivalled boost to the film he had himself starred in just as the practice of
"lecturing to pictures" was on the wane. By 1913/14, other narrative, aesthetic,
performance, and commercial agendas had combined to configure the presence of a
lecturer a symbolic admission that the cinematic images themselves lacked sufficient
clarity or eloquence to be able to communicate without supplementation. As popular,
and sometimes as narratively necessary, as he had been through the transitional era,
the figure of the lecturer had become, in effect, an industry anachronism.

With his demise, films had to shoulder their own story-telling obligations
without external assistance. The result was a coming-of-age for the industry and,
in particular, for the industry's approach to literary adaptations which had been
some of the chief beneficiaries (and principal victims) of the lecturer's art. Through
the latter half of the silent era (post-1913), and in amongst more ordinary fare, the
film industry went on to produce many literary adaptations of vigor, clarity, imagination and considerable influence. From the provocative casting of Theda Bara in
Romeo and Juliet (1916) to the delicious eeriness of Hitchcock's *The Lodger* (1926);
from the brilliantly executed actor doubling and touching introspection of Fox's *A
Tale of Two Cities* (1917) to the entertaining excess of Cecil B. DeMille's *The Ten
Commandments* (1923); from the comically nuanced performance of Asta Nielsen in
Hamlet (1920) to the uncompromising spectacle of MGM's *Ben Hur* (1925); from
the dramatic ambition of Pastrone's *Cabiria* (1914) to the dreamy extravagance of
Douglas Fairbanks' *The Thief of Bagdad* (1924); from the titillating spirituality
of Blanche Sweet in D. W. Griffith's *Judith of Bethulia* (1914) to the striking expressionist aesthetic of F. W. Murnau's *Nosferatu* (1922)[10] – the silent era witnessed
literary adaptations of dynamism, invention, visual drama, emotional weight and
interpretive import. But, as my select list of some personal adaptation highlights
from the era also suggests, these resist homogenizing claims, collectively presenting
a sample snapshot of filmmaking in the period nearly as varied in tone and character
as the broader cinema histories from which they emerged and to which they
vibrantly contributed.

NOTES

1   King John is commercially available on the BFI DVD *Silent Shakespeare* (hereafter *Silent Shakespeare*).

2   Though predominantly true, there were exceptions. *Scrooge; or, Marley's Ghost* (Paul's Animatograph Works: dir. W. R. Booth, 1901), for example, was 620 feet in length on release, with a runtime of c. eleven minutes, and ambitious in terms of narrative coherence. It is commercially available on the BFI DVD *Dickens Before Sound* (hereafter *Dickens Before Sound*).

3   The Vitagraph *Oliver Twist* is commercially available on *Dickens Before Sound*.

4   George du Maurier was both author and illustrator of *Trilby* (1894).

5   A print of the Bentley *Oliver Twist* is available to view at the Library of Congress, Washington DC. The Bentley *David Copperfield* is commercially available on *Dickens Before Sound*. The other titles are presumed lost.

6   The Clarendon *Tempest* is commercially available on *Silent Shakespeare*.

7   Kalem's *From the Manger to the Cross* is commercially available on Image Entertainment DVD.

8   The name of the reviewer is not given. However, it seems likely, both from probable review allocation practice on one trade journal, and from the similarity of the terms employed across reviews, that this was the same reviewer who had also previously been assigned Bentley's earlier Dickens films.

9   *Richard III* is commercially available on Kino International DVD.

10 The 1916 Fox *Romeo and Juliet* starring Bara is presumed lost (Buchanan, 2009: 202–16); Hitchcock's *The Lodger* (1926) is commercially available (GMVS); the Fox *A Tale of Two Cities* (1917) starring William Farnum as both Carton and Darnay is intermittently available (Masterpiece Collection VHS) (see Buchanan with Newhouse, 2009); Cecil B. DeMille's *The Ten Commandments* (1923) is commercially available in a boxed set with the 1956 version (Paramount Home Entertainment); the Asta Nielsen *Hamlet* (1920) is available (Edition Filmmuseum) (see Howard, 2009; Buchanan, 2009: 217–40); MGM's *Ben Hur* (1925) is available in a boxed set with the 1959 version (Warner Brothers Home Entertainment); Pastrone's *Cabiria* (1914) is available on Region 1 DVD (Kino); Raoul Walsh's *The Thief of Bagdad* (1924) starring Fairbanks is commercially available (Elstree Hill); D. W. Griffith's *Judith of Bethulia* (1914) starring Blanche Sweet is commercially available (Bach Films) (see Buchanan, forthcoming); Murnau's *Nosferatu* (1922) is multiply commercially available (including on Elstree Hill).

REFERENCES

Altman, Rick. *Silent Film Sound*. New York: Columbia University Press, 2004.

Andrew, Dudley. *Concepts in Film Theory*. Oxford: Oxford University Press, 1984.

The Bioscope, 22:379, January 15, 1914, 217.

Brown, Richard and Barry Anthony. *A Victorian Film Enterprise: The History of the British Biograph and Mutoscope Company, 1897–1915*. Trowbridge: Flicks Books, 1999.

Buchanan, Judith. "Gospel Narratives on Silent Film." In *The Cambridge Companion to Literature on Screen*. Eds. Deborah Cartmell and Imelda Whelehan. Cambridge: Cambridge University Press, 2007, 47–60.

Buchanan, Judith with Alex Newhouse. "Sanguine Mirages, Cinematic Dreams: Things Seen and Things Imagined in the 1917 Fox *A Tale of Two Cities*." In *Charles Dickens, "A Tale of Two Cities" and the French Revolution*. Eds. Colin Jones, Josephine McDonagh, and Jon Mee. Basingstoke: Palgrave Macmillan, 2009, 146–65.

Buchanan, Judith. *Shakespeare on Silent Film: An Excellent Dumb Discourse*. Cambridge: Cambridge University Press, 2009.

Buchanan, Judith. "Judith's Vampish Virtue and its Double Market Appeal." In *The Ancient World in Silent Cinema*. Eds. Maria Wyke and Pantelis Michelakis. Cambridge: Cambridge University Press, forthcoming 2013.

Bush, W. Stephen. "Lectures on Moving Pictures." *Moving Picture World*, 3:8, 1908, 136–7.

Bush, W. Stephen. "Special Lectures on Notable Films." *Moving Picture World*, 6:1, 1910, 19.

Gifford, Denis. *Books and Plays in Films 1896–1915: Literary, Theatrical and Artistic Sources of the First Twenty Years of Motion Pictures*. London: McFarland and Mansell, 1991.

Gunning, Tom. "An Aesthetic of Astonishment: Early Film and the (In)credulous Spectator." *Art and Text*, 34, 1989, 31–45.

Gunning, Tom. "The Intertextuality of Early Cinema." In *A Companion to Literature and Film*. Eds. Robert Stam and Alessandra Raengo. Oxford: Blackwell, 2004, 127–43.

Herbert, Stephen, Colin Harding and Simon Popple. Eds. *Victorian Film Catalogues: A Facsimile Collection*. London: The Projection Box, 1996.

Howard, Tony. *Women as Hamlet: Performance and Interpretation in Theatre, Film and Fiction*. Cambridge: Cambridge University Press, 2009.

Keil, Charles. "'From the Manger to the Cross': The New Testament Narrative and the Question of Stylistic Retardation." In *Une Invention du Diable? Cinéma des Premiers Temps et Religion*. Eds. Roland Cosandey, André Gaudreault,

and Tom Gunning. Sainte-Foy: Les Presses de l'Université Laval, 1992, 112–20.

"The Lasky 'Oliver Twist': J. D. Walker Presents a Genuine Masterpiece." *The Bioscope*, February 1, 1917, 429.

Lindsay, Vachel. *The Art of the Motion Picture*, Rev. edn. 1922. New York: Liveright Publishing Corporation, 1970.

MacFarlane, Brian. Ed. *The Encyclopedia of British Film*. London: Methuen, 2003.

McKernan, Luke. "A Scene – 'King John' – Now Playing at Her Majesty's Theatre." In *Moving Performance: British Stage and Screen, 1890s–1920s*. Eds. Linda Fitzsimmons and Sarah Street. Trowbridge: Flicks Books, 2000, 56–68.

Merritt, Russell. "Rescued from a Perilous Nest: D. W. Griffith's Escape from Theatre into Film." *Cinema Journal*, 21:1, 1981, 2–30.

Monaco, James. *How to Read a Film: Movies, Media, and Beyond*, 4th edn. Oxford: Oxford University Press, 2009.

Musser, Charles. "The Nickelodeon Era Begins: Establishing the Framework for Hollywood's Mode of Representation." In *Early Cinema: Space, Frame, Narrative*. Ed. Thomas Elsaesser. London: BFI Publishing, 1990a, 256–73.

Musser, Charles. *The Emergence of Cinema: The American Screen to 1907*. New York: Simon Schuster and Prentice-Hall, 1990b.

"'Oliver Twist': The Hepworth Company's Splendid Long Film." *The Bioscope*, 16:302, July 25, 1912, 279, 281.

"Review of New Films." *New York Dramatic Mirror*, December 12, 1908, 6.

Uricchio, William and Roberta Pearson. *Reframing Culture: The Case of the Vitagraph Quality Films*. Princeton, NJ: Princeton University Press, 1993.

2
Writing on the Silent Screen

Gregory Robinson

The use of intertitles in silent cinema to further the narrative or convey dialogue is one of the cinematic arts that died almost entirely with the adoption of synchronized sound. However, while speaking characters and voiceover narration certainly replaced much of the need for intertitles, they did not replace all of the functions that filmed text provided. When text and image inhabit the same narrative but not the same narrative space, a productive tension often results, where image and text "speak" both to the audience and to each other. This dynamic is one of the pleasures that modern viewers experience when they rediscover silent cinema. Academically, the same dynamic presents a path for exploration. For example, metaphors such as "reading a film" or "literature on screen" are popular ways of considering the relationship of text and moving images, but with intertitles, the same concepts appear almost literal: audiences are actually (rather than figuratively) reading the screen. Guided by the conventional wisdom that the best stories need no text at all, most silent filmmakers tended to ignore the potential this combination offered and chose to keep text safely in the margins of the moving images. Yet, as with any convention, there were exceptions, experiments where filmmakers challenged the accepted role of text and inverted its supplemental status. This chapter tells the story of these experiments, the writing on the screen that played an essential role in developing the unique character of silent cinema.

A Companion to Literature, Film, and Adaptation, First Edition. Edited by Deborah Cartmell.
© 2012 Blackwell Publishing Ltd. Published 2012 by Blackwell Publishing Ltd.

Step Write Up – A Cinema of Textual Attractions

Pinpointing the absolute first use of printed text in silent cinema is a difficult task, considering the instability of early films and the early attitudes towards preservation. One attempt comes from *The British Film Catalogue 1895–1985,* which notes that R. W. Paul's *Our New General Servant* (1898) is the first British film to feature intertitles (Gifford, 2000: 3). At 320 feet, it was remarkably long for its time, a feat enabled by using intertitles to link its four scenes together. Another British filmmaker, G. A. Smith, provides two more early examples. His 1898 film, *The Santa Claus,* features a single filmed title card with the film's name in large, decorative letters, and his 1900 film, *The House That Jack Built,* uses an intertitle reading "reversed." This single word signals the film's "trick," where the toy house that was destroyed in the opening sequence is now shown backwards, making it appear as if the house were being rebuilt.

In the same year, a particularly fascinating and innovative use of text in film occurs in Cecil Hepworth's *How It Feels to Be Run Over*, a forty-second film depicting a car crash. Like many early films, it self-consciously plays with the boundaries of film and reality; the car literally crashes into the camera, but it figuratively crashes into the theater viewers. As the collision occurs, the screen goes blank for a moment, and as the image shifts from the outside world to the mind's eye, a series of punctuation marks appears ("? ? !!! !"), followed by a burst of jagged, flickering text: "Oh! Mother <u>will</u> be pleased." The words are jagged, fast, and scratched directly into the celluloid, giving them an eerie appearance (see Figure 2.1).

Surprisingly, Hepworth did not seem to think that the text in his film was anything special. In his biography, he notes only that the film was particularly difficult because it was shot outside (Hepworth, 1951: 55). The catalogue produced by the Hepworth Company dismisses the text as the "stars" one sees after a traumatic accident (Hepworth & Co., 1903: 26). Yet, several contemporary film scholars have

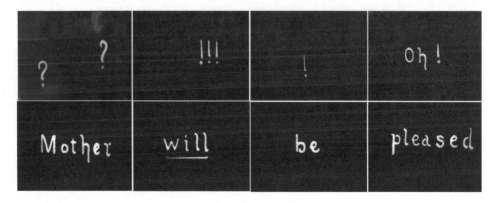

Figure 2.1 The ending text of Hepworth's *How It Feels to Be Run Over*. Dir. Cecil M. Hepworth. UK: Hepworth, 1900.

written lengthy treatises on the film and its curious ending, speculating as to what the words might mean.[1] They all focus on a single question: Why would mother be pleased? The fact that debate continues speaks to the power and potential of filmed text to inspire viewers as much as, if not more than, filmed images do.

Furthermore, the very shape and presentation of the words suggest a cinematic possibility that contemporary cinema rarely explores. Historically, words, the symbol of foundation, stability, and law, exist in books, and remain in the place where they were created until their host medium is destroyed. The end of *How It Feels* highlights a new textual power: mobility. The text does not temporally exist for as long as the reader wishes it to do so. Instead, the will of the projector replaces the will of the reader. Movies give text a mobile surface and a newfound freedom, the ability to appear and disappear without the reader's control. In this case, the words flash onto the screen so quickly that it is almost impossible to read them at a comfortable pace. The entire phrase has appeared and disappeared in less than two seconds. Although there is no evidence to suggest that Hepworth was making a statement about the possibilities of text within his emerging medium, it seems to have coincidentally emerged with the accident the film implies. Eighty years after *How It Feels*, Michael Snow, one of Canada's most important experimental filmmakers, shot *So Is This*, a work made entirely of filmed text. This challenging film presents words in a way that is remarkably similar to the ending text of *How It Feels*, showing one word at a time, using large white lettering on a black background that completely fills the frame. The resemblance becomes truly striking when *So Is This* increases its pace, matching not only the style but also the speed of *How It Feels* and challenging the reader's visual control of the text in exactly the same way.

Perhaps what the text *means* in *How It Feels* is not as important as what the text *does*. Both the crash and the text attract our attention; the words seem to crash into the viewer with the same force and intensity as the filmed car. The text does little, if anything, to further the film's narrative in the manner that conventional intertitles do. However, it does a great deal to enhance the film's overall effect of shock, horror, and black humor.

As film evolved in the silent period, filmmakers were progressively more interested in integrating text into the film so cleanly that a viewer could watch a film without paying much attention to the fact that reading was involved. Text grew smaller and more standardized. Conventions emerged, allowing viewers to intuitively understand the difference between spoken and expository titles. These conventions, which are now definitive of silent cinema, sharply contrast the textual presentation of films such as *How It Feels*. In the earliest days of movies, text was untamed, a feature evident in *Uncle Tom's Cabin* (1903) where the text's exuberant presentation flies in the face of the tale itself. The movie depicts one of America's greatest horrors, but the intertitles (which cover the entire screen in large, hand-painted letters) are unapologetic. Other early texts, including Ferdinand Zecca's bright red-lettered intertitles, display the same sort of disregard for the conventions that later developed. They refuse to do what later critics attempted to force text to do: quietly help the image along without breaking the narrative flow. Instead, these intertitles shout. In the process, they give us a hint of what cinema could have been if it had taken a different turn.

Filming Text

It is worth noting that intertitles were not the only way of mixing text with moving images in the late nineteenth and early twentieth century. Amongst other tools, exhibitionists often projected slides to introduce films, offer messages (e.g., "Ladies, please remove your hats"), or assist with narrative continuity. Early exhibitors could purchase these slides from film suppliers, or the exhibitor could create them. Since slides were not included in the cost of movies, there was a financial incentive for the exhibitor to make his own. Inserting material into movies seems alien by contemporary standards, but whereas modern films are the artistic property of the studios, movies in the early period served more as raw material for the exhibitors. The first real "stars" of moving pictures were these exhibitors, who had a great deal of creative freedom with the films they either bought or rented from film exchanges. Like vaudevillian showmen, their role was to turn films into a spectacle for their viewers (Musser, 1991: 123). Therefore, exhibitors often ran a movie projector and a slide projector concurrently, and a skilled projectionist could switch between the two quite quickly.

For an excellent example of one use of slides (and even a shot of an exhibitor), see Edwin Porter's 1902 *Uncle Josh at the Moving Picture Show*. The film begins with Uncle Josh (a repeating character in Porter films) on the left, watching movies on the right. The slide "The Edison Projecting Kinetoscope" appears in large letters, filling the screen-inside-the-screen. Showing the company name, rather than the film, highlights the practice of billing the equipment and the name rather than a theme or an overarching title. The practice also makes an important statement about the way text can act to assert ownership. *Uncle Josh at the Moving Picture Show* recreates R. W. Paul's *Countryman and the Cinematograph* (1901) scene for scene, using Edison's shorts. The slides, however, make a point of identifying every work as an Edison product, staking a claim to it, and discouraging any later efforts to remake the film. Porter used a distinctive font to introduce internal films until 1906, when die-cast letters replaced the hand-drawn cards. It is a unique font that stamped an identifiable ownership on a film simply by its appearance, and even Porter films that did not use intertitles often used the same font in internal signage, such as on the door of the dentist's office in *Laughing Gas* (1907). In this fashion, the text itself, even without specific copyright language, became a symbol of ownership.

The second slide in *Uncle Josh* that introduces an internal film reads "Parisian Dancer." It is cleverly labeled to look like "Parisian Danger," which is exactly what it turns out to be for Uncle Josh. When the film begins, he jumps out of his seat, excited by the provocative dance he sees on the screen. After a short clip of the dancer, another slide is projected, "The Black Diamond Express," and the 1896 Edison short about an oncoming train begins. Uncle Josh, caught up in the illusion and pulled out of his seat by the dancer, thinks the train is real and jumps out of the way. The final title reads "A Country Couple," and is followed by a comic narrative of a couple who attempt to kiss, which gets Josh so upset that he attacks the screen. There is a rhythm created by the title/scene/title/scene structure that *Uncle Josh* uses, but it does not provide thematic continuity. The slides tell us what to expect, and the clips show how that expectation is enacted, but each clip is thematically disparate. When filmmakers began to ship their films with filmed intertitles already in place, the title/clip pattern displayed in *Uncle Josh at the Moving Picture Show* remained essentially constant. The only difference was that the titles were now part of the reel, and they linked together a more cohesive narrative. Three early examples from three different countries appeared nearly concurrently. In France, Ferdinand Zecca used this pattern in *Victimes de l'alcoolisme* (1902) and *Ali Baba et les quarante voleurs* (1902). In the latter, bold red letters on a black background give each section a title, much like chapters in a book: "Seseme Ouvre Tou/Open Sesame", "Le Tresor des voleurs/The Robber's Treasure," etc. Following each title, a short scene occurs, shot from a fixed camera. The following year (1903), English director George Albert Smith released *Dorothy's Dream*, which used filmed text to introduce each scene. This work may have influenced American director Edwin Porter, who released *Uncle Tom's Cabin* the same year and used filmed text in a similar manner (Musser, 1991: 243). Each scene is introduced with an ornate title that fills the entire screen with giant, hand-drawn lettering, more like a poster or a main title than the tamer intertitles that came to be the norm in later silent cinema. These intertitles, such as "St. Clair Defends Uncle Tom" and "Tom Refuses to Flog Emaline," offer a hint as to what will follow and then allow the images to provide the details. In part, this was possible because there was some expectation on the part of the filmmakers that moviegoers would have already been familiar with the story.

In a 1903 Edison catalogue, this practice is cited as a technical achievement: "In this film we have made a departure from the old method of dissolving one scene into another by inserting announcements with brief descriptions as they appear in succession" (Bordwell, Staiger, and Thompson, 1985: 98). This kind of intertitle, often called a "leader" since it leads the scene, was gradually replaced with dialogue titles and short continuity titles that blended into the narrative more seamlessly. Ironically, unlike dialogue and continuity titles, leaders still enjoy some use in contemporary movies. Avant-garde filmmaker Jean-Luc Godard uses leaders in films like *Masculin Féminin: 15 Faits Précis* (1966) and *Le Weekend* (1967) primarily to disrupt rather than clarify, providing an example of how the accepted role of intertitles can be altered for artistic purposes. Conversely, contemporary films such as David Fincher's *Se7en* (1995), Quentin Tarantino's *Kill Bill* (2003), and Wes Anderson's *The Fantastic Mr. Fox* (2009) use leaders that function exactly as the earliest leaders did: they break the action and provide "chapter titles" for the various sections. Interestingly, the leaders in these movies are not particularly evocative or "literary," but they are functional. They provide some order to nonlinear plot elements as well as stylistic pauses. In doing so, they use text in a way that was never replaced after the integration of synchronized sound, and their financial success shows that intertitles can still function in mainstream works without necessitating the artistic challenges found in more avant-garde uses of intertitles.

Textual Standardization and Experimentation

Ultimately, what this use of text provides Fincher, Tarantino, and Anderson is a way of putting in order what audiences may perceive as a series of unconnected images. There is some evidence that audiences wanted this order quite early in cinema's history, starting around 1906 when movies began to grow in both length and narrative complexity. The vast majority of films in the first decade of the twentieth century used intertitles sparingly or not at all, relying on either the audience's knowledge of the story or a paid employee in the theater who could explain the films as the images appeared. In 1908, an early viewer named W. M. Rhodes wrote in to *Moving Picture World* proposing that if films could provide text at every "20 or 30 feet (or at every place on film wherein an explanation was necessary), then the theater manager would have no use for a lecturer" (1908: 143). He was promptly lambasted in an editorial reply, which argued that this act would unnecessarily make films more expensive and that a "perfectly thought out plot, well put together, should tell its own story" ("Editorial Reply", 1908: 143). The editor's response summarizes the most commonly adopted stance taken by the trade journals and the screenwriting manuals of the early twentieth century: the best use of intertitles was the most minimal use of intertitles. That said, not all critics shared this opinion, and many altered their opinions or established different positions for different genres. In Torey Liepa's excellent survey of this debate, he notes "that trade criticism not only argued for or against intertitles, but also advocated particular intertitle styles, critiquing some forms and applauding others" (2008: 143). The filmmakers' attitudes varied even within particular studios. For example, Edison's *The Seven Ages* (1905) uses the same kind of hand-painted, poster-like titles that were present in earlier Edison films such as *Uncle Tom's Cabin*, *The European Rest Cure*, and *The Ex-Convict*. The same year, Edison films such as *The Life of an American Policeman* and *The Miller's Daughter* began using a more standardized model, where die-cut letters are attached to a felt board and displayed under the Edison logo. These titles appear less frequently than previously used intertitles (often only for the main title).

A third approach was introduced by Edison director Edwin Porter, who began experimenting with moving text in intertitles, a process he called "jumble announcements." Films like *How Jones Lost His Roll* (1905) and *The Whole Dam Family and the Dam Dog* (1905) use a stop–action technique to make die-cut letters move into place and form words. Porter uses the same technique with great success in *College Chums* (1907), where two characters are superimposed over the image of a city. When they speak, the swirling letters travel across an image of the city from person to person. The letters move in a fashion that is evocative of the characters' emotions, and as they begin to argue, the words speed up. As their argument grows more heated, the letters start crashing into one another, physically enacting a metaphorical battle of words.

Despite Porter's innovations, it was the more conventional option (mechanically rather than artistically produced intertitles) that came to dominate cinema in the 1910s. Historian and former title writer Terry Ramsaye notes that, around 1910, every 1,000-foot reel of film averaged about 80 feet of intertitle, or 8%. Many of these intertitles were made to be reused in multiple films and "included all such vital expressions as, 'The next day,' 'Ten years elapse,' 'Happy ever afterward,' 'Forgiven,' 'Wedding bells,' and 'One hour later'" (Stempel, 2000: 36). In an article in the *New York Times* entitled "Title Work Years Ago," Jack Natteford tells of his experience in the early 1910s as an intertitle writer, which he describes as "the period of the 'that night' and 'the following day' period of title writing."[2] As an experiment, he attempted to break away from this school and compose poetic titles for an animated film. In this early attempt to use the literary over the straightforward, the intertitles flopped. Noting an overall lack of audience sophistication, Natteford vowed never to stray from straightforward titles again (1923: X5).

Around 1910, another change in titling was also taking place: dialogue intertitles. Although titles that reproduced speech exist as early as Zacca's *Ali Baba et les quarante voleurs* (1902) and Edison's *The Convict* (1904), the dominant intertitle type from 1900–1910 was an expository title that helped establish narrative continuity. A cinemetric study performed by Torey Liepa shows that dialogue titles accounted for 2% of the total text found in his sample set of films from 1908.[3] This number rises to 18% by 1910, 30% by 1913, and 50% by 1916 (Liepa, 2008: 108). In a similar survey, Barry Salt found that in his sample the percentage of dialogue titles had risen to 50% by 1913 (1992: 108). In both instances, the shift is dramatic. After 1913, dialogue titles typically appeared more frequently, whereas continuity titles appeared less often, presumably because dialogue titles furthered the film's narrative in a way that was ostensibly less obtrusive.

Although dialogue titles were a functional method of representing speech, there were some interesting attempts to do so using alternative methods. Two fascinating examples come from Charles Felton Pidgin, a statistician and novelist who had patented several devices for computing statistical data. In 1916, he submitted a patent for a method of replicating dialogue in silent films using special balloons. These balloons had text written on them and, at the appropriate time, the actors would blow into the balloons, inflating them at the pace of regular speech and allowing text to "unfold" just as normal dialogue does. Pidgin's justification is as follows: "It often becomes necessary to add to the pictures themselves certain features, words, letters, and so forth, which are shown on a separate screen. This

separation of speech and action must necessarily be ineffective to a great degree"
(Pidgin, 1917: 1). Pidgin's solution seems a bit comical by today's standards, as
does his second device, which attaches to the actor's head and uses a pump hidden
under the actor's arm. When the actor was ready to speak, he could move his
arm in such a way as to activate the pump and inflate the words (see Figures 2.2
and 2.3).

Not surprisingly, having actors blow up balloons with their mouths or pump
their arms during dramatic moments never found its way into actual movies.
However, Pidgin's premise that speech could be represented as a balloon seemed to
solve one of the intertitle's problems, in that the balloon could exist on the screen
with the actor. As early as 1906, two Biograph films, *Nurse Wanted* and *Looking for
John Smith*, attempted to use speech balloons, although Biograph ultimately abandoned the technique. Animated shorts such as the 1917 *Abie Kabibble Outwits His
Rivals* and the 1920 *Mutt and Jeff Go on Strike* also experimented with dialogue
balloons, but even these works, which ostensibly had more graphic freedom, tended
to use intertitles just as film did. Attempts by later movies to use the dialogue
balloon idea were rare, but worth noting for their attempt to break the boundaries
of silent film's textual conventions. One small example of a dialogue balloon is used
in a single scene of the 1925 Lon Chaney film *The Unholy Three,* where a parakeet
speaks by way of a nearby ventriloquist. Interestingly, a similar device (albeit
lacking the actual balloon) occurs in Harold Lloyd's 1919 *Just Neighbors,* when a
conversation enacted through intertitles is interrupted by a parrot that appears to
say "Liar" when the word is placed over his head.

The most sustained and oft-cited use of dialogue balloons in silent cinema is
Abraham Schomer's *The Chamber Mystery* (1920), where oval-shaped black balloons
appear onscreen next to the characters who are speaking (see Figure 2.4). Because
the balloons appear to have been created on glass and superimposed between the
camera and the actor, there has to be a cutaway before a character can be shown
again with a dialogue balloon and "speak." A cut must also occur for the dialogue
to end. This makes for a somewhat jumpy presentation of dialogue, in addition to
the distracting shadows cast by the dialogue balloons. When cuts like this are
impossible, the film uses traditional intertitles.

Interestingly enough, audiences did not seem to react positively or negatively to
this innovation. The reviews in *Moving Picture World* and *Exhibitor's Trade Review* are
lackluster, but only mention the film's technical innovation briefly (Deutelbaum,
1975: 20). Judging from these responses, it is possible that this technique, which
seems somewhat absurd by contemporary standards, did not seem nearly as odd to
1920s moviegoers. Given our current acceptance of subtitles in foreign films, one
might question why superimposition over moving images never became more than
a minor gimmick in silent cinema. As *The Chamber Mystery* shows, it is certainly
possible to add words to the screen without halting the flow of the images, and it
is conceivable that audiences could have adjusted just as they had already adjusted
to the use of intertitles.

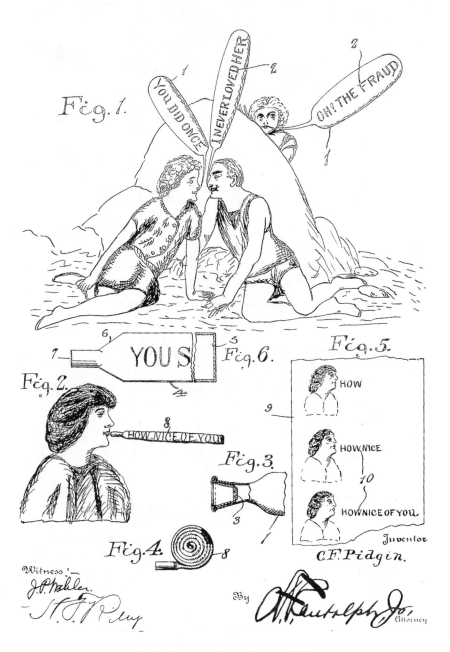

Figure 2.2 Charles Pidgin's inflatable dialogue device. Patent 1917.

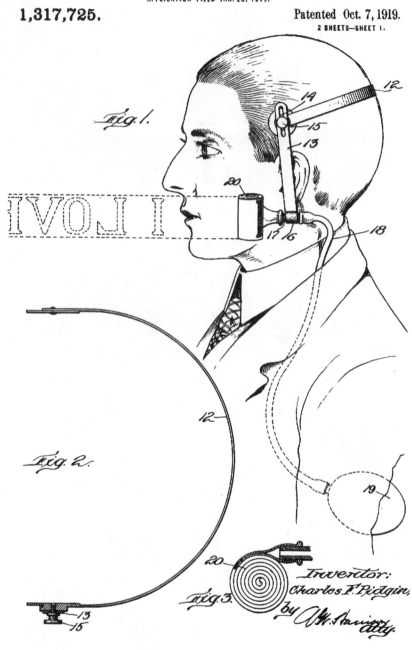

Figure 2.3 Pidgin's revision of his dialogue device. Patent 1917.

Figure 2.4 Dialogue balloons in *The Chamber Mystery*. Dir. Abraham S. Schomer. USA: Schomer-Ross Productions, 1920.

The most likely explanation is a financial one. Intertitles were inexpensive, easy to produce, and accepted by most moviegoers. A separate department of the studio could create them (often after the film was completed) in a way that supported Hollywood's growing trend towards an assembly-line model of production. Furthermore, as international cinema became more important for studio profits, the ability to quickly replace intertitles became increasingly important because a studio could release the same film in multiple countries by simply changing the titles. Finally, intertitles provided a legal space that superimposed text could not, since the studio logos could be placed on each card to establish copyright.

There is little indication that aesthetic considerations played a role in maintaining the intertitle convention. Although using more text had helped establish cinema as a more "respectable" art form by 1915, as evidenced by *Cambiria* (1914) and *Birth of a Nation* (1915), most attitudes towards the use of text were consistent with the editor's 1908 lambasting of W. M. Rhodes in *Moving Picture World*. Echoing this sentiment, two of the earliest books of film criticism that argued for the artistic value of movies, Lindsay's *Art of the Moving Picture* (1915) and Münsterberg's *The Photoplay: A Psychological Study* (1916), claimed that the use of text usually lowers the aesthetic value of a film. Lindsay argued that, while intertitles remained a commercial necessity, "the fewer words printed on the screen the better, and that the ideal film has no words printed on it at all" (Lindsay, 1915: 10). Münsterberg was somewhat more tolerant of leaders that functioned like chapter titles, but his ideal was still pure images. "[Intertitles] have no right to existence" he stated, "in a work of art which is composed of pictures" (Münsterberg, 1916: 201).

The counter to Lindsay and Münsterberg's argument appeared in the form of Anita Loos, a young writer from New York City. She was the single figure bold enough to impress Vachel Lindsay, who claimed that " 'Title writing' remains a commercial necessity. In this field there is but one person who has won distinction – Anita Loos" (Lindsay, 1915: 15). By celebrating text and expressing an opinion that was exactly the opposite of Lindsay and Münsterberg's, she became the intertitle's first champion. With her came a significant counter-movement in film aesthetics: the literary intertitle.

Literary Intertitles and Title Writers

Although D. W. Griffith was accustomed to using intertitles containing a good amount of text,[4] he once famously argued with John Emerson against using text in films, stating that "People don't go to the movies to read. They go to look at pictures" (Norman, 2007: 37). Ironically, Griffith and Emerson were actually discussing the scripts of Anita Loos, whom they had newly hired to write titles, though she had been selling scripts to Griffith since the 1912 film *The New York Hat*. She would soon champion the idea that people *do* go to the movies to read and that, in fact, movies could not succeed as an art form without asking audiences to do so. Her first performative evidence of this claim came in the form of her 1916 Triangle film *His Picture in the Papers*, which starred Douglas Fairbanks as Pete Prindle, the rebellious son of a health food mogul. The intertitles cleverly comment on the film with lines like: "Having banqueted at home, Pete sneaks off to get something to eat." Importantly, the humor is not self-contained in the intertitle, but rather dependent on how those words fit into the context of the film. In this case, the intertitle seems to show rather than tell how Pete does not care much for the food products that are so important to his family, inverting the traditional roles of image and text. In another telling scene, the female lead gets a kiss from Pete after she has recently kissed a vegetarian. The title that follows reads: "Wherein it is shown that beefsteak produces a different style of love-making from prunes." Again, the humor does not rely on the kind of gags that would later come to dominate intertitle writing, but instead comes from a deeper mix of playfulness, double entendre, and poetic presentation.

Audiences appreciated Loos' titles so much that Griffith hired Loos to write intertitles for his epic film *Intolerance*.[5] In the same year, Douglas Fairbanks announced that Loos would be writing the intertitles for all of his films. Fairbanks noted that:

> I have sat through plays by Miss Loos and have heard the audience applaud her subtitles as héartily as the liveliest scenes. There have even been cases I could mention where her comments out-shone the scenes themselves. This has convinced me of the great value of the kind of work she does (Schmidt, 1917: 622).

In the Fairbanks' films *His Picture in the Papers* (1916), *American Aristocracy* (1917), and *Wild and Wooly* (1917), Loos pioneered a bold writing style. It rejects the sparse aesthetic that catered to uneducated audiences in favor of lengthy and frequent titles that are rife with double entendre. More importantly, she stood up to detractors in defense of this approach. Faced with a *New York Times* reporter who adhered to the more conventional minimalism, Loos convincingly argued that images alone simply were not enough to raise the artistic status of cinema. "If the photoplay is to become a fine art," she states, "the author must be permitted to express in words the finer shades of meaning and the subtleties of character which lie too far beneath the surface for pantomime portrayal" ("The Emerson–Loos Way," 1920: X7). Using text like this seems somewhat tame by today's standards, but even as late as 1920, books such as *Careers for Women* were arguing that female title writers ought to write as simply as possible, given that "the proportion of highly educated people who attend picture shows is exceedingly small" (de Lissa Berg, 1920: 338). Loos actively fought against this stereotype. In fact, she seemed to believe that the future of movies depended upon audiences that could actively participate in the viewing process.

In a recent article reexamining Loos' writing, Laura Frost notes that Loos' inter-titles "presumed and even created an active audience to whom they offered a new kind of pleasure: literary visual pleasure" (2010: 297). This "visual pleasure" relied on transforming the supplemental role of intertitles and placing both text and image on equal ground. In a medium that strove for purely visual storytelling, Loos argued that words would actually elevate films rather than detract from them. Her claim is bold and idealistic, but its practice would prove to be a challenge, even to modern audiences.

Unfortunately, Loos' literary style of title writing never found another champion. Few other writers had Loos' gift for mixing text and images, and the critics' demand for a pure, image-driven cinema could not be swayed. Writers who made up for lack of talent with shear bulk and overly dramatic diction became known as the "Rosy-Fingered Dawn" school of title writing, a phrase that implied haughty and archaic intertitles that pretentiously tried to elevate film beyond its lower and middle class audiences.[6] Ultimately, such attempts seemed so pompous that they strengthened arguments for a more minimal use of intertitles.

The style that did more readily appeal to these audiences and did manage to persevere through the end of silent cinema was much closer to the quick, sharp gags of Loos' contemporary, H. M. "Beanie" Walker. In many ways, Walker was Loos' opposite; he was not particularly literary, nor was he a darling of the press. Yet, what he lacked in media exposure, he made up for in bulk and one-liners, an accom-plishment and a skill that earned him the title "Dean of the Art" (Davis, 2008: 378). His style of writing helped establish and codify the rhythm of the comic intertitle so that it became a kind of cliché in silent cinema. It is immediately recognizable in his work in all of the silent Laurel and Hardy films, the silent Little Rascal films, and Harold Lloyd's famous *Safety Last* (1923). Walker's writing pro-vided a shape, a rhythm, and even a tone that could be anticipated, where one line would be relatively straightforward, followed by a dash, and then followed by a line which played off the mock-seriousness of the first, usually with a pun of some sort.

A good example comes from the Laurel and Hardy film *Do Detectives Think?* (1927) where the judge is introduced as: "Judge Foozle had charged the Jury ~ He always charged everything~~." The first line is the "straight" one invoking the judge's role, where the follow-up line twists it into humor with a pun on "charged," implying that the judge prefers credit to cash. As one might imagine, this type of writing was more popular than the somewhat high-brow musings of Loos. The titles served as jokes in themselves, funny even outside of the context of the film. With Walker's help, "title writer" and "gag man" became interchangeable in early magazines and periodicals.

From 1917 to 1929, Walker wrote titles almost exclusively, producing over 100,000 title cards for over 200 films (Davis, 2008: 379). Despite this success, he was not granted a place in title writing's first fraternity, a group that self-consciously played on their role as wordsmiths by calling themselves the "Titular Bishops." Malcolm Stewart Boylan, himself a member, comically describes the group as "Nine men of assorted waistlines, accents, and origins [that] are titling practically all the big pictures." Boylan continues by noting that "Until three years ago, the title writer was a nice young man of no importance. Today he is a personage at the studios, a man to be reckoned with, both before and after payday" (1928: 102). In an earlier article in the *New York Times*, Jack Natteford explains that in the late silent period "hack" title writers wrote the basic titles (e.g., "The Next Day"), while these "literary specialists" were "summoned at the last moment and paid $1,000 or $1,500 for giving just the right verbal flavor to a production" (1923: X5).

Although Natteford refers to these writers as "literary specialists," none of the members of this association came from literary backgrounds. In fact, eight of the nine members had backgrounds in newspaper journalism, a field that empha-sized attention-grabbing headlines. Katherine Hilliker, one of the few female authors to earn recognition as a title writer,[7] notes that

> An excellent training camp for the embryo titler is the local room of a newspaper office, for there, as nowhere else is he taught to prune his garden of literature – his mental sunflowers are cruelly cropped – and the faculty of being able to express much in little is one of the first rules of the titling game (Stempel, 2000: 37).

In this "literary pruning," we see Hollywood's rejection of the philosophy that Loos had attempted to transform into an accepted convention. That said, this rejec-tion did not negate the idea that title writers could be "artists" or "specialists," only that the title writer's art was distinct from the literary author's.

Not surprisingly, most title writers who used the "newspaper headline" model found little external recognition for their work. The one exception was Ralph Spence. His fame derived from his clever and often funny intertitles, such as this character introduction from *Tillie the Toiler* (1917): "B. F. Whipple – a brain worker who had forgotten his tools" and this description of a nightclub from *Orchids and Ermine* (1926): "A good night at the club – where there is nothing pre-war but the chorus." Although he clearly had a talent for comedy, Spence's truly remarkable (and marketable) skill was his ability to work as a "film doctor," someone who could use the right words to take an unsuccessful movie and make it profitable. According to a story in the *New York Times*, the 1920 film *Molly and I* (Fox Studios) had flopped and, as an experiment, the studio agreed to give Spence $150 to rework the titles. Spence changed the film from an emotional drama to a comedy through creative titling, and the film was ultimately successful ("Captioneer Turns Subtle," 1928: 110). Spence promoted himself in this fashion, taking out full-page ads in the *Film Daily Year Book*, with headlines such as "All bad little movies when they die go to Ralph Spence" ("All Bad Little," 1926: 1501). (See Figure 2.5.)

By most accounts, he was the first and only title writer to achieve the kind of "star" status usually reserved for actors. According to *Motion Picture World* he was the "highest-paid title writer in the world at $5/word" (1926: 279). In 1929, he became the first title writer to receive separate billing on theater marquees (Gale, 2003: 389). He lived the lifestyle of a star as well, doing publicity events

Figure 2.5 Ralph Spence. 1926 advertisement in the *Film Daily Year Book*.

with other stars (including a fountain drink making contest with Lew Cody), traveling frequently, and drinking to excess. Oddly, when the nominations were made for the first and only Academy Award for Best Title Writing, Spence was not selected.

Interestingly, most modern viewers are surprised to learn that there actually was an Academy Award given for Best Title Writing. It was awarded during the first Academy Awards Ceremony in 1929. The candidates were George Marion, Jr., Gerald Duffy, and Joseph Farnham, two of whom were members of the Titular Bishops. The writer who was not a member, Gerald Duffy, is the most intriguing nominee. First, he was the only nominee to be deceased. He had died earlier that year, making him the first Academy Award nominee to be given a posthumous nomination. Furthermore, he was the only nominee to have a specific film, *The Private Life of Helen of Troy*, associated with the nomination. The other writers were nominated for their overall body of work. However, although Duffy had a long history of writing and titling, his primary role in *The Private Life of Helen of Troy* was adapting the play, not writing the titles. The primary title writer was Casey Robinson, whose titles did not go over well with initial audiences. As was the practice, the studio called in Ralph Spence to rework the titles, an act which ultimately made the movie successful (Stempel, 2000: 39). Therefore, Duffy was nominated, at least in part, for Spence's work.

The second candidate was George Marion, Jr., who seemed much more promising. Almost fifty years after talkies became the norm, Billy Wilder still remembered enthusiastically that Marion Jr.:

> . . . got twenty five hundred a week for writing titles in the silents! He was the most sought after; the producers would bring him a picture with all the scenes finished – they wouldn't even know yet whether it was a comedy, very often, or whether they had a drama – until Marion finished writing the titles! (Wilk, 2004: 16).

A quick survey of Marion's work shows why. Like the other major title writers, Marion built his fame on comedy titles. He wrote titles for several films starring the comic Colleen Moore and wrote the titles that appear in Clara Bow's star vehicle *It*. Importantly, while he could write humorously, he was also capable of producing extremely moving passages that coincided both in tone and rhythm with the film itself. This opening title from Joseph Von Sternberg's 1927 film *Underworld* provides an excellent example: "A great city in the dead of night. . . . streets lonely, moon-flooded. . . . buildings empty as the cliff-dwellings of a forgotten age."

Looking back at Marion's success, reputation, and breadth, he seems to be an easy choice for the Academy Award, especially since the judges were looking at his body of work rather than a particular film. However, there was one other nomination, Joseph Farnham, the chief title writer at MGM. Farnham was the somewhat infamous editor who had chopped Von Stroheim's *Greed* from five hours to two hours, reportedly without reading the script. Like Walker, Spence, and Marion, Farnham spent years titling films, and was regarded as an expert. Of the group of nominees, Farnham proves to be one of the least interesting, if for no other reason than because he openly preached writing towards the lowest common denominator, claiming that the best title writing "appeals to every type of audience" ("Good Psychologist," 1927: 29). Essentially, Farnham's philosophy was to make intertitles as unnoticeable as possible, negating the traces of his own presence. So why, exactly, might he have won the first and only Academy Award for title writing? Justifying his extraordinary talents would be difficult, although life-time achievement was certainly a factor. The most likely reason stems from the Academy itself, of which Farnham was a founding member. Before the award process became democratized, a panel of judges made the selections. It was a panel that MGM had substantial influence over, and MGM, not surprisingly, won several early awards. Farnham had joined the right group and was working for the right company, making him the obvious choice for multiple reasons other than the artistic merit of his work.

In the same year, the Academy gave Warner Bros. an award for their work with *The Jazz Singer,* one of the early milestones in movies with synchronized sound. Intertitles would continue to be used as long as silent films were made, but it was clear that their necessity in film had a limited lifespan. After Farnham's win, the award for Best Title Writing was never offered again. Interestingly, when title writing was no longer a full-time occupation, there were few complaints from the title writers. They seemed ready to let it go. Ralph Spence continued writing screenplays and plays, and Anita Loos went on to write *Gentlemen Prefer Blondes*, the work that would ultimately be her most popular. Herman Mankiewicz, a title writer and Titular Bishop, went on to work as the main screenwriter for the film *Citizen Kane.*

Of course, intertitles and filmed text did not end with the implementation of synchronized sound. Inserts (text within the diegesis such as signs, newspaper articles, and letters) continue to be used as a continuity device. Shorter titles, such as the ones found in *Se7en* (1995) and *The Fantastic Mr. Fox* (2009), also continue to serve as an accepted means of ordering a narrative. What did end almost entirely was the frequent interaction between text and images that makes intertitles such a fascinating aspect of silent cinema. I say "almost entirely," because there are several post-silent films that show how text can productively interact with images. Certainly there are artistic films like *So Is This*, and nostalgic silents like Guy Maddin's *Heart of the World* (2000). Yet, the more interesting examples are mainstream films like Peter Greenaway's *The Pillow Book* (1996), where text is often superimposed across the background, and Tony Scott's *Man on Fire* (2004), where subtitles take on the character of what is being said. Rather than using text to challenge the nature of film (as avant-garde films might), these movies integrate text in a way that makes them richer and more evocative. The text works with the film's images rather than simply supporting them or organizing them, and it does so without alienating the mainstream audience. These two examples show that the functionality of intertitles continues to offer a potential area of exploration for contemporary filmmakers, a way of making a film register on multiple levels and creating a productive tension that may not be lost, but certainly has been undervalued.[8]

NOTES

1 See Arthurs and Grant (2003); Cahill (2008); and Robinson (2011).

2 The article is listed as by a "Hack Title Writer." I'm guessing the author is Jack Natteford, because the author claims to have re-titled Griffith's *The Battle at Elderbush Gulch* and *The Massacre*, which were re-edited and re-titled by M. G. Cohn and J. F. Natteford.

3 "Cinemetrics" is a way of studying cinema empirically, timing the shots and shot types. Several cinemetric studies are posted here: www.cinemetrics.lv/.

4 Note the paragraph-length intertitle that begins *His Trust Fulfilled* in 1911.

5 Tom Stempel, in *Framework: A History of Screenwriting in the American Film*, argues that the title writing in *Intolerance* was most likely a collaborative process between Anita Loos,

Frank Woods, D. W. Griffith, and Joseph Henabery.

6 For a performative critique of the "Rosy-Fingered Dawn" style, see pages 102–3 of A. M. Nornes' *Cinema Babel: Translating Global Cinema*.

7 Katherine Hilliker wrote the intertitles for several important films, including *Ben Hur* (1925) and *Sunrise* (1928).

8 Further exploration of text and moving images could also explore advances in new media writing (see dreamingmethods.com), video games (a good example is the textual thoughts which appear in *Splinter Cell: Conviction*), and even television commercials (there is a tremendous similarity between Hepworth's *How It Feels* and a recent Liberty Mutual Insurance commercial that depicts a crash and shows the text "Am I okay?").

REFERENCES

"All Bad Little Movies When They Die Go to Ralph Spence." *Film Daily Year Book*, 1927, 1501.

Arthurs, Jane and Iain Grant. Eds. "How It Feels." *Crash Cultures: Modernity, Mediation and the Material*. London: Intellect Books, 2003.

Bordwell, D., J. Staiger, and K. Thompson. *The Classical Hollywood Cinema: Film Style and Mode of Production to 1960*. New York: Columbia University Press, 1985.

Boylan, M. S. "Nine Star Title Writers." *New York Times*, June 17, 1928, 102.

Cahill, J. L. "How It Feels to Be Run Over: Early Film Accidents." *Discourse*, 30:3, 2008, 289–316.

"Captioneer Turns Subtle." *New York Times*, May 6, 1928, 110.

Davis, L. *Silent Lives*. Albany: Bear Manor Media, 2008.

Deutelbaum, M. "Trial Balloons." *Image*, 18:1, 1975, 20.

"Editorial Reply." *Moving Picture World*, February 22, 1908, 143.

"The Emerson–Loos Way." *New York Times*, February 29, 1920, X7.

Frost, L. "Blondes Have More Fun: Anita Loos and the Language of Silent Cinema." *Modernism/Modernity*, 17:2, 2010, 291–311.

Gale, S. H. *Sharp Cut: Harold Pinter's Screenplays and the Artistic Process*. Lexington: University Press of Kentucky, 2003.

Gifford, D. *The British Film Catalogue 1895–1985*. London: Fitzroy Dearborn, 2000.

"Good Psychologist Needed to Title Motion Pictures." *Los Angeles Times*, October 27, 1927, 29.

Hepworth, C. *Came the Dawn*. London: Phoenix, 1951.

Hepworth & Co. *A Selected Catalogue of the Best and Most Interesting "Hepwix" Films*. London, 1903.

Liepa, T. *Figures of Silent Speech: Silent Film Dialogue and the American Vernacular, 1909–1916*. New York: New York University Press, 2008.

Lindsay, V. *The Art of the Moving Picture*. New York: Macmillan, 1915.

de Lissa Berg, C. "The Title Editor." In *Careers for Women*. Ed. Catherine Filene. Boston: Houghton, 1920, 337–8.

Motion Picture World, July 31, 1926.

Münsterberg, H. *The Photoplay: A Psychological Study*. New York: D. Appleton, 1916.

Musser, C. *Before the Nickelodeon: Edwin S. Porter and the Edison Manufacturing Company*. Berkeley: University of California Press, 1991.

Natteford, J. F. "Title Work Years Ago." *New York Times*, December 2, 1923, X5.

Norman, Marc. *What Happens Next: A History of American Screenwriting*. New York: Three Rivers Press, 2008.

Nornes, A. M. *Cinema Babel: Translating Global Cinema*. Minnesota: University of Minnesota Press, 2007.

Pidgin, C. F. "Patent 1240774." September 18, 1917.

Rhodes, W. M. "Letter to the Editor." *Moving Picture World*, February 22, 1908, 143.

Robinson, Gregory. "Oh! Mother Will Be Pleased: Cinema Writes Back in Hepworth's *How It Feels to Be Run Over*." *Literature/Film Quarterly*, 39:3, 2011, 218–30.

Salt, B. *Film Style and Technology: History and Analysis*. London: Starword, 1992.

Schmidt, K. "The Handwriting on the Screen." *Everybody's Magazine*, May, 1917, 622–3.

Stempel, T. *Framework: A History of Screenwriting in the American Film*. New York: Syracuse University Press, 2000.

Wilk, M. *Schmucks with Underwoods: Conversations with Hollywood's Classic Screenwriters*. New York: Applause, 2004.

3

Adaptation and Modernism

Richard J. Hand

Defining the "Modern"

The word "modern" finds its root in the Latin word *modernus* which means "just now". The word appears towards the end of the fifth century AD and was used for centuries in order to differentiate between what is "here and now" and what has become "the past." Even the past was once modern, but there was never any problem in distinguishing or allowing a smooth shift from one status to the next. However, in the twentieth century it does become a problem. Suddenly "Modern" becomes a fixed label for the period from the early twentieth century until soon after 1945 or even more precisely the inter-war period. Within this period, works of culture were produced which have become regarded as examples of Modernism, reflecting the era of Modernity. This is culture in the broadest sense: Modernism appertains to painting, sculpture, music, architecture, design, theater, literature, and cinema – and more besides. It is important to acknowledge, however, that cultural Modernism did not just "happen." In the context of literature, for example, a number of earlier writers could be held up as forerunners who embody the "aesthetic spirit" of Modernity. The British novelist Laurence Sterne (1713–68), the American writer Edgar Allan Poe (1809–49), and the French poet Charles Baudelaire (1821–67) may all have died before the historical era of Modernism and yet their work contains aspects that could in many respects be described as Modernist.

So what characterizes the Modern so thoroughly that a general term becomes indelibly associated with a specific cultural period? Here are several definitions

A Companion to Literature, Film, and Adaptation, First Edition. Edited by Deborah Cartmell.
© 2012 Blackwell Publishing Ltd. Published 2012 by Blackwell Publishing Ltd.

of Modernism and Modernity from a diverse selection of literary critics and philosophers:

> Herbert Read: "an abrupt break with all tradition . . . The aim of five centuries of European effort is openly abandoned" (Bradbury and McFarlane, 1978: 20).
>
> J. A. Cuddon: "a breaking away from established rules, traditions and conventions" (1979: 399).
>
> M. H. Abrams: "a deliberate and radical break with some of the traditional bases not only of Western art, but of Western culture in general" (2009: 202).
>
> Roger Fowler: "the artist's freedom from realism, materialism, traditional genre and form" (1987: 151).
>
> Chris Baldick: "a rejection of nineteenth-century traditions and of their consensus between author and reader" (1991: 159).
>
> Jürgen Habermas: "Modernity revolts against the normalizing functions of tradition" (1981: 5).
>
> Michel Foucault: "Modernity is often characterized in terms of consciousness of the discontinuity of time: a break with tradition, a feeling of novelty, of vertigo in the face of the passing moment" (1984: 39).

These critics have different interests and foci and yet there is one shared feature to all those definitions: the word *tradition*. More precisely, each account defines the Modern as taking an active role *against* tradition. Whether it is abandoned, broken from, freed from, revolted against or rejected, it is clear that there is no place for "tradition" in Modern culture. Indeed, let us add an eighth definition, the most radical of all: Theodor W. Adorno believes that whereas "previously, styles and artistic practices were negated by new styles and practices," Modernism "negates tradition itself" (Osborne, 1989: 38).

In order to be liberated from tradition (or to annihilate it altogether), one has to take an active role against it. There is, however, more than one way to do this. This is why Modernism must not be regarded as a fixed movement, but rather as a "spirit" that encompasses a myriad of approaches. Broad cultural movements such as Symbolism, Cubism, Futurism, Expressionism, Constructivism, Imagism, Vorticism, Dadaism, and Surrealism have, to greater or lesser extents, irreconcilable differences between them and yet they are unified under the umbrella of Modernism. It is the diffuse condition of the era of Modernism, the lack of a consensus in approach beyond a revolt against tradition, which is one reason that *dissonance* is a concept that so successfully captures the mood of the epoch. It is not just heard in the cacophony of the jostling artistic movements of the period, but the aesthetics of dissonance frequently occurs within individual cultural works. We might think of the atonal music of Arnold Schoenberg, the abstract art of Wassily Kandinsky, the experimental writings of Gertrude Stein, and the use of stream-of-consciousness in the fiction of James Joyce. In all of these examples, we can find the traditional conventions of harmony and structure replaced by fragmentation and diffusion. It is also a radical period of technical innovation, which reflects and exacerbates the experimental dimension to the Modern. New inventions such as cinema and radio broadcasting not only offer a forum for Modernist exploration, they have a major impact on the zeitgeist and the artist's and audience's sense of self.

Despite Modernism's denunciation of tradition, captured so effectively in the title of Ezra Pound's essay collection *Make It New* (1934), there is at least one traditional practice that continues unabated within this radical era: *adaptation*. In the Modernist world, the "old" process of adaptation continues to be a key practice within the "new" performing arts of cinema and radio. In fact, one could even argue that in the epoch of Modernism, adaptation becomes an obsession. Furthermore, as could only befit the spirit of this most exciting historical period, adaptation takes on a thrilling and profound resonance.

In order to make sense of adaptation in the era of Modernism, it is helpful to look back to the period immediately preceding the Modern era. The nineteenth century brings the achievement of Modernist adaptation into sharp relief. After all, it was the technology of the nineteenth century that invented cinema and ultimately made radio possible. Likewise, certain proto-Modernist Victorian and Edwardian writers (some of whom survived into the Modernist era) had experiences in adaptation with aesthetic and legal consequences that help make sense of Modernism and adaptation.

Adaptation and Pre-Modernism

During the nineteenth century, adaptation became ubiquitous on the British stage. It can be found in the craze for the tableau interpretation of famous works of pictorial art and also in the popular theater form of the pantomime – socially inclusive and variety-based entertainments based on legends and fairy tales – which remains a distinctly recognizable form into the present day. In addition, the translation/ adaptation of "foreign" melodramas and the dramatization of narrative fiction into stage drama were extremely popular industries. As examples, we need only consider Tom Taylor's adaptations of Victor Hugo's 1830s plays *Lucrèce Borgia* and *Le Roi s'amuse* (significantly bowdlerized of anything politically or morally controversial), the numerous adaptations of Walter Scott's novels, or C. H. Hazlewood's phenomenally successful 1863 stage version of Mary Elizabeth Braddon's novel *Lady Audley's Secret* (1862). However, despite its prevalence, the perception of the cultural process of adaptation was not without its complexities. For some writers it was a process and art form that was unproblematic to understand, primarily because of the close relationship that was perceived as existing between the sister arts of fiction and drama. Hence we find William Harrison Ainsworth, in the "Preface" to his 1837 novel *Rookwood*, declaring that a novel "is a drama, with descriptions to supply the place of scenery" (xxviii). Similarly, in his 1858 speech to the Royal General Theatre Fund, Charles Dickens asserts that "every good author, and every writer of fiction, though he may not adopt the dramatic form, writes in effect for the stage" (1988: 262). These descriptions perhaps suggest that it was considered easy for an artist – and audience – to step between the realms of fiction and drama which, by default, must surely be at their closest when an adaptation is being created.

However, some writers thought that not only were adaptations all too easy to produce, the resulting products were an inferior form of art that deserved nothing but scorn. This is demonstrated by Brander Matthews' 1880s poetic satire "The Ballade of Adaptation." Towards the end of the nineteenth century there was a sense from some quarters of the theatrical and literary establishment that the Anglo-American theater was in crisis. Although the novel and poetry were regarded as being in triumphant condition, the stage seemed to be moribund. The popular theaters of melodrama or music hall were perceived as being far away from literature and the examples from the Renaissance repertoire tirelessly staged by Henry Irving or Ellen Terry merely rubbed salt into the wound that English, the language of Shakespeare, lacked a contemporary literary theater. George Steiner describes the situation as one in which "the Shakespearean shadow" (1961: 150) fell between the knowledge that English drama desperately needed to be rejuvenated and the actual process of writing these new plays. In his satire, Brander Matthews takes the familiar lament about contemporary theater and proposes that redemption is to be found in adaptation:

> The native drama's sick and dying,
> So say the cynic critic crew:
> The native dramatist is crying
>
> "Bring me the paste! Bring me the glue!
> Bring me the pen, and scissors, too!
> Bring me the works of E. Augier!
> Bring me the works of V. Sardou!
> I am the man to write a play!"
>
> For want of plays the stage is sighing,
> Such is the song the wide world through:
> The native dramatist is crying
>
> "Behold the comedies I brew!
> Behold my dramas not a few!
> On German farces I can prey,
> And English novels I can hew;
> I am the man to write a play!"
>
> There is, indeed, no use denying
> That fashion's turned from old to new:
> The native dramatist is crying
>
> "Moliere, good-bye! Shakespeare adieu!
> I do not think so much of you.

Although not bad, you've had your day,
And for the present you won't do.
I am the man to write a play!" (White, 1888: 38)

Matthews delights in presenting adaptors as comically false prophets whose craft of "writing" consists of butchering the pre-existing achievements of foreign drama-tists and English novelists. Perhaps most profoundly, the new playwright's rejection of Shakespeare as passé is meant to reflect a sorry state of affairs whereby *tradition* and creativity have become less important than scissors and glue.

Although Ainsworth and Dickens regard fiction and theater as fundamentally intertwined and Brander Matthews sees the adaptation industry as being ripe for satire, it is not an overstatement to say that some writers were incensed by adapta-tion – not least for legal reasons. Due to the shortcomings of the copyright laws of the period, a novelist's legal control over his or her work did not extend to dramatizations of it. Hence we find a furious Charles Reade complaining about the phenomenal success of "piratical" versions of his 1856 novel *It is Never too Late to Mend*:

Saloons rose into theatres by my brains, stolen. Managers made at least seventy thou-sand pounds out of my brains, stolen: but not one would pay the inventor a shilling (Reade and Reade, 1887: 164–5).

In March 1838, Charles Dickens writes in a letter that he plans "to dramatize *Oliver [Twist]* for the first night of the next season" (Churchill, 1975: 189). Although this production never came to pass, London's theater-going public was not denied seeing *Oliver Twist* on stage: there were five different dramatizations of the novel in 1838 alone, none of which needed the original author's permission and none of which netted him a penny.

It was not until 1911 – interestingly, in the Modern age and the era of cinema – that the Copyright Act was passed through Parliament which amended the law relating to copyright and protected writers with regard to, amongst other things, the dramatization of narrative works. The Act states:

For the purposes of this Act, "copyright" means the sole right to produce or repro-duce the work or any substantial part thereof in any material form whatsoever, to perform the work or any substantial part thereof in public; if the work is unpublished, to publish the work or any substantial part thereof; and shall include the sole right,

   (a)   to produce, reproduce, perform, or publish any translation of the work;
   (b)   in the case of a dramatic work, to convert it into a novel or other non-dramatic work;
   (c)   in the case of a novel or other non-dramatic work, or of an artistic work, to convert it into a dramatic work, by way of performance in public or otherwise;

(d)   in the case of a literary, dramatic, or musical work, to make any record, per-
forated roll, cinematograph film, or other contrivance by means of which the
work may be mechanically performed or delivered, and to authorise any such
acts as aforesaid ("Copyright Act 1911").

As can be seen, the Act protects writers against adaptation "in any material form
whatsoever," whether translation, or adaptation into drama or film. Before the 1911
Copyright Act, the somewhat absurd situation reigned whereby novelists could only
protect their works against adaptation if they dramatized it themselves. In an 1899
essay, George Bernard Shaw explains how "every prudent novelist whose book contains valuable dramatic material takes the precaution to put together some sort of
stage version, no matter how brief or inept" (1958: 68) simply so that by obtaining
a theatrical license they were in a stronger position to protect their intellectual
property. The consolidation of authors' rights through the adequate regulation of
copyright was only one fundamental change which had implications for adaptation
as culture moved into the Modern epoch. As well as legal changes there were major
technological advances, including the invention of cinema and developments in
sound, which would ultimately lead to radio broadcasting. Before we look at these
media and their close relationship with adaptation, it is beneficial to consider writers
who could be considered "proto-Modernist."

Adaptation and Proto-Modernism

Writers such as Thomas Hardy, Henry James, and Joseph Conrad are "proto-
Modernist" or "transitional" figures whose careers extended from the nineteenth
century into the Modern period. All three of these artists had experience of adaptation. In 1894, during the pre-Copyright Act era, Hardy adapted his 1891 novel
Tess of the D'Urbervilles. The script was not staged at the time but three decades later
there was a revival of interest in the play when the Dorset-based theater company
the Hardy Players learnt of its existence. The ensuing regional production enjoyed
enough success for a London staging to be proposed. However, it was made clear to
Hardy that his 1890s adaptation would need to be substantially revised for a 1925
London audience. When the noted playwright and critic St John Ervine – a young
child when *Tess* was published – is proposed to, as it were, adapt the adaptation,
Hardy writes to him directly to decline his services:

> My consolation in giving up your assistance is that, according to my experience of
> the theater, provided a play has a good story at the back of it, the details of construc-
> tion are not important. . . . The dramatization of a novel is really only an ingenious
> piece of carpentry (1987: 312).

For Hardy, adaptation is merely a technical craft: it may be "ingenious," but it is
nothing more than "carpentry."

Hardy's contemporary Henry James uses a similar "technical" metaphor in describing the playwright as a "joiner" who has made a box and then must pack it:

> The five-act drama – serious or humorous, poetic or prosaic – is like a box of fixed dimensions and inelastic material, into which a mass of precious things are to be packed away. It is a problem in ingenuity and a problem of the most interesting kind. . . . The false dramatist either knocks out the sides of his box, or plays the deuce with the contents; the real one gets down on his knees, disposes of his goods tentatively, this, that, and the other way, loses his temper but keeps his ideal, and at last rises in triumph, having packed his coffer in the one way that is mathematically right (1949a: 35)

It is evident that James, the great Formalist, was fascinated by the ingenious, mathematical exercise of the dramatist and he did write a large number of plays including adaptations of several of his own novels including *Daisy Miller* (novella 1878; play 1882) and *The American* (novel 1877; play 1891). In an 1877 essay on "The London Theatres," James confesses that he is "very much like a Francisque Sarcey" (1949b: 96), the influential French theater critic who extolled the importance of technical perfection and would acclaim the prolific dramatists of the "well-made play," Eugène Scribe and Victorien Sardou, as standing amongst the greatest of playwrights. However, James' own attempts prove to be largely catastrophic. When staged, the plays were unsuccessful with audiences who could even be openly hostile: James writes to his brother after the premiere of *Guy Domville* (1895) shocked by the heckling and jeering audience which he likens to a "a cage of beasts at some infernal 'zoo'" (W. James, 1993: 337). There are several reasons why James' plays were so unsuccessful. For George Bernard Shaw, the problem was a linguistic one that afflicted many novelists who attempted to "adapt" themselves into playwrights, as he explains in a letter to the *Times Literary Supplement* on May 17, 1923:

> . . . there is a literary language which is perfectly intelligible to the eye, yet utterly unintelligible to the ear even when it is easily speakable by the mouth . . . The disastrous plays of James, and the stage failures of novelists obviously much more richly endowed by nature and culture than many of the successful playwrights with whom they have tried to compete, suggest that they might have succeeded if only they had understood that as the pen and the *viva vox* are different instruments, their parts must be scored accordingly.

Another reason for James' failure is his obsession with the "technical" aspects of drama and adaptation which is at odds with a contradictory "protectionism" whereby he attempts to squeeze as much of the original fiction into the play. For instance, in his *Daisy Miller* adaptation James feels obliged to give the story a happy ending with Daisy surviving malaria, thus turning his tragic novella into a formulaic stage comedy. At the same time, James abuses dramatic techniques in trying to find equivalent ways to present the exposition and characterization so important in his fiction. Analyzing *Daisy Miller*, Bernd Lenz reaches a conclusion with profound implications:

> Was in der Erzählung gelingt – die Abstimmung von Dialog- und Erzählpassagen, der Handlungsablauf mit dem notwendig tragischen Ende, die sprachliche Darstellung, Charakterisierungs- und Erzähltechnik – , funktioniert im Drama nicht mehr. Simple Dialoge, ein melodramatisches *happy ending*, Auslassen von dramatisch wirksamen Szenen aus der Vorlage, die bis zum Überdruß praktizierte Technik des >aside< und flache Charaktere lassen Erzählung und Drama trotz der bisweilen wörtlichen Übereinstimmungen wie zwei völlig unterschiedliche Texte wirken (1985: 170).
>
> What works in fiction – the harmonization of dialogue and narrative passages, the plot with the necessarily tragic ending, the language, techniques of characterization and narrative – does not work any longer in drama. Simple dialogues, a melodramatic happy ending, omission of dramatic scenes, the over-use of the aside and two-dimensional characters make narrative and drama appear as two entirely different texts, despite frequent identical passages.

Lenz suggests there is a fundamental difference between fiction and drama even when some of the text is identical. We are a world away from the pronouncements of Ainsworth and Dickens and the effortless symbiosis of fiction and drama.

There is something disappointingly backward-looking in James's adherence to the traditional Scribe and Sardou formulae of plot, sentiment, and stagecraft. However, despite his naiveté as a playwright, in another context James can be nothing short of an early Modernist in the assessment of the performing arts. In the novel *The Tragic Muse* (1890) – James' most ambitious exploration of the world of theater – he accounts for the need for change in the contemporary theater, and highlights the major difficulties that will have to be surmounted, when he writes that "Today we are so infinitely more reflective and complicated and diffuse" (1978: 51). By implication, if an authentic reflection of contemporary consciousness is to be achieved, the traditional principles of artistic, self-contained completion, and perfection will need to be challenged if not rejected in a broader acceptance of ambiguity, fragmentation, and variation. In short, the type of work James came towards creating in some of his narrative fiction.

The sense of crisis (or "vertigo" as Foucault describes it) implicit in this mood of cultural uncertainty finds striking manifestation in a final example of proto-Modernism: Joseph Conrad. Conrad died in 1924, but in the last few years of his life he embarked on a number of experiments in the adaptation of his fiction for the stage and cinema. The key year for Conrad as adaptor was 1919 inasmuch as there were two contemporaneous versions of his 1915 novel *Victory*: the Hollywood film of *Victory* directed by Maurice Tourneur and featuring Lon Chaney; and the dramatization *Victory: A Play in Three Acts* written by Basil Macdonald Hastings and produced in the West End by the actor-manager Marie Löhr. Tourneur's influential film was the first screen adaptation of Conrad, and Löhr's production remains the longest-running stage production of a Conrad adaptation. In the light of the success of these, we find Conrad venturing to picture houses with his literary agent to learn the craft of cinematic adaptation and exploring the possibilities of writing plays for London's experimental Grand Guignol theater and the mainstream West End. Conrad secured a contract with Famous Players- Lasky (which would become Paramount) to produce a number of screenplays based on his own fiction. Conrad only completed one – *Gaspar the Strong Man* (1920) – a "film-play" based on the short story "Gaspar Ruiz" (1908) and this was never produced. Similarly, his example of "horror" theater, *Laughing Anne* (1920), based on the short story "Because of the Dollars" (1915), was rejected by the Grand Guignol. In contrast, Conrad's most ambitious adaptation – the dramatization of his 1907 novel *The Secret Agent* in 1919 – received a West End production in 1922.

The experience of adapting *The Secret Agent* proves to be a profoundly shocking experience for Conrad. As he is writing the play in November 1919, he describes in a letter that he finds the process of adaptation to be an eviscerating experience. The irony and meticulously constructed narrative of the novel disintegrates, leaving what Conrad can only describe as "a merely horrible and sordid tale" (Conrad, 2002: 520). In the same letter, Conrad makes an astonishing confession: "I myself had no idea what the story under the writing was till I came to grips with it in this process of dramatization." It is remarkable that Conrad, an artist so famous for his artistic precision and control, finds that adaptation does not merely transform his novel into a monster, but reveals that it always was a monster. It is an intriguing situation as ironic as any in Conrad's oeuvre: an adaptor called Joseph Conrad sits in the Modern world attempting to tackle a classic of Edwardian fiction, written by the same man. In discussing the concept and practice of adaptation, Arrigo Subiotto identifies it as a central process in Modern culture whereby writers as diverse as Bertolt Brecht or T. S. Eliot are aware that "the writer can find his own identity and meaning only through an active relationship with the past" (1975: 191). In addition to the Modern writers Subiotto cites, we can add Conrad as an example of a writer who turns to the past – in his case the deeply personal past of his literary achievements – to make sense of the present. However, if the process of adaptation is a fruitful enterprise for Brecht and Eliot, for Conrad it is an experiment that evidently places him in a creative heart of darkness. Ironically – and aptly – Conrad's disconcerting experience captures the Modernist era's zeitgeist of alienation and dissonance.

Adaptation and Modernist Cinema

It is significant that the two great technological inventions with cultural impact – cinema and radio broadcasting – occur within the Modern period of the 1890s and 1920s. In fact, what this reflects is how essential these innovations were in capturing, shaping, and determining the culture of the period. For the contemporary artist, it was impossible to ignore these media and for some (such as Salvador

Dali and other Surrealists; Bertolt Brecht and other Epic/Expressionists; W. H. Auden and other Modern English writers) they would be irresistible as creative outlets. The late Modernist writer, Graham Greene (whose first novel *The Man Within* was published in 1929), seems to embody the spirit of the era most impressively through his successful combination of careers as film critic, screenwriter, and novelist. Moreover, Greene's narrative fiction (a compelling source for adaptation in its own right) frequently utilizes cinematic effects such as flashback, the deliberate manipulation of point of view, and so on.

Despite various precursors and other contested beginnings, the Auguste and Louis Lumière film screenings in Paris in 1895 are normally taken as marking the inauguration of the cinema age. In the first years after the invention of the motion picture, the medium was seen as having primarily a "scientific" use, fulfilling what we would see as a "documentary" function. Eventually, there were examples of cinema producing short entertainments and playful novelties. However, Eileen Bowser argues that, after 1907, U.S. cinema no longer had a solely scientific or "novelty" status and there was an increasing demand for more sophisticated narratives, and the adaptation of literary works provided one solution (1990: 42–3). In 1908 there was a flurry of Shakespeare adaptations across the film industry after which the Edison Company produced one-reel versions of Goethe's *Faust* in 1909 and Dickens' *A Christmas Carol* and Mary Shelley's *Frankenstein* in 1910. In addition, there was also an element of "moral panic" at play. The cinema was an irresistible target for those seeking a root cause for the social calamities they saw infecting the newly arrived twentieth century, as Guy Phelps explains: "the cinema had been blamed for almost every social calamity of the preceding decade" (Petrie, 1997: 62). Interestingly, the 1909 Cinematograph Act in Britain was passed ostensibly to safeguard the physical environment of buildings where (highly inflammable) films were exhibited, but it was also the beginning of film censorship. In the United States, Thomas Edison warned in July 1907 that the success and future of the cinema industry depended upon it establishing a "good moral tone" (Bowser, 1990: 37).

Cinema therefore attempted to protect itself by using "the prestige of the classics" (Bowser, 1990: 43) through adaptation. Indeed, some film exhibitors at the time would meet with local schools to encourage teachers to use soon-to-be-adapted literary texts on their curricula. However, what is interesting is how adaptation is approached. If we consider the Edison *Frankenstein*, for example, we find a film that is attempting to capitalize on the prestige of adapting a classic novel, but all is not straightforward. As Winston Wheeler Dixon reveals: "Many exhibitors found the film too horrid to show" (2000: 117). Interestingly, in Mary Shelley's original novel, the creation of Frankenstein's monster occurs in ellipsis. However, a quarter of the Edison one-reel film is devoted to the creation scene. This sequence is, in fact, the dramatic highpoint and narrative focus of the film. It is a set-piece that is special effects-driven: we see the creature's skeleton gathering flesh until it is a fully formed monstrosity. It is undoubtedly this sequence that was deemed "too horrid" for audiences. Modern technology determined Edison's *Frankenstein*. Shelley may have kept the creation in ellipsis in order to avoid providing a scientific explanation or to adhere to the tradition of Greek tragedy wherein shocking events occur off-stage. The Edison film puts the lengthy creation sequence center-screen not only because it is an exciting dramatic sequence but also because Modern film effects mean that it can be realized convincingly. The Edison *Frankenstein* demonstrates that Modern film technology is capable of capturing the fullest ramifications of uncanny literature. In fact, the place of the adaptation of horror literature in the context of Modernist cinema as a whole is especially significant. This is particularly the case if we turn to one of the most pioneering cinematic movements to emerge from cultural Modernism: Expressionism.

The term "Expressionism" emerged in relation to the German visual arts shortly before the First World War. Expressionist art does not present a uniform technique or style but was a broad movement committed to the exploration of emotional subjectivity and the revelation of inner reality. To look at it another way, Expressionism's particular spirit of Modernist anti-traditionalism sought to reject conventional "realism" and its mimetic approach to the surface realities of the world. The paradigmatic film of Expressionism is *Das Cabinet des Dr. Caligari* (Robert Wiene, 1920). Although the film is not an adaptation, it unmistakably draws on German folk tale and Gothic traditions. In addition, as a landmark in cinematic art *Das Cabinet des Dr. Caligari* proved highly influential as a point of reference and source for adaptation. The film's elaborate sets, distorted angles, and chiaroscuro represent one of the most ambitious and profound examples of cinematic Modernism. In addition, not only did *Das Cabinet des Dr. Caligari* demonstrate the possibilities of cinema in the era of Modernism, it also achieved, impressively, international critical and popular success. The techniques of narrative, point of view, and visual design in *Das Cabinet des Dr. Caligari* made the film highly influential and a work that has been frequently "returned to" by subsequent generations. The fact that it is a pre-sound era work has meant that there have been numerous re-imaginings of music and soundscape for the film, while the central characters, Dr. Caligari (Emil Jennings) and Cesare (Conrad Veidt), have become icons of Modernist performance. David Lee Fisher remade the film (*The Cabinet of Dr. Caligari*, 2005) with a contemporary cast but its use of "green screen" incorporated visuals from the original. Although not the adaptations they sound like they should be, the Expressionist masterpiece is name-checked in two extremely kitsch but nonetheless stylishly designed movies, the Robert Bloch-penned psychological thriller *The Cabinet of Caligari* (Roger Kay, 1962) and the high camp sci-fi comedy, *Dr. Caligari* (Stephen Sayadian, 1989).

As a whole, adaptation has an important place in German Expressionist cinema. *Faust* (F. W. Murnau, 1926), based on Goethe's version of the legend of the scholar who sells his soul to the Devil, combines melodramatic performance with a genuinely epic design. Various special effects including superimposition are used to make Faust's summoning scene a vision of lightning, fire, and apocalyptic horsemen. The most iconic image from the film is the spectacle of a literally gargantuan Mephisto (Emil Jennings) lowering over Faust's village. The film builds on the achievement of the designs seen in the productions of Expressionist theater directors such as Leopold Jessner, but cinematic technology permits an even more ambitious revelation. Other adaptations include *Der Golem* (Paul Wegener and Henrik Galeen, 1915) and its prequel *Der Golem, wie er in die Welt kam* (Carl Boese and Paul Wegener, 1920), based on the Yiddish legend of the animated man of clay, which would have a major influence on subsequent cinematic adaptations of *Frankenstein*.

The most abiding adaptation to emerge from Expressionist cinema is *Nosferatu, eine Symphonie des Grauens* (F. W. Murnau, 1922), the first film version of Bram Stoker's *Dracula* (1898). Ironically, this masterpiece of Modernist adaptation was compelled to become more oblique than intended: the film version was unauthorized and when Stoker's widow took legal action over copyright, the studio was forced to change the names of the characters and omit direct references to "vampires." Florence Stoker was still not content and secured an injunction demanding that all copies of *Nosferatu* be destroyed (fortunately, copies survived). The fact that *Nosferatu* remains one of the most revolutionary adaptations of *Dracula* bears testament to the liberating spirit of Modernism. The radical nature of the adaptation is embodied most profoundly in the form of Count Orlok (Max Schreck) himself. Far from being the moustached vampire from Stoker's novel or the suave and virile noble in most film versions ever since, Orlok is a terrifying personification of death: his skull-like head contains rodent teeth and Modern film technology enables him to move with frightening speed, in negative image or with physical impossibility. Just as Stoker's popular novel provides a fascinating insight into late Victorian anxieties, *Nosferatu* is a nightmare vision befitting its immediate post-First World War context. The combination of location filming with abstract set-pieces of technical experimentation, make it one of the most potent adaptations of the era. Expressionism rejected the aesthetic of realism and through their Modernistic experimentation, if not audacity, these works were able to convey a profundity to match or excel their source texts.

The lure of Hollywood was irresistible (or, by the time Adolf Hitler came to power in the 1930s, unavoidable) to many Expressionists and other Modernists. Therefore, for example, filmmaker Paul Leni imports an element of Expressionist flair to his 1927 adaptation of John Willard's phenomenally popular – and conventional – stage melodrama *The Cat and the Canary* (1922). Other veterans of German Expressionist cinema would bring a distinctive Modernist style to popular Hollywood cinema from Universal horror movies through to film noir. Karl Freund directed *The Mummy* (1932), adapted from Nina Wilcox Putnam and Richard Schayer's story scenario by John L. Balderston, whose 1927 revision of Hamilton Deane's 1924 stage adaptation of *Dracula* formed the basis of Universal's *Dracula* (Tod Browning, 1931). Freund also directed Peter Lorre in *Mad Love* (1935), an adaptation of Maurice Renard's 1920 novel *The Hands of Orlac*. The aesthetic of the pioneering Expressionists became part of the Universal house style in certain set-pieces and, often most evidently, the chiaroscuro and shadow play opening title sequences of, for example, the Edgar Allan Poe adaptations, *Murders in the Rue Morgue* (Robert Florey, 1932), *The Black Cat* (Edgar G. Ulmer, 1934) and *The Raven* (Lew Landers, 1935).

It is notable that Poe, the American Gothic writer whose experiments in point of view and fragmented, intertextual narrative would prove so influential on Modernist literature, would also prove a key source for Modernist film. Before Universal's stylish horror melodramas, other attempts to adapt Poe include the short U.S. film *The Fall of the House of Usher* (James Sibley Watson and Melville Webber, 1928), a work that remains remarkable for its use of abstract imagery and technique; and, also in 1928, a longer adaptation of the same story, *La chute de la maison Usher* by the French filmmaker Jean Epstein. Epstein was a key influence on the development of the cinema of Surrealism, a movement as integral to French Modernism as Expressionism is to German Modernism. However, rather like Poe himself, Epstein's own inspirations and choice of methods are particularly diverse. His aesthetic alludes to the experiments of proto-Modernists such as Baudelaire and Poe, while his filmmaking techniques draw on the methods of Russian montage and German Expressionism as much as the French cinematic avant-garde. To this end, in *La chute de la maison Usher* we are presented with exterior location filming and studio chiaroscuro; rapid editing and dreamlike languidness. Guy Crucianelli goes so far to contend that in Epstein's adaptation of "The Fall of the House of Usher" we find "the ultimate synthesis of Jean Epstein's theories on cinematic expression and a culmination of the director's tendency to weave 'diverse strands' of source material into a puzzle-like whole" (2007: 21) with the result that the work not only stands as "a classic of the 'first avant-garde' but as the culmination and adaptation of many avant-gardes" (34).

Epstein employed the young Luis Buñuel to adapt Poe's short story and work as assistant director on *La chute de la maison Usher*. Buñuel, who would become the Surrealist film director *par excellence*, resigned from the production due to what he perceived as Epstein's increasing departure away from Poe's original story. This is ironic given Buñuel's own radical approach to adaptation in later works such as *Le Journal d'une femme de chambre* (1964), his cinematic interpretation of Octave Mirbeau's 1900 Decadent – and proto-Modernist – novel of the same title. However, what is more ironic is that in shifting away from a strict adherence to the narrative of Poe's "The Fall of the House of Usher," Epstein produces a work that comes closer to the eclectic aesthetic of the U.S. writer. Even if Epstein's approach to adaptation in creating *La chute de la maison Usher* did not appeal to Buñuel, it can be seen as providing an inspiration to other avant-garde filmmakers. For example, Jean Cocteau's *La Belle et la Bête* (1946), an adaptation of Jeanne Marie Le Prince de Beaumont's eighteenth-century fairy tale, combines evocative location filming, extraordinary studio sequences, and technical effects such as slow motion. Cocteau "animates" the Beast's castle with fireplaces coming to life and, most iconically, arms and hands emerging from walls and tabletops to hold candles and fulfill other servile tasks. Over all, Cocteau's avant-garde adaptation creates a dreamlike fantasy which combines meticulous historical detail with unsettling Surrealism. *La Belle et la Bête*, like *Das Cabinet des Dr. Caligari*, achieved popular and critical success and it is a tribute to Cocteau's sensibility that he succeeded in creating a work that is simultaneously a pioneering "fantasy movie" and an abiding achievement in cinematic Modernism.

Adaptation and Modernist Radio

We have seen how important technology was in helping to determine and facilitate the vision of cultural Modernism. If creating performing arts adaptations in the context of Modernism proved vertiginous for a transitional writer such as Joseph Conrad, for the new generation of artists as diverse as F. W. Murnau, Jean Epstein and Jean Cocteau, a genuinely radical approach to adaptation provided an opportunity to make paradigmatic achievements in cinematic Modernism. However, cinema was not the only new technology invented in the era of Modernism. As Douglas Kahn writes, "Modernism has been read and looked at in detail but rarely heard" (1999: 4). Just as cinema offered an exciting forum for artistic experimentation, nineteenth-century inventions such as the telephone, the telegraph, and various technologies to record sound proved fascinating to the avant-garde of the Modernist era. The importance of Modernist sound in relation to adaptation came to its most prominent position with the development of radio broadcasting. Theories and experiments regarding radio waves in the nineteenth century culminated in a working system of "wireless telegraphy" primarily used for shipping and then, in the early 1920s, the inauguration of the first radio stations. Just as cinema was perceived as being an invention of scientific use before its creative potential became clear, radio developed from an instrument for communicating information to being a forum for creativity.

The earliest radio "narratives" – described by Leonard Maltin as the first radio "institution" (2000: 13) – were on-air readings of children's stories. Similarly, the first examples of radio drama were recited versions of stage plays. These examples were developed in the United States, but the UK followed a similar pattern. BBC radio drama began with the broadcasting of extracts from Shakespeare in February 1923, which led to a full-length recitation of *Twelfth Night* on May 28, 1923. However, it was not long before the phenomenal success of radio demanded more material and the adaptation of fiction into drama provided an obvious solution. Commencing with the dramatization of Charles Kingsley's *Westward Ho!* in April 1925, the adaptation of fiction became a central feature of British radio drama and has remained so to the present day.

Radio was an all-live medium with prerecording for broadcast on magnetic tape only coming in after the Second World War. To this end, the sensational popularity of radio made huge demands on its producers, above all in the United States where competing networks strove to attract and keep their audiences. In the area of radio drama, the U.S. networks had to become prolific as "repeats" would have to be full-scale "revivals" with a live cast, musicians, and sound effects technicians, let alone the fact that the audience would be expecting something "new" each evening. The issue of repertoire is important when we consider a long-running U.S. series such as *The Witch's Tale* (1931–38), radio's first horror drama series. Although the show's writer-director Alonzo Deen Cole produced many original works, he also made significant use of adaptation. In its first year, *The Witch's Tale* produced a radio version of Mary Shelley's *Frankenstein* (August 3, 1931). In November 1931, Universal released its film version of the novel and although *The Witch's Tale* pre-empted this, its revivals of the radio play (March 7, 1932 and July 17, 1935) doubtlessly exploited the success of the film. Indeed, as Jeffrey Richards observes, "a richly symbiotic relationship developed between Hollywood and radio" (2010: 1), a fact most emphatically evident in *Lux Radio Theater* (1934–55), a hugely popular show which broadcast radio adaptations of popular movies, usually featuring the original film stars. To return to *The Witch's Tale*, other classics of horror it adapted include *Dr. Jekyll and Mr. Hyde* in both a one-part (November 23, 1931) and two-part version (August 19 and 26, 1937); and versions of legends such as "The Flying Dutchman" (February 1, 1932 and April 26, 1934) and "The Golem" (September 24, 1936; September 25 and October 9, 1933). In addition to these classics of the uncanny, *The Witch's Tale* – in meeting the demands that its popularity placed on its repertoire – also adapted many neglected works such as John William Polidori's *The Vampyre* (June 5 and 12, 1933); Prosper Mérimée's "The Venus of Ille" (July 2, 1931; July 18, 1932 and August 22, 1935); and Théophile Gautier's "Clarimonde" (August 16, 1932 and November 26, 1935) and *Jettature* (August 27, 1931; July 3, 1933 and July 6, 1936). We can thus find in radio drama examples of adaptation that venture impressively wide for their source material.

Despite its impressive range of source texts, *The Witch's Tale* tends to be somewhat conventional and melodramatic in treatment. Other examples from the early years of radio adaptation can yield examples extremely experimental in technique in a manner that reflects its Modernist context. For example, radio drama pioneers such as Wyllis Cooper, Norman Corwin, and Arch Oboler used the all-live nature of broadcasting to produce radical works that exploited the *form* of radio to its full potential. Sometimes ground-breaking radio work used the adaptation of fiction to innovative ends. For example, Arch Oboler produced a thirty-minute play entitled "Johnny Got His Gun" (March 9, 1940), an adaptation of Dalton Trumbo's 1939 antiwar novel of the same title. The work is centered on a severely wounded soldier who lies paralyzed on a hospital bed and we are privy to his thoughts, his despair, and his memories. Oboler's dramatization – starring James Cagney – is a masterpiece of Modernist radio, a live and compelling stream-of-consciousness that combines voice and soundscape into what is simultaneously an emotive and political experience. As another example, the popular series *Suspense* (1942–62) typically produced half-hour whodunits adhering to the conventions of the crime genre.

However, even *Suspense* could be surprisingly experimental: in "One Hundred in the Dark" (September 30, 1942), an adaptation of Owen M. Johnson's 1913 short story, there is an extraordinary set-piece in which a character slowly counts from one to a hundred. The live broadcast comes across less like a generic piece than a work of Dadaism.

The importance of radio drama pioneers' contribution to adaptation and Modernism has tended to be marginalized, with one major exception: Orson Welles. John Houseman and Orson Welles had established the Mercury Theatre in New York City in 1937 and were subsequently approached by CBS to launch what was intended to be a quality "intellectual" drama series "to ward off federal investigations into radio's overcommercialization" (Hilmes, 2002: 104). Houseman and Welles decided to make adaptation the *Mercury Theatre on the Air*'s specialty. Their premiere performance on July 11, 1938 was an adaptation of Bram Stoker's *Dracula*. Despite the success of Universal's *Dracula* and its key source, the melodramatic play by Hamilton Deane and John L. Balderston, the *Mercury Theatre on the Air* returns to Stoker's novel, including aspects of its epistolary style. Houseman and Welles' *Dracula* becomes a gripping, eclectic narrative of different voices (including Welles as both Dracula and Dr. Seward). This demonstrates Welles' development of the "first person singular" technique which made radio drama *intimate* and even *interiorized* in a way that reflected both the domestic location of radio and its Modernist context. In short, just as Jean Epstein's radical re-visioning of Poe took him closer to the source author's aesthetic, the *Mercury Theatre on the Air*'s closer adherence to the style and narrative of the original novel comes across as a radical technique, more experimental than most other adaptations.

The most famous *Mercury Theatre on the Air* adaptation is, of course, "War of the Worlds" (October 30, 1938). If their *Dracula* adheres closely to Stoker's words and structure, their version of H. G. Wells' *The War of the Worlds* (1898) takes the simple idea at the heart of Wells' story and subjects it to a complete reimagining. After the opening monologue, which is closely modeled on the first page of Wells' novel, "War of the Worlds" becomes a work about radio. The play emulates the style of "breaking news" (including the dissonance of confusion, hesitation, and interruption), exploiting the very medium it is using – live radio – to convey the Martian conquest of the earth. The furor after the broadcast has become legendary but despite the repercussions – for instance, "Dramatizations of simulated news bulletins became verboten" (Douglas, 1999: 165) – the production was Orson Welles' ticket to Hollywood. Welles, this great "interpreter of literary modernism" (DeBona, 2010: 67), would arrive in the film industry with the desire to adapt: his first film proposal was an adaptation of Conrad's *Heart of Darkness* but this was rejected and he made *Citizen Kane* (1941) instead. When one considers the contribution that Welles made to Modernism and adaptation through radio drama, it is unfortunate – and puzzling – that this failed to materialize in his early film work. But as Guerric DeBona concludes, Welles was never suited to "Hollywood – or its practices of film adaptation" (2010: 93).

Conclusion

We have seen how the uncomplicated, albeit maligned or legally frustrating, position of adaptation amongst some nineteenth-century writers became problematic with the dawn of Modernism. For some proto-Modernists, a traditional, formulaic approach to dramatization fails to produce authentic work. For Joseph Conrad, immersing himself into adaptation pushes him into an abysmal crisis which, ironically, captures precisely the vertigo and dissonance of Modernism. In the cinema and radio drama of Modernism we can find eclectic and (sometimes inadvertently) iconoclastic achievements – artists fascinated by the *forms* of new technologies and their potential to realize their artistic visions. Theodor W. Adorno defines Modernism as art "groping for objectivity in a framework of open-endedness and insecurity" (Osborne, 1989: 38). In other words, Modern existence is seen as precarious and lacking in closure; and so art attempts to devise ways of "capturing" this essence, despite the fact that this essence is impossible to catch in a way that would be unanimously approved. Adaptation provided a springboard into creativity for a diverse range of artists of the Modern period, yielding experiments and explorations that remain exciting and innovative to the present day.

References

Abrams, M. H. *A Glossary of Literary Terms*, 9th edn. Boston: Wadsworth, 2009.

Ainsworth, W. H. *Rookwood*. London: Bentley, 1837.

Baldick, C. *The Concise Oxford Dictionary of Literary Terms*. Oxford: Oxford University Press, 1991.

Bowser, E. *The Transformation of Cinema: 1907–15*. New York: Scribner, 1990.

Bradbury, M. and J. W. McFarlane. *Modernism, 1890–1930*. Brighton: Harvester, 1978.

Churchill, R. C. Ed. *A Bibliography of Dickensian Criticism 1836–1975*. London: Macmillan, 1975.

Conrad, J. *The Collected Letters of Joseph Conrad Volume 6: 1917–1919*. Eds. Frederick R. Karl and Laurence Davies. Cambridge: Cambridge University Press, 2002.

"Copyright Act 1911." Legislation.gov.uk. Original version. (n.d.). The National Archives. January 30, 2011. www.legislation.gov.uk/ukpga/Geo5/1-2/46/section/1/enacted.

Crucianelli, G. "Painting the Life Out of Her: Aesthetic Integration and Disintegration in Jean Epstein's *La Chute de la maison Usher*. In *Monstrous Adaptations: Generic and Thematic Transmutations in Horror Film*. Eds. Richard J. Hand and Jay McRoy Manchester: Manchester University Press, 2007, 20–34.

Cuddon, J. A. *A Dictionary of Literary Terms*. Harmondsworth: Penguin, 1979.

DeBona, G. *Film Adaptation in the Hollywood Studio Era*. Urbana: University of Illinois Press, 2010.

Dickens, C. *The Speeches of Charles Dickens: A Complete Edition*. Ed. K. J. Fielding. Hemel Hempstead: Harvester Wheatsheaf, 1988.

Dixon, W. W. "Transferring the Novel's Gothic Sensibilities to the Screen." In *Readings on Frankenstein*. Ed. D. Nardo. San Diego: Greenhaven, 2000, 115–28.

Douglas, S. J. *Listening In*. New York: Times Books, 1999.

Foucault, M. *The Foucault Reader*. Ed. Paul Rabinow. New York: Pantheon, 1984.

Fowler, R. *A Dictionary of Modern Critical Terms*. London: Routledge, 1987.

Habermas, J. "Modernity versus Postmodernity." *New German Critique*, 22, 1981, 3–14.

Hardy, T. *The Collected Letters of Thomas Hardy: Volume 6: 1920–1925*. Eds. Richard Little Purdy and Michael Millgate. Oxford: Oxford University Press, 1987.

Hilmes, M. *Radio Reader: Essays in the Cultural History of Radio*. New York: Routledge, 2002.

James, H. *The Complete Plays of Henry James*. Ed. L. Edel. London: Rupert Hart-Davis, 1949a.

James, H. *The Scenic Art*. London: Rupert Hart-Davis, 1949b.

James, H. *The Tragic Muse*. Harmondsworth: Penguin, 1978.

James, W. *The Correspondence of William James: Volume 2*. Eds. Ignas K. Skrupskelis, Elizabeth M. Berkeley, and John J. McDermott. Charlottesville: University of Virginia Press, 1993.

Kahn, D. *Noise, Water, Meat: A History of Sound in the Arts*. Cambridge, MA: MIT Press, 1999.

Lenz, B. "Intertextualität und Gattungswechsel." ["Intertextuality and Generic Change"]. In *Intertextualität: Formen, Funktionen, anglistische Fallstudie*. [Intertextuality: Case Study of Forms, Functions and English Language Studies]. Eds. U. Broich and M. Pfister. Tübingen: Niemeyer, 1985, 158–78.

Maltin, L. *The Great American Broadcast*. New York: Penguin Putnam, 2000.

Osborne, P. "Adorno and the Metaphysics of Modernism: The Problem of a 'Postmodern' Art." In *The Problems of Modernity: Adorno and Benjamin*. Ed. Andrew Benjamin. London: Routledge, 1989, 23–48.

Petrie, R. Ed. *Film and Censorship: The Index Reader*. London: Cassell, 1997.

Pound, E. *Make It New*. London: Faber, 1934.

Reade, C. L. and C. Reade. Eds. *Charles Reade: A Memoir Volumes I and II*. London: Chapman and Hall, 1887.

Richards, J. *Cinema and Radio in Britain and America, 1920–60*. Manchester: Manchester University Press, 2010.

Shaw. G. B. "Mr. Shaw on Printed Plays." *Times Literary Supplement*. May 17, 1923, 339.

Shaw, G. B. "The Censorship of the Stage in England." In *Shaw on Theatre*. Ed. E. J. West. London: MacGibbon and Kee, 1958, 68.

Steiner, G. *The Death of Tragedy*. London: Faber, 1961.

Subiotto, A. *Bertolt Brecht's Adaptations for the Berliner Ensemble*. London: Modern Humanities Research Association, 1975.

White, G. *Ballades and Rondeaus: Chants Royal, Sestinas, Villanelles, &c. Selected, with Chapter on the Various Forms*. New York: D. Appleton and Co., 1888.

4

Sound Adaptation

Sam Taylor's *The Taming of the Shrew*

Deborah Cartmell

It is remarkable that so little has been written about the significant impact the introduction of sound had on adaptations: in relation to both how adaptations were conceived and received by the general public, film and literary critics. There is no disputing that the coming of sound heralded a new era for adaptations. While there was a substantial degree of skepticism in the late 1920s and early 1930s about the advantages of sound, what we would call technophobia today, the inclusion of speech in screen versions of literary and theatrical works, undeniably revised what it was to be an adaptation: words. While Guerric DeBona rightly regards the rise of adaptations in the 1930s as resulting from both the economic conditions of the Great Depression and the advent of the Production Code (2010: 25), the introduction of sound has to be a major factor in this increase in films based on plays and novels or, to put it more bluntly and obviously, films based on words. The advent of sound led not only to a transformation of the adaptation, but also to a "rebirth" or to a reinvention of the form itself, with authors ignored by the silent screen, such as Jane Austen, adapted for the first time. Indeed Shakespeare, in spite of the hundreds of silent adaptations of his work, was also seen to be adapted for the *first* time. This chapter considers the damage done to the reputation of the adaptation, even in spite of its best efforts to defend itself, due to an almost hysterical promotion and privileging of sound, focusing on the first mainstream Shakespeare "talkie," Sam Taylor's *The Taming of the Shrew* (1929).[1]

There is surprisingly little critical attention given to the coming of sound in this movie. While clearly chosen as a star vehicle for the most famous couple of the

A Companion to Literature, Film, and Adaptation, First Edition. Edited by Deborah Cartmell.
© 2012 Blackwell Publishing Ltd. Published 2012 by Blackwell Publishing Ltd.

silent period, Mary Pickford and Douglas Fairbanks, as a play ultimately concerned with the silencing of a woman, it can be regarded as both a peculiar and appropriate choice for the first mainstream film to give Shakespeare back (some of) his words. The fetishization of this adaptation through its employment of Shakespeare's language becomes the unique selling point of the film in its publicity materials, a feature that bestows upon this adaptation, and its successors, perhaps for the first time, its very credentials as an adaptation.

A reasonable assumption today is that the coming of sound, the bringing "back" of Shakespeare's words, would have been welcome to Shakespeare critics and film reviewers alike, but, on the whole, it was greeted in the late 1920s/early 1930s with fear and loathing from both film and literary communities. The initial hostility and the gradual conversion of writers to sound has been well documented by Laura Marcus (2007), but it is possible that the reputation of the adaptation never entirely recovered from the inclusion of speech, and it was the amount of words left in or left out that tended to dominate an adaptation's reception. Concerns that film adaptation was regressing to its theatrical origins and that the talking film would be a much inferior version of both film and theater were highly prevalent, most famously recalled in *Singin' in the Rain* (1952, an adaption of Moss Hart and George S. Kaufman's *Once in a Lifetime,* 1930, first adapted to film in 1932) in which the emergence of sound is dismissed as vulgar, something that will never catch on, like the horseless carriage.

One of the sound film's more famous opponents was Aldous Huxley who outspokenly attacked the talkies in his journalism as well as in his novel *Brave New World* (1932). While inviting comparisons with Shakespeare's *Tempest* in its title, implicitly identifying itself as an adaptation of Shakespeare, Huxley's novel savages film adaptation of Shakespeare through "the feelies" (or the recently introduced "talkies"); *Othello* becomes debased and unrecognizable as *"Three Weeks in a Helicopter,* 'AN ALL-SUPER-SINGING, SYNTHETIC-TALKING, COLOURED, STEREO-SCOPIC FEELY. WITH SYNCHRONIZED SCENT-ORGAN ACCOMPANI-MENT" (Huxley, 2004: 145). Following from what many of Huxley's contemporaries regarded as the debasing vulgarity of the "talkies" were the "smellies," enthusiastically anticipated by an author or authors writing under the pseudonym "John Scotland" in a monograph, published in 1930, welcoming and explaining the technology of the talkies: "In America the 'Smellies' have actually arrived, and the firm of Metro Goldwin Meyer are claiming to be the pioneers of the latest pandering to yet a further sense." According to Scotland, the idea of "'atmospheric' cinema theatres is taking hold and just around the corner" (1930: 149). The "smellies" were a long way off – and mercifully forgotten today – but the "talkies" were beginning to take hold and given that Taylor's film was the only mainstream Shakespeare talkie released at the time in which Huxley is writing, it is possible that it is *The Shrew* that is being satirized here as part of the "brave new world." The repulsively seductive and debasing experience caused by this adaptation echoes Aldous Huxley's disgust, followed by self-loathing upon experiencing *The Jazz Singer* – "I felt ashamed of myself for listening to such things, for even being a member of the species to which such things are addressed" (1972: 73). In spite of his initial repugnance to the talkies, within a few years Huxley, like most of his contemporaries, warmed to the art of screenwriting, even settling down in Hollywood, adapting, with some pride, the likes of Jane Austen (see Clark, 1984).

It is hard to imagine why someone would feel quite so offended by the advent of the sound film, but Huxley was not alone in his initial abhorrence of the talkies. The use of sound, words in particular, made an adaptation more "literary" or "theatrical" and therefore less "filmic." Hard-line opponents of sound were largely those who campaigned for cinema to be regarded as art, and were concerned that sound would both throw film back to a dependence on theater and be used for commercial rather than artistic reasons. Cultural commentator, Gilbert Seldes distinguished between "movies" and "talkies," the latter often "a chaos distasteful to the orderly mind" (1929: 8). Film critic Paul Rotha divided films into two categories: one good, one bad; one silent, one talking: "Cinematography today seems to be distinguished by parallel courses of development. On the one hand, there is the cinema proper, compounded from the elements of the medium, discovered and built up by the Russians up till the beginning of the dialogue era; whilst on the other, there is the vast output of ordinary narrative talking films of sensational interest that occupies the capitalist studio organizations of Western Europe and America" (1931: 15). The talking narrative film was not allowed entrance into "cinema proper" and was regarded in this transitional period as "impure cinema" in its double reliance on literature and theater. Expanding on his essay in the inaugural issue of F. R. Leavis' *Scrutiny,* William Hunter identified the sound film as addictively infantilizing while mourning the loss of "the efficacy of words." The film, in particular the talkie, which he describes as the "talking, singing and dancing monstrosity" (1932: 61) was effectively banned from any serious literary journal, having no part to play in the Leavisite "great tradition." Hunter's attack on the narrative talking film, significantly, in the first volume of *Scrutiny*, perhaps reveals a latent anxiety among literary scholars that there may be something like "Adaptation Studies" looming on the horizon, something that clearly needs to be nipped in the bud. *Scrutiny* was clearly not having anything to do with film and more particularly, adaptations of literary and dramatic texts. Writing earlier in *Mass Civilisation and Minority Culture* F. R. Leavis perceives cinema to be incontrovertibly threatening an overthrow of culture: films "provide now the main form of recreation in the civilized world; and they involve surrender, under conditions of hypnotic receptivity, to the cheapest emotional appeals, appeals the more insidious because they are associated with a compellingly vivid illusion of actual life" (1930: 10). Leavis does not mention film adaptations explicitly in the body of his text, presumably because they represent the lowest of the low, undeserving even of mention in this tirade against popular culture. In a footnote, however, he quotes a letter from Edgar Rice Burroughs (creator of Tarzan):

It has been discovered through repeated experiments that pictures that require thought for appreciation have invariably been box-office failures. The general public does not wish to think. This fact, probably more than any other, accounts for the success of my stories, for without this specific idea in mind I have, nevertheless endeavoured to make all of my descriptions so clear that each situation could be visualised readily by any reader precisely as I saw it (1930: 10).

Leavis' almost unspeakable contempt for an author admitting that he writes with an eye to adaptation is revealed in his perfunctory dismissal of Burroughs' position: "The significance of this for my argument does not need comment" (1930: 10). Likewise, Q. D. Leavis regards film as a coarsening opiate, like bestselling novels but worse, appealing to the lowest denominator in society, a form of "uplift" entertainment that she describes as "largely masturbatory" (1932: 165). The imagery of warfare in F. R. Leavis' references to cinema in *Mass Civilisation and Minority Culture* is revealing of his steadfast position, which has become part of his legacy: film is indeed the enemy and it will not be allowed to invade the terrain of literary studies.

Not all literary critics saw cinema, in particular, the talkie, as threatening, parasitic, and patronizing. In 1936, Renaissance scholar Allardyce Nicoll optimistically saw film, not just as The New Literature, but as "the New Shakespeare," and in sound, new possibilities for cinema. Paraphrasing Will Hays, Nicoll claims that the recognition of film "by the great universities" will mark "the beginning of a new day in motion picture work, paving the way for the motion picture's Shakespeares" (1936: 163). For Nicoll, cinema, especially, the talkie, potentially offers a window into the past, in the uncertain age of modernity, a vehicle for a return to an "authentic" version of Shakespeare. At the time, Nicoll, as an academic, was in a minority in his enthusiasm for introducing film studies into academia and in his defense of the talking picture, indeed of the Shakespeare adaptation. The bringing of words to Shakespeare films occurred within a climate in which both adaptations and talkies were met with scorn from literary and film critics alike. An adaptation, as Nicoll observes, is doomed as impure cinema (124): too popular, too commercial, and too dependent upon literature and theatrical traditions to be of any value as "art." This labeling of adaptation as "impure cinema" condemned the adaptation (alongside its offspring, the biopic) as the most derided of all film genres.

Huxley was not the only one to identify Shakespeare "talkies" as implicitly the most despicable form of film. As Neil Forsyth has argued, so too did art historian Erwin Panofsky in the much discussed essay, "Style and Medium in the Moving Pictures" (revised version published in 1947). Panofsky, like Nicoll, singled out the Reinhardt–Dieterle film of *A Midsummer Night's Dream* (1935), which he condemns at great length as "the most unfortunate film ever produced" (1974: 238) in its falling victim to the pitfalls of the "talkies," in its over-reliance on theatrical rather than filmic traditions (Forsyth, 2006). Rather than provide film with artistic kudos, the use of Shakespeare's language (and by implication, that of other canonical writers) is seen not to uplift (as has often been argued), but to devalue cinema. Curiously, there's little, if no mention of an earlier Shakespeare film in academic debates on the talkie adaptation. Sam Taylor's *The Taming of the Shrew* (1929) is the first feature length Shakespeare "talkie" and as such deserves a very special place within the canon of Shakespeare on screen.[2]

Overshadowed by the Rheinhardt–Dieterle film of 1935, surprisingly Taylor's *Shrew* has not been read in relation to its use of sound in the little scholarship devoted to it, a peculiarity given the context in which it was produced. The film's notoriety is down to its infamous credit line, "by William Shakespeare with additional dialogue by Samuel Taylor," and, possibly, for this reason, largely overlooked in Shakespeare and film scholarship. Roger Manvell, in *Shakespeare & the Film* (1971), devotes only two and a half pages to it, citing anecdotal evidence of the film's designer, Laurence Irving's (son of the famous Henry Irving) attempts to persuade Taylor not to make himself a laughing-stock by adopting the credit (24–5). While the film is still best known for its credit line, there is no evidence that it was ever used and close scrutiny of the film reveals only a few "additional" lines (Pendleton, 1993: 152–3).[3] Samuel Crowl gives it short shrift in his survey of Shakespeare on screen preferring like those before him to concentrate on the 1935 *Midsummer Night's Dream* (2008). The little work that has been done on Taylor's film, rather than contextualizing it within the new sound era, instead focuses on gender. Russell Jackson has argued that Mary Pickford's wink to Bianca at the end of her lecture on wifely obedience brings Katherine into the twentieth century, making Petruchio the one who is duped (1994: 112). Barbara Hodgdon, on the other hand, sees Katherine's momentary triumph allayed by the alleged cruel treatment of her by her co-star (her husband, Douglas Fairbanks) while on set and in the final moments when Petruchio "stops her mouth" (to paraphrase from *Much Ado*) with a final forced kiss (1998: 15). Diana E. Henderson is somewhere in the middle in her reading: Katherine becomes "the sneaky servant rather than the Stepford wife of patriarchy" (2004: 125). Taylor uses leading actors Mary Pickford and Douglas Fairbanks in the title roles for the first time together. Undeniably a star vehicle, the film can be seen to voyeuristically expose and exploit their well-known relationship (which, unknown to the audience, was troubled at the time of shooting). The actors' success in the silent period (Pickford was exceedingly well known as "America's sweetheart," while Fairbanks' fame was based on his death-defying athleticism and masculinity) is referenced throughout the film. Fairbanks runs everywhere at amazing pace, demonstrates superhuman strength and agility in restraining Katherine, and picks up and hurls his servants around as if they're made of feathers. Pickford is continually shown in quintessentially Pickford-esqe poses, especially in close-up, emphasizing her famous bow-shaped lips and with quivering eyes looking pleadingly at the camera.

Released simultaneously as a talkie and a silent film (Willson, 2000: 19–20), this is a very pared down version of Shakespeare's play. In the film, the central pair find that their love of brandishing whips is something that they have in common; upon

Figure 4.1 Douglas Fairbanks and Mary Pickford in *The Taming of the Shrew*. Dir. Sam Taylor. USA: United Artists, 1929.

meeting Petruchio for the first time, Katherine gazes at Petruchio's exceptionally long and heavy whip and instantaneously hides her much smaller weapon behind her back (Figure 4.1);[4] or as the pressbook stresses: "Her whip, which had lashed the back of many a suitor, looked small and puny when compared to his blacksnake" (10). The whips functions as visual correlatives to the whip-like tongues of the central pair, with undeniably phallic associations.

As Ann Thompson has observed in the Cambridge edition of *The Taming of the Shrew*, David Garrick's 1754 adaptation, which prevailed until the mid-nineteenth century (and upon which this film is based), included a line indicating that Petruchio "shook his Whip in Token of his Love" and a whip was later added as a property by John Kemble in his 1788 production (1984: 19). According to Thompson, the whip became a standard property for future stage performances, but the Taylor film extends the significance of the whips by including the property in virtually every frame of the movie. Katherine carries hers around as if it is a handbag. Easily recalled as "the film with the whips," these seemingly gratuitous strips of leather are the dominant image of the film, and while the whips can be explained as signifiers of the central characters' sadomasochistic sexuality, their use can be explained literally as a means of achieving discipline and silence: a whip, of course, is a word used to refer to both a person who ensures discipline and a call issued to stamp out deviance in the interests of harmony. It seems a peculiar accident, if it is an accident, that the first mainstream Shakespeare "talkie" is an adaptation of a play concerned not with the celebration of words but with the suppression of words, and that it makes this theme blatantly apparent through the extensive use of the silence-inducing whips.

But the film's pressbook repeatedly emphasizes that this is a talkie. While contemporary "so-called serious" writers on film condemn sound movies as popular, formulaic, and infantilizing, unsurprisingly the writers of the pressbook, whose motives are purely to sell the movie, continually stress the uplifting quality of sound. Numerous articles in the very detailed pressbook for the film, while overly keen to praise, inadvertently allude to anxieties about the film's reception in its capacity as an "all-talking" adaptation of Shakespeare. Indeed, the publicity materials covertly address the anticipated criticisms of the likes of Aldous Huxley and Erwin Panofsky. The book arms itself against purist objections to the production of a talking Shakespeare film by directly and audaciously addressing the question of fidelity. In brief, the message of the pressbook is that sound allows for the first time fidelity on screen to an author's work and, by extension, to the period in which it was produced.

Perhaps the most striking notion to emerge from the pressbook is its perception of *The Taming of the Shrew* not just as the first mainstream talking adaptation of Shakespeare but as *the first* adaptation of Shakespeare (obliterating all silent predecessors). The pressbook reiterates in its summaries that this is the first film adaptation of the play: "in this screen story of the Bard's immortal comedy, brought to the screen for *the first* time in the history of motion pictures" (9 – my italics) or "the glorious comedy which has come finally to motion pictures after four centuries of success on the legitimate stage" (10). It could be argued that the publicity writers failed to do their research or refused to acknowledge earlier adaptations of the play (1908, 1911, 1923, the first directed by D. W. Griffith). But it is more likely that these adaptations were not forgotten but cunningly disqualified as adaptations due to their lack of words. Mary Pickford herself echoes the repeated assertion – "Shakespeare brought to the screen for the first time" (10) – in an interview by Julian Arthur:

> Also there is another reason why we wanted to be the first to bring Shakespeare to the screen. It somehow seems an advance toward a higher standard in talkie dialogue, and there is something really worthwhile and constructive in this idea. The great mass of people who are unfamiliar with Shakespeare will be introduced to him in a manner that will make his work attractive. We have spared no pains to preserve authenticity in every detail and we have lost none of the spirit of the play in the transcription (15).

Pickford (or someone pretending to be Pickford) claims that Taylor, Fairbanks, and herself are "the first to bring Shakespeare to the screen," implying again that what went before wasn't Shakespeare at all. The pressbook repeatedly declares that this is an adaptation for the very reason that it contains the words of the adapted text.

Figure 4.2 From *The Taming of the Shrew* pressbook (1929).

Pickford's reported speech contains a number of well-known arguments for the justification of filming Shakespeare: to uplift the value of film; to bring culture to the masses; and to somehow capture "the spirit" of "the original." Clearly the film's producers anticipated the latter point would be contentious and the pressbook has a number of articles reassuring us of the film's authenticity. In short, it is the words that constitute the film's "authenticity." Beginning with the catchline, "The big three – Mary, Doug, and Bill" (4), the pressbook features an imaginary interview with "the big three" illustrated with Pickford, Fairbanks and Shakespeare drinking tea, discussing the movie (Figure 4.2).

Fairbanks opens with the introduction, "Mary, this is Bill Shakespeare. He wrote our last picture" (5) and goes on, with the help of Mary, to convince Shakespeare that if he were alive in 1929, he would be writing for the movies and that this film of his play is "better the way we have shortened it" (5). The imaginary interview alleviates any fears that the film is a departure from the "real Shakespeare" with Shakespeare himself giving it the thumbs up and Fairbanks concluding: "a lot of people have said they wondered what Shakespeare would say about our doing him on the screen. I am certainly glad he dropped in and now I can tell everybody that he is perfectly satisfied" (5). In another article in the pressbook, "Adapting Shakespeare to the Talking Picture Screen," Arthur J. Zellner declares that "orthodox worshippers of Shakespeare who clothe his every word with an aura of sanctity should not take offense" (30)[5] and goes onto question the authorship of the play and point out some examples of successful theatrical truncated versions, such as Garrick's (whose eighteenth-century production, *Catherine and Petruchio*, is claimed as inspiration for the film). Critic James Agate writing in *The London Pavilion* (November 11, 1929) introduces the film to cinema audiences, confidently averring that "it is safe to say that if the cinema had been known in Shakespeare's day, there is nothing in the present picture which Shakespeare would have disowned."

The pressbook mixes pseudo scholarship with tabloid-style journalism, clearly in anticipation of attacks from Shakespearean "purists," the likes of Aldous Huxley, who will not abide Shakespeare's words being spoken on film. As mentioned earlier, the dominant theme of the pressbook is the film's fidelity to Shakespeare, a subject quite clearly instigated by the use of sound in this production. Repeatedly, we are told that all the words are Shakespeare's:

> . . . not one bit of the glorious Shakespearean dialogue has been sacrificed when in keeping with the fast moving comedy, director Sam Taylor has re-told the story with the deftness so characteristic of his work . . . (10).
>
> Every line of dialogue used in the picture stands as written by the Bard himself (10).
>
> . . . every bit of dialogue spoken in the film was taken from the original Shakespeare and every bit of atmosphere, from the characters to the sets, is in keeping with the customs of the fifteenth century (10).

These repeated assertions of pure authenticity seem to have been swallowed by contemporary reviewers, in spite of the publicists' ignorance (in the passage quoted above) of the very period in which Shakespeare was writing.

Without doubt, the sound by today's standards is dreadful, with Pickford and Fairbanks shouting out all their lines with little trace of emotion. Pickford claimed to be disappointed with her own performance, retiring from acting shortly after the film; rather than presenting Katherine as an equal to Petruchio in strength and wit, she felt that she played the part like a "spitting kitten" (Willson, 2000: 26). Most critics have claimed that Fairbanks steals the show, with Pickford looking uncomfortable and out of place throughout (Hodgdon, 1998). But this discomfort is with the spoken words and strikingly, all the emotion in the film is conveyed in the nonspeaking sections, as Taylor's film oscillates between the talkie and silent modes, very much a film aware of its transitional and dual status. Given the talkie was seen as a purely commercial enterprise and despised by those advocates of pure cinema and literary critics who saw the coming of sound as a further invasion and violation of their artistic territory, the contrasting styles, the talkie and the silent, are indeed pertinent. It is worth noting that the film is framed by much talking while the middle section of the film is dominated by silence that "upstages" the overly theatrical opening and close. The shouting of the central actors is in sharp contrast to the superiority of their silent performances.

Significantly the first mainstream Shakespeare talkie is a play about the "successful" suppression of the dangerous female tongue, as mentioned, blatantly visualized by the whips in this production. But it is a success that is not altogether unqualified, given that Katherine finds a voice (albeit one that is music to the ears of a patriarchal society) at the end of the play. The film on one level exploits the fame of the central couple while on another self-consciously juxtaposes the visual with the verbal, the silent film with the talkie. Surprisingly, aesthetically, silence wins over words in the final impression of the film as Katherine's spectating is far more eloquent than Petruchio's verbal declarations. Take the scene in which Petruchio sends Katherine to bed and returns to eat the rejected food. Diana E. Henderson's observation that Katherine "remains the one who sees more than her husband, creating a silent connection between her perspective and the filmmaker's own" (Henderson, 2004: 125) can be extended into regarding the film's oppositional aesthetics: Katherine sees and Petruchio talks, reflecting the debate, here a veritable battle, between silent and talking cinema.

Katherine, after miraculously undergoing a makeover from a mud-soaked and bedraggled wreck to a perfectly groomed starlet complete with diaphanous white peignoir, opens the bedroom door and gazes down at Petruchio who is at the table with his dog, Troilus. At this point of the film, Katherine has been transformed from bad to good girl, symbolized in the change of costume from black riding suit (worn at the outset of the film) to pure white. Positioned at the top of the staircase, she literally and metaphorically looks down at Petruchio. Unable to speak, she is visually superior and given a voice in her enforced silence, and in contrast to Shakespeare's Katherine her tactical advantage enables her to triumph over this Petruchio's unguarded scheming:

PETRUCHIO:
Troilus, good dog for a hearty meal
Thus have I politicly begun my reign,
And *it is* my hope to end successfully.
Today she ate no meat *and today she shall not sleep.*
Last night she slept not, nor tonight she shall not.
As with the meat, some fault
I'll find about the making of the bed,
And here I'll fling the pillow, there the bolster,
This way the coverlet, another way the sheets.
And *amidst* this hurly I *pretend*
That all is done in *loving* care of her.
And then *forsooth she'll* watch all night,
And if she chance to nod I'll rail and *sing*,
And with my *singing* keep her still awake.
This is *the* way to kill a wife with kindness,
And thus I'll curb her mad and headstrong humour.
Does thou know better how to tame a shrew?

[Dog barks]
Nay, good Troilus, nay. (*The Taming of the Shrew,* 1939)[6]

The eavesdropping Katherine speaks visually throughout the sequence, gradually moving from the shock of the spectacle to plotting revenge (in anticipation of the finale, concluding with a knowing wink to the camera). Petruchio, oblivious to the fact he is being watched and overheard, brags to the dog (which has physically and symbolically taken Katherine's place at the table). The juxtaposition of the two characters, one silent, one carelessly and unnecessarily wordy, reflects the film's transitional status between silent cinema and talkie. Clearly the more eloquent of the two is Katherine and in the debate between what Gilbert Seldes refers to as "the talkies" and "the movies," the talkie is shown to be vastly inferior: stupid, infantile, and lacking in subtlety due to its unnecessary wordiness. Against the grain of the pressbook's valorization of the wordiness of Taylor's *The Taming of the Shrew,* the film seems to be at pains to reinforce the old adage that a picture speaks louder than words or that the central pair, especially Pickford, are making a final and fruitless plea for the survival of silent cinema in anticipation that the new talkie will end both careers. Retrospectively, Pickford lamented in her autobiography: "The making of that film was my finish. My confidence was completely shattered, and I was never again at ease before the camera or microphone" (quoted in Henderson, 2004: 124).

This is Shakespeare with and without words: Katherine is "silenced" (as Pickford writes in her autobiography she was asked to adopt Pickfordian characteristics in her portrayal of Kate)[7] and while Petruchio's words are victorious, sound is vastly outplayed by silence and the end product is in direct opposition to the publicity surrounding it. (Significantly, Sam Taylor himself makes no contribution to the pressbook and its valorization of words.) Claims that this is the first ever Shakespeare film and declarations about its fidelity to Shakespeare in its preservation of the words are contradicted by the primacy of the visual over the verbal, or the silent film over the talking adaptation. Indeed the film itself, contrary to the message of the pressbook, seems to fight against its status as an adaptation, or as an "all-talking" film.

The Taming of the Shrew's pressbook audaciously reveals that the coming of sound enabled the birth of adaptation and while the promoters of the film do their utmost to proclaim the film as an adaptation, indeed the first Shakespeare adaptation ever, the film itself does the opposite, demonstrating the superior eloquence of silence. Sound is the basis for claims of fidelity (and acknowledgment of lack of originality) resulting in adaptation's exclusion from the accolade of "art." Obviously, the talkie was eventually accepted as the way forward but sound, or more precisely, words, continued to stigmatize critical appreciation of adaptations. While the pressbook of *The Taming of the Shrew* repeatedly marvels at Shakespeare's words on screen, the image of the whips suggests throughout that this is a film that fiercely asks its characters to "shut up."

Sam Taylor's *The Taming of the Shrew* is remarkable in enacting the debate between sound and silence (to adapt or not to adapt?) in this transitional phase of film history. The film's pressbook boldly claims that the coming of sound reinvented what constitutes an adaptation: fidelity to the words of the author and authenticity to the period in which the text was produced. Seemingly, in spite of the oppositional aesthetics presented in the film itself, the film's promotional materials proclaim it as the "first" adaptation of Shakespeare and since its release, until the late twentieth/ early twenty-first century, few writers on adaptation bothered to mention adaptations of the silent period, implicitly averring that to be an adaptation the film must have words. It seems no accident that the first full-length study of screen adaptations, George Bluestone's *Novels into Film* (1957), while arguing that sound should serve the visuals rather than the other way around, like most of its successors and unlike work in general film studies, restricts itself to case studies of films in the sound era. Significantly, Geoffrey Wagner, in *The Novel and the Cinema* (1975), begins with the sentence: "Sound cinema is literate" (9). Such a perspective produces unprofitable "word-counting" exercises of fidelity criticism, often judging the quality of an adaptation by the amount of words retained.

The pre-eminence of sound, or the misleading and unwitting prioritization of words in adaptation studies, is a significant factor contributing to the exclusion of film adaptations of literary and dramatic texts from a place in the history of art as well as within literary and film studies, for most of the twentieth century. Adaptations, at least for many in the last century, are identified and doomed by their initial selling point: "all talking," dismissed for either saying too much or not enough.

Notes

1 This chapter, in part, develops material in Cartmell (2010), reproduced with permission of Palgrave Macmillan (September 21, 2011).

2 As Kenneth Rothwell points out, the first "talkie" of a Shakespeare play was a ten-minute trial scene from *The Merchant of Venice* in 1927 (1999: 29).

3 Thomas A. Pendleton notes that the print of the film in the Museum of Modern Art (Fairbanks' copy) contains no tagline and very little additional dialogue. According to Pendleton, additions include "O Petruchio, beloved" (after Katherine hurls a stool at Petruchio's head), her howl passing for "I do" at the wedding, and lines lifted from Garrick's adaptation of the play. At the end

of the wooing scene and after arriving at Petruchio's estate, Katherine states: "Look to your seat, Petruchio, or I throw you / Cath'rine shall tame this haggard; or if she fails / Shall tie her tongue up and pare down her nails."

4 Maria Jones (2000) has pointed out some confusion over the whips in the film. Jackson argues that Katherine throws Petruchio's whip into the fire, thereby disarming him while Hodgdon sees Katherine as throwing her own whip into the fire in an act of capitulation.

5 He loses some credibility when he refers to "the stilted phrases of the 15th century" (16).

6 The italics indicate where words have been changed or added. For instance "pretend"

replaces "intend,", "loving" replaces "reverend," and "sing" replaces "brawl." The text is taken from the soundtrack and compared to *The Taming of the Shrew*, 4.1, 175–98. This speech is not in *Catherine and Petruchio*.

7   As Jackson (1994: 120) and Henderson (2004: 124) note, Pickford claims in her autobiography, *Sunshine and Shadow* (1956), that she was told to rely on her silent tricks rather than attempt something more dramatic.

References

Agate, James. *London Pavilion*, no. 768, November 11, 1929.

Bluestone, George. *Novels into Film: The Metamorphosis of Fiction into Cinema*. Berkeley: University of California Press, 1957.

Cartmell, Deborah. "The First Adaptation of Shakespeare and the Recovery of the 'Renaissance' Voice: Sam Taylor's *The Taming of the Shrew*." In *The English Renaissance in Popular Culture*. Ed. Greg Colón Semenza. New York: Palgrave, 2010, 129–42.

Clark, Virginia M. *Aldous Huxley and Film*. London: Scarecrow, 1984.

Crowl, Samuel. *Shakespeare and Film: A Norton Critical Guide*. New York: Norton, 2008.

DeBona, Guerric. *Film Adaptation in the Hollywood Studio Era*. Urbana: University of Illinois Press, 2010.

Forsyth, Neil. "Shakespeare and the Talkies." In *The Seeming and the Seen: Essays in Modern Visual and Literary Culture*. Eds. Beverly Maeder, Jürg Schwyter, Ilona Sigrist, and Boris Vejdovsky. Bern: Peter Lang, 2006, 79–102.

Garrick, David. *Catherine and Petruchio. A Comedy. Altered from Shakespeare, by David Garrick, Esq. Taken from the manager's book at the Theatre Royal Covent-Garden*. Reproduction from Bodleian Library (Oxford). London: Gale, n.d.

Henderson, Diana E. "A Shrew for the Times, Revisited." In *Shakespeare the Movie II: Popularizing the Plays on Film, TV, Video and DVD*. Eds. Richard Burt and Lydna E. Boose. New York: Routledge, 2004, 120–39.

Hodgdon, Barbara. *The Shakespeare Trade: Performances & Appropriations*. Philadelphia: University of Pennsylvania Press, 1998.

Hunter, William. *Scrutiny of Cinema*. London: Wishart & Co., 1932.

Huxley, Aldous. "Silence is Golden." In *Authors on Film*. Ed. Harry M. Geduld. Bloomington: Indiana University Press, 1972, 68–76.

Huxley, Aldous. *Brave New World*. London: Vintage Press, 2004.

Jackson, Russell. "Shakespeare's Comedies on Film." In *Shakespeare and the Moving Image*. Eds. Anthony Davies and Stanley Wells. Cambridge: Cambridge University Press, 1994, 99–120.

Jones, Maria. " 'His' or 'Hers?' The Whips in Sam Taylor's *The Taming of the Shrew*." *Shakespeare Bulletin*, 18, 2000, 36–7.

Leavis, F. R. *Mass Civilisation and Minority Culture*. 1930 rpt. London: Arden, 1979.

Leavis, Q. D. *Fiction and the Reading Public*. 1932 rpt. London: Pimlico, 2000.

Manvell, Roger. *Shakespeare & the Film*. London: J. M. Dent, 1971.

Marcus, Laura. *The Tenth Muse: Writing about Cinema in the Modernist Period*. Oxford: Oxford University Press, 2007.

Nicoll, Allardyce. *Film and Theatre*. London: George G. Harrap, 1936.

Pendleton, Thomas A. "*The Taming of the Shrew*, by Shakespeare and Others." *PMLA*, 108, 1993, 152–3.

Panofsky, Erwin. "Style and Medium in the Moving Pictures." In *Film Theory and Film Criticism: Introductory Essays*, 4th edn. Eds. Gerald Mast, Marshall Cohen, and Leo Braudy. 1974, 233–48. Oxford: Oxford University Press, 1974, 233–48.

Rotha, Paul. *Celluloid: The Film Today*. London: Longmans, Green and Co., 1931.

Rothwell, Kenneth. *A History of Shakespeare on Screen: A Century of Film and Television*. Cambridge: Cambridge University Press, 1999.

Scotland, John. *The Talkies*. London: Crosby Lockwood and Son, 1930.

Seldes, Gilbert. *An Hour with the Movies and the Talkies*. London: J. P. Lippincott Co., 1929.

Shakespeare, William. *The Taming of the Shrew*. Ed. Brian Morris. London: Thomson, 2006.

Taming of the Shrew, The. Pressbook, 1929.

Taming of the Shrew, The. Dir. Sam Taylor. USA: United Artists, 1929.

Thompson, Ann. *The Taming of the Shrew*. Cambridge: Cambridge University Press, 1984.

Wagner, Geoffrey. *The Novel and the Cinema*. Rutherford, NJ: Fairleigh Dickinson University Press, 1975.

Willson, Robert F. Jr. *Shakespeare in Hollywood, 1929–1956*. Madison, Teaneck: Fairleigh Dickinson University Press, 2000.

Part II
Approaches

5

Adaptation and Intertextuality, or, What isn't an Adaptation, and What Does it Matter?

Thomas Leitch

In the final chapter of *A Theory of Adaptation,* Linda Hutcheon, after defining an adaptation as "an extended, deliberate, announced revisitation of a particular work of art" (Hutcheon, 2006: 170), asks what isn't an adaptation – that is, which kinds of intertexts do and do not count as adaptations. Following John Bryant's analysis in *The Fluid Text,* she argues that "no text is a fixed thing: there are always a variety of manuscript versions, revisions, and print editions" (170), just as there are inevitable variations in performances of *Hamlet* or *Turandot* or *Swan Lake* or "The Star-Spangled Banner." Distinguishing between "the kinds of fluidity determined by (a) the production process (writing, editing, publishing, and performing) and (b) those created by reception, by people . . . who censor, translate, bowdlerize, and adapt [texts] further" (170), she places these latter modes of revision on "a continuum of fluid relationships between prior works and later . . . revisitations of them" that constitute a "system of diffusion" (171). This continuum runs from those recreations that put an aesthetic premium on fidelity to the original text like literary translations and transcriptions of orchestral music for piano to condensations and abridgments to what Hutcheon calls "adaptation proper" (171), which conveniently occupies a position in the middle of the spectrum. At the other end are spin-offs like *Play It Again, Sam,* reviews and academic criticism that follow the film in "offer[ing] an overt and critical commentary" (171) on earlier works, sequels and prequels, fanzines and slash fiction, and Galadriel Barbie and Legolas Ken. Hutcheon specifically rules that brief allusions, "bits of sampled music" (170), and "museum exhibits" (172) are not adaptations, but these exceptions apart, the field sounds invitingly broad.

A Companion to Literature, Film, and Adaptation, First Edition. Edited by Deborah Cartmell.
© 2012 Blackwell Publishing Ltd. Published 2012 by Blackwell Publishing Ltd.

Hutcheon's formulation leaves several important questions unresolved. Why do adaptations have to be extended and announced as such? Is every performance an adaptation? Is every critical commentary, including this one? If all texts are fluid, multiple, and indeterminate – that is, if every text is an intertext whose stability and integrity are social and political rather than ontological – then what are the differences between adaptations and the whole vast range of intertexts? In short, where does adaptation proper cross the boundary and become adaptation improper? Brief and suggestive as it is, Hutcheon's analysis raises so many problems and leads to so many questionable calls that it goes a long way toward explaining why other writers on adaptation don't even attempt to distinguish adaptation from other modes of intertextuality. The most striking recent example, Julie Sanders' admirable *Adaptation and Appropriation,* begins with a section entitled "Defining Terms" consisting of two chapters, "What is Adaptation?" and "What is Appropriation?" Yet Sanders declines to draw a categorical distinction between the two terms, even though that is exactly what students consulting a volume in Routledge's New Critical Idiom series are presumably most likely to be seeking. Instead she distinguishes them only in terms of the degrees of closeness they exhibit to the texts that inform them:

> An adaptation signals *a relationship* with an informing sourcetext or original. . . . On the other hand, appropriation *frequently* effects a *more decisive journey away* from the informing text into a wholly new cultural product and domain. This *may or may not* involve a generic shift, and it *may* still require the intellectual juxtaposition of (at least) one text against another. . . . But the appropriated text or texts are *not always as clearly signaled or acknowledged* as in the adaptive process. They *may* occur in a far less straightforward context than is evident in making a film version of a canonical play (2005: 26, my emphasis).

Other recent theorists of adaptation have been equally reluctant to define their field of study. Neither Robert Stam nor Christine Geraghty defines adaptation, and Sarah Cardwell's definition – "the gradual development of a 'meta-text'" (2002: 25) – though highly successful in providing an alternative to what Cardwell calls "the centre-based model of adaptation" (15) that sees a novel like *Emma* as the only begetter of a series of reworkings all closely connected to it but not to each other – is much less successful in distinguishing adaptation from intertextuality in general.

Even though it would seem to be the first order of business for anyone writing on adaptation either to cite the consensually accepted definition of the term or, if there is no such definition, to provide a definition that explained how adaptations differed from the other modes of intertextual relations that were most like them, academic commentators do neither of these things. They cite earlier definitions only to take exception to them and generally decline to provide more watertight definitions because they are more concerned to distinguish their accounts of adaptation from errant earlier accounts, as Stam and Cardwell do, than to distinguish adaptations from the other intertextual modes that most closely resemble them. Given the widespread failure to make this distinction, we might conclude that Hutcheon is asking the wrong question. But if I take issue with parts of her answer, I deeply sympathize with her question, though I wonder if she asks it in the best way. The question "What isn't an adaptation?" implies that somewhere in the intertextual jungle is a bright line that separates adaptation from everything else. Even though I agree with Hutcheon that adaptation exists on a continuum of intertextual relations, her failure to locate this bright line suggests that there may be a less frustrating way to pose her question.

So I propose to transform Hutcheon's indispensable but unanswerable question into a series of questions that sound much less epigrammatic but may have the virtue of being answerable. Instead of asking what isn't an adaptation, I propose to ask where the line between adaptations proper and improper might plausibly be drawn, why we would want to draw it in one place rather than another, and what is the point of drawing it at all. I am especially interested in the implications for adaptation theory of drawing the line in different places: the advantages each line offers; the problems it raises; and the disciplinary consequences it has for adaptation studies. I begin with the axiom that adaptation is a subset of intertextuality – all adaptations are obviously intertexts, but it is much less obvious that all intertexts are adaptations – and review nine different accounts of the relation between adaptation and intertextuality. Though these nine different accounts are intended to be suggestive, not exhaustive, each of them has something valuable to offer the discourse on adaptation, and considering them all together provides more illumination than any one of them alone can offer.

1. Adaptations are exclusively cinematic, involving only films that are based on novels or plays or stories. I begin with this premise because it provided the dominant model in the field of adaptation studies for some forty years, from the publication of George Bluestone's *Novels into Film* in 1957 to the appearance in 1999 of *Adaptations: From Text to Screen, Screen to Text,* edited by Deborah Cartmell and Imelda Whelehan. This groundbreaking collection expanded the range of intertextual relations considered adaptations to include television programs, films based on comic strips, novelizations, and films like *The Piano* that feel like literary adaptations even though they are not. But although Cartmell and Whelehan argue persuasively against "the idea that literary adaptations are one-way translations from text – especially 'classic' texts – to screen" (23), the intertextual account of adaptation they provide is still fundamentally dualistic. It continues to be organized around articulations of and departures from a normative model involving literary originals and audio-visual adaptations that harkens back to Bluestone's observation that "the novel . . . [is] a medium antithetical to film" (1957: 23). Until September 2008, when it became the Association of Adaptation Studies, the Association of Literature on Screen Studies faithfully reflected this dualism in its very name.

This dualistic, bimedial account of adaptation has been extraordinarily powerful and persistent for several reasons. It offers both conceptual simplicity – the cinematic and televisual texts it considers as adaptations are counterpoised to their literary originals – and disciplinary neatness. Although its foundational dualities are so readily oversimplified that a whole generation of adaptation scholars – Morris Beja, Geoffrey Wagner, Keith Cohen, Dudley Andrew, Joy Gould Boyum, James Griffiths, Brian McFarlane – established their positions by quarreling with these dualities, none of them succeeded in replacing or decentering them. Even today, as McFarlane mourned a few years ago, the comment most frequently and depressingly heard when English teachers discuss literary adaptations is that "it wasn't like that in the book" (2007: 3).

The most obvious limitation of this approach to adaptation studies is that in an age of explosive new media, it excludes adaptations in virtually all media from consideration. Operas, ballets, theatrical plays, web pages, YouTube videos based on earlier texts – everything but film is eliminated from the field of study. Apart from this glaring and untimely parochialism, the page-to-screen approach – or, as it is generally practiced, the novel-to-film approach – is rife with conceptual fallacies. The problems it raises have been reviewed many times, perhaps most comprehensively and illuminatingly by Kamilla Elliott. In *Rethinking the Novel/Film Debate,* Elliott points out that it is based on a "designation of novels as 'words' and of films as 'images' [which] is neither empirically nor logically sustainable" (2003: 14) since many novels depend on images, either inscribed or implicit, and even more films depend on words, written as well as spoken. Both novels and films, to stick with the two modes on which Elliott focuses, are hybrid modes that "put pressure on . . . the temporal and spatial dichotomy of words and images" (18) that adaptation theory inherits from Gotthold Ephraim Lessing's 1766 *Laocoön,* his essay on the limits of painting and poetry, a dichotomy freighted with value judgments that invariably elevate original verbal texts above parasitic visual texts, which, as Bluestone famously asseverated, "cannot render thought" (1957: 47–8). As Rochelle Hurst has demonstrated, Bluestone's iron binary of novel and film, which ought logically to make "fidelity . . . an impossible ideal" that "should thereby be excluded as a means of critical assessment," ends up "paradoxically perpetuat[ing] the preoccupation with fidelity" because "the novel/film binary simultaneously bifurcates and hierarchizes the binaric pair, locating the novel as the superior, preferred locus in direct opposition to the film" (2008: 185).

At the same time, Elliott's close analysis of the text and reception of *Vanity Fair* in editions that included Thackeray's illustrations and illuminated chapter headings along with his words "reveal[s] dynamics that are far more aesthetically fecund than the deceptive, railroaded, agenda-driven rhetorical analogies of 'prose painting'" (76). Elliott's quarrel with oversimplified, loaded dichotomies between allegedly verbal and visual texts shows just how potentially productive these dualities can be despite the most staunch intentions of their proponents. Theories of adaptation rooted in the even more loaded dualities between literary and cinematic texts carry both the promise and the limitations of other fields defined by structuring dualities. By providing two possible disciplinary homes for adaptation studies, departments of literature and of cinema, they guarantee that adaptation studies will never be central or fully accepted by either one. This very lack of disciplinary comfort in a field contested by two reluctant disciplines has the potential, in the hands of a scholar like Elliott, to become adaptation studies' greatest strength.

2. **Adaptations are exclusively intermedial, involving the transfer of narrative elements from one medium to another.** This is a more generous version of the first model because it does not specify the two media as literature and film and therefore avoids the problems of weighing two media with such fraught histories against each other. It has been blessed by a most unexpected source, the Academy of Motion Picture Arts and Sciences, which since its 1958 awards ceremony has made a sharp distinction between films eligible for an Oscar for Best Original Screenplay and those eligible for an Oscar for Best Screenplay Based on Material from Another Medium. In fact, the Academy eerily prefigures contemporary scholarship in intermediality by declining to specify the other medium in question. Best Adapted Screenplays can be based on novels, plays, stories, operas, ballets, comic books, video games, or popular songs. Nor does the Academy require that the story have a specifically narrative basis in the earlier medium. The early James Bond movies, for example, were all eligible for the Best Adapted Screenplay Oscar because they were based on Ian Fleming's novels, the later movies because they were based on a franchise character who had floated free of any specific novelistic incarnation but still prevented them from being considered Best Original Screenplays.

If we follow Eckart Voigts-Virchow in tracing the genealogy of the term *intermediality* to both Julia Kristeva's anti-intentionalist notion of intertextuality and Dick Higgins's distinction "between intermedia (which fuses aesthetic practices) and multimedia or mixed media (which combine discrete media)" (2005: 83), we can see both the benefits of this framing of adaptation and some of the problems it raises. Two great advantages the intermedial model has over the page-to-screen model are the neutrality of its language and its corresponding freedom from the necessity of dogmatic evaluation. In principle, theorists of intermediality can be just as dogmatic in their value judgments as anyone else, but their terminology does not automatically imply such judgments, and their cultural studies approach generally waives evaluative questions. In addition, to the extent that its proponents remember that intermediality is not reducible to bimediality, this approach is free from the dualistic problems that beset page-to-screen theories of adaptation. Like the Academy Awards, intermedial models are hospitable to media that are neglected by the focus on novels and movies: oral storytelling, radio, television, and hypermedia. Perhaps because of their quest for a scientifically neutral language, intermedial studies have flourished in Europe. Indeed the United States is the only industrialized nation in which media study is not a required part of the public school curriculum. So an emphasis on intermediality would unite adaptation studies to a powerful disciplinary ally whose power is growing and spreading, one that could go far to promote the centrality of adaptation studies to education in media literacy.

For all its scientific precision and disciplinary power, however, an intermedial account of adaptation faces two formidable problems. One is the difficulty in differentiating between adaptation and other intermedial practices. Voigts-Virchow addresses this problem by distinguishing between "media combination, media transfer, and media contact," the second of which is the domain of adaptations, but the third of which encapsulates a "narrow notion of intermediality" (85–6). As he acknowledges, all these activities "may appear together in an individual media product" (86). So his taxonomy applies to relations and activities, not to texts themselves.

A complementary problem is the widespread existence of adaptations that are intramedial rather than intermedial. Chaucer borrows the stories for *The Knight's Tale, The Reeve's Tale,* and *Troilus and Criseyde* from Boccaccio without changing the medium – unless a change from prose to poetry, or from Italian to Middle English, is considered intermedial. Shakespeare plunders Holinshed and Plutarch for his history plays and bases *Henry V* on the earlier play *The Famous Victories of Henry V.* Numberless novels like *The Wind Done Gone* and films like the 1992 remake *The Last of the Mohicans* have been inspired by earlier novels and films. Voigts-Virchow, who is well aware of such examples, is at pains in his discussion of monster movies to distinguish between their status as "*trans*medial myths . . . *intra*medial meta-films . . . [and] *inter*medial references" (85). The result is to parcel out adaptation among transmedial, intramedial, and intermedial operations instead of considering it as a unified set of texts or textual operations or a unified disciplinary field. And it may well be that this is the most accurate way to define adaptation. It seems clear, however, that the price of an intermedial account of adaptation is to dissolve the operations it involves into a more comprehensive study of intermediality that sets itself against adaptation as a distinctive practice. It is no wonder that Hutcheon dissents from this view, asserting bluntly that "not every adaptation is necessarily a remediation" (2006: 170).

3. **Adaptations are counter-ekphrases.** This mouth-filling third formulation, which is closely linked to the second, sounds as if it has come out of left field because students of adaptation have declined to profit from the centuries-old study of ekphrasis. The earliest accounts of ekphrasis, dating from the third and fourth centuries C.E., define it as "an extended description . . . intrud[ing] upon the flow of discourse and, for its duration, . . . suspend[ing] the argument of the rhetor or the action of the poet" (Krieger, 1992: 7). In time the definition came to focus on the representation of artworks in one medium by artworks in another, as in Rembrandt's *Aristotle Contemplating the Bust of Homer,* and eventually on literary representations of the plastic arts, or "*the verbal representation of visual representation*" (Heffernan, 1993: 3) like Wallace Stevens' anecdote of the jar, Keats' Grecian urn, and the shield of

Achilles in the *Iliad*. The motto of ekphrasis is Horace's dictum *ut pictura poesis*: as pictures, so poetry.

The history of commentary on ekphrasis would be refreshing for adaptation theorists to read because it is one long confession of literature's hopeless inferiority to the visual arts. Although it anticipates adaptation study's prejudice in favor of the original artwork's anteriority over the copy's belatedness, it inverts what was until recently the customary assumption of adaptation theory by contending that words have to struggle to capture the power of images, rather than the other way around. Although adaptation could be defined as ekphrasis under the trope's earlier, broader definition of artworks that imitate artworks in another mode, it is far more suggestive to adopt the narrower definition, which has been prevalent since the Renaissance, and consider adaptation as counter-ekphrasis instead.

The consequent inversion of the hierarchy of representational modes so firmly entrenched in adaptation study from its beginnings is the most striking contribution the analogy between adaptation and ekphrasis has to offer the field. But considering adaptation as an inversion of ekphrasis raises other provocative implications as well. Murray Krieger, noting that neither Achilles' shield nor Keats' urn actually exists, describes ekphrasis not merely as the representation of a representation but as "the illusionary representation of the unrepresentable, even while that representation is allowed to masquerade as a natural sign" (1992: xv). In the case of Homer and Keats, ekphrasis creates the objects whose representations it purports to represent. The closest parallel in adaptation studies are films I have described as based on a true story, films that create nonexistent progenitor texts through the gesture of invoking them (Leitch, 2005: 289–90). Even though these films do not label themselves as adaptations, their invocation of sources they textualize by identifying them with "a true story" helps illuminate the process by which every adaptation, like every ekphrasis, both contests and confirms the status of its source by identifying it as a source.

In ages in which the visual sign is assumed to have an intimate, iconic link with its referent beyond the power of any verbal sign, ekphrasis underscores poetry's yearning toward a union with physical nature it cannot achieve. Even under semiotic analyses that read both verbal and visual representations as conventionally coded, ekphrasis continues to express "the dream of a return to the idyll of the natural sign" (Krieger, 1992: 22). From this point, it is a short step to considering "the visual emblem and the verbal emblem . . . complementary languages for seeking the representation of the unrepresentable. Ekphrasis is the poet's marriage of the two within the verbal art" (22). This account emphasizes what theorists have increasingly considered the hybrid nature of adaptation, which adds one language to another in an exhilarating, exasperating attempt to represent experiences that can only be invoked.

Refreshing as this inverted perspective is to contemplate, it is not easy to shoehorn adaptation into the mold of ekphrasis, or even of counter-ekphrasis. Ekphrasis involves embedded representation, not a point-by-point simulacrum of an earlier work that is coextensive with a later work. Homer's description of Achilles' shield has long stood as a model of ekphrasis not only because it represents a visual image of a nonexistent object but because it is so obviously digressive, stopping both the argument and the narrative of the *Iliad* in their tracks for the sake of a tour de force of detailed description. Ekphrasis, as James Heffernan asserts, "is the unruly antagonist of narrative, the ornamental digression that refuses to be merely ornamental" (1993: 5). This antagonistic refusal of narrative seems remote from the impulse toward adaptation in ways that cannot be recuperated by labeling adaptation counter-ekphrasis.

More important, the benefits of comparing adaptation to ekphrasis lie mostly in the past, in the form of a missed opportunity. Ten years ago, it would have been tonic for students of film adaptation, taking example from the study of ekphrasis, to attack the alleged superiority of literature as a representational medium. These students could have pointed to the winding road of ekphrasis studies, which began by proclaiming the superiority of the natural, visual sign before "celebrat[ing] the incapacity of words to yield natural signs and, instead, relat[ing] poetry to the temporal condition of our inner life" (Krieger, 1992: 24) and ultimately, beginning with Nietzsche, reversing the hierarchy of the arts, placing music, the most abstract and least obviously mimetic, at the top, literature in the middle, and the iconic visual arts at the bottom. As if summoned by this reordering, cinema arrived on the scene, quickly spawning theories of adaptation that accepted the recent denigration of visual representation as permanent and immutable. The history of ekphrasis studies would have provided valuable ammunition for adaptation theory ten years ago. But now that students of adaptation have spent so much of that period liberating their field, without any apparent awareness of ekphrasis, from the assumption that verbal representations are superior to visual representations, the other legacy of the motto *ut pictura poesis* – its inscription of a visual/verbal dichotomy most adaptation theorists would reject out of hand – so poisons it that it is hardly worth claiming.

4. Adaptations are texts whose status depends on the audience's acceptance of a deliberate invitation to read them as adaptations. The advantages of this position, which is Hutcheon's own, are surprisingly similar to those of the intermedial models to which it is opposed. By waiving questions of fidelity and evaluation as irrelevant to a definition of adaptation, it also frees adaptations from a good deal of invidious baggage. And by focusing on the practice of creating and interpreting adaptations, it too redirects attention from a hypostasized medium-specific duality to the relations between different texts and different processes of reading and writing. Although an older generation of critics might complain that this account of adaptation commits both the intentional and the affective fallacies, it would surely find a hospitable home, like intermedial studies, within the broader discipline of reception studies.

Problems arise from this account's double focus on production and reception. In order for an adaptation to count as an adaptation for Hutcheon, it has to meet two conditions: its creators must intend it to be perceived as an adaptation; and its audience must so perceive it. Under this model, the status of unacknowledged adaptations like *Torrid Zone* (1940), an unofficial remake of *His Girl Friday* (1940) in the tropics, is ambiguous. Such examples might seem marginal, but very few Hollywood remakes, from *Body Heat* (1981), which borrows its premise and much of its plot from *Double Indemnity* (1944), to *Swing Vote* (2008), widely compared by reviewers to *The Great Man Votes* (1939), explicitly credit their cinematic forbears. In fact, film remakes raise the most persistent problems for this account, since most remakes depend on what I have called "a triangular notion of intertextuality" (Leitch, 2002: 54) that positions them as readaptations of a common literary source while masking their debt to earlier film adaptations of that source. Since Hutcheon considers all remakes adaptations, it is fair to ask whether remakes that seek to conceal their status as remakes are still adaptations, and for whom.

These last three words raise other problems with this account. If a given audience misses the intertextual reference of a particular adaptation, does it still count as an adaptation? Clearly not for that audience. So the question of whether a particular adaptation counts as an adaptation rests not with any properties of the adaptation as such but with its audience – which would be fine if we hadn't just agreed that it rested with its creators. Nor will it resolve this problem to define adaptation as the product of a negotiation between creators and audiences, since this account specifically excludes from consideration the properties of that negotiation's site – the text of the adaptation itself. A particularly troublesome example for this account to handle is Gus Van Sant's virtually shot-by-shot 1998 remake of *Psycho*. None of the many commentators I have read on Van Sant's film, which duly includes the credit "Based on the novel by Robert Bloch," considers it an adaptation of the novel; they all treat it as a remake of Alfred Hitchcock's 1960 film adaptation, which its credits nowhere mention (though the closing credits include an acknowledgment to Hitchcock's daughter). Because Van Sant's film was a box-office failure, it has become a beau ideal of Hutcheon's position that what makes an adaptation an adaptation is that it is "seen *as an adaptation*" (Hutcheon, 2006: 6), since virtually everyone who has paid the slightest attention to the film has seen it in Hitchcock's shadow. At the same time, critical consensus on the film, which is invariably dismissed as a pale imitation of Hitchcock, would seem to make it a decisive exception to Hutcheon's rule that "an adaptation is a derivation that is not derivative – a work that is second without being secondary" (7).

The simplest way to contextualize Hutcheon's analysis is to consider which sorts of intertexts it most usefully distinguishes from adaptations. In Hutcheon's account, adaptation is not distinct from parody, pastiche, sequels, prequels, performance, orchestration, summary, or critical commentary, because it includes all these modes. The main modes that Hutcheon's criteria of a deliberate invitation to consider the adaptation's intertextuality and the conscious acceptance of that invitation are two kinds of intertexts: those that are literally indistinguishable from the originals, like photographic images and audiotaped performances; and those that misleadingly attempt to pass themselves off as original, like plagiarism and forgery. A definition of adaptation that emphasizes intentionality and reception is fundamentally economic because it inevitably focuses on the motives and interests that provide legal, moral, and aesthetic sanction for some kinds of copies, the derivations that are not derivative, but not others. Instead of seeking the scientific neutrality of terms like "intermediality," this model accepts the metaphorical baggage that comes with the term "adaptation" as a problem to be addressed head-on.

5. Adaptations are examples of a distinctive mode of transtextuality. This account comes from Gérard Genette's *Palimpsests,* which propounds five modes of transtextuality characteristic of "literature in the second degree": the intertextuality marked by quotation and allusion; the paratextuality indicated by "secondary signals" (1997: 3) like titles, prefaces, epigraphs, blurbs, and book jackets; the metatextuality of commentary and allusion; the "silent" architextuality implicit in paratextual generic markers like John Donne's title *Songs and Sonets* or Edwin Abbot's subtitle to *Flatland: A Romance of Many Dimensions*; and the hypertextuality that links one text to a hypotext "upon which it is grafted in a manner that is not commentary" (2008: 5). Of these five modes, hypertextuality, as Robert Stam points out, "is perhaps the type most clearly relevant to adaptation" (2005: 31).

The precision of Genette's categories, the richness and thoroughness of his commentary on a wide range of particular texts, with a heavy emphasis on the most "palimpsestuous" (1997: 399), and his patient discriminations between, for example, Jean de Meun's "unfaithful" (192) continuation of *The Romance of the Rose* and D. H. Lawrence's "murderous" (198) continuation of the Gospels in *The Man Who Died* – all these features compel close attention to his taxonomy. But if adaptation theorists paid Genette the attention he deserves, they would notice the problems his categories pose for adaptation studies.

The most obvious of these problems is that Genette nowhere discusses adaptation as a transtextual mode, or in any other connection either. He concludes his discussion of the 1972 film *Play It Again, Sam,* which he calls "a contract of cinematographic hypertextuality (hyperfilmicity)" and "a cinematic equivalent of the antinovel" whose final scene transforms it "from antinovel to travesty" and an example of "parodic art at its best" (156, 157), with the rueful remark: "This sort of 'stuff' is a bit out of my field" (157). Adaptation theorists looking to Genette for an authoritative system of classification that can distinguish adaptation from other modes of intertextuality – or, as Genette would say, transtextuality – are building on a shaky foundation.

This shakiness is largely intentional. Despite his reliance on the jargon of his taxonomy, Genette's attitude toward both his material and his project is consistently playful, as when he describes "the present book . . . that which thou, indefatigable

Reader, art supposedly holding in hand – is nothing other than the faithful transcription of a no less faithful nightmare, stemming from a hasty and, I fear, sketchy reading, in the dubious light of a few pages by Borges, or I know not what Dictionary of Works from All Times and All Countries" (394). Far from claiming that his transtextual categories are mutually exclusive, he warns at the outset that "one must not view the five types of transtextuality as separate and absolute categories without any reciprocal contact or overlapping" (7). He even declines to distinguish absolutely between hypertexts and hypotexts, arguing instead that "every successive state of a written text functions like a hypertext in relation to the state that precedes it and like a hypotext in relation to the one that follows" (395) and agreeing with Jean Giraudoux that allegedly original texts like the *Iliad* and *The Song of Roland* are simply "hypertexts whose hypotexts are unknown" (381). Despite the distinction implied by the subtitle of *Palimpsests – Literature in the Second Degree –* its power of discrimination is limited by the possibility that there may be no such thing as literature in the first degree, especially since the very category "literature" is already an architextual marker.

The only categorical distinction Genette upholds categorically is that between "the two fundamental types of hypertextual derivation: transformation and imitation" (394). But this distinction is useless in classifying adaptation, which clearly depends on both activities. Scarcely more helpful is his more tentative distinction between "two types of functions" within what he calls "the serious mode" of hypertextuality – including "practical" hypertexts like summaries and translations – that "responds to a social demand and legitimately endeavors to draw a profit from the service it renders," and a "more nobly aesthetic" mode in which "a writer leans on one or more preceding works to construct that which will give expression to his thought or his artistic sensibility" (395), since most cinematic adaptations seek both artistic and commercial success. Genette is on firmer ground when he is most elusive, as in his conclusion that "[t]he hypertext at its best is an indeterminate compound, unpredictable in its specifics, of seriousness and playfulness (lucidity and ludicity)" (400). *Palimpsests* provides a great deal of inspiration to adaptation theorists, but its author would be the first to disclaim any authority of its system of classification to distinguish adaptation from anything else.

6. **Adaptations are translations.** In setting forth this model, Linda Costanzo Cahir, its leading contemporary exponent, follows Bluestone (1957: 62) in distinguishing sharply between adaptation and translation, though she reverses the force of Bluestone's distinction:

While literature-based films are often, customarily and understandably, referred to as adaptations, the term "to adapt" means to alter the structure or function of an entity so that it is better fitted to survive and to multiply in its new environment. To adapt is to move *that same entity* into a new environment. In the process of adaptation, the same substantive entity which entered the process exits, even as it undergoes

modification – sometimes radical mutation – in its efforts to *accommodate* itself to its
new environment.

"To translate," in contrast to "to adapt," is to move a text from one language to
another. It is a *process of language,* not a process of survival and generation. Through
the process of translation a fully new text – *a materially different entity* – is made, one
that simultaneously has a strong relationship with its original source, yet is fully
independent from it. Simply put: we are able to read and appreciate the translation
without reading the original source (2006: 14).

For Cahir, it is not literally true that adaptations are translations. Instead, the
differences between the two are so crucial that what we mistakenly call adaptations
are more accurately described as translations.

This approach to adaptation, which insists on the textual and aesthetic integrity
of both the earlier and later incarnations of the text in question, offers two advantages. Its redefinition of adaptations as translations allies adaptations with the literal
translations of Chaucer and Shakespeare and other intramedial adaptations that pose
such taxonomic problems to intermedial theories of adaptation. And it places questions of fidelity in an illuminating new context familiar to students of translation,
who "have strong presumptions and predilections regarding the proper activities of
translators" (14). Cahir's translation model, like the traditional criteria for translations from one language to another, places a premium amounting virtually to an
ethical imperative on fidelity but asks, "To what . . . should the translator be *most*
faithful? The question is not that of the translation's faithfulness, but of its *faithfulness to what?*" (15).

Cahir aptly notes that "[e]*very act of translation* is simultaneously an act of interpretation" (14). But this observation reveals the deepest flaw in her account of
adaptation: its incompatibility with prevailing theories of translation, which are as
concerned to break down the integrity of individual textual manifestations as her
theory of adaptation is to maintain them. George Steiner, for example, introduces
the 1992 edition of his influential study *After Babel* by summarizing a "general
postulate" he judges to have been "widely accepted" since his monograph's first
publication in 1975:

> [T]ranslation is formally and pragmatically implicit in *every* act of communica-
> tion. . . . To understand is to decipher. To hear significance is to translate. Thus the
> essential structural and executive means and problems of the act of translation are
> fully present in acts of speech, of writing, of pictorial encoding inside any given
> language. Translation between different languages is a particular application of a con-
> figuration and model fundamental to human speech even where it is monoglot (xii).

Steiner's project, from his opening up of the textual and lexical indeterminacies
in Posthumus' philippic against women in *Cymbeline* to his prophecy of a Kabbalistic
future in which "translation is not only unnecessary but inconceivable" because
"[w]ords will rebel against man. They will shake off the servitude of meaning"

(499), is a sustained assault on the stability and integrity of the texts Cahir confidently assumes to be bearers of determinate meanings. Hence her theory raises several terminological problems she does not resolve. If adaptation is actually translation, then what is the precise relation between linguistic and medium-specific (not just cinematic) coding and decoding? Does recoding always involve repurposing? Does decoding? How does a shift to the medium of a new language compare to shifts in other media of communication? What are the advantages and disadvantages of adopting the first as an analogy – or is it a homology – for the second? The main problem with considering adaptation as translation, however, is that recent theories of translation, which have dramatically deepened Steiner's suspicion of the unitary pre-translated text, seem to run directly counter to the conclusions this model is presumably designed to support.

7. **Adaptations are performances.** If all adaptations are indeed interpretations, then it may be possible to take the opposite tack from Cahir and argue that all adaptations are performances. On the face of it, this suggestion sounds absurd, for adaptations are surely texts of one sort or another rather than realizations of texts. Robert Stam's celebrated list of nineteen different synonyms for adaptation, from rewriting to incarnation (2005: 25), does not include performance. Although James Griffiths has argued that a given adaptation can most usefully be seen as "an imitation [that] tries to capture some qualities of the object without perversely trying to capture them all" (1997: 41), no leading theorist has defined adaptation as performance. Even Hutcheon, whose survey considers "musical arrangements and song covers, visual art revisitations of prior works and comic book versions of history, poems put to music and remakes of films, and videogames and interactive art" (Hutcheon, 2006: 9), is content to observe that "live performance works" like musical scores represent a "parallel" case in which inevitable changes from performance to performance are determined by "the production process" rather than "by reception, by the people who 'materially alter texts'" (170; cf. Bryant, 2002: 7).

It would seem less improbable to call adaptations performances if the play rather than the novel were considered the unmarked source of cinematic adaptations, as it was in both the United States and France for the first forty years of the cinema. But it would be even more accurate to define adaptations as works that treat their forbears as performance texts, whether or not those forbears were originally so intended. The most servile adaptation implicitly proclaims its progenitor incomplete and in need of realization; otherwise why produce the adaptation at all? Even adaptations in the same medium as their alleged originals, like translations into a new language, pose as bringing these original works to new life by supplying something they notably lack. Such a forward-looking attitude, in which the performance text is treated as a recipe for a new creation rather than a court that has issued a restraining order anticipating any possible infractions by future realizations, could go far to correct the deplorably archeological tendency of adaptation study as it continues to be practiced.

Although all film adaptations are performances of their screenplays, Jack Boozer is surely correct in observing that the screenplay, widely discounted as an interloper in the novel/movie binary, "has been deemed merely a skeletal blueprint for the adapted film and thus unworthy of serious consideration in its own right" (2008: 2). Approaching adaptations as performances would direct closer attention to their screenplays as performance texts, and in the process productively complicate prevailing notions of authorship and text. A concomitant result would be to provide a new analytical context for film adaptations based on the relationship between other adaptations that clearly depend on performance and the texts they perform: operas and their librettos; ballets and their musical scores; popular songs and their words; pieces of liturgical music and the sacred texts they set; radio programs and the scripts on which they are based; even, at the far end of the spectrum, each new performance of Beethoven's Fifth Symphony.

This reorientation, however, would come at a price, for virtually all movies, not just adaptations, are performances of their screenplays. So the same reorientation that would draw closer attention to the vital features film adaptations share with ballets and radio programs would seriously muddle the difference hallowed for fifty years by the Academy of Motion Picture Arts and Sciences between those films that are written directly for the screen and those films that are not. Defining adaptation as congruent with all performance would open the floodgates to thousands of works that have never before been considered adaptations.

One way to distinguish adaptations from other performances would be to define adaptations not as performances but as recordings or transcriptions of performances. This rule would distinguish film adaptations, Top 40 recordings of pop music, and translations into a new language, on the one hand, from, for example, the innumerable separate performances of "Happy Birthday to You." Unfortunately, it would also distinguish canned theater, recorded music, and filmed opera and ballet, all of which would count as adaptations, from live performances of plays and operas and ballets and music, which would not. And surely there is a case to be made for every single performance of "Happy Birthday to You" as a new adaptation of the same performance text to specific performers and listeners and circumstances. Although it may well be impossible to define adaptation as a particular kind of performance practice, the analogy is valuable for the new light it throws on old problems, even if the cost is still more intransigent new problems of its own.

8. Adaptations are quintessential examples of intertextual practice. The effect of this claim would be to establish adaptation as not just a bustling metropolis but the capital city of the realm of intertextuality. The distinctive feature of this model is its emphasis on adaptation as a center rather than a congruence. Adaptation becomes in this account a locus that helps determine the shape of the field in which it is located but not its size or its boundaries. To adopt this model would amount to a triumph for adaptation scholars, whose principles and practices would become presumptive models for the whole range of intertextual studies.

Apart from the aggrandizing of adaptation studies, what would be gained by anointing adaptations – rather than parodies, sequels, commentaries, or the dialogized narrative Mikhail Bakhtin considered the novel's most distinctive quality – as the quintessential intertexts? Rochelle Hurst provides the basis for a defense of this position in her essay "Adaptation as an Undecidable: Fidelity and Binarity from Bluestone to Derrida." Reviewing the problems of fidelity discourse, which first rules faithfulness to source texts impossible and then castigates adaptations for failing to achieve it, Hurst invokes Jacques Derrida's notion of "undecidables" – "'false' verbal properties . . . that can no longer be included within philosophical (binary) opposition, but which, however, *inhabit* philosophical opposition, resisting and disorganizing it, *without ever* constituting a third term, without ever leaving room for a solution in the form of speculative dialectics" (2008: 186; cf. Derrida, 1981: 43). For Hurst, adaptation is a stellar example of a Derridean undecidable that "inhabits *both* sides of the binary" (186). Every reference in scholarly and popular writing to an adaptation as a "version" of an earlier text – every assertion that "the adaptation, in a sense, *is* the novel – albeit the novel in filmic guise" (188) – underlines adaptation's status as "a hybrid, an amalgam of media – at once a cinematized novel *and* a literary film, confusing, bridging, and rejecting the alleged discordance between page and screen, both insisting upon and occupying the overlap" (187).

There are many other texts, of course, that call the potency of such binaries into question. Derrida himself cites Plato's pharmacy, the hymen, the zombie, and the androgyne as scandalous undecidables. What makes adaptation an especially powerful member of this company is that it calls into question the very dichotomies concerning texts, textuality, and cultural status that John Tibbetts and Jim Welsh have listed as constitutive of the field: "art and commerce, individual creativity and collaborative fabrication, culture and mass culture, the verbal and the visual" (2005: xv). The metaphorical dichotomy posed by Tibbetts and Welsh's opening question – "Literature and film: is this a natural marriage or a shotgun wedding?" (xv) – encapsulates both the epigrammatic advantages and the conceptual pitfalls of the dualistic thinking adaptation simultaneously encourages and challenges. Adaptation is the mode of intertextuality that has been defined from its beginnings as a problem child, a mode whose definition has focused on its challenge to the binaries on which both it and its critical discourse have depended.

Hutcheon's definition of adaptation as "repetition without replication" (2006: 7) would seem to make adaptation central to both intertextual and intermedial theory, where its manifest problems would be welcomed as precisely the kind of material around which scholarly disciplines are organized. Indeed adaptation offers serious advantages in this regard over both literature and cinema, which both have to settle for a canon of works rather than a series of productive problems as their disciplines' weaker organizing principles. Yet it is Hutcheon who provides the ammunition for the sharpest critique of this model.

9. Adaptations are a distinctive instance, but not a central or quintessential instance, of intertextuality. This model amounts to a confession of failure, or at least a fallback position, from the previous model. It is not a model that Hutcheon espouses, but it is implicit in her earlier work on intertextuality, as when she observes that

> [w]hile we need to expand the concept of adaptation to include the extended "refunc-tioning" (as the Russian formalists called it) that is characteristic of the art of our time, we also need to restrict its focus in the sense that adaptation's "target" text is always another work of art or, more generally, another form of coded discourse (Hutch-eon, 1985: 16).

As she concludes her earlier monograph, Hutcheon reviews her survey by noting that

> [i]n the last five chapters, the "worldly" or ideological status of adaptation has been touched on a number of times. Much adaptation, we saw, turned out to be conserva-tive or normative in its critical function. . . . According to a Romantic aesthetic, such forms of art are by definition parasitic. Even today, this same negative evaluation exists and its basis, as betrayed by its language, is often ideological in a very general sense: we are told that adaptation seeks to dominate texts, but that it is still ultimately peripheral and parasitic (Stierle, 1983, 19–20).
>
> We have also seen, however, that there is another type of adaptation. . . . This other kind or mode has a wider range of pragmatic ethos and its form is considerably more extended. Adaptation in much twentieth-century art is a major mode of thematic and formal structuring, involving what I earlier called integrated modeling processes. As such, it is one of the most frequent forms taken by textual self-reflexivity in our century. It marks the intersection of creation and re-creation, of invention and critique (Hutcheon, 1985: 100–1)

The claims Hutcheon makes here for adaptation as the quintessential mode of intertextuality would be very broad indeed if she were actually talking about adap-tation. But in fact she is talking about parody. My only alteration to these two quoted passages, to substitute "adaptation" for "parody" every time the latter word appears, indicates how seductively easy it is to make precisely the same global and normative claims for any of a number of intertextual modes of which adaptation is only one contender, and by no means clearly the strongest.

If adaptation, however, is challenged by partisans of translation and parody for centrality in the field, the resulting debates can only be good for intertextual studies. Even if adaptation is ultimately dethroned by another contender, its textual status, readily summarized as the-same-but-different, can serve as a powerful way to organize genre theory. Both the production and marketing of best-sellers, which depend on creating and satisfying the demand for a reliable product that is con-stantly improving, depend on this claim, as in publisher Stephen Rubin's blurb for an aspiring blockbuster: "Linda Fairstein always comes up with an intriguing hook for her Alex Cooper thrillers. In *Lethal Legacy* she has outdone herself" (2009: i). As I have suggested elsewhere, adaptation, "the master Hollywood genre that sets the pattern for all the others" (Leitch, 2008: 117), can provide as much insight into the reception of genres as into their production and distribution.

This final model, which leaves the work of distinguishing adaptations from other intertextual modes as a central task for the discipline of intertextual studies, is a good place to conclude my survey because it is so inconclusive. Instead of offering a logical conclusion, I'd prefer to close this essay by distinguishing three futures for the field of adaptation studies that depend on whether its practitioners define adaptation itself from the center or the edges.

If we begin by proposing a central rationale for adaptation, a single definition intended to apply to all and only adaptations or an analogy that explains why some texts but not others are to be considered adaptations, our attempt to define the field from the inside out leaves us with the problems of establishing its coherence, its consistency, and its boundaries with other competing fields. If, by contrast, we begin with the question of how to distinguish adaptations from the other texts they most closely resemble and then attempt to define the genus of which adaptations are a species, our choice of boundaries will define the field from the outside in, and we face the problem of rationalizing the field we have fenced in and demonstrating its integrity. In the spirit of confounding binaries, however, I propose a third alternative based on the fact that the field has been marked over the past ten years by a notable lack of consensus about the extent, the methodology, and the boundaries appropriate to its objects of study – except, of course, for the near-unanimous rejection of fidelity discourse, the bad object of adaptation studies – and an equally notable efflorescence of provocative scholarship. After reviewing the problems involved in organizing the discipline more rigorously, adaptation scholars may well decide to defer the question of what isn't an adaptation indefinitely. After all, no matter how they answer that question, they will be imposing new disciplinary constraints on a field that may well flourish more successfully when a thousand flowers bloom.

REFERENCES

Abbot, Edward. *Flatland: A Romance of Many Dimensions*. Ed. Rosemary Jann. New York: Oxford University Press, 2008. (Original work published 1884.)

Bluestone, George. *Novels into Film: The Metamorphosis of Fiction into Cinema*. Baltimore: Johns Hopkins University Press, 1957.

Body Heat. Dir. Lawrence Kasdan. USA: Ladd/ Warner Bros., 1981.

Boozer, Jack. "Introduction: The Screenplay and Authorship in Adaptation." In *Authorship in Film Adaptation*. Ed. Jack Boozer. Austin: University of Texas Press, 2008, 1–30.

Bryant, John. *The Fluid Text: A Theory of Revision and Editing for Book and Screen*. Ann Arbor: University of Michigan Press, 2002.

Cahir, Linda Costanzo. *Literature into Film: Theory and Practical Applications*. Jefferson, NC: McFarland, 2006.

Cardwell, Sarah. *Adaptation Revisited: Television and the Classic Novel*. Manchester: Manchester University Press, 2002.

Cartmell, Deborah. "Introduction to Part 2." In *Adaptations: From Text to Screen, Screen to Text.* Eds. Deborah Cartmell and Imelda Whelehan. London: Routledge, 1999, 23–8.

de Loris, Guillaume, and Jean de Meun. *The Romance of the Rose.* Trans. Frances Horgan. New York: Oxford University Press, 1999. (Original work published 1230/1275.)

Derrida, Jacques. *Positions.* Trans. Alan Bass. Chicago: University of Chicago Press, 1981.

Donne, John. *The Songs and Sonnets of John Donne.* 2nd edn. Ed. Theodore Redpath. Cambridge: Harvard University Press, 2009. (Original published 1635.)

Double Indemnity. Dir. Billy Wilder. USA: Paramount, 1944.

Elliott, Kamilla. *Rethinking the Novel/Film Debate.* Cambridge: Cambridge University Press, 2003.

Genette, Gérard. *Palimpsests: Literature in the Second Degree.* Trans. Channa Newman and Claude Doubinsky. Lincoln: University of Nebraska Press, 1997. (Original work published 1982.)

The Great Man Votes. Dir. Garson Kanin. USA: RKO, 1939.

Griffiths, James. *Adaptations as Imitations.* Newark: University of Delaware Press, 1997.

Heffernan, James A. W. *Museum of Words: The Poetics of Ekphrasis from Homer to Ashbery.* Chicago: University of Chicago Press, 1993.

His Girl Friday. Dir. Howard Hawks. USA: Columbia, 1940.

Hurst, Rochelle. Adaptation as an Undecidable: Fidelity and Binarity from Bluestone to Derrida. In *In/Fidelity: Essays on Film Adaptation.* Eds. David L. Kranz and Nancy C. Mellerski. Cambridge: Cambridge Scholars Press, 2008, 172–96.

Hutcheon, Linda. *A Theory of Parody: The Teachings of Twentieth-Century Art Forms.* New York: Methuen, 1985.

Hutcheon, Linda. *A Theory of Adaptation.* New York: Routledge, 2006.

Krieger, Murray. *Ekphrasis: The Illusion of the Natural Sign.* Baltimore: Johns Hopkins University Press, 1992.

Lawrence, D. H. *The Man Who Died.* London: Secker, 1931.

Leitch, Thomas. "Twice-Told Tales: Disavowal and the Rhetoric of the Remake." In *Dead Ringers: The Remake in Theory and Practice.* Ed. Jennifer Forrest and Leonard Koos. Albany: SUNY Press, 2002, 37–62.

Leitch, Thomas. *Film Adaptation and its Discontents: From* Gone with the Wind *to* The Passion of the Christ. Baltimore: Johns Hopkins University Press, 2005.

Leitch, Thomas. "Adaptation, the Genre." *Adaptation,* 1.2, 2008, 106–20.

McFarlane, Brian. "It wasn't like that in the book. . . ." *Literature/Film Quarterly,* 28, 2000, 163–9. Rev. and rpt. in *The Literature/Film Reader.* Eds. James M. Welsch and Peter Lev Lanham, MD: Scarecrow, 2007, 3–14.

Play It Again, Sam. Dir. Herbert Ross. USA: Paramount, 1972.

Psycho. Dir. Alfred Hitchcock. USA: Paramount, 1960.

Psycho. Dir. Gus Van Sant. USA: Universal. 1998.

Rubin, Stephen. "Dear Bookseller." introductory letter prefacing Advance Reading Copies of Linda Fairstein, *Lethal Legacy.* (Unpaged front matter [p. i]). New York: Doubleday, 2009.

Sanders, Julie. *Adaptation and Appropriation.* London: Routledge, 2005.

Stam, Robert. "Introduction: The Theory and Practice of Adaptation." *Literature and Film: A Guide to the Theory and Practice of Film Adaptation.* Malden, MA: Blackwell, 2005, 1–52.

Steiner, George. *After Babel: Aspects of Language and Translation.* 2nd edn. Oxford: Oxford University Press, 1992.

Stierle, Karlheinz. "Werk und Intertextualität." [Work and Intertextuality] In *Dialog der Texte: Hamburger Kolloquium zur Intertextualität.* [Dialogue of Texts: Hamburg Colloquia to Intertexuality]. Eds. Wolf Schmid and Wolf-Dieter Stempel Vienna: Wiener Slawistischer Almanach, 1983, 7–26.

Tibbetts, John C., and James M. Welsh. Eds. *The Encyclopedia of Novels into Film.* 2nd edn. New York: Checkmark/Facts on File, 2005.

Torrid Zone. Dir. William Keighley. USA: Warner Bros., 1940.

Voigts-Virchow, Eckart. *Introduction to Media Studies.* Stuttgart: Klett, 2005.

6
Film Authorship and Adaptation

Shelley Cobb

The 2002 film *Adaptation* written by Charlie Kaufman (with additional credit for his fictitious twin brother Donald Kaufman) and directed by Spike Jonze stands out among film adaptations, as other adaptation critics and scholars have noted, in that it is a self-conscious and self-reflexive film about the adaptation process (Hutcheon, 2006: 15; Stam, 2004: 1). The narrative centers on Charlie Kaufman's attempt to adapt Susan Orlean's *The Orchid Thief*, a nonfiction book about Florida plant dealer John Laroche who (illegally) collects and sells rare orchids. Charlie struggles with the process of writing the adaptation but also struggles with questions about what it means to be a scriptwriter and the author of an adaptation. He fights an inferiority complex while watching his less talented twin brother Donald use a formulaic how-to-write-a-script course to make a success of his first screenplay. The film also shows Orlean writing and researching her book and developing a relationship with Laroche, which leads to the two of them getting high and stealing orchids. These two narratives ultimately intertwine when Kaufman sees the drugs, and Orlean trips out, declaring "we have to kill him . . . before he murders my book!" The film culminates in a standoff between Laroche and Orlean against the Kaufmans. Laroche and Orlean chase the Kaufmans through the Florida swamps, and they kill Donald who was trying to save his brother. As they chase Charlie deeper into the swamp, an alligator attacks and kills Laroche. Orlean breaks down over Laroche's body and says, "I want my life back . . . before it got all fucked up. Let me be a baby again. Let me be new." The film then cuts to Charlie in a blanket leaning against a cop car. Orlean's breakdown is the last time she appears on screen. Charlie's narrative is resolved by a romantic reunion with the woman he loves and a revelation about

A Companion to Literature, Film, and Adaptation, First Edition. Edited by Deborah Cartmell.
© 2012 Blackwell Publishing Ltd. Published 2012 by Blackwell Publishing Ltd.

how to conclude the script of his adaptation, while Orlean is left wishing for a new beginning.

Drafts of the script available online have more satisfying, if disturbing, conclusions to Orlean's narrative. In a draft from 1999, Orlean, after Laroche's death, shouts at Charlie that he is a fat pig and Donald comes to his defense, attacking Orlean.[1] A gun goes off and both Orlean and Donald die. In a draft dated 2000, Orlean says the lines about being new and then she shoots herself with a gun in front of Kaufman before the police arrive. No matter how her narrative ends, Orlean will not be returning to seek her revenge on the scriptwriter, or filmmakers, who adapt her book into something unrecognizable, essentially "murdering" it. Orlean must disappear for Kaufman to have his happy ending. Still, she does try to kill him first, to save her story, to save herself. After the alligator kills Laroche, it is clear that they cannot both make it to the end. The showdown between Orlean and Kaufman, the novelist and the scriptwriter of an adaptation, acts out a central but often covert concern of adaptation studies, criticism, and reviews: authorship and its relation to ownership. In a culture where authority, originality, and ownership still construct the meanings, uses, and appreciation of art and cultural texts (despite all our postmodern views and poststructuralist theorizing to the contrary), adaptation complicates and challenges these values. The confrontation between Orlean and Kaufman and the narrative logic that requires that only one can be the surviving author plays out our cultural repression of the fact that adaptation requires two authors, if not more. Moreover, *Adaptation* never considers the director's role as an author of the film adaptation, an omission, I would argue, that further exposes, within the narrative, our cultural fears of multiple authors and the impossibility of imagining those fears in a battle between more than two. In contradiction of the film's narrative, screenwriters have struggled to hold a place in the on-again/off-again debates about authorship in film studies, a fact that exposes the institutionalized repression of that same fear.[2]

The film's imagining of adaptation as a battle of violence (and death) amongst authors is not unique. Consider John Patterson's tirade in the *Guardian* for his article titled "Pass the pillow. If only . . . great writers could stop their stories being made into dull movies":

> There is no more wretched or ephemeral an endeavour than the adaptation of a great novel to celluloid . . . . The problem resurfaces again and again throughout Hollywood history like an unconquerable strain of bibliophobic herpes. Name me an unparalleled masterpiece of literature and I will show you at least one film version of it (and in some cases seven or eight) so atrocious it's likely to reanimate the corpse of the writer and have them shuffling zombie-like toward Beverly Hills with vengeance in mind. *War and Peace? The Brothers Karamazov?* Rubbishy movies. *The Godfather? Gone with the Wind?* That's more like it! (Patterson, 2007).

The passage typifies the way that the biases around authorship, outlined above, often play out in the reception of adaptations in a binary between high culture and low culture. Accepting a cultural cliché of formalism that "true Art" can only exist in one form, he argues that high culture texts like *War and Peace* and *The Brothers Karamazov* never make good films.[3] He also suggests that only popular novels like *Gone with the Wind* and *The Godfather* can be adapted, reinforcing the formalist cliché and its elitism. The high culture/low culture binary has meant that adaptation studies, historically, tended to focus on the literary author – evidenced by the myriad books organized around adaptations of a single author (Henry James, Jane Austen, Shakespeare) – and sidelined adaptations of popular novels as not adaptations per se. Recently, scholars like James Naremore and Timothy Corrigan have argued that auteurs avoid the restrictions of fidelity in their adaptations because the required faithfulness is to their own authorial identities, putting an emphasis on the performative nature of adaptation (Naremore, 2001: 8). Alfred Hitchcock makes similar claims alongside François Truffaut in their interviews from 1967. In this chapter, I analyze their conversation closely in order to examine how the establishment of the film auteur depended upon formalist aesthetics and the distinction between high and low art forms understood specifically through adaptation. Cinema's historical struggle to be accepted as an art in its own right has been well documented, as well as auteur theory's central role in that struggle. I would not be the first to suggest that auteur theory made its mark on that struggle by constructing the cinema auteur as the equivalent of the (paternal) literary author and, in effect, elevating (some) cinema above mass production and mass culture. However, the role of adaptation in that move has been little commented on.

One of my main points in this chapter is that elevation of the film auteur is effected through a gendered language (Cobb, 2011). Hitchcock's ability to recode adaptation from reproduction to production is a claim to artistic paternity. In her work on the fidelity metaphor in translation studies, Lori Chamberlain argues that "in the metaphoric system [of fidelity] . . . what the translator [adaptor] claims for 'himself' is precisely the right of paternity; he claims a phallus because this is the only way, in a patriarchal code, to claim legitimacy for the text" (Chamberlain, 1992: 67). Chamberlain goes on to argue, "to claim that translating is like writing, then, is to make it a creative – rather than merely re-creative – activity" (1992: 67). Alexandre Astruc (a *Cahiers du Cinéma* critic associated with the auteur theory) also claimed cinema as a form of writing in his article "The Birth of a New Avant-Garde: Le caméra-stylo." He argues that auteur cinema, which rejects the scriptwriter as a role distinct from the director, moves beyond filmmaking as simply "illustrating a scene" and becomes "a true act of writing." For Astruc, "The film-maker/author writes with his camera as a writer writes with his pen" (Astruc, 1968: 17). Of course, Sandra Gilbert and Susan Gubar, in their book *Madwoman in the Attic* (1979), have made the link between the phallus and the pen clear. Therefore when an auteur, with his caméra-stylo, makes an adaptation, the process can be recoded into masculine production rather than feminine reproduction. The recoding of adaptation into production often entails violence, and discursively, the relationship between the film auteur and the literary author becomes a kind of battle that is often meta-phorically haunted by the specter of death (much like the showdown between Kaufman and Orlean).

Adaptation and the Authority of the Auteur

The language of fidelity that has traditionally plagued adaptation criticism has coded adaptation as a form of artistic reproduction rather than production. However, some adaptations can be recoded from reproduction to production. For these films, their authority, originality, and paternity have been so definitively produced by the filmmaker that they are hardly understood as adaptations at all (even if marked with legal and cultural signs of adaptation), and they are received as the artistic products of their film authors. This transfer of ownership, gained by the recoding of adaptation into a productive activity, becomes a signifier of authority and originality – two signs central to the image of the auteur.

In his interviews with Alfred Hitchcock, François Truffaut makes this recoding of reproduction into production and transfer of ownership very clear when he says to Hitchcock, "your own works include a great many adaptations, but mostly they are popular or light entertainment novels, which are so freely refashioned in your own manner that they ultimately become a Hitchcock creation" (Truffaut, 1983: 71). Truffaut's phrase "freely refashioned" implies that Hitchcock rejects any obligations toward fidelity in his adaptations so that instead of reproducing a film version of a novel or short story, he produces something new, something in his "own manner" that effectively eradicates the original author's authority and gives Hitchcock full ownership of the adaptation. His ownership then becomes a signifier of his auteur status: "a Hitchcock creation."[4] However, Truffaut offhandedly concedes that this depends on a lack of cultural status for the originals. As "popular and light entertainment" Hitchcock's source texts always/already have a "weakened" author because they are non-canonical, popular literature, often genre fiction that depends on the modified repetition of generic codes for its identity rather than a recogniz-able author-artist. Outside the "great tradition" of any national literary culture and nearly as mass-produced as classical cinema itself, historically (before the influence of cultural studies on literary studies) these narratives have been dismissed as art by critics in the same terms that those critics have dismissed classical Hollywood cinema. Most influentially, Q. D. Leavis describes the reading of popular fiction as "a drug addiction" (1978: 152), and her husband F. R. Leavis describes the watching of cinema as equally dangerous: "[films] involve surrender, under conditions of hypnotic receptivity, to the cheapest emotional appeals" (2006: 14). Truffaut's comment asserts the authority of the cinematic auteur by juxtaposing Hitchcock's authorial status to the absent authorial status of "popular and light entertainment" literature, pitting one mass culture form against another with the apparent intent to situate cinema as culturally superior. Below, he further distances cinema from popular literature by aligning it with the authorial status of the classical, canonical, literary author:

> F. T.: Many of your admirers would like to see you undertake the screen version of such a major classic as Dostoyevsky's *Crime and Punishment*, for instance.
>
> A. H.: Well, I shall never do that, precisely because *Crime and Punishment* is somebody else's achievement. There's been a lot of talk about the way in which Hollywood directors distort literary masterpieces. I'll have no part of that! What I do is to read a story only once, and if I like the basic idea. I just forget all about the book and start to create cinema. Today I would be unable to tell you the story of Daphne du Maurier's *The Birds*. I read it only once, and very quickly at that. An author takes three or four years to write a fine novel; it's his whole life. Then other people take it over completely. Craftsmen and technicians fiddle around with it and eventually someone winds up as a candidate for an Oscar, while the author is entirely forgotten. I simply can't see that (Truffaut, 1983: 71).

Hitchcock's response tells us much about his own views and, as we shall see, Truffaut's views, on authorship, both literary and cinematic. He immediately declines the idea that he might adapt *Crime and Punishment* because it is an "achievement," and it is clear that he does not simply mean a finished product but an accomplishment of high quality that requires significant personal investment, and it belongs to someone else, namely Dostoevsky, the author of a "literary masterpiece." His language reflects that of *The Great Tradition* when Leavis explains that his project entails asserting which authors do (and, by extension, which do not) "belong to the realm of significant creative achievement" (Leavis F. R., 1948: 2). Hitchcock's exclamation, "I'll have no part of that!" suggests that, according to his standards, the adaptation of a literary masterpiece by a revered author borders on the illegal and definitely stands outside the bounds of artistic propriety. It is only "craftsmen and technicians" who engage in such objectionable behavior. Hitchcock's labeling of filmmakers who adapt classics as such excludes them from any authorial or proprietary pretensions, and by having declared that he would never "fiddle" with another man's achievement, he sets himself apart from the journeyman status that he bestows on them. His final disparagement, "somebody winds up as a candidate for an Oscar," works to undermine the significance of Hollywood's institutional awards while simultaneously linking his lack of Oscars with his refusal to tamper with another's authorial masterpiece. Ultimately he seems to be suggesting that he never received an Oscar because he is not a "craftsman" but something more: an author who creates masterpieces (Truffaut, 1983: 133).[5] Finally, in order to protect the authority of his own masterpieces he must also protect other authors' masterpieces by not adapting them. In this way, Hitchcock performs his identity as an auteur in distinction to the *metteur-en-scène* that Truffaut articulates in his essay "A Certain Tendency in French Cinema" (2009).

To make the equation definitively clear, in the introduction to the printed interviews, Truffaut writes,

If, in the era of Ingmar Bergman, one accepts the premise that cinema is an art form, on a par with literature, I suggest that Hitchcock belongs – and why classify him at all? – among such artists of anxiety as Kafka, Dostoyevsky, and Poe (Truffaut, 1983: 20).

From our vantage point, the answer to Truffaut's question about classification seems fairly obvious: the intent is to align Hitchcock and his films with the untouchable and masterly Dostoyevsky rather than the forgettable and "light" Daphne du Maurier. His quick and thoughtless consumption of *The Birds* may be, in part, because it is a short story, but his consumption of it acts as the example of how he treats all "books" that he adapts. These books along with *The Birds* are outside the category of a "fine novel" by an author who gives his "whole life." They are, as popular novels and stories have generally been understood, formulaic, generic, quick reads, lacking depth and complexity. They are not masterpieces:

> F. T.: I take it then that you'll never do a screen version of *Crime and Punishment*.
> A. H.: Even if I did, it probably wouldn't be any good.
> F. T.: Why not?
> A.H.: Well, in Dostoyevsky's novel there are many, many words and all of them have a function.
> F.T.: That's right. Theoretically, a masterpiece is something that has already found its perfect form, its definitive form (Truffaut, 1983: 69–72).

By definition then, masterpieces are unadaptable; the inevitable circular reasoning implicit in these comments is that anything that is adaptable or that is an adaptation is not a masterpiece.[6] Ultimately, though, the importance of this configuration for the auteur is that any filmmaker who can adapt successfully, recoding reproduction into production, is a master.

More recently, in his article, "Which Shakespeare to Love? Film, Fidelity, and the Performance of Literature," Timothy Corrigan has argued that in postmodern popular culture, the filmmaker can now master a literary master. He suggests that in this "post-cultural" age when the unity of texts has been fragmented and canonical writers "have come to represent an illusory and fossilized sense of individuality" the "vision, style, and signature of the filmmaker as auteur supplants the missing literary author as controlling and defining agency" (Corrigan, 2002: 158, 165). Therefore, the current commerce of auteurism no longer requires a popular, mass-culture source text for its lack of authority, but can now consume the classical, canonical author whose cultural status has diminished in this postmodern, post-structural, post-death-of-the-author culture. Corrigan cites Gus Van Sant's *My Own Private Idaho* (1991) and Scorsese's *The Age of Innocence* (1993) as examples, but his example par excellence is Kenneth Branagh and his multiple Shakespeare adaptations: "he draws attention away from the text and to the performative virtuosity that we, the audience, are invited to participate in as a shared recognition not of textual Shakespeare, lost to time, but of the performative Branagh as an agent of the dead, overcoming time" (Corrigan, 2002: 176). Corrigan argues that "fidelity has become a fully archaic aesthetic measure, except as one can be faithful to one's own self, desire, tastes, imagination, and inclinations" (Corrigan, 2002: 167). The "one" is of course the auteur, and it is only the auteur who can restore the viewer's "faith in the fidelity of individual vision and idiosyncrasies of self-expression" (Corrigan, 2002: 168). For Corrigan, then, fidelity is concerned with the textuality of the auteur's repeatable signature.

Although I find Corrigan's argument about the performance of literary adaptations to be compelling, ultimately its limitation lies in its dependence on a catholic understanding of the auteur who has the opportunity, the resources, and the cultural authority to repeat that signature in multiple films. Feminist film theorists have shown that industrially, economically, and culturally female filmmakers have been excluded from this elite masculine club.[7] Feminist psychoanalytic theorists have also shown that the process of individuation necessary for the expression of "individual vision" within a patriarchal culture requires the demonization of all things feminine, whether that be the female, the queer male, the transsexual, or any other gendered identity that troubles the boundaries and the hierarchies between the masculine and its others.[8] However, as Tania Modleski (1989) has shown, particularly in the instance of Hitchcock's *Rebecca*, masculine, and therefore authoritative, "individual vision" and expression is not necessarily hermetically sealed off from the forces of the feminine.

As evidence of the persistence of the feminine in Hitchcock's work and identity as an auteur, in her book *The Women Who Knew Too Much: Hitchcock and Feminist Theory*, Modleski cites the following: Hitchcock's declaration of *Rebecca* that "it's not a Hitchcock picture;" the evidence from David O. Selznick's infamous memo that he insisted Hitchcock keep "the little feminine things;" Robin Wood's declaration that "the film fails either to assimilate or to vomit out the indigestible novelettish ingredients of Daphne du Maurier's book;" and Truffaut's supposition that *Rebecca* inspired Hitchcock to "enrich" later films "with the psychological ingredients . . . in the Daphne du Maurier novel" in order to argue that:

> Such are the paradoxes of auteurship: by being forced to maintain a close identification with du Maurier's "feminine" text to the point where he felt that the picture could not be considered his own . . . Hitchcock found one of his "proper" subjects – the potential terror and loss of self involved *in* identification, especially identification with a woman.
>
> *Rebecca* thus provides one final ironic instance of the notion that the feminine is that which subverts identity – in this case, the identity of the auteur, the Master of the labyrinth himself (Modleski, 1989: 43).

Modleski seems, to me, to make a point about auteurship that Corrigan misses because of his delight in "the power of film and its embodied authors to luxuriate in a blasphemous disregard for literary, historical, textual, or even logical accuracy,

[and] the ability to stage and perform one's inclinations and desires as a way to salvage a romantic fidelity" (Corrigan, 2002: 178). The possibility of performing faithfully only to one's self-expression and individual vision requires the possibility of being unfaithful to one's self-expression and individual vision. Within an adaptation, the act or moment of unfaithfulness to one's auteur self is when the filmmaker's identification with the author of the adapted text supersedes the auteur's faithfulness to himself. In fact, the unfaithful moments make possible the auteur's ability to be faithful to himself in the process of adaptation. In other words, if, as Corrigan argues, Shakespeare and other classical authors are "literary ghosts [who] need spokespersons to articulate and perform their lost secrets," and these spokespersons are the auteurs who perform their own embodied agency and identities in their adaptations, then the performance of the auteur identity and the enactment of his embodied agency through adaptation requires some faithfulness to the continuing, although fragmented, presence of the ghost who holds onto the lost secrets the auteur chooses to perform.

I would argue then, with Modleski, that Hitchcock's inability fully to consume du Maurier and her novel is not a failure, but that the coexisting presence of both Hitchcock's and du Maurier's signatures on the film is the nature of adaptation. It is also impossible to discount other authorial imprints such as that of the producer, scriptwriter, and others. In the case of *Rebecca*, Elisabeth Bronfen in her book, *Home in Hollywood: The Imaginary Geography of Cinema*, points out that the remaining presence of the feminine authorial voice in the film owes its existence to Hitchcock's paternal and authoritative producer David O. Selznick. Selznick's paternal power and agency in forcing Hitchcock to retain "all the little feminine things" would seem to undermine Modleski's argument that it is the feminine itself that subverts identity because, in Bronfen's words, "the punitive law of a paternal authority figure remains" (2004: 62). However, as Modleski shows, Selznick insisted on changes to Hitchcock's original script "in order to remain true to what he considered the feminine spirit of the book" (Modleski, 1989: 43). The unanswerable questions, then, are with which authorial signature does the adaptation's authority and ownership lie? With Selznick's protection of the feminine identity of the novel? With Hitchcock's submission to Selznick's authority? Or with Hitchcock's discovery of his own auteur identity and his "proper subjects" in a film that he felt was not his own? Or with the female author who keeps reappearing despite the auteur discourse's attempts to excise her? The point is that Western culture's masculine version of individual authorship as the signifier of originality, authority, and ownership is troubled by adaptation and its threat of multiple authors and fragmented identities.

A Jane Campion Film without a Life of its Own

Jane Campion is one of the few English-language women filmmakers who, after one feature film and several shorts, had a viable auteur status so that fidelity to her repeatable signature was searched for in her adaptation of Henry James' *The Portrait of a Lady*. I also show how her auteur status, as it is circumscribed by her femaleness, cannot overcome the "textual author, lost to time." After the success of *The Piano* (1993), interviewers and reviewers remarked upon the "immense anticipation for [Campion's] next film" (Saccoccia, 1999: 201). There was some split feeling in the reception discourse about the source text being very different from *The Piano* and the source text having much in common with *The Piano*. However, in a *Literature/Film Quarterly* article written before the U.S. release of Campion's adaptation, Jeanne Dapkus argues for the value of comparing the two works with an eye to both their similarities and differences; for her, "in spite of the fact that the two works do not resemble one another in style or tone, *Piano* seems to echo *Portrait* structurally, and the heroines experience revelations related to strikingly similar struggles between their natural selves . . . and their position within . . . Victorian society" (Dapkus, 1997: 177). Dapkus declares in the opening sentences of her article that she "had already decided to write up an analysis of a relationship of the two works" before she learned of Campion's adaptation of *Portrait*. Her premonitory insight into the affinities between the two works, corroborated by the subsequent revelation that Campion would be adapting *Portrait*, encourages Dapkus to speculate about the director's own thoughts. Dapkus says, "it is with some pleasure that I can hypothesize that Campion may have sensed a connection between *Portrait* and *Piano*, because her efforts to direct a film version of *Portrait* immediately follow in the wake of *Piano*'s huge success" (Dapkus, 1997: 177). Dapkus's pleasure about her own intuition into Campion's mind and career choices may seem slightly quaint but her enthusiasm about the connections and oppositions between the texts alongside the comments by the interviewers about the same concerns point to the implicit but strong desire for the art cinema auteur whose varying films are linked by thematic and stylistic similarities.

The apparent similarities between Campion's Ada and James' Isabel suggest that an adaptation creates the difficulty of how the art cinema director will insert herself, in David Bordwell's terms, as the "overriding intelligence" organizing a film based on material with the signature of another "overriding intelligence" (Bordwell, 1999: 719). Truffaut and other New Wave directors, and art cinema directors throughout cinema history, have made adaptations of literary sources, many of which are pulp fiction, and some of which are canonical texts. And yet, our understandings of the art cinema director as auteur depend on our cultural values for originality and authority that I elaborated for the auteur in general, especially as it was foundationally and quintessentially conceived in the character of Alfred Hitchcock above. What we must remember here is the "notion that the art-film director has a creative freedom denied to her/his Hollywood counterpart," and that the Hollywood auteur exerts originality, authority, and ownership in spite of an oppressive system that, nevertheless, he remains firmly within, expressing his individuality within the codes of the classical norm (Bordwell, 1999: 719). Bordwell argues that the art cinema auteur expresses his individuality through "recurrent violations of the classical norm" (720). The difference creates a consistent perception in auteur discourse that the signs of authorship within Hollywood cinema have to be searched for, hidden as they are within the classical system, and that the signs of authorship within art cinema are readily apparent, as they are attributed to "any breakdown of the motivation of cinematic space and time by cause-effect logic" (Bordwell, 1999: 720). This means that the Hollywood director's claims to auteur status must be proven by the critic, whereas the art cinema director's claims to auteur status are built into the formal conventions of art cinema.

Of course, the variety of films that circulate as art cinema do not all have the textual characteristics that Bordwell defines, nor are they exclusively defined by or received as art cinema based on formal conventions alone. National identity often serves as an identifying feature of art cinema in that it differentiates an art film as other than Hollywood. By virtue of being non-Hollywood, some non-American films circulate as art cinema despite having few of the aesthetic qualities and formal conventions Bordwell articulates. John Hill makes this argument for British cinema arguing that "even relatively conventional, or artistically conservative, works have tended to circulate as 'art cinema'" (1999: 65). The important point to note about the circulation of heritage films as a kind of art cinema is that they do so without the expectation of individual expression that constructs art film auteurism, while often making up for that lack by trading on the cultural and artistic prestige of a literary source. Richard Dyer defines heritage cinema as such: "Films that may be characterised by use of a canonical source from the national literature . . . conventional filmic narrative style, with the pace and tone of 'European art cinema' but without its symbolisms and personal directorial voices" (1995: 204). Dyer's description is corroborated by John Hill: "The heritage film is a kind of 'art cinema' but one which derives its 'art' from extra-textual sources rather than its employment of the strategies of self-conscious narration and expressive style" (1999: 79).

The expectations of faithfulness have been around for a long time, but by the 1990s had become associated particularly with the late twentieth-century heritage film and its "museum aesthetic," exemplified by the popular Merchant Ivory productions. Heritage films have a potential lack of authorship that allows the authorship of the novel to dominate the adaptation's identity. John Hill makes this point well: "the heritage film . . . avoids overt interference with the original and strives to suggest faithful reproduction. This may not always entail strict fidelity to the original text . . . but it does involve fidelity to the popular idea of 'great literature' or literary worthiness" (1999: 80). This is the prominent idea of faithful adapting. The heritage film appears to fulfill the need of the discourse of fidelity to protect, preserve, and submit to the canonical novel. What all of the above adds up to is that we expect an auteur (like Hitchcock) to adapt novels that will not infringe on his authority as auteur, and we expect canonical novels to be adapted within the parameters of a reverential heritage cinema that will not undermine the authority of the novel's authorship. In more crude terms, auteur discourse expects that if

Hitchcock has enough sense of the dynamics of authority, originality, and authorship not to adapt *Crime and Punishment* in order to maintain and further his own auteur identity, then Campion should have enough sense not to adapt *The Portrait of a Lady* for the same reasons. We expect this because we expect auteurs to know how to and to choose to protect and develop their identity and status as authors.

The reception of *The Portrait of a Lady* (1996) reflects this tension between our expectations of fidelity to the authority of a canonical novel and our expectations for the originality of the art cinema auteur. The concern at stake for the discourse of Campion as auteur is the maintenance of Campion's authorship, authority, and originality: her own faithfulness to her discursive auteurism.[9] In contrast to other reviews of Campion's *Portrait* that berated her for not being faithful to James, many reviewers were most concerned about Campion's faithfulness to her own career development, auteur identity, and audience expectations. The extraordinary success of *The Piano*, as Dana Polan comments after the fact, inevitably, "set high standards and expectations that Campion's subsequent productions would be judged against" (Polan, 2001: 124), and there is palpable dismay in the tone of the reviewer who wrote, "It's possible that if Jane Campion's 'The Piano' hadn't been such a vivid wonder of a film, 'The Portrait of a Lady' . . . wouldn't be such a letdown. But I doubt it" (Guthman, 1997: D3). Somewhat more philosophically, another reviewer concedes.

> It was always difficult to see how Jane Campion could trump the ace of *The Piano*, so successful in its wide appeal although it looked like a specialised project. *The Portrait of a Lady*, based on the Henry James novel but retold by a woman film-maker with rather different concerns, looks very unlikely to match its success (Malcolm, 1997).

Other reviewers wrote, "Her film is the bold interpretation of a classic, not a freestanding work on its own" (Maslin, 1996) and "as an adaptation of a classic novel, *Portrait* refreshingly refuses the manicured nostalgia of a Merchant Ivory show or a BBC serial. But as a Jane Campion film, it lacks texture, resonance and a life of its own" (Brown, 1997). All these reviews deal in a sense of loss, in the idea of what could have, or really *should have*, been. The last two quotations explicitly make the point that the loss is one of ownership and auteurism, played out in the language that the film ought to be "its own" entity. It might seem then that any auteur who adapts a canonical novel would encounter the same kind of criticisms to a similar degree. However, what it means to be a canonical author or a cinema auteur is not the same for everyone who acquires that status. The possibility of a female film-maker acquiring auteur status is limited for many reasons, including the masculinized discourse of auteurism. This is illustrated in a comparison with a film released the same year of Campion's *The Piano*: Martin Scorsese's adaptation of Edith Wharton's *The Age of Innocence*. The reviews for his film are nearly unanimously full of praise, and many of them find a language to fit the idea of a classic novel adaptation into the idea of Scorsese as auteur:

> Instead of "Masterpiece Theatre-style fawning, he fills this movie with visual flow, masterful cinematography and assured direction. There's an alert, thinking presence behind the camera (Howe, 1993).
>
> Taking "The Age of Innocence," Edith Wharton's sad and elegantly funny novel about New York's highest society in the 1870s, Martin Scorsese has made a gorgeously uncharacteristic Scorsese film. Yet with a fine cast headed by Daniel Day-Lewis, Michelle Pfeiffer and Winona Ryder, Mr. Scorsese has made a big, intelligent movie that functions as if it were a window on a world he had just discovered, and about which he can't wait to spread the news (Canby, 1993).
>
> Without bloodshed or a holler of "fuck you," Scorsese – the raging bull of directors – bursts into the china shop that is Edith Wharton's 1920 novel, *The Age of Innocence*. He roughs things up a bit, though nothing gets shattered except our preconceptions (Travers, 1993).

It is tempting to blame gender stereotypes only for the positive reception of a male auteur's adaptation of a classic novel by a female author and the more troubled reception of a female auteur's adaptation of a classic novel by a male author, as if the auteur discourse constructs the authorial power relations so that any male film-maker can claim authority over an adaptation of a woman-authored novel and any female filmmaker will fail to claim authority over an adaptation of a novel authored by a man. This, of course, would elide the very real differences between Scorsese and Campion. These include their production and distribution contexts (Hollywood/ International Art Cinema) and their career longevity (Scorsese's first feature film was released in 1967 and Campion's first feature was 1989). It seems unfair to compare them. And yet, there is no female filmmaker in Hollywood with the career longevity and auteur status that compares with Scorsese. However, male auteurs are allowed a discourse of authority that is largely kept from women authors or only allowed them in tangential, tenuous, and temporary ways. It is Scorsese who is read as remaining faithful to his auteur identity, an identity structured not only by the films themselves but also by the discursive authority embedded in the popular and academic reception of his work and the way that reception is constructed by the discursive authority of the auteur. With this in mind, it is difficult to see how Campion could have mastered Henry James (the Master) in any similar way to Scorsese's mastery of Wharton's novel, his oeuvre, and cinema itself.

Trademark or Signature?

The most consistent and productive response to the academic concern that "the question of the aesthetic primacy of literature or film is the key debate" (MacCabe, 2011: 7) has come from Robert Stam and his promotion of Bakhtinian theories to open up the study of adaptations beyond a simple one-to-one correspondence between book and film: "Notions of 'dialogism' and 'intertextuality', then, help us to transcend the aporias of 'fidelity' and of a dyadic source/adaptation model which excludes not only all sorts of supplementary texts but also the dialogical response of the reader/spectator" (Stam, 2004: 27). Stam does not say much about authorship except in order to discount literary authorial intent as any possible guide for an adaptor:

> Bakhtin's notion of author and character as multi-discursive and resistant to unifica-
> tion . . . problematized both author and character as stable unitary identities . . . And
> if authors are fissured, fragmented, multi-discursive, hardly "present" even to them-
> selves, the analyst may inquire, how can an adaptation communicate the "spirit" or
> "self-presence" of authorial intention? (Stam, 2004: 9).

More recent work on adaptation has started to claim space for the author-adaptor. In his introduction to *True to the Spirit: Film Adaptation and the Question of Fidelity*, Colin MacCabe declares that "To forget that a text is based in an individual body or bodies with their specific historical trajectories is to engage in the worst kind of academic idealism" (MacCabe, 2011: 22). And in her chapter "Max Ophul's Autuerist Adaptations," Laura Mulvey argues for the "autuerist adaptation," showing how Ophul's "films' divergence from their original texts has a consistency" (2011: 76). Consistent themes, tropes, and iconography across a director's oeuvre are, of course, signs and signifiers of auteur identity and the director's signature on each film.

In the chapter "Adapter as Auteur" in his book *Adaptation and its Discontents*, Thomas Leitch analyses the auteur status of three filmmakers (Alfred Hitchcock, Walt Disney, and Stanley Kubrick) who have acquired some of the authority of authorship by making adaptations and, in my terms, asserting their ownership over the adaptations by coding them as productions rather than reproductions. He argues:

> Rising from the ranks of metteurs-en-scène to the status of auteur depends on
> an alignment of several marketable factors: thematic consistency, association with a
> popular genre, an appetite for the coordination and control of outsized projects, sen-
> sitivity to the possibility of broad appeal in such disparate media as movies, television,
> books, magazines, and T-shirts (Leitch, 2007: 256).

Campion fits this criteria fairly well as she has a clear thematic consistency in women's narratives, has been associated with the traditionally popular genre of the woman's film, exhibits an appetite for outsized projects by adapting Henry James and the life and death of John Keats, as well as her sensitivity to the broad appeal of television and books. Indeed, Kathleen McHugh argues that Campion has achieved this move from reproduction to production:

Campion's placement of her literal signature within cinematic sequences that theorize the logic of her subsequent adaptation effectively appropriates and signs their imaginative work as her own. As a result, it is precisely the mediation of the authorship and signatures of *others* in her adaptations that operates to render these films the ones in which her signature and auteurist identity most clearly and forcefully emerges (2009: 139).

Through a feminist critical analysis of Campion's texts, intertexts, and authorial signature, McHugh's claims are more than valid, but, as I have suggested, reception is the place where auteur authority and authorial identity is made, sustained, and fought for. Importantly, it is not, of course, just academic reception that constructs the discourse of auteurism; popular film criticism plays a significant role, as do press releases, interviews, and advertising. Linda Hutcheon makes the important point that "it is evident from both studio press releases and critical response that the director is ultimately held responsible for the overall vision and therefore for the adaptation as adaptation" (2006: 85). Campion was held responsible for the adaptation as adaptation and for her own auteur identity by the popular press and, for many, she and her film came short of their expectations. It would be of benefit to both adaptation studies and feminist film studies to consider the disconnects between popular and academic reception in regards to auteurism.

In his 1992 book *A Cinema without Walls: Movies and Culture after Vietnam*, Corrigan makes it clear that marketing and reception have always been at the heart of the auteur's power. He argues that critiques of auteur theory ignore the importance of the "auteur as a commercial strategy for organizing audience reception [and] as a critical concept bound to distribution and marketing aims that identify and address the potential cult status of an auteur" (Corrigan, 1992: 103). Recognizing the commerce of auteurism as a function of capitalism means that we must take into account the element of competition. In terms that invoke the authorial duel in *Adaptation*, Leitch's final comment in his chapter on authorship and adaptation suggests that the adaptor's auteur identity fights for authority with the original text's author in the sphere of marketing: "Perhaps the most indispensable of these factors is a public persona . . . that can be converted to a trademark more powerful than the other authorial trademarks with which it will inevitably compete" (2007: 256). Those other authorial trademarks with which an adaptation must contest are innumerable; they exist both outside the adaptation and inside it. Most importantly, as I have shown, they exist within authorship theories and histories as well. Frederic Jameson articulates the competition within the texts as an "active-tension" in which "the individual works, and even the oeuvre of the individual modern artists, seek each other's death, in the sense in which they brook no other gods besides themselves" (Jameson, 2011: 231). He argues that this is true of literary authors and film auteurs, both amongst themselves and between each other. This modernist view of authorship as a signature of ownership that must compete with others is inevitably complicit with the commercial view of authorship as a trademark that must compete with others. Jameson's language takes us back to the violence in the film *Adaptation*, and the inevitable specters of loss and authorial death that haunt the study of adaptation. It seems the only way to exorcise these ghosts is to pay close attention to those "individual bodies" in which texts are based, and to remember that not all bodies, and therefore, not all authors, are equal.

NOTES

1 Both scripts were downloaded from the website BeingCharlieKaufman.com. www. beingcharliekaufman.com/index.htm?top. htm&0. Accessed January 12, 2008.
2 See Boozer (2008) for more on the screenwriter as author of an adaptation.
3 Patterson is a regular contributor to the *Guardian*'s film section, and his work often has a polemical tone.
4 The following analysis of Hitchcock's and Truffaut's conversation was inspired by James Naremore's comments on this same section of the interviews in his introduction to *Film Adaptation*. He notes that it is "commonplace to observe that some of the best movie directors deliberately avoid adaptations of great literature in order to foreground their own artistry" (7).
5 The Academy nominated Hitchcock as Best Director seven times; famously, he never won. *Rebecca* did win Best Picture, but, as Hitchcock himself makes very clear, that Oscar goes to the producer.
6 Their rhetoric mimics the modernist aesthetics of literary criticism, exemplified by Brooks (1949) and Booth (1961).
7 See Lane (2004) and Tasker (2010).
8 See, for example, Doane (1999) and Mayne (2003).
9 I have discussed Campion's auteur identity and *The Portrait of a Lady* previously. See Cobb (2010).

REFERENCES

Astruc, Alexandre. "The Birth of a New Avant-Garde: Le camera-stylo." In *The New Wave: Critical Landmarks*. Ed. Peter Graham. Garden City: Doubleday, 1968, 17–23.

Booth, Wayne C. *The Rhetoric of Fiction*. Chicago: Chicago University Press, 1961.

Boozer, Jack. "Introduction: The Screenplay and Authorship in Adaptation." In *Authorship in Film Adaptation*. Ed. Jack Boozer. Austin: University of Texas Press, 2008, 1–30.

Bordwell, David. "The Art Cinema as Mode of Film Practice." In *Film Theory and Criticism: Introductory Readings*. Eds. Leo Braudy and Marshall Cohen. Oxford: Oxford University Press, 1999, 715–24.

Bronfen, Elisabeth. *Home in Hollywood: The Imaginary Geography of Cinema*. New York: Columbia University Press, 2004.

Brooks, Cleanth. *The Well-Wrought Urn*. London: Dennis Dobson, 1949.

Brown, Geoff. "Politeness forbids." *The Times*, February 27, 1997.

Canby, Vincent. "*The Age of Innocence*: Grand Passions and Good Manners." *New York Times*, September 17, 1993.

Chamberlain, Lori. "Gender and the Metaphorics of Translation." In *Rethinking Translation: Discourse, Subjectivity, Ideology*. Ed. Lawrence Venuti. London: Routledge, 1992, 57–74.

Cobb, Shelley. "Jane Campion's Women's Films: Art Cinema and the Post-feminist Rape Narrative. In *Rape in Art Cinema*. Ed. Dominique Russell. London: Continuum Press, 2010.

Cobb, Shelley. "Adaptation, Fidelity and Gendered Discourse." *Adaptation*, 4:1, 2011, 28–37.

Corrigan, Timothy. *A Cinema without Walls: Movies and Culture after Vietnam*. London: Routledge, 1992.

Corrigan, Timothy. "What Shakespeare to Love? Film, Fidelity, and the Performance of Literature." In *High Pop: Making Culture into Popular Entertainment*. Ed. Jim Collins. Oxford: Blackwell, 2002, 155–81.

Dapkus, Jeanne. "Sloughing off the Burdens: Ada's and Isabel's Parallel/Antithetical Quests for Self-actualization in Jane Campion's Film *The Piano* and Henry James's Novel *The Portrait of a Lady*." *Literature/Film Quarterly*, 25:3, 1997, 177–87.

Doane, Mary Anne. "Caught and Rebecca: The Inscription of Femininity as Absence." In *Feminist Film Theory: A Reader*. Ed. Sue Thornaham. Edinburgh: Edinburgh University Press, 1999, 70–82.

Dyer, Richard. "Heritage Cinema in Europe." In *Encyclopedia of European Cinema*. Ed. Ginnette Vincendeau. Facts on File Inc., 1995, 204–5.

Gilbert, Sandra and Susan Gubar. *Madwoman in the Attic: The Woman Writer and the Nineteenth Century Literary Imagination*. New Haven: Yale University Press, 1979.

Guthman, Edward. "Arty *Portrait* Loaded with Heavy Symbolism," *San Francisco Chronicle*, January 17, 1997, Section D3.

Hill, John. *British Cinema in the 1980s*. Oxford: Oxford University Press, 1999.

Howe, Desson. *"The Age of Innocence." Washington Post*, September 17, 1993.

Hutcheon, Linda. *A Theory of Adaptation*. London: Routledge, 2006.

Jameson, Fredric. "Afterword". In *True to the Spirit: Film Adaptation and the Question of Fidelity*. Eds Colin MacCabe, Kathleen Murray ,and Rick Warner. Oxford: Oxford University Press, 2011, 215–33.

Lane, Christina. "Just Another Girl Outside the Neo-Indie." In *Contemporary American Independent Film: From the Margins to the Mainstream*. Eds. Chris Holmlund and Justin Wyatt. New York: Routledge, 2004, 193–210.

Leitch, Thomas. *Film Adaptation and its Discontents: From* Gone with the Wind *to* The Passion of the Christ. Baltimore: Johns Hopkins University Press, 2007.

Leavis, F. R. *The Great Tradition*. New York: Stewart, 1948.

Leavis, F. R. "Mass Civilization and Minority Culture." In *Cultural Theory and Popular Culture: A Reader*. Ed. John Storey. Edinburgh: Pearson, 2006, 12–19.

Leavis, Q. D. *Fiction and the Reading Public*. London: Chatto and Windus, 1978.

MacCabe, Colin. "Introduction: Bazinian Adaptation: *The Butcher Boy* as Example." In *True to the Spirit: Film Adaptation and the Question of Fidelity*. Eds. Colin MacCabe, Kathleen Murray, and Rick Warner. Oxford: Oxford University Press, 2011, 3–26.

McHugh, Kathleen. "Jane Campion: Adaptation, Signature, Authority." In *Jane Campion: Cinema, Nation, Identity*. Eds. Hilary Radner, Alistair Fox, and Iréne Bessiére. Detroit: Wayne State University Press, 2009, 139–56.

Malcolm, Derek. "Maid in a Cold Climate." *The Guardian*, February 28, 1997.

Maslin, Janet. "Henry James, Not Too Literally." *New York Times*, December 27, 1996.

Mayne, Judith. "A Parallax View of Lesbian Authorship." In *Film and Authorship*. Ed. Virginia Wright Wexman. New Brunswick: Rutgers University Press, 2003, 76–88.

Modleski, Tania. *The Women Who Knew Too Much: Hitchcock and Feminist Theory*. London: Routledge, 1989.

Mulvey, Laura. "Max Ophul's Autuerist Adaptations." In *True to the Spirit: Film Adaptation and the Question of Fidelity*. Eds. Colin MacCabe, Kathleen Murray, and Rick Warner. Oxford: Oxford University Press, 2011, 75–90.

Naremore, James. "Introduction: Film and the Reign of Adaptation." In *Film Adaptation*. Ed. James Naremore. New Brunswick: Rutgers, 2001, 1–18.

Orlean, Susan. *The Orchid Thief: A True Story of Beauty and Obsession*. London: Vintage, 2000.

Patterson, John. "Pass the Pillow. If only . . . great writers could stop their stories being made into dull movies." *The Guardian*, September 1, 2007.

Polan, Dana. *Jane Campion*. London: BFI, 2001.

Stam, Robert. "Introduction." In *Literature and Film: A Guide to the Theory and Practice of Adaptation*. Eds. Robert Stam and Alessandro Raengo. Oxford: Blackwell, 2004, 1–52.

Saccoccia, Susan. "Portrait of a Lady and Her Films." In *Jane Campion: Interviews*. Ed. Virginia Wright Wexman. Jackson: University of Mississippi Press, 1999, 201–4.

Tasker, Yvonne. "Vision and Visibility: Women Filmmakers, Contemporary Authorship, and Feminist Film Studies." In *Reclaiming the Archive: Feminism and Film History*. Ed. Vicki Callahan. Detroit: Wayne State University Press, 2010, 213–30.

Travers, Peter. *"The Age of Innocence." Rolling Stone*, September 16, 1993.

Truffaut, François. *Hitchcock*. New York: Touchstone, 1983.

Truffaut, François. "A Certain Tendency in French Cinema." In *Auteurs and Authorship: A Film Reader*. Ed. Keith Barry Grant. Oxford: Blackwell Publishing, 2009, 9–18.

7

The Business of Adaptation

Reading the Market

Simone Murray

There's nothing unique about adaptation. How could there be? Apart from the fact that adaptations appear ubiquitous, popping up everywhere you turn in modern life, there is the logical inconsistency of the very idea: classification as an adaptation necessarily draws attention to a work's *lack* of uniqueness, foregrounding its borrowings from elsewhere, its indebtedness to a preceding text/s, and its location amongst a raft of similarly themed textual reworkings of particular narratives, characters, or worlds. Hence adaptation studies has from its inception evidenced a subversive bias against literary studies' long-valorized talisman of uniqueness. Despite this, it is striking how the study of adaptations has declined to push this contextual understanding of the adapted text to its logical conclusion. For each film that screens at the local multiplex or art-house cinema, each classic-novel miniseries broadcast on television or purchased on DVD, and every tie-in edition, novelization, published screenplay, or companion book appearing on the shelves of a local bookstore represents only the most tangible manifestation of an underlying adaptation industry responsible for creating, disseminating, and guiding consumption of adapted material. Hence, in answering the question of how do adaptations come to be, it is imperative to move beyond exclusive preoccupation with issues of creative influence (intertextuality or the idea of cultural memes) and to consider adaptations also in more concrete industrial, commercial, and legal terms. In short, adaptations constitute not discrete *sui generis* artifacts, but outcomes of an encompassing economic system.

Reconceptualizing adaptation as a business prompts adaptation studies along enticing new scholarly paths that have the potential to reframe standard approaches

A Companion to Literature, Film, and Adaptation, First Edition. Edited by Deborah Cartmell.
© 2012 Blackwell Publishing Ltd. Published 2012 by Blackwell Publishing Ltd.

to adaptation. Specifically they can provide fresh insights into the remarkable instability of adaptation, as manifest in the adapted text which can itself be reused and recycled, as where successful adapted products spawn further spin-offs in other media formats. Similarly, in an adaptation economy itself characterized by instability, projects can be as easily hyped one moment, and put into the limbo of turnaround the next. By extension too, the range of individuals responsible for an adaptation – the number of hands which metaphorically "shape" the creative output – needs to be revised radically upward from the traditionally valorized creative figures of the author and film director to include less visible industry players such as agents, rights managers, book fair conveners, film festival programmers, cultural prize judges, screenwriters, casting agents, publicists, marketers, producers, distributors, broadcast schedulers, reviewers, and the like. All of these industrial agents have stakes (albeit unequal) in the evaluation of an adaptation's success, and their early responses crucially influence which adaptations are taken up within the academy for detailed analysis in books such as this one.

The goal of this chapter in approaching adaptation socioeconomically is to engender self-reflexivity in readers as consumers and analysts of adaptation by encouraging them to look beneath the textual surface of specific adapted works to perceive traces of the industrial system which makes possible such works' existence. Adaptations are not only meaningful in themselves (as textually oriented approaches bountifully elaborate) but they are also emblematic of larger social and economic formations here dubbed for shorthand "the adaptation industry" (Murray, 2011). I ask readers to put aside temporarily adaptation studies' habitual primary concern with aesthetic evaluation and to suspend familiar humanities-style suspicion of commercial imperatives as always necessarily debasing and destructive of creative impulses. Instead, this chapter provides an introduction to conceptualizing adaptations as the outcome of a vast, transnational, constantly mutating, and frequently internally conflictual socioeconomic system with tremendous influence in shaping the contours of contemporary culture.

Elements of the Adaptation Industry

Peering beneath the surface of any given adaptation to ask how it came to exist immediately provokes the question of who originates adaptations. In the early decades after adaptation studies' emergence in the late 1950s, the answer to this question (where it was even posed) would have been reflex: the author (Bluestone [1957], 2003). Yet from the 1980s onwards, as adaptation studies came to terms with an increasingly two-way flow between print and screen media, the answer may have been revised to include the director (nominated, through heavy borrowing from auteur theory, as film's dominant creative consciousness) (Cartmell and Whelehan, 1999). But the most recent and exciting wave of adaptation studies, evident since around the turn of the twenty-first century, embraces the contemporary reality that adaptations may originate in any media format and migrate to any other (or even the same media format, albeit in a different incarnation). Hence nontraditional adaptations sources such as theater (often, despite myriad studies of Shakespeare on screen, subordinated to the novel), opera, stage musicals, comics, artworks, and computer games increasingly supply case studies for academic monographs and conference papers; as do nonfiction sources such as biographies, memoirs, feature-length journalism, how-to guides, and more (Hutcheon, 2006; Leitch, 2007; Sanders, 2006). In the twenty-first century, an adaptation may originate from any sector of the creative industries (conceived broadly) and migrate to any other sector or sectors, frequently simultaneously.

Such a near-infinite array of industrial contexts for an economically oriented study of adaptation quickly threatens to become impossibly unwieldy, perhaps intimidating would-be adaptation industry analysts into seeking refuge in the comparative familiarity of textual analysis. But it need not be so. French sociologist Pierre Bourdieu's productive concept of the cultural field (*champ*) offers a useful tool for conceptualizing an abstract space in which adaptation industry interests innovate, react and above all compete to garner maximum "cultural capital" (another useful Bourdieusian coinage denoting cultural prestige or social esteem) (1993). Bourdieu's characteristic interest in the material dimensions of cultural life ensures that the commercial and industrial interests of adaptation-industry stakeholders are fore-grounded in such a model, but Marxism's riptide of economic reductionism is avoided through Bourdieu's equal attention to more abstract cultural questions of hierarchy, evaluation, and shifts in critical fashion. The "field" comprises both the totality of economic interests at stake as well as the various cultural and educational strategies through which these arrangements are normalized, justified, and ritually reproduced. That said, Bourdieu's characteristic positioning of the field of high-art ("restricted") production as in dialectical opposition to the lucrative sector of mass-market commodities is open to question in twenty-first-century Anglophone settings.

To provide a more concrete example of this, and of the route a contemporary adaptation might take (developed at greater length in the case study comprising the second half of this chapter), we could take the still common case of an acclaimed literary novel adapted to film. Such an adaptation project might pass through a sequence of industry stakeholders such as author, agent, publisher, book prize committee, producer, screenwriter, distributor, and audience member. Note, however, that whereas similar models in the discipline of book history have characterized such communication pathways in relation to literature as "circuits," suggesting unidirectional flow, contemporary adaptation is avowedly *multi*directional and better represented by a network model: any node in the network may initiate an adaptation project in any direction (Darnton, 1990). The flip-side of such a proliferation of adaptation originators, however, is that each of these stakeholders also potentially acts as gatekeeper, stymieing or rejecting an adaptation project at any point in its development. Salient also is the fact that territorial disputes are frequent and ongoing between stakeholders in the adaptation network, such as decades-long tensions between agents and editors over who is the appropriate guardian of authors' rights; between screenwriters and producers over the integrity of the shooting script in feature film production; and even between producers and distributors over their respective cut of a film's box-office takings (Murray, 2011).

The principal benefit of Bourdieusian field theory for conceptualizing the adaptation industry is its central premise that cultural value is not innate in any work, but is socially constructed, perpetuated, or challenged. This realization makes possible an analysis of how each element in the adaptation network inflates or decreases a cultural text's stocks of critical esteem. Hence, award of – or even shortlisting for – a significant literary prize massively increases the chances of a book's adaptation in the affiliated sectors of film and television, just as Academy-Award consecration of a film registers an immediate impact upon publishers' decisions to reprint and re-jacket adapted backlist titles. But equally, and again drawing attention to the inherent fluidity and instability of the adaptation industry, elevation of a text's cultural stocks in one sector may conversely diminish its prestige for specific audiences in another, such as self-identified literary readers' aversion to tie-in editions of filmed novels, or ardent comic fans who decry Hollywoodization of an underground classic.

The Rights Economy

Bourdieu's abstract model derives further argumentative impetus from changes which have occurred since roughly the early 1980s in real-world media industries. A combination of deregulation of national media systems, an influx of investment capital into international markets, and technological advancements within the media themselves triggered successive waves of mergers and acquisitions across the international media sector, resulting in the creation of a small number of vastly capitalized, transnational, multimedia conglomerates. The modish business theory of "synergy" advocated ownership of media holdings across traditional industry sectors such as film, television, book publishing, newspapers and magazines and – increasingly as the twentieth century drew to a close – computer gaming, internet service provision, and social-networking media as well. The convergent interests and vast revenues of such media conglomerates facilitated the multipurposing of packages of "content" (note the medium-neutrality of the term) between media divisions or, increasingly, the incubation of media projects designed from inception to span media platforms – what cultural critic Henry Jenkins refers to as the practice of "transmedia storytelling" (2006: 93). Changeover from analogue to digital formats occurred at different rates amongst the various media industries (it is still underway, for example, in book publishing and terrestrial television), but the longer-term future was clear: all media formats would share an underpinning digital platform based on binary code. Such a unifying technological basis makes reformatting of a given content package for different media substantially less time- and labor-intensive than previously. As a result of these broadly contemporaneous regulatory, commercial, and technological shifts, by the turn of the millennium both business and academic analysts talked not of separate media industries but rather of different sectors of an all-encompassing mediasphere – transnational, highly concentrated, and culturally pervasive.

Within this massified industrial context, adaptations were incubated in much the same way they had been from the earliest decades of the twentieth century: through trading in intellectual property (IP) rights. But the increased traffic in adapted content, and the alertness from projects' inception to their proto-adaptive potential, caused an explosion in the range and value of media rights. This was especially true of so-called "subsidiary rights" clauses in book contracts (i.e. those governing the adaptation of a text into film, television, stage-play, radio-play and audiobook formats, inter alia, as well as rights to serialize or create licensed merchandise from a work). Such rights went from virtual contractual addenda to potentially highly lucrative sources of income for author and/or publisher, especially in relation to established bestsellers. Directly concomitant with the growth in the rights economy from the 1980s onwards was the rise of the agent as the creator's key rights-management advisor. Agents – whether traditional literary agents or the more audiovisual-focused talent agents – work on commission and thus have direct motivation to monetize the maximum range of their clients' rights in content properties. In the most recent sectoral development, larger agencies are themselves increasingly consolidating into a small number of multinational, cross-sectoral agencies capable of representing clients' works across the full gamut of media industries – known as "360-degree" representation. In the contemporary adaptation industry, control over creative IP has become the dominant business currency. For this reason, IP disputes such as unauthorized adaptations by fans, which are distributed virally online, attract such rhetorical heat because, for corporations, they seem to strike at the adaptation industry's very legal foundations. Conversely, the many analysts of adaptation who have noted the upswing of classic-novel adaptations of writers such as Austen and Dickens from the 1990s onwards should factor in these properties' public-domain status as a key aspect of their commercial appeal for producers.

Geographies of Adaptation

When considering the contemporary Anglophone adaptation industry, the first thing to note is its fundamentally transnational character: just as content may now originate in any medium and migrate to any other, a particular narrative, character, or motif may arise from any Anglophone market (or, somewhat less commonly, in translation) and be taken up for adaptation in other national markets. Indeed, the highly transnational nature of contemporary feature film and television financing, production, and distribution makes such international appeal virtually a prerequisite for any large-scale adaptation project. That said, the cultural geography of the contemporary adaptation industry features a number of dominant hubs and many peripheral outlier regions. Issues of proximity and access to these crucial nexuses around which adaptation transactions cluster hence profoundly influence the range of texts selected for adaptation, and the marketing prominence resultant adaptations receive. Like Bourdieu's concept of the "field," a useful model for conceptualizing the geographical contours of the adaptation industry is the circuit: an annual round of sequentially organized meetings in various prominent international locales at which adaptation industry stakeholders meet to pitch projects, make deals, and showcase recently completed works.

One such dominant circuit within the international adaptation industry is the round of major book fairs convened annually in, in calendar order, Bologna (focusing on children's books and held each March); London (April); New York City (where BookExpo America convenes biannually in May, with various other U.S. cities hosting in alternate years); and – the biggest of them all – the Frankfurt Book Fair (October). These vast trade events are predominantly organized around the buying and selling of foreign and translation rights in book titles, but in recent years Frankfurt, in a move swiftly imitated by other major fairs, has established a Film and Media Forum specifically to promote the Fair as a venue for trading in audio-visual rights in book properties.[1] This sidebar event attracts agents, publishers, producers, and screenwriters to a series of expert speaker presentations and themed panel seminars, and programs one-on-one pitching sessions between buyers and sellers of film, television, and increasingly also computer gaming and social-networking rights in books. In a further attempt to enhance its profile within international book and media sectors, Frankfurt has recently also established a dedicated Comics Centre, showcasing work of graphic novelists and comics artists and facilitating rights trade between comics publishers and other media industries (Bologna had for some decades hosted its own, more children-focused, Illustrators Exhibition). In fostering such events, Frankfurt appears to be drawing also on the pre-existing model of the Cinema and Literature International Forum (CLIF), a far smaller event convened annually in Monaco, which brings together Francophone and Anglophone book, film, and television personnel to incubate adaptation rights trading, and which culminates in award of a series of prizes for the best adapted (and even adaptable) projects.[2]

In highlighting its Côte d'Azur location in its advertising, Monaco's CLIF delib-erately evokes the glamour of a different cultural circuit: the annual round of A-list film festivals headed by Cannes at which films are premiered, distribution deals brokered, and influential critical prizes awarded. Interestingly, one of the oldest and most prestigious international film festivals, the Berlin International Film Festival, has in recent years formalized a partnership with the Frankfurt Book Fair centered upon adaptation. "Berlinale Day," scheduled each October at the Book Fair, screens films adapted from print sources alongside accompanying expert discussions; conversely each February's "Books at Berlinale" event selects twelve promisingly adaptable titles and pitches these to film producers. This strategy of attracting nontraditional delegates to film-centric events and facilitating creative encounters between rights-trading personnel across the various media has been imitated already at other film festivals internationally. For example, the Melbourne International Film Festival (MIFF) annually hosts "Books at MIFF," uniting book and screen industry personnel with a focus on stimulating adaptation of Australian cultural content. Adaptations will, doubtless, continue to be brokered more informally outside of such dedicated book- and screen-industry circuits. But such fora catalyze and regularize cross-industry conversations between those responsible for project commissioning in diverse media formats. As adaptation industry traffic is increasingly conducted through such key sites, it is worth pondering how the underlying infrastructure of adaptation industry circuits maximizes the likelihood of content from certain parts of the world reaching international audiences, and how cultural producers from outlining regions (whether national, sub-national, or linguistic in composition) face significant challenges in attracting global attention for home-grown work in even its original format, let alone in cross-media adaptation.

The Potential of Socioeconomic Approaches to Adaptation

Adaptation studies has, since its emergence, been prone to bouts of academic self-doubt. Such successive waves of methodological self-examination are unsurprising given adaptation studies' relative youth and intellectually precarious siting in the hinterlands of literary and screen studies. It is true to say, however, that disciplinary self-reflection has revolved almost exclusively around aestheticist debates over the range of texts appropriate for study, as defined along more or less inclusive generic, linguistic, or medial lines. Voices advocating that a more contextually focused, sociological or economic lens be used to view the phenomenon of adaptation have been rarely heard. Often cited is influential film theorist Dudley Andrew's statement that "It is time for adaptation studies to take a sociological turn" (1980: 14), and James Naremore's echoing *cri de coeur* a full twenty years later that "what we need . . . is a broader definition of adaptation and a sociology that takes into account the commercial apparatus, the audience, and the academic culture industry (2000: 10). Yet despite some scholars since heeding the call for context – such as R. Barton Palmer in his analysis of film noir adaptations (2004), Linda Hutcheon in a chapter of her monograph *A Theory of Adaptation* (2006), as well as the heartening evidence provided by several articles in the recently launched journal *Adaptation* – the textual analysis approach remains resolutely dominant. Where information about a given adaptation's industrial, economic, legal, or reception contexts is incorporated into academic analysis, it is frequently introduced as a preliminary framing device to set up the ensuing textual analysis, rather than being presented as any form of challenge to the terms of aestheticist evaluation or as constituting a viable methodological alternative. A glance at adaptation studies' academic genealogy quickly reveals why:

its two sponsoring disciplines are both located firmly in the humanities, as opposed to social sciences, camp with courses in the sociology of literature having been always emphatically marginalized within studies of print culture, and political economic approaches to film always threatening to undercut film studies' originative claims to cinema as an art form worthy of academic connoisseurship.

My claim in this chapter, and elsewhere, is not that socioeconomic approaches to adaptation represent a wholesale replacement for textual analysis but that they constitute a necessary complement because in compelling and exciting ways they widen the frame of what adaptation analysts can consider. For example, contextual approaches to adaptation can help illuminate:

- the industrial conditions for the creation (or, equally, non-appearance) of an adaptation;
- connections between adaptations at levels other than source text, author, director, or genre;
- influences of contextual issues on textual form (such as directors' cuts, differing versions for specific markets, test-audience responses to films, alternative endings, draft scripts, user-generated content);
- paratexts of adaptation (e.g. film trailers, posters, websites, DVD extras, marketing materials, film festival imagery, trade commentary, online discussion);
- reasons for textual afterlives beyond the cultural resonance of specific narratives (such as box-office imitation, studio image makeovers, star or director vanity projects, shifting audience demographics, regulatory changes, industry restructuring).

Such interests connect a still lingeringly insular adaptation studies with currently energetic debates within cultural studies, media studies, book history, critical legal studies, and media history disciplines. Rather than threatening to subordinate adaptation studies to any one of these disciplines (understandably unpalatable for a discipline having only recently cast off the opprobrium of mainstream literary and screen studies colleagues), contextually alert approaches to adaptations promise to map the interconnections between multiple areas of the so-called "new humanities" disciplines. The phenomenon of adaptation may, in short, come to be seen as comprising the unifying logic of the contemporary cultural scene.

To emblematize exactly what a socioeconomic approach to adaptation stands to offer, the second half of this chapter comprises an adaptation industry case study of a specific text: German novelist Bernhard Schlink's *The Reader* (1995, trans. 1997) and The Weinstein Company's film of the same name (2008). In tracing the movement of this specific text through the adaptation industry networks outlined earlier in this chapter, I could be accused of intellectual timidity: choice of a literary novel (albeit translated) and an Oscar-aspirant arthouse film might appear pretty standard adaptation studies fare, flying in the face of recent interventions seeking to expand the definition of what adaptation is by embracing both popular culture texts and media beyond the traditional book/film dyad. But this case study is in no way presented as definitive, but rather merely illustrative. The methodology showcased here could equally be applied to content deriving from any creative medium, in any genre, in any language/s, arising from any geographical area, and dating just as well from the historical, as opposed to the recent, past. It is presented as an enticement to readers to experiment with socioeconomic approaches rather than as any sort of exclusivist template. In so doing, this chapter's main contention is that cultural politics do not inhere only in textual representations, awaiting the interrogative, savvy eye of the modern cultural critic. Cultural politics in fact play out every bit as powerfully in the circumstances of texts' creation, their routes of circulation, and their various modes of consumption. If anything, cultural assumptions and norms may be more potent in these contexts because adaptation scholars have for so long refrained from analyzing them.

The Reader: "The Little Book that Could"[3]

In academic anthologies such as this one, adaptation case studies are typically selected for their uniqueness – not of a specific adapted work (which is, as alluded to earlier, by definition anything but unique) but because some notable aspect of the text's adaptation particularly invites critical attention. By contrast, what interests me most about *The Reader* is less any unique qualities than its typicality: it serves almost as an exemplar of the processes by which an acclaimed contemporary literary novel is adapted into an arthouse film, and thus illustrates the workings of what may at first encounter seem the impossibly abstract concept of the adaptation industry in a usefully empirical way.

Bernhard Schlink's novel *The Reader* narrates the story of a transformative liaison between a fifteen-year-old schoolboy, Michael, and an emotionally distant, thirty-something former concentration camp guard, Hanna, who meet in a chance encounter in 1950s West Germany and form a passionate relationship, before Hanna's abrupt departure and then unexpected reappearance in Michael's life years later. The novel's core cross-generational relationship – at first sexually charged and later a cause of fraught self-reflection on the essentially unknowable nature of the beloved – has been widely interpreted, including by Schlink, as an allegory for the troubled attempts of Germany's post-war generation to come to terms with the atrocities committed by their parent's generational cohort during the era of the Third Reich. *The Reader* was first published under its original title, *Der Vorleser*, in 1995 by Zurich-based German-language publisher Diogenes. It was subsequently translated into English by Knopf rights director Carol Brown Janeway (who, unusually, is also Schlink's U.S. agent) and published in the United States in 1997 as a hardback by Random House's respected highbrow imprint Pantheon, though it received minimal critical or marketing notice at the time. It was the February 1999 selection of *The Reader* for Oprah's Book Club which first attracted intense media attention and generated substantial sales for Schlink's novel. This initiated prompt re-jacketing of the paperback by Random House's upscale fiction imprint Vintage, whose cover design now combined its earlier tastefully halftone image of an open book and bouquet with Oprah's characteristic O logo superimposed in vivid yellow and red. The U.S. Oprah edition was sold alongside the more literary-identified "pre-Oprah" standard English-language cover design to cater for those whom UK publishing trade journal the *Bookseller* rather delightfully terms "cover-look snobs" (Richardson, 2008: 22). Oprah's choice of *The Reader* – her first foreign-language selection – for mainstream television audiences was somewhat surprising, partly, in terms of content, because of the novel's explicit accounts of underage sex, and partly, in terms of genre, because of the decidedly moral-philosophical, *Mitteleuropa* tenor of Schlink's deceptively simple prose style.

During this phase of increasing international profile for *The Reader*, a theatrical adaptation was staged at the Edinburgh Fringe Festival by Scotland's Borderline Theatre Company in August 2000 – the story's first transcendence of the book form. That Borderline managed to secure stage rights is surprising, given that in 1996 British screen director Anthony Minghella, flush with Academy Award success for his adaptation of Michael Ondaatje's *The English Patient* (1996), had secured film rights to *The Reader*, intending at that time to direct it himself. Because Schlink's novel was first published in German, the film's producers were required to purchase the film rights to both the German original as well as to the English-language translation in order to secure the property and prevent any rival adaptation stealing a march on their project's release. The specifics of the rights deal surrounding the stage adaptation of *The Reader* bear out the complexities of adaptation rights-trading and corporations' avidity to secure the maximum tranche of IP rights in an adaptable property. As UK journalist Susan Mansfield noted in an article about Borderline's production of *The Reader*: "It is almost unprecedented for a theatre company to be granted performance rights while a film is in production" (2000). Generous to the small-scale theater company though the producers' actions might seem, the terms of the grant included a ban on any other theatrical adaptations of the novel for a twenty-year period. In the event, Minghella's other film commitments over subsequent years saw him acquiesce to British director Stephen Daldry's pleas to direct the film himself, under the production and distribution umbrella of The Weinstein Company (TWC). Meanwhile, the story's transcendence of the book form was already well underway in a fourth medium – sound, with an audiobook version having been released in 2001 by HarperCollins AudioBooks, and a rerecorded, unabridged version festooned with film tie-in artwork being subsequently issued by Random House Audio to coincide with release of the movie (2008). In addition, the Oscar-winning critical prestige of the ensuing film was reconverted back into print form via TWC's publishing subsidiary, Weinstein Books, which published David Hare's screenplay (2009). Again capitalizing on publicity surrounding Winslet's award of Best Actress Oscar for her performance as the enigmatic

Hanna, TWC subsequently began movement of *The Reader* through its various post-cinema exhibition "windows," starting with release of the DVD in 2009. During the late 2008–9 period and for some time afterwards therefore, all of these products coexisted in the cultural marketplace, cross-promoting each other, reinforcing *The Reader's* brand identity with both existing and new audiences. Collectively they contributed to maintaining the profile of a lucrative, high-tone cultural franchise founded on the phenomenon of adaptation.

Miramax and the Weinstein Brothers: "Campaigning for Oscar nominations"[4]

Any discussion of arthouse literary adaptation over the preceding twenty years must, inevitably, make some mention of film distributor Miramax, and of its semi-legendary founders, the Weinstein brothers. Heavyweight Hollywood producer-distributors Harvey and Bob Weinstein began Miramax as a specialist distributor in New York state in 1979, focusing on rock documentaries, filmed stand-up comedy, foreign-language features, and assorted cult fare for the college and repertory circuits. A string of successes from the late 1980s through to the mid-1990s – including *Scandal* (1989), *The Cook, The Thief, His Wife and Her Lover* (1989), *The Crying Game* (1992), and *Pulp Fiction* (1994) – made the Miramax brand virtually synonymous with artistically ambitious, often arthouse films which managed to cross-over into mainstream, blockbuster successes. Film scholar Alisa Perren proposes three criteria evident in Miramax's choice of films: strong potential for festival-circuit and critical acclaim; edgy, boundary-pushing subject matter and/or avant-garde cinematic styles; and the ability to sustain marketing campaigns centered upon sensational, exploitation-style publicity (2001: 31–4). Former film marketing analyst and prominent scholar of the political economy of contemporary Hollywood, Justin Wyatt, concurs with Perren's interpretation, arguing that Miramax's success is built upon "selling a product which lends itself to media-induced controversy," especially regarding a film's sexual explicitness (1998: 80). The highly publicity-friendly contretemps surrounding Miramax releases such as *Priest* (1994, dealing with themes of clerical homosexuality and incest) and *Kids* (1995, depicting underage sex and drug-taking) support the contention that, for Miramax, pretty much any publicity was good publicity. Beginning with the break-through success of Steven Soderbergh's Palme d'Or win at the Cannes Film Festival in 1989 for enticingly titled and alive-to-the-Zeitgeist *sex, lies and videotape*, the Weinsteins shepherded a record number of arthouse productions to mainstream success, amongst them the adaptations *Trainspotting* (1996), *The English Patient* (1996), *Chocolat* (2000), *The Lord of the Rings* trilogy (2001–3), and *Chicago* (2002). The need to capitalize rapid expansion prompted the Weinsteins to sign a co-distribution deal with unlikely corporate partner Disney in 1993 – although care was taken to keep the corporate brands distinct in the public mind – prior to outright sale of Miramax to Disney in 2005. Shortly after, the Weinsteins founded and continue to lead their own production and distribution outfit, TWC – the major financier of *The Reader*, and the film's distributor in the key U.S. domestic market.

Given the current discussion's concern with the adaptation industry as a field of interdependent commercial and cultural interests, the main question prompted by the Weinsteins is: why do producers of arthouse literary adaptations assiduously court book-world institutions and loyal readers? Certainly it is not for box-office revenue alone; as U.S. trade journal *Publishers Weekly* remarks, "When you look at what a big book in publishing is versus how many people you need to go to a movie for it to be successful, the numbers are very different" (Maas, 2001: 25). Granted, a bestselling and critically praised book comes with the advantage of built-in name recognition as a proven property, which in turn facilitates raising of production finance and securing of advance distribution deals. UK literary agent Julian Friedmann, in a London Book Fair industry seminar about adaptation, confirmed that, "If the writer is already a brand name . . . it's much easier for [the producer] to raise money. So financiers feel comfort." But the Weinsteins' motivation is rather more complex than this would, on the face of it, suggest. It in fact breaks down into an intricately coordinated three-phase marketing and publicity strategy. Firstly, loyal readers of an acclaimed novel are important chiefly as key, opinion-setting early adopters, whose positive responses to a film adaptation can be used as a launching pad for a broader distribution and publicity campaign. It is for this reason that rights sales contracts can forbid authors from engaging in negative publicity about a film adaptation, as critical fan–author internet exchanges could generate damaging early publicity, suggesting that a beloved author's book had been "betrayed" by Hollywood. In the second phase of producers' strategy, fan approval can be used as a basis for critical and reviewer praise at key festivals and in the build-up to the awards season. Compared with the television and print advertising outlay required for a typical saturation-release blockbuster, such specialist reviewer and awards plaudits also present as relatively affordable. Finally, nominations, and especially Academy Award wins, can be leveraged into a mainstream publicity campaign and distribution strategy targeting the mass audience. For most literary screen adaptations this mass audience should not be thought of as coterminous with the mass audience for a typical summer blockbuster. Rather, it represents an accumulation of multiple niche audiences on an international scale. If successful, this third and final phase realizes what has long been the ultimate goal of the Weinsteins' business strategy: the arthouse/mainstream quality indie cross-over.

Just such cultivation of fan readers of a literary (and, courtesy of Oprah's intervention, also a bestselling mass-market) novel is clearly demonstrated by the release pattern of incremental expansion implemented by TWC for *The Reader*. The highly anticipated film premiered in limited release in New York City on December 10, 2008, a tactic known in film marketing parlance as a "platform" release because revenue per screen statistics matter less at this stage than generating critical "heat" or "buzz" about a film's awards prospects in a major metropolitan locale. *The Reader* then expanded on December 25 for the post-Christmas build-up to the new year's Academy Award nominations, opening across the United States on January 9, 2009. Upon release of Oscar nominations in late January (*The Reader* scored five), Weinstein announced his intention to "expand the flick to play on 1,100 screens" and "we'll go to 2,000 if that goes well" (presumably code for heated speculation of an Academy win in one of the major categories of Best Film, Best Actress, or Best Director) (Grover, 2009). Thus, far from assuming that readers of a book will simply discover a film adaptation of their own accord, successful producer-distributors of literary adaptations elaborately stage-manage audiences' exposure to screen releases, both in terms of a film's seasonal as well as geographical roll-out. As befits one of the few film distributors with a public profile, Weinstein has repeatedly emphasized that great filmmaking and screen performances are, of themselves, never sufficient to "make" a film. Also required are marketing chutzpah and a nose for publicity that virtually pressgangs patrons into cinema attendance through hyping a film as a cultural phenomenon, a "must-see" event:

> Other distributors slap out a movie, put an ad in the newspaper – usually not a very good one – and hope the audience will find it by a miracle. And most often they don't. It's the distributors' responsibility to find the audience (quoted in Perren, 2001: 34).

"An Oscar contender before filming begins":[5] Cultivating *The Reader*'s Readers

The release pattern of *The Reader* clearly evidences a strategy of incremental familiarization amongst opinion-setting audiences. But in fact the Weinsteins' cultivation of *The Reader*'s readers began as much as two years prior to the film's formal premiere. During the pre-production phase, key personnel were assembled whose cinematic track records, as well as their combined clout with the literary community, were designed to maximize the film's chances of critical – and through this commercial – success. British director Stephen Daldry, though a relatively new hand at screen directing, had previously guided Nicole Kidman to an Oscar-winning performance in his adaptation of Michael Cunningham's Pulitzer Prize-winning *The Hours* (2002), itself an intertextual homage to Virginia Woolf's *Mrs Dalloway* (1925) and thus a film with impeccable literary credentials. The screenwriter of both *The Hours* and *The Reader* was British theater giant Sir David Hare, arguably the UK's most esteemed living playwright and a major figure within Britain's cultural establishment. Buttressing the heavyweight cultural capital of both director and screenwriter, Bernhard Schlink was also closely involved in the film's development over several years. The three undertook a lengthy tour of Germany to explore issues of the long-term historical legacy of the Holocaust, German war guilt, and the ambiguous feelings of Germany's post-war generation towards that of their parents. Schlink's strong imprimatur for the adaptation even registers in the finished film itself: the author makes a cameo appearance as one of the customers in the beer garden/cycling holiday sequence.[6] All this marshalling of literary community endorsement for the film as a "faithful" adaptation of Schlink's novel comes together in the film's elaborate website which, as is now standard, went live well prior to the film's release to build publicity and allay qualms amongst "purist" book fans. Not only does the website prominently flag that the film is "based on the best-selling novel," the website design itself consciously remediates the format of the codex book for the quite differently proportioned computer screen.[7] The webpage's various menus guide browsers through a fluid series of paper-textured, deckle-edged codex pages, as though better to reassure the book's millions of fans that – despite the evidence contained in the lengthy production notes – the film represents a minimally mediated version of the book come to life.

The Weinsteins' campaign of literary community cultivation accelerated through-out post-production and upon *The Reader*'s release, with the clear goal of establishing the film amongst this culturally powerful grouping as a prelude to a concentrically expanding mainstream campaign. Even prior to the film's much-disputed final cut, Weinstein arranged a special pre-release *Reader* preview with the New York City-based Accompanied Literary Society (ALS), an invitation-only group of New York celebrities, literati, and cultural industries scene-makers. Daldry, as well as other notables such as novelist Michael Cunningham and *Angela's Ashes* author the late Frank McCourt, were in attendance, and select media outlets such as celebrity bible *Vanity Fair* were granted press access to build positive pre-release buzz regarding the film's artistic merit. The ALS's stated mission is to "extend the range and reach of literature," specifically by promoting writing in the context of other art forms, and facilitating liaison between creators and the corporate world.[8] How appropriate then that this ideal forum for show-casing an awards-aspirant literary adaptation should count both Harvey Weinstein and TWC amongst its sponsors.[9]

In the pressure-cooker December–January season in which studios now release their prime Oscar-contending films, TWC continued relentlessly to court literary-critical endorsement for their screen adaptation. At the film's formal premiere in New York City (note, not the more typical film industry choice of Los Angeles), Bernhard Schlink attended the standing-room-only question and answer session following a showing of the film's final cut. *Business Week*'s correspondent interpreted this unusual premiere format as motivated by the fact that "Some academy members were likely in the audience" (Grover, 2009). In February 2009, shortly after *The Reader*'s Oscar nominations, Schlink, Daldry, Hare, and the film's major stars gave a joint press conference at the Berlin Film Festival. Daldry has previously remarked that "you can't find a German who hasn't read the book" (Kaminer, 2008). Hence establishing critical endorsement of the adaptation in this most sensitive foreign market, and one of Europe's most populous at that, was always going to be crucial for the Weinsteins' overarching strategy. In the feverish speculation of Oscars' season, *The Reader*'s multiple book, film, audiobook, and published screenplay ver-sions endlessly cross-promoted and reinforced each other's market presence, each helping to build maximum public consciousness of *The Reader*'s media brand. Nor did this deliberate blurring of the various print- and screen-format incarnations of *The Reader* abate in the wake of the film's wide cinema release and subsequent DVD issue: at the 2009 Melbourne Writers Festival Bernhard Schlink introduced a special screening of *The Reader*, afterwards answering audience questions raised by the film.[10] Such combined author–film sessions are becoming increasingly prominent in the programming of cultural festivals such as the UK's famed Hay Festival (dubbed "the Woodstock of the mind") as writers' festivals extend the ambit of their interests beyond the codex format itself to encompass a much broader, medium-neutral conception of writerliness (Murray, 2011). In doing so they moreover prolong the cultural circulation of an adaptation franchise.

But despite all the intricately coordinated cross-sectoral planning recorded in the trade press around the production and release of *The Reader*, not everything went according to plan – the adaptation industry contains too many fractious elements and is too characterized by fraught instability to be solely pliable to marketing departments' will. In fact, the most widely publicized aspect of *The Reader*'s distribution campaign concerned the deaths of two of the film's esteemed producers, Anthony Minghella and Sydney Pollack, and the subsequent titanic clash of egos that flared between remaining executive producers, Harvey Weinstein and Scott Rudin. Roiling conflict over *The Reader*'s final cut and release date had become the dominant media story about the film from September 2008, threatening to eclipse TWC's carefully designed campaign of literary cultivation. Briefly, the dispute arose over whether Daldry, finetuning the Broadway musical adaptation of his earlier film *Billy Elliot* (2000) by day while editing *The Reader* by night, would have a final cut of the film ready in time for 2008 Golden Globe contention. Harvey Weinstein, with TWC's financial situation foremost in mind, was agitating strongly for a November 2008 release. Meanwhile, Scott Rudin already had both *Revolutionary Road* and *Doubt* in contention for the 2008 Oscar season, and supported Daldry's request for more post-production time and thus a 2009 release date. Rudin's threat (subsequently enacted) to take his name off *The Reader*'s credits opened up a further front in the dispute. Moreover, the question of whether Kate Winslet would secure Oscar nominations for both *Revolutionary Road* (directed by her then husband Sam Mendes) and *The Reader*, and would thus be competing against herself, added an extra celebrity frisson to a story previously confined to the trade press. Eventually, a compromise U.S. release date of December 12, 2008 was hammered out, making the film eligible for the all-important 2008 Academy Award competition.

Conclusion

I have delved into the production, distribution, and critical reception histories of *The Reader* at some length to demonstrate the possibilities for enhanced understanding of adaptation to be gained through close attention to the workings of the encompassing adaptation industry. Too often and for too long in adaptation studies, production – let alone the more emphatically marginalized topic of distribution – have been largely absent. Reception histories, fashionable since the impact of post-structuralist and cultural studies concepts of audience agency since the 1980s, have tended more often towards critical generalizations about audience responses, usually also analyzed from considerable historical distance, or they have drawn conclusions about reception of a given adaptation from other producers' subsequent reworkings of similar material, rather than basing their conclusions on empirically supported analysis of what *contemporary* audiences made of a given screen text immediately upon, or following hard on the heels of, its cinema release.

In doing so, adaptation studies has through its practice rather than by decree deemed contextual, and especially material, concerns mere framing for detailed textual analyses. This implicit devaluation of context demotes it to a mere pre-condition for the creation of great cinema art (in cases where the critical verdict on an adaptation is positive) or presents it as merely the sordidly commercial environment against which genius directors must lamentably struggle (where an adaptation is judged unsuccessful). Both views are misleading and unrepresentative because they fundamentally underestimate the ways in which legal, economic, industrial and systemic concerns dramatically influence which texts are considered for adaptation, within which sectors of global screen culture, and how the institutional apparatus equally facilitates creation of certain kinds of adaptations. Moreover, mainstream adaptation critics underestimate the continuing impact contextual factors have on determining matters of textual form. Here the alleged mere "frame" could itself just as easily comprise the main focus of academic interest. Or, because such either/or conceptions of context/text relations are both arid and tedious, better that the two categories be held together and interrelated to illuminate how context frequently influences form and, conversely, how ground-breaking content may trigger widespread and long-running industrial shifts in imitation or counter-reaction.

Another surprise: such multi-perspectival approaches are relatively common in the disciplines which gave rise to the hybrid undertaking that has become adaptation studies. Introductory screen studies textbooks have long included sections on production and contextual issues, even during the long imperium of "high theory;" whereas in literary studies, the disciplines of bibliography and book history have, although marginalized, always insisted upon the importance of books as material objects and social actors in wider political, intellectual, and social domains. It is puzzling then that the academic cross-breed of adaptation studies should have sheared off the materialist elements present in both of its parent disciplines and elevated the text almost to a critical fetish. This has occurred despite (or perhaps *because of*) the fact that of all filmmaking, economic motivations are often most readily evident in relation to adaptation. Rather than commercial motivations constituting a source of continuing shame for the still coalescing discipline of adaptation studies, they provide a key to the future development of the field, highlighting how much comprehension of the economic bases of culture enhances our understanding of the texts around us. Such speculations might also prompt researchers to question whether it has become an anachronism in the twenty-first century even to talk about delimited book, film and television industries, as though they were any longer entities discreet from the encompassing mediasphere. And at the broadest level, an economic approach to adaptation could lead scholars in the humanities and social sciences generally to question the inherited divide between these two academic camps, and to ask whether their bifurcated theoretical, methodological, and institutional formations may inhibit current understandings of cultural phenomena as much as they attempt to explicate them.

Notes

1 www.frankfurt-book-fair.com/en/fbf/topics/film_media/. Accessed November 30, 2010.

2 www.forum-cinema-litterature.com/accueil/accueil.php. Accessed November 30, 2010.

3 Nicholas Latimer, Knopf Associate Publicity Director, describing *The Reader* upon its announcement as Oprah's Book Club selection for March 1999 (quoted in Maryles and Donahue, 1999: 20).

4 Grover (2009).

5 http://entertainment.timesonline.co.uk/tol/arts_and_entertainment/film/article2295884.ece. July 11, 2011.

6 "From Book to Film." http://thereader-movie.com/site. July 11, 2011.

7 www.thereader-movie.com. July 19, 2009.

8 www.accompaniedliterarysociety.org. July 19, 2009.

9 www.accompaniedliterarysociety.org. July 19, 2009.

10 www.mwf.com.au/2009/content/mwf_2009_events.asp?name=2237. July 19, 2009.

References

Andrew, Dudley. "The Well-Worn Muse: Adaptation in Film History and Theory." In *Narrative Strategies: Original Essays in Film and Prose Fiction*. Eds. S. M. Conger and J. R. Welsch. Macomb, IL: Western Illinois University, 1980, 9–17.

Bluestone, George. *Novels into Film*. [1957]. Baltimore, MD: Johns Hopkins University Press, 2003.

Bourdieu, Pierre. *The Field of Cultural Production: Essays on Art and Literature*. Ed. Randal Johnson. Cambridge: Polity, 1993.

Cartmell, Deborah, and Imelda Whelehan. Eds. *Adaptations: From Text to Screen, Screen to Text*. London: Routledge, 1999.

Darnton, Robert. "What is the History of Books?" [1982]. In *The Kiss of Lamourette*. Robert Darnton London: Faber & Faber, 1990, 107–35.

Grover, Ronald. "Harvey Weinstein Builds Business with *The Reader*." *Business Week*, February 2, 2009. www.businessweek.com/bwdaily/dnflash/content/jan2009/db20090130_143403.htm. Accessed November 3, 2010.

Hutcheon, Linda. *A Theory of Adaptation*. New York: Routledge, 2006.

Jenkins, Henry. *Convergence Culture: Where Old and New Media Collide*. New York: New York University Press, 2006.

Kaminer, Ariel. "Translating Love and the Unspeakable." Review of *The Reader* (2008). *New York Times*, December 7, 2008. www.nytimes.com/2008/12/07/movies/07kami.html. Accessed January 24, 2011.

Leitch, Thomas. *Film Adaptation and its Discontents: From* Gone with the Wind *to* The Passion of the Christ. Baltimore, MD: Johns Hopkins University Press, 2007.

Maas, John-Michael. "Writing off into the Sunset." *Publishers Weekly*, March 26, 2001, 25.

Mansfield, Susan. "Coming to Terms with the Past." *Aberdeen Press and Journal*, August 26, 2000.

Maryles, Daisy and Dick Donahue. "Oprah Goes International." *Publishers Weekly*, March 1, 1999, 20.

Murray, Simone. *The Adaptation Industry: The Cultural Economy of Contemporary Literary Adaptation*. New York: Routledge, 2011.

Naremore, James. "Introduction: Film and the Reign of Adaptation." In *Film Adaptation*. Ed. James Naremore. London: Athlone Press, 2000, 1–16.

Palmer, R. Barton. "The Sociological Turn of Adaptation Studies: The Example of *Film Noir*. In *A Companion to Literature and Film*. Eds. Robert Stam and Alessandra Raengo. Malden, MA: Blackwell, 2004, 258–77.

Perren, Alisa. "sex, lies and marketing: Miramax and the Development of the Quality Indie Blockbuster." *Film Quarterly*, 55:2, 2001, 30–9.

Richardson, Anna. "A Shot in the Backlist." *Bookseller*, February 22, 2008, 22–3.

Sanders, Julie. *Adaptation and Appropriation*. New Critical Idiom. Abingdon, UK: Routledge, 2006.

Schlink, Bernard. *The Reader*. Trans. Carol Brown Janeway. New York: Pantheon Books, 1997.

Wyatt, Justin. "The Formation of the 'Major Independent': Miramax, New Line and the New Hollywood." In *Contemporary Hollywood Cinema*. Eds. Steve Neale and Murray Smith. London: Routledge, 1998, 74–90.

Part III
Genre: Film, Television

8

Adapting the X-Men

Comic-Book Narratives in Film Franchises

Martin Zeller-Jacques

During the past decade, comic-book adaptations have become an increasingly familiar sight on our movie screens. In addition to the blockbuster outings of classic DC and Marvel superheroes, which are now a regular part of Hollywood's seasonal schedule, less well-known comic books have also given us *Ghost World* (2001), *The Road to Perdition* (2002), *Persepolis* (2007), *American Splendor* (2003), and many other films not immediately recognizable as comic-book adaptations. However, superhero films still make up the majority of comic-book adaptations, and have become a substantial part of our contemporary film industry. In part this is due to their value as texts with a built-in audience. The enduring popularity of superhero narratives all but guarantees financial safety, and the critical success of films like Christopher Nolan's *Batman Begins* (2005) and *The Dark Knight* (2008) has proven that such films can aspire to the highest aesthetic standards. However, superhero films can pose particular problems to the theorist of adaptation. The plethora of comic books, films, television shows, radio programs, advertisements, toys, video-games, and novels which comprise even a moderately well-established superhero's textual history problematize the process of adaptation in ways that are productive for thinking about adaptations in general. Such variety encourages us to think of adaptation not as a binary with "source" on one side and "adaptation" on the other, but instead as an ongoing process through which new adaptations continually (re)develop an ever-growing metatext – an intangible "ideal" text formed by the agglomeration and interrelationship of all the texts which deal with a particular superhero's narrative universe. Moreover, as superhero films become increasingly well established and develop into film franchises, they stretch our conception of adaptation even

A Companion to Literature, Film, and Adaptation, First Edition. Edited by Deborah Cartmell.
© 2012 Blackwell Publishing Ltd. Published 2012 by Blackwell Publishing Ltd.

further, and arguably work to supplant their superheroic narrative "sources" by creating alternative metatexts of their own. This chapter follows the development of one film franchise through this process, discussing the inherent problems of adapting superhero narratives, and conceptualizing how superhero films have begun to move beyond adaptation.

Underlying any adaptation of a superhero comic book is an exceptional problem of fidelity. Adaptation studies has historically been keen to distance itself from questions of fidelity, rejecting the popular complaint that an adaptation isn't "as good as the book" as a subjective aesthetic preference which tends to obfuscate the theoretical and practical issues at play in the process of adaptation. Without contradicting this, however, we must make room for the fact that an audience's desire for fidelity may be a powerful motivating factor for those producing or viewing an adaptation. For a film's producers, the appeal of a comic-book adaptation is its potential as a pre-sold franchise with a ready-made audience. Such an audience's response to the text will be heavily dependent upon its engagement with its source(s), and the adaptation risks ignoring this at its peril. However, as we shall see, conceptualizing a source in a narrative as complex and long running as an established superhero comic book is even more fraught than in literary adaptation studies. Every fan will have a different conception of what constitutes fidelity and will be able to point to ample textual evidence supporting his or her claim. However, superhero films are more widely disseminated than superhero comics, and also seek to attract new audiences unfamiliar with the characters they portray. Johnson points out that, "a clear discrepancy exists between the cultural status of comic books and their filmic counterparts, one that certainly contributes to the subordination of the former at the industrial level" (2007: 66). However, it is not only cultural convention which subordinates comic books, but also their industrial position as seed properties for much more profitable film, television, and video-game franchises. During the past several decades a series of media mergers has brought the two most substantial comic-book publishers within the multimedia conglomerates of Time-Warner (DC) and Disney (Marvel). The vast majority of new superhero adaptations are made from properties belonging to one of these two companies, and these films are shaped by the parallel pressures of appealing to a fan audience while providing an accessible and exciting narrative experience for a wide audience. Disney has openly stated its intention to offset the potential risk of producing many new superhero films by making the characters "as commercial as possible," showing that it clearly desires a broad audience for these films (McAllister et al., 2006: 111). Moreover, because superhero adaptations exist as part of an ongoing cycle of multimedia production, which continually contests and revises them as new texts and products are created, new superhero adaptations continue to complicate the processes underlying their own creation. Indeed, the reach and scale of contemporary superhero blockbuster franchises allows them the potential to supplant the narratives from which they are notionally adapted, so that they become the "source" of future adaptations and sequels. This chapter will explore these problems of adaptation through a detailed look at the longest-standing superhero film franchise which remains in production: the X-Men.

One of the flagship properties of Marvel Comics, the X-Men have existed, in one form or another, since 1963. Within the Marvel Universe, the X-Men are mutants, humans whose genetic structure has changed, and granted them superpowers, or bizarre handicaps, or occasionally both. Although the portrayal of mutation has shifted over the long lives of the characters, one constant element has been the use of the X-Men, and mutants in general, as a way of exploring issues of prejudice and identity politics in contemporary society. As I will suggest below, this element of "real-world" relevance made the X-Men ideal subjects for Marvel's initial twenty-first century superhero adaptation. Moreover, the ongoing success of the film franchise spawned by the X-Men has allowed it to become one of the first examples of a film series with a narrative depth and breadth comparable to that of the metatext it adapts.

Adapting Superhero Narratives

At first glance, the problem of visualizing a superhero's world on screen and the problem of condensing the vast serialized narratives of superhero comics into a two-hour movie (or even a multi-part movie franchise) appear to be different in nature. Initially, the adaptation of a comic book's visual elements appears to be relatively easy, given the superficial similarities between comic books, with their panel-by-panel images, and strips of film. In practice, however, the adaptation of comic-book images is problematic. As Leitch points out, "though their individual panels are more likely to correspond to individual shots . . . [comic books] comprise discontinuous tableaux rather than streaming video" (2007: 194). As still images, comic books excel at presenting evocative character poses and expressive single images, such as Clark Kent ripping open his shirt to reveal the Superman emblem beneath, or Peter Parker walking away from a garbage can out of which protrudes his discarded Spiderman costume. However, they must rely on a visual shorthand, or else written verbal cues, to portray significant movement across space or time. Films, on the other hand, excel at portraying movement, but often try to evoke their comic-book "sources" through the direct adaptation of evocative single images like the ones described above, both of which appear in recent film adaptations. Yet while many comic-book adaptations transfer such visual "moments" onto the screen, very few even attempt to represent the stylized visual world of a comic book.[1] However, superhero comic books often have particular visual tropes which are so much a part of their characters that the film cannot help but address them directly. Costumes, utility belts, secret lairs, and the other trappings of superheroism tend to be so intrinsic to these characters that they must be represented in film adaptations. Yet, while some of these features are so iconic as to be unambiguous (beyond rendering it in material instead of ink, there is little room to change Superman's costume without fundamentally altering the character), most have been represented in a variety of different ways. There have been dozens of different looking Arkham Asylums and Batmobiles; many varied Cerebros and Danger Rooms. In practice, then, except in the few films which explicitly attempt to mimic comic-book style, only iconic images, locations and props tend to be drawn from the visual element of comic books when superhero texts are adapted, and even these often have a number of possible sources on which they may be based.

Adapting the story/ies of superhero narratives is, if anything, even more problematic. A serialized narrative of fifty years' duration, the various stories which comprise the metatext of *The X-Men* would be complicated enough as the source for an adaptation if they maintained a consistent style or tone. However, just as every different illustrator or animator has adapted *The X-Men*, creating numerous different visual styles reflecting various period fashions and authorial interpretations, so each new issue or graphic novel adds to the array of stories which have been told about the X-Men, many of them more than once. The X-Men have saved the world from aliens, fought racial prejudice, worked out teenage angst, teamed up with leprechauns, and tussled with Dracula. The sheer size and variety of a metatextual world, like that inhabited by the X-Men, can render it confusing and contradictory in ways which even the most self-conscious literary fiction cannot approach. A film calling itself *Moby Dick* could hardly portray Captain Ahab as a recluse who moved to Kansas because he was sick to death of whales, but a film about the X-Men could, with ample textual justification, present Magneto as a disillusioned separatist, living in peace on a secluded island, or, just as validly, as a genocidal sociopath. With their variety of visual styles and their abundance of overlapping, intertwining narratives, long-running superhero comics like *The X-Men* are among the most varied and complex, or perhaps contradictory and over-determined, texts ever to have existed. Thus the central question which should be asked of any new superhero adaptation, in terms of both its visual and its narrative qualities, is the same: what, exactly, is being adapted?

The scale of this question is perhaps best encapsulated by the simple observation that *The X-Men*, while the name of a movie and a set of characters, has only occasionally been the name of a comic book. Marvel has published titles including: *The Uncanny X-Men; The X-Men; X-Men Unlimited; The Astonishing X-Men; Ultimate X-Men; X-Men: Age of Apocalypse; The New X-Men*; to say nothing of related titles like *X-Force, X-Calibur*, and *The New Mutants*, as well as the many other titles in which characters from the X-Men appear as guest-stars.[2] Most of these titles have yielded dozens, some hundreds of issues. The longest running, *The Uncanny X-Men*, has been published since 1963 and (to date) consists of more than 500 issues. These comics have also spawned previous adaptations, including a highly regarded and widely syndicated animated series with a seventy-six episode run (1992–7), and numerous video-games. In short, the past fifty years have seen the unbroken, and typically accelerating, production of new X-Men stories across a variety of media. Moreover, while these stories have shared characters and events, they have not shared precisely the same diegesis – the same narrative world. Because of this they often revise, nullify or simply contradict one another, but they also build on one another, incorporating ideas which cross various continuities and media. Moreover, every reader brings to each of these new texts his or her own level of previous engagement with other *X-Men* texts, and thus his or her own knowledge and expectations of the new text.

Of course, however bewildering the implications of adapting such a complex text may be, it is not only the narrative and the images which are being adapted. Grouping comic-book adaptations together with board-game, song and video-game adaptations, as "post-literary adaptations," Leitch suggests that "Whatever particular features they borrow, the feature that is most important is the marketing aura of the original . . . Whether or not this aura invokes literary cachet, it always betokens commercial value from whatever associations are most likely to be profitable" (2007: 260). While Leitch sees post-literary adaptations as a way to move beyond what he calls "the chimerical quest for fidelity" (258), comic-book adaptations are, in fact, rarely forgetful of their many, many sources. Moreover, the "originals" involved in comic-book adaptation continue to exist as live, circulating commodities, in the form of downloadable e-zines and trade paperbacks, and, in some cases, DVDs and syndicated television series, and thus continue to have monetary value which new adaptations will seek to exploit, or at least, not to devalue. In order to fully address the adaptation of superhero narratives, we need to acknowledge that such narratives are neither only commodities nor only texts, but that they are simultaneously part of a wide-ranging and multifaceted metatext, and of a network of multimedia entertainment properties. As part of their wider superheroic metatexts, most superhero films are latecomers attempting to retell stories told many times before, or to find new ways to treat old material. However, as part of multimedia entertainment properties, they are increasingly becoming the flagship of their brands – the shop window through which all other facets of the property are displayed. When examining a superhero adaptation, then, we are examining a text marked by contradictory forces: by the pressure to reimagine an old narrative for an established audience, and the pressure to repackage old properties for a new audience.

Both aspects of these texts are addressed by Sarah Cardwell's approach to adaptation studies, which envisages any new adaptation (whether literary, post-literary, or otherwise) as contributing to an ever expanding metatext. Cardwell notes the way that new adaptations of classic fiction inevitably draw on older ones. Characterizing the "fidelity" discourse, as well as many critical refutations of it, as a "centre-based model of adaptation," where "each subsequent adaptation is understood to hold a direct relationship with the culturally established original," she points out that although this model may accept that the source text has a complicated, historically situated genesis, when considering the adaptation: "it denies the linear, textual history of adaptation available to each new adapter . . . ," decontextualizing the adaptation by preferring its relation to its "source" over the other discourses which may determine its final shape (2002: 14–15). Cardwell suggests that we instead see "adaptation as the gradual development of a "metatext," recognizing that, "a later adaptation may draw upon any earlier adaptations, as well as upon the primary source text" (25). Importantly, Cardwell's model of adaptation leaves open the possibility that a new adaptation is influenced not only by previous adaptations comprising parts of the same metatext, but also by other contexts, such as generic affiliation, contemporary filmmaking fashion, and market positioning.

As blockbuster films with substantial budgets and the expectation of equally substantial profits, superhero films are certainly subject to a variety of influences ranging beyond their supposed comic-book "sources." Indeed, in many aspects of their presentation, the need for superhero adaptations to compete with other blockbuster action films supersedes their relationship with their sources. As a result such films have tended to appeal to a discourse of "realism" which has not often troubled superhero comic books, discarding elements of the fantastic or macabre which are not strictly necessary to the thrust of the story. Thomas Leitch has noted a similar trend in adaptations of Sherlock Holmes, perhaps the only literary character with as rich and varied a history of adaptations as an established superhero, and his explanation of this phenomenon is useful in understanding superhero adaptations. Writing of one episode of Granada's television adaptation of Sherlock Holmes, Leitch suggests that it "changes so many elements in Conan Doyle's story of a scientist's unwise experiments with monkey glands that it raises the question of why the producers . . . chose the story in the first place." He concludes that, "In rewriting Doyle, the adaptations are choosing fidelity to the appealing macrotext of the Victorian milieu and to a selection of powerful microtexts" (2007: 228–9). As a result, the Granada adaptation discards elements of the Holmes mythos which feel dated, or implausible, or simply those which do not tally with the contemporary public's expectations of Holmes' Victorian setting. Likewise, superhero adaptations often focus upon the appealing macrotext of the special-effects-driven blockbuster, while selectively drawing upon the iconic microtexts of costumes, powers, team-ups, and villains.

At one level, this approach is not unique to superhero adaptations, but can be found in any new superhero text, in any medium. As Geoff Klock has suggested, because a comic-book superhero's narrative is "a serial narrative that has been running for more than sixty years, reinterpretation becomes part of its survival code..." (2002: 13). Thus any new superhero text positions itself in relation to those which have come before it. For Klock, this creates a problem of influence in superhero narratives, and it is chiefly through Harold Bloom's paradigm of the Anxiety of Influence (1997) that he approaches them, arguing that in the dreamlike climate of superhero narratives, "strong work comes to define truth, as narrative continuity is fuzzy at best" (13). In other words, the organizing principle of superhero narratives is not sequence or causality – events are not required to follow one another according to the logical rules which govern other realist narratives – but rather strength of influence. As evidence for this, Klock offers close textual readings of several "strong" works from the history of superhero comic books, including Frank Miller's *The Dark Knight Returns* and Alan Moore's *Watchmen*, and demonstrates the way that these stories retroactively revise what has come before them and influence what has come after them. In Bloom's terms, they perform a misprision, a productive *mis*-reading of previous superhero work, recasting that tradition in their own terms.

However, both Bloom and Klock conceive of strength as something emanating from the author, and influence as a process taking place between powerful creative imaginations. They neglect to ask the place of the audience in this relationship, and when dealing with narratives which reach as wide and varied an audience as contemporary superhero adaptations, this is a crucial omission. Klock's concern is chiefly with those superhero works he calls "revisionary," those which comprise "an organization of a host of contradictory weak readings of a single, overdetermined character," turning them into one "strong vision" (29). However, I would suggest that the structure of misprision Klock identifies is visible not only in the work of strong authors, but in most or all new superhero texts, and the strength of a new text should not only be conceived in terms of the breadth of its vision, or depth of its invention, but also in the size of its audience. The 1960s Adam West *Batman* television series (1966–8) may be a critically reviled pop-culture joke, but it remains a strong influence on the production of new Batman texts, which invariably seek to avoid any resemblance to it. The size of its audience and its resulting place in our collective cultural memory render it as a strong work within the tradition of Batman, and superheroes in general.

Today, when every new superhero film is positioned in the market as a wide-release blockbuster, each one potentially functions as a strong work – definitively restructuring the previous superhero tradition or metatext from which it is adapted. I have suggested elsewhere (Zeller-Jacques, forthcoming) that this role as strong work leads to a "crisis of adaptation" in new superhero films, in which their relationship to the metatexts from which they have been adapted is made visible "as they attempt to position themselves as authentic through the explicit reinscription or rejection of what they regard as the metatext's essential tropes." While this crisis of adaptation remains visible across most contemporary superhero adaptations, it has been further complicated by the increasing size and scope of superhero film franchises, which, without approaching the size or complexity of existing superhero metatexts, circulate so widely that they threaten to displace the very stories they adapt. Although such franchises continue to enact the crisis of adaptation, reinscribing and restructuring their source metatext in order to make room for themselves, they do so on a large scale, incorporating multiple films, along with television and video-game tie-ins. Each of these functions as an adaptation in its own right, but simultaneously reinforces the interpretative primacy of the earlier texts in its own franchise.

One company has done more than any other to merge these two sets of concerns in its superhero adaptations. Formerly the largest single publisher of superhero comics, Marvel Comics now increasingly focuses its efforts on the production of feature films. According to McAllister et al., "Increasingly, comic book companies see themselves in the character licensing business (at the very least) and perhaps more specifically in the filmed entertainment industry" (2006: 111). Indeed, for several years, Marvel produced its own feature films, so as to ensure that its licensing revenue remained in-house (Johnson, 2007). The company's recent purchase by Disney has allied an enormous stable of pre-sold superhero properties to one of the most expansive multimedia distribution networks of the present day (Graser, 2009). And while Marvel's chief rival, DC Comics, has a similar place within the Time-Warner media group, it has not yet produced anything like the same concentration of superhero films as Marvel. Nor does Marvel simply produce standalone films. Since the second *X-Men* film, and most notably with the recent *Iron Man* (2008, 2010), *Hulk* (2008), *Thor* (2011) and *Captain America* (2011) films, Marvel has attempted to establish narrative connections between their films. *The X-Men* films have been produced by 20th Century Fox, in association with Marvel Entertainment, and were not necessarily planned as a franchise. However, following the success of the first three films, the franchise has begun to expand by focusing on one or two characters at a time in films like *X-Men Origins: Wolverine* (2009) and *X-Men: First Class* (2011). Meanwhile, *The Avengers* is being produced in house by Marvel/Disney, and will only be released once each of the major characters in the film has had a solo film outing. Both of these strategies ally a concern with the narrative of the film adaptations, which are designed to be expansive and embracing enough to rival the comic-book/television/film metatexts from which they are drawn, and the potential of these adaptations as brand-leading tentpoles which can continue to attract audiences for long periods with extensive franchises. In the following examination of the *X-Men* franchise, we will discuss both of these sets of concerns and see how they work to shape the finished films.

Establishing X-Pectations for *The X-Men* – Crisis of Adaptation and Creating a Visual Language

Released in 2000, Bryan Singer's *X-Men* was the first of a new generation of superhero films. Although there had been notable precedents, including Donner's *Superman* (1978) and Burton's *Batman* (1989), the genre had been stumbling throughout the 1990s and was widely considered to have collapsed with *Batman and Robin* (1997). This is not merely an aesthetic observation, but a comment on the range of devices available to a filmmaker working within the superhero genre. In 2000 the potential audience for superhero films was still to be constituted, and thus *X-Men* aims widely, hoping to incorporate the existing audience for X-Men comic books with elements of the audience for any effects-driven blockbuster, while also adding some A-list respectability by placing Singer, director of the critically and popularly lauded *The Usual Suspects* (1995), at the helm. In this regard, *X-Men* established a pattern followed by later auteur-driven superhero blockbusters such as Raimi's *Spiderman* (2002) and Ang Lee's *Hulk* (2003). As a film, then, *X-Men* is conditioned not only by its status as a superhero adaptation, but also by the limited visual and narrative languages as yet established for the telling of superhero narratives as blockbuster films, and the need to find a lucrative and widespread audience. At the same time, Singer has acknowledged that he felt the fan audience was particularly important to the success of the film, since the X-Men are not household names in the way that Superman and Batman are: "Ultimately, the comic book fans are your first core audience, the ones that are going to embrace it and talk about it and embrace it or reject it . . . They were the first people we worried about" (quoted in Boucher, 2010). At the center of the X-Men's crisis of adaptation, then, lies an appeal towards two arguably competing forms of authenticity: the film tries to please the established fan-base by adhering to what it regards as essentially important about the source metatext, but it simultaneously strives to adhere to the "realistic" milieu of the contemporary action-blockbuster, and downplays the more outlandish aspects of the X-Men metatext from which it is adapted: *The Uncanny X-Men* of the comic books become merely *The X-Men*. In both its visual style and its narrative, *The X-Men* reflects the generic conventions of action cinema even as it develops a visual and narrative vocabulary that will enable later installments to become ever more self-reliant and expansive.

This dynamic is at its most visible in the opening scenes of *The X-Men*, which work to situate the film within a familiar world and to establish the realistic emotional and narrative frameworks of the story. *The X-Men* opens with two young mutants discovering their powers under difficult circumstances. After the credit sequence, the first image of the film shows a gray-clad concentration camp guard training his gun on a distant column of people in drab, mud-stained clothing. The caption reads: "Poland, 1944." We watch the column file through the camp, their clothes prominently marked with yellow Stars of David. The adults are separated from the children, and as one young boy (Erik Lensher/Magneto) screams for his mother, the strength of his desire to rejoin her twists and distorts the metal gates of the prison, nearly tearing them down before he is subdued by the guards. The action then shifts to the United States, in "The not too distant future." We watch a teenage girl (Marie/Rogue) map out her planned trip across the States with her boyfriend. As the two kiss a close-up shows the boy's face drained of color as he begins to convulse. The girl screams and backs away while the boy lies writhing on the bed.

Singer's choice to foreground Magneto's past as a concentration camp survivor and Rogue's teenage anxieties offer viewers footholds in other discourses than that of the costumed superhero. While the idea of superpowers resulting from evolution may be difficult to grasp, the near-universal emotional trigger of a concentration camp allows Magneto's power to be read metaphorically, as a manifestation of his will to fight back against the oppression he has suffered. One of the film's producers, Lauren Shuler Donner, has acknowledged that, "The opening, it really was a declaration of intent. . . . It said to the audience this is a serious film, grounded in the realistic and the historic and somewhat dark" (quoted in Boucher, 2010). The scene with Rogue, who, apart from her "power" and her accent, shares little with her comic-book incarnations, allows the viewers to understand mutation through the traumas of coming of age. Portraying Rogue as confused and frightened, "a merger of . . . younger X-characters [like Jubilee and Kitty Pryde]," instead of the powerhouse she is in the comic books,[3] allows her to act as a surrogate for the audience (Singer quoted in Hughes, 2003: 178). Thus the audience is not required to identify with the costumed heroes and villains of the story, but with the potential victim in the midst of the conflict. A similar device is also used to orient the audience early on in *X-Men 3: The Last Stand*. Warren Worthington III, better known to X-Men fans as Angel, is shown as a teenager, locked in the bathroom, attempting to file off the nubs of the wings that have begun to grow on his back; with him we experience not the uncanny glory of flight, but instead, when his father walks in, the pain of parental disappointment and rejection. Moreover, this mundane emotional motivation underpins the film's central plot, as it is Warren's father who funds the research which leads to the development of the mutant cure, and Warren's choice to continue living as a mutant which inspires the X-Men to continue fighting on.

At least since the publication of the graphic novel, *God Loves, Man Kills* (Claremont, 1982), itself the explicit inspiration for much of the plot of *X2: X-Men United,* the X-Men have often been used to comment on identity politics, with mutants acting as a convenient parallel for any race, gender, sexuality, or political affiliation on which the authors have wished to comment. The choice to focus on Magneto and Rogue as just such figures is further aided by the inclusion of Senator Kelly. Early in the film we see Senator Kelly, the chief advocate of a "Mutant Registration Act," which would require all mutants to make themselves known to the federal government, questioning Jean Grey during a U.S. Senate Hearing. In a speech recalling McCarthy's HUAC hearings, Kelly claims to have "a list of names of identified mutants, living right here in the United States," and carries on to paint a frightening picture of the implications of allowing mutants to go on living unchecked, arguing that "The American people deserve the right to decide whether they want their children to be at school with mutants, to be taught by mutants. . . . We must know who they are, and above all we must know what they can do." As the film's voice of the politics of fear which drives human opposition to all mutants, Senator Kelly acts as a realistic counterpoint to the superpowered action set-pieces and his rhetoric emphasizes the parallels between Magneto's experiences in Nazi Germany and the situation facing mutants. While this parallel does not originate with the adaptation, the choice to adhere to this aspect of the "orthodox" continuity is significant for what it leaves out. In the comics, Senator Kelly has a long history involving alternate timelines and evil "masonic" societies, and the Mutant Registration Act was the first step towards Project Wideawake, a government-funded program which used giant robots called Sentinels to capture and sometimes execute mutants. As it does on other occasions, *The X-Men* leaves out such uncanny elements in order to avoid alienating non-fan viewers, abandoning the Sentinels but keeping Senator Kelly.

It is not only the narrative of *X-Men* which attempts to situate the film as realistic. Elements of the look of the characters, especially their costumes, are also presented in a manner which draws on the film's generic associations with other blockbuster action films in preference to its superheroic sources. The costumes worn by the X-Men during the film consist of plain black leather with discreet X-symbols on the shoulders and belts. These costumes have no direct precedent in X-Men comic books, though they went on to influence the black and yellow leather costumes worn by the team in Grant Morrison's *New X-Men* series (2001–4), which de-emphasizes the characters' roles as superheroes in favor of a more explicit focus on identity politics. Singer's explanation for the costumes, however, attributes his choice of costume to his concern with "realism," saying, "It had to be black leather . . . it's durable, it's the kind of thing that if they got hit with it on, it would bounce off" (Singer quoted in Hughes, 2003: 180). The film itself mocks established conventions of superhero costuming in a brief exchange between Wolverine (Hugh Jackman) and Cyclops (James Marsden). Chafing uncomfortably the first time he wears his leather combat-suit, Wolverine complains: "You actually go outside in these things?" to which Cyclops responds with a self-conscious quip about the teams' original costumes: "What would you prefer, yellow spandex?" At this level, the costumes used in the film attempt to distance *The X-Men* from its origins as a comic-book narrative. In addition, they serve to reinforce its connection with contemporary non-superhero action blockbusters. Most notably, the all-black outfits worn by the X-Men recall the cyber-punk aesthetic of the then-recent hit, *The Matrix* (1999). This hardly amounts to a wholesale repudiation of the superhero genre – *The Matrix*, after all, is replete with superheroism – but it nevertheless represents a further separation of The Uncanny from *The X-Men*, a preference for the stylized realism and established genre conventions of the action film over the superhero tradition of the existing X-Men metatext.

However, there is more at work here than a desire to cash in on proven genre success. Costumes in *The X-Men* franchise play an important part in expressing the ideologies of the characters who wear them. Karaminas writes that, "As part of an iconic signifier, [the superhero wardrobe] . . . separates those with superhuman strength from 'mere' mortals and sets the costume-wearer apart from conventional society" (2005: 1; 5). In *The X-Men* the superheroes' costumes are discreet in comparison to their comic-book incarnations, but more importantly, in comparison to the villains. The integrationist politics of Xavier and his X-Men are mirrored in the clothes they wear: simple, plain, and practical. Capes, helmets, and armor are the symbols of the villains; they are the ones whose costumes declare them separate from "mere mortals" and "conventional society." Thus Magneto is often seen wearing a cape and helmet; Sabretooth dresses in layers of animal skins; Juggernaught wears a harness and helmet, Mystique prefers to stay in her scaly, mutant form rather than "passing" as human, and a group of mutant street toughs mark themselves with elaborate tattoos proclaiming their mutant heritage. As the franchise continues, this dynamic is complicated by characters like Nightcrawler and Beast, both of whom have bestial features, blue skin, and, in Nightcrawler's case, a prehensile tail. Yet these characters consistently seek out integration, and the difference marked on their bodies thus plays poignantly, emphasizing the injustice of surface judgments rather than their separation from humanity. (In a direct reversal of the tattooed mutant-pride brigade, the fervently Catholic Nightcrawler carves his skin with designs to represent his own sins.).

These ideas find their clearest expression in a scene from Singer's second X-Men film, *X2: X-Men United*. Just prior to the film's climax, a running confrontation which takes place in a secret military base, the mutant separatist, Magneto (Ian MacKellan) finds a moment to speak with the hotheaded teenage mutant, John Allardyce (Aaron Stanford). Already feeling unappreciated by the adult X-Men, John is intrigued by Magneto, and asks him about his distinctive helmet – a recognizable version of the one worn by Magneto in the X-Men comics. Magneto responds by saying that the helmet, "is the only thing that's going to protect [him] from the real bad guys." As he says this, he uses his power to float John's lighter, a keepsake which he is never without, towards himself, and asks the boy's name. When John responds, Magneto asks again, in a hushed voice: "What's your *real* name, John?" Using his power to draw the flame from his lighter to his hand, John responds, "Pyro." John's mix of vulnerability and confidence helps the moment to play as a kind of coming out, a perception reinforced by McKellan's well-publicized homosexuality. However, it also serves to induct John into Magneto's separatist politics, as the older man assures John that, "You are a god among insects. Never let anyone tell you different," and hands the lighter back in a shot framed to recall the image of *The Creation of Adam* on the ceiling of the Sistine Chapel.

In this exchange, both the costume and the codenames of superpowered beings function as signs of their difference. In contrast to an earlier scene in the first *X-Men* film, in which Wolverine and Rogue reveal their real (i.e. human) names to one another in a gesture of mutual trust, in the exchange between the once and future villains, Magneto and Pyro, the codename further signifies the difference already indicated by their powers and costumes. Through this trope the films manage to reconcile part of their crisis of adaptation, simultaneously accommodating "canonical" elements of the metatext in the form of the villains' costumes, yet still contributing to the realistic presentation of the rest of the film by using these elements to comment on the franchise's allegorical treatment of identity politics.

The early *X-Men* films were relatively conservative in their scale, and in their presentation of the fantastic world they portrayed, carefully condensing a sprawling, fifty-year-old metatext into a few short, comprehensible hours of linear narrative. However, their judicious development of narrative strands and visual tropes allowed the later films in the franchise to expand more freely. Once these first films had created some of the conventions of "realistic" superheroic storytelling, the franchise could begin to stretch itself to incorporate a much wider array of characters, ideas, and storylines. Leaving aside the aesthetic achievements of the later films, which are, to put it generously, questionable, this broadening begins to suggest the expansive possibilities which occur when the de-serialized narratives of a superhero adaptation are opened up to becoming re-serialized.

The X-Panding Universe: *X-Men 3, X-Men Origins: Wolverine*

While the first two *X-Men* films exemplify the crisis of adaptation in the way that they seek to establish themselves simultaneously as authentic X-Men texts and as authentic summer blockbusters, then the more recent X-Men films have increasingly built upon the earlier films, often in preference to the wider X-Men metatext. In Klock's terms, the longer the X-Men film franchise continues, the more it constitutes strong work within the X-Men metatext. As a result the newer films are positioned as following on from or explaining the events and situations of the previous films, which largely take up the position of "source" texts from which the newer films spring. This does not mean that they cease entirely to adapt material from other parts of the metatext, only that this is no longer their primary source. Even more than adaptations, these later films are sequels and prequels – expansions of a franchise which positions itself as a sufficient and separate alternative to the metatext it adapts. In these films, the crisis of adaptation finds its fullest expression, as the serialized superhero film franchise begins to mimic the density of the metatext it adapts, and positions itself as an authentic and complete replacement for that metatext.

Following on from the earlier X-Men films, *X3* situates its characters in a realistic world. Its central plot, involving a "cure" for mutation, developed by the geneticist, Dr. Kavita Rao, is drawn from Joss Whedon's *The Astonishing X-Men* (2004–7), a series which had begun running just two years before the film was released. The use of a relatively contemporary source text by the creator of *Buffy the Vampire Slayer* might serve to broaden the appeal of the franchise, but as with previous installments, the uncanny elements are removed. So, instead of gaining the "cure" from an alien, as she does in the comic, Dr. Rao develops it from the essence of a young mutant whose ability cancels out the powers of other mutants, allowing the film to choose not to tax the credulity of its audience beyond what its basic premise requires. The same pattern is also repeated in *Wolverine*, which draws its opening scenes from the 2001 comic book, *Origin*, a gothic fantasy which owes a heavy debt to the Brontës, but quickly establishes its realist aesthetic through a montage of the various wars (U.S. Civil, First World War, Second World War, Vietnam, etc.) in which Wolverine has fought during his preternaturally long life.

Each of these films draws primarily upon a single, prominently authored source, combining this with the already established film franchise, in order to create a simple, accessible story. However, both also vastly expand the territory of the franchise, introducing numerous new characters and references to the wider X-Men metatext. Although these elements are included, at least in part, in order to gratify a fan audience waiting to see their favorite characters or moments dramatized, their effect is to create a sense of density, of unexplored territory within the franchise. In *X3*, for instance, we learn that Beast used to be one of the X-Men, before serving in the U.S. Cabinet, and we glimpse the severed head of a Sentinel robot in a Danger Room simulation, while in *Wolverine* we meet a whole roster of mutants with whom Wolverine once served on a secret commando unit. In many cases, these new pieces of information require us to retroactively rewrite what we have already learned within the franchise. Beast, for example, appears on a television interview in the first X-Men film, sans blue skin and fur, as ordinary Hank McCoy, yet no explanation is given for the change in his appearance, and he is now played by a different actor. Of course, part of the reason for this discrepancy, is that the first X-Men film was an untested commodity; there was no guarantee that it would ever have a sequel, or that Beast would appear as a character if it did. Nevertheless, his prominence in *X3* encourages us to read this as the "stronger" text in relation to Beast, and to write him into our understanding of the time period before the first film was set, either erasing our earlier glimpse of the character, or rationalizing the change as a story yet to be told.

Although there are numerous similar examples, they all tend to serve a dual purpose. Teasing glimpses like the view of the Sentinel's head, or the Phoenix-shaped shadow above the water at the end of *X2*, reward existing fans with narrative buds which can be parsed for significance, and savored in the anticipation of future satisfaction. Meanwhile, for new fans they provide the sense of a densely populated fictional world, full of further possibilities. Through the incorporation, however briefly, of elements of the expanded X-Men metatext, these later films lay claim to all of the metatext, and seek to establish their franchises as strong, definitive versions of that metatext. Indeed, the later installments of the franchise, through their persistent widening of the territory they cover, contrive to suggest a complete narrative world connecting all of the films, establishing an increasingly comprehensive alternative to the existing X-Men metatext the more films are added to the franchise.

Conclusion

As more superhero films fill our screens, and more of them become interconnected parts of their own franchises and metatexts, superhero narratives on screen are gradually becoming self-sustaining. No longer tied to the comic-book medium which initially brought them to a mass audience, they circulate with increasing freedom, and at most, a selective eye for their "original" predecessors. This shift in the superhero genre, from one which is primarily based in comic books and adapted into other media, to one which is most visible on film and to which comic books are a minor appendage, is still in process. However, it has already become apparent that any critical treatment of comic-book adaptations must take account not only of their status as adaptations, but also of the commercial logic underlying the reasons for that adaptation, as well as their generic and franchise relationships to other films.

NOTES

1   The most notable exceptions are *Dick Tracy* (1990), *Sin City* (2005), and *300* (2006). It should be noted that, certainly in the case of the latter two comics, and arguably in the case of *Dick Tracy* as well, the comics from which the films were adapted were notable for their stylized, expressionistic artwork, and this may have relieved the films of the burdensome expectation of realism.

2   For a relatively comprehensive list of the various X-Men titles and their associated his-tories, see the marvel.wikia.com Bibliography of X-Men Titles, http://marvel.wikia.com/Bibliography_of_X-Men_titles.

3   Rogue began her career as a villain, using her mutant power to temporarily drain and utilize the powers of other mutants. Early in her history she permanently absorbed the powers of a rather old-fashioned hero called Ms. Marvel. Consequently, in any comics written after the early 1980s, she flies and has super-strength as well as her mutant ability.

REFERENCES

300. Dir. Z. Snyder. USA: Warner Bros., 2006.

American Splendor. Dir. S. Berman and R. Pulcini. USA: Fine Line, 2003.

Avengers, The. Dir. J. Whedon. USA: Marvel Enterprises, 2012.

Batman and Robin. Dir. J. Schumacher. USA: Warner Bros., 1997.

Batman. 20th Century Fox Television, 1966–8. Creator. B. Kane.

Bloom, H. *The Anxiety of Influence*. 2nd edn. New York: Oxford University Press, 1997.

Boucher, G. "Bryan Singer on 'X-Men: First Class': It's got to be about Magneto and Professor X." *L.A. Times Online*, March 18, 2010. *Los Angeles Times*, December 12, 2010. http://herocomplex.latimes.com/2010/03/18/bryan-singer-and-the-xmen-together-again/.

Buffy the Vampire Slayer. Mutant Enemy. Dir. J. Whedon. 1997–2003.

Captain America: The First Avenger. Dir. J. Johnston. USA: Marvel Enterprises, 2011.

Cardwell, S. *Adaptation Revisited*. Manchester: Palgrave, 2002.

Claremont, C. *God Loves, Man Kills*. New York: Marvel Comics, 1982.

Dick Tracy. Dir. W. Beatty. USA: Touchstone, 1990.

Ghost World. Dir. T. Zwigoff. USA: United Artists, 2001.

Graser, M. "A Hero Sandwich." *Variety*. September 4, 2009, 1.

X-Men Origins: Wolverine. Dir. G. Hood. USA: 20th Century Fox, 2009.

Hughes, D. *Comic Book Movies*. London: Virgin Books, 2003.

Hulk. Dir. A. Lee. USA: Universal, 2003.

Incredible Hulk, The. Dir. L. Leterrier. USA: Universal Pictures, 2008.

Iron Man. Dir. J. Favreau. USA: Paramount, 2008.

Iron Man 2. Dir. J. Favreau. USA: Paramount, 2010.

Johnson, D. "Will the Real Wolverine Please Stand Up? Marvel's Mutation from Monthlies to Movies." In *Film and Comic Books*. Eds. I. Gordon, M. Jancovich, and M. McAllister.

Jackson: University of Missouri Press, 2007, 64–85.

Karaminas, V. " 'No Capes!' Uber Fashion and How "Luck Favours the Prepared'. Constructing Contemporary Superhero Identities in American Popular Culture." *Proceedings of "Imaginary Worlds: Image and Space" International Symposium*, October 14, 2005, University of Technology, Sydney. May 1, 2008. www.dab.uts.edu.au/research/conferences/imaginary-worlds/no_capes.pdf.

Klock, G. *How to Read Superhero Comics and Why*. London: Continuum, 2002.

Leitch, T. *Film Adaptation and its Discontents: From Gone With the Wind to The Passion of the Christ*. Baltimore: Johns Hopkins University Press, 2007.

Matrix, The. Dir. Wachowski, A. and L. Wachowski. USA: Warner Bros., 1999.

McAllister, M., I. Gordon, and M. Jancovich. "Blockbuster Meets Superhero Comic, or Arthouse Meets Graphic Novel?" *Journal of Popular Film and Television*, 34:3, 2006, 108–14.

Morrison, G. *The New X-Men*. New York: Marvel Comics, 2001–4.

Persepolis. Dir. V. Parronaud and M. Satrapi. France/USA: 2.4.7 Films, 2007.

Road to Perdition, The. Dir. S. Mendes. USA: Dreamworks, 2002.

Spiderman. Dir. S. Raimi. USA: Columbia Pictures, 2002.

Superman. Dir. R. Donner. USA: Warner Bros., 1978.

The Usual Suspects. Dir. B. Singer. USA: Poly-Gram Filmed Entertainment, 1995.

Thor. Dir. K. Branagh. USA: Marvel Studios, 2011.

Whedon, J. *The Astonishing X-Men*. New York: Marvel Comics, 2004–7.

Wright, Bradford. *Comic Book Nation: The Transformation of Youth Culture in America*. Baltimore, MD: Johns Hopkins University Press, 2003.

X-Men: First Class. Dir. M. Vaughn. USA: 20th Century Fox, 2011.

X-Men. Genesis Entertainment, 1992–7. Creator: A. Lee. Television series.

Zeller-Jacques, M. " 'Everything Begins With Superman': Infinite Crises in an Expanding Metatext." In *Science Fiction across Media: Adaptation/Novelization*. Eds. T. Van Parys and I. Hunter. Gylphi: Canterbury, forthcoming.

9

The Classic Novel on British Television

Richard Butt

Introduction

Adaptations of classic novels have been a significant component of British television drama since the earliest days of broadcasting. While they no longer dominate drama production as they did up until the 1960s, they continue to deliver substantial domestic audiences, and are a key export commodity for international markets. The classic serial, which became the most common form for adaptations of classic novels on British television, is recognized as a distinct television genre by producers, critics and audiences, comprising an unusually stable set of expectations central to which is the relationship between each serial and its particular literary source. The classic serial also exhibits what commentators have identified as the "textual markers" of the adaptation genre (Cartmell, 2010; Leitch, 2008). A period setting and the deployment of period music; a preoccupation with authors, books, and words; and the incorporation of fine art into the program's mise-en-scène, all work to foreground the classic serial's status as an adaptation and form part of the genre's claim to television's cultural high ground.

The classic serial has informed popular perceptions of the key attributes of quality television drama since the 1980s. Charlotte Brunsdon argues that in discussions of television quality, the Granada Television adaptations *Brideshead Revisited* and *The Jewel in the Crown* were "repeatedly invoked to carry the meaning of quality television" (Brunsdon, 1990: 84). In those discussions, she argues, the four components that were consistently identified as signifying quality in a television drama were that they were: based on a literary, often "middle-brow," source; featured the

A Companion to Literature, Film, and Adaptation, First Edition. Edited by Deborah Cartmell.
© 2012 Blackwell Publishing Ltd. Published 2012 by Blackwell Publishing Ltd.

"Best of British Acting," particularly actors from theater; manifested high production values, where the money is "spent according to upper-middle class taste codes whether to represent upper-class lifestyles or exotic poverty" (85); and could be classed as heritage exports (86). To a large extent, all four of these components continue to form part of the classic serial's generic regime.

As various commentators have observed, however (Cardwell, 2002; Caughie, 2000), adaptations of classic novels on British television have been as unpopular with academic writers as they have been popular with their television audiences. In discussions of television drama and in the field of adaptation studies, classic novel adaptations are consistently critiqued as overly theatrical, formulaic, commercially driven commodities that are aesthetically unimaginative, conservative, and nostalgic. "Formally unchallenging, while nevertheless replete with visual strategies that signify 'art' their only specifically televisual demand is that the viewer switch on at the right time and watch" (Brunsdon, 1990: 86). Even the critically acclaimed and widely popular Austen adaptations in the mid-1990s are not exempt from this unusually vitriolic academic assessment. In offering an account of the classic novel on British television, this chapter engages with the key terms of this debate, challenging some of its argument and opening up other lines of inquiry. It begins by locating the emergence of the form within the development of British television drama, a development in which it played a key role.

Emergence and Development

Much of the early evolution of British television was initially determined by the various institutional, technological, and programming practices that had already developed in BBC radio in the 1920s, and this was certainly the case for adaptations of the classics. Given that John Reith, the BBC's first Director-General, believed that radio should inform, educate and entertain, and that a significant part of that objective would be delivered by bringing culture to a mass audience, it was entirely consistent with his philosophy that readings of scenes from classic literature, including Dickens, Austen, Scott and Trollope, featured in the earliest years of radio broadcasting. A relationship with theater was quick to develop, as some of these scenes were performed in the radio studio by stage actors such as Bransby Williams, who was known for his enactments of Dickens' characters and scenes (Giddings and Selby, 2001: 9). More generally, radio adaptations became commonly referred to as "plays." While there were serialized readings of classic novels, particularly those of Dickens, the classic serial or the "serial play" as it was known, took longer to emerge. In the mid-1930s radio adaptations were often broadcast across two nights, such as Louise Drury's adaptation of Charles Kingsley's *Westward Ho!*, split across the evenings of Friday, 30 October and Sunday, 1 November, 1936. In the following year these serial plays were further extended, with adaptations of classic novels running across twelve regular parts.

Early television drama followed the formats established by radio. In the first few months of broadcasting, classic novel adaptations were largely limited to enactments of scenes from those novels. A more expanded form of televised drama was Outside Broadcasts of full-length theater productions, such as *Twelfth Night* with Peggy Ashcroft and Michael Redgrave, which was "televised" from London's Phoenix Theatre on the evening of Monday January 2, 1938. But counter to the prevailing view that theater played an over-determining role in the development of television drama, and that adaptations of classic novels failed to develop a properly televisual aesthetic, Jason Jacobs argues that "developing the 'art' of television drama was seen as a distinct project, separate from the relay and extraction of theatrical forms, and found in the third drama format: the adaptations" (Jacobs, 2000: 35). Adaptations, that is, became the primary vehicle for the creation of a distinct form of television narrative that combined the liveness and intimacy of theater with film's mobility of camera and ability to cut between scenes. Producers and screenwriters, some drawn from the film industry itself, sought to overcome the technological and spatial limitations of Alexandra Palace to develop a drama aesthetic appropriate to the television form.

By 1938, drama planning became increasingly standardized and the television play (as opposed to the televised play) was established as the major television event on Sunday evenings; the May 20, 1938 edition of the *Radio Times*, for instance, highlights the Sunday evening broadcast of *Pride and Prejudice*. Up until the late 1950s, televised plays were almost overwhelmingly adaptations rather than original scripts. With broadcast television suspended during the Second World War, it was left to radio to continue with the adaptation of classic novels, with narratives increasingly delivered in serial form.

After the war the form of television drama continued to develop as its production became increasingly departmentalized and its programming consolidated into a standardized, familiar schedule. Central to this regular schedule, and derived from radio, was the Saturday serial drama, a format which included adaptations of the classics, the earliest of which included "*The Warden* (six parts, May 1951) and *Pride and Prejudice* (six parts, February 1952)" (Jacobs, 2000: 111–12).

To accommodate the constraints of live broadcasting, these adaptations were shot in a single large studio featuring a number of sets, normally covered by two pedestal cameras and two mobile cameras, with the pictures' vision mixed live in the gallery. From 1952 filmed inserts were cut into this live broadcast, and from 1954, filmed serials began to be scheduled. By 1958 the corporation began to use videotape to record its programs, a significant innovation for television drama that had implications both for the way in which drama production was organized and for its aesthetic regime (Jacobs, 2000: 24). Part of the motivation for these developments was the end of the BBC's television monopoly with the impending arrival of ITV. Launched in 1955, the commercial channel's first week of broadcast included an adaptation of *The Scarlet Letter*, an audacious piece of scheduling that both challenged the BBC's monopoly of the classic novel adaptation and differentiated ITV from its rival through its adaptation of a mid-nineteenth century American novel that dealt with adultery, sin, and repentance. However, adaptations of classic novels were an expensive, risky and therefore occasional venture for the commercial channel, whereas for the BBC they remained a regular part of its schedules, its output including classic novel adaptations such as *Pride and Prejudice* (1958, 1967), *Jane Eyre* (1956, 1963, 1973), *Vanity Fair* (1956, 1967) *Great Expectations* (1959, 1967), *Martin Chuzzlewit* (1966), and *Middlemarch* (1953, 1962, 1968). By 1963, "Serials" was a distinct division within BBC Drama with its own head of department.

While the classic serial during this period primarily remained studio and interior based, there were further noteworthy developments. The launch of BBC2 in 1964 included the first episode of a serial adaptation of *Madame Bovary* in its first week of programming, and when it began broadcasting in color it was with another classic serial, *Vanity Fair* (Kerr, 1982: 15). As both BBC1 and ITV moved to color in 1969, period costume and location shooting became an increasingly significant part of the form. Despite these developments, the BBC classic serial throughout this period exhibited a distinct and recognizable generic identity that was to be maintained well into the 1980s. This in itself presented a problem for its critics. Writing in 1982, Paul Kerr argued that:

> careful comparison between the novels in question, for example *Wuthering Heights* and *Vanity Fair*, and their tele-versions, reveals the tendency towards homogenization in television adaptation. The very profound formal differences that [Raymond] Williams identifies between such novels became all but invisible on television (11).

Twenty-one years later, David Monaghan similarly argued that "because so many classic novels have been transformed into television serials during the last thirty years, a certain normativeness has attached itself to the BBC classic drama format" (Monaghan, 2003: 225). To some extent these statements depend on a slightly restrictive selection of classic serials for their evidence, a canon of classic novel adaptations discussed later. However, the volume of classic serials produced by the BBC between the late 1950s and the late 1980s demanded relatively standardized production practices which inevitably manifested themselves in the consistencies of narrative structure and pacing, set design and iconography, that enabled the classic serial to function as a recognizable genre with a distinct set of conventions and audience expectations. Moreover, the very frequency with which adaptations of classic novels appeared on television further undermined their aesthetic status, as quality is usually recognized as residing in those programs which distinguish themselves from the regularity of television programming, a regularity the classic novel adaptation had become a familiar part of. Breaking the apparent homogeneity or normativeness of the classic novel adaptation would require a significant institutional shift, and it was ITV, rather than the BBC, that provided it in the early 1980s with Granada's expansive adaptations of the "modern classics" *Brideshead Revisited* and *Jewel in the Crown*. The languid pace, fidelitous script, and nostalgic gaze of

Brideshead, Sarah Cardwell argues, became the benchmark for all subsequent classic serials (2002: 108), a benchmark that was consolidated by the adaptation of Scott's Raj Quartet novels three years later. It was not until the mid-1990s that the BBC firmly re-established its cultural authority in the adaptation of the classic novel with its productions of *Middlemarch* (1994), *Martin Chuzzlewit* (1994), and, in particular, *Pride and Prejudice* (1995). For Cardwell, this *Pride and Prejudice* is a "generic archetype" of the classic serial, exhibiting and developing the generic conventions established by *Brideshead*: "conventions of content (the display of 'heritage' as representative of 'the past'), style (a languorous pace and filmic use of the camera) and mood (nostalgia)" (133). Fidelity, heritage, and nostalgia remain key terms in the academic critique of adaptations of the classic novel on British television, and it is to these that this chapter now turns.

Heritage and Authenticity

Most commentators agree that the classic serial is an innately conservative genre. They argue, as Julian North notes, that "the form of classic adaptation itself will ensure the failure of challenges to conservative orthodoxy" (1999: 38). Because of their status as classic novels, television aims for a high level of textual fidelity in their adaptation, a fidelity which consequently reproduces the traditional values that, it is argued, are articulated in the novels themselves. Whereas cinema has demonstrated an enthusiasm for quite radical adaptations of the classics, in the field of television production, fidelity is "the critical standard that monitors the effectiveness of literary adaptation in articulating [...] the literary values associated with the concept of public service broadcasting" (Sheen, 2000: 14). The continued use of fidelity as the critical standard for television adaptations of classic novels persists moreover, because it feeds "on publicity detailing the pains taken by adapters and production teams to be faithful and authentic" (North, 1999: 39). While the study of adaptation has abandoned the concept of fidelity as a measure of a text's cultural value, the classic serial, by virtue of the logic of the systems in which it is caught up, is still bound by it. The rather homogenizing characterization of all classic novels as ideologically reactionary is not without its critics. North for instance argues that the conservative perception of Austen is not unproblematic, but she accepts that "Austen has become something of a conservative icon in popular culture" (38). Narelle Campbell similarly argues that in Austen's *Pride and Prejudice*, Elizabeth resists both the limitations imposed on women by that society's established systems of power and the objectification of women by men. However, "despite the [1995] adaptation's (seemingly) liberated interpretation of sexual attraction in *Pride and Prejudice*, the repeated motifs of the gaze and display both function to reassert patriarchal paradigms of power" (2009: 159).

While the concern for textual fidelity is apparent in the ways in which the adaptations minimize, as far as is possible, changes to the adapted novel's plot, the desire for historical fidelity manifests itself in the care taken by production teams to ensure their costumes, set design, and locations are "authentic." Such care has long been rooted in the production practices of television costume drama more generally. But since *Brideshead Revisited* and *Jewel in the Crown* raised the bar on the production values associated with the classic serial's generic regime, the costs involved in attaining those visibly high values have required broadcasters to market their adaptations internationally. For the BBC, this has long involved co-production with WGBH, whose "Masterpiece Theater" is networked by the Public Broadcasting System; *Bleak House* (2005), *Jane Eyre* (2006), and *Cranford* (2007), for instance, were all BBC/WGBH co-productions. For critics, such co-production compromises the selection of novels and their adaptation, ensuring they are prestigious but noncontroversial vehicles for the export of a marketable version of English culture.

Theorists argue that the classic serials' recruitment of historical detail to authenticate its representation of the past is problematic. As Kerr argues, "props are employed specifically as signifiers of the past and its faithful and meticulous reconstruction. Such ambitions of authenticity function to factify the fiction, literally to prop it up, performing a positivist role as the tangible trace of a lost era" (1982: 13). Monaghan similarly argues that "the 'verisimilitude' carefully cultivated by televisual renderings of the Austen canon is usually 'superficial' and serves as a substitute for any attempt to point up the complexities of character and theme that lie beneath the polished surface of her novels" (2003: 197). Sarah Cardwell, in her extensive consideration of the subject, argues that "the extent of temporal fidelity within this genre suggests that it is more than a stylistic choice or convention, and that there is some other, more fundamental motive for the over-emphasis on the "accurate" portrayal of (mostly) nineteenth-century England" (2002: 115). Cardwell, drawing on the academic literature on the representation of the past, argues that the fundamental motive driving the classic serial's temporal fidelity is our cultural need to connect to our past, the response to which has been the construction of a particular version of national heritage. Fred Inglis, for instance, describes *Brideshead Revisited* as "an architectural education and a celebration of cultivated tourism such as Waugh would have despised, yet which he in much of his writing inaugurated" (2000: 192). Charlotte Brunsdon similarly argues that "just like the National Trust and advertisements for wholemeal bread, they [*Brideshead* and *Jewel in the Crown*] produce a certain image of England and Englishness which is untroubled by contemporary division and guaranteed aesthetic legitimacy" (1990: 86). Further, it is argued that English heritage is displayed in film and television narratives in a manner which makes possible, and encourages, a specifically nostalgic engagement with that display on the part of the viewer. Cardwell argues that Austen's novels, which dominated film and television adaptations of classic novels in the 1990s, "can be fairly easily recruited into a nostalgic portrayal of the past" (2002: 135). Monaghan agrees, lamenting "the nostalgic, English Heritage version of the British past that most film and television adaptations substitute for the richly nuanced world that Austen actually creates" (2003: 203). Cardwell argues that central to the production of this nostalgic gaze are establishing shot sequences of large country houses, and that the BBC 1995 *Pride and Prejudice*, with its long shots of expansive country estates, is typical of both the heritage film and the television classic novel adaptation in this regard. But, she argues, unlike the heritage film, the gaze in the television serials is not an anonymous one, as the shot is usually preceded by that of one of the narrative's characters gazing at the building. The shots, that is, are part of the economy of point-of-view shots, such that our reading of the answering establishing shot of the building is guided by the way in which the character gazes upon it: "Elizabeth looks with awe upon Rosings and with wonderment, longing and wistful regret upon Pemberley" (2002: 140). She argues that, along with the dancing scenes, shots of the countryside, and of characters traveling in carriages, these scenes constitute a stylistic pattern designed to orientate the audience to the serial's nostalgic mood (141–52).

While television adaptations of classic novels do exhibit some of the generic features of the heritage film, and while they can offer the opportunity of a nostalgic gaze, they are not unambiguously nostalgic, and they offer viewing pleasures in addition to those offered by the spectacle of heritage. Jane Pidduck argues that "viewed in relation to earlier costume drama, contemporary cinematic and television projects increasingly shift settings from the written texts' emphasis on dialogue and mannered interiors to a more dramatic emphasis on the picturesque outdoors" (1998: 386). Analyzing the gendered coding of interior and exterior spaces in these adaptations, she argues that adaptations of Jane Austen's novels made in the 1990s "may be read as evocative dramatizations of female desire and transgressive sexuality" (384). Rather than viewing them as part of the clichéd generic iconography of the classic novel adaptation, she argues that "coach rides, horse rides, picnics and especially country walks are important in the spatial economy of these texts, offering moments of respite and respiration away from the pressures of social convention" (387). Images of movement, tracked with a mobile camera, strikingly contrast with the more static interior shots, particularly shots of women waiting at windows, an image she reads as one of constrained desire. For Pidduck, "the mobilization of the female figure in the landscape stands out most resoundingly in *Pride and Prejudice*, where Elizabeth (Jennifer Ehle) consistently strides, cheerful and apple-cheeked, through the idyllic countryside" (392). Such images, she argues "evoke an audiovisual and corporeal pleasure in movement and possibility" (392). Contrary to the arguments that these adaptations either reproduce the conservatism of Austen's novels or undermine the radical feminist undercurrent of those novels, Pidduck argues that they "map out the *limits* of historical feminine middle-class mobility and aspiration, while at the same time seeking to overcome them" (390). In his analysis of the BBC's 2007 adaptation of *Cranford*, Chris Louttit identifies a similar retention of Elizabeth Gaskell's progressive politics. The confrontations between Lady Ludlow and her

estate manager, Mr. Carter, over Carter's investment in the education of the
son of a poacher reproduce Gaskell's views on the importance of working-class
education (2009: 41). Moreover, Louttit argues, Gaskell's radicalism is amplified
through the changes the adaptation makes to the character of Miss Galindo, particularly "the development of her forthrightness into a much more strident kind
of proto-feminism" (42).

The Classic

The classic serial has been the dominant form in which classic novels have been
adapted for television since 1951. While the previous discussion has articulated
some of the key features of its generic regime, the two terms that make up the title
of the genre merit further attention. Since at least the 1980s, the literary canon has
been challenged, demystified and delegitimized within literary and cultural criticism, critiqued as an institution exercising hegemonic power through the process
of the inclusion and exclusion of authors and works. A television genre whose very
title foregrounds its relation to the concept of a canon of literary classics is thus
immediately caught up within this critique, not least because each classic novel
adaptation might be seen to maintain and legitimize an illegitimate concept.
Brunsdon, for instance, argues that "the most currently accessible idea of quality,
which I have designated *Brideshead/Jewel,* so clearly represents the historical and
cultural privilege with which aesthetic judgment is encrusted" (1990: 89).

Pierre Bourdieu argues that the literary "classic" is produced as one of the outcomes of a literary field which values originality. Consequently:

> schools, artists and words which are inevitably associated with a moment in the history
> of art, which have "marked a date" or which "become dated", are condemned to fall
> into the past and to become *classic* or *outdated*, to drop into the "dustbin" of history
> or become part of history, in the eternal present of *culture*, where schools and tenden-
> cies that were totally incompatible "in their time" can peacefully coexist because they
> have been canonized, academicized and neutralized (1993: 105–6).

This partly explains why, despite the heterogeneity of authors and works selected
for television adaptation, discussions of those adaptations homogenize them as a
consequence of their prior designation as "classic." The differences between these
adapted texts at the time of their original publication, the different contexts in
which they were produced, the different literary genres to which they belong and
their occupation of different sectors of the literary field, all these differences fall
out, Bourdieu argues, when the novels are canonized as "classics." Canonized, they
are also homogenized, and this homogenization is assumed to carry over to the
classic television serial itself despite the differences that persist between those adap-

tations, differences which are at least partly rooted in the differences between the novels from which they are adapted.

It is the case, however, that the genre exhibits its own hegemonic tendencies, manifest in its selection and repeated adaptation of particular classics over others. In British television we can identify the privileging of particular authors, notably but not exclusively Austen and Dickens, privileging of works written during a particular period, around 1811 (*Sense and Sensibility*) to 1874 (*Middlemarch*), set in particular places, London and "pastoral" England, and the privileging of works of "English literature." This later term works to marginalize not only other English language authors, but also all the other "classics" of world literature. It is not that novels regarded as "classics" within the literary field that fall outside these categories do not get adapted, but their adaptation is a rarer occurrence, and their narratives challenge dominant conceptions of the genre. For instance the BBC's 1997 adaptation of Sir Walter Scott's *Ivanhoe* and its 2005 adaptation of Robert Louis Stevenson's *Kidnapped* are both based on the form of the quest-romance, a form which dates back to *Beowulf* but which had fallen out of vogue by the seventeenth century until Scott reestablished it in 1819 with *Ivanhoe*. Both the novels and their adaptations are set outside the nineteenth century, in the reign of Richard I and the post-Jacobite Scotland of 1751 respectively, and their heroic narratives directly engage with the cause of the political unrest of the time and some of its key actors. While they therefore offer entirely different generic pleasures to the adaptations of Austen and Dickens, they are nonetheless classic serials. However, the hostile critical reception with which they were received was at least partly a consequence of their failure to conform to what are commonly regarded as the classic serial's generic attributes.

A more recent drama which throws further light on the dynamic relationship between canonization and the classic serial is the BBC's 2011 adaptation of Winifred Holtby's 1936 novel *South Riding*. The three-part drama exhibits many of the features common to the classic serial. It was broadcast on BBC1 on Sunday evenings at 9pm, the familiar classic television serial slot; it was adapted by the prolific and highly regarded classic serial auteur Andrew Davies; its lead roles were played by two actors associated with previous classic television series, Anna Maxwell Martin (*Bleak House*, 2005) and David Morrisey (*Our Mutual Friend*, 1998). Like many classic serials, it had previously been adapted for film (in 1938), radio (in 1999 and 2005), and television (in 1974). The book was both critically well received and a best-seller when it was first published, and it has never been out of print, reissued as a Virago Modern Classic in 1988. In common with most television serials the adaptation was accompanied by a tie-in publication of the book which featured images from the serial on the front cover, accompanied by the words "now a major BBC drama" and "a twentieth-century classic". The adaptation featured the typically high production values, concern for period authenticity, and cinematic style of other recent classic serials. Its opening title sequence foregrounded both its status as an adaptation and the adapted author's name, suggesting Holtby carries the literary authority to guarantee the cultural value of the serial. But the book's status as a classic is rather ambivalent, and this had consequences for the way in which it was positioned. The *Radio Times* previewed the program as both "a period drama" and a "contemporary costume drama," but not as a classic serial, and although the BBC website accompanying the program referred to the story as "Winifred Holtby's classic novel" (BBC, 2011), the BBC's publicity material also described it as "little-known." In a series of interviews with the production team for the website, the adaptation is positioned as both similar to but different from the "standard" classic serial. Andrew Davies states that "I think people will find *South Riding* a nice change from some of the dramas which have been done in the past. It's nice to have something that isn't all upper class and set in a big country house," and director Diarmid Lawrence similarly observes that for the Yorkshire community of South Riding in the 1930s "there's nothing over their shoulders to be nostalgic about" (BBC, 2011).

Citing Raymond Williams' canonization of Elizabeth Gaskell in 1961, and F. R. Leavis's canonization of Emily Brontë in 1979, Bridget Fowler argues that "in the case of women's writing, canonization can often occur late, and may be the work of a pioneering critic working outside the politics of the mainstream" (1997: 147). The lateness of the canonization of women writers can mean that particular series are regarded as adaptations of classics only retrospectively, after their moment of broadcast. Fowler argues that Winifred Holtby, along with other inter-war women writers such as Margaret Kennedy and Rebecca West "were suspect in literary terms precisely because, despite the freshness of their subjects, they sold well" (148). "Many of these uncanonized novels have their origins in the great impulse towards radicalism of the inter-war period with its manifestations in the democratization of education, the seizure of power at local level to extend popular housing and the feminization of the public sphere" (149); concerns which are visibly manifest in this most recent adaptation, but concerns which demonstrate its distance from the alleged conservatism and heritage concerns of the classic serial genre. Moreover, the serial, like the novel, refuses to offer a romantic resolution. As Fowler writes, "tradition no longer works either, its harsh loss signified by the rejection of the romance form, for the unfulfilled love between the gentleman farmer and the young head-teacher is cut short by his death: passion and social position are doomed to be at war" (149).

The Serial

Much of the writing on the classic serial acknowledges that the television adaptations of classic novels serialize what was in many cases originally released in serial form, and that the extended time frame of the television serial provides an accommodating space for these frequently extensive narratives. Dickens' *Bleak House*, for instance, was first published in twenty monthly installments between March 1852 and September 1853, each installment comprising a one shilling "part" of three to four chapters. Only after all the parts had been published was the novel published in volume form. Similarly, the 2005 BBC adaptation of *Bleak House* was broadcast weekly across fifteen episodes on Thursday and Friday evenings, and only subsequently released as a DVD box set. The part publication of the novel and the episodic broadcast of its adaptation are driven by the same commercial logic. The weekly or monthly installment structure of Victorian part publication emerged during "the period in which English publishing was being transformed from a pre-capitalist, petty commodity mode to a fully capitalist literary mode of production" (Feltes, 1986: x). Central to this transformation was the creation of a mass market for serial fiction which worked by attracting a readership with the first part installment and then hooking that readership into investing their money into the subsequent parts through a narrative structure designed to achieve precisely that end. In broadcasting, serial adaptations of classic novels employ the same narrative devices for the same commercial end, to create and sustain a mass television audience (ideally for broadcasters around seven million viewers) over the duration of the serial's broadcast. Serial adaptations are, to use Feltes' term for their literary equivalent, "commodity-texts," the cultural logic of a specific economic (and, for the BBC, political) environment.

Serials are structured as a series of narrative parts that end temporarily before being resumed in the following episode, a structure of anticipation and suspense. For instance, the discovery of the body of the law writer, Nemo, occurs at the end of Dickens' second published installment of *Bleak House* and at the end of the 2005 BBC adaptation's first episode, the discovery in each case generating a series of suspense questions, questions about his relationship to other characters, the precise nature of his demise, its consequences for Tulkinghorn's investigations and so on; questions whose answer is delayed until at least the next installment or episode. But there is a structure of recollection at work too. We recall past events and episodes and compare them with current ones; our framing of suspense hypotheses about the future is dependent on our memory of events that occurred in the past. The opening scene of the *Bleak House* adaptation features a flashback to a key memory from Esther's childhood, generating the anticipation that her childhood question, "who am I exactly" and why am I my mother's disgrace, will be answered in future installments. Later in that episode, Lady Dedlock (Gillian Anderson) sees her former lover Captain Hawdon's handwriting amongst Tulkinghorn's (Charles Dance) Chancery papers. Observing her reaction, Tulkinghorn detects a secret from Lady Dedlock's past and determines to track it down for his own financial profit. This plot turning point triggers a chain of recollections and anticipations for characters and viewers, whereby past actions will have future consequences. The serial's temporal structure, stretched across time, looks both backward and forward. Similarly in the adaptation of *Cranford*, Miss Matty (Judi Dench) recalls Thomas Holbrook's (Michael Gambon) proposal to her in her youth, and it is partly this memory which makes her determined to ensure that history does not repeat itself in the case of Captain Brown's daughter. Another fragment from this past, Miss Matty's dance card, leads to the successful recovering of the past in the Christmas special when she leads her friends in restoring the dance hall and organizing a Christmas show for the villagers; we spend our Christmas with the inhabitants of Cranford in their Christmas.

The serial structure is not, however, uniform, and variations on that structure can offer subtly different forms of narrative pleasure. The twice-weekly scheduling of *Bleak House*, for instance, was unusual in the context of other recent classic novel adaptations, but it was an approach that was employed in classic novel adaptations and costume dramas in the 1970s. While the BBC 2007 adaptation of *Cranford* was broadcast in the more generically typical form of weekly hour-long parts on Sunday evenings, it too offered its own variations to the classic serial. The adaptation incorporated not only Elizabeth Gaskell's *Cranford*, itself first published in eight irregularly distributed parts in Dickens' *Household Words* between 1851 and 1853, but also material from three additional Gaskell stories published across a nine-year period. Moreover, the serial was followed by a two-part sequel, *Return to Cranford*, broadcast over Christmas 2009, a sequel in which the characters' lives, like those of the audience, had moved on by two years.

Both adaptations feature a wide cast of characters, introduced early on in the serials and distributed across multi-threaded flexi-narratives which converge around specific spaces: London's Chancery and its environs in *Bleak House* and the main street of the village of Cranford. *Bleak House* maintains an overarching emotional spine that derives from the conflict between Lady Dedlock and Tulkinghorn. While the episodes of *Cranford* are framed by the romance between Doctor Harrison and Miss Sophy, a story that draws not on *Cranford* but on "Mr. Harrison's Confessions," a short story Gaskell published anonymously in *The Ladies Companion and Monthly Magazine* in 1851, *Cranford* doesn't display the same strong narrative arc as *Bleak House* and its episodes lack the cliffhanger endings of the Dickens' adaptation. As its ability to maintain a significant audience share attests, however, this is not a narrative failing. Rather, the differing narrative structures of the adaptations echo the disagreement between Dickens and Gaskell concerning the most effective way to structure individual parts in serial publications. Linda Hughes and Michael Lund argue that "this battle about editorial policy involved different narrative aims and rival assumptions about readers' pleasure. While Dickens wanted each part to be self-contained – with a clear climax and resolution – Gaskell wanted a more leisurely pace for the development of plot and the entanglement of her audience" (1995: 151). *Cranford*, they argue, is "an unusually clear instance of 'arousal' and 'desire' in plot emerging in patterns contrary to traditional concepts" (152).

What difference does it make that we watch the serialization of a classic novel spread across up to fifteen episodes or two months? The broadcast scheduling of the classic serial imposes a particular temporality on the telling of the story and thus on our engagement with it. Time passes for us as it passes for the characters in the narrative. It is a form which works with the rhythms of daily life that structure broadcast television scheduling. In doing so, it both replicates the temporal structure of our own lived experience, of being-in-time, to use Heidegger's formulation, and becomes caught up in it. While the primary drive of the classic serial as a commodity text is to capture and hold on to a mass audience, that audience's extended entanglement with the lives of the serial's characters engenders a sustained familiarity and intimacy between the fictional world and the world of its audience, an intimacy enabled by the extended duration and temporal structure of the serial form and the way in which that both reproduces, and becomes part of, the temporal pattern of our own daily lives.

Recent Developments

In this final section I want to consider the current place of the classic novel adaptation on British television, positioning it within the context of both contemporary television drama and British broadcasting. The classic serial continues to reach a significant audience share, viewing figures for *Bleak House* (2005) peaked at 7.2 million, and for *Cranford* (2007) at 7.8 million, and continues to be credited with manifesting the hallmarks of quality television. *Cranford*, for instance, won widespread recognition for the caliber of its production: a Broadcasting Press Guild Award and Radio Industries Club Award for Best Drama Series/Best Drama Programme; BAFTA, Primetime Emmy, and Broadcasting Press Guild Award for Eileen Atkins as Best Actress; Broadcasting Press Guild Award and the Royal Television Society Award for Heidi Thomas as Best Writer; and BAFTA Craft Award for production design for Donal Woods. Writing in 2000, Erica Sheen states that "until recently, one might have asserted categorically that the television classic serial reflected a continuing commitment to the essentially literary values associated with the concept of public service broadcasting" (14). However, she suggests that "since the mid-1980s, when its claim to a license fee began to be based on its ability to attract a mass audience, the BBC has become subject to the need to produce texts that create value not for 'culture,' but for its own system of production" (15). Certainly, in successive BBC Annual Reports between 2005 and 2008, BBC Director-General Mark Thompson consistently began his summary of significant achievements by drawing attention to that year's classic serial as an example of "outstanding television drama," his 2008/9 report arguing that costume dramas, from *Pride and Prejudice* to *Cranford*, were only made possible by the broadcaster's license fee funding.

As Sheen's comment suggests, post-1995 the classic serial has been located within a significantly changed institutional, technological, and aesthetic television context, what various commentators now refer to as "TV3." For Robin Nelson, one of the consequences for television drama in this new environment has been an aesthetic turn towards the cinematic. The "cinematic," in this context, implies:

> an enhanced visual means of story-telling in place of the dialogue-led television play with its theatrical, rather than filmic, heritage. Today's high budgets for "high-end" TV drama approximate to (though do not quite reach) those of cinema, affording a single camera with post-production editing approach, using 16mm, and exceptionally 35mm stock (or now HDTV) for recording its imagery, rather than magnetic tape. High budgets also afford highly paid star performers (2007: 11).

Our Mutual Friend (1998), serialized across four ninety-minute episodes on BBC2, illustrates something of this enhanced visual style, the production team drawing on their film and television experience to develop the serial's strikingly cinematic realist aesthetic: director Julian Farino and director of photography David Odd had both worked in documentary; composer Adrian Johnston had scored three of Michael Winterbottom's feature films including *Jude*; and editor Fran Parker had worked with Dennis Potter. The publicity material that accompanied the series makes clear their intention to do things differently, particularly to distance themselves from earlier picturesque adaptations of Dickens, and to focus the production design on the emotional drive and melancholy tone of the story rather than historically accurate period detail. Together the team created a distinct and consistent visual style, established from the opening scene in which Lizzie rows her father, Gaffer Hexam, on the Thames at night as he scavenges the river for its detritus and its dead. The mise-en-scène closely corresponds to Marcus Stone's illustration "The Bird of Prey" printed in the first monthly number of *Our Mutual Friend* in its original part publication. For the serial's production design Thornton studied "David Lean's *Great Expectations* and *Oliver Twist* for their 'visual economy' but also [drew] inspiration from Gustave Doré, Victorian photographs and the illustrations to Henry Mayhew's *London Labour* and *London Poor*" (Giddings and Selby, 2001: 163). His selection of design sources, and their influence on the production's carefully controlled lighting and color palette, particularly in the selectively lit grainy interior shots, produced a visual style that is both cinematic and evokes a documentary realism. The adaptation also reworks some of the novel's literary devices. The opening scene, for instance, establishes the river as both a metaphor that runs through the serial and a narrative device that brings its various strands together. As in the novel, the river is used as a symbol of life and death, resurrection and rebirth: John Harmon and Eugene Wrayburn are both reborn in the Thames, Harmon escapes death to forge a new identity, while Wrayburn, pulled out of the river by Lizzie, marries her; Wrayburn's rival for Lizzie, and his would be murderer, later drowns in its waters.

A strikingly different aesthetic was achieved in the BBC's 2005 adaptation of *Bleak House*. As has been already touched on, the serial was scheduled in the manner of a soap opera, running in two half-hour episodes a week, directly after *Eastenders*, with an omnibus edition at weekends. Nelson points to the way in which in the new television environment broadcasters construct selected programs as "Event TV," and notes that *Bleak House* was "flagged" in this manner on the first night of its broadcast (2007: 56). Such positioning marked the serial out as quality television, different from the regular flow of television content. Again, its difference was articulated not only by its unusual scheduling but also by its distinct visual style. With a budget of around £8 million, *Bleak House* was the first classic serial to be shot on High Definition tape. Producer Nigel Stafford-Clark explained that "I'd always planned to shoot with two cameras, hand-held – the way Steven Soderbergh shot *Traffic*. It suited both the fast-moving, multi-story approach that Andrew [Davies] was writing, and the need to shoot far more quickly than on any previous period adaptation if we were to fit within the available budget" (BBC, 2007). Production designer Simon Elliott describes how rather than taking the standard classic serial approach of employing various locations on what he refers to as "the Stately Home circuit," much of the series was shot at Balls Park, an empty period mansion near Hertford. The team saved time and money by designing and setting the different spaces in its interior to serve as the serial's various locations: Bleak House itself, Chesney Wold, Tulkinghorn's office, and the garrets above Krook's shop that are home to Nemo and Miss Flite (BBC, 2007).

Iris Kleinecke-Bates argues that the promotional material accompanying the series and its DVD release "indicates a shift in emphasis from adaptation to television drama; *Bleak House*, or so we are to believe, is more than an adaptation, more than a literary masterpiece – it is now on television, an edgy, modern drama that sweeps the viewer along at a fast pace" (2009: 113). Such edginess, Robin Nelson argues, is a particular feature of "high-end" television drama in the TV3 era (2007: 20). Kleinecke-Bates describes how the opening scene's:

> carriages, wet cobble-stones and costume are recognizable as the visual tropes of the classic serial and in particular the Dickens adaptation, but these familiar sights are undercut by fast and self-conscious editing which draws attention to itself through odd camera angles, extreme close-ups, and sudden cuts which give the impression of hurry and confusion and frustrate the viewer's desire to linger and see (2009: 115).

Nelson argues that such "a snappy editing rhythm yielding a strong visual dynamic is perhaps a cultural feature of contemporary TV drama as much as a technological one" (2007: 117). Director Justin Chadwick, who had previously directed the counter-espionage thriller series *Spooks*, replaced the long establishing shot of the country house regarded as central to the heritage effect of the classic serial, with the radically dynamic "crash zoom" to drive the pace of the complex multistrand narrative of the serial (Nelson, 2007: 117).

In this chapter, I have sketched out the emergence and development of the classic novel adaptation on British television, from early dramatized extracts of the works of canonical authors to the international commodity form of the classic serial. In doing so, I have sought to identify the form's key generic features and the critical debates they have engendered. I hope to have established that the classic serial is not as innately conservative or homogenous a genre as it has often been regarded, and that its textual pleasures are not restricted to those of nostalgia and heritage. In an increasingly risk-averse financial environment, adaptations have downsized to shorter three- to four-part hour-long serials, of which the BBC now commission only three or four a year, and have varied their literary and historical subjects. Some of these manifest a serious aesthetic and social ambition. Chris Louttit for instance argues that the result of *Cranford*'s " 'painterly' use of lighting and careful composition is to lend the small and sometimes ridiculously comic lives of women like Miss Matty, Miss Deborah and Miss Pole a sense of quiet importance (2009: 43). Others, such as *Lost in Austen* (ITV, 2008), exhibit the subversive playfulness and knowing performativity that Sarah Cardwell first identified in *The Fortunes and Misfortunes of Moll Flanders* (ITV, 1996) (2002: 160–84). All these examples suggest that the classic novel will continue to occupy its significant position on British television and in the lives of its audiences for the foreseeable future.

REFERENCES

BBC. *Bleak House Behind the Scenes.* May 2007. BBC. January 2010. www.bbc.co.uk/drama/bleakhouse/behindthescenes/.

BBC. *South Riding.* 2011. BBC. March 10, 2011. www.bbc.co.uk/programmes/b00y5gm3.

Bourdieu, P. *The Field of Cultural Production.* Cambridge: Polity, 1993.

Brunsdon, C. "Problems with Quality." *Screen,* 31:1, 1990, 67–90.

Campbell, N. "An Object of Interest: Observing Elizabeth in Andrew Davies' *Pride and Prejudice.*" *Adaptation,* 2:2. 2009, 149–60.

Cardwell, S. *Adaptation Revisited: Television and the Classic Novel.* Manchester: Manchester University Press, 2002.

Cartmell, D. "*Pride and Prejudice* and the adaptation genre." *Adaptation in Film and Performance,* 3:3, 2010, 227–43.

Caughie, J. *Television Drama: Drama, Modernism, and British Culture.* Oxford: Oxford University Press, 2000.

Fowler, B. *Pierre Bourdieu: Critical Investigations.* London: Sage, 1997.

Feltes, N. *Modes of Production of Victorian Novels.* Chicago: University of Chicago Press, 1986.

Giddings, R. and K. Selby. *The Classic Serial on Television and Radio.* Basingstoke: Palgrave, 2001.

Hughes, L. and M. Lund. "Textual/Sexual Pleasure and Serial Publication." In *Literature in the Market Place: Nineteenth-Century British Publishing and Reading Practices.* Eds. J. O. Jordan and R. L. Patten. Cambridge: Cambridge University Press, 1995, 143–64.

Inglis, F. "*Brideshead Revisited* Revisited." In *The Classic Novel: From Page to Screen.* Eds. R. Giddings and E. Sheen. Manchester: Manchester University Press, 2000, 179–96.

Jacobs, J. *The Intimate Screen: Early British Television Drama.* Oxford: Oxford University Press, 2000.

Kerr, P. "Classic Serials: To Be Continued." *Screen,* 23:1, 1982, 6–19.

Kleinecke-Bates, I. "Historicizing the Classic Novel Adaptation: *Bleak House* (2005) and British Television Contexts." In *Adaptation in Contemporary Culture: Textual Infidelities.* Ed. R. Carroll. London: Continuum, 2009, 111–22.

Leitch, T. "Adaptation, the Genre." *Adaptation,* 1:2, 2008, 106–20.

Louttit, C. "*Cranford*, Popular Culture, and the Politics of Adapting the Victorian Novel for Television." *Adaptation*, 2:1, 2009, 34–48.

Monaghan, D. "*Emma* and the Art of Adaptation." In *Jane Austen on Screen*. Eds. G. MacDonald and A. MacDonald. Cambridge: Cambridge University Press, 2003, 197–227.

Nelson, R. *State of Play: Contemporary "High-end" TV Drama*. Manchester: Manchester University Press, 2007.

North, J. "Conservative Austen, Radical Austen: *Sense and Sensibility* from Text to Screen." In *Adaptations: From Text to Screen, Screen to Text*. Eds. D. Cartmell and I. Whelehan. London: Routledge, 1999, 38–50.

Pidduck, J. "Of Windows and Country Walks: Frames of Space and Movement in 1990s Austen Adaptations." *Screen*, 39:4, 1998, 381–400.

Sheen, E. "Where the Garment Gapes": Faithfulness and Promiscuity in the 1995 BBC *Pride and Prejudice*. In *The Classic Novel: From Page to Screen*. Eds. R. Giddings and E. Sheen. Manchester: Manchester University Press, 2000, 14–30.

Part IV
Authors and Periods

10
Screened Writers

Kamilla Elliott

Much literature-film criticism has focused on the adaptation of canonical British literature to film; this essay considers the adaptation of canonical British literary authors to film. Writers have been screened in many forms, media, and genres; this chapter concentrates on representations of authors *in films that adapt their writings*. In so doing, it probes a rhetorical tradition that conflates author names and works: one that extends from literary criticism to adaptation studies. Indeed, when nineteenth- and early twentieth-century critics write of "reading Dickens" (Powell, 1849: 300), "reading Miss Austen" (Richardson, 1877: 254), or "reading Shakespeare" (Scott, 1909: 143), they do not refer to reading their biographies, letters, or diaries; they refer to reading their fictional literary works. Such conflations derive in part from Romantic theories of expressive authorship. In 1883, Algernon Swinburne insisted that *Wuthering Heights* "is what it is because the author was what she was; this is the main and central fact to be remembered" (762–3). Yet conflations of author names and literary writings have persisted across psychoanalytic, formalist, structuralist, poststructuralist, and New Historicist literary criticism and are thus not reducible to Romantic theories. For example, book titles bearing the phrase "reading Shakespeare" appear in almost every decade from the 1870s to the 2010s; Google Books attests that in May 2012, nearly 80,000 books carried the term within their titles or pages.

Although the rhetorical tradition has persisted across critical movements, its uses have varied. Psychoanalytic critics and biographers perceive that literary works manifest the latent content of author psyches; formalist, structuralist, and poststructuralist traditions conflate author names and works to express a *displacement* of

A Companion to Literature, Film, and Adaptation, First Edition. Edited by Deborah Cartmell.
© 2012 Blackwell Publishing Ltd. Published 2012 by Blackwell Publishing Ltd.

authors by their works, whether claiming works to be organic forms with independent lives, or independent manifestations of intertextuality, or markers of writing, deemed "a space into which the writing subject constantly disappears" (Foucault, 1988: 283). Roland Barthes, who announced the death of the Romantic author and the birth of the poststructuralist reader (1977a), maintains the rhetorical conflation of author name and works in *Roland Barthes by Roland Barthes* (1977b); Michel Foucault cemented the link by locating "the author function" in the author's proper name (1988: 292).

The conflation of author names and writings extends from literary criticism and theory to adaptation studies. *Dickens on Screen* (Glavin, 2003), *Jane Austen on Screen* (MacDonald and MacDonald, 2003), and *A History of Shakespeare on Screen* (Rothwell, 2004) do not refer to filmic representations of these authors, but to films of their fictive writings, as the publishers' descriptions attest: "*Dickens on Screen* is a broad ranging investigation of over a century of film adaptations of Dickens's works"; "*Jane Austen on Screen* is a collection of essays exploring the literary and cinematic implications of translating Austen's prose into film"; "*A History of Shakespeare on Screen* chronicles how film-makers have re-imagined Shakespeare's plays from the earliest exhibitions in music halls and nickelodeons to today's multi-million dollar productions show in megaplexes." Yet some of these adaptations screen the writers as well as their works, positing new concepts of how authors relate to their works, as well as to readers, film audiences, and their own narrators and fictional characters. More broadly, these representations illuminate relations between literature and film.

Screened writers do not conform neatly to philosophical paradigms or theoretical schools. Few films subscribe to a single theory of authorship; most support, contest, undermine, and parody various theories simultaneously. My account therefore subscribes to an intertextuality in which philosophical theories of authorship are intertexts rather than master narratives through which screened writers must be read or to which they must conform. Far too much cultural information would be suppressed, distorted, ignored, and lost were philosophy to be the dominant discourse of this chapter; moreover, such an approach allows screened writers to challenge and demonstrate the limitations of philosophy in accounting for cultural practice.

That said, theories of authorship remain crucial intertexts for screened writers. Histories of author theory (e.g. Bennett, 2005) identify a major paradigm shift with Barthes' "The Death of the Author," published in 1967. This resounding obituary for Romantic theories of transcendent, original, individual, expressive authorship reconfigures relations among authors, texts, and readers:

> [W]riting is the destruction of every voice, of every point of origin . . . the voice loses its origin, the author enters into his own death, [when] writing begins . . . [There is] no other origin than language itself, language which ceaselessly calls into question all origins . . . it is language which speaks, not the author . . . [A] text is not a line of words releasing a single "theological" meaning (the "message" of the Author-God) but a multi-dimensional space in which a variety of writings, none of them original,

blend and clash . . . a text is made of multiple writings, drawn from many cultures and entering into mutual relations of dialogue, parody, contestation, but there is one place where this multiplicity is focused and that place is the reader, not . . . the author (Barthes, 1977a: 142, 143, 146, 148).

Such claims have significant implications for theories of literary-film adaptation as well as authorship, deposing literary authors as sole points of origin for film adaptations of their works, positioning them as always already adaptors of other texts and their adaptations as always already adaptors of other texts besides their literary sources. Conversely, the cultural practice of adaptation has implications for Barthes' dichotomy of readers and authors. Although the rhetorical tradition of "reading" Shakespeare, Dickens, or Austen continues in accounts of Shakespeare, Dickens, and Austen "on screen," adaptations are not exactly readings; they occupy a liminal position as both readings and (re)writings. As writings growing out of readings, as writings that are interpretive readings, they complicate and deconstruct distinctions made by philosophers and theorists among authors, readers, and texts and between the production and consumption of texts.

The second greatest paradigm shift in theories of authorship came in 1969, with Michel Foucault's "What is an Author?" Foucault partially resurrected Barthes's dead author, but only as language – as a proper name:

[T]he author's name, unlike other proper names, does not pass from the interior of a discourse to the real and exterior individual who produced it; instead, the name seems always to be present, marking off the edges of the text, revealing, or at least character-izing, its mode of being. The author's name manifests the appearance of a certain discursive set and indicates the status of this discourse within a society and a culture (1988: 285).

For Foucault, the author function is located in the proper name, which subjects it to discourses, beliefs, and practices surrounding and attaching to that proper name, governing the production, circulation, classification, and consumption of texts. Yet to locate the author function in his or her name is *itself* a discourse of authorship that expresses beliefs about authorship which are too narrowly linguistic, literary, and discursive and do not sufficiently account for some cultural practices. For millennia, the author function has manifested in *images* of authorial bodies as well as proper names – in portraits, statues, photographs, film, television, and digital media.

Images of authorial bodies in early cinema grew out of eighteenth- and nineteenth-century print media. In his preface to *Portraits of Illustrious Personages of Great Britain* (1823), a highly popular, widely reprinted, multi-volume publication, Edmund Lodge explains why "illustrious personages" require representation by images as well as discourses:

As in contemplating the portrait of an eminent person we long to be instructed in his history, so in reading of his actions we are anxious to behold his countenance. So earnest is this desire, that the imagination is ready to coin a set of features, or to conceive a character, to supply the painful absence of the one or the other (2).

For Lodge, words and images are incomplete separately: so much so, that they create reciprocal, inextricable consumer desire. His volumes, he claims, give "to biography and portraits, by uniting them, what may very properly be called their natural and best moral direction" (2). While we are skeptical of claims to nature and morality today, our most common forms of social identification globally – picture IDs – still combine proper names and images of bodies. Representation does not live by the word alone.

Authors not only joined other "illustrious personages" as named faces in nineteenth-century print galleries, their named portraits also began to displace illustration conventions that privileged fictional protagonists. In 1838, a portrait of Charles Dickens usurped the expected frontispiece of *Nicholas Nickleby*'s protagonist (Patten, 2001: 32). The displacement ties the novel's title to the image of its author rather than to the image of the protagonist it names; it grounds the text in the author's picture identification rather than the titular character's. Images of authors thus played a part in tying author names to their works in cultural perception. By mid-century, the images of authors circulated apart from books in the "steady demand for [their] carte-de-visite portraits" (Matthews, 1974: 54).

Silent Cinema and the Dead Canonical Author

Early cinema built upon print media practices, co-opting the author function manifested in pictures (not just proper names and verbal discourses) for cinematic purposes. The 1922 British film of Thackeray's *Vanity Fair*, produced in the *Tense Moments with Great Authors* series, opens with a few moments with the "Great Author." Its establishing shot, depicting the novel's first-edition title page (1848), ties the author name to the novel's title. The author name functions to establish the film in keeping with Foucault's author function. But the next shot presents the *image* of the author, his face carved out in filmic close-up from the three-quarter-length portrait that forms the frontispiece to the 1898 edition of his collected works. Together, they form a filmic picture-ID, identifying not only the author by his works and the works by their author, but also the *name* of the author by the *face* of the author. The author is picture-identified not so much to authenticate his own literary authorial identity as to confer it on the film. The film thus engages in identity theft, using Thackeray's picture identification to identify and legitimate *itself*. The first edition copyright page, for all its claims of authorial authority and textual origin, blazons a copyright that has expired, swallowed up by the film's titles and copyright claims, which precede the image of the book's title page. The novel's copyright page thus becomes complicit with declaring the film's rights and the expiration of its own.[1]

Even as the author is *screened*, rendered pictorially present, he is, in another sense of the word, screened *off* from the very film screening him. Still portraits in film, even at this early date, conventionally signal a dead or absent person. The author's portrait, then, declares him dead and absent by contrast to the moving images of the film. Taken in revered old age rather than at the time of *Vanity Fair*'s first edition, the portrait too presses the author closer to his death. Since the death of the author is used to determine the legal date on which a copyright ends, this affirms the film's birth through the death of the author.

The next shot serves as tombstone; it depicts the entrance to one of Thackeray's former residences with this plaque above it:

W. M. Thackeray
1811–1863
Novelist
Lived here.

The endpoint of Thackeray's life (1863) is declared before his "Lived here"; it declares his present absence along with his past presence.

Shots of first editions, frontispiece portraits, and preserved buildings in this and other similar films place dead authors in filmic shrines of literary relics, icons, and temples. These imagistic traditions grow out of contemporaneous print biographies. The illustrations to Keim's and Lumet's biography of Dickens, published in 1914, include a frontispiece of the author and photographs of "Houses made famous by Dickens" (1914: vii).[2] Even as such hagiography supports literary canonization, it co-opts it for other works, for biographies and films. This is less a matter of birthing ordinary readers through the deaths of canonical authors than of birthing and legitimating other *works* and other *authors* through the death of the author. Authorial meaning is neither maintained intact nor widely dispersed as gathered and conferred upon works that he did *not* produce. The dead author has not disappeared into writing; he has been mummified *as* dead author, as authorial corpse, displayed as filmic property in a filmic museum. *The Bioscope* review of the series perceives this when it decrees the films "admirably produced, with the atmosphere of the period, country, *and author faithfully preserved*." The review goes further to posit the film as a medium for authors as well as their texts:

> [T]hese carefully chosen selections from literary masterpieces will appeal alike to those who are intimate with the books, and will be gratified to see the characters so reverently brought to life, and the others, who from such excellent short entertainments, will surely desire *a better acquaintance with the authors* (1922: 59, my emphases).

The conflation of author names and texts in reading extends to film viewing; the books' mediation of authors and readers extends to the films' mediation of authors and film audiences. Bringing fictional characters to life extends to bringing dead authors to life for reader-viewers who already know the author through his books; indeed, the film claims to bring readers into "a *better* acquaintance with the authors" than the book. Again, the author function does not live by words alone, as film carries readers beyond verbally inculcated "intuition" to the knowledge of visual perception. Reviewing a re-edition of Lodge's volumes, a periodical writer claims that

> There are minute traits and delicate shades of mental and moral character, which may be more correctly estimated on seeing the countenance, than they can be from a mere perusal of what the individual has written, said, or done (Review of *Portraits and Memoirs*, 1832: no page numbers).

Deemed both resurrecting and fecund, the *Tense Moments with Great Authors* series is seen to animate past reading and produce future reading. The film and its review concur with Walter Pater:

> There are some to whom nothing has any real interest, or real meaning, except as operative in a given person; and it is they who best appreciate the quality of soul in literary art. They seem to know a person, in a book, and make way by intuition (2004: 18).

Yet even as the author lends authority to the film, subjecting the author's name, portrait, books, and residence to filmic modes of representation means that "the author" takes on filmic properties. The title page and frontispiece vacillate between authorizing literary and biographical origins and props photographed on a film set; the shot of the author's former residence oscillates between literary shrine and filmic establishing shot.

Yet in the end, the interchange of literary and filmic crediting and representation is not mutual and reciprocal. Just as the film shows the entrance to Thackeray's residence, but does not allow viewers to enter it, so too it presents the title pages of *Vanity Fair*, but denies viewers access to its inner pages. Only a few snippets of the novel's text appear on title cards; new text has been written for the film; the vast majority of the film unfolds wordlessly. The film thereby not only pronounces the author dead in a historical sense, but also in a Barthesean sense. Barthes is not so much concerned with the physical death of authors and their subsequent canonization as with the death of interpretive traditions that make author intent the final authority. The film goes further than Barthes to declare the death of the *text* as well as of the author. In 1911, G. K. Chesterton adduced that "the whole substance and spirit of Thackeray might be gathered under the general title *Vanity Fair*" (51). As the film screens far more of *Vanity Fair from* view than it screens *to* view, the body of the text dies along with the body of the author. Released from the constraints of copyright in the Copyright Act of 1911, the "general title *Vanity Fair*" became the property of the general public and "the substance and spirit of Thackeray" were gathered for new media. Thus the film subscribes to Romantic theories of authorship only to dislocate and co-opt them.

Silent Cinema and the Undead Author

Early American films take a more vivacious approach to screened writers than British films, adding the technological animation of authorial bodies to the mythical mediation of authorial spirits. In "The Death of the Author," Barthes perceives "Writing [as] that neutral, composite, oblique space where our subject slips away, the negative where all identity is lost, starting with the very identity *of the body writing*" (142, my emphasis). Barthes rejects the body of the author – the authorial "voice" and the "body writing," and castrates the writing hand from both voice and body as "a pure gesture of inscription" (1977a: 146). By contrast, Edison's *Vanity Fair* (1915) foregrounds the authorial body in the act of writing; indeed, a preview promises audiences "a prologue which will show Thackeray, in all verity, in his study starting to write the novel." Thackeray "in all verity" refers to the dead author's filmic simulation by an actor; a title card announces "William Makepeace Thackeray," but bears the subscript, "Harold Hubert." Although Jean Baudrillard's work on simulation comes to mind, the claim to verity is a transparent one, with no attempt at deception. Like *cinema verité* later in the century, the film adopts the "verity" to express a documentary style.

In American silent films of canonical British literature, the death of the author, the disappearance of the authorial subject and body into writing, is held at bay by acts of live screened writing, in which the writing subject does not disappear, but remains highly visible. More than this, although Barthes pronounced that "the birth of the reader must be at the cost of the death of the Author" (1977a: 148), reader-viewers are born inextricably from acts of writing in these films, reading the words formed in wet ink on blank pages. In Zenith's *Scrooge* (1913), the audience sees the words that "Dickens" writes, reading "A Christmas Carol. Marley was" as they are formed. In one sense, the writing hand is not cut off from the body; in another sense, it is. The close-up shot that renders the writing legible to readers *does* cut the writing hand off from the body and subsequently, both the image of the author writing and his writing are displaced by film scenes and title cards. But it is not so much the birth of the reader that produces the death of the author as the beginning of the filmed novel.

Whereas *Scrooge* portrays Dickens writing only at its start, Edison's *Vanity Fair* returns to the writing Thackeray at its end. As the final film scene fades, the final words of the novel appear as live writing on a hand-held, handwritten, legible manuscript. "Thackeray's" hand places a full stop at the end of the novel's last sentence. The film cuts to a long shot of the "author" in his study, piling up sheaves of manuscript and placing this last sheet on top with an air of satisfaction. The clear implication is that, as the audience has been watching the film, "Thackeray–Hubert" has been writing it. We discover that "Thackeray" did not die after the prologue to birth this film; he is still writing at its end. As live writing both frames and contains the film, film viewing is presented as a live reading of live writing. Film keeps the ink wet; every screening shows Thackeray beginning to write the novel and does not allow the final period to be placed until the film ends. Such live writing simultaneously literalizes and undermines Barthes' argument that "every text is eternally written here and now" (1977a: 145). The film frame presents its text as written here and now, not by reader-audiences, but by the novel's author. Such simulations figure authors as neither alive nor dead, but rather as *undead*, eternally writing, rising from their graves at each screening to author the films that screen them.

Undead screened writers lie somewhere between Slavoj Žižek's two authorial bodies ("a terrestrial body subject to the cycle of generation and corruption" and "a sublime, immaterial, sacred body" – 1991: 254) and as such dismantle the opposition. Through the quasi-immortality of celluloid, cinema produces terrestrial authorial bodies not subject to corruption at the same time it materializes the "sublime, immaterial, sacred" bodies of canonical literary authors. Such representations and such acts of undead writing do not allow a final death of the author. Rather, resurrecting authors at each screening keeps writings attached to and emerging from undead authorial bodies.

Filmic animations of dead authors disrupt Romantic ideas of dead canonical authors as well as Barthesean ones. Instead of communing with readers as disembodied spirits through the body of their works, undead writers insist on manifesting as bodies and their words do not appear apart from those bodies. The undead screened writer nevertheless allows for a *partial* death of the author that enables the film to claim the dead literary author and animate him as an undead filmic writer. In scenes of authorial inscription, screened writing is always already the language of film, a language that constructs the author constructing the language of the book as the language of the film. At the same time, because literary authors are cast, costumed, enacted, directed, filmed, edited, and credited, they are subjected to the same modes of representation as their adapted fictional characters in these films, thereby undermining their authorial identity, biographical actuality, authorial omniscience, interpretive authority, autonomy, and agency.

Beyond these diminutions, the "verity" of the screened literary author turns out to be a lie. Neither Thackeray nor Thackeray played by Harold Hubert has written the Edison film. An uncredited Charles Sumner Williams wrote the scenario; no one knows who wrote the intertitles. Each intertitle is headed "The Edison Studios," claiming that text as studio property. If the author is undead, the screenwriter is a ghostwriter who does not manifest at all. If the literary author is a simulation, the film's writer is unseen and his name untold.

Film, Television, and the Name of the Author

In adaptations of canonical literature made in the 1930s and 1940s, the bodies of authors too become unseen, appearing solely as names in film credits and on the covers and title pages of books. These representations support Foucault's view that the author function is located in the proper name and make proper names complicit with Barthes' declaration of the author's death. As authorial names and bodies of work displace images of authorial bodies, author names function as epitaphs on the tombstones of their texts.

Photographed book covers and pages in this period "turn" in two senses of that word: they turn book pages into film scenes in a parody of flip-book animation (Elliott, 2003: 96); they equally turn from the authorial name and its declarations of authority, origin, creation, and copyright, to the collaborative authorship of film credits. Unlike *Vanity Fair* (1922) before it and *Great Expectations* (1946) after it, Monogram's 1934 adaptation of *Jane Eyre* does not photograph the novel's title page but instead creates a film-book that places film credits on the pages of a book. The photographed book looks like an edition of *Jane Eyre*, but it is not. It puts film production credits where books place publisher information and claims copyright for the film where books display theirs. It further ruptures the literary relationship between author and text, inserting "based on the novel" between "*Jane Eyre*" and "by Charlotte Brontë". The book's title pages, then, belong and refer to the film.

Subsequent pages break from Romantic notions of solitary authors to credit the film's other authors – actors, director, cinematographer, costumer, production designer, editor, composer, etc. The chief actors are credited twice; once in prose and again in picture identifications resembling moving "book" illustrations. Displacing the authorial frontispiece, these images restore the very conventions that Dickens had displaced in *Nicholas Nickleby* and which silent films had perpetuated.

In the 1950s, as the *auteur* movement took hold in academic and high art film circles, the director became the "author" of the film, a notion that persists to the present day. The literary author's name gradually left its home on filmed book covers and title pages and became subject to film and television crediting practices. The opening prologue of *Tom Jones* (1963) attaches the film's title to an image of the title character rather than to the author's name. The first and only credit to the novel's author appears divorced from the title of the book and subordinated to a screenwriting credit:

Screenplay by
JOHN OSBORNE
Based on the novel by
HENRY FIELDING

Size matters. While the screenwriter shares a large font size with the director, producer, and lead actors, the author shares a smaller font size with the composer, production designer, art director, cinematographer, editor, assistant director, script editor, various minor producers, and the voiceover narrator. (The significance of font size is established early on, when supporting actors appear in smaller font than leading actors.) Appearing mid-credits further diminishes the prominence of the literary author: the film's stars are credited first; the climactic credit goes to the film's director-producer, Tony Richardson.

Apocalypse Now (1979) does not credit Joseph Conrad or *Heart of Darkness* at all, even though it adapts much of the novel's plot, character names, relations, dialogue, and colonial setting. When asked why Conrad was not credited, screenwriter John Milius protested: "If *Apocalypse Now* is based on *Heart of Darkness*, then *Moby Dick* is based on the Book of Job!" (quoted in Phillips, 1995: 35–6). Milius reflects a Bakhtinian, Barthsean view of adaptation as intertextuality, but uses it as a pretext for screening the literary author *from* view rather than *to* view. Far from the democratizing effect that Barthes championed, the death of the author enables new authorial hierarchies.

The more conservative 1980s witnessed both a retreat from and an accentuation of authorial discreditings. Some *auteur* directors actively harnessed author names to their own rather than screening them off or burying them mid-credits. In the opening title, "David Lean's film of *A Passage to India* by E. M. Forster," the author's name follows the director's name, but uncharacteristically precedes star names; moreover, the names share a font size. The title hovers ambivalently between film title and book title; the pronouns too are ambiguous, "of" indicating both possession and derivation.

The idea that the director possesses both author and book culminated in the 1990s with a new titling trend that made the author's name part of the film title, as in such films as *Bram Stoker's Dracula* (1992), *Mary Shelley's Frankenstein* (1994), *Emily Brontë's Wuthering Heights* (1992, 1998), *William Shakespeare's Hamlet* (1996), *William Shakespeare's Romeo + Juliet* (1996), and *William Shakespeare's A Midsummer Night's Dream* (1999). The expanded titles of promotions, reviews, and posters extend the possessive construction, making directors and production companies the authors' keepers rather than editors and literary critics, as in "Francis Ford Coppola's *Bram Stoker's Dracula*," "Kenneth Branagh's *Mary Shelley's Frankenstein*," "Peter Kosminsky's *Emily Brontë's Wuthering Heights*," and Baz Luhrmann's *William Shakespeare's Romeo + Juliet*." These redoubled possessives assert not only the film's authentication by the literary author, but also the director's or production company's ownership of that authorial authenticating power. The film *auteur* now authors the literary author at the same time s/he is authorized by him/her (Elliott, 2003: 141).[3]

Yet this practice was instituted as much to differentiate new film and television adaptations from prior ones as to affirm film and television via canonical literature. Russell Baker confidently asserted in his introduction to the U.S. broadcast of London Weekend Television's *Emily Brontë's Wuthering Heights* (1998) that it "finishes the story just as Emily Brontë wrote it," suggesting that prior adaptations had not.[4] If in the early decades of the twentieth century film adaptations invoke the images and names of canonical authors to define film via literature synonymically, as writings produced live by dead authors or as film-books, in the century's latter decades they do so to define themselves as *not* literature. In the final decade, adaptations further attach to, possess, and identify with author names in order to define themselves differently from *other adaptations*. Complicating Foucault's argument that the author function is lost at the moment an author is proven not to have written the texts attributed to him or her, in adaptation, the author name and function extend to those works s/he is known *not* to have written, as well as to differentiating works s/he has not written from other works s/he has not written.

The Return of the Authorial Body:
The Author as Narrator, Character, Audience

In the wake of the *auteur* movement and the cultural revolution of the 1960s, film and television adaptations turn from representing authors as screened writers to positioning them diversely as narrators, audiences, and characters of their own works. Such representations fragment and diminish their authorial authority.

From the early nineteenth century, authors and literary critics have taken great pains to distinguish authors from their narrators. In the latter twentieth century, literary film and television adaptations blur such distinctions. "The Great Gonzo as Charles Dickens" (voiced by Dave Goelz) contravenes formal literary distinctions between author and narrator in *The Muppet Christmas Carol* (1992), parodying the problems of omniscient narration for embodied author-narrators, problems especially heightened when they are puppets who must mask the hands, strings, and rods manipulating them. If *The Muppet Christmas Carol* heightens the constructedness of screened writer-narrators, *Wuthering Heights* (1992) works to obscure it. The film opens with Emily Brontë (played by an uncredited Sinead O'Connor) wandering the moors and beginning to "imagine" her novel:

> First I found the place. I wondered who had lived there – what their lives were like. Something whispered to my mind and I began to write. My pen creates stories of a world that might have been, a world of my imagining. And here is one I'm going to tell. But take care not to smile at any part of it.

In this scene of pre-writing, cinematic voiceover restores the voice of the author that Barthes and Foucault, following Derrida, had pronounced dead at the moment of writing. As she speaks of writing without being seen writing, the scene renders writing unseen and foregrounds the voice.

The scene of pre-writing is equally a scene of pre-production, since "Brontë" does what filmmakers do before they begin shooting: she scouts out a location before she begins writing. More broadly significant, figuring vision and sound as the bases of writing inverts traditional, linear concepts of literary film adaptation that make writing the basis of audiovisual representation. Adaptation is rendered a cyclical affair, as writing derives from and returns to sounds and images. The scene of pre-writing furthermore inverts adaptation sequencing, as

> the last stage in the chain of literary film adaptation – the film – dramatizes the first – pre-textual authorial imagination and inspiration. Such a preface touts the film as more comprehensive of the novel's origins than the novel itself and authenticates the film with a dramatized incarnation of the author caught in the very act of inspiration (Elliott, 2003: 137).

While Kosminsky's film co-opts Romantic theories of imagination to dismantle linear sequences of adaptation and posit written and audiovisual representation as the origin and end of writing, other films tie literary inspiration to dreaming and the unconscious. Identifications of film and dream evolved through the twentieth century. In 1907, Georges Méliès released a short film, "Le Rêve de Shakespeare": literally, "Shakespeare's Dream," but translated, "Shakespeare Writing Julius Caesar." The slippage is significant, as the film presents a cause-and-effect relationship between dreaming and writing. Shakespeare (played by Méliès) struggles to write the murder of Julius Caesar. He falls asleep and the scene appears to him in a dream, positioning him as its audience. The film-dream is presented as the source of literary inspiration; again, what comes last in the chain of adaptation (the film within the film) is positioned as a scene of pre-writing. Waking, "Shakespeare" re-enacts the dream *before* he writes it down; pre-writing is thus figured as a performance adapting the film-dream. These retroactively prefigure the bases of his literary celebrity: "the scene dissolves into a bust of William Shakespeare, around which all the nations wave flags and garlands" (Star Film Catalogue, quoted in Ball, 1968: 36).

The idea that inspired writing can derive from dreaming is an ancient one; in the Judeo-Christian bible, dreams produce written prophecies and, at the start of Méliès' Shakespearean dream, he is visited by classical muses. In 1892, Robert Louis Stevenson suggested that writing inspired by dreams may not be divine or heroic, but amoral and antisocial. Of *The Strange Case of Dr. Jekyll and Mr. Hyde* (1886), he recounts:

> I dreamed the scene at the window, and a scene afterward split in two, in which Hyde, pursued for some crime, took the powder and underwent the change in the presence of his pursuers. All the rest was made awake, and consciously . . . I do most of the morality . . . my Brownies have not a rudiment of what we call a conscience (Stevenson, 1892: 264).

Like dreams, film adaptations from the 1980s on were often transgressive and parodic of canonical texts and authors. At the end of *Jekyll and Hyde . . . Together Again* (1982), the camera pans to a tombstone announcing the death of the author:

> Robert Louis Stevenson
> 1850–1894
> Famed Author of
> The Strange Case
> of
> Dr. Jekyll and Mr. Hyde

The filmic tombstone marks both the biographical and Barthesean death of the author of *Jekyll and Hyde*. Yet what lies beneath undercuts both deaths: the tombstone begins to shake and the camera pans below ground to reveal a skeleton in rags rolling in his grave, growling, "Ruined! The bastards, the bastards! My story ruined!" The decomposing, seething, undead, yet resoundingly buried author is represented as audience of the film, relegated to an impotent, bitterly critical afterword, protesting the illegitimacy of his "bastard" adaptors. The author returns to life to condemn the birth of these readers as illegitimate. Furthermore, in literalizing and incarnating a cultural expression, "rolling in his grave," the film embodies conventional language *as* the (un)dead author, parodying Barthes' distinctions between dead authors and living language.

Salome's Last Dance (1988) positions its screened writer, Oscar Wilde, more ambivalently. The film belongs to a subgroup of adaptations that dramatize the staging of canonical plays,[5] depicting Wilde watching a performance of *Salome*. Here too the screened writer is represented as audience rather than author of his text. His conflicted response to the play indicates its power over him as audience, again blurring the lines between authors and readers, between playwrights and audiences. The author is constructed by his text not solely in Foucault's sense, but by the ways in which watching it performed construct and reveal his desires and sexuality.

Dream, film, desire, and sexuality conflate in psychoanalysis. Film and psychoanalysis have been aligned throughout the twentieth century into the twenty-first. Films of the 1990s and 2000s seize on and parody pop-cultural theories of libido, repression, and language in their representations of screened writers, eroticizing Romantic theories of creation, libidinizing inspiration, aligning writer's block with sexual impotence, and carnalizing literary production. *Tromeo and Juliet* (1996) epitomizes and parodies these trends. In a filmic preface, its writer-director, Lloyd Kaufman, and co-writer, James Gunn, discuss their inspiration for this satiric, schlock horror adaptation:

> Shakespeare's spirit entered my body. I can't tell you which orifice Shakespeare's spirit exited my body, but the result is *Tromeo and Juliet* . . . One of the things few people

know . . . scholars know this, but most people don't . . . is that on William Shake-speare's deathbed, he had a dream. Troma was able to find out and actually fulfill Shakespeare's dream by adding a three-foot penis monster in *Tromeo and Juliet*. . . . I think Shakespeare is smiling down from above and very happy with the Troma team. . . . We've given Shakespeare the car crashes, the kinky sex, the dismember-ment, all of the wonderful things that Shakespeare wanted but never had.

The implication that Shakespeare enters as spirit and exits as sperm is reinforced by the unsubtle "three-foot penis monster." The adaptation claims to fulfill unreal-ized authorial desire; the carnalization of his play paradoxically makes the spirit of Shakespeare "very happy." In contrast to the parodied Stevenson, this author is silently "smiling down from above" rather than rolling below ground as a cursing corpse.

Two years later, *Shakespeare in Love* (1998) libidinizes literary inspiration so bla-tantly that even the most casual observer cannot fail to observe it. Lying back on an anachronistic, pseudo-psychoanalytic alchemist's couch, Shakespeare (Joseph Fiennes) describes writer's block in metaphors of sexual impotence:

I have lost my gift. . . . It is as if my quill is broken, as if the organ of my imagina-tion is dried up, as if the tower of my proud genius has collapsed. . . . Nothing comes. It's like trying to pick a lock with a wet herring.

The scene parodies Lacanian psychology, which conflates linguistic and sexual power. Many critics have discussed Viola's (Gwyneth Paltrow) revival of Shakespeare's pen and penis, but none more eloquently than Courtney Lehmann:

[A]s dress rehearsals from "The Rose Theatre" are intercut with *un*-dressed rehearsals in "Viola's bedroom" . . . rhymed couplets emerge from the rhythms of orgasm, and the seminal work of *Romeo and Juliet* is born . . . the more they play, the more *of* the play . . . they produce . . . the authorial body [is] the privileged site of the adaptation process . . . authorship is anchored in and made accountable to the body – in all its vulnerability and virility . . . quite literally raising Shakespeare from the ranks of death and its perpetual paramour: impotence. This bedroom farce thus reimagines the "death of the Author" as a "little death" by playfully linking poetic labor to sexual expenditure (2002: 223, 213).

And yet the play does not derive solely from the private worlds of love-making and closed rehearsals. In spite of its parody of Barthes' "The Death of the Author" as a little death, it supports his view that any

text is a tissue of quotations drawn from the innumerable centres of culture . . . the writer can only imitate a gesture that is always anterior, never original. His only power is to mix writings, to counter the ones with the others, in such a way as never to rest on any one of them (1977a: 146).

Throughout the film, characters speak lines from *Romeo and Juliet* apart from and prior to its writing. Shakespeare overhears an anti-theater cleric declaiming, "The Rose smells thusly rank by any name. I say a plague on both their houses!"; he takes lines and plotlines from Marlowe (Rupert Everett); he adapts lines spoken by friends and lover; when he cannot find language spoken by others, he adapts lines that he himself speaks in the course of his daily life.

But even as the film supports Barthes' view that authors recycle existing texts, it astonishingly omits any credit to Shakespeare's actual *written* sources. Its Shakespeare adapts speech, not texts; it restores the voices and "the body writing" that Barthes and Foucault had claimed writing destroys (Barthes, 1977a: 142; Foucault, 1988: 283). Here, just as it partly validates and partly rebuts Barthes' and Foucault's theories of authorship, the film affirms Romantic theories of expressive authorship while denying Romantic notions of originality when it figures both *Romeo and Juliet* and *Twelfth Night* as adaptations of Shakespeare's life. The second play is particularly significant in this regard, since it is deemed a rare instance of an "original" Shakespeare play.

But Shakespeare's "life" here *is* the film and the film is fictional; therefore, the extradiegetic claim is that the plays adapt the film. The film and its assertions of biography, an eternal present tense, and Hollywood realism lay claim to Shakespeare's life as the origin of Shakespeare's writings. Barthes argues that "life never does more than imitate the book" (1977a: 147); the film incongruously and anachronistically presents the author's life and books as imitating the film. Claiming to show Shakespeare's sources, the film proposes itself as Shakespeare's source.

And yet the film has been adapted from Shakespeare's writings and other writings and films. The film thus paradoxically harnesses multiple texts to lay claim to origin. Although screenwriter Tom Stoppard claimed in interview that the film "was an original" (Teeman, 2008) and although the screenplay won the Oscar for best original screenplay, *Shakespeare in Love* adapts *Romeo and Juliet*. When it stages the play at the Globe, it joins the body of Shakespearean adaptations about the making of play performances; more centrally, it adapts the *writing* of the play.

In representing the writing of *Romeo and Juliet* as deriving from its own subsequent writing, the screenplay not only hides Shakespeare's written sources and Shakespeare as its own source, it also hides its other written sources. There is no credit to the novel, *No Bed for Bacon* (Brahms and Simon, 1941), even though Stoppard admits that he read it and Fidelis Morgan submitted a screenplay of *No Bed for Bacon* to *Shakespeare in Love*'s producer, which co-screenwriter Marc Norman may have read (Sherrin, 2000: 7–8). The film is clearly indebted to the novel's plot, which the 1986 reprint summarizes:

> Lady Viola Compton, a young girl from the Queen's Court, visits the theatre and is so infatuated by Shakespeare and his plays that she disguises herself as a boy player and inspires *Twelfth Night* and the playwright's affection (quoted in Offman, 1999).

Offman attests that

> Both versions feature the same grand scene, in which a troubled production of Shakespeare's play finally reaches the stage after many disasters (in both cases, connived by a rival theater owner) – only to have one of the first actors on stage struggle to spit out his lines.

Even more specifically, the novel opens with its Shakespeare struggling with his authorial name:

> [A] melancholy figure sat tracing its signature on a pad.
> *Shakesper*
> *Shakspere*
> *Shekspar*
> He always practised tracing his signature when he was bored. He was always hoping that one of these days he would come to a firm decision upon which of them he liked the best (13).

The film adapts this episode, carrying it into a poststructuralist parody of Foucault's author function, as this author struggles to produce a proper authorial name on which to pin his author function. Carrying the novel's experiments beyond phonetics to semantics, the film deconstructs the proper name into improper or common nouns, as Derrida had done in 1976:

> Will Shakespeare
> Willm Shakesbear [or Willm Shakesbeer? – a blot renders the letters indeterminate]
> W Shake
> Willm Shaksebee
> William Shakepen
> ~~Will Shagswell~~
> ~~Will Shagsbeard~~

The author name is further incomplete, crossed out, and overwritten, techniques that Derrida and other poststructuralists have used to represent their theories of language. In a film about impotence and about an author whose authorship has been hotly contested, the double strike through "Will Shagswell" is doubly resonant.

This film further deconstructs Shakespeare as author by making him a biographical character who speaks his fictional characters' lines and an actor in his own play. The following year, Patricia Rozema's *Mansfield Park*, "based on Jane Austen's *Mansfield Park*, her letters, and early journals," deconstructs the author name and function. In this "portrait of Austen and her work" (Rozema quoted in Berardinelli, 1999), Rozema goes beyond the usual conflations of author name and works. In her merger of Jane Austen and *Mansfield Park*'s fictional protagonist, Fanny Price, the character name displaces the author name and it is Price who authors Austen's juvenilia and biographical letters. The film's opening further deconstructs poststructuralist oppositions between writing, bodies, and voices. Extreme close-ups align the paper's tiny hairs with human skin and the pen scratching that skin slides through a sound dissolve into a whispered story. Since the extreme close-ups render the text illegible, the narrative depends upon the voice. The film joins others that have deconstructed divisions between authors and readers, as the character-author is the main reader of her texts, reading them to other characters and, looking at the camera, to the film audience.

On film, Shakespeare, Austen, and numerous screened writers in biopics that lie outside the scope of this chapter regularly crumple, tear, and burn their writings. Screened writers not only destroy canonical literature's master narratives; they also destroy literary criticism's new master narratives – its philosophies and theories of authorship. Foucault argues that the author

> is a certain functional principle by which, in our culture, one limits, excludes, and chooses; in short, by which one impedes the free circulation, the free manipulation, the free composition, decomposition, and recomposition of fiction. . . . The author is therefore the ideological figure by which one marks the manner in which we fear the proliferation of meaning (1988: 292).

Screened writers upend Foucault's argument; on film and television, the figure of the author proliferates and redistributes meaning, including the meanings of literature and film in relation to each other, and the meanings of philosophical theories of authorship. While Dudley Andrew has argued that "The problematic of adaptation is the signature of the author" (2011: 27), the body of the screened writer proves problematic for mainstream theories of authorship in the humanities.

NOTES

1 The UK Copyright Act of 1911 set the expiration of copyright at fifty years past an author's death (which would be 1913 for Thackeray's works) and protected literature from new technological incursions upon copyright, including "cinematographic" productions.

2 Four of the twelve short films made in the *Tense Moments with Great Authors* series derive from Dickensian novels. No other author appears more than once.

3 The tradition continues with BBC's *Bram Stoker's Dracula* (2006).

4 The trailer to the 1992 film of the same title had made a similar claim. Neither is accurate; Kiju Yoshida had adapted both generations of the novel in 1988.

5 These include *A Double Life* (1947), *Kiss Me Kate* (1953), *A Midwinter's Tale* (1995), and *Shakespeare in Love* (1998).

REFERENCES

"Le rêve de Shakespeare." ["Shakespeare writing Julius Caesar."] Dir. Georges Méliès. France: Méliès, 1907.

Andrew, Dudley. "The Economies of Adaptation." In *True to the Spirit: Film Adaptation and the Question of Fidelity*. Eds. Colin MacCabe, Rick Warner, and Kathleen Murray. Oxford: Oxford University Press, 2011.

Ball, Robert Hamilton. *Shakespeare on Silent Film.* London: Allen & Unwin, 1968.

Barthes, Roland. "The Death of the Author." Trans. Stephen Heath. *Image – Music – Text.* New York: Hill & Wang, 1977a, 142–8. (Original essay published 1967.)

Barthes, Roland. *Roland Barthes by Roland Barthes.* Trans. Richard Howard. New York: Hill & Wang, 1977b.

Bennett, Andrew. *The Author.* London: Routledge, 2005.

Berardinelli, James. "The Darker Side of Jane Austen: Patricia Rozema Talks about *Mansfield Park*." Reelviews, November 15, 1999. www.reelviews.net/comment/111599.html. Accessed January 31, 2011.

Brahms, Caryl and S. J. Simon. *No Bed for Bacon.* Pleasantville, NY: Akadine Press, 2000. (Originally published 1941.)

Chesterton, G. K. *Appreciations and Criticisms of the Works of Charles Dickens.* New York: Dent, 1911.

Derrida, Jacques. *Signéponge/Signsponge.* Trans. Richard Rand. New York: Columbia University Press, 1984. (Originally published in French 1976.)

Elliott, Kamilla. *Rethinking the Novel/Film Debate.* Cambridge: Cambridge University Press, 2003.

Foucault, Michel. "What is an Author?" In *Modern Criticism and Theory: A Reader.* Eds. David Lodge and Nigel Wood. Edinburgh: Pearson Education, 1988, 280–93. (Original essay published 1969.)

Glavin, John, Ed. *Dickens on Screen.* Cambridge: Cambridge University Press, 2003.

Jekyll and Hyde . . . Together Again. Dir. Jerry Belsen. USA: Paramount, 1982.

Keim, Albert and Louis Lumet. *Charles Dickens, 1812–1870.* Trans. Frederic Tabor

Cooper. New York: Frederick A. Stokes, 1914.

Lehmann, Courtney. *Shakespeare Remains: Theater to Film, Early Modern to Postmodern.* Ithaca, NY: Cornell University Press, 2002.

Lodge, Edmund. *Portraits of Illustrious Personages of Great Britain, Engraved from Authentic Pictures in the Galleries of the Nobility and the Public Collections of the Country with Biographical and Historical Memoirs of Their Lives and Actions.* Vol. 1. London: Harding, Mavor and Lepard, 1823. (Originally published 1821.)

MacDonald, Gina and Andrew MacDonald, Eds. *Jane Austen on Screen.* Cambridge: Cambridge University Press, 2003.

Mansfield Park. Dir. Patricia Rozema. USA/UK: Miramax/BBC, 1999.

Matthews, Oliver. *The Album of carte-de-visite and Cabinet Portrait Photographs, 1854–1914.* London: Reedminster, 1974.

Offman, Craig. "Neither a borrower. . . ." *Salon,* February 5, 1999. www.salon.com/entertainment/feature/1999/02/05feature.html. Accessed January 20, 2011.

Pater, Walter. *Appreciations, with an Essay on Style.* Rockville, MD: Manor, 2004. (Originally published 1888.)

Patten, Robert L. "From *Sketches* to *Nickleby*." In *The Cambridge Companion to Charles Dickens.* Ed. John O. Jordan. Cambridge: Cambridge University Press, 2001, 16–33.

Phillips, Gene D. *Conrad and Cinema: The Art of Adaptation.* New York: Peter Lang, 1995.

Powell, Thomas. *The Living Authors of England.* New York: D. Appleton & Co., 1849.

Review of Edison's *Vanity Fair. Motography,* July 10, 1915, 51.

Review of *Portraits and Memoirs of the Most Illustrious Personages of British History. The Leeds Mercury.* June 2, 1832. Issue 33090, n.p.

"Review of *Tense Moments with Great Authors* series." *The Bioscope,* January 26, 1922, 59.

Richardson, Anna Deborah. *Memoir of Anna Deborah Richardson: With Extracts from Her Letters.* Ed. J. W. Richardson. Charleston, SC: Bibliobazaar, 2010. (Originally published 1877.)

Rothwell, Kenneth Sprague. *A History of Shakespeare on Screen: A Century of Film and Televi-*

sion. Cambridge: Cambridge University Press, 2004.

Scott, Temple. *The Pleasure of Reading.* New York: M. Kennerley, 1909.

Shakespeare in Love. Dir. John Madden. USA/UK: Universal/Miramax, 1998.

Sherrin, Ned. "Introduction." In *No Bed for Bacon.* Caryl Brahams and S. J. Simon. Pleasantville, NY: Akadine Press, 2000, 7–17. (Introduction dated 1999.)

Stevenson, Robert Louis. "A Chapter on Dreams." In *Across the Plains & Homeward through America.* London: Chattus and Windus, 1892.

Swinburne, Charles Algernon. "Emily Brontë," *Athenaeum*, June 16, 1883, 762–3.

Teeman, Tim. "Sir Tom Stoppard on Writing *Shakespeare in Love.*" *The Times* Online. February 11, 2008. http://entertainment.timesonline.co.uk/tol/arts_and_entertainment/film/article3349213.ece>.AccessedJanuary20,2011.

The Muppet Christmas Carol. Dir. Brian Henson. USA: Jim Henson Productions/Walt Disney, 1992.

Tom Jones. Dir. Tony Richardson. UK: Woodfall, 1963.

Tromeo and Juliet. Dir. Lloyd Kaufman. USA: Troma, 1996.

Vanity Fair. Dir. W. C. Rowden. UK: *Tense Moments with Great Authors* series, 1922.

Vanity Fair. Dirs. Charles J. Brabin and Eugene Nowland. USA: Edison, 1915.

Žižek, Slavoj. *For They Know Not What They Do: Enjoyment as a Political Factor.* London: Verso, 1991.

11
Murdering *Othello*

Douglas M. Lanier

At the end of Thomas Kyd's *Spanish Tragedy*, written between 1582 and 1592, the disillusioned hero Hieronimo, anguished at the death of his son Horatio, engineers a spectacular revenge upon his nemeses, the princes Balthasar and Lorenzo. That revenge takes the form of a play about treachery at the Persian court which Hieronimo, Lorenzo, Balthasar, and the wronged princess Bel-Imperia act out before gathered Spanish and Portuguese royalty. This play-within-the-play concerns the murder of an innocent husband by the lusty sultan Suleiman, but Hieronimo's performance ends with a twist: the murder of two characters played by Balthasar and Lorenzo becomes Hieronimo's opportunity to kill the two for real, in full view of unknowing spectators. In this shocking revenge spectacle, representation crosses the boundary between fiction and reality, and with deadly ferocity. In *The Spanish Tragedy* Hieronimo discovers that the court's professed commitment to justice is actually a sham, nothing more than a public performance, a form of Machiavellian theater to be taken for reality. What gives his play-within-a-play such savage irony is that Hieronimo appropriates one form of courtly theater – the masque – to take revenge upon the corrupt theater the court has become. In the process, Hieronimo rejects his own co-optation by the court and re-establishes theater's moral capacity to be an agent of justice, though he does both with an excessive, half-mad glee. The revenge spectacle in Kyd's play thus makes a deeply equivocal case for the cultural authority of the stage. By amplifying precisely what anti-theatricalists most feared – the capacity for stage performance to become uncannily *real* – this scene engages in multiple forms of transgression. It performs the forbidden act of murder, but more important, it breaks the boundary between fiction and reality and by so doing

A Companion to Literature, Film, and Adaptation, First Edition. Edited by Deborah Cartmell.
© 2012 Blackwell Publishing Ltd. Published 2012 by Blackwell Publishing Ltd.

re-establishes Hieronimo's poetic and political independence, qualities essential to his integrity as a humanist intellectual. This murderous masque is, in short, intended as a defense of theater, as potent as it is troubling.

Hieronimo's embedded play, one of the early modern English theater's key scenes, establishes a link between metatheater and murder that reverberated throughout English revenge tragedy, including the most famous instance, Shakespeare's *Hamlet*. We might expect, then, that the motif of the embedded revenge play would survive on film in adaptations of *Hamlet*. Yet though a few film adaptations of *Hamlet* have engaged this link, *Othello* has been by far the more prominent vehicle for filmmakers to consider this theme. One reason may be that the *Othello* narrative, turning as it does on Iago's ability to make convincing the fictional tale of Desdemona's infidelity, demonstrates the capacity of a skilled performer to compel belief in what is ultimately an empty fiction and the capacity for even an initially skeptical spectator to mistake fiction for reality. What is more, the sheer intensity of the *Othello* narrative and the identification it encourages with Othello work to blur the boundary between reality and fiction. Theatrical anecdotes suggest that Othello's assault on the innocent Desdemona has so horrified spectators that some have tried to intervene, and several actors playing Othello have become so caught up in their parts that they have injured their Desdemonas or themselves. This effect springs, Lois Potter argues, from "a sense that the intensity of [the play's] effect is inappropriate for something known to be merely fictional"; "the history of playing Othello," she claims, "is the history of a desire for a degree of identification between hero and role that might almost seem to rule out the need to act at all" (2002: 1).

This last point may offer a third reason why the cinema has been so attracted to backstage narratives which involve Othello and real murder. For, to extend Potter's point, the performance of Othello's murder of Desdemona is the place where the power of the theater is most terrifyingly intense and at the same time where the theater's theatricality is extinguished, where fictional performance of murder becomes (or threatens to become) the thing itself, with Desdemona's dead body serving as the grim signifier of the Real. Just as the final play-within-the-play of early modern drama is the place where theater fantasizes about its own political and aesthetic power, in a scenario where fictionality falls away if only momentarily, so these *Othello* adaptations and the threat of theatrical murder becoming real are sites where cinema engages the theater, its closest artistic forebear, and reconceptualizes the stage's aesthetic power. This act of intermedial appropriation is extraordinarily conflicted. These films amplify the power of stage performance, presenting the *Othello* narrative as an almost irresistible text which seems to possess the actor as he performs his part. These films evoke an ideal of cinematic realism – the disappearance of the actor into the role, the erasure of staginess – but the terms of that ideal become pathologically reversed – the theatrical role erases the actor, uncannily bringing to the surface unconscious fantasies, anxieties, and aggression that "play" him rather than he playing them. The aesthetic power of theater, recoded in terms of a cinematic ideal of "total acting," is thereby retained and even enhanced, making it an all the more attractive object for cinematic appropriation, while at the same time theater is pathologized, the extravagant theatricality and semiotically over-saturated language of the classical stage treated as a trigger for psychological excess and aberration, so that theater thereby becomes a dangerously mad unconscious that must be purged or repressed. The murdering Othello trope thus offers a deeply contradictory engagement with the residual cultural authority of the theater, demonizing it and paradoxically rendering it available for appropriation by the cinema *sous rature*.

The murdering Othello motif has had a durable presence in Shakespeare film history, existing in two phases. The first extends from the silent era to postwar *noir*, including such films as August Blom's *Desdemona* (1911), *A Modern Othello* (1917), Harley Knoles' *Carnival* (1921), Herbert Wilcox's *Venetian Nights* (a.k.a. *Carnival*, 1931), Walter Reisch's *Men Are Not Gods* (1936), and George Cukor's *A Double Life* (1947). After existing in campy or parodic form in horror films (like Pete Walker's *The Flesh and Blood Show*, 1972 or Douglas Hickox's *Theatre of Blood*, 1973, which expands the trope to other Shakespeare plays) and sitcoms (like "Lamont Does Othello," an episode of *The Redd Foxx Show*, 1973, or "Homicidal Ham," an episode of *Cheers*, 1983), the motif returned with revival of interest in screen Shakespeare in the 1990s and after. Variations appear in films like Juan Luis Iborra's *Valentín* (2002), Roysten Abel's *In Othello* (2003), Richard Eyre's *Stage Beauty* (2004), and Ivan Lipkies' *Huapango* (2004). In this chapter, I will focus on the first phase of this motif, in particular on *Men Are Not Gods* and *A Double Life*. Strictly speaking, none of these films are thoroughgoing adaptations of Shakespeare, though each incorporates substantial material from *Othello*. In each film, an actor involved with a theatrical production of *Othello* murders or attempts to murder a co-star while playing out a Shakespearean scene; typically — and unlike most revenge play scenarios — the crime is not fully within the actor's control. In her perceptive discussion of several films in this early sequence, Barbara Hodgdon has noted how they work to "des-demonize" the Desdemona figures, presenting them as sexually culpable in some fashion (1991: 232–8). By rewriting the basic terms of Desdemona's characterization — the women in these films seem to be genuine adulterers — and by presenting Shakespeare's play as unleashing uncontrollable dark impulses in performance, these narratives rationalize the men's revenge against their unfaithful lovers by adopting the excuse "*Othello* made me do it." While I find Hodgdon's analysis persuasive, I want also to observe that the psychodynamics of the actor-Othello figures in these films typically revolve around anxieties about class status, anxieties which play out in allegorized form the competition for cultural status between theater and film. The central issue in these adaptations is class, not race, mapped back upon *Othello* in various ways. These films tap into Othello's status as an *arriviste*, an aspirant to full cultural citizenship in the upper echelons of Venetian society. The plots of these films turn on masculine sexual anxiety to be sure, but that anxiety is closely bound up with insecurities about the protagonist-actor's class or cultural status, his rival often being a gentleman or man of means. This insecurity about class partakes of long-standing uncertainties about the cultural stature of actors, at once objects of respect and moral suspicion, but more specifically it also addresses the uncertain status of classical theater in an age of cinema and mass media. The psychodynamics of racial identity in *Othello* is thereby transformed into psychodramas of class anxiety which themselves prismatically articulate cinema's cultural unease when standing in the shadow of the stage.

August Blom's *Desdemona* (a.k.a. *For Åbent Tæppe*, 1911) establishes the basic contours of the murdering Othello trope. Einar Lowe, an actor, discovers that his wife and co-star Maria is having an affair, and under the spell of the play, he kills her onstage as the two act the murder scene from *Othello*. Several elements developed in later films make their first appearance here: Einar's rival is Brisson, a dapper, top-hatted gentleman, clearly his superior in status; Einar uses theatrical craft to verify his wife's infidelity, in this case by disguising himself as Brisson; the film encourages the viewer to empathize with Einar, the Othello figure of the scenario; at first Einar struggles against the violence that *Othello* encourages him to indulge, just as Othello struggles against killing Desdemona in the murder scene. One of the most remarkable features of this film is its ending. This is the only film in this cycle where the actor playing Othello actually murders his wife onstage, but even more striking is Einar's action afterward. He walks downstage and still under the spell of Othello points accusingly at Brisson in his box seat; at this the audience immediately turns on Brisson, and he is forced to exit in shame, leaving Einar to collapse in grief over his wife's dead body as he comes to his senses. This startling deferral of guilt from actor to gentleman comes as a surprise and is central to the film's effect. The finger pointed at Brisson identifies him with elite cultural status and the capacity to seduce, of which Shakespeare is also a potent emblem and of which Einar is figured as a double victim. Brisson's expulsion from the box resonates with the film's recoding of "proper" high-culture theatrical Shakespeare as powerful yet dangerous and threatening.

Harley Knoles' *Carnival* (1921) and Herbert Wilcox's 1932 sound remake *Venetian Nights* can trace their origins to the Italian play *Sirocco* by Alexander Siegmund Pordes-Milo, adapted by H. C. M. Hardinge and Matheson Lang. *Carnival* was intended as a star vehicle for Lang, a well-established Shakespearean and matinee idol beginning to make the transition from stage to screen. *Carnival* was ideal for Lang's cinematic ambitions, for it traded on his substantial Shakespearean credentials[1] while recasting Shakespeare in terms of contemporary melodrama, a genre with mass-market appeal, and providing glimpses of Venice with its location shooting. The storyline concerns Italian actor Silvio Steno, who is rehearsing *Othello* with his actress-wife, vain, neglected Simonetta. When Silvio is called away on carnival night, Simonetta succumbs to the charms of an Italian count and attends the carnival in his company, abandoning their child Nino who Silvio upon his return finds alone and crying. When the two perform the death scene in *Othello* the next day, Silvio nearly strangles his wife as he falls under his part's spell, but at the last second he relents and she is saved. Both chastened, the two reconcile. As is Einar in *Desdemona*, the film presents Silvio as a double victim of elite power: of Count Scipio, his aristocratic friend and romantic rival; and of Shakespeare's script, which preoccupies his attention and stirs up impulses he cannot control. A crucial context for Silvio's actions is a speech early in the film where he discusses the part of Othello with Scipio. Silvio complains that Othello is a flawed role, irrational, preposterous, overly theatrical, for, so he claims, no enlightened modern man could ever be led into jealousy over a spouse's straying affections; he dismisses the play in favor of the kind of modern naturalism demanded by the cinema. Silvio's discovery that he too is capable of jealous rage thus confirms the psychological truth that gives Shakespeare's play such power, though that power is figured as dangerously seductive and fundamentally pathological. Unlike *Desdemona*, however, Knoles' silent version ends with Silvio pulling back from the murder of Simonetta (as Desdemona) at the last second. When she recovers backstage, Simonetta reveals in flashback that she fended off Scipio's advances in the gondola and so remained faithful to Silvio after all. This revelation toys with the viewer's expectations – we have been encouraged to assume that Simonetta has indeed been unfaithful, and we expect Silvio to follow through with the Othello role he has been pursuing. Though this double twist allows for a happy ending that preserves the Steno family, it still prompts a deeply ambivalent stance toward Shakespeare, at once a source of universal "truth" about human nature but also of an uncanny performative power which overwhelms and bewitches. Both the count and Shakespeare's play stir up forbidden passions that threaten the bourgeois family.

Herbert Wilcox's sound remake in 1931, *Venetian Nights*, announces its concern with fiction and reality in the opening sequence. Borrowing a device from Hitchcock, Wilcox opens with a close-up of Simonetta being strangled and screaming, followed by a reverse shot of Silvio speaking "Not dead? Not yet quite dead? . . . I would not have thee linger in thy pain" (5.2.95, 97).[2] Only after we reach the word "thee" and see a bored girl touching up her lipstick does the camera reveal that we have been watching a rehearsal, not a real murder. This short sequence enacts in miniature the appropriative strategy of the film as a whole, drawing us into the stage fiction and demonstrating its horrifying power only then to establish the cinematic fiction as the genuine reality. Noteworthy is the splitting of perspectives between Silvio and Simonetta, motivated in part because *Venetian Nights* was a star vehicle for the two leads, Matheson Lang reprising his earlier role, and Dorothy "Chili" Bouchier, at the time billed as Britain's answer to "It" girl Clara Bow (see Grantside, 1998). The part of Simonetta was expanded from the earlier silent version, with Bouchier playing Simonetta as a flirtatious, sometimes petulant coquette, a negative version of the "new woman" she had earlier been identified as; the carnival scenes were substantially extended, fleshed out with location shots of Venetian fireworks and bacchanalian revelry that euphemistically suggest the consummation of Simonetta's relationship with the count. The condemnation of

Simonetta's behavior in this sequence is undoubtedly also a condemnation of financial excess in this mid-Depression film.

The divergence of narrative perspectives widens when Silvio and Simonetta arrive at the theater for the performance of *Othello* at the film's end. When Silvio arrives at the theater he is preoccupied and disturbingly quiet, a man struggling to contain himself, but as he blacks up and sees Othello's image in the mirror, he becomes unhinged, haunted by the voice of his sister Italia – "sooner or later there's bound to be someone, it's only natural" – which obliquely echoes Iago's words to Othello. His reaction is to stare at his hands, which involuntarily ball up in rage before he momentarily recovers. Othello becomes Silvio's *doppelgänger*, allowing him to express the rage he struggles to contain, but also fueling it. Just as he is about to go onstage, Silvio intercepts an incriminating note from Simonetta, prompting him suddenly to speak in Othello's voice, "O now do I see 'tis true . . . [thou] art so lovely fair . . . that the sense aches at thee – would'st thou had ne'er been born!" (3.3.449, 4.1.70–1). From this point on, his intense performance of Othello – we see him in 4.2 and in 5.2 – reflects what he believes Simonetta has done. To magnify the subtextual dynamics of the performance, we see the first scene, in which Othello accuses Desdemona of adultery, from the count's viewpoint. Uniquely positioned to grasp what Silvio's speeches reveal, he reacts with embarrassment, lowering his eyes at Desdemona's denial that she is a strumpet. Between the two *Othello* scenes, Silvio discovers that the count was Simonetta's companion at the carnival when the star he plucked from her costume falls from his handkerchief. Ever the aristocrat, the count does not flinch. His officious exit – he snaps to attention and proclaims "If you want me, you know where to find me" – leaves Silvio without redress, except through the *Othello* narrative.

Set against Silvio's perspective is Simonetta's. Although she is frantic to placate Silvio, in the theater scenes Simonetta is far less childlike and self-absorbed than earlier, submitting to the performance of *Othello* with growing awareness that it may lead to disaster. Her newly "mature" submissiveness and remorse may indeed reflect her acceptance of the des-demonization of the "new woman," but she also uses *Othello* to give voice to her own subjectivity, something denied the wives in *Desdemona* and *Carnival*. As Silvio broods offstage, Simonetta sings Desdemona's "willow song" so intensely that even the count is moved, her isolation punctuated by a single spotlight on the darkened stage. Even in the final scene the camera repeatedly cuts away to Simonetta in bed struggling to remain in character, in the passive posture of Desdemona, as she awaits her husband's approach. As Silvio plays Othello, he begins to substitute the name "Simonetta" for "Desdemona"; when he strangles her, her scream and the shot of Silvio looking down upon her reminds us of the film's opening sequence, replaying the blurring of reality and theater now in deadly fashion, without tricking the viewer. Indeed, the movement of the camera from long to medium to close-up shots draws us into the couple's private reality – visually, the scene becomes cinematic rather than filmed theater.

As in earlier versions the inset murder scene involves the surfacing of repressed rage against women's sexual independence. Here, however, Silvio's backstage horror – he stares at his blacked-up hands as if they were instruments of an Other within – suggests a recognition of split male subjectivity absent in earlier versions. When he tries to repress this recognition and pushes Simonetta away, she takes command. In the longest speech of the film, she tells him that he mustn't feel guilty, for she too gave in to the carnival, though she was never unfaithful. Her latter assertion, somewhat contradicted by the evidence we've seen, has the effect of complicating what constitutes infidelity, and that is the point – the replacement of a standard of absolute sexual purity with one of steadfast commitment. Here Simonetta acknowledges her own erotic Other within, providing Silvio the model to break out of his male rage, guilt, and repression.

The final scene provides several signs of their mutual acceptance of what might otherwise be destructive passions. Hearing carnival music from afar, at Silvio's prompting Simonetta opens the window to let the sounds enter their room. As the two embrace, Silvio lovingly strokes Simonetta's face, rubbing off his black make-up on her face; where before Silvio's seeing his blacked-up face in the makeup mirror catalyzed his murderous rage, now the mirror image of himself and Simonetta in smeared blackface prompts their mutual laughter. This final comic moment reads in several ways at once: as a transformation of Silvio's impulse to eradicate Simonetta's beauty into something comically benign; as a sign of Silvio's (and Simonetta's) acceptance of the stain of the passionate Other within their characters; as a reduction of Silvio's Othello *doppelgänger* to nothing more than insubstantial greasepaint. *Venetian Nights* opens with an image of murder we momentarily take as cinematically real but which turns out to be theater, a reversal that allows us temporarily to deny the truth that play-acted murder reveals. The film ends on a second visual reversal, an image of the two in a mirror with streaked makeup that dispels theatrical illusion.

Men Are Not Gods (1937), the next film in the cycle, takes a strikingly different approach to the murdering Othello motif. It focuses on women's experience, a focus announced as early as the credit sequence where we hear the "willow song"; it also focuses not on the stage actor but on the theatrical spectator. The encounter of working-class secretary Ann Williams with Shakespearean theater subjects the mystique of the stage to thoroughgoing critique while insisting upon its utter irresistibility. Having lost her job at the *Post* because she rewrote a devastating review of a new *Othello* at the request of the star Edmond Davey's wife, Ann decides to attend the show she saved but has never seen. Upon hearing Davey perform Othello's self-defense in 1.2, "I fetch my life and being / From men of royal siege, and my demerits / may speak unbonneted to as proud a fortune / As this that I have reach'd" (1.2.21–4), lines that, we soon learn, speak to Davey's upper-class bearing, she quickly falls under the play's and the actor's spell. Tellingly, she takes her seat in the gallery as Brabantio complains about his daughter being "corrupted / By spells" (1.3.60–1). With her opera glasses she focuses on Davey as he delivers the

"Most potent, grave and reverend signors" speech, listening intently as he declaims about "what charms, / What conjuration, and what mighty magic . . . I won his daughter" (1.3.91–2, 93). Even as he denies he has used witchcraft, Ann's broad smile reveals that Davey as Othello has bewitched her with his aristocratic manner and heroic grandiloquence. Although the excerpts from 3.3, 3.4, and 5.2 that follow (and Ann's reactions to them) illustrate the capacity of Shakespearean performance to enthrall the inexperienced theatergoer, they also hint at problems to come. Othello's farewell to "the tranquil mind" and "content" speaks to what will soon become her obsession with Davey; Desdemona's line "men are not gods" stresses the folly of idealizing men; and Othello's exit line, "No way but this: / Killing myself, to die upon a kiss" (5.2.368–9), suggests the self-destructive quality of Ann's growing passion for the actor and the theater as well as Davey's as-yet-unseen capacity for murder. Taken together, the troubling resonances of these excerpts, mere hints at first, establish both the extraordinary power of Shakespearean performance but also the danger that power poses for Ann. It is noteworthy that much of that power is here attributed to Shakespeare's uncannily resonant language, a theme developed in *A Double Life.*

After the first *Othello* performance the film veers from screwball comedy into increasingly tragic melodrama. Ann's first encounter with Davey – he, Ann, and his wife dine at the Savoy – makes clear that her attraction springs from his upper-class status, reinforced by the glamour of the Shakespearean stage. Davey's foil is Tom, Ann's fast-talking, working-class colleague from the *Post* who, despite his sincere affection for her and sheer persistence, lacks Davey's class mystique. When Tom out of frustration begins to spout Brabantio's lines, "She is abused, stol'n from me, and corrupted / By spells and medicines bought of mountebanks" (1.3.60–1), his street performance yields him nothing but a pelting by fruit and flower-pots. His choice of text suggests that Ann's cross-class adoration of Davey has the same socially unsettling quality as Desdemona's cross-racial love for Othello, a point reinforced by the next scene in which Ann goes to the Royal Academy to stare adoringly at a portrait of Davey as Othello, pictured at the moment he parts the bed-curtain to murder Desdemona.

It is not long before Davey exploits Ann's devotion to his high-cultural image. At another rendezvous at the Savoy, Davey suddenly confesses his love for her and his desire to be free of his overbearing wife Barbara who manages his career. Davey's failure to recognize that his star status actually depended on Barbara's initial action at the newspaper reeks of elitist privilege, and it is compounded by his reason for being attracted to Ann: her "simplicity," her passion and capacity for romanticization, qualities he links to her working-class status. For him Ann epitomizes the mass audience who regards him as a star, "the great public, the symbol of the unreserved seat, the gallery, with its capacity for enthusiasm." If posh Barbara sees Davey as a man-child whose high status needs careful maintenance, Ann simply idolizes him as "a great artist." Davey proposes that he and Ann have an affair, a suggestion she at first rejects. This sequence recasts the relationship between high (theatrical)

culture and its mass audience in terms of a cross-cultural love story gone sour.
Where before the mass audience might worship high culture from afar, here that
adulation is soon revealed to be misplaced, for high culture is all too willing to
abuse its position of cultural supremacy, here in the form of sexual exploitation. In
this, *Men Are Not Gods* anticipates films like Powell and Pressburger's *The Life and
Death of Colonel Blimp* (1943) and Reed's *The Fallen Idol* (1948) in which once idealized male authority figures are revealed to have feet of clay.

In *Men Are Not Gods*, the malignant side of that authority comes to the fore when
Ann tries to break off her attachment to Davey and the theater, mewing herself up
in her flat. But when she turns on the radio to distract herself, she hears Davey's
voice performing the Senate speech, the very speech that so captivated her in the
theater. Discovering that it is a broadcast of *Othello*, she turns it off, but then she
hears Davey's voice from the window, then from the ceiling above, then from a truck
outside as she pleads "no, no, no!" This memorable sequence illustrates the ubiquity
of the now uncannily oppressive authority of *Othello* (and Shakespeare) over her, a
power that invades her private space by allying itself with mass media, a power she
cannot deny or escape. The triumphal lines with which this sequence ends, "This
only is the witchcraft I have used!" (1.3.168), articulates the uncanny effect Shakespeare's words have over her, words quickly followed by images of storm clouds.
Unable to resist, Ann gives in to Davey's blandishments, but when Barbara, having
discovered the affair, reveals she is pregnant, Ann breaks off the relationship, ending
her Dear John note with the fateful line, "You belong to Barbara as long as she
lives." With Ann having resisted Davey's upper-class charms and Shakespeare's
cultural cachet, the plot would seem to have nowhere to go, but in the film's final
act the power of *Othello* returns, now in homicidal form. The focus shifts from Ann
to Davey as he falls under Othello's spell, prompted by the last line in her letter
which hangs in his memory. If before Othello had been for Ann a figure of heroic
nobility, now Othello becomes for Davey a conduit for seething rage at his sense of
privilege being denied. To get one last look at Davey, Ann attends a performance
of Davey's *Othello,* and her presence, along with Shakespeare's script, prompts Davey
to give himself over to homicidal passions.

Barbara's willow song scene, the vignette which opens the film's final *Othello*
sequence, establishes the sense of romantic betrayal, guilt, and foreboding which
hangs over the performance. As she sings the camera focuses on Davey as Othello
listening backstage, puffing on a cigarette, a symbol of his inward fuming. As
Barbara sings "let nobody blame him, his scorn I approve" (4.3.50), we see Ann in
the gallery, lowering her eyes with regret; at "I called my love my false love"
(4.3.53), she sinks into tears. This film features the longest excerpt from the murder
scene of any of the films I'm discussing (5.2.1–44, 54–62, 85–92), but the fact that
it excises mention of Cassio and the handkerchief makes Davey/Othello's rage seem
all the more unjustified, the eruption of an unconscious misogynistic impulse, a raw
assertion of power. At first Davey's approach to the murder scene is stylized and
theatrical, but after he breaks the relative calm by shouting "Yet she must die, else

she'll betray more men" (5.2.6), he becomes a man possessed, running about the stage, leaping on the bed, his eyes bulging, his delivery filled with outbursts. As he contemplates murder while Desdemona sleeps, he briefly glances up at Ann in the audience, revealing that his rage is as much directed at her as at Barbara (both Ann and Desdemona are blondes). More and more he seems like a cinematic monster – his threatening shadow on the wall, straight out of horror film clichés, prompts Barbara to give an unnervingly realistic scream. And yet for all the focus on Davey's unhinged mental state, the film gives considerable attention to the spectators' (and especially Ann's) developing realization that something is wrong. As Davey moves to strangle Barbara on the line "it is too late" (5.2.92), Ann hysterically screams "stop, stop!", stopping the play and breaking its spell. With her outburst Ann finally understands the sinister power she has been under as well as the destructiveness beneath Davey's debonair veneer. In Davey's case, Ann's scream exposes his murderous intent, to himself and particularly to Barbara. As Barbara runs to safety, he is frozen onstage in the posture of a bug-eyed strangler, the tableau of the victimizer. Only then does Davey acknowledge what he was capable of and collapses in shame.

After this catharsis, the film moves quickly to a backstage reconciliation between Ann, Barbara, and Davey, the improbabilities of which mark the film's struggle to return to class and gender conventionality and the realm of comedy. After telling Davey of her pregnancy, Barbara forgives him, observing "there's so much truth I say in the words I say each night on the stage. Men are not gods." If, as this line suggests, the film's central theme is the de-idealization of gentlemanly mystique and theatrical stardom, the terms of Barbara's forgiveness – she explicitly blames herself for his dalliance – suggests that she is willing to go only so far in addressing the sordid gender politics the narrative have exposed. For her, it is enough to have purged Davey's violation of marital fidelity. In Ann's case, when Davey thanks her for saving him from doing something terrible, she re-accepts her subordinate class status, saying "I shall go on being what you once said I was, representative of the gallery, the symbol of the unreserved seat, the enthusiastic audience, and applaud." Despite these women's quiescence, however, there is a tentative hint of resistance to the reinstitution of masculine, upper-class authority. The film aligns Shakespeare and theatrical glamour with that authority, but at the end the stage manager tells the audience that because of Ann's outburst the play cannot go on to its seemingly inevitable conclusion: "I hope that you, I hope that even perhaps Shakespeare will forgive us if on this occasion only we allow Desdemona to live." By so explicitly refusing Desdemona's scripted demise, *Men Are Not Gods* completes its reimagining of the murderous Othello trope in terms of the protocols of a "woman's picture,"[3] exposing the mechanisms of male sexual and class privilege for what they are, self-serving hypocrisy.

Of this group of films, George Cukor's *A Double Life* (1947) offers the most thorough consideration of the vexed authority of Shakespearean theater in the cinematic age. The film chronicles the psychological deterioration of Anthony John, a

Broadway star who takes up the role of Othello and cannot keep it separated from his disintegrating love life. Eventually, like Othello, he strangles the woman he loves and, as the police close in, he stabs himself as he performs the final scene of *Othello*, a new variation on the murdering Othello trope. *A Double Life* is a *film noir* meditation upon postwar social dislocation and fractured masculine selfhood. Othello's crisis of racial identity becomes metaphor and catalyst for the American stage actor's crisis of class status. We first see Anthony as he confronts his portrait in the theater foyer, one of many portraits, posters and busts that establish his public image as an up-market icon. As his female fans reveal, that dashing public image, all cocked hat and pencil-thin moustache, defines Tony's appeal. And yet Tony's turn away from his admirers betrays his discomfort with his image as a "gentleman's gentleman," the title of the boulevard farce in which he stars as the film begins. This sequence announces the complex interplay between Tony's class status, erotic desire, and masculine identity. In conversation with his agent, Tony reveals that for all his seeming *savoir-faire*, he sprang from working-class stock. His aristocratic charm is assembled from the upper-class parts he's played and from his own efforts to teach himself how to talk and move, to make himself "Tony," efforts that have forced him "to tear [him]self apart and put [him]self together again and again." His father, an actor who ended up as a doorman, emblematizes the precarious state of Tony's achievement. Just below Tony's genteel surface lurks profound anxiety about his "genuine" identity. The "double life" of the title thus comes to signify not only the life of the actor but also the life of the upwardly-mobile American male who for all his achievements cannot escape a sense of inauthenticity and fear of falling, the awareness that his status depends upon repression of his darker, "essential" lower-class character.

The pivotal figure in Tony's biography is his wife (actually, ex-wife) Brita, the European sophisticate who, he says, awakened his ambition to become a great actor.[4] As with Othello and Desdemona, Tony's insecurity about cultural legitimacy becomes intertwined with his romantic obsession with Brita, who signifies his precarious membership in a high-cultural caste. As the film opens, Tony and Brita are divorced, the result of Tony's obsessiveness when involved in "deep" parts, yet the two continue to act – literally and figuratively – as husband and wife. Only by hanging on to this relationship long after it is over can Tony maintain an illusion of security; when Brita refuses his proposal of remarriage, Tony's carefully managed "double life" begins to unravel and he descends into homicidal psychosis. Understandably, for Tony the role of Othello holds a particular terror and perverse fascination.[5] When his agent suggests he take up the part, Tony senses the play's unsettling parallels to his own life and Shakespeare's uncanny potential to overwhelm him, and he demurs, "Some parts give me the willies, on the stage and off." Yet doing Shakespeare offers him a chance to establish himself as a man of class, a "real actor," and so he consents. In a montage of rehearsal and performance scenes intercut with Tony's dreams and accompanied by his anxious voiceover, Cukor invests Shakespearean theater with the power to invade Tony's psyche through the words themselves.

Indeed, Shakespearean tragedy – "deep," serious theater as opposed to the popular farce Tony normally plays – is so potent that, for a method actor like Tony, the part of Othello comes to possess him.

Early on when Tony, reviewing the play, reads "Haply, for I am black / And have not those soft parts of conversation / That chamberers have" (3.3.267–9), the lines uncannily give voice to his working-class insecurities. As soon as he speaks them, he is prompted to leave the posh Empire Theater and enter the dreamworld of nighttime New York City. Here the connection between Othello, American Shakespeare, and masculine crisis becomes clearest, for Tony's wandering through the bleak cityscape becomes a visual correlative for what he has repressed, the seedy streets from which he had escaped and to which he is drawn. As Tony stares into a shop window, his reflection is replaced by Othello's, his *noir* alter-ego, the vehicle he intends to use to establish his artistic legitimacy but also the image of his inescapable social otherness. Soon he takes up with Pat Kroll, a blue-collar waitress at the Venezia Café who dreams of becoming a model, an illusion that masks her downward spiral into poverty and promiscuity. Tony regards her as a kindred spirit, a working-class figure with fantasies of upward mobility. Cukor hints at the connection between the two when Tony briefly toys with Pat's earrings in the mirror and when he answers her comment, "I've handled lines all my life," with the telling quip, "So have I." Their tryst reveals once again Tony's attraction to the working-class identity he is at pains to deny. The danger of his being overcome by that attraction is indicated aurally, by the roar of an El train at the scene's beginning and end. Each time Tony walks to Pat's apartment, we see the El pass behind his head, as if we could see the forbidden desire literally pass through his mind.

Set in motion by Brita's rejection, Tony's murder of Pat is a desperate act of displacement filtered through *Othello*. The play is so psychologically powerful that it becomes an uncanny script for Tony's insecurities. In rehearsal he nearly strangles Brita as they perform *Othello*'s final scene, and later he explodes with jealousy at her mention of Bill Friend, the theater press agent. Friend – his name describes his bland relationship with Brita – provides contrast to Tony. Where Shakespearean Tony is haunted by doubts about class identity, Bill is quintessentially middlebrow, a well-adjusted "regular Joe" who alone is prescient about Tony's guilt. Despite his fury, Tony cannot bring himself to follow through on his impulse to kill Brita, so Pat becomes the substitute, the wanton woman he jealously imagines Brita to be. But Pat's murder is also the fruit of Tony's class insecurities. Having assayed Shakespeare, Tony has by all rights established himself as a "real actor," a "gentleman's gentleman" worthy of Brita's admiration. Her rejection thus confirms how insurmountable his real identity is, and it activates a fear of artistic and sexual impotence that intensifies as Tony interrogates Brita about what it is Bill does better than he. Pat, the sexually fallen woman, is then punished for the imagined sins of the angelic Brita. But in killing Pat Tony is also trying to destroy his alter-ego, the mirror image of his working-class status that even Shakespeare cannot mitigate. Cued by her innocent request to "put out the light," Tony falls uncontrollably into his role as Othello and strangles Pat Desdemona-style with a kiss, the El thundering in his ears, Pat's struggling hand and the fluttering curtain replicating the details of the onstage *Othello*. The murder in this film plays out with horrifying ambivalence the symbolic violence of Shakespearean theater. The authority of Shakespearean theater is such that the least verbal allusion to *Othello* triggers its transformation from fiction to reality, particularly in the hands of a "real" actor such as Tony. Tony's murder of Pat makes Shakespeare's aesthetic power visible, literal, and lethal, establishing a relationship between highbrow culture and psychological pathology. At the same time, the tawdry circumstances of Pat's murder end up transposing *Othello* in that most lowbrow of modes, the tabloid sensationalism of the B-movie thriller, the very act of transposition that *A Double Life* is engaged in. In short, Pat's Desdemona-style death marks the film's simultaneous appropriation and disavowal of the power of Shakespearean performance.

From Pat's murder on, the plot becomes a detective story in which Friend unmasks Tony's villainy. Unlike Tony, Bill is untroubled by the cultural divide that so torments his Shakespearean counterpart. He too pursues Brita, but when it's clear Brita is out of his league, he "nobly" bows out, his pride and identity intact. He all too willingly accepts the tabloid tie-in with *Othello* he's offered by a sleazy reporter, a lurid front-page story about the killer's Othello-like "kiss of death," in an effort to bolster the show's commercial success. When the story appears, Tony reacts with fury at this blow to his Shakespearean "dignity," and he tries to strangle Bill while once again involuntarily launching into Othello's speeches. That maniacal reaction raises Bill's suspicions, and when Tony's alibi turns out to be empty, Bill decides to test him with theater, in a version of the disguise test from Blom's *Desdemona*. He hires an actress to play a blonde waitress like Pat, with the idea that, Claudius-like, Tony, seeing her, will reveal his guilt.

What is striking is how completely this crucial sequence recasts the nature of the theater. The scene that precedes Tony's "confession" focuses on the mechanics of visual illusion, how Bill's makeup artist can use the tricks of his trade to make an actress look exactly like Pat. What matters most is physical resemblance, not affinities of social class or psychology. In fact, Bill rejects the first actress, much more a match for Pat's personality, in favor of the higher-class choice, a richly-coutured actress who his makeup man then proceeds to remake "downward" in Pat's image. The scene pointedly converts theater from an art of the word to an art of the image. Earlier Tony presented the rehearsal process for *Othello* as a grand battle between the dark imagination and fragile reality, triggered by the uncanny power of the Shakespearean text and the actor's anxieties. That process is repeatedly represented by Tony's distorted or transformed reflection in mirrors accompanied by ominous voiceovers of Shakespeare's text. By contrast the theater Bill employs is all cosmetics and visual legerdemain, a theater of surfaces, not psyches, the "healthy" alternative to the tortured symbolic violence of high Shakespearean drama. It is, in short, theater accommodated to the condition of mass-market film. Though *A Double Life* certainly seeks to borrow the cultural prestige of Shakespearean theater by preserving it on film, the institutional imperatives of its homage require that classical theater be pathologized under the murderous sign of the Shakespearean word and replaced by stagecraft aligned with the cinematic image.

Bill's "mousetrap," handled as a wordless sequence of guilty close-ups, sets in motion Tony's self-destruction. The Empire's backstage, now a shadowy labyrinth of curtains and flats, has come to mirror Tony's unconscious. Haunted by onstage voices and shrouded in gloom, Tony has become unnerved at performing *Othello*'s final scene yet again; glancing warily at the light he will later put out, he despairs that "it's reached the nightmare stage." It is as if Shakespeare's textual authority compels Tony to return obsessively to revisiting the self-division of his own identity, all under the unrelenting eye of the public. Once Tony takes the stage, Cukor oscillates between Tony's subjective point of view (highly imbalanced compositions, distorted close-ups, double exposure, nondiegetic sound) and the audience's "objective" perspective (shot so as to emphasize the claustrophobia of the stage). Increasingly the camera shares Tony's perceptual dislocation and identifies with his plight, particularly as he comes to Othello's final speech. With an incriminating witness waiting in the wings, Tony's final moments as Othello play like some dream-like police interrogation, with spotlights glaring in his eyes and the sound of the El train ringing in his ears. Shakespeare's words now compel Tony to offer an involuntary confession for his crimes. His entreaty to "speak of me as I am" (5.2.351) is spoken not as Othello but as himself, as the bewildered plea of the typical *noir* protagonist who finds himself lost in a maze of fatal ambition and desire he only half understands. Like Othello, he can find no escape from the nightmare of self-division except through suicide, which he commits as part of the play, unbeknownst to his audience.[6]

Dying backstage, Tony speaks once again in his own voice. He imagines meeting Pat, first "up there" and then, correcting himself, "down there," a destination rife with class as well as moral connotations. Marveling at "the things that go through one's head," he recalls the tale of Kirby, an actor so effective at dying that the audience would request that he die again, which Kirby would do, over and over. Kirby represents for Tony his own horrifying fate as a Shakespearean, doomed by his success as Othello to voice his own self-division night after night as a condition of having become a "real actor." The grim irony is that for all his skill at dying, Kirby is now forgotten, a fate Tony fears will be his own. Though he begs Bill, "don't let them say I was a bad actor," what remains of Tony's Shakespearean greatness is what the film's poignant final shot records. As the curtains part, a spotlight illuminates a small empty space in the darkness, the space where in his first show of Othello Tony stood taking his bows. Like Kirby before him, Tony's fame comes through repeated reenactment of his own self-erasure, and as if to darken the irony, the audience's applause rises at the image of Tony's absence onstage.

This final image neatly epitomizes the film's strategy in depicting Shakespearean theater. At its heart is Shakespeare's massive, indelible, and, for American audiences, problematic cultural authority. In that regard, Olivier's *Henry V*, released in the United States in the summer of 1946 and still in circulation when *A Double Life* hit the screens, provides a crucial context. Olivier's adaptation became the most successful Shakespeare film yet made, its marketplace viability in America dependent on the film's much-trumpeted "prestige." What vexed marketers was its Shakespearean language, regarded since the Shakespeare films of the 1930s as box-office poison, and so the American advertising campaign sought to refocus attention on the film's Technicolor spectacle and its depiction of "one of the great-est love scenes in literature." The difficulty was, in other words, how to convert Shakespearean cultural authority, still associated in Olivier's *Henry V* with the theater and "merrie old England," to terms more amenable to Hollywood's Ameri-can populism. *A Double Life* lays claims to Shakespearean prestige to be sure, but it represents that prestige as overwhelming, uncontrollable, dangerous. Through Tony we experience the vexed place of Shakespearean theater in postwar American film, caught between the desire to co-opt the class-coded power of high culture represented by the unattainable Brita(in) and the Empire Theater, and the homi-cidal reverse-image of that power, its desire for and horror at the lower-class mass audience represented by the prole Pat Kroll. The film partially recuperates what it problematizes by transposing *Othello* into a distinctively cinematic genre, in effect establishing American mass-market film – or a mode of theater largely indistinguishable from film – as rightful heir to the cultural preeminence of the Shakespearean stage. *A Double Life* doesn't simply reject Shakespearean cultural authority; it celebrates that authority under (self-) erasure, as a greatness the on-film theater audience cheers in its absence.

That this strategy confers a form of prestige that is not entirely ironic can be illustrated by the example of Ronald Colman, the actor who portrayed Tony. The part of Anthony John was originally intended for Laurence Olivier who was "una-vailable for the part" (McGilligan, 1997: 194). Colman, several biographers report, worried about his performance as Othello, since he "had never felt either the desire or ability to tackle" Shakespeare before (Colman, 1975: 224–5; Levy, 1994: 164–7; McGilligan, 1997: 195); Patrick McGilligan reports that to put Colman in the proper mood, George Cukor "talked to [him] at length about his struggling early days as an actor in the United States, kindling the memory of hardship and bitter-ness" (1997: 195). In an interesting metacinematic way, then, Colman's struggle with the part unintentionally replicated the dynamic of legitimation within the film. Before *A Double Life* was released Colman was widely regarded as a gracefully aging matinee star. Yet the cachet of the Shakespearean stage *sous rature* was such that for this, his one foray into Shakespeare, Colman won the Golden Globe and Academy Awards in 1948, in the latter case beating out Michael Redgrave (*Mourn-ing Becomes Elektra*) and Gregory Peck (*Gentleman's Agreement*). In the same year, Olivier released his *Hamlet*. Unlike his *Henry V*, this film was shot in black-and-white, and it exploited motifs typical of *film noir*, including expressionistic sets, chiaroscuro lighting, voiceovers, subjective camera perspectives, themes of madness and paranoia, and a final shot that comments ironically on the film's fallen protagonist. There is no evidence that *A Double Life* exerted influence on Olivier's *Hamlet*. And yet the conjunction of Shakespeare and *noir* made possible an exchange of legitimation between Hollywood and classic theater. Intended or not, that conjunction recalibrated the cultural register of Shakespearean prestige, taking it out of the tradition of the theater and a specific national-cultural heritage and allowing it to be received within codes of reception more amenable to cinema audiences. Whereas the Academy of Motion Picture Arts and Sciences (AMPAS) had recognized Olivier's *Henry V* with a special honorary award in 1946, his *Hamlet* was to bring Olivier Academy Awards for best actor and director in 1949, the only Oscar wins of his much-nominated career.

What does this film cycle reveal about screen adaptation of Shakespeare in the first half of the twentieth century? Transposing Shakespeare from stage to screen is not merely a matter of making the plays less stage-bound by opening them up with lavish sets or locations, not merely a matter of learning how to deliver Shakespearean dialogue believably in a medium which favors photographic naturalism, not merely a matter of finding suitable correlatives among established cinematic genres for the theatrical genres within which Shakespeare worked. Adapting Shakespeare for film involved all of these elements, but the films under consideration here suggest that it also involved a transfer and a transformation of the kind of cultural capital Shakespeare represented to early twentieth-century film audiences. As the twentieth century began, Shakespeare's artistic prestige and reputation for rhetorical power, an inheritance from the nineteenth century, was bound up with the stage, the cinema's rival and sister medium. For the cinema fully to appropriate Shakespeare's cultural authority, filmmakers needed to re-present the nature of Shakespearean stage performance, to redefine its capacity to enthrall theatergoers and to create mystique and prestige for actors, and it needed to redefine that capacity in terms that served dual, contradictory interests of the nascent film industry: to establish film as a bona fide artistic medium, heir to the legitimate stage, and to establish it as the predominant mass-market performance medium, identified with the interests of the general public and distinguished from what it often characterized as the elitism of the theater. *Othello*, with its anecdotal history of performances so compelling they become homicidal, provided a ready-made vehicle for effecting that transformation of cultural capital, for tales of murdering Othello demonstrated both the extraordinary power of Shakespeare and its imbrication in symbolic violence, and in storylines that make for compelling modern film melodramas, where the camera gives us special access to the darker truth of what we might see performed onstage. To be sure, these films are often troublingly misogynistic, though as the cycle develops increasingly they insist upon the pathology of male psychology. But they are also extraordinary documents of metacinematic discourse, in which stage Shakespeare, like Desdemona, a figure both loathed and beatified, can be embraced only at the moment of its death.

NOTES

1 Lang had played Othello as early as 1907 in
   Manchester, and he played a revival of his
   Othello in rotation with his stage version of
   Carnival when the latter premiered at the
   New London Theatre in 1920. Ironically,
   while *Carnival* was a hit, his *Othello* got poor
   reviews because critics assumed that because
   it played as a matinee show, it must have been
   substandard (see Lang, 1940: 130–7).

2 All citations from *Othello* are taken from
   Wells and Taylor (1998).

3 For more on the "woman's film" as a genre,
   see Basinger (1993), the introduction to Gledhill (1987), Mercer and Shingler (2004:
   78–98), and especially Landy (1991). Landy
   notes that British film melodramas of the
   1930s are heavily weighted toward crises of
   male rather than female identity, whereas
   Hollywood produced a large group of films
   focused on women in the same period (1991:
   194). *Men Are Not Gods* may also reflect
   changes in cinematic portrayals of adultery in
   the mid-1930s. Before the Hays Code took
   root in Hollywood in 1934, "a disproportion-
   ate number of adultery movies were told from
   the standpoint of the 'other woman,'" but
   afterward such films "usually focused on the
   moral dilemma of the cheating spouse"
   (Lasalle, 2000: 178).

4 Cukor cast actress Signe Hasso in the role of
   Brita, one of several Swedish actresses (Greta
   Garbo, Ingrid Bergman) who seemed to fascinate Cukor as symbols of European elegance. In Levy's biography of Cukor, Hasso is
   reported to recall that Cukor thought European actresses were exotic and extraordinary:
   "'Oh, you strange women,' he would say"
   (1994: 164).

5 For a short discussion of *A Double Life*'s relationship to *Othello*, see Willson (1986).

6 McGilligan's (1997) account of George
   Cukor's closeted homosexuality suggests
   another set of resonances for this final
   scene. Tony's secret and guilty erotic life,
   his desire to resolve the tortured double life
   he is forced to lead, the association of
   homosexuality in the period with the
   theater and upper-class refinement: all
   suggest that the film might be read as a
   highly coded portrait of the anguished closeted homosexual in the period. Cukor had
   earlier engaged the theme of doomed love
   with the suicide of washed-up actor Larry
   Renault (played by John Barrymore, with
   obvious Shakespearean resonance) in *Dinner
   at Eight* (1933) and again in his *Romeo and
   Juliet* (1936).

REFERENCES

Basinger, Jeanne. *A Woman's View: How Hollywood
   Spoke to Women, 1930–1960*. Hanover, NH:
   Wesleyan University Press, 1993.

Carnival. Dir. Harley Knoles. UK: Alliance
   Films, 1921.

Colman, Juliet Benita. *Ronald Colman: A Very
   Private Person*. New York: William Morrow and
   Co, 1975.

Desdemona (a.k.a. *For Åbent Tæppe*). Dir. August
   Blom. Denmark: Nordisk Film, 1911.

Dinner at Eight. Dir. George Cukor. USA: MGM,
   1933.

A Double Life. Dir. George Cukor. USA: Kanin
   Productions, 1947.

The Fallen Idol. Dir. Carol Reed. UK: London
   Film Productions, 1948.

Gledhill, Christine. Ed. *Home is Where the Heart
   is: Studies in Melodrama and the Woman's Film*.
   London: BFI, 1987.

Grantside, Michael. "Chili Bouchier: Britain's 'It'
   Girl." *Classic Images*, 276, June, 1998, 20–4.

Hamlet, Dir. Laurence Olivier. UK: Two Cities
   Films, 1948.

Hardinge, H. C. M. and Matheson Lang. *Carnival: A Play in Three Acts*. London: Samuel
   French, 1927.

Henry V. Dir. Laurence Olivier. UK: Two Cities
   Films, 1940.

Hodgdon, Barbara. "Kiss Me Deadly; Or, The Des/Demonized Spectacle." In *Othello: New Perspectives*. Eds. Virginia Vaughan and Kent Cartwright. Cranbury, NJ: Associated Ups, 1991, 214–55.

Kyd, Thomas. *The Spanish Tragedy*. Ed. J. R. Mulryne. London: New Mermaids, 2nd edn, 1989.

Landy, Marcia. *British Genres: Cinema and Society, 1930–1960*. Princeton, NJ: Princeton University Press. 1991.

Lang, Matheson. *Mr. Wu Looks Back*. London: Stanley Paul and Co, 1940.

Lasalle, Mick. *Complicated Women: Sex and Power in Pre-Code Hollywood*. New York: St. Martin's, 2000.

Levy, Emanuel. *George Cukor, Master of Elegance*. New York: William Morrow and Co., 1994.

The Life and Death of Colonel Blimp. Dirs. Michael Powell and Emeric Pressburger. UK: Rank Film Producers and The Archers, 1943.

McGilligan, Patrick. *George Cukor: A Double Life*. New York: St. Martin's, 1997.

Men Are Not Gods. Dir. Walter Reisch. UK: London Film Productions, 1936.

Mercer, John, and Martin Shingler. *Melodrama: Genre, Style, Sensibility*. London: Wallflower Press, 2004.

Pordes-Milo, Alexander Siegmund. *Sirocco*. Leipzig: Wigand, 1912.

Potter, Lois. Ed. *Othello. Shakespeare in Performance Series*. Manchester: Manchester University Press, 2002.

Romeo and Juliet. Dir. George Cukor. USA: MGM, 1936.

Venetian Nights (a.k.a. *Carnival*). Dir. Herbert Wilcox. UK: British & Dominions Films, 1931.

Wells, Stanley, and Gary Taylor. Eds, *The Oxford Shakespeare: The Complete Works*. Oxford: Clarendon, 1998.

Willson, Robert F., Jr. "A Double Life: *Othello* as Film Noir Thriller." *Shakespeare on Film Newsletter*, 11, 1986, 3, 10.

12

Hamlet's Hauntographology

Film Philology, Facsimiles, and Textual Faux-rensics

Richard Burt

The medium of the media themselves (news, the press, tele-communications, techno-tele-discursivity, techno-tele-iconicity, that which in general assures and determines the *spacing* of public space, the very possibility of the *res publica* and the phenomenality of the political), this element itself is neither living nor dead, present nor absent: it spectralizes. It does not belong to ontology, to the discourse on the Being of beings, or to the essence of life or death. It requires, then, what we call . . . *hauntology*.
Jacques Derrida (1994: 50–1)

Photography has killed editing. Period. (*Someone* has to tell the editors.)[1]
Randall McLeod (1999: 72, 154)

That would be scann'd.
Hamlet 3.3.75[2]

Signing Your Own Death Warrant: *Hamlet*'s Specters of Provenance

"A *Hamlet* in Flames," an episode of a British television series entitled *The New Adventures of Charlie Chan* (1957), begins with a prologue about the provenance of a rare book: a Nazi officer steals an imaginary First Folio of *Hamlet* (dated 1603) from its present owner, a French count, in whose castle the Nazi is now billeted.

The Nazi occupier forces the count to "sell" what I will henceforth call the Fauxlio *Hamlet* for a fraction of its market value and demands that he sign a bill of

A Companion to Literature, Film, and Adaptation, First Edition. Edited by Deborah Cartmell.
© 2012 Blackwell Publishing Ltd. Published 2012 by Blackwell Publishing Ltd.

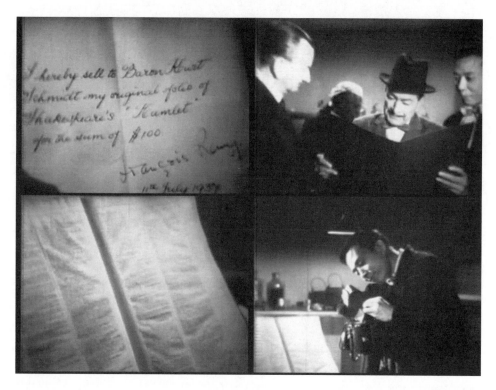

Figure 12.1 "A *Hamlet* in Flames," from *The New Adventures of Charlie Chan*. Dir. Don Chaffey. 1957.

sale backdated to 1937 in exchange for his life. (Figure 12.1(a)). After the count leaves the room, the Nazi owner of *Hamlet* signs an order for the count's execution and telephones it in. The "bill of sale" establishing the edition's provenance occurs in occupied France in 1940. Flash-forward to Belgium, 1957. The ex-Nazi has now put the *Hamlet* Fauxlio up for sale. In the prologue, the count had rather archly asked the Nazi officer if he were sure about the 1937 date. Now we discover why. The count had not owned the edition until 1940. The bill is therefore evidence of a criminal transaction.

Charlie Chan (J. Carrol Naish), accompanied by his "Number One" son, Barry (James Hong), is called in to investigate. Shortly after he examines the Fauxlio, it is stolen, and the bookshop where it was kept is burned; the Nazi officer is murdered by friends of the count who find him out through the bill of sale; Chan discovers the murderer; and the Fauxlio is returned to the police who will in return send it to the British Library.

An intriguing subplot involving Barry develops within this rather prosaic Chan episode. Barry wants to photograph the *Hamlet* edition, one of only three remaining copies, to provide a facsimile edition for the college he attends (Figure 12.1(c) and 12.1(d)) He manages to begin doing so, but is called away by the thief

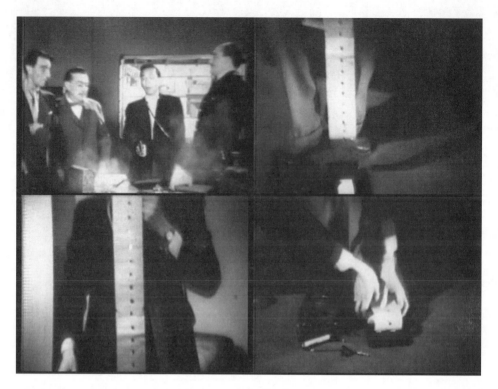

Figure 12.2 "A *Hamlet* in Flames," from *The New Adventures of Charlie Chan*. Dir. Don Chaffey. 1957.

impersonating the police to come to his father's aid. The thief then steals the book that the son has left open and unguarded. At the end of the film, after the Fauxlio is in the hands of the French police, Barry thanks the police captain for letting him photograph the entire faux Folio. Adding a somewhat comic touch to the ending, Barry takes out a gun he recovered at the crime scene, which Chan tells him to return to the police (Figure 12.2(a)). Barry obliges, but the gun accidentally goes off and the bullet hits his camera, sitting on the police captain's desk. Picking up the remains of shattered camera from the floor, Barry discovers to his dismay that the entire roll of film is ruined: every photo has a hole through it (Figure 12.2(b–d)).

I begin with this account of "A *Hamlet* in Flames" not because of the episode's aesthetic merits (which are few) but because it raises broad questions about what D. A. Greetham calls "textual forensics" (1997), questions which turn on the facsimile and photography: a murder involving a rare imaginary edition of *Hamlet* and a subplot about literally shooting film of it becomes a kind of crime scene after the real crime of murder in the main plot has been committed, when subplot and main plot merge in an epilogue. The evenly and neatly distributed holes in the undeveloped roll of film evince a kind of cinematic seriality, a punctuation of the otherwise blank, scrolling space of undeveloped film.

Just the Facs(imiles), Ma'am

The Charlie Chan *Hamlet* Fauxlio has a curious status: it is a film prop that has no extra-filmic referent; furthermore, the facsimile stage prop stands diegetically outside of evidence, subject neither to legal nor to textual forensics within a television series about a detective. The bill of sale is the evidence, not the *Hamlet* edition; and the edition cannot be photographed and used as textual evidence by scholars either. The title page of the *Hamlet* edition is undated (the son says it was published in 1603), in contrast both to the conspicuously dated bill of sale the count signs and to the prominent dates establishing the years of the narrative events, 1940 and 1957. The *Hamlet* First Fauxlio is haunted because it cannot be read or reproduced and entered into evidence or laid to rest, just given a sendoff across the "Franglish" Channel. Initially, the Charlie Chan *Hamlet* Fauxlio is haunted by the bill of sale tying the rare book to its dead, true owner. But by the end of the episode, the edition of *Hamlet* is itself haunted: with the count dead and the Nazi exposed, its provenance has become spectral. The edition will be sent to the British Library, but only because it has reached the end of the line, fully resistant to reading as an image or as a text, a backing that backs up nothing. Narrative closure is figured by a medium that does not provide closure: the roll of film cannot be developed and hence cannot be sequenced, developed, divided into photo-facsimiles of pages to be studied; just as no one in the episode who reads the edition ever gets beyond the title page. Unanchored in a kind of "dead waste *Hamlet*," the Charlie Chan *Hamlet* Fauxlio floats between the zones of auratic genuine Quarto and First Folio *Hamlet*s and their re/productions as film props and textual facsimiles. On the basis of this *Charlie Chan* episode I hazard the generalization that a criminological textual forensics depends on what I call a "hauntographology," a supplemental, spectral backing of evidence that is not itself regarded as evidence: textual forensics is always "textual faux-rensics."

Un/Editing *Hamlet*, the Media of Adaptation, and the Un/Evident Facsimile

Though not an adaptation in the strict sense of the word, "A *Hamlet* in Flames" provides a productive introduction into questions about text and film that are perhaps best raised under the rubric of film adaptation studies. Since the mid-1990s, criticism of Shakespeare film adaptations has divorced attention to the film from attention to the text in order to analyze the film as a film and on its own terms. While in many ways a salutary turn, the divorce that made it possible has come with a price, namely, that one reads a film the same way one would read a literary text, namely, by historicizing it. Moreover, film adaptations and print editions are both regarded the same way, as divisible units, material things, commodities.

It is worth putting some deconstructive pressure on the distinction between a facsimile edition and a modern edition from the perspective of film adaptation studies. Paradoxically, the facsimile is related to a specific medium (lithography photography, digital scanning) yet is a reproduction that appears indifferent to its media platform (whether the image is analogue or digital does not matter, whereas video and Blu-ray editions of a film do matter because they produce vastly different image and sound qualities). Necessarily engaged with media translations (language also being understood as a medium) and technologies, "hauntographology" allows us to put text and film into dialogue without returning to unproductive comparisons between original and adaptation because it raises philosophical, philological, and technological questions about the limits of a "textual forensics" of print editions and film adaptations with respect to their ontology, media specificity, and legibility. *Hamlet*'s hauntographology involves a "film forensics" that exceeds, I will show, any crime scene graphology that reduces evidence to so-called material traces.

This chapter makes two broad claims: the first concerns cognitive problems in un/editing *Hamlet* (textual forensics and the facsimile); the second concerns how these cognitive problems become a political problem of reading that arises when the sovereign is dead but not gone, when the referent is indistinguishable from spectrality (neither here nor there, neither alive nor dead) and when spectrality becomes co-extensive with techno-tele-media, or what Jacques Derrida calls "spectrographics."[3] When referent effects are indistinguishable from spectral effects in *Hamlet* editions (language in the play is itself mediatized through print) and film adaptations (the skulls in Branagh's film), a strong sense of narrative closure does not arrive because the ending can only repeat/echo the structure of the "wait and (what did we/what will we) see" beginning of the play.[4]

The end of *Hamlet* reroutes this structure through Horatio, Hamlet, and other "txt" messengers. Fortinbras tries to decide Hamlet's optative future past ("he would have proved most royal"), but Fortinbras' decision itself requires a decision, when read or acted, because it involves a crux (does he say "royal" or "royally"?). Even when edited, Fortinbras' decision only defers questions of a forensics sort – who is guilty of what? – about the past as answerable only in the future. Horatio's account of what has happened is announced as a prequel – "So shall you hear" (5.2.335) – that could also serve as a sequel. The logic of Horatio's deferral of an answer derives from the logic of reference in the play: referents are produced both through spectral media effects (notes, writing tables, skulls, and so on) and through testimonies of eye-wit/less/nesses who may or may not report aright what happened (or didn't) in *Hamlet*.

The continual deferral of questions of cognition in *Hamlet*, I maintain, registers the play's serial structure (the ending echoes the beginning; the mousetrap repeats the dumb-show; "twice two months" becomes "twice two hours"; the Second Quarto becomes the First Folio, if we assume, as virtually all editors now do, that the First Quarto is less reliable). This serial structure is not reducible to a textual forensics "crime scene" in that editing and reading are not quantitative (do we have all the empirical evidence we need to draw a correct and just conclusion?). Techno-tele-media do not function in *Hamlet* as they (may seem to) do in courts of law: they do not exorcize media from evidence so as to make possible a juridical decision about provenance, ownership, restitution, restoration, and the return of property (see Burt, 2012a). By trying to reconstruct a narrative about what did or did not happen in the composition, transmission, and printing of *Hamlet* Quarto 1, Quarto 2, and Folio from an extratemporal standpoint, editors repeat the serial structure of each of *Hamlet*'s multiple editions whether they wish to edit relatively conservatively, at will, or somewhere in between. Since characters in *Hamlet* cannot look back without looking forward to a time of revelation that never arrives, since the sovereign's decision itself is spectralized, sovereignty can at most forestall perdition; it cannot provide salvation. Branagh attempts (and fails, perhaps deliberately), I maintain, to give his *Hamlet* narrative closure by adding a two-part epilogue first showing Hamlet's funeral and then showing the destruction of Old Hamlet's statue. As a coda to this chapter, I will return to the cognitive problems of editing *Hamlet* in order to show how the "techo-tele-media" (Derrida, 1994: 79, 102) network and paradoxically both weakened and strengthened spectralized sovereignty of *Hamlet* complicate the delivery of what Derrida calls the a-utopian promise of a democracy "to come" (see Burt, 2012b, forthcoming).

Pointing the Finger: Film Prints and Finger Prints

Unlike textual criticism, which philologically reconstructs texts through a forensics model to determine the genesis, if not the origins of a text's publication, film adaptation studies takes literature – a modernized and edited text – as its point of departure. Film philology as such does not (yet) exist. The facsimile is nevertheless crucial to our sense of what an adaptation is, if an adaptation is not to be devalued as a secondary version, a copy of a model. Thompson and Taylor distinguish facsimile editions from modernized editions in terms of their relative readability "When the edition is more than a facsimile but intended for use by general readers, students or actors, it is one of an editor's duties to correct obvious errors in the text" (2006a: 540). The contrast Thompson and Taylor draw is well illustrated by Stephen Booth's (1979) edition of Shakespeare's *Sonnets* which prints a facsimile of the 1609 Quarto in parallel with a modernized text. Yet facsimiles of pages of Shakespeare Quartos and Folios are far from being excluded in most editions even if their number usually falls short of Booth's complete facsimile edition. The cost of reproducing images on paper does not account for the fact that Booth's edition is not the default for editing and criticism. Even though facsimile editions of Shakespeare's works have been available online for some time, they are usually not read together with a modernized edition created by a critic at his computer screen and printed text (to create a virtual, Booth-like edition) nor are facsimile editions assigned in Shakespeare classes or cited by critics even though some Arden editions include facsimile editions.[5]

Why, then, do modern Shakespeare editors almost universally use facsimiles in their paratextual supplements to produce readable (less error-ridden) editions?[6] While textual matters such as spelling, punctuation, quotation marks, and so on get the immediate attention of ("anti-" or "un-")editors and literary critics, facsimiles of facsimiles or facsimiles of pages of genuine Shakespeare editions tend to be used uncritically as evidence by editors and by anti-editing scholars to edit, "unedit," conflate, or deconflate editions of Shakespeare's plays: the facsimile, like the film still or screen capture in film criticism, serves in all cases as an unexamined backup for positivist and empiricist notions of textual forensics and textual evidence.[7]

This point holds true as well for props like the Charlie Chan *Hamlet* Fauxlio and facsimiles of non-existent editions such as the *Reproduction in Facsimile of HAMLET from the First Folio of 1623*. This facsimile of a non-existent edition of *Hamlet* requires not only the inclusions of paratextual pages from the *First Folio* but also the addition of new paratexts in the form of an introduction and a textual apparatus. Yet no one would think to call this or any other facsimile a forgery or a fraud. Some textual critics might even consider teaching it, along with online and print facsimiles, in a class concerned with editing *Hamlet*. There is no such thing as a "fauxsimile" (or a fake prop). By the same token, there is no such thing as a genuine facsimile (or a genuine prop).

What consequences for film adaptation studies (and textual criticism) follow from textual faux-rensics? Before we can answer that question, further preliminary questions need to be raised: Why has the widespread reproduction of facsimiles of print editions and in criticism escaped critical attention from bibliographers and philosophers? Why is there as yet no history of the facsimile? Why has the facsimile escaped historians of the book? Why, in short, do editors, textual critics, and deconstructive critics tend to put on hold the ways in which *Hamlet* editions and film adaptations are penetrated by textual and visual media, as facsimiles (that also serve to "prop" up their arguments)? Now let me return to the question at the top of this paragraph. Two consequences follow: first, the concept of unediting is subsumed by the broader concept of unreading (see Burt 2012c and Burt and Yates, 2012, forthcoming); second, the definitive edition or complete works are always in crucial ways unfinished and incomplete (not because any edition is provisional but because the moment when one stops editing – the moment one stops reading – is necessarily a moment of crisis, if not madness: one must make a decision that cuts out or cuts off variants or meanings by implicitly declaring an editorial or interpretive state of emergency. In editing, the state of exception, or suspension of the rules of evidence, is the norm.[8] Though facsimiles often reproduce details of specific pages, facsimiles are not themselves considered by editors to be readable as details, clues, or symptoms, or even other kinds of mute speech that might bear on one's reading of a particular edition or work of criticism. One might say that the purpose of facsimiles is precisely to block reading by making reading unnecessary not only for the editor but also for the reader of the edited text. Whereas graphic designers have debated whether typography and page layout should be invisible to the reader or draw attention to themselves, they have not debated facsimiles since they are supposed to be visible. And like any technology, facsimiles become visible when they break down, when the image quality is so degraded as to require apology or comment.

Facsimiles in modern editions are generally taken to be self-evident because they are there to be looked at, not read, if they are to serve as evidence. Standing in for the text as thing, facsimiles are hidden reproductions that become invisible while seeming to present the already visible referent. Facsimiles gain their rhetorical power by seeming to present the original, to make it edible and tasty, not just to reproduce it. The apparently self-evident definition of an edition as a material, physical text (a book or DVD) widely adopted in book history is, like that of the stage prop, guaranteed only through hallucinations of past readers and genuine texts, hallucinations made possible by the facsimile's translation of language into image.

Handwriting and printed text are translated into indexical icons; facsimiles of images become "graphic" illustrations. As such, facsimiles constitute the limits of the forensics, the possibility of identifying a specter. As Derrida writes of ghost hunting in *Specters of Marx*, "one must have the ghost's hide and to do that, one must have it. To have it, one must see it, situate it, identify it. One must possess it without letting oneself be possessed of it. But does not a specter consist insofar as it exists, in forbidding or blurring this distinction? In consisting of this very indiscernability?" (1994: 132). The in/distinctness of the facsimile fore*ground*s the "hauntographological" groundless grounds of *Hamlet* editions and adaptations. On the one hand, the facsimile is like a ghost that may be identified since it is there on the page just waiting to arrest you; but, on the other hand, it is like a ghost you cannot bust since you see what it shows, not it itself. The facsimile is an image, but it functions like a metonymy since a page stands implicitly for the whole text. (You seem to get the whole thing at a major discount.)

Hamlet's Photo-Finish

Although Shakespeare's works are not always the subject of Randall McLeod's highly influential and random essays on "un-editing," they will be the focus of my discussion not only because McLeod uses an unusually high number of photographs, facsimiles, diagrams, and on one occasion even a drawing, but also because his essays have been often overlooked both by editors and textual critics (Burt and Yates, 2012, forthcoming). Why? Because his reliance on facsimiles both reinforces the norms of textual forensics and relentlessly resists the norms of editing and reading: McLeod "photoquotes," to cite his neologism, images of printed pages not to produce a better edition of a literary text or to produce a new, closer or somehow more accurate reading of a literary text.

In his (dis)seminal essay, "Un-Editing Shakespeare," McLeod initially links textual evidence to the medium that conveys it in a positivist manner typical of modern editors:

> For us to witness the vast difference between the evidence of text conveyed by fac-similes and what stands revealed as editorial rumors and irrelevant improvements of it, is immediately to unedit Shakespeare. Thus the camera anchors our perception of Shakespeare's text in historical evidence untrammeled with ideal projections of its meaning. Beginning over a century ago **facsimiles** of Shakespeare's earliest editions started to bypass the compositorial and editorial bottlenecks between textual evidence and consumer, and to present the authoritative texts **very much** as they appeared to Shakespeare's contemporaries (McLeod, 1982: 37, my emphasis in bold).[9]

McLeod's initial positivist proposition that facsimiles anchor textual evidence and reveal rumor gives way to a concession that photographs may sometimes lie.

McLeod subtly corrodes the positivism of his first assertion even further as he continues: "In the age of letterpress, from the cradle of printing to this century, when photo- and photo-electronic technology is transforming it 'beyond recognition,' textual transmission from manuscript to print or from print to reprint involved an approximately linear processing of text; it was read (absurdly) bit by bit, or (semantically) phrase by phrase, left to right, line by line; and remembered in these small units by a compositor, who reconstituted it in an array of types, from the faces of which a new version of the text was eventually printed. Such processing is ato-mistic, sequential, and linear; but the textual object exists as a simultaneous whole, a thing in itself – but a *thing* – however tradition dictates our unraveling it" (1982: 37, my emphasis). If "textual transmission . . . involved approximately linear processing of text," its medial transmission has transformed that process "'beyond recognition'." In later essays on Renaissance literature, McLeod grants even more importance to facsimiles and "photoquoting," yet at the same time he permanently defers reading the text in favor of "gazing" at it: the book becomes a roll of film, a reel of celluloid, that he projects as "a magic lantern show" (1991: 66). The text as thing cannot be unraveled, just blown up into non-radioactive fragments at which one may gaze but not reconstruct and narrate, put into a temporal sequence, like the enlarged photos that possibly establish evidence of a crime developed by an art photographer in Michelangelo Antonioni's *Blow-Up* (1966).

As the reader may have already glimpsed, the facsimile in the "A *Hamlet* in Flames" episode entirely empties out the positivism that McLeod, like the less criti-cal editors he writes against, assumes clings to the facsimile. For editors and un/editors, the facsimile serves as an unexamined referent for textual reference. There may be no textual authority, that is, but the photograph always has an unquestioned authority, however suspect its truth-value may be (Didi-Huberman, 2004: 299–71).

The crime scene detected by textual forensics has to exclude from evidence the media condition that makes its narratives possible: the reproducibility of its photographic exhibits and, more broadly, the media that deliver reference effects. For editors and un/editors, the facsimile serves as an unexamined referent for textual reference. If necessary, permissions are given for copyright reasons, usually in endnotes, and sometimes the photographer is credited, but the provenance and dimensions of the text are only rarely given. The date of the photograph is never given, even when it is reproduced to establish a date as in the case of a painting that may be a forgery or part of a diptych. The facsimile props up historicism, as it were, because it appears as a transparency, not an apparition, to the reader and editor. Although textual critics and editors tend to see their work as fundamentally opposed, their common use of facsimiles is one instance of their shared empiricist and historicist criminological practices of "textual forensics."

Heil *Hamlet*: Spectral Photography/Spirit Photography

Any negation of the photo-facsimile's evidentiary status does not exhaust it, however. The facsimile becomes a kind of photo-negative that keeps on returning. When reduced to physical matter, exorcized of spectrality, one might even say, the facsimile may show up as a new kind of evidence in the form of spirit photography.[10] Consider a pair of spirit photographs taken in 1914, one a portrait of Jesus and the other a portrait of Shakespeare. (12.3(a) and (b)). The photos are in some ways specular images. Both images are drawings made to look like photos; similarly, Jesus looks to his right, Shakespeare to his left at nearly the same angles, and both portraits are surrounded by a series of much smaller photographs.

The only major difference between the two portraits is the nimbus that surrounds Jesus' head, which overexposes some of the faces above his head beyond recognition. The small difference that the halo around Jesus inscribes between two sacred figures, Shakespeare and Jesus, is collapsed in the mall comedy *Hamlet 2* (dir. Andrew Fleming, 2008). At the beginning of the stage production of *Hamlet 2*, Jesus, played by Dana Marchz (Steve Coogan), failed-actor turned teacher who has written and directed the play, returns from the dead and gives Hamlet a time machine so that he may go back in time to save the lives of Gertrude, Laertes, and Ophelia, whom Hamlet also marries. Claudius is left out of the plot, but Old Hamlet turns up on a huge movie screen near the end to tell Hamlet he forgives him. After Hamlet forgives his father, Jesus in turn forgives his "higher Father." The only difference is that God does not respond, but his silence is in effect replaced by the audience's enthusiastic applause.

Yet an excess of specters haunts Marchz's salvific sequel. A visual quotation of 33 A.D., the time Jesus tells Hamlet to set his time machine for, appears on a large screen at the back of the stage just as Hamlet starts the machine, namely Leni Riefenstahl's 1933 film *Triumph of the Will* (Figure 12.4(a) and (b)). Adolf Hitler

Figure 12.3 Spirit photographs: W. Fitz-Hugh Smith. (a) "The Master" and (b) "Shakespeare." 1901.

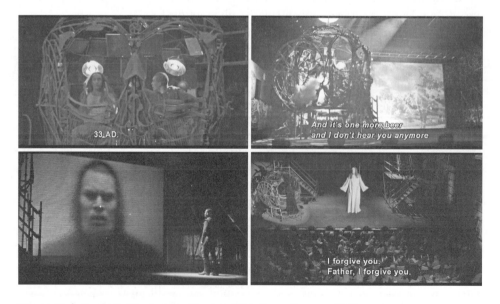

Figure 12.4 *Hamlet 2*. Dir. Andrew Fleming. USA: Focus Features, 2008.

appears in the second of three shots, as if "Heiling" Jesus and Hamlet. This footage, however, is effectively hidden both because of its brevity and because our attention is directed to the action in the left side of the frame. *Hamlet 2* splits the screen in half, letting in, though effectively making invisible, a spectralization that haunts the apparently successful revisitation of Old Hamlet that would exorcize past traumas. A negative of negation, a "NotSee" res-insurrection of two world historical crime scenes, the Riefenstahl footage links the crucifixion of Jesus and the Holocaust, structures the narrative sequencing of *Hamlet* and *Hamlet 2* as unhappy play and then happy sequel (as a do-over of the play) even if it is not evident and not evidence.[11] The silent and invisible God Jesus addresses at the end of the stage production is the flip side of the footage from *Triumph of the Will*. The negative of negation is in turn negated as theological evidence, however, the ghost of Old Hamlet does not spectralize enough: he appears as a father speaking entirely new lines, but he cannot double as an invisible and inaudible and never incarnated higher Father (Figure 12.4(c) and (d)).

> "Thus twice before, and jump at this dead hour, / stalk hath he gone by our watch." The vigilance of the watching guard, the very watch of consciousness, is also a maddened watch or timepiece that, turning on itself, does not know how to guard or regard the hour of this "dead hour." It is delivered over to another time for which the timeclock and the calendar are no longer the law. . . . Dates have become unhinged" (Derrida, 1995: 19).

The Instants of Hamlet's Death: The Spectralization of the Specter

Before turning to Kenneth Branagh's *Hamlet*, we need first to work through the status of spectrality in *Hamlet* and that means engaging Jacques Derrida's account of the play in *Specters of Marx*. As Derrida observes, dating is a problem from the beginning of *Hamlet*. How many times has the ghost appeared before the play begins? When did Old Hamlet die?[12] There is no "crowner's" [coroner's] (5.1.4) report for Old Hamlet's death as there is for Ophelia, just a "forged process" given out by unnamed sources to "the whole ear of Denmark" (1.4. 36–37). No death certificate is ever issued, and, as Derrida points out (1994: 48), the desire to produce one only grants the dead even greater power over the living. Derrida's brilliant account of the specter and power of the techno-tele-media is limited, however, by his rather narrow focus on the ghost of old Hamlet and Hamlet's response to him in the first Act of *Hamlet*.[13] Derrida's area of concerns in *Hamlet* includes the "visor effect" of seeing without being seen, even though the Ghost's helmet is raised; the becoming corporeal of the Ghost; the disjunctive temporality of "the time is out of joint"; and the first time and its repetition.[14]

Indeed, Derrida's separates his deconstructive account of media spectrality from his account of specters in *Hamlet*. Media "spectralize," according to Derrida.[15]

Moreover, spectrality is not defined by the return of the dead but extends to media: "the experience of ghosts is not tied to a bygone historical period, like the landscape of Scottish manors, etc., but on the contrary, is accentuated, accelerated by modern technologies like film, television, the telephone. These technologies inhabit, as it were, a phantom structure. Cinema is the art of phantoms; it is neither image nor perception. It is unlike photography or perception. And a voice on the telephone also possesses a phantom aspect: something neither real nor unreal that recurs, is reproduced for you and in the final analysis, is reproduction. When the very *first* perception of an image is linked to a structure of reproduction, then we are dealing with the realm of phantoms" (Derrida, 1989, 61).[16]

Despite his often philological close and acute readings of variants between literary and philosophical texts, Derrida reads *Hamlet* without any attention to the history of its editing or to its media.[17] Derrida cites each of the four French translations he uses, but he does not cite the English edition from which he quotes in English. Moreover, when he cites indented passages from his unidentified English edition of *Hamlet*, he always cites the text without modernizing the spelling and punctuation. When Derrida discusses *Hamlet* in the body of his text, he tends to modernize the text. The English translation of *Spectres de Marx* does not supply any bibliographical information about the English edition Derrida uses and introduces some minor errors of its own: the translator changes Derrida's attribution of "the time is out of joint" from Hamlet to *Hamlet*, assigns the line a page of its own, and omits Derrida's last note to a French translator (Derrida, 1993: 19 154 n1).

*Hamlet*s With/Out *Hamlet*[18]

My hauntographological reading of *Hamlet* editions and adaptations puts through a call to *Hamlet* that Derrida put on hold in *Spectres of Marx*.[19] If we understand the Ghost's spectrality in *Hamlet* as a problem of reference arising from an irreducibly linguistic link between sovereignty and the image of the King, we may also understand that the sovereign's power to decide the exception is necessarily a power both weakened and strengthened by the spectralization of the already spectral royal image.[20]

Hamlet wants grounds to prove that Claudius is guilty because he comes to doubt whether the spirit he encounters is his father. But just what is the Ghost? The Ghost is in one sense a simulacrum, repeatedly referred to as being "like" the King: "In the same figure, like the King that's dead" (1.1. 40); "Look's a not like the King" (1.1. 42); "Is it not like the King?" (1.1. 59); "Comes armed through our watch so like the King" (1.1. 109). The Ghost is referred to with gendered and neutered pronouns: "it" recurs frequently and used interchangeably with "him." Similarly, "ghost" and "spirit" are used interchangeably. Horatio tells Hamlet he saw his father ("I think I saw him yesternight; / Saw? who? / My lord, the king your father. / The king my father!" 1.2. 188–90). Yet Horatio then qualifies his assertion by seeming to correct himself: "A figure like your father" (1.2. 198). Hamlet offers a number of names for the Ghost: "That I will speak to thee: I'll call thee Hamlet, / King, father, royal Dane: O, answer me!" And the Ghost does not distinguish between referring to himself as a spirit and as King: "I am thy Father's spirit" and refers to himself in the third person before speaking in the first person: "Our last King, / Whose image even now appeared to us" (1.1. 79–80).

The Ghost spectralizes the specter, making the Ghost's referent in excess of any identification of his body or spirit by collapsing both into an image. Consider Horatio's line "Our last king, / Whose image even but now appear'd to us." The adjective "last" rather than "late" works in two contradictory ways: on the one hand, it opposes king to image in order to differentiate them, making "image" synonymous with "ghost" and "spirit"; on the other hand, "last" does not limit the referent of "image" to the meaning of "ghost" since the last King had an image before he was murdered. Moreover, Claudius is technically the last King of Denmark. The image that "even but now appeared" would thus be the same image they had seen before, that would have appeared earlier.

This spectralization of the ghost's referent as an image of an image returns after Hamlet is dead in Fortinbras' speech about him at the end of the play: "Bear Hamlet, like a solider to the stage / For he was likely, had he been put on, to have proved most royally" [First Quarto; Folio has "royall"]. The political force of the spectralization of the specter becomes clear as "like" takes the form of a simile and hence a concrete referent: "soldier" becomes the default model for Hamlet's corpse from the perspective of the ghost of a Hamlet that would have proved to have been.

Fortinbras' sovereignty over the play is of course limited. When does the play end? Many film adaptations, including Laurence Olivier's (1948) and Gregory Doran's (2009) stop at Horatio's "good night sweet Prince / And flights of angels sing thee to thy rest" (5.2. 344) and reduce Fortinbras to a specter by omitting his role entirely.[21] Fortinbras' sovereignty is spectralized in the Second Quarto and Folio editions. Consider the crux in the Folio and Second Quarto in Horatio's lines "Of that I shall also cause to speak / And from his mouth whose will draw on [no] more." Is it "draw on" or "draw no" more? As Horatio becomes Hamlet's mouthpiece ("Not from his mouth" (337)) Horatio's delivery is subjected to static interference: is Horatio referring to Hamlet's death or to Fortinbras' right to succeed? This toggle switch of the palindrome "no" and "on" put the editor on call waiting. Moreover, it self-deconstructs Horatio's last lines, both commanding and advising Fortinbras:

> Let this same be presently performed
> Even whiles men's minds are wild, lest more mischance
> On plots and errors happen (5.2. 346–8).

Horatio's ability to prevent more mischance and errors from happening depends on a performance that must wait until the play is over, even if that ending happens "presently." What is it that Horatio wants to be performed, exactly? The noun for the demonstrative adjective "this," namely, "same" has no clear referent: are we to infer that Horatio means a dialogue between Horatio and Fortinbras based on their mutual partly-line conversation with the noblest of the audience? And how will its performance act in an apotropaic manner? Whatever prophylactic purpose Horatio thinks will be fulfilled if "this same" is "presently performed" not only involves yet another deferral, but also is put on hold by the text's unreliable tele-textual-phonics, subject to interruptions in the form of a cruces. The on and off "on" and "no" crux registers *Hamlet*'s self-corrupting textual status, a status arising from its, perhaps hasty, translation from one medium platform to another: stage to page or manuscript to page, and so on, calling up the possibility that Horatio is part of a cover up.

Fortinbras is mostly on stage during what may reasonably be considered the play's epilogue: he occupies a weakened place in the narrative structure already weakened by the play's lack of clarity over the moment of Hamlet's death. In their note to Hamlet's "I am dead" (5.2. 317), Ann Thompson and Neil Taylor write "If Hamlet is already dead when he kills the King, this may be Shakespeare's solution to the moral dilemma of the blood-guilt of the successful revenger" (2006: 457, n.317). Even if we accept the possibility that a dead person can commit murder, the final moments of the play leave the instant of Hamlet's death uncertain by multiplying them: "Horatio, I am dead" (5.2. 322); "O, I die, Horatio" (5.2. 337); "He hath my / Dying voice" (5.2. 340); the stage direction that follows "The rest is silence." [Dies] (5.2. 342); and the letters "O, o, o, o" that the First Folio inserts between Hamlet's final word, "silence," and "Dyes."[22] Are the letters "O, o, o, o" the addition of a previously missing stage direction? Or have they been added with the reader of the Folio in mind? In any case, only an editor can produce the moment of death in the form of a stage direction, "Dies."

Hamlet's spectralization of the specter of the King extends from the Ghost to Claudius, young Hamlet, young and Old Fortinbras, and the King of England: all are caught up in a discourse and telephonic network in which the medium of the image – text as facsimile or as a prop – interrupts transmissions and in which life and death are not reducible to the distinction between organic and inorganic matter or to questions of forgery, counterfeiting, rumor, process, and so on. The multimedia-capable fauxsimile structures the hauntographological status of all sovereigns in the play, living or dead, bloats Hamlet's narrative structures in ways that forestall closure because they make decision impossible.[23] Hamlet's pronouncements of his death cannot be distinguished from announcements of it.

Kenneth Branagh's "Definitive Film Adaptation" of *Hamlet* (1996)

Having put through a hauntographological connection of media spectrality to the text(s) of *Hamlet*, we may now turn to Kenneth Branagh's *William's Shakespeare's*

Hamlet (1996) to examine how the film produces referent effects by bringing back the dead in ways that both tighten and loosen the hold the martyr/sovereign has over the living. More broadly, Branagh's film will make it possible to see how fac-similes of Shakespeare editions in scholarly and popular publications resemble props in film and video adaptations of Shakespeare plays, in advance: like facsimiles, props are referents without a referent. Branagh's inset film-within-the-film sequences in his *Hamlet* (sometimes working as a flashback, sometimes as a hallucination, as in the Player King's speech) are more like the facing-page images in Folger paperback editions than they are in illustrated editions.

I will limit my discussion to three sequencess in the film: the gravedigger's scene; the engraved "Hamlet" seen at the beginning and end of the film; and the sup-plementary epilogue of Branagh's own invention making Hamlet into a Jesus figure. Consider Branagh's inset sequence in the gravedigger scene. A shot of Yorick still alive playing with Hamlet as a child follows the gravedigger's identification of Yorick's skull by the buckteeth that still remain in it: baring his teeth in imita-tion of the buckteeth of the skull, the gravedigger (Billy Crystal) hands the skull to Hamlet. In the next shot, a face-on close-up of the skull held in Hamlet's left hand begins with Hamlet saying "alas poor Yorick" and then dissolves into a match-out close-up of Yorick's face (and the buckteeth of the actor – Ken Dodd – who plays Yorick) as Hamlet continues speaking. This is the last of *Hamlet*'s many flashbacks.

The testimonial force of the flashback diminishes the longer it continues beyond the initial match-out cut, illustrating a story in excess of the memories Hamlet relates to Horatio. As he does frequently in the film, Branagh comes out of the flashback the same way he got in, with a match-out from Yorick's face to his skull.[24] The flashback device has by this point been further drained by Branagh's frequent recycling of the same footage in different flashbacks or illustrations of different speeches in the film.[25]

As if anticipating the exhaustion of this match-out device, Branagh has the gravedigger conspicuously exhume more skulls than the play demands. The gravedig-ger has lined up a neat row of six skulls on ground level at one edge of the grave he has just dug. In the next three shot reverse shots of the gravedigger and Hamlet, the number of skulls mysteriously decreases. We understand why when we see the gravedigger furtively put the last two skulls into a sackcloth bag to his right, leaving only Yorick's in front of him. In a kind of vanishing act, Branagh disappears an excessive number of skulls, leaving the viewer to wonder what the gravedigger will do with his sack of skulls.

Branagh both heightens and exhausts the cinematic ways he produces reference effects in the double epilogue. In the first epilogue, Hamlet is carried out of the palace and given a full military funeral (Figure 12.5). Branagh returns to Laurence Olivier's *Hamlet* (1948), the film he apparently regards as his rival, for a final time here (Figure 12.6). In Olivier's long epilogue, Hamlet is not a messianic figure. His corpse instead passes by the empty chair and lingers again over the shot of the King

Figure 12.5 *William Shakespeare's Hamlet*. Dir. Kenneth Branagh. USA: Columbia Pictures, 1996.

Figure 12.6 *Hamlet*. Dir. Laurence Olivier. USA: Universal Pictures, 1948.

and Queen's bed we saw near the beginning of the film. In the final long shot, Hamlet is put "most high" with nowhere to go but "The End."

By contrast, Branagh turns Hamlet into a martyr whose death seems clearly meant to be viewed as redemptive (a chorale and full orchestration version of the theme music plays on the soundtrack to cue us). Branagh's salvific epilogue works only by leaving things open: Hamlet has to have an open casket funeral if we are to see him as a martyr Prince, a messianic figure resembling Jesus (as the red color "drains out" of the corpse like blood). In order to provide a stronger sense of closure, Branagh separates the shots of Hamlet's funeral in Olivier's version from the shots of the bed and the chair that return like ghosts. Branagh ends the second epilogue by returning to the opening shot of the film: the name "Hamlet" bookends the film and introduces an additional linear narrative structure by ending the destruction of Old Hamlet's statue. The title of the film, "Hamlet," follows two paratextual shots, first "Castle Rock Presents" and then "William Shakespeare's" printed in red against a black background. The first shot of the film shows the name "Hamlet" carved on stone. The sound of a bell chiming begins with the first shot and continues into the third shot, when we discover, as the camera slowly tracks left from "Hamlet" and the camera racks the palace behind the statue into focus, that the film title becomes diegetic as a name on a statue. In response to Bernardo's question "Who's there?," Branagh cuts to a medium close-up of the head of Old Hamlet's statue, and we are to infer that the name "Hamlet" we saw as the film's title appears on the bottom of this statute, and a few shots later, we understand that the ghost is indeed in the statue when the hand on the sword moves. Branagh's integrated and very brief paratext makes the title do double work, assigning it first to Shakespeare and then to the statue.

The second epilogue showing the destruction of Old Hamlet's statue, as I will demonstrate presently, marks clearly how difficult it is for Branagh to dis/place *Hamlet*, link the title and name of Hamlet to an image of Hamlet or the name of an author. On the one hand, the opening sequence and the second epilogue provide narrative structure: just as we move from reading Hamlet as the title and then as the name of the statue, so we move from the (animated) statue at the beginning of the film to its destruction at the end. On the other hand, Branagh always keeps the shot of the name "Hamlet" separate from shots of the statue. In the film's opening sequence, Branagh does not show Hamlet's face and name in the same shot, instead filming it (and the guards frequently as well) only in close-up and soft focus. Even before we see the head of the statue, the slow tracking shot leaves "Hamlet" a "wounded name" (5.2. 328) by momentarily making legible words within the name "Hamlet" that may be read as unwitting commentary on the film, first "Ham" and then "Ha."[26]

An inverse corollary covering of the wounded name occurs in the second epilogue. The film cuts to the same shot of Hamlet's name at the base of the statue that we saw at the beginning of the film in the statue title at 18:52–3; and then 1:18:55–6

Figure 12.7 *William Shakespeare's Hamlet*. Dir. Kenneth Branagh. USA: Columbia Pictures, 1996.

and 1:18:58 showing pieces of the statue falling in front of its base as the film crosscuts the shots of the engraved name "Hamlet" with shots of the soldiers putting nooses around the head, knocking the head with a hammer twice, and smashing parts of the statue, including the hand holding the sword we saw move near the start of the film (Figure 12.7).

At 1:19:04, the statue's head falls to the ground and lies horizontally, taking up almost the entire screen. At 1:19:10, the last shot of the film fades to black.

The pieces that we do see fall no longer resemble the body parts – arms or hands – we just saw being smashed. But neither Hamlet's image nor his name is destroyed. No shot of the head being struck off appears: we only see it being hammered twice in close up. The name of Hamlet is left intact. The name of the father, "Hamlet," is not scratched out, just hidden by the fallen head of the statue (rather than matched to it) that, like Hamlet's corpse when carried out of the palace, has its eyes open, suggesting that its "perturbed spirit" (1.4) has at best been arrested above ground and whose sovereignty can be read as both weaker and more powerful than ever. Unlike Olivier, Branagh does not conclude his film with the words "The End."

> In the experience of the end, in its insistent, instant, always imminently eschatological coming, at the extremity of the extreme today, there would thus be announced the future of what comes. More than ever, for the future-to-come can announce itself and in its purity only on the basis of a past end: beyond, if that's possible, the last extremity . . . is there not a messianic extremity, an *eskhaton* whose ultimate event (immediate rupture, unheard-of interruption, untimeliness of the infinite surprise, heterogeneity without accomplishment) can exceed, at each moment, the final term of a *phusis*, such as work, the production, the *telos* of any history? (Derrida, 1994: 37).

Spectrographies and Textual Faux-rensics: Return of the Pre-Crime Seen, or No End to Editing *Hamlet*

At the end of his "Little [*Kleinen*] History of Photography," Walter Benjamin makes a remark about crime scenes based on his understanding of the task of the photographer:

> It is no accident that Atget's photographs have been likened to those of a crime scene. But isn't every square inch of our cities a crime scene? Every passer-by a culprit? Isn't the task of the photographer – descendant of the augurs and haruspices – to reveal guilt and to point out guilt in his pictures? The "illiteracy of the future," someone has said, "will not be ignorance of reading or writing, but of photography." But shouldn't a photographer who cannot read his own pictures be no less accounted an illiterate? Won't inscription become the most important part of the photograph? (1999: 527).

Photography has to become a kind of writing for it to become readable, according to Benjamin. I conclude this chapter with a glance at the role photographs play in the remarkably "unedited" Third Arden edition of *Hamlet*. The edition was published in two volumes: one titled *Hamlet* (2006a); the other *Hamlet: The Texts of 1603 and 1623* (2006b).

Both covers have the same design, apparently based on a beautiful silver nitrate photograph of the dead Ophelia, underwater, dressed in a smock and holding in her left hand, a branch with flowers, near her crotch, in a shadowy area of her smock. Ophelia's head is not fully in the shot; a black band at the top of the cover branding the book "The Arden Shakespeare" crops her face at her open mouth. Ophelia's cropped body serves as an icon of (blocked) mourning by simulating a very old kind of black and white photography. The covers of both volumes of *Hamlet* double as works of art and (possibly) crime scenes.

In addition to the subtitle, *The Texts of 1603 and 1623*, the two volumes differ in two key aspects: the cover of *Hamlet: The Texts of 1603 and 1623* is a photographic negative of the unsubtitled and undated *Hamlet* cover. *Hamlet* is in white type and *Hamlet: The Texts of 1603 and 1625* is in black type. The bleached or faded version of Ophelia's image on the cover of *Hamlet: The Texts of 1603 and 1623* looks like a photographic "negative" of the *Hamlet* cover. Do these covers show the publisher's (and perhaps the editors' too) "crime scene"? Perhaps. The "negative" cover makes it clear that the branch Ophelia appears to be holding has been photoshopped into the "positive" cover image. Yet the covers would probably never be entered into evidence precisely because book covers are generally not read, in Benjamin's sense, except by reviewers.[27] Moreover, the Arden covers become potentially readable because there are two of them, a positive and a negative. The covers of the Arden *Hamlet* Third Series phenomenalize the spectralization of the specter in *Hamlet*, giving the three editions a new linear sequence in which one edition haunts the other's haunting image of Ophelia. Yet the covers render textual forensics inoperable in ways that ultimately reflect politico-juridical movements, because any textual forensics depends on images or facsimiles that have no real status as evidence. The mismatch between titles (*Hamlet*) and image (Ophelia) provide a last example for the purposes of this chapter on *Hamlet*'s hauntographology: split into a negative and a photograph, Ophelia's death remains, as it does in the text(s), an open case, or what Walter Benjamin would call the multi-media of the involuntarily remembered image:

> On the knowledge of the *memoire involuntaire*. Not only do its images come when they are summoned, but they appear rather as images that we have never seen before we remember them. This is clearest in the case of images in which – as in some dreams – we see ourselves. We stand before ourselves just as we once stood in an originary past (*Urvergangenheit*) but as we have never stood before our gaze. And precisely the most important images – those developed in the darkroom of the lived moment – are the ones we get to see. One could say that our deepest moments, like some cigarette packs, are given to us together with a little image, a little photo of ourselves. And the "whole life" that is said to pass before the eyes of the person who is dying or those people who are hovering in danger of dying is composed out of precisely these little images. They present a rapid succession, like those precursors of the cinematograph, the little booklets in which we, as children, could admire the skills of a boxer, a swimmer, or a tennis player in action (Benjamin, "From a Small Speech on Proust Given on My Fortieth Birthday." Cited by Agamben, 1999: 159).

ACKNOWLEDGMENTS

For their comments on earlier drafts of the present essay, I would like to thank John Michael Archer, Elizabeth Burt, Peter Fenves, Judith Haber, Scott Newstok, Stephen Orgel, Neil Taylor, Ann Thompson, and especially Julian Yates.

NOTES

1 The editors already do know what McLeod (1994), cited in the second epigraph, thinks they do not. See Taylor (1973).
2 All citations are to Ann Thompson and Neil Taylor's edition of *Hamlet*, Arden Third Series. London: Thomson, 2006.
3 On "techno- tele-media," see Derrida (1994: 79–81, 102); for Derrida, "media power" is always and above all a "signifying power."
4 On skepticism in Hamlet, see Kottman (2007: 139–64); Cavell (1987: 179–91); and Ratcliffe (2009).
5 See the facsimile of the 1600 Quarto of *Henry the Fifth* in the back of Tom Craik's 1995 Arden edition and Quarto facsimiles in 2H6, 3H6, *The Merry Wives of Windsor*, and *The Taming of the Shrew* (*A Shrew*) Arden Third Series editions. Ann Thompson tells me that the forthcoming R&J will also have a Q facsimile, explaining that the facsimiles "are, apart from anything else, a good way to prevent the textual notes being completely clogged with Q variants, but the rationale is different in each case" (Email, January 5, 2011).

6 Whenever I use the word "facsimile" in this chapter, I exclude the sometimes interchangeably used "diplomatic facsimile," or transcription, and the photograph of a text. I am interested in what Randall McLeod (1994) aptly calls the "photoquoting" of facsimiles in the textual apparatus of modernized editions.

7 See the "unedited" two-volume Arden Third Series edition of *Hamlet* (Eds. Ann Thompson and Neil Taylor) for example. The editors use facsimiles of sample passages (536–9). In their introduction, Thompson and Taylor list the ways in which Shakespeare's texts can be edited: "1. A photographic, or diplomatic, facsimile of a particular copy of a particular printed book . . . ; 2. An old-spelling, or modernized, edition of such a copy of *Hamlet*; 3. An old-spelling, or modernized, edition of an 'ideal' . . . printed edition of a text . . . ; 4. An old-spelling, or modernized, edition of the reconstructed text of a lost manuscript assumed to lie behind a printed edition . . . ; 5. An old-spelling, or modernized, edition of a play (e.g. Shakespeare's *Hamlet*).

8 I explore other consequences regarding cinema in Burt (2012c forthcoming).

9 See McLeod (1982, 1990, 1991, 1994, 1999, 2000).

10 On a trial held in 1862 involving fraud, *Hamlet*, and spirit photography, see Kaplan (2008: 215–16; see 254, n.14 for references to newspaper accounts of the trial).

11 Accounts of the holocaust are typically accompanied by assertions that the crimes cannot be adequately represented on film, photography, and literature. See, for example, Derrida (2008: 26, 80). For more on the Nazis and Shakespeare, see Burt (2005).

12 Derrida (1994: 185, n.20) notes that "it is not clear whether the Ghost's 'foule crimes' that happened in his 'dayes of Nature' were his or not." See also Derrida (1995: 14–40).

13 Even if there were a coroner's report for Old Hamlet's time and cause of death, the report would not set the time for Hamlet, just as the coroner's report about Ophelia doesn't settle anything for Laertes. On the sentence "I am dead," see Blanchot and Derrida (2000: 68).

14 See Derrida (1994: 7–8) and Warren Montag (1999: 67–82).

15 See Derrida (1994: 50–1).

16 See also Derrida (2001a: 74–85 and 2005); Derrida and Fathy (2000).

17 See, for example, Derrida's (2001b: 283–5, 295–6, 305, 316–21, 336, 342–7) stellar close readings of variants in Rousseau's *Confessions* and omissions in one of two versions of Paul de Man's essay "Excuses, Confessions."

18 I allude here to Margreta De Grazia (2007), a study I take to be a failed attempt to exorcize the "materiality" of the text from all spectrality, if not all editing. On the "x without x" formulation De Grazia uses in her title, see Blanchot and Derrida (2000: 88–9); the "community without community" see Derrida (1997: 37, 42, 46–7, n.15; 1999: 250–2); where Derrida explains the meaning of his formulation "messianicity without messianism" see Derrida (1999: 265, n.29 and 267, n.69, where the translator supplies a helpful commentary on Derrida's phrases "death without death" and "relation without relations(s)"); and see Derrida's discussion of what he calls a "materiality without matter" (2001b).

19 In broader terms, this would mean putting through a call from Avital Ronell's, *Telephone Book* (1989), which I take to be a reading of *Hamlet*, to Derrida's reading of *Hamlet* in *Specters of Marx* (1994).

20 See Carl Schmitt's formulation, "sovereign is he who decides the exception" (1985: 5). See also Schmitt (2009) and Derrida (1997: 165, 169–70, n.2). See also Derrida's (1997) discussions of the "The Phantom Friend Returning" and the "Specter of the Political" in chapters four and five, respectively.

21 See also the somewhat paradoxical line Horatio offers near the end of the First Quarto: "I'll show to all the ground, / The first beginning of this tragedy" (17. 120–1).

22 On the sentence "I am dead," see Blanchot and Derrida (2000: 68); and on the spectral

virtuality that makes truthful testimony possible, see 72, 75, and 92. In an endnote to *Specters of Marx* (1994: 189, n.3), Derrida also cites his discussion of the implication of death ("I am dead") in the declaration of "I am" in his earlier book, *Speech and Phenomena* (1973). Though Derrida returns in a number of his writings to what he calls Hamlet's "visor effect" (seeing without being seen) in *Specters of Marx*, he never notes, cites, or discusses Hamlet's twice-repeated line "I am dead" (5.2. 317 and 322). See Derrida (2002: 120–1 and 2009: 26, 392). For related remarks on Hamlet, see Derrida (2008: 45, 75) and 2010: 39–41, 233) Derrida cites *Specters of Marx* in a footnote on this page.

23 On Hamlet's narrative structure, see Weber (2004) and Fenves (1997). Like Derrida, Weber and Fenves do not engage in Hamlet's editing history. Weber cites Harold Jenkins' *Hamlet* (Arden Second Series).

24 The first of many such mirroring repetitions is seen in the opening shots of the name "Hamlet." The camera tracks left the first time we see it, and then tracks right at the same speed the second time we see it. Branagh also repeatedly circles the

actors in a given scene with the camera in a long take.

25 The device works less and less well to insure a visual referent for the language of the play. The recycled film clips-within-the-film do not match the framing play-within-the-play structure of *Hamlet*, itself famous for the puzzling replication of the dumb show by *The Murder of Gonzago*. Branagh clumsily tries to produce fact-similes through his interpolations whereas Shakespeare produces the Mousetrap as a fauxsimile of the dumb-show, itself a re-enactment of Claudius's murder.

26 See Marc Shell (2006) for a discussion of Hamlet being a "little ham" akin to Porky Pig. See also the citations of Hamlet in *The King's Speech* (dir. Tom Hooper, 2010), a film about King George VI learning not to stutter.

27 Reviewers occasionally do "read" book covers, and "in reviews, of the two volume Arden Third Series *Hamlet*, have tended to comment on (a) the featuring of Ophelia and (b) the positioning of her hand. If you look at that hand on the Q2 cover you will see that the design is not in fact based on a photograph." Email to the author from Ann Thompson, December 20, 2010.

References

Agamben, Giorgio. "Benjamin and the Demonic: Happiness and Historical Redemption." *Potentialities: Collected Essays in Philosophy*. Trans. Daniel Heller Rozan. Stanford, CA: Stanford University Press, 1999, 138–59.

Benjamin, Walter. *Walter Benjamin: Selected Writings Volume 2 1931–34*. Eds. Howard W. Eiland and Michael W. Jennings. Cambridge, MA: Harvard University Press, 1999.

Blanchot, Maurice and Jacques Derrida. *The Instant of My Death* and *Demeure: Fiction and Testimony*. Trans. Elizabeth Rottenberg. Stanford, CA: Stanford University Press, 2000.

Booth, Stephen. Ed. *Shakespeare's Sonnets*. New Haven, CT: Yale University Press, 1979.

Burt, Richard. "SShockspeare: (Nazi) Shakespeare Goes Heil-lywood." In *A Companion to Shake-speare in Performance*. Eds. Barbara Hodgdon and W. B. Worthen. Oxford: Blackwell, 2005, 437–56.

Burt, Richard. "Shakespeare Reverbatin': Spectral Media, Unread-ability, and the Weak Sovereignty of the In/Definitive Edition." In *Shakespeare and Culture*. Ed. Bearice Lei. National Taiwan University Press, 2012a, 117–52.

Burt, Richard. "Duly Noted or Off the Record? Sovereignty and the Secrecy of the Law in Cinema." In *Secrets of the Law. Amherst Series in Law, Jurisprudence, and Social Thought*. Eds. Martha Umphrey, Austin Sarat, and Lawrence Douglas. Stanford, CA: Stanford University Press, forthcoming, 2012b.

Burt, Richard. Sh k es e re Cin-Offs Beyond Wreckognition: Film Philology and Abbas

Kiarostami's *Where is My Romeo*. In Any Scott-Douglas (Ed) *Shakespeare Spin-Offs*. Palgrave Macmillan, forthcoming 2012c.

Burt, Richard and Julian Yates. "What's the Worst Thing You Can Do to Shakespeare?" In *Renaissance Drama* n.s. 40. Special issue on "The Field of Early Modern Drama." Ed. William West, 2012, forthcoming.

Craik, Tom. Ed. *Henry the Fifth*. Arden Third Series. London: Thomson, 1995.

De Grazia, Margreta. *Hamlet without Hamlet*. Cambridge: Cambridge University Press, 2007.

Derrida, Jacques. *Speech and Phenomena: And Other Essays on Husserl's Theory of Signs*. Trans. David B. Allison. Chicago: Northwestern University Press, 1973.

Derrida, Jacques. "The Ghost Dance: An Interview with Jacques Derrida by Andrew Payne and Mark Lewis." Trans. Jean-Luc Svoboda. *Public* 2, 1989, 60–73.

Derrida, Jacques. *Spectres de Marx: l'état de la dette, le travail du deuil et la nouvelle Internationale*. Paris: Galilee, 1993.

Derrida, Jacques. *Specters of Marx: The State of the Debt, the Work of Mourning, and the New International*. Trans. Peggy Kamuf. New York: Routledge, 1994.

Derrida, Jacques. "The Time is Out of Joint." In *Deconstruction is/in America: A New Sense of the Political*. Ed. Anselm Haverkamp. New York: New York University Press, 1995, 14–40.

Derrida, Jacques. *The Politics of Friendship*. Trans. George Collins. London: Verso, 1997.

Derrida, Jacques. "Marx & Sons." In *Ghostly Demarcations: A Symposium on Derrida's Specters of Marx*. Ed. Michael Sprinker. New York: Verso, 1999, 213–69.

Derrida, Jacques. "Interview: Le cinema et ses fantômes." *Cahiers du Cinéma*, April, 2001a, 74–85.

Derrida, Jacques. "Typewriter Ribbon: Limited Ink (2) ('within such limits')." In *Material Events: Paul de Man and the Afterlife of Theory*. Eds. Tom Cohen et al. Minneapolis: University of Minnesota Press, 2001b, 277–360.

Derrida, Jacques. "Spectographies." In *Echographies of Television: Film Interviews*. Eds. Jacques Derrida and Bernhard Stiegler. New York: Polity, 2002, 113–34.

Derrida, Jacques. *Paper Machine*. Trans. Rachel Bowlby. Stanford, CA: Stanford University Press, 2005.

Derrida, Jacques. *The Animal That Therefore I Am*. Ed. Marie-Louise Mallet. Trans. David Wills. New York: Fordham University Press, 2008.

Derrida, Jacques. *The Beast and the Sovereign. Vol. 1*. Trans. Geoff Bennington and Peggy Kamuf. Chicago: Chicago University Press, 2009.

Derrida, Jacques. *Séminaire La bête et le souverain. Vol. II (2002–2003)*. Paris: Galilee, 2010.

Derrida, Jacques. *The Beast and the Sovereign. Vol. 2*. Trans. Geoff Bennington and Peggy Kamuf. Chicago: Chicago University Press, 2011.

Derrida, Jacques and Safaa Fathy. *Tourner les mots: Au bord d'un film*. Paris: Galilee, 2000.

Didi-Huberman, Georges. "Appendix: The Detail and the Pan: The Aporia of the Detail." In *Confronting Images: Questioning the Ends of a Certain History of Art*. Pennsylvania Penn State Press, 2004, 229–71.

Fenves, Peter. "Marx, Mourning, Messianicity." In *Violence, Identity, and Self-Determination*. Eds. S. Weber and H. de Vries. Stanford: Stanford University Press, 1997, 253–70.

Kaplan, Louis. *The Strange Case of William Mumler, Spirit Photographer*. Fesler-Lampert: Minnesota Heritage Books, 2008.

Kottman, Paul. "Speaking as One Witness to Another: *Hamlet* and the 'Coming of the Scene'." In *A Politics of the Scene*. Stanford, CA: Stanford University Press, 2007, 139–64.

McLeod, Randall [Random Cloud; Randall M. Leod]. "UN Editing Shak-speare." *Sub-stance*, 33/34, 1982, 26–55.

McLeod, Randall. "From *Tranceformations in the Text of Orlando Furioso*." In *The Library Chronicle of the University of Texas at Austin*. 20. Eds. Dave Oliphant and Robin Bradford. 1990, 60–85.

McLeod, Randall. "Information upon Information." *TEXT* 5, 1991, 241–81.

McLeod, Randall. "FIAT *f*LUX." In *Crisis in Editing: Texts of the English Renaissance*. Ed. Randall McLeod. Brooklyn: AMS Press, 1994, 61–72.

McLeod, Randall. "Enter Reader." *The Editorial Gaze*. New York: Garland, 1999, 60–85.

McLeod, Randall. "Where Angels Fear to Read." In *M(a)rking the Text*. Eds. Joe Bray, Miriam Hadley, and Anne C. Henry. Burlington, VT: Ashgate, 2000, 144–92.

Montag, Warren. "Spirits Armed and Unarmed: Derrida's Specters." In *Ghostly Demarcations: A Symposium on Derrida's Specters of Marx*. Ed. Michael Sprinker. New York: Verso, 1999, 67–82).

Ratcliffe, Stephen. *Reading the Unseen: (Off-stage) Hamlet*. Denver, CO: Counterpath Press, 2009.

Ronell, Avital. *The Telephone Book: Technology, Schizophrenia, Electric Speech*. Lincoln: Nebraska University Press, 1989.

Schmitt, Carl. *Political Theology: Four Chapters on the Concept of Sovereignty*. Trans. George Schwab. Chicago: Chicago University Press, 1985.

Schmitt, Carl. *Hamlet or Hecuba: The Intrusion of the Time into the Play*. Trans. David Pan and Jennifer R. Rust. New York: Telos Press, 2009. (Original published 1956.)

Shell, Marc. *Stutter*. Cambridge, MA: Harvard University Press, 2006.

Taylor, Neil. "'Correcting 'Misprints' in *Henry IV Part Two*." *Notes and Queries*, 20:4, 1973, 134–6.

Thompson, Ann and Neil Taylor. Eds. *Hamlet*. Arden Third Series. London: Thomson, 2006a.

Thompson, Ann and Neil Taylor. Eds. *Hamlet: The Texts of 1602 and 1623*. Arden Third Series. London: Thomson, 2006b.

Weber, Samuel. "'Ibi et uique': The Incontinent Plot (*Hamlet*)." In *Theatricality as Medium*. New York: Fordham University Press, 2004, 181–99.

13
Shakespeare to Austen on Screen

Lisa Hopkins

As cinematic phenomena, Shakespeare adaptations and Austen adaptations have a lot in common, with links and similarities ranging from the small and incidental (as when James Stewart's character in *Harvey* (dir. Henry Koster, 1950) reads aloud from Austen's *Sense and Sensibility* to a pooka who owes much to Shakespeare's *A Midsummer Night's Dream*) to the very much larger and more structural. Both obviously benefit from the very considerable cultural capital of their respective authors, and as a result production values are often very high and both cast and crew may well have strength in depth. Shakespeare adaptations have traditionally been more willing to experiment with unexpected casting choices, such as Toyah Wilcox in Derek Jarman's version of *The Tempest* (1979) or Russell Brand in Julie Taymor's (2010), but Austen adaptations too have been willing to be adventurous, as witnessed by the choice of Alicia Silverstone for Amy Heckerling's *Clueless* (1995) or the presence of two future *Doctor Who* companions, Billie Piper and Michelle Ryan, as Fanny Price and Maria Bertram in *Mansfield Park* (dir. Iain B. MacDonald, 2007). As *Clueless* also bears witness, both authors have also proved able to adapt with ease to updating, and indeed in the case of *Lost in Austen* (dir. Dan Zeff, 2008) to actual time travel, as a twenty-first-century fan of *Pride and Prejudice* finds herself swapping places with Elizabeth Bennet. Shakespeare and Austen adaptations have also flourished in new cultures: Vishal Bharadwaj's *Omkara* (2006), for instance, retells *Othello* as a story of Indian culture, and Gurinder Chadha's *Bride and Prejudice* (2004) does the same for *Pride and Prejudice*, as too does Rajiv Menon's Tamil-language *Kandukondain Kandukondain* (2000) for *Sense and Sensibility*, even if Linda Troost and Sayre

A Companion to Literature, Film, and Adaptation, First Edition. Edited by Deborah Cartmell.
© 2012 Blackwell Publishing Ltd. Published 2012 by Blackwell Publishing Ltd.

Greenfield suggest that Menon's film is based rather more closely on Emma Thompson's adaptation than on Austen's novel (Troost and Greenfield, 2008: 5), while Rajshree Ojha's *Aisha* (2010), which closely followed *Clueless*, gave a similar treatment to *Emma*. Both Shakespeare and Austen have also fared well in Spain, where a number of early film adaptations of Austen included the first ever version of *Northanger Abbey* on screen (*La Abadía de Northanger*, dir. Pedro Amalio López, 1968) (Sánchez and Carmen, 2008), and there were versions of *Taming of the Shrew* (*La fierecilla domada*, dir. Antonio Roman, 1956), *Hamlet* (dir. Claudio Guerin, 1970), and *Richard III* (dir. Claudio Guerin, 1967) (Calvo, 2009: 948).

In a less obviously logical move, both Shakespeare and Austen have, even if in varying degrees, been appropriated by the screen primarily as authors of love stories. In the case of Austen this is readily understandable, though Austen herself might be surprised at the extent to which her strong impulses to satire and social comedy have been subordinated to a stress on the erotic appeal of a wet-shirted Mr. Darcy or a Colonel Brandon as played by Alan Rickman. In the case of Shakespeare this is a less predictable emphasis, but it is remarkable that the Zeffirelli and the Luhrmann versions of *Romeo and Juliet* (1968 and 1996) have been two of the most prominent and popular of Shakespeare adaptations, while adaptations of tragedies such as *Hamlet* and *Macbeth* routinely maximize the attention paid to the erotic relationship between the hero and heroine (or sometimes in the case of *Hamlet* between the hero and his mother). Perhaps less surprisingly, both authors have also been deployed on screen for exclusively heterosexual purposes: Celestino Deleyto argues that in Kenneth Branagh's *Much Ado About Nothing* (1993) the relationship between Don John and his followers is eroticized to the point that "any distinction between homoerotic desire and villainy has totally disappeared" (1997: 96), while many critics have complained that *Shakespeare in Love* (dir. John Madden, 1998) resolutely refuses to engage with any suggestion that Shakespeare might have been bisexual (when Viola observes that it is the first time she has undressed a man, Joseph Fiennes' Shakespeare says " 'Tis strange to me too"), and Patricia Rozema's *Mansfield Park* (1999) and Dan Zeff's *Lost in Austen* (2008) are rare exceptions among Austen adaptations or biopics in hinting at the possibility of conscious or unconscious eroticism which some critics have floated.[1]

Both authors have also lent themselves well to much looser appropriation: in both the Merchant Ivory team's *Jane Austen in Manhattan* (1980) and Kenneth Branagh's *In the Bleak Midwinter* (1995; *A Midwinter's Tale* in the States), Austen and Shakespeare function in effect as sites of cultural contestation rather than as authors of the frame narratives themselves. Similarly both *Lost in Austen* and *Bridget Jones's Diary* (dir. Sharon Maguire, 2001) transpose Austen rather than adapt her, as too does Whit Stillman's *Metropolitan* (1990), while the radically modernized version of *Othello* scripted by Andrew Davies (dir. Geoffrey Sax, 2001) and Akiro Kurosawa's *Theatre of Blood* (1973) perform much the same cultural work on Shakespeare. Both have also recently been the subject of very similar biopics (Burt, 2008: 58; Cano López and García-Periago, 2008; Cartmell, 2010), though where the two films part company, inevitably, is when it comes to the question of consummation of the relationship: just as there is no sex in Austen's own novels, so there can be no sex in anything that purports to be a representation of her life.

The lack of sex is not the only difference; there are other respects in which Shakespeare and Austen adaptations are more generally dissimilar. There is not (to the best of my knowledge) a vogue in Austen-based porn films, as Richard Burt has shown there is in Shakespeare's case (Burt, 2004), although Arielle Eckstut's *Pride and Promiscuity: The Lost Sex Scenes of Jane Austen* offers soft-porn vignettes of both some likely couplings and some less likely ones (including Henry and Mary Crawford and Frank Churchill suggesting a little light sodomy to Mr. Knightley), and Mitzi Szereto's *Pride and Prejudice: Hidden Lusts* did the same. The inventive and often very beautiful animated versions of several of Shakespeare's plays put together by an unlikely combination of Russian animators and the Welsh TV channel S4C find no counterparts in Austen. More systematically, I think there is a difference in the way that Shakespeare adaptations and Austen adaptations intersect with other modes of film. In 2006, Deborah Cartmell declared that "Shakespeare on film seems to have established itself as an area in its own right, with little or no heed of the wider context of studies in literature on screen" (1150). Cartmell was speaking specifically of the *study* of Shakespeare on film, but the Shakespeare films of Laurence Olivier and Kenneth Branagh might indeed seem to inhabit their own entirely separate genre not of film pure and simple but of "Shakespeare film," with a prominence afforded to the language quite unlike the approach to dialogue generally found in film *tout court*; there is, for example a marked contrast with *Revengers Tragedy* (dir. Alex Cox, 2002), *The Changeling* (dir. Marcus Thompson, 1998) and *Hotel* (dir. Mike Figgis, 2001), which have with varying degrees of comfort all spliced Renaissance texts roughly contemporary with Shakespeare to modern dialogue and setting, and which Gordon McMullan calls "each in its different way postmodern, spectacular" (2009: 124), although he ultimately suggests that they "share a basic premise with *Shakespeare in Love*: that 'Jacobean' equals 'decadent', that Jacobean revenge tragedy was a degraded, unhealthy successor to the vigorous splendours of Shakespeare" (134). Indeed of the non-Shakespearean canon of Renaissance plays only one, John Ford's *'Tis Pity She's a Whore*, has been adapted into a major film (dir. Giuseppe Patroni Griffi, 1971) into which no modernizing element has been injected. By contrast, the abstract of Pamela Church Gibson's article "Jane Austen on Screen – Overlapping Dialogues, Different Takes," published in the second volume of *Adaptation*, announces that it is a review article which "examines some of the recent essay collections devoted to cinematic and televisual adaptations of Jane Austen's novels, locating them within the 'Austen on Screen' discipline" (2009). Though there may once have been a "Shakespeare on Screen" discipline, the Shakespeare film has broadened both its cultural aspirations and its field of reference and is now more likely to affiliate itself with and locate itself within other genres rather than to seek to assert its exclusivity, as when we find an article title like Yvonne Griggs' " 'Humanity must perforce prey upon itself like monsters of the deep': *King Lear* and the Urban Gangster Movie" (2008), also in *Adaptation*.

The interconnectedness of Shakespeare films with other genres has a number of manifestations. Sometimes similarities can be seen within the work of one director: thus Robert Hapgood points out that when casting his *Hamlet* (1990) "Zeffirelli has never tired of recounting the moment of decision when he saw a parallel between Hamlet's abortive meditation on suicide in the 'to be or not to be' soliloquy and the scene in *Lethal Weapon* when [Mel] Gibson as Martin Riggs cannot bring himself to pull the trigger that would end his life," which ultimately led him to cast Gibson as the hero (1997: 83). Even more markedly, both Michael Hoffman's *A Midsummer Night's Dream* (1999) and his earlier *One Fine Day* (1996) tell a story which centers on the bridging of two worlds – in the case of *A Midsummer Night's Dream* that of the fairies versus that of the Athenian court and in the case of *One Fine Day* the heroine's organized day versus the hero's scatty day – with a concomitant interest in a dichotomy of work versus play. Both too are totally governed by time: *A Midsummer Night's Dream* operates within a tightly defined timeframe presided over by the changing moon, and in *One Fine Day* we recurrently see a digital clockface. There are also other similarities. In *A Midsummer Night's Dream*, the nineteenth-century setting could be seen as increasing a sense of women's limited roles, an idea underlined by Hippolita's strongly marked sympathy for Hermia, while in *One Fine Day* there is a clear difference between what men and women can get away with: the George Clooney character's child is much more readily tolerated at his place of work than the Michelle Pfeiffer character's is at hers. Indeed throughout the film much is made of the incompatibility between the world of children and the world of work, and it is clear that the world of work is in turn a hostile place which paradoxically results in the infantilization of adults: Pfeiffer's character tells Clooney's that he has a Peter Pan complex, to which she retorts that she has a Captain Hook one, and her clients want to build an "upscale amusement park for adults." The fairies' fascination with technology in *A Midsummer Night's Dream* echoes the dependence on cell phones in *One Fine Day*, while Bottom is like Clooney's and Pfeiffer's characters in that he has a glimmering of a truer art and more aspirational values than those which govern most of the other characters, as in the architectural model made by the Pfeiffer character and the anti-corruption campaign of the Clooney character. Above all, both films are centrally interested in relationships between adults and children. In *A Midsummer Night's Dream* a lot of the dialogue is cut, but not that which pertains to the changeling boy; in *One Fine Day* Michelle Pfeiffer is a single parent estranged from the father of her child, who is a musician and not committed to the child. (*One Fine Day* further prefigures *A Midsummer Night's Dream* in that it opens at night, with the child disturbed; he says he has had a bad dream.) George Clooney's character, also a separated single parent, is a journalist whose ex says she always has to be the grown-up in their relationship. In *A Midsummer Night's Dream*, whose setting in a rainy Italy makes it seem like a deliberately darker version of the glamorized Tuscany of Branagh's *Much Ado About Nothing*, Hoffman again introduces a motif of marital unhappiness with the wordless war between Bottom and his wife. These two stories might be set a world apart, but to Hoffman, they both speak of much the same set of concerns.

It is not only when the same director is involved that one can see similarities between Shakespearean and non-Shakespearean films. There is, for instance, a strongly marked kinship between the brutal, image-obsessed Rome of Julie Taymor's *Titus* (1999) and the brutal, image-obsessed Rome of Ridley Scott's *Gladiator* (2000), and I have argued elsewhere that there are also parallels between the dark, menacing New York of Michael Almereyda's *Hamlet* (2000) and the dark, menacing New York of Tim Burton's *Batman* (1989),[2] while in *Love's Labour's Lost* (2000) Kenneth Branagh is paying obvious homage to the well-established genre of the musical. Perhaps most striking of all is the Royal Shakespeare Company's 2008 production of *Hamlet*, directed by Gregory Doran and starring David Tennant, first broadcast on BBC2 on December 26, 2009 and thus neatly sandwiched between the two parts of Tennant's final ever *Doctor Who* episode, "The End of Time," which had begun on Christmas Day and was to conclude on New Year's Day. In the 1965 *Doctor Who* episode "The Time Meddler," a rogue Time Lord begs the Doctor to let him engineer a win for Harold at the Battle of Hastings because progress would be accelerated and "Shakespeare'd be able to put *Hamlet* on television." William Hartnell's Doctor puts paid to that idea, but David Tennant's makes it possible, and does so in ways that rarely allow us to forget his Whovian history. The first screening was preceded by a BBC announcer promising "Another side of David Tennant," and was followed by an advert for the second part of "The End of Time." Tennant had insisted on distancing his Doctor persona during the initial stage run in Stratford and London, refusing to sign anything other than *Hamlet* programs; by the time the stage production transferred to the screen, however, a number of factors both within and beyond its control had conspired to link *Doctor Who* and *Hamlet* so strongly that it became impossible not to see the one in the light of the other. When the production first appeared onstage, there were only two instances of casting overlap with *Doctor Who*, Tennant himself and John Woodvine, who had appeared with Tom Baker in *The Armageddon Factor*, where he, like many Hamlets, spends a lot of time looking in what appears to be a mirror (it is in fact two-way) and where Baker's Doctor quotes *Richard II* at him. By the time the stage production had transferred to screen, however, both Penelope Wilton, who played Harriet Jones in *Doctor Who*, and Gugu Mbatha-Raw, who played Martha's sister Tish, had appeared in the Jude Law *Hamlet* at the Wyndham in the summer of 2009, and John Simm had just been announced as a future Hamlet at the Crucible Theatre, Sheffield, in autumn 2010.

Other ties also bound *Doctor Who* and the telefilm version of *Hamlet* into a shared nexus. At the time of filming, Patrick Stewart, who plays Claudius, was appearing in *Waiting for Godot* with Ian McKellen, and *The Lord of the Rings* films, in which McKellen starred as Gandalf, have been an obvious influence on the resurrected *Doctor Who* series as a whole, perhaps most obviously when Simm's Master calls

Tennant's Doctor "Gandalf." The repeated jokes in *Doctor Who* about how thin Tennant is find an echo in the change of Gertrude's line to "He's hot and scant of breath" (from "he's fat"), and in both *Hamlet* and "The End of Time" we hear the noise of a helicopter overhead and see the shadows of rotors, in the case of *Hamlet* for the scene with Fortinbras' troops and in "The End of Time" when the Doctor is talking to the Master. Finally, at the beginning of "The End of Time," part one, Timothy Dalton says in voiceover, "It is said that in the final days of Planet Earth everyone had bad dreams," echoing what Hamlet says to Rosencrantz and Guildenstern. Reviewing *Hamlet* in *The Times* and commenting on the similarity with the *Doctor Who* episodes, Helen Rumbelow argued that

> What it does is highlight the Doctor Who-ishmess of *Hamlet* in a way that scholars have never before considered. In an early scene Tennant's Hamlet was crouched on a stone floor, reaching his hand before him in the B-movie posture of "disbelieving horror", as he was terrorised by a ghost with smoke billowing behind him. Viewers who had just tuned in would have been scanning the next frame for Billie Piper. And when Tennant's character says, "I could be bounded in a nutshell, and count myself a king of infinite space", I thought to myself: hmmn, Tardis?

Rumbelow attributed this entirely to Tennant himself – "Quickly though, you realise that what you are picking up on is the constants in Tennant's acting" (2009: 12). In fact, though, it is more fundamental than that: the juxtaposition makes us see both a Doctor who is Hamletesque, unable to decide whom or indeed whether to shoot when he finds himself faced with a Master who, Laertes-like, was once a peer but has since done something bad and a Rassilon who, Claudius-like, represents a corrupted father figure (in "The Five Doctors" we are told that there are some very dark rumors about him), and also a Hamlet who, like the Doctor, is essentially an action hero. Tennant maintained in interview that "it's not the story of a man who can't make up his mind, it's about a man who keeps making his mind up and becomes full of energy and certainty and then hits brick walls here and there . . . when he sees a crack in his prison's walls he just leaps at it" – or, as his interlocutor summarized, "I suppose it means that other characters or circumstances create your obstacles, rather than you creating them for yourself" (Rokison, 2009: 298), just as the Doctor's enemies are almost always external monsters rather than inner demons. Both also drew attention to parental relationships: Rassilon is by way of being the father of all the Time Lords, and in a straw poll of family and colleagues, roughly half identified the unnamed woman in white as probably or certainly the Doctor's mother, a speculation which has also proved popular in internet discussion sites.

Films of Jane Austen books, however, are more likely to inhabit a secure, unified genre, or to be criticized if they do not, especially if the Austen text at stake has been or is perceived to have been adapted without due sensitivity to the very specific cultural codes and social restrictions within which her characters operate. This applies particularly to her women, who cannot simply act as their modern counterparts might: Rebecca Dickson argues that in the Roger Michell *Persuasion* (1995), for instance, "Elizabeth's portrayal misleads viewers about the nature of women's roles in the early nineteenth century" in terms of "her heavily exaggerated coarseness" (1998: 45). The very specific criteria by which Jane Austen adaptations are generally judged can perhaps be seen most interestingly in the frosty reception afforded to Jim O'Hanlon's 2009 four-part adaptation of *Emma* for the BBC, which filled its prestigious autumn classic serial slot. Before its screening the adaptation was hailed in *The Times Playlist* as a new departure in Austen adaptations, with columnist Melissa Katsoulis, who began by observing that "I have to say, I've never much liked the novels of Jane Austen," declaring her approval of TV adaptations because of "the endless parade of handsome actors necessitated by Austen's trademark boy-crazy plotting" and rhapsodizing that "What the producers are most proud of in this adaptation is the rehabilitation of Austen's stuffy characters and relationships for a contemporary audience" (2009). However, by the time it had reached the third of its four weeks Jonathan Brown of *The Independent* was asking "Has the costume drama had its day?", because "the second part of the prime-time Sunday-night costume drama pulled in only 3.5 million viewers – down nearly 1 million on the opening episode the previous week – while the third episode saw another 200,000 switch off" (2009), while the many negative comments by Jane Austen bloggers included the caustic observation that the trees are in full leaf on Christmas Eve (it might also be noted that Mr. Elton leaves immediately after Christmas and stays away until there are bluebells, during which time the spiritual needs of the parish can presumably go hang). In similar vein, Charles Moore in *The Daily Telegraph* asked "Why . . . on a single day of the story, were we offered the horticultural miracle of daffodils out, oak in full leaf and mature wistaria flowering (the last did not even acquire its name until two years after the book was published in 1816)?"; he also caustically observed that "Emma says, 'Our collection of romantic riddles is building up nicely'. There are at least three reasons why that sentence could not have been uttered in 1816" (2009), while Laurie Kaplan complained that "Emma Woodhouse (Romola Garai), like Maria (Julie Andrews) in *The Sound of Music*, swings her arms, swirls her eyes, and seems unable to stop smiling" (2009: 1–2). Kaplan's reference to *The Sound of Music* neatly illustrates how when Austen adaptations are like other films they are less well received than when Shakespeare ones are.

Perhaps part of the problem was that O'Hanlon's adaptation, like Donald Hounam's script for Betsan Morris Evans' 2000 adaptation of *Lady Audley's Secret*, dramatizes what it sees as the subtext of the novel, with the result that points are woefully labored in a script that can't leave well alone. For example, having checked with the twenty-one-year-old Emma that she no longer plays with her dolls, Mr. Knightley helpfully suggests for the benefit of the less acute members of the audience that perhaps she is using Harriet Smith as her doll instead, and later, when she visits Donwell, he says "I was thinking how at home you look. You might be mistress of this house," just in case anyone hasn't worked out yet that that might be the direction in which we're heading. What was even more noticeable was how glum this adaptation was. It opens with Emma as a baby and her mother dying. Mrs. Weston then dies and we see Frank taken away in the rain, followed by Jane Fairfax being taken by the Campbells, and though Miss Bates assures small Jane that "Captain Campbell is not frightening," the camera looks up at an unsmiling man in a red coat. Later, when Emma suggests that Miss Taylor might have a child, Mr. Woodhouse says "Mothers die, and that is a fact."

It is certainly true that there is a dark side to *Emma*. Although in *Mansfield Park* Jane Austen famously wrote "Let other pens dwell on guilt and misery" (1966: 446), there are some miseries which she does sketch in *Emma*, even if she does not dwell on them, and which indeed serve to offset all the more sharply the comedy which supplies the dominant tone of the novel. Indeed the opening of the novel has something of the atmosphere of the funereal: we are told that "Sorrow came – a gentle sorrow – but not at all in the shape of any disagreeable consciousness. – Miss Taylor married," and the second paragraph of the book informs us of the death of Mrs. Woodhouse (1966: 37). This is in fact only the first of a number of deaths associated with the story. The most famous is of course the death of Mrs. Churchill (379), something which is made significantly grimmer when we are told of "the departure of the funeral for Yorkshire" (380) – this in high summer, and when we have already had the heat several times remarked on, suggesting that a long journey with a corpse is not going to be pleasant. In addition, the first Mrs. Weston died young (43), as too did both Jane Fairfax's parents, and David Lodge notes that "According to tradition, [Jane Austen] predicted that Mr Woodhouse would live for two years after his daughter's marriage, and that Mrs Frank Churchill would die young" (1968: 17), making a savage mockery of Mr. Knightley's remark of Frank Churchill "What years of felicity that man, in all human calculation, has before him!" (Austen, *Emma*, 1966: 415). In the circumstances it might seem ironically appropriate that Randalls Park on the outskirts of Leatherhead, the estate that was almost certainly the model for the Randalls of *Emma* (Edwards, 1985: 158; McAleer, 1991), is now a crematorium.

Emma is also a narrative that is haunted by possible tragic versions of itself. Not only is there clearly the potential for social unrest, as indicated by the actions of the gypsies (Austen, *Emma*, 1966: 330–1) and the poultry thieves (464), but there are two allusions to *Romeo and Juliet*: "The course of true love never did run smooth" (100) and "Of such, one may almost say, that 'the world is not their's, nor the world's law'" (391). We hear the shadow of possible tragedy within the narrative itself when we are told that Emma "had resolved to defer the disclosure till Mrs Weston were safe and well" (436), and again this would resonate particularly sharply in the context of Jane Austen's own family: two of her sisters-in-law, the wife of her brother Edward and the first wife of her brother Charles, died in childbirth, so Austen was well aware of the risks. Jon Spence has also argued that while writing *Emma* Jane Austen was even more aware of pregnancy than ever before because both her sister-in-law Mary, wife of her brother Frank, and her niece Anna were pregnant and, for the first time, living close by (2003: 212). The malleable and impressionable Harriet could almost be seen as a forbear of Frankenstein's Monster, and we are reminded that a grim fate might well have been lying in wait for her when we are told that she "would be placed in the midst of those who loved her, and who had better sense than herself; retired enough for safety, and occupied enough for cheerfulness. She would be never led into temptation, nor left for it to find her out" (463): implicit here is what might have happened if temptation had found her.

Nevertheless, the last words of the novel are "the perfect happiness of the union" (465), and they do not ring hollow. This is achieved above all by Jane Austen's use of comic style. No sooner have we read the gloomy "in living constantly with her father, and in no house of his own, there would be much, very much, to be borne with" (433) than we switch to the comedy of "It is remarkable that Emma, in the many, very many, points of view in which she was now beginning to consider Donwell Abbey, was never struck with any sense of injury to her nephew Henry" (433–4). Similarly, the rather muted rapture of Mr. Knightley's feeling "something so like perfect happiness, that it could bear no other name" (419) is followed by the comedy of "Frank Churchill was a villain. – He heard her declare that she had never loved him. Frank Churchill's character was not desperate" (420), while the dark of "all those duties and cares to which time must be giving increase of melancholy!" (434) is relieved by the shade of "it really was too much to hope even of Harriet, that she could be in love with more than *three* men in one year" further down the page. O'Hanlon's adaptation misses this overall comic structure.

Most noticeably, though, there are moments in the O'Hanlon adaptation that indicate astonishing insensitivity to early nineteenth-century *mores*, presumably because, as Laurie Kaplan notes, the principal concern of those involved was to make the adaptation "modern" in feel: Kaplan quotes the producer George Ormond as calling it "an *Emma* for a contemporary audience" (2009: 3) and the director himself as saying that the aim was "to create a modern spirit by reflecting the present" and to achieve an adaptation that is "bright, funny, colorful, energetic, modern, vivacious, and completely of the period." Actors will use "slightly modern body language," and Emma herself will be "very, very modern," a young woman full of "physical energy" (3). The effect of this, as Kaplan justly observes, is that "physical activity and restlessness are transformed in this modern adaptation into familiarity and intimacy, resulting in shocking breaches of the early nineteenth-century codes for decorous behaviour" (7). There are plenty of infelicities in other respects too. Emma calls the gypsies "travellers"; Mr. Knightley snubs Mr. Woodhouse, and villagers snub Emma after she is rude to Miss Bates; Mrs. Elton is not just impertinent but impossibly rude; and Frank kisses Jane in the middle of the village. There is an omniscient narrator, but it is one who offers us neither Austen's text nor Austen's voice; Miss Taylor is referred to as "Anne Taylor"; Isabella and John Knightley are seen as young and skittish; and Mr. Knightley informs us that he was at the births of Isabella's children. Jane Fairfax is not just reserved – she doesn't have a personality. (She is very keen on having a ball though, and indeed becomes positively silly about it.) Mr. Woodhouse, who presciently warns against Box Hill specifically on the grounds that a disaster might occur, says with astonishing self-knowledge "I am a foolish man, aren't I?"; he and Emma then have a completely impossible conversation when they should fail to understand each other. There is in fact a general dumbing-down: Mrs. Elton refers to her sister's having "the latest carriage" rather than a barouche-landau, and we are informed that Emma tries to read *Paradise Lost* rather than being allowed to guess for ourselves what books might find their way onto her reading list. Emma says of the question of Jane Fairfax's post "there is the issue of privacy," Frank says of Jane "How awful her hair looks," and when the alphabet letters are put out they are not too muddled – Dixno, blunred – so that even the slow-witted should be able to decode them. There are some shoddy shortcuts, as when Mr. Elton's proposal sequence contains borrowings from Mr. Collins or when we are left with no idea why Emma comes running into Mrs. Weston asking what the matter is. There are other inexplicable moments too: Frank has already been riding round the neighborhood before his public arrival, and Miss Bates exclaims "Isn't it marvellous? Mother has found her voice!", though there is no indication of why she should ever have lost it. Most notably, there are no servants, entirely erasing Austen's carefully nuanced exploration of the nature of work in this society: Mr. Weston goes to see after the dinner, Mr. Elton leads his wife's donkey to Donwell, everyone seems to walk to Box Hill, and Emma does her own gardening. Finally after the proposal scene Emma has hysterics about moving, completely disrupting the rhythm, and Mr. John Knightley has to come to stay "to protect the chickens," which have never previously been mentioned. This is, then, not only a "modern" but an essentially incoherent version of Austen, and since Austen is valued for her rationality as well as her romance, it is not surprising that this adaptation sank like a stone.

Another Austen adaptation which has not been universally well received is the Joe Wright *Pride & Prejudice* (2005). Unlike *Emma*, this has polarized opinion and gained fans as well as foes, but here too it is instructive to consider the grounds on which it has attracted critical disfavor from those who dislike it. Here the issue centers on the difference between exterior and interior scenes. Subtle and nuanced differences are generally found in the treatment of landscape in Shakespeare and Austen adaptations. Many Austen films have fed directly into the heritage and tourism industries, as attested by Marcia McLuckie's glossy, large-format *Jane Austen TV and Film Locations Guide*.[3] At Lyme Park, visitor numbers rocketed after it appeared as Pemberley in the 1995 version; at Chatsworth, the Pemberley of 2005, the bust of Matthew Macfadyen remained on display for some time. Shakespeare, though, is different: even where an iconic building such as Blenheim Palace is used in a Shakespeare film no similar effect is discernible. It is true that settings are often an important part of Branagh's Shakespearean *oeuvre*, as with the use of Blenheim for *Hamlet* or the odd choice of Japan for *As You Like It* (2006), but only in *Much Ado About Nothing* is the landscape really prominent, creating a very strongly marked contrast between the sketchily indicated "Messina" of the play and the rolling Tuscan landscapes of the Branagh film; it is for instance notable that the Prince, Benedick, and Claudio discuss love outdoors while Don John plots indoors, and the only time he ventures outside to do so, there is lightning. Indeed so wedded is this film to making maximum use of the scenic possibilities of its setting that even the "church scene" is set outdoors.

The effect of choices about setting is, however, very different when it comes to the two different authors. In Shakespeare films, it sometimes feels as if the director's first question has been "Where can I move it to?"; thus Kenneth Branagh gives us an *As You Like It* set in Japan and Ralph Fiennes' *Coriolanus* was filmed in Serbia, in ways which partly build on Julie Taymor's use of Croatia in *Titus*. But when it comes to Austen adaptations even the tiniest-seeming adjustment can lead to complaints, as is most clearly illustrated by the Joe Wright *Pride & Prejudice*, of which Laurie Kaplan laments that "The shifting of Austen's iconic scenes from exterior to interior spaces, or from interior to exterior spaces, breaks the rhythm of the drama, pulls apart the imagistic structure Austen so carefully set up, and creates an anti-Austenian environment by forcing a Brontëan darkness on a novel of manners" (2007).[4] Indeed Kaplan complains that "Even the rain is loud . . . Moments of strong feeling in Austen belong to the characters, not to the weather" (2007), though Sarah Ailwood does try to defend the Wright film by arguing that some of its uses of the tension between interior and exterior are creative: "The camera . . . takes Elizabeth's visual perspective as she looks out the window at the Pemberley gardens: the change in focus from translucent to clear glass reflects her new clarity of understanding of Darcy's character"; "When we first see Darcy at Rosings, he is framed by a window and standing adjacent to a caged bird, signifying his enclosure within a social order which seeks to control not only women but also men," which she sees as communicating "Austen's concern with the commodification of men in the early nineteenth-century marriage market" (2007). Nevertheless, there is clearly a strongly felt sense amongst critics that there is in Jane Austen a well-defined tension between the use of interior spaces characterized as domestic and exterior ones characterized as representing nature and/or freedom from social convention, and this is something not felt when it comes to Shakespeare films and the critical response to them.

However, Emma Thompson was responsible for additional uncredited dialogue in the Joe Wright *Pride & Prejudice* (Deborah Moggach makes it clear that others were employed to work on the script, but Moggach got a ruling crediting her as sole writer [Brosnan, n.d.]), and there is I think a greater kinship than seems to have been noticed between those Austen films in which Emma Thompson was involved and the Shakespeare films of Kenneth Branagh (to whom she was of course once married and with whom she starred in *Much Ado*), which is particularly marked in the use of settings. *Pride & Prejudice*, as we have seen, has not been universally well received; Ang Lee's *Sense and Sensibility* (1995), for which Thompson wrote the script, has generally found more favor with critics and may well appear very different from the Wright. It opens in a dark room, illuminated only by a single candle, in which Mr. Dashwood lies dying; then we cut to the outside of a house in town before moving inside to see Fanny dissuade Mr. John Dashwood from honoring his promise to his father. However, *Sense and Sensibility* too is sensitive to the lure of lush scenery, and indeed while the credits are still rolling we see Fanny and John in the carriage on a lonely road en route to Norland, showcasing all three of the location types which the film deploys later. At Norland itself, Margaret escapes to a tree house and we see Edward arriving on horseback, an image of freedom. It is in the garden that Edward expresses to Elinor his dislike of London and his wish for a country parish, and they bond further on horseback, riding past sheep, while Fanny intimates her disapproval to Mrs. Dashwood as they stand framed by the building. When the Dashwoods move to Barton Cottage, we are repeatedly reminded of its country setting and the landscape around it. In Devonshire, Marianne and Willoughby are almost always out of doors, though in London he snubs her in a house.

The prominence of landscape is not the only link between *Sense and Sensibility*, the Wright *Pride & Prejudice*, and *Much Ado About Nothing*. In *Pride & Prejudice*, Elizabeth circles on a swing in the garden; in *Much Ado About Nothing*, Beatrice soars on a swing after hearing that Benedick loves her – and there is even a direct echo of *Sense and Sensibility* where one sister says to another "Your feet are cold" as they share a bed, just as Elizabeth says to Darcy, "Your hands are cold." Moreover, Sally B. Palmer suggests that "This re-seeing of the Bennet family resembles an Anglicized version of Louisa May Alcott's *Little Women*" (2007), and the original UK video release of *Sense and Sensibility* was prefaced by trailers for *The Swan Princess* and *Little Women*. The Wright *Pride & Prejudice* is not, then, as different as one might suppose from other adaptations which have been much better received; the difference, I think, lies not in its use of landscape *per se* but in its use of it in a way that entails perceived insensitivity to the social codes and constraints which govern the lives of Austen's heroines.

A final question is whether these films tell men's stories or women's, and here there is I think a strong kinship between adaptations of Shakespeare and adaptations of Austen. In Laura Mulvey's formulation (1989), women are offered as the subject of the male gaze. However, I have argued elsewhere that in the 1995 *Pride and Prejudice* it is Darcy, not Lizzy, who is looked at (Hopkins, 1998), and that is also how the 2005 version is received by Sharon Lathan, author of the Darcy Saga books, which are openly inspired by the Wright film. Obviously adaptations of Shakespeare plays such as *Hamlet*, *Henry V*, *Othello*, *Titus*, and *King Lear* tell men's stories; other films, though, are less clear-cut. In *Much Ado About Nothing*, Beatrice has a backstory with Benedick, and Celestino Deleyto argues that "*Much Ado* continues a general trend in Shakespearean romantic comedy in that it overtly hinges on Beatrice, the female protagonist, as the main point of identification for the audience" (1997: 92) since "The proud group of men in leather who dominate the first few minutes of *Much Ado* soon starts crumbling under the influence of the 'female space' of Messina" (93). Equally, though, Don Pedro seems genuinely affected when he asks Beatrice if she will marry him, in a way that foregrounds his emotional state rather than hers, and Kenneth Branagh's Benedick certainly has a well-developed subjectivity; even Robert Sean Leonard's Claudio is less self-assured and potentially more sympathetic than he might be. In the case of *Pride & Prejudice*, Catherine Stewart-Beer argues that "It can be seen as a refreshing feminine counterpoint to a tendency in much period adaptation to ramp up the masculine viewpoint" (Stewart-Beer, 2007) and Sarah Ailwood writes of "the film's almost exclusive focus on Elizabeth's subjectivity and its privileging of her visual perspective" and notes that "Initially, Wright's representation of Darcy departs from Austen's method of constructing his character in the novel, as the viewer learns about Darcy only as Elizabeth's knowledge and experience of him increases" (2007). In the 1995 *Pride and Prejudice* we see Darcy and Bingley alone together discussing Bingley's feelings for Jane, while in *Sense and Sensibility* we see Sir John and Brandon talking alone together about Marianne. We observe Brandon looking at Marianne when he first sees her and that it becomes for a moment his story; later, Willoughby watches the wedding and it briefly becomes his story. Shakespeare may be a male author and Austen a female one, but in these adaptations at least each offers a sympathetic insight into the subject position of the other sex, and perhaps that is another reason which allows films of their work to enter into such fruitful dialogue with each other.

ACKNOWLEDGMENTS

With thanks to Jonathan Grover and Deborah Cartmell.

NOTES

1 See Castle (1995a and 1995b).
2 See Hopkins (2009: 73–5).
3 See Parrill (1999).
4 See Chan (2007), who comments that "interior spaces reify the social constraints that all Austen characters operate under," and Ailwood (2007), who argues that "Wright's use of the visual capabilities of film attributes to Austen a greater investment in Romantic imagery than can be supported by the novel itself."

REFERENCES

Ailwood, Sarah. "'What are men to rocks and mountains?': Romanticism in Joe Wright's *Pride & Prejudice*." *Persuasions On-Line*, 27:2, 2007. www.jasna.org/persuasions/on-line/vol27no2/ailwood.htm. Accessed November 7, 2011.

Austen, Jane. *Emma*. Ed. Ronald Blythe. Harmondsworth: Penguin, 1966.

Austen, Jane. *Mansfield Park*. Ed. Tony Tanner. Harmondsworth: Penguin, 1966.

Brosnan, Edel. "From Hampstead to Hollywood" (Interview with Deborah Moggach). n.d. Writers Guild of Great Britain. www.writersguild.org.uk/public/008_Featurearticl/023_DeborahMoggac.html. Accessed November 7, 2011.

Brown, Jonathan. "Has the Costume Drama had its Day?" *The Independent*. October 22, 2009.

Burt, Richard. "What the Puck? Screening the (Ob)scene in Bardcore *Midsummer Night's Dreams* and the Transmediatic Technologies of Tactility." In *Shakespeare on Screen: A Midsummer Night's Dream*. Eds. Sarah Hatchuel and Nathalie Vienne-Guerin. Rouen: Publications de l'Université de Rouen, 2004, 57–86.

Burt, Richard. "Becoming Literary, Becoming Historical: The Scale of Female Authorship in *Becoming Jane*." *Adaptation*, 1:1, 2008, 58–62.

Calvo, Clara. "Shakespeare in Spain: Current Research Trends." *Literature Compass*, 6:4, 2009, 942–56.

Cano López, Marina and Rosa María García-Periago. "Becoming Shakespeare and Jane Austen in Love: An Intertextual Dialogue Between Two Biopics." *Persuasions On-Line*, 29:1, 2008. www.jasna.org/persuasions/on-line/vol29no1/cano-garcia.html. Accessed November 7, 2011.

Cartmell, Deborah. "Film as the New Shakespeare and Film on Shakespeare: Reversing the Shakespeare/Film Trajectory." *Literature Compass*, 3:5, 2006, 1150–9.

Cartmell, Deborah. "*Pride and Prejudice* and the Adaptation Genre." *Journal of Adaptation in Film and Performance*, 3:3, 2010, 227–44.

Castle, Terry. "Letter." *London Review of Books*, 17:16, 1995a, 7 November, 2011. www.lrb.co.uk/v17/n15/terry-castle/sister-sister.

Castle, Terry. "Sister-Sister." *London Review of Books*, 17:15, 1995, 3–6.

Chan, Mary M. "Location, Location, Location: The Spaces of *Pride & Prejudice*." *Persuasions On-Line*, 27:2, 2007. www.jasna.org/persuasions/on-line/vol27no2/chan.htm. Accessed November 7, 2011.

Deleyto, Celestino. "Men in Leather: Kenneth Branagh's *Much Ado about Nothing* and Romantic Comedy." *Cinema Journal*, 36:3, 1997, 91–105.

Dickson, Rebecca. "Misrepresenting Jane Austen's Ladies: Revising Texts (and History) to Sell Films. In *Jane Austen in Hollywood*. Eds. Linda Troost and Sayre Greenfield. Lexington: The University Press of Kentucky, 1998, 44–57.

Eckstut, Arielle. *Pride and Promiscuity: The Lost Sex Scenes of Jane Austen*. Edinburgh: Canongate, 2003.

Edwards, Anne-Marie. *In the Steps of Jane Austen*. 2nd edn. Southampton: Arcady, 1985.

Gibson, Pamela Church. "Jane Austen on Screen – Overlapping Dialogues, Different Takes." *Adaptations*, 2:2, 2009, 180–90.

Griggs, Yvonne. " 'Humanity must perforce prey upon itself like monsters of the deep:' *King Lear* and the Urban Gangster Movie." *Adaptation*, 1:2, 2008, 121–39.

Hapgood, Robert. "Popularizing Shakespeare: The Artistry of Franco Zeffirelli." In *Shakespeare, the Movie: Popularizing the Plays on Film, TV and Video*. Eds. Lynda E. Boose and Richard Burt. London: Routledge, 1997, 80–94.

Hopkins, Lisa. "Mr. Darcy's Body: Privileging the Female Gaze." In *Jane Austen in Hollywood*. Eds. Linda Troost and Sayre Greenfield. Kentucky: The University Press of Kentucky, 1998, 111–21.

Hopkins, Lisa. *Relocating Shakespeare and Austen on Screen*. Basingstoke: Palgrave Macmillan, 2009.

Kaplan, Laurie. "Inside Out/Outside In: *Pride & Prejudice* on Film 2005." *Persuasions On-Line*, 27:2, 2007. www.jasna.org/persuasions/on-line/vol27no2/kaplan.htm. Accessed November 7, 2011.

Kaplan, Laurie. "Adapting *Emma* for the Twenty-First Century: An Emma No One Will Like." *Persuasions On-Line*, 30:1, 2009. www.jasna.org/persuasions/on-line/vol30no1/kaplan.html. Accessed November 7, 2011.

Katsoulis, Melissa. "Match Made in Heaven." The Times Playlist. October 3–9, 2009.

Lodge, David. Ed. *Jane Austen, Emma: A Casebook*. Basingstoke: Macmillan, 1968.

McAleer, John. "What a Biographer Can Learn About Jane Austen From *Emma*." *Persuasions*, 13, 1991. www.jasna.org/persuasions/printed/number13/mcaleer.htm. Accessed November 7, 2011.

McMullan, Gordon. " 'Plenty of blood. That's the only writing:' (Mis)representing Jacobean Tragedy in Turn-Of-The Century Cinema." In *The Spectacular In and Around Shakespeare*. Ed. Pascale Drouet. Newcastle upon Tyne: Cambridge Scholars Publishing, 2009, 123–36.

Moore, Charles. "This Misjudged 'Emma' is a Pedant's Dream." *The Daily Telegraph*, October

27, 2009. www.telegraph.co.uk/comment/columnists/charlesmoore/6443318/This-misjudged-Emma-is-a-pedants-dream.html. Accessed November 7, 2011.

Mulvey, Laura. *Visual and Other Pleasures*. Bloomington: Indiana University Press, 1989.

Palmer, Sally B. "*Little Women* at Longbourn: The Re-Wrighting of *Pride and Prejudice*." *Persuasions On-Line*, 27:2, 2007. www.jasna.org/persuasions/on-line/vol27no2/palmer.htm. Accessed November 7, 2011.

Parrill, Sue. "What Meets the Eye: Landscape in the Films *Pride and Prejudice* and *Sense and Sensibility*." *Persuasions*, 21, 1999, 32–43.

Rokison, Abigail. "Interview: David Tennant on *Hamlet*." *Shakespeare*, 5:3, 2009, 291–303.

Rumbelow, Helen. "Tennant's Extra." *The Times*, section 2, December 28, 2009.

Sánchez, Romero and Mari Carmen. "A la Señorita Austen: An Overview of Spanish Adaptations." *Persuasions On-Line*, 28:2, 2008. www.jasna.org/persuasions/on-line/vol28no2/sanchez.htm. Accessed November 7, 2011.

Spence, Jon. *Becoming Jane Austen*. London: Hambledon, 2003.

Stewart-Beer, Catherine. "Style over Substance? *Pride & Prejudice* (2005) Proves itself a Film for Our Time." *Persuasions On-Line*, 27:2, 2007. www.jasna.org/persuasions/on-line/vol27no2/stewart-beer.htm. Accessed November 7, 2011.

Troost, Linda and Sayre Greenfield. "Appropriating Austen: Localism on the Global Scene." *Persuasions On-Line*, 28:2, 2008. www.jasna.org/persuasions/on-line/vol28no2/troost-greenfield.htm. Accessed November 7, 2011.

14
Austen and Sterne: Beyond Heritage

Ariane Hudelet

Associating Austen and Sterne in an article on film adaptation may seem odd. Whereas the former has enjoyed cinematic fame ever since the beginning of the cinematic "Austenmania" in 1995, so that the heading "Austen films" is now considered as a subgenre within film adaptations of literary classics, Sterne's work was for a long time deemed unfilmable – until the first, and so far only, adaptation of his most famous work *Tristram Shandy* was directed by Michael Winterbottom in 2005. Austen's novels are love stories and present the evolution of a young woman moving towards self-knowledge and marriage; they follow a neat, fairy-tale-like, three-part structure, and are delivered in a crisp and ironical third-person narrative voice. Tristram's story, on the contrary, is told by a first-person narrator who keeps digressing and lamenting the fact that his life is quicker than his writing; the narrative also plays with an apparently loose and jumbled structure and is devoid of any sense of closure. "Austen films" are commonly considered as the epitome of the heritage film genre (a conservative, nostalgic representation of the past which relishes in the splendor of great mansions, impeccable manners, and exotic period detail in a fantasy of authenticity, while obliterating any social or political criticism), so much so that many people keep associating them with the productions of Merchant Ivory, although James Ivory never adapted any Austen novel.[1] For the time being, there is no such thing as "Sterne films."

Yet, Michael Winterbottom's feature film *A Cock and Bull Story* (2005) and one of the latest television adaptations of Austen, *Lost in Austen* (ITV, 2008), a miniseries written by Guy Andrews and directed by Dan Zeff, have a lot in common, and what they share allows us to reflect on a new type of adaptation, one that could be called

A Companion to Literature, Film, and Adaptation, First Edition. Edited by Deborah Cartmell.
© 2012 Blackwell Publishing Ltd. Published 2012 by Blackwell Publishing Ltd.

postmodern or metafictional, and to examine how more and more films today tend to both acknowledge and circumvent "the problem with adaptation," that is to say the irreducible expectations of a substantial part of the audience to experience "their" reading of the novel when watching the film adaptation, which inevitably leads to disappointment.[2] Both films manage to integrate in their own substance, structure and aesthetics, a reflection on how contemporary technologies and new modes of producing and consuming culture influence the way films are made, texts are received, and fiction is perceived. Austen and Sterne themselves experimented with a relatively new form – the modern novel as it developed in eighteenth-century Britain in a specific economic and social context which conditioned the emergence of a different kind of fiction writing. According to Ian Watt, they could be considered each in their own way, as successful syntheses of the achievements of the most influential novelists of the early eighteenth century, both using and subverting the conventions of the genre (1987: 290–301). Today, these adaptations of classics illustrate how, by associating features of traditional heritage films and a reflection on images, texts and representation in our postmodern era, one can still use some of the conventions of heritage films while subverting them at the same time, just as Austen and Sterne themselves already played with the conventions of the form they were using.

Technological Changes, the Status of the Image, and "a New Province of Adaptation"

At the beginning of the twenty-first century, new technological developments in the film industry and in media and communication in general, are changing our modes of perception and representation, our ways of seeing and watching, and our relationship with reality and art. We are undergoing a "digital revolution" in which the widespread development of computer-generated images and the possible replacement of celluloid film by digital technologies shed a new light on our understanding of what an image is.[3] Cinema has always been associated with both realism and imagination, as Robert Stam explains: from the very first films of the Lumière brothers and Georges Méliès, cinema has "conjugate[d] the realistic and the fantastical" (2005: 13) and is thus inscribed in the history of all art, which is "nourished by the tension between magic and realism, reflexivity and illusionism" (2). Yet, even in the cinematic works that developed the magic side of the form, the technical process of shooting on celluloid film still implied that the filmic image was a mechanical "print" of the light that had struck the objects in front of the camera. André Bazin provided what is probably the most influential analysis of the "realistic," or "ontological" nature of the film image (1967: 9–16), and Bernardo Bertolucci claimed that "every film, even fictional, was also a documentary" (Nowell-Smith and Halberstadt, 2000: 248).[4] It is this mechanical, documentary nature of the cinematic image that seems to be gradually giving way to an image that bears no mechanical, indexical relationship with the referential "real," a filmic image which can be created *ex nihilo* by a computer. The "realism" of the celluloid film is gradually replaced by the "hyperreality" of the digital image, and the widespread use of digital imagery, sometimes combined with celluloid footage, casts doubt on the "documentary" status of the filmic image; in Robert Stam's words, it "de-ontologizes the indexical, Bazinian image" (Stam and Raengo, 2005: 12). This is what Stam calls "adaptation in a post-celluloid world," pointing out that "film production and consumption – and adaptation theory – will be irrevocably changed by the digital revolution." The latter "undermine(s) the question of 'original' and 'copy'" and thus questions the hierarchy that has long presided over adaptation studies (Stam and Raengo, 2005: 11–12). Indeed, although the term "fidelity" is today generally dismissed as an inadequate criterion for serious study, the relation to the "source" text seems to come back with a vengeance in many case studies and the spontaneous reaction to an adaptation inevitably brings up the comparative approach with the "original" work. But, as Stam points out, if there is no longer any "original," or any "copy," this idea of "fidelity" can no longer exist. We could thus draw a parallel between the belief in the essential "realism" of the film image and the belief in a possible "fidelity" of a film adaptation to the text it is adapted from. Just as one believes that film is an indexical image of the real, one can believe that a film adaptation ought to be, or could be, an indexical image of "the reality" of the text. This idea of a "real" nature or interpretation of a text was already greatly criticized in the days of Roland Barthes and Umberto Eco, who developed the idea that a text was something incomplete that became actual only through a specific reading, an "open work" susceptible to many diverse, and possibly antagonistic, but equally valid, interpretations (Barthes, 1978; Eco, 1987). Yet, in spite of the critical debate, the questions of "fidelity" and "truth" still commonly appear, for instance, in the avowed ambitions of certain films, especially heritage films. In interviews of the film crew, or passages from the press kits, one can still read about the ideal of "authenticity," or the need to remain "true to the spirit of the author."[5] Even the titles of the films themselves can sometimes convey the idea that new adaptations can pretend to be closer than ever to the texts they are adapted from: from *Bram Stoker's Dracula* (1992) to *Mary Shelley's Frankenstein* (1994) or *Jane Austen's Emma* (ITV, 1996), it is as if recent films, with their elaborate audiovisual techniques, claimed this greater definition, this historical accuracy, and an ability to get closer to the characters. The simulacrum – to use Baudrillard's concept – becomes "more real" than the real (Baudrillard, 1994).

Yet such ambitions often lead to dissatisfaction or disappointment: it is not *Jane Austen's Emma*, just another *Emma*. It is not *Bram Stoker's Dracula* but Coppola's *Dracula*. This dissatisfaction and the acknowledgment of the "aporias" of fidelity (Stam and Raengo, 2005: 14) have paved the way to another type of adaptation. Instead of pretending that the possibilities of film have expanded thanks to these technological innovations, other films seem to integrate within their construction and choices the essential blurring of the limits between the real and the fictional, and the impossibility or the non-desirability of producing a cinematic "copy" of a literary antecedent. Metafictional or self-referential adaptations, films which reflect on their own mode of representation rather than pretend to reproduce the story and characters from the source, are not a radically new phenomenon. Zeff's and Winterbottom's films can be placed in the tradition of movies based on literary texts produced in the past two decades, which do not try to provide a definitive version of the text, but instead attempt to represent rather our relationship to literary works, to capture a specific type of reception at a specific moment. Al Pacino's *Looking for Richard* (1996) for instance represents Pacino himself preparing his adaptation of Shakespeare's *Richard III*, doing research on the period, asking people in the streets of Manhattan what they thought of William Shakespeare, interviewing scholars and performers, casting his actors, and rehearsing the scenes. Charlie Kaufman's script for Spike Jonze's *Adaptation* (2002) represents the difficulty of a screenwriter (named Charlie Kaufman) faced with the daunting task of adapting Susan Orlean's nonfiction novel *The Orchid Thief*. More indirectly they can be also placed in the line of the numerous adaptations which transpose works from the past into a late twentieth-century or early twenty-first-century context, such as Amy Heckerling's *Clueless* (1995), Baz Lurhmann's *Romeo + Juliet* (1996), or Tim Blake Nelson's *O* (2001), and thus, simultaneously, represent a dialogue between a story from the past and our own present reality.

But the specificity of *Lost in Austen* and *A Cock and Bull Story* is the way their metafictional approaches are also shaped by changes in media and modes of production and consumption of culture, and the way they manage to play with the conventions of heritage films, neither completely endorsing nor disavowing the genre. Just as another eighteenth-century novelist, Henry Fielding, in his novel *Tom Jones*, claims that he was venturing into a "new province of writing,"[6] we could go as far as to say that the two films which we will now focus on reflect a "new province of adaptation," which could correspond to what Thomas Leitch calls "the postliterary adaptation" (2007: 257–79). These films, even if they are without a doubt adapted from Austen or Sterne, are also, to a large extent, adapted from other visual rather than written texts: video-games, previous heritage films, television series, documentaries, and popular culture items. Both stretch the meaning of adaptation to its furthest limits, and shift it to what Stam calls a logic of "cut'n mix and sampling" (Stam and Raengo, 2005: 12) rather than copying, reproducing, or recreating.

Lost in Austen: Hyperreal Austen or the Ultimate Fantasy

The very beginning of the first episode of the ITV miniseries *Lost in Austen* can be seen as the representation of the fantasy of "Austenites," those avid readers who cherish the works of the novelist so much that they sometimes tend to consider the world and characters of the novels as a happy alternative to their own. The first shot is an extreme close-up on the Penguin edition of *Pride and Prejudice*, before we discover a modern woman in her early thirties, dressed in a leather jacket and jeans, opening the book and settling down in her comfortable couch to read it, while her voiceover explains: "It is a truth generally acknowledged that we're all longing to escape." The sequence dissolves from her intent look at the pages of the book to the way her imagination stages the diegetic world of the novel: a carriage driving through the countryside, an elegant assembly at a ball, a dark silhouette on horseback standing out against the sunset, which dissolves to the words written on the page while the voiceover continues: "I escape *always* to my favorite book, *Pride and Prejudice*. I've read it so many times now the words just say themselves in my head and it's like a window opening." When another dissolve presents a medium shot of the back of a tall gentleman who is standing in his garden and surveying the vast expanse of his elegant park, her narration becomes more specific: "It's like I'm actually there! It's become a place I know so . . . *intimately*. I can *see* that world, I can . . . *touch* it." After a brief subjective point-of-view shot of a large alley, we discover the reader herself, in an empire-line dress, now inscribed in her fantasy (an idealized world, suffused in glowing sunlight, and made unreal by the soft blurring of the edges of the frame, the use of slow motion, and by the replacement of direct sound by the voiceover and the nondiegetic music). She appears to be looking for someone, running towards the tall gentleman, until a final subjective point-of-view shot shows us the latter about to turn around towards us ("I can see Darcy"). But before we can discover his face, the editing jerks us back to the present, cutting to the reader quickly shutting her book as if overwhelmed by the excitement of such a fantasy ("Wow . . . Amanda!"), and pausing, out of breath, before returning to her solitary pleasure of reading Austen ("Now . . . where was I?").

This representation of the powerful sense of identification the novel still produces in contemporary readers leads to a magical story in which Amanda Price, the modern-day reader, is accidentally stranded in the diegetic world of *Pride and Prejudice*. Amanda is interrupted in her reading by the arrival of her uncouth and drunk boyfriend who delivers a very unromantic proposal before falling asleep in front of the television. She hears some noise in her bathroom and discovers an intruder, who turns out to be Elizabeth Bennet. The explanation that is provided – a secret door that is "entirely without sense in the attic at Longbourn," and that would not open until then – very quickly indicates that any idea of realism or verisimilitude is out of the question. On their second encounter, Amanda ventures into the passage, the door closes behind her, and she is forced to remain in Longbourn and to take her place among the Bennets at the beginning of the plot of *Pride and Prejudice* which she knows by heart. Elizabeth, meanwhile, will be following her own, off-screen adventure, in early twenty-first century London. The series feeds on the extreme phenomenon of identification and projection that Jane

Austen's novels and their very popular screen adaptations create. Ever since it began with three film adaptations in 1995, "Austenmania" has waxed and waned, but never disappeared. The cinematic and television popularity of the author went together with a surge of Austen websites and forums on the internet. The readers and viewers could pursue the stories online, and share their reactions, questions and interpretations with fellow e-Austenites.[7] The web was the perfect imaginary space to give shape to this tendency among many readers to consider these novels as alternate worlds in which one can "escape," a substitute reality that is a salutary alternative to ours.

Lost in Austen thus seems to be an adaptation of many things other than Austen's text. It also adapts a kind of textual reception and appropriation, and it offers insight into this new imaginary space in which literary texts are received, transformed, appropriated, and re-imagined, a space which is informed by the original stories and characters of course, but also by the numerous film adaptations of this specific novel and other Austen adaptations, by other heritage films, and by the entire cultural environment of contemporary readers, whether cultural productions or artifacts. It does indeed, as Laurie Kaplan observes, use the device of the magical door (2008), but what Amanda finds behind this door when she enters the fictional space of *Pride and Prejudice* is clearly identified as her *own* imaginary representation of the novel. Several shots from the pre-credits sequence I described above are indeed repeated later on in the film – in episodes 3 and 4, for instance when Amanda, wearing the same dress, does indeed run through the gardens of Pemberley towards Darcy, once she has decided to remain in the diegetic world of *Pride and Prejudice* in Elizabeth's stead, who also finds it preferable to follow her destiny in the age of computers and electrical appliances. The only difference, when the shots are associated with Amanda's "real" presence in the world of *Pride and Prejudice*, is that the blurry edges are replaced with a clear focus, that there is no slow motion any more, and that Darcy does turn back to face her and accept this "intimacy" that Amanda had already been experiencing before physically entering *Pride and Prejudice*.

The series can thus be placed in the tradition of recent narratives such as Philip Pullman's *His Dark Materials*, a trilogy (1995, 1997, 2000) based on the existence of parallel worlds, or novels such as Jasper Fforde's *The Eyre Affair* (2001), in which characters can "book jump" and penetrate the texts of classical literature. Just as the intervention of Fforde's heroine, Thursday Next, in the plot of *Jane Eyre*, eventually changes the ending of Brontë's novel, Amanda Price also changes the ending of *Pride and Prejudice*. The fantasy comes full circle, appropriation is absolute, and *Pride and Prejudice* has actually become her story. But the visual representation of this alternate universe of the literary story owes a lot to other, nonliterary forms among which video-games are probably the most influential. *Lost in Austen* was originally the title of a "choose your own adventure" book; the series also relies on the same principle of interactivity and appropriation of the plot, although its treatment is humorous and somewhat ironical. The point of interactivity is supposed to be the relative autonomy of the user or player: in an interactive story such as video-games, you can choose the direction the story is going to go because you make some key choices; you are in charge of some aspects of the plot. Yet here, what matters most for Amanda is to stick to the original plotline which she knows by heart, and she tries her best to keep the plot on track in spite of Elizabeth's absence, but her well-meaning efforts, as we expect, quickly lead to disaster and perfect chaos, until she finally accepts to endorse her autonomy in the plot. She decides, in the end, to replace Elizabeth – Darcy falls in love with her, and she has now become the heroine of the story.

The aesthetic choices and mise-en-scène do indeed reflect the influence of video-games. In the opening sequence, the several subjective point-of-view shots posit Amanda as our avatar. She is present in almost all the scenes, and our identification with her is stressed by the framing in which we see part of the back of her head or shoulder, blurred in the foreground, and in the use of fluid continuous tracking shots commonly used in video-games (such as those shots we have in the gardens at Pemberley). In order to increase our identification with her, and in accordance with the kinaesthetic experience that video-games provide, the film stresses the physical exoticism of that world and what it means for a contemporary body to find itself in that context, thus stressing the "reality" of that world which becomes tangible, concrete, and matter of fact. Just as Amanda claimed at the beginning that she could "see" and "touch" that world, the film stresses the sensual relation-ship she has with that world later on through a focus on physical and material detail. Close-ups on the plates served at Netherfield stress the discrepancy of culinary tastes between then and now; when, on her first night at Longbourn, Amanda tells her hosts that she would like to brush her teeth, they point to her a little wooden case with a bunch of twigs, some salt and chalk. Part of the pleasure of following Amanda is to feel what it is like to actually exist, physically, in that world, thus adopting what Joyce Goggin calls "the video game aesthetic, frequently mobilized to com-municate an intensified state of mind or sensory perception and to invite viewer involvement" (2007).

This trend is not radically new – the influence of interactivity and video-games was already present in Joe Wright's 2005 adaptation of *Pride and Prejudice*, a point Goggin thoroughly explored:

> the film continuously stresses Elizabeth's gaze and reinforces the viewer's identification with her viewpoint through the same techniques: continuous tracking shots, subjec-tive point of view shots, and the implication of the viewer through the kinesthetic illusion that they have entered a projected space and may explore and participate in this technologically mediated space (Goggin, 2007).

Many sequences in Wright's picture (the Netherfield ball and the sequence in the sculpture gallery at Pemberley being the most striking) rely on the breaking of the 180-degree rule that traditionally preserves visual illusion in film. Goggin explains that "video games hold out the illusion of having the freedom to move one's avatar a full 360 degrees at any given time" (2007), a freedom reproduced by the long, continuous, steadicam takes of *Pride & Prejudice*, the likes of which one can also find in *Lost in Austen*, notably for the scene of the final kiss between Amanda and Darcy, in which the camera revolves around the two before settling on a close-up of Amanda as she looks directly at the camera.

The use of video-game aesthetics is not the only link between *Lost in Austen* and earlier adaptations of Austen. The virtual reality in which Amanda evolves is presented as something extremely familiar to audiences, not just because of its use of the plot and characters of *Pride and Prejudice*, but because of the innumerable references (explicit and implicit) to film adaptations of her novels, and to heritage films in general. The series makes it very clear that today "Jane Austen" exists in the collective imagination maybe as much through her different incarnations as through her texts. The variety of references allows the film to appeal to very diverse types of audience (see Kaplan, 2008). Austen "purists" will probably be sensitive to the carefully crafted dialogues and successful pastiche of Austen lingo (for instance, when Elizabeth retorts to Amanda, who had just argued that she was not real but merely a character in a book: "It grieves me, Miss Price, that I must presume to dispute with you. I have my fleshy envelope as you yours"), or references to her other texts (as when, towards the end of episode 2, Amanda scolds Mr. Bingley and tells him, "It was badly done, Mr. Bingley. Badly done!", literally using Mr. Knightley's words of reproach to Emma in the eponymous novel). Fans of the Austen films will appreciate the innumerable references to previous adaptations: the pig "Lady Ambrosia" evokes the conspicuous presence of the animal in the Bennet household in Wright's film; and in episode 2, a shot of Mrs. Bennet and her daughters sitting next to each other on a couch is also a visual quotation from a similar shot at Netherfield, in Wright's film. Andrew Davies' seminal and widely popular BBC miniseries (1995) is also a constant subtext, from the similar piano tune that accompanies the opening credits to the bedroom scene in which Jane brushes Amanda's hair (a similar scene stressed the intimacy between Jane and Elizabeth in the miniseries), and of course the numerous references to Colin Firth's memorable interpretation of Darcy (which culminates in the moment when Elliot Cowan as Darcy, obliging a request from Amanda, is seen emerging from a pond, his white shirt sticking to his chest *à la* Firth, while Amanda gazes longingly and declares: "I'm having a bit of a strange postmodern moment here").[8] More generally, the attention to period detail, the stress on the manners of the time, the mise-en-scène of the balls, and the choice of pictorial framings offer a synthesis of the more traditional features of the heritage film genre, but unlike what is expected from a traditional heritage film, the whole point of the miniseries is indeed to be "unfaithful" to the novel, and Amanda's progress leads to independence from Austen; what matters is this new story constructed by the modern reader.

The remaining audience would of course be those who are not familiar with the story of *Pride and Prejudice*, whether text or film adaptations. For those, *Lost in Austen* also provides the simple pleasure of time-traveling, feeding on modern fiction, especially the popular television series *Doctor Who* (through the glimpse of a Tardis) or *Life on Mars*. The latter is indeed often mentioned by reviewers when they attempt to pitch *Lost in Austen* ("Jane Austen meets *Life on Mars*[9]"). In order to imply that the sentimental issues and existential worries of these characters are as modern as those, let's say, of contemporary women in an upper-class Californian suburb, the opening credits adopt a design that clearly resembles that of *Desperate Housewives*, with two-dimensional figures being propped up and down in front of a stylized background, with a quick editing between one little tableau and the next, and humorous connections between them. Finally, the title itself could be seen either as an echo to Sophia Coppola's *Lost in Translation* or even to the TV series *Lost*, which all depict characters taken out of their familiar surrounding and confronted with an alien environment.

Thus, while still insisting on the "authenticity" of this fictional world, as heritage films do, the series multiplies the confrontations between contemporary references and cultural artifacts (cell phones, cigarettes, or the tube travelcard that serves as a bookmark in the very first shot of the film – her journey being as simple as a daily commute) to establish what Laurie Kaplan calls "cultural connectedness" which makes the series "appealing to a young audience" (2008: 11). This cultural connectedness reaches a climax when Amanda and Darcy return to modern-day London and discover Elizabeth perfectly attuned to her new surroundings. On learning the name of Amanda's companion, Elizabeth exclaims "We have been married for two hundred years," and proves her point by "googling" him (Darcy played by Colin Firth) right in front of his eyes. We see here that "Jane Austen" exists as much on the internet as in her books today – and maybe more. The easy mix between reality and fiction presented in this tale, and the quick dismissal of verisimilitude or realism, can also be related to the increasing invasion of the fictional into our daily life, and of the related de-realization that tends to bring our daily life closer to the fictional. The ubiquity of virtual, computerized reality, the quickness of communication and exchanges, the absolute accessibility of the entire world from one's computer screen, all this leads to a redefinition of what the real is. The experience of a novel through film adaptation becomes an avatar of these daily fictional activities which tend to fill our lives, and since human contacts are more and more dematerialized by the new means of communication, the "reality" of the fictional world becomes greater, even if its shape is fluctuating and unstable since the principle of interactivity implies that readers have more and more control over the material and can refashion it as they please.

A Cock and Bull Story and the "(un)making-of"

Lost and Austen and *A Cock and Bull Story* both question the relationship between reality and fiction, albeit in a very different manner. The absolute "wish fulfillment" that we find in the miniseries is a far cry from the overall tone of *A Cock and Bull Story*. In order to adapt this reputably "unfilmable" novel, the filmmaker chooses to present a shooting crew trying to complete the production of *Tristram Shandy*, the movie, but not really succeeding in doing so, just as Tristram never succeeds in telling the story of his life in the novel. The film thus transforms a metatext into a metafilm by adopting the form of a mock-documentary, or mockumentary alternating sequences taken from the novel (shot in costumes and on period sets) and sequences showing the trivial stories of the actors and members of the crew, the difficult shooting conditions or financial problems of production. The main actors play their own parts: Steve Coogan plays Steve Coogan who plays Tristram Shandy and his father Walter Shandy, Rob Brydon plays Rob Brydon who plays Uncle Toby, Gillian Anderson plays Gillian Anderson who plays Widow Wadman. But the system is not rigid since other actors also play the part of the director (Jeremy Northam for instance plays the director, Mark, who is not named Michael Winterbottom). The scenes that are directly adapted from the novel are not very numerous, and yet we do get the "sense" or the nonsense of the novel better than in any adaptation which would have tried to remain close to the seemingly chaotic plot construction of the novel. Beside the major plot moments such as the conception of Tristram, his birth, his accidental circumcision, or Uncle Toby's reconstitution of the battle of Namur in the garden of Shandy Hall – the film manages to transpose the "digressive and progressive" (Sterne, 1985: 95) nature of Sterne's novel, and to cinematically recreate this heterogeneous, overwhelming nature of the novel, thus translating the novel's refusal of closure and of a cohesive form.

The influence of new technologies and the changing status of the image on *A Cock and Bull Story* may be harder to decipher. There is no use of video-game aesthetics, nor are there many references to the internet or to contemporary popular culture, and the technique of the film within the film is something that has been done before, as the numerous filmic references within the film indicate. *A Cock and Bull Story* is perhaps more a palimpsest than an adaptation. Just as *Lost in Austen* multiplied the references to previous films, Winterbottom incorporates other films in his own substance: well-known scores are recycled, such as Nino Rota's music for Fellini's *8 ½* (1963), another film in which a film crew finds it hard to complete their project. When Steve Coogan first appears on the screen as Tristram Shandy, Michael Nyman's pastiche of Purcell composed for Peter Greenaway's *The Draughtsman's Contract* accompanies a wide-angle shot of the façade of a grand estate such as the one in Greenaway's film.[10] In the "fictional parts," Tristram, the narrator, speaks directly to the camera as has been the fashion recently to adapt intrusive narrators – we saw Henry Fielding impersonated and directly addressing us in the 1997 BBC/A&E miniseries *The History of Tom Jones*, or Alex Kingston as *Moll Flanders* recurrently breaking the fictional illusion to call upon the viewer in the Granada miniseries *Moll Flanders* (1996). This palimpsestic dimension shows that Winterbottom's film is also about the abundance of images. By contrasting a "fictional part" and a "documentary part," the film presents itself as a making of, in which we have the pleasure of seeing "behind the scenes," as if we were privy to what supposedly happens "off-screen." The film thus invites us to reflect on the fact that almost everything today can be recorded, and that not only are fictional films constantly recycling elements from previous works (here more explicitly than in others), but they are also surrounded by a multitude of images supposedly revealing the "reality" of the filmmaking beyond the fiction. Almost every film today has its own "making of" that will be included on the DVD or broadcast after or before the film on cable channels, but here the making of has blended with the film itself.

Considering that Sterne's novel is a parody of the conventions of realism as they were established in the eighteenth-century novel, a scathing review in *Eighteenth-Century Studies* considered the film to be irrelevant and simplistic because of this apparent opposition between a "real" and a "fictional" world in the adaptation:

> None of this succeeds – in large part because the director rests satisfied with the belief that these scenes represent "reality" as opposed to the "fiction" he is filming. But of course, these actors are no more real than the characters in *Tristram Shandy*, and probably a great deal less (New, 2006: 579).

But this accusation misses the point since the film does indeed subtly question the separation between fiction and reality, and examines the pleasure as well as the limits of artistic representation, by adopting and undermining at the same time the techniques associated with the documentary, and more specifically the "making of." The criticism is based on the degree of "reality" of these actors or characters whereas *A Cock and Bull Story* precisely manages to question the "documentary" status of the film image and the different levels of fiction and of spectatorial belief. The film delights in making us lose our bearings, notably by associating this documentary style with many cinematic techniques that stress the artificiality of editing: wipes, irises, freeze-frames, split-screens, voiceover narration, flashbacks and flash forwards, etc., which are used to mimic the pervading and self-conscious narration of the novel. Conversely, the film chooses to preserve a continuity between the "fictional" and the "real" sequences, as Michael Winterbottom explains in an interview:

> [...] there was the choice of keeping the two halves very separate or merging them together and this way the film becomes more coherent and people are encouraged to make connections. It was the same with the shooting: we decided to do both parts handheld, with available light, so instead of emphasizing the difference we kept things relatively close (Spencer, 2006: 17).

The choice of actor Steven Coogan to perform Tristram and Walter Shandy also contributes to this dizzying blurring of the fictional and the real. The film focuses on the central competition and bickering between leading actors Steve Coogan and Rob Brydon, and on their respective personae. The public persona of Steve Coogan reinforces this uncertainty between fiction and reality since he is famous in the UK for his character of Alan Partridge, a fictional television and radio presenter who has acquired a sort of autonomous existence and has remained intimately associated with Coogan's own personality. When the film shows Steve Coogan interviewed by Tony Wilson, they first begin to discuss Coogan's past as Alan Partridge. When asked about the influence of Alan Partridge over his performance as Tristram, Coogan answers that, although people have seen some Alan Partridge in all his impersonations, "there was a character who came before Alan Partridge, and that character was called . . . Steve Coogan." Thus, Steve Coogan, asked about his interpretation of a character called Steve Coogan, refers to himself as first and foremost a "character." And since the character in the film is directly based on the "real" Steve Coogan (his well-known ambition, his aborted career in Hollywood, and even his scandalous affair with a prostitute are all elements from reality that are taken up by the film script), confusing what is real and what is fictional is inevitable. One can also argue that what the general audience knows about the "real" Steve Coogan could also be considered as fictional, since it's a public persona that is constructed by the media and possibly by the actor himself. So this highly postmodern construction is also based on the question of the truth conveyed by images and on the impossibility of knowing this truth through representation, be it a fictional film or public opinion. It thus resonates magnificently with Sterne's novel, which is also about the impossibility of knowing oneself, of establishing one's identity through the process of writing. In Winterbottom's film, the issue is acting, appearances, and public image. What is our "reality" when it is transposed in today's society where everything is visible and recordable, but where the sense of "truth" constantly evades us – just as truth through literary fiction evades Tristram because life is quicker than writing? When Tristram, in Sterne's novel, attempts to draw his uncle Toby's character, he expresses this aporia, the fact we can never depict anyone accurately, whatever means we choose to adopt (music, science, or painting):

> Others, to mend the matter, will make a drawing of you in the *Camera*; – that is most unfair of all,– because *there* you are sure to be represented in some of your most ridiculous attitudes.
>
> To avoid all and every one of these errors, in giving you my uncle Toby's character, I am determined to draw it by no mechanical help whatever –. . . in a word, I will draw my uncle Toby's character from his Hobby-Horse (Sterne, 1985: 98).

Winterbottom's own *camera* does not try to capture the novel directly either; it manages to *draw* its story indirectly. And the complex interrogations it raises as to the truth of characters and the identity of these actors resonates perfectly with Sterne's questioning of textual representation.

Sterne's book materially included this investigation into the limits of textual representation. The formal experiments of the novel are famous: such as changes in typography, the insertion of a black page after the death of Parson Yorick, or the graphic representation of his storylines and digressions through serpentine lines.

They have led some to consider this novel, as Steve Coogan declares in a mock interview included in the film, "a postmodern classic written before there was any modernism to be post about" – a catchy presentation of the novel that "sounds" nice in a promotional interview but which would probably be considered simplistic by scholarly experts. In his film, Winterbottom also includes a reflexion on the new means of access to the film and on the way they influence our reception of it. The film is no longer only a fixed, single object that is watched in a theater. It is now more commonly watched on DVD, or on the internet. The DVD edition of *A Cock and Bull Story* reflects this careful attention to the object as part of the film product itself. Today film viewing is preceded or followed by other modes of "consumption," and there is a multitude of byproducts which contribute to its reception. The DVD special features for instance generally provide interviews of the cast, a making-of, deleted or extended scenes. Here, we see that these bonuses work to increase the uncertainty as to what is real and what is fictional. We never know when the actors answering questions are in earnest or continuing to play their parts, because the characters in the film are so much inspired by their supposedly "real" person (again, a tricky issue when dealing with public figures submitted to artificial media exposure).

A good example would be the bonus on the premiere of the film, which mainly consists in footage of the party which followed the projection, and in brief interviews of members of the crew or other guests that seem to remain in the same tongue-in-cheek tone as the film. We never know how much credence to give to statements made about the difficult personality of Steve Coogan, or about the competition between him and Brydon. It contrasts greatly with the usual special features on DVDs that are extremely codified and follow marketing rules dictating a very stereotypical kind of expression – one that is rather simplistic, and overwhelmingly positive. Here, we have the opposite since the palpable tension between Steve Coogan and Rob Brydon that was at the center of the film continues, whereas we know (from other articles and interviews – but then, does that mean it is "true"?) that the two actors are friends "in real life."

Other special features on the DVD edition are the "deleted scenes," "scene extensions," and "behind the scene footage," the latter category being difficult to understand since *A Cock and Bull Story* already presents itself as a "making of." The most puzzling example is probably "the complete Tony Wilson interview," to which we already alluded. Steve Coogan indeed performed the part of Tony Wilson (the famous Manchester music mogul) in a previous Winterbottom film, *24-Hour Party People* (2002), but now the "real" Tony Wilson faces the actor who impersonated him in a previous film and interviews him about the new film being made. At the beginning of the interview sequence in the film, an unidentified voiceover – which we hear only once – announces "If you want to see the EPK interview, it will part of the DVD package, along with extended versions of many of the scenes, which should act as footnotes to the main film," thus openly placing the relationship between the film and these satellite films in the line of the relationship between the text and its "para-text" (Sterne also plays repeatedly with footnotes, see Sterne, 1985: 83, 164, 184, etc.). Now, in the special features, the interview is thus presented as the "reality" behind the fictional or maybe as an "extended scene" — we cannot be certain as the footage was not placed in the other categories in which it may have fitted. In spite of the time clock underneath the frame and the rather poor quality of the sound, the documentary status of the footage is dubious: it is not the version that was supposedly "shot" by Tony Wilson's crew but a final editing of different footage. Some was apparently shot by the camera that stands next to the interviewer but we also have many reverse shots, from different angles, notably shots of Tony Wilson himself or his soundman. Coogan's attitude is also paradoxical, since he "plays" the role of the interviewee in an artificial manner — at one point, for instance, he interrupts his answer and lets out a strange, unnatural laugh as if he had forgotten his lines.

The film thus subtly deals with the evanescent limit between reality and fiction in the domain of public record and images. A somewhat unsettling film, *A Cock and Bull Story* takes up the ultimate challenge for realism: that of chaos. It is no use pretending we can give artificial form to the chaotic real; we can just mimic its lack of order and laugh about it, before we die. The time of the shooting has replaced the time of the writing, and the personal ambition of the actor substitutes itself for that of the character-narrator, but in the end both the novel and the film are about the same vanity of life and of artistic representation, as a French reviewer of the film pointed out:

> [...] *Tristram Shandy* presents a mise en abyme of the essential incapacity of literature to grasp life, and mimics this incapacity from page to page. Well, likewise, cinema grasps life, but on a substance that vanishes: its body remains fluid, a film that unrolls, a ray of light which disappears, immaterial images which float away in our memory. The feelings of persistence and loss are simultaneous (Baumann, 2006: 119, my translation).

Both films therefore illustrate the evolution of the status of "reality" in film in the age of computer-generated images, new media, and new modes of cultural consumption. If *Lost in Austen* erases the limit between the fictional and the real by embracing the romantic idea that fiction is just another possible world, *A Cock and Bull Story* prefers to focus on doubt and uncertainty, showing that film can no longer be seen as a believable document of reality because the degree of staging and acting (and digital manipulation) can never clearly be established. In spite of their differences, both films comment on the naive belief of the value of reality over fiction and reassert the sheer pleasure of fiction, be it romantic and wish-fulfilling, or, above all, frustrating and puzzling. A long way from traditional heritage films, they force us to relocate the issues of adaptation in a totally different realm from that of duplication, copy or fidelity, but reassert fictional or cinematic pleasure, and a sense of continuity between the literary world, the cinematic or television world, and our own.

NOTES

1 This is with the possible exception of *Jane Austen in Manhattan* which can hardly be considered as an adaptation, and certainly not a heritage film since it represents the competition between two New York theatrical companies to stage a recently retrieved manuscript of Austen's adaptation of Richardson's *Sir Charles Grandison*.

2 "It is hard to suppress a sort of yearning for a faithful rendering of one's own version of the literary text" (McFarlane, 2007: 15).

3 See Prince (1996: 27).

4 Both Bazin and Bertolucci are quoted in Burgoyne (2003: 220–1).

5 See for instance the interview of Joe Wright by Sara Michelle Fetters: "I wanted to be respectful to this 21-year-old girl who sat in a parlor in the south of England and wrote this book. I wanted to be true to her. [...] I was interested in being true to her spirit and the spirit in her stories." January, 2011. www.moviefreak.com/features/interviews/

joewright.htm. Accessed November 8, 2011.

6 "[...] as I am in reality, the founder of a new province of writing, so I am at liberty to make what laws I please therein" (Fielding, 1994: 65).

7 The Republic of Pemberley is probably the first, and the most imposing of these websites. See www.pemberley.com. November 8, 2011.

8 This also evokes *Bridget Jones's Diary* (novel by Helen Fielding, 1996, film directed by Sharon Maguire, 2001) and its representation of Darcymania.

9 See for instance Rifkind (2008) or Anita Singh (2008).

10 The French title for Winterbottom's film developed this reference since the film was released as *Tournage dans un Jardin Anglais/Shooting in an English Garden*, a parody of the French title of Greenaway's picture, *Meurtre dans un Jardin Anglais/Murder in an English Garden*.

REFERENCES

Austen, Jane. *Pride and Prejudice*. London: Norton, 2001. (Original published 1813.)

Baudrillard, Jean. *Simulacra and Simulation*. Trans. Sheila Glaser. Ann Arbor: University of Michigan Press, 1994. (Original published 1981.)

Baumann, Fabien. "*Tournage dans un jardin anglais*: la trace sur le film." [Shooting in an English Garden.] *Positif*, 545–6, 2006, 118–19.

Barthes, Roland. "The Death of the Author." In *Image, Music, Text*. Trans. Stephen Heath. New York: Hill and Wang, 1978, 142–8. (Original published 1968.)

Bazin, André. "The Ontology of the Photographic Image." In *André Bazin. What Is Cinema?* Vol.

1. Trans. Hugh Gray. Berkeley: University of California Press, 1967, 9–16. (Original published 1958.)

Burgoyne, Robert. "Memory, History and Digital Imagery in Contemporary Film. In *Memory and Popular Film*. Ed. Paul Grainge. Manchester: Manchester University Press, 2003, 220–36.

A Cock and Bull Story. Dir. Michael Winterbottom. Screenplay by Frank Cottrell Boyce. UK: BBC, 2005.

Eco, Umberto. *The Open Work*. Trans. Anna Cancogni. Harvard: Harvard University Press, 1987. (Original published 1962.)

Fielding, Henry. *Tom Jones*. Harmondsworth: Penguin, 1994. (Original published 1748.)

Goggin, Joyce. "*Pride and Prejudice* Reloaded: Navigating the Space of Pemberley." *Persuasion Online*, 27:2, 2007. January 2011. www.jasna.org/persuasions/on-line/vol27no2/goggin.htm.

Kaplan, Laurie. "Completely Without Sense: *Lost in Austen*." *Persuasions*, 30, 2008, 241–54.

Leitch, Thomas. *Film Adaptation and its Discontents: From* Gone with the Wind *to* The Passion of the Christ. Baltimore: Johns Hopkins University Press, 2007.

Lost in Austen. Dir. Dan Zeff. Screenplay by Guy Andrews. UK: ITV, 4 episodes, 2008.

McFarlane, Brian. "Reading Film and Literature." In *The Cambridge Companion to Literature on Screen*. Eds. Deborah Cartmell and Imelda Whelehan. Cambridge: Cambridge University Press, 2007, 15–28.

New, Melvyn. "Tristram Shandy: A Cock and Bull Story." *Eighteenth-Century Studies*, 39:4, 2006, 579–81.

Nowell-Smith, Geoffrey and Ilona Halberstadt. "Interview with Bernardo Bertolucci." In *Bernardo Bertolucci: Interviews*. Eds. Fabien S. Gerard, T. Jefferson Kline, and Bruce Sklarew. Jackson: University Press of Mississippi, 2000.

Prince, Stephen. "True Lies: Perceptual Realism, Digital Images and Film Theory." *Film Quarterly*, 49:3, 1996, 27.

Rifkind, Hugo. "*Pride and Prejudice* Meets *Life on Mars* in ITV1's *Lost in Austen*." *The Times*, August 30, 2008. http://entertainment.timesonline.co.uk/tol/arts_and_entertainment/tv_and_radio/article4613100.ece. January, 2011.

Singh, Anita. "Jane Austen Meets *Life on Mars* in New ITV Drama." *The Telegraph*, August 5, 2008. www.telegraph.co.uk/news/uknews/2505190/Jane-Austen-meets-Life-On-Mars-in-new-ITV-drama.html. January, 2011.

Spencer, Liese. "The Postmodernist Always Wings it Twice." *Sight and Sound*, 2, 2006, 14–17.

Stam, Robert. *Literature through Film, Realism Magic and the Art of Adaptation*. Oxford: Blackwell, 2005.

Stam, Robert and Alessandra Raengo. Eds. *Literature and Film: A Guide to the Theory and Practice of Film Adaptation*. Oxford: Blackwell, 2005.

Sterne, Laurence. *The Life and Opinions of Tristram Shandy*. Harmondsworth: Penguin, 1985. (Original published 1761–7.)

Watt, Ian. "Realism and the Later Tradition: A Note." In *The Rise of the Novel*. Ian Watt. London: Hogarth, 1987, 290–301. (Original published 1957.)

15
Neo-Victorian Adaptations

Imelda Whelehan

Neo-Victorian studies has "arrived" and its progression to academic respectability has taken a similar path to adaptation studies. While screen adaptations of literature are as old as film technology and take momentum from the rage for theatrical adaptations, neo-Victorian studies reflect on the more contemporary phenomenon of the recent increase in novels which exploit the idea of the Victorian period, either by rewriting classic texts (such as *Great Expectations* (1861) or *Jane Eyre* (1847)), pastiching a Victorian narrative style, and/or a focus on topics that promise to expose the less seemly underside of Victorian culture. Given the newness of the area as academic study[1] it has garnered an astonishing amount of interest and yet, in common with adaptations, the area inspires fascination and loathing in equal parts. Mark Llewellyn observes that neo-Victorian studies "has the potential to help us think through the ways in which we teach, research and publish on the Victorians themselves" (2008: 165), suggesting that its presence within and beyond Victorian studies has paradigm-shifting potential. I begin this chapter with such comparisons in order to state the obvious and get it out of way: neo-Victorian literary texts are themselves adaptations; even when they do not refer back to a single Urtext, they remain compatible with contemporary definitions of adaptation and appropriation.

In *A Theory of Adaptation* (2006) Linda Hutcheon observes that adaptations are "inherently 'palimpsestuous' works, haunted at all times by their adapted texts" (6), and this also offers a broad definition of the neo-Victorian novel. This continues her earlier exploration of "historiographic metafiction" as a postmodern tendency which

A Companion to Literature, Film, and Adaptation, First Edition. Edited by Deborah Cartmell.
© 2012 Blackwell Publishing Ltd. Published 2012 by Blackwell Publishing Ltd.

narrates the past self-consciously and with an acceptance that what constitutes "history" is fluid, changing and contested, and underscores many neo-Victorian authors' ambition to "rewrite the past in a new context" (1988: 118). Hutcheon's delineation of the protagonists of such fiction as "anything but proper types: they are the ex-centrics, the marginalized, the peripheral figures of fictional history" (1988: 113–14), has particular relevance as such characters can be found in abundance in the most popular examples of the genre, which focus on reimagining the Victorian period's crusty underbelly.

Even though there is a general acceptance among scholars of the neo-Victorian that the novels are in some sense works of adaptation and that theoretical perspectives such as Hutcheon's have useful application, few consider *screen* adaptations in equal terms, but rather as an illustration of a lesser achievement, or even as doing an active disservice to the book. Therefore even though adaptation criticism finds a place in neo-Victorian studies (and vice versa) there are glimpses of a retroactive return to the "not-as-good-as-the-book" premise of approaches to adaptations twenty or more years ago. This chapter will examine such tendencies by considering a selection of neo-Victorian novels and screen texts, including the two which as novels have achieved near canonical status –*The French Lieutenant's Woman* (1969; 1981) and *Possession* (1990; 2002). Both were able to deploy the ideas of neo-Victorianism in film by the visual juxtaposition of two historical periods. I will then discuss *Tipping the Velvet* (1998; 2002) and *The Crimson Petal and the White* (2002; 2011), two striking television adaptations of phenomenally popular novels which demonstrate a key thread in modern neo-Victorian fiction as making visible the underside of Victorian Britain. Neither deploys overt visual references to the contemporary period and the neo-Victorian perspective is supplied by anti-realist camerawork and characters acting contrary to their costumes. Finally this chapter will consider whether an analysis of the novel and film adaptation of *Fanny by Gaslight* (1940; 1945) allows us to re-evaluate neo-Victorianism as a developing thread throughout post-Victorian society, rather than purely a post-1960s phenomenon. The choice of text is prompted by Jonathan Loesberg's view that the novel "despite it being in most ways just a romantic melodrama with a certain literary wit . . . establishes the three elements of post-Victorian narrative shared by its more self-consciously postmodern successors" (2007: 364). In his author's note Michael Sadleir anticipates the key concerns of heritage adaptation: "care has been taken to maintain period-accuracy and to give invention a basis of fact" (1947: vi); and as a well-known Victorian collector and bibliophile, his interests are not so far from those of A. S. Byatt or John Fowles. The consideration of a novel and film from the 1940s facilitates reflection upon the extent to which changing historical contexts influence what can be said about Victoriana, as well as what kinds of Victorian literary styles, themes, and sentiments are to be adapted.

This chapter will also reflect on the differing reception of neo-Victorian novels and their adaptations. In the case of screen adaptations there is a view that they blunt the edge of the neo-Victorian fictional project with a tendency to visual blurring between that which is depicted as "Victorian" and neo-Victorian. It is the case that contemporary screen adaptations of Victorian texts often offer critical interventions or re-readings that might be relocated onto a neo-Victorian terrain in their own right and this reinforces a blurring effect. I am not concerned about whether print or screen text is *superior*, although I note that this question is implicitly raised in neo-Victorian studies. I will conclude by returning to the idea that costume adaptations and neo-Victorian fiction may be mutually strengthening; and that the success of such print fiction may owe as much to the reception of period screen adaptations and the commercial will of publishers to sell by the logic of genre or category rather than by individual author.

Neo-Victorian texts are testament to the interface between scholarly trends and reading, and, importantly, the academic credentials of authors such as Sarah Waters and A. S. Byatt add authenticity to their work and herald a new interest in fiction which deals in popular history and literary criticism. Such books do not actually require a deep reading of Victorian classics; neither is a familiarity with queer theory essential, though an acquaintance with both (through reading, academia, broadsheet newspapers, screen adaptations) is seen as enhancing readerly pleasure. This is true of the double register at which much fiction of this category works, where the pleasures of recognition are available to those with knowledge of Victorian "Urtexts" pastiched or otherwise quoted, but equally a knowledge of Victorian hypertexts may suffice. The key obstacle for screen adaptations of the *neo*-Victorian novel is, in a nutshell, how they may be distinguished from the *Victorian* on screen if the text does not visually juxtapose a narrative perspective of both past and present. There is the relative difficulty in offering visual challenges to traditional motifs which have become codified as shorthand for the historical period. The dominant styles and aesthetics of costume and heritage drama may seem to dull the edge of the narrative with a twee coziness of familiarity, a dominance that even a leather dildo cannot ultimately unsettle for long. Both print and screen neo-Victorian productions are testimony to the powerful legacy of the Victorian age and its fiction, but also to the impact of the costume drama in television and film over the past half-century or more: they display history through the lens with which we are most comfortable at the present time. The pleasures of neo-Victorian novels are similar to the well-conceived screen adaptation of a classic novel – a seeming return to well-turned plots, laced with a knowingness of the ideologies which underpin and therefore destabilize classic realism: so that in some cases, as will be seen in the discussion of *The Crimson Petal and the White*, expectations are thwarted.

Concise definitions of the neo-Victorian are hard to come by, and unsurprisingly, there is no consensus about the boundaries of the genre and the focus has been predominantly on print fiction. It is a term which "usefully categorises a vast range and variety of modern publications, from David Lodge's *Nice Work* (1988) to later productions investing in the Victorian Age, either comically – Jasper Fforde's *The Eyre Affair* is a good example – or more generally in other genres such as detective fiction – D.J. Tayor's *Kept: A Victorian Mystery* (2006) for instance – or more straightforwardly historically – nuanced fiction such as Peter Carey's *Jack Maggs* (1997)" (Johnston and Waters, 2008: 2–3). Often the focus is upon the responses awakened in us as critics and readers, as well as upon their status as readings of and interventions into Victorian texts which offer a new model of reading or re-reading what might only very problematically be called the "original." Louisa Hadley defines such texts as "contemporary fiction that engages with the Victoria era, either at the level of plot, structure, or both" (2010: 4); and most critics agree that the earliest neo-Victorian novels are John Fowles' *The French Lieutenant's Woman* (1969), A. S. Byatt's *Possession* (1990), and Jean Rhys' *Wide Sargasso Sea* (1966). Such fiction is significantly inflected by revisionary history of the period, and this is most obvious in narratives that focus on the dispossessed, and those traditionally viewed to have been "hidden from history." To the skeptical, the focus on sex and the abject might suggest that any critiques or new insights into the Victorian period take second place to sensationalism and prurience.

As has already been remarked, by its nature the neo-Victorian novel is an act of adaptation; Victorian fiction is often the source of appropriation, but crucially the period itself – what is known and understood as well as what is misunderstood – is to be adapted and refunctioned to embrace the concerns of our own period. In the process what is most important is the *idea* of the "original" to be adapted rather than any perceivable *reality*, so the dominant attributes of the Victorian age – whether it be perceptions of sexual repression, crushing poverty, fog, or so forth – are deployed and integrated with those of the millennium – queer or gender concerns, and wider disquisitions on empire, social freedom, and individual choice. The examples under discussion show novelists concerned with evoking the period, but also self-consciously reflecting upon their incapacity to do so. Additionally, the Victorian period is situated as an era that can never be retrieved, only reconstructed by fictional means, borne out by the frequency of researchers or investigators populating the pages of such novels. For Mark Llewellyn neo-Victorian texts are "processes of writing that act out the results of reading the Victorians and their literary productions" (2008: 168), and this emphasis on re-reading, reimagining and re-voicing invokes Barthes' concept of readerly and writerly texts and the notion that a writerly text elevates the reader to the status of producer of that text.[2] Thus far we can see that definitions emphasize the neo-Victorian writer as an historian and social commentator as well as creative artist; the reader participates in an event that evokes the pleasures of popular-historical fascination with Victoriana as well as the gratifications of an essentially contemporary work of fiction.

Neo-Victorian writers, it is implied, can look back at the Victorian period with a colder eye than their literary forebears: "[r]emoved by a generation, we escape the 'anxiety of influence' that characterized the Modernists' reaction to the Victorians and prompted the disparagement of writers like Lytton Strachey and Virginia Woolf" (Hadley, 2010: 7). For screen adaptors, the Victorian period also marks the birth of film and the increasing significance of a democratized visual culture through more widespread use of photography. There is arguably little "anxiety of influence" here, and adaptors hark back to another significant tradition where, as Hutcheon notes, "[t]he Victorians had a habit of adapting just about everything – and in just about every possible direction" (2006: xi). Where neo-Victorians make specific use of classic Victorian texts, it is very likely that such texts have been adapted and remodeled many times before. For Rohan McWilliam, the specific attraction of the neo-Victorian novel is that it "offers an alternative kind of 'history from below'" which might be seen to fill in what is unsaid in Victorian writings, featuring "plenty of hysteria, prostitution, consumerism, spiritualism, uppity servants, cross-dressing, and transgression of boundaries" (2009: 108, 107). This contemporary genre is thus conceived as giving voice to the voiceless; whether the net effect is to remind us of rigid social divisions, as if such divisions no longer have any social relevance, is open to question.

Screen adaptors of Victorian literature who choose a period setting confront questions of historical authenticity and the most visible indications of "pastness" are choices of location, props, and costumes, as well as, depending on author, weather systems, quantity of dirt, and non-diegetic sounds such as carriages hurtling past and barrow boys selling wares. In neo-Victorian novels various narrative strategies are deployed to remind the reader how people lived in the Victorian period, from an intrusive contemporary narrator who guides, instructs, and interferes such as that of *The French Lieutenant's Woman*, to *Possession* where we encounter scholars of the Victorian period reconstructing literary lives. We learn about fictional poets, Randolph Ash and Christabel LaMotte, through their relative positions in the literary canon, the methodologies of those who study them, their personal correspondence, and their literary writings. Later they are described in Victorian *situ* – all the more surprising in the sudden shift to omniscient narration – where the reader comes to hold privileged information only guessed at by the scholars who seek to reconstruct their relationship through words. In *The Crimson Petal and the White* a Fowlesian narrator promises an enthralling narrative journey, not simply through the past but upwards through social classes to follow the destiny of Sugar once she leaves the house of her mother and madam, Mrs. Castaway. Such readerly prompts do not work so well on screen and Reisz's solution in adapting *The French Lieutenant's Woman* is to show the actors becoming "Victorian" by reading Fowles' novel, with the result that by the end one senses Mike's yearning for a "past" that he has had a part in creating. The film *Possession* exploits the novel's split narrative and depictions of Ash and LaMotte shadow the story of investigation of their interconnected lives as the two young scholars Roland Michell and Maud Bailey race against time to expose the shabby practices of scholar/collector Cropper, who, in league with Ash's ancestor, exhumes the poet's body in the search for final truths. In these cases, the present day identifies and positions itself in relation to the past. Mike looks back nostalgically in place of Fowles-as-narrator who haunts the pages (and even shares a railway carriage with his characters); Maud's discovery of her direct lineage to LaMotte and Ash changes her academic and personal sense of self and exposes contrary shifting canon formations.

The narrator of *The Crimson Petal* represents the contemporary, situating the past as alien territory and highlighting the treacherous path the reader is taking. In the BBC TV adaptation the opening voiceover becomes Sugar's macabre and sensationalist novel, itself a project in wish-fulfillment, and this voice obliterates any straightforward sense of the viewer's present.

In addition to the pressures on adaptors to interpret such novels in ways that appeal to an audience is the challenge of imagined historical "authenticity" constructed by the authors. There are other tensions too which determine how neo-Victorian and Victorian projects collide as adaptations become more inventive. One such adaptation is *The Way We Live Now* (David Yates, 2001) where David Suchet portrays Augustus Melmotte as an allusion to Robert Maxwell, thereby visually uniting financial scandals of the 1870s with ongoing mismanagement in the past two decades. The costumes and properties signify Victorian Britain, but the narrative celebrates historical anachronism and the pleasures of reading contemporary scandal as if it were a three-decker novel. The challenge for such adaptors of the Victorian is the correct blend of authentic period setting with contemporary critical sentiments to achieve neo-Victorian effects. The filthy London portrayed in novels such as *The Crimson Petal* is as much a response to the "muddy hem" aesthetic of recent screen adaptations, a backlash against relatively sanitized "lifestyle" period dramas of the mid-1990s. I am arguing that the neo-Victorian approach is the resulting cross-fertilization of narrative styles from fiction and film and television and that the nature of screen adaptations of this literary form have been neglected, or seen as a devaluation of its fictional aesthetic because eras, authors, and styles are cheerfully mashed up and blended.

Neo-Victorian fiction alerts us to its contemporaneity, by its focus on underclasses and underworlds, on sex and socialism; adapting the Victorian in the past two decades has been all about sexing up the past, so that risqué content is almost routine and rarely shocking. One effect of textual cross-fertilization between neo-Victorian fiction and adaptations of the Victorian has been that adaptations of neo-Victorian novels themselves have somewhat lagged behind, because the "neo" is already interpolated in the act of adaptation. Bucking this trend, Sarah Waters' three neo-Victorian novels have all been adapted for television (and the BBC adapted her Second World War novel, *The Night Watch* (2006), in 2011). Waters is highly regarded for offering a new angle on the myth of a sexually repressed society, interweaving lesbian themes into Victorian culture. But the adaptations are seen as "sexed up" in less positive terms, and Andrew Davies' role as scriptwriter on two of them is controversial, exacerbated by voyeurist newspaper previews which "foreclose on notions of female spectatorship by coding their audiences as heterosexual and male" (Emmens, 2009: 143). Topics ripe for novelistic revaluation through the lens of queer theory do not always strike the same tone in visual culture, and the lesbian "romps," certainly no more evident in the adaptation than in the novel in the case of *Tipping the Velvet,* play into well-known soft-porn tropes and obscure other visual attempts to queer our perspective on sexuality through distanciation

– such as the penis point-of-view shot of Nan's face as she opens the fly of a paying customer.

The academic study of neo-Victorian writing has the inevitable effect of rendering "serious" a range of novels with a mixture of social or critical intentions. Where there is a "mission" on these authors' part it can most easily be identified as that of engaging with dominant historiographical perspectives on the Victorian as well as literary critical ones. However, given most readers are not Victorianists, readerly response is primarily to challenges to dominant ideas about the period. Matthew Sweet is one critic who has debunked many characteristics we associate with the Victorians, adding that "most of the pleasures we imagine to be our own, the Victorians enjoyed first" (2001: x). He notes too, how screen adaptations of Victorian literature begin in the last years of this period, and a number of authors lived to see, or at least to profit financially from them, including Thomas Hardy and Mary Braddon – still alive when *Aurora Floyd* became a two-reel movie in 1913 (2001: 25). Sweet's lively and evocative book implies that there are hundreds of hidden histories of Victorian life waiting to be rediscovered or reimagined; and neo-Victorian texts give credence to this view, affecting the way we understand Victorian life and culture, but equally shaped by what we think we already know.

In considering what happens to the neo-Victorian text in the process of adaptation, it is salutary to consider what happens to our sense of history in the act of reconstruction; as Kate Mitchell observes, novelists have to confront "the question of whether history is equated, in fiction, with superficial detail; an accumulation of references to clothing, furniture, décor and the like, that produces the past in terms of its objects, as a series of clichés" and she asks, "[c]an these novels recreate the past in a meaningful way or are they playing nineteenth-century dress-ups?" (2010: 3). As suggested earlier our main access to Victorian periodicity on screen is through nineteenth-century dress-ups; our relationship to history in adaptations is one of filling in the gaps that documented history leaves and with those additions we recognize the weight of our contemporary concerns. Neo-Victorian novels' recent explosive popularity confirm that immersing ourselves in things Victorian is a continuous site of pleasure, and in adaptation that means watching our social and psychological concerns performed in costume.

Commentators on neo-Victorian fiction can associate screen adaptation with a conservative analytical perspective so that 1990s Austen adaptations are summarized by Diane Sadoff as glorifying "class-appropriate courtship and marital choice even as they celebrate female resistance to such arrangements, enabling safe examination of gender and sexual relations" (2010: 70). One might argue much neo-Victorian fiction offers a similarly "safe" examination of gender, class, and other social concerns depending on whether narrative strategies are interpreted as involving a challenging reflection on our own times, or whether transplanting gender and class politics to a previous era neutralizes current political issues. As Voigts-Virchow remarks, "it is less painful to attack, and easier to understand, the patriarchal orthodoxies of the Victorians than it is to achieve understanding for or to pass judgement on existing contemporary moral fundamentalisms" (2009: 113). While this might not detract from the power of such critiques, it reminds us of the pitfalls of using the Victorians as a lens for our own concerns.

While distinctively wrapped neo-Victorian novels are a highly visible presence on bookstore shelves, the recent successes of *Tipping the Velvet* and *The Crimson Petal and the White* on television have yet to spawn a mass of other adaptations, perhaps because in the novels the work of "adaptation" and refunctioning is seen as already done; or, as is the case with Fowles' *The French Lieutenant's Woman*, it was regarded initially as unfilmable. The latter novel was written at a time when literary study was beginning to feel the tremors of European theory; socially, debates on class and gender were similarly moving to the fore. From the start it is emphasized that the narrator exists in a different historical period from that which is being narrated and acts as both guide and instructor. At times the narrator-character will pause to convey facts and opinions which flesh out character choices; an understanding of the social context reminds us that Charles, the gentleman, is moving with the times in his liaison with Ernestina, the wealthy draper's daughter. In the oft-quoted thirteenth chapter, the omnipresent time-traveling narrator both demystifies the process of Victorian realism and then re-mystifies it by claiming he has little control over the doings of his characters. This disingenuous double-narration where one perspective on writing and creativity is pitted against an opposing one gestures to the key pleasures of the neo-Victorian novel in reading a "Victorian" novel in a contemporary register. When Fowles' narrator-character stops narrative time winding his watch back fifteen minutes to usher in the second alternative ending we are allowed to celebrate the human themes of the great Victorian novels whilst choosing, if we wish, a distinctly postmodern ending.

Reisz's film dramatizes the historical slippages between the Victorian and contemporary periods by setting, location and costume, emphasized by the opening scene where Meryl Streep plays actress Anna getting ready to perform Sarah Woodruff in the film-within-the-film. Lyme Regis and its Cobb offer the perfect setting for this historical/anti-historical film as this actual location retains its periodicity to the extent that it can play the Victorian/twentieth-century with little adjustment. The characters move between past and present and in and out of character by a telephone ringing, or a vehicle pulling into shot. The film allows us to enjoy the picturesque features of the historical drama whilst keeping its critical distance from the costume drama. It also uses visual cues common to period adaptations, most notably the association of interiors as social performative spaces set against the liberties afforded by nature. This is affirmed and exploited to good effect in the final "Victorian" scene of the film where the camera looks through the stone arch of the boathouse as Charles rows Sarah into Windermere and they seem at home in the natural world which surrounds them. Compare this to the subsequent twentieth-century scene where Mike returns to the room where the reunion between Charles and Sarah is filmed to find Anna has left; her car pulls away as he looks out, framed by the window, still confined, in a whisper of gender reversal. At this point too, Carl Davis' "nineteenth-century" score blurs into the twentieth-century scene (the diegetic music has previously been that of a band playing at the party) as the Victorian period invades the present, rather than the reverse.

The demystification of the filming process (showing characters getting ready for shot, rehearsing lines, juxtaposing character's relationships with those between the actors) does not actually taint the illusion that the film is being shot chronologically, so that the final scene coincides with the cast's end-of-film party, a technique which echoes Fowles' thirteenth chapter. Charles and Sarah's potentially happy Victorian ending heralds the end of Mike and Anna's affair and Mike's anguish. Watching Streep as Anna rehearse the role of Sarah strengthens rather than undermines the spectacle with which we are then presented and performs for the knowing spectator classic fidelity debates, as if Anna must channel Sarah by an intimate connection with the novel, about which Mike and her are seen sharing ideas. In the closing scene Mike calls for "Sarah" rather than Anna and we are returned to the shot of Sarah and Charles on the lake which ended the Victorian film within the film. For Mary Lynn Dodson, "the heart of the movie is the nineteenth-century love story" (1998: 300); but the focus on Meryl Streep in performance as Anna/Sarah and Jeremy Irons as Mike/Charles, attends to the act of imagining and inhabiting Victorian spaces.

Possession, the novel, celebrates excavation and exploration and the ways gaps and silences cannot always be filled in. Maud Bailey and Roland Michell represent academic researchers whose work on past artifacts takes on more meaning than their current existence. Bailey re-reads the Victorian age through her feminist championing of the critically ignored poet Christabel LaMotte, also a relative, and her scholarship is inflected with both her sexual politics and personal background. Her Women's Resources Centre is a haven from mainstream scholarship as well as testimony to the possibilities of feminist work, even while the bullish U.S. feminist Leonora Stern is treated with less narrative sympathy. The enigma which structures the novel is the discovery of a love affair between poets Randolph Ash and LaMotte, impelling the plot forward like a detective story, initiated by Roland's academic crime of stealing a letter discovered by chance in the London Library. The similarities between the work of the literary historian and the detective are exploited, while moral questions of how we read and what information and critical strategies we deploy are foregrounded. The various academics offer different models of research, and the "truth" about these poets, such as it is, has to be gleaned by the collective knowledge of all. In addition to Bailey, Michell and Stern, there is Mortimer Cropper, the author-fetishist who creates a museum to Ash; the underfunded, scatty UK Ash scholar Professor Blackadder with his camp of young post-docs in the British Library; and Beatrice Nest, the enigmatic keeper of Ash's wife's diary protective of her subject and cynical about feminist re-readings of the diaries. Ash as canonical writer is set against LaMotte as neglected one and questions of quality and worth are mediated by issues of gender, emphasized by the glimpses into the lives of the two writers in the omnisciently narrated sections of the book.

Maud and Leonora's championing of LaMotte is ultimately legitimated when comparative readings of the two poets show their mutual indebtedness, and Byatt's *tour de force* is to take on the mantle of author-ventriloquist, creating literary works which recall writings of the period and show off her Victorianist scholarly credentials. For Jonathan Loesberg we "share the scholarly act of learning the past through the interpretation of its documents," which emphasizes the strangeness of the directly narrated sections that "cannot any longer be known by the modern characters and is available to the reader only magically" (2007: 379, 380). The book concludes in sensationalist fashion culminating in a grave-robbing finale when all the suspects are brought together. There are obvious parallels between the relationship of LaMotte and Ash and Michell and Bailey, and a revelation about Mrs. Ash's inability to engage in sexual relations with her husband casts Ash's affair in a different light. The true nature of the relationship between Christabel and Blanche Glover remains veiled, although in the omniscient narrative Ash is surprised at the intensity of virgin Christabel's sexual response.

For Dana Shiller, novels like *Possession* and *The French Lieutenant's Woman* "emphasize the textualization of the past, demonstrating the great extent to which the late twentieth-century sense of 'Victorianism' comes to us already emplotted by the nineteenth-century novel," adding that "*Possession* consistently works to undermine its characters' assumption that given access to enough documents, the scholar can attain complete knowledge of his or her subject" (1997: 546, 548). This reliance on documents is something Ellen Ash tries to thwart in burying Christabel's last letter to Ash, which reveals that they have a child. Locations emphasize conflicting ideas of "pastness:" Seal Court, LaMotte's ancestral home, is decaying, with its present residents confined to the ground floor, a happy accident of such neglect being that Ash and LaMotte's correspondence remains undisturbed. This old ruin can be contrasted to the Richmond home LaMotte shared with Glover, which has been restored lovingly to Victorian pristineness, except as Michell notes, "It would have been sootier. It would have looked older. When it was younger" (1991: 211). At this point we are reminded of the post-Thatcher heritage boon and the increasing popularity of Victorian homes, fixtures, and fittings so that "'History' becomes its tangible objects, which are bought and sold to decorate homes, or to boost tourism. The past becomes a possession" (Mitchell, 2010: 94).

The film starts with Ash walking alone in the countryside, his voiceover recitation of a love poem abruptly changing to a different voice in the cut to a contemporary auction house selling his manuscripts. This scene gathers several key protagonists with a parallel one tracking Michell's discovery in the library. Critical differences transform into cultural ones with Michell portrayed, in the words of the librarian, as "The American," to which he retorts, "you're one of our favourite colonies." His Americanness is the foil to Maud's Englishness, and Jennifer Jeffers perceives the casting choice as reterritorialization, making him more singular as an "outcast" and obliterating the class dynamics between him and Maud (2006). The fact that American actress Gwyneth Paltrow reprises the received English tones she deployed in McGrath's *Emma* (1996), while Trevor Eve assumes an American accent as Cropper, further muddies the sense of nationhood even while the Englishness of Ash and LaMotte and of period adaptation are fetishized by both the costume-drama element, the casting of Jennifer Ehles and Jeremy Northam, and by Maud's beautifully restored Victorian home. Maud remains keeper of LaMotte's memory and reputation; but her relationship to the Lincolnshire Baileys is closer; moreover, the grandeur of the stately home is visually exploited, even under dust covers.

Visually the legacy of *The French Lieutenant's Woman* is most apparent in the doubling of locations populated by both past and present, so that as Ash and LaMotte leave their hotel room at Whitby, Bailey and Michell enter and sort out more complicated sleeping arrangements. Such scenes capitalize on Victorian locations as well as the love of Victoriana in the setting of Maud's home; but other meanings emerge in juxtaposition: while the contemporary critics might be following in these writers' footsteps their relationship is more complex. Maud's ironic declaration, "aren't we modern!" sums up their crucial difference from the Victorian pair. This shadowing of LaMotte and Ash does most of the interpretive work as their writing, so crucial to the movement of the novel, appears rarely and then as artifacts, such as the love poem LaMotte tears up as she and Ash leave Whitby. Roland's dreary relationship with Val is supplanted by his lone tenancy with a solicitor friend who serves the twin purpose of reminding us of the enormity of his crime in stealing the letter as well as its impact: "It'll rewrite history, old chap!" Blanche and Christabel's lesbian relationship is depicted as "romantic friendship" via scenes of domestic intimacy; Blanche's pictures, hung about their home, cast her as a lost female pre-Raphaelite and underline the arbitrariness of who or what becomes significant, as we recall that in the novel her paintings are lost. The tragedy of Blanche's death is dwelt upon, reinforced by a lengthy intercut scene of her Woolfian suicide by drowning. Further visual links to *The French Lieutenant's Woman* occur as Christabel's hooded cloak recalls that of Sarah Woodruff, and resemblances between Jeremy Northam's Randolph Ash and Jeremy Irons' Charles Smithson are marked by costume. Physical shots of letters and artifacts remind us of their role as carriers of secrets and truths and the final scene completes the opening one as Ash encounters his daughter and gives her a letter to convey to Christabel, which is promptly dropped and left blowing in the wind.

Michel Faber and Sarah Waters are concerned with Victorian subcultures and sexuality in a way that Voigts-Virchow describes as "in-yer-face" (2009: 110) – deliberately confrontational and even shocking to the reader. For others this is faux-Victorian writing: an insertion of stories which could not be written and cannot be easily validated through historical research. In the case of *Tipping the Velvet* Waters eschews the dual-time narrative in favor of first-person confessional "to *invent* a past that links to the present" (Mitchell, 2010: 120); links between this Victorian story and the reader's present are emphasized by the repetition of the word "queer," a word which has passed from derogatory to itself challenging, theoretically informed, and "in-yer-face" in our own time. Nan's journey from "boy" performer, to cross-dressing rent-boy, to lesbian sex object, and finally to domesticated lesbian with a social conscience allows a vivid portrayal of a life of unspeakable desires in the period, as it asserts a diverse range of lesbian and queer identities in the present time. The naturalness and inevitability of Nan's desire for Kitty and Florence is reminiscent of Jeanette Winterson's depiction of coming out in *Oranges Are Not the Only Fruit* (1985), but lesbian fiction has grown up in the years separating the novels and queer performances substitute for any notion of singular authentic lesbian identity. There is pity too for Nan's clients as she recognizes theirs "was a love so fierce and so secret it must be satisfied, with a stranger" (Waters, 1999: 200). Waters' positioning of her lesbian *rite de passage* in the Victorian period, so richly drawn, allows the reader the dual pleasures of eroticized love story and realist story-telling, so that for gay and straight readers alike there is perhaps an element of making strange.

The very public sexual identity of the author and the popularity of the book meant that the ethics of a male scriptwriter and director were scrutinized closely. Sex on screen can dangerously tilt into soft-porn readings, just as neo-Victorianism collides with Victorian costume drama mise-en-scène. Furthermore the portrayal of gay relationships on screen is a minefield, given that they are mainly connoted by the act of sex, and its portrayal can invite criticisms of satisfying, or more often failing to satisfy, heteronormative voyeuristic curiosity. Clearly Andrew Davies' reputation for "sexing up" the classics creates certain expectations, as alluded to earlier, but the emphasis throughout is on the libidinous and liberating world of the theater and the performative roles of Nan. The spectator is also seduced by Kitty's performance and the bustle of the theater, both among the audience (with a period-dressed Sarah Waters among them) and backstage. Anna Chancellor as Mrs. Lethaby offers a powerful portrayal of the lesbian dominatrix who is part of a thriving butch/femme culture existing comfortably within society, in opposition to the discreet Cavendish Ladies' Club of the novel. Nan and Kitty's lovemaking is intercut by scenes of their drag king performances, communicating the audience's love of the spectacle and subversive possibilities of cross-dressing, but also the underlying risks of lesbian identity beyond the theater: as Nan and Kitty kiss on the lips on stage, the cut to the audience reaction says it all. Nan's journey towards self-knowledge in both novel and film is also a journey towards social conscience and life with Florence, her brother and orphaned baby Cyril, appearing as Waters' celebration of "pretend family relationships," an antidote to the 1980s repression of alternative lifestyles in the UK's Section 28.[3]

Michel Faber's *The Crimson Petal and the White* deploys a disembodied narrator who acts as a guide, and this immersive technique is both reassuring and a reminder to the reader that they traverse a breach between their present era and that of the novel. This is a novel of especially gargantuan proportions: "[r]eviewers repeatedly point out its 800-page girth, as if its size alone positions the novel belatedly, with Dickens or Dumas, even before the spine is cracked" (Palmer, 2009: 90). Within its pages we are not just whisked into the underworld of the Victorian brothel, but also into the unspeakable realm of bodily functions and excreta. Human effluvia floods the novel – from William Rackham's soiling of himself the first time he visits Sugar, through semen, vomit, excrement, and even the aftermath of an induced abortion. Not content to have us confront the abject via constant reminders of human effluence, the novel focuses on smells – both good and bad so that "[o]lfactory ghosts often intervene in this narrative to disturb the calm surface of realistic and visual representations" (Colella, 2010: 86); whereas the scent of lavender and eau de cologne connote pastness, associated as they are now with musty old age. The stink of humanity overwhelms everything in Faber's attempt to convey dirty nineteenth-century London, and William Rackham's perfume factory expresses one attempt to obscure smell, just as characters' vices and vulnerabilities are barely beneath the surface.

This novel evokes the use of all of the senses and suggests, perhaps, that this unites us with our forebears. Yet by undermining genre expectations of narrative resolution it baffles readers "because it does not live up to their expectations of a (neo-)Victorian novel; they feel intellectually and financially conned because they have bought into a version of the Victorian that the author seems to play along with only to renegotiate the terms of the contract in the final pages" (Heilmann and Llewellyn, 2010: 13). Faber's playing with plot expectations results in a muddle of cul-de-sacs, whether intentional or not. Agnes' diary entries are one example of curiosity frustrated as Sugar unearths them hoping to find out the truth about Rackham's wife, only to be confronted with tedium and vacuity. Agnes is a study in the logical extension of what might happen if women are entirely ignorant of the world and their bodies, but the extent of her ignorance becomes bewildering. Sugar understands Agnes' plight better than most when she observes that all such women are children: "they grow taller and gain a few 'accomplishments' until, at fifteen or sixteen, still accustomed to being made to sit in a corner for failing to conjugate a verb or refusing to eat their pudding, they go home to their suitors" (2002: 553). Stories within stories suggest endless intertextual possibilities as Agnes, a "madwoman" of sorts, if not in the attic, encounters her maid reading *Jane Eyre* and thinks "there's something very wicked about a lady's-maid savouring this horrid tale of a wife driven mad by illness and shut up in a tower by her husband while he attempts to marry another woman" (2002: 440). Frustrating too is the pointlessness of Sugar's novel, which is fed to the winds at the conclusion, as a teasing glimpse envisaged by Sugar for the end of her own novel, "death for the heroine" (2002: 229), is yet another red herring.

This lack of coherence, or at least conclusiveness, is dealt with in the television adaptation by resolving the narrative voice into Sugar's voiceover, as if she is reading aloud her novel of revenge against her customers, "a tale of embraces charged with hatred and kisses laced with disgust, of practised submission and a secret longing for vengeance" (2002: 229). Faber's response to this adaptation is one of surprise to have "seen something on TV that I feel has its own artistic integrity and its own emotional power. It's someone else's baby, but damn it, I care how it gets treated" (2011). Despite it being some else's baby, and despite his evident uninterest in television in general, he recognizes his own themes emerging beyond the central focus on Sugar, that it is "about grownups who are really overgrown children in search of lost or absent mothers, and the children that they in turn produce" (2011). In the absence of a conclusive ending for the novel the screen adaptation strengthens textual causality and character motivation so that Sugar is more obviously a protector and savior to Agnes and a mother to Sophie. Her vitriolic novel of violent revenge against her erstwhile customers is lost to the elements as she escapes Rackham's house with Sophie; but in the closing scene she unwraps and opens a pristine new journal as if to begin work on a sequel denied us by Faber, who instead teases his readers with snippets in the collection *The Apple* (2006).

Reading Sadleir's *Fanny by Gaslight* using contemporary neo-Victorian novels as a context reveals shared themes and narrative devices. As in *The French Lieutenant's Woman* and *Possession* the narrative flits between the present and the Victorian past, but the gap between is narrowed to the length of Fanny Hooper's life. The elderly Fanny, retired to an isolated French hotel, is encouraged by impending poverty to sell her memoirs to a visiting Englishman who, like Sadleir himself, is "one-third author to two-thirds publisher" (1947: 7). The means by which Fanny's story is able to be told comprises an introductory chapter in the third person, followed by first-person narration initially from Fanny's perspective, then from that of her lover Harry Somerford, with a third part concluding the memoir in Fanny's voice once more. A concluding third-person chapter describes Gerald Warbeck's attempt to shape her memoirs into a structured manuscript: "He hit on the device of making Harry Somerford the recorder of the all-important epoch in Fanny Hooper's life when they two were together. This device, he argued defensively, was a favourite with certain famous novelists of the Victorian period, and could therefore suitably be revived for a book with a Victorian setting" (1947: 381). Warbeck's agonizing over the ordering of the narrative, coupled with Sadleir's preceding author's note mimics strategies used by contemporary neo-Victorianists and shows a shared understanding of the challenge of representing pastness.

Fanny's story (like Sugar's or Nan's) is of the Victorian underworld, both a class-based critique of the wealthy and privileged whilst being a testimony to Fanny's survival despite tragedy and her unorthodox life choices. Fanny's stepfather, William "the Duke" Hopwood, keeps a tavern and below that, "a gambling-hell,

a drinking-den, a house of assignation, a theatre of obscene burlesque, even –
within the limits of its accommodation – a knocking-shop. Practically nothing
was too scandalous to be tolerated; virtually no taste too wanton to be catered for"
(1947: 57). As a child Fanny stumbles upon this underworld, appropriately named
"Hopwood's Hades," and learns of the Duke's involvement in organized crime as
well as his own code of honor: "he refused to take part in any undertaking which
permitted cruelty as an element in sex-traffic, and he was resolutely opposed to
the victimization of young children" (1947: 65). This results in a confrontation
with the wealthy Lord Manderstoke after his brutal killing of an underage prostitute whose body he deliberately plants in Hopwood's establishment, resulting in
the Duke's criminal conviction and eventual death. Fanny's knowledge of Hopwood's business sees her grow up practical and non-judgmental; her lover Harry
Somerford is also a debunker of hypocrisy, tutored well by Kitty Cairns at whose
brothel he was once a customer, and where his friendship with Fanny develops.
But their romance is thwarted by Fanny's refusal to marry him, and they cohabit
instead with the full knowledge of their friends and neighbors. This aside, Fanny
is the stuff of historical romance, as the product of a loving union between her
mother and local aristocrat, Sir Clive Seymore; but Sir Clive also refuses to encourage his natural daughter to marry having "some reason for not regarding marriage
as the element in a love-affair which is made in Heaven" (1947: 282), because he
was forced to give up his lover and marry within his class.

The novel brims with descriptions of London's underworld of discreetly maintained brothels and burlesques, inviting comparisons with *The Crimson Petal*.
Sadleir's work was informed by his professional interests as a publisher and a Victorian book collector; as John Sutherland asserts, "Sadleir made academic study of
the Victorian novel, in all its many commercial mutations, respectable" (2001:
146) and his tastes ran to writers considered minor at the time, such as Anthony
Trollope, as well as gothic romance. As Sutherland further observes Sadleir incorporated "a daring amount of eroticism, as well as researched information about
Victorian sexuality and about the Victorian metropolitan underworld" to make him
"arguably the precursor of other contemporary-Victorian romances" (2001: 151,
152). This can be exemplified by his description of Rosherville pleasure gardens
(actually located in Gravesend, Kent, but accessible to Londoners by steamer) so
that "[n]owadays when the despised Victorians are labelled as tyrannical and
prudish, the freedom of Rosherville would simply be disbelieved. But I can assure
you that the sweet-smelling luxuriant gardens were for lovers to use as they
wished, and with no one to interfere save to prevent rowdiness or breaches of peace"
(1947: 137).

Gainsborough pictures adapted the novel[4] as a very English melodrama complete
with a happy ending, where Harry survives his duel with Lord Manderstoke. While
it is a costume drama, it takes the freer interpretation of period deployed in classic
Hollywood movies as well as offering direct visual homage, most obviously when
Fanny helps Lady Seymore tighten her corset, the mise-en-scène evoking the iconic

Gone with the Wind (1939). Whilst Sadleir intends to write the novel that the Victorians could not, much of its content was too rich for popular film and even the subsequent production would not be shown in the United States until 1948, not least because the heroine was an illegitimate child (on release it was renamed *Man of Evil* as "Fanny" was a proscribed word). The film situates Fanny and friend Lucy as childhood rivals and opposites, Lucy marked out as the "fast" one. Fanny's discovery of her stepfather's club earns her several years in boarding school in the film, but the spectator is treated to scenes of Hopwood's club where debauchery is implied by women draped across men, while a vigorous can-can is performed. As the drunken Lord Manderstoke (James Mason) is ejected from the club, he pushes Hopwood under a passing cab, his death rapidly followed by that of Fanny's mother (who lives to old age in the book), leaving Fanny to discover the secret of her true parentage via Sir Clive. Lord Manderstoke reemerges as the beau of Mrs. Seymore and, rather than be blackmailed into revealing the truth about Fanny, Sir Clive throws himself under a train. Manderstoke's links with Fanny are visually reinforced throughout the film and he soon returns as the lover of Lucy, now a burlesque dancer. While Lucy is rendered simplistically sluttish, Harry and Fanny are rehabilitated into respectability, the friendship developing through Harry's (Stewart Granger) working relationship with deeply respected politician Sir Clive. Despite the overlay of respectability, the film retains vestiges of the novel's amorality, particularly in its portrayal of colorful clubs and the Parisian theater, even while its surface moral frame is tightened by the swift disposal of both Fanny's natural parents and her stepfather. Fanny's reluctance to marry becomes a principled desire to preserve Harry's professional reputation in the face of his family's objection to her, and despite his insistence that in "a hundred years from now they'll be no such thing" as class distinctions.

The melodrama culminates in Harry accepting Manderstoke's challenge to a duel, because of his belief that the corrupt aristocrat has an evil influence over Fanny's life. Having killed Manderstoke outright, Harry is dangerously wounded and his puritanical sister arrives to claim him. At the finale Fanny recognizes spinsterish jealousy in his sister's callousness and the film ends hopefully with Fanny asserting, "you're going to live. Harry do you hear? You're going to live. . . . we're going to have a home and children". Instead of Fanny looking back on a few snatched years of happiness and the subsequent tragedy of a daughter killed in the Great War as in the novel, the young couple look forward to a joint future beyond the petty divisions of class; seriously ill and lying in a French convent, Harry sums up the wished-for safe return of England's many war wounded from the continent.

Though sanitized of course, this postwar film surprises in its focus on London's underworld and on a heroine at home with both cheerfully honorable crooks and her aristocratic father, whilst Sadleir's attempted authentic Victorianism is blended with the Gainsborough aesthetic. Forgotten and out of print for at least 20 years, the novel traces common threads with the ambitions of neo-Victorian novelists today. *Fanny by Gaslight* certainly conforms to Heilmann and Llewellyn's definition of neo-Victorian fiction as novels which are *"self-consciously engaged with the act of (re) interpretation, (re)discovery and (re)vision concerning the Victorians"* (2010: 4 – italics in original). Their play on words here, with parenthetical prefixes, emphasizes both a sense of return and repetition, but also the project of intervention in the themes, form, and/or politics of Victorian literature, and the way readers are made conscious that their own knowledge of the period might be incomplete or inaccurate. Sadleir, in common with these contemporary writers, made money out of a novel unashamedly aimed at the popular market as well as later enjoying the spectacle of his work adapted to screen.

Critic's responses to adaptations of neo-Victorian novels are considerably more skeptical. Of Andrew Davies' adaptation of *Tipping the Velvet,* Heilmann and Llewellyn observe that the fact it "will be remembered as much for the golden phallus/dildo as anything about the narrative of women's rights presented in the novel is surely problematic" (2010: 243). Successful adaptations are often remembered for a striking visual moment, such as a wet shirt, and this can be interpreted as reductive or evocative depending on the perspective of the viewer, but their main contention is that Davies has disturbed core meanings in the original texts even while his involvement in the adaptation of Waters is acknowledged to broaden the appeal of the neo-Victorian. They are not alone in suggesting that a heteronormative reading of Waters' novel tends to prevail and there may be some justification for that criticism, as noted earlier. They are also right to remark on the potential blurring of the Victorian and neo-Victorian in adaptation, but their argument flounders where it seems to be based on a conviction of the inferiority of the screen narrative and where they see slippage between texts as necessarily negative, rather than another facet of the neo-Victorian approach. For example, they observe that in *Affinity* (2008) Davies revisits his lesbian reading of the relationship between *Little Dorrit*'s Miss Wade and Tattycoram; and that the BBC's marketing of *Cranford* (2007) and *Lark Rise to Candleford* (2008) depicts them as a joint "brand" implying historical proximity; while David Suchet's role in the drama *Maxwell* (2007) recalls his Maxwellesque performance of Melmotte proliferating meanings and readings across genre and period.

Neo-Victorian scholars sense a threat that the Victorian is collapsed into some kind of nameless past without sense/respect for historical distance, leading to a question of whether there is a right and wrong way to acknowledge the Victorians in the present day, and display a quite overt tendency to prefer the adaptive potentialities of prose over the power of the screened adaptation. While celebrating the palimpsestuous and intertextual and acknowledging the relevance of adaptation theory and criticism to the work of neo-Victorian scholars, Heilmann and Llewellyn remain skeptical about recent perspectives such as Robert Stam's. They particularly object to what they see as his account of the limitless "liberties" that a screen adaptation can take: "[w]hile we have sympathy for Stam's critique, there does remain nevertheless the uneasy sense that this provides a potential blank slate for the developments of adaptations that bear little but the name of the original, which is then used for trading and commercial rather than aesthetic and innovative reasons" (2010: 233). Robert Stam has usefully examined ongoing tensions between the valuing of literary versus screen intertextuality, and the possible overvaluing of literary at the expense of film and television analysis with the result that "[a]daptation becomes a zero-sum game where film is perceived as the upstart enemy storming the ramparts of literature" and where "the inter-art relation is seen as a Darwinian struggle to the death rather than a dialogue offering mutual benefit and cross-fertilization" (2005: 4). Even in Heilmann and Llewellyn's generally inclusive approach, the opposition of aesthetic against commercial summarizes the core tension between screen culture and literature. "Screen adaptation has to be scrutinized with the question, is it seeking to provide a new angle on the nineteenth century, or to make a fast buck?" (2010: 232) while literature's seedy commercial identity remains suppressed.

Given the omnivorous consumption of contemporary literary and screen texts, there is good reason to suspect that the spectacle of Victorians on screen contributed to the neo-Victorian genre as much as groundbreaking novels such as *The French Lieutenant's Woman*. A number of critics, however, still want to draw a line in the sand when it comes to defining what is and is not neo-Victorian, particularly in response to screen adaptations. What they find exciting about neo-Victorian fiction – its appropriation of Victorian narrative typologies, the focus on hidden histories, the challenging of certainties about our recent ancestors' lives and concerns – reminds us of the sheer promiscuity of the genre, so that it seems a little harsh to expect such a degree of fidelity on the part of screen adaptations. Neo-Victorian novels engage the reader primarily through the promise of pleasure, and that pleasure derives mainly from a recognition of shadows of past classic novels, half-remembered ideas about Victorian culture, and the contemporary habit of bringing sex and bodily functions into just about everything. Thanks to the proliferation of adaptations of nineteenth-century staples, readers are blessed with a Victorian frame of reference whether or not they've read the books, and authors can gainfully exploit their readers' general visual literacy.

The act of reading is reified in neo-Victorian writing, so that in *Possession* "the afterlife of the texts of the past is achieved through the process of reading texts, a process which brings the past imaginatively to life in the present" (Hadley, 2010: 123). A favoring of reading over spectating and a nagging belief that reading is better because "adaptations often flatten out the complexities of Victorian fiction" (Hadley, 2010: 142) positions screen adaptation as the ersatz "nineteenth-century dress-ups," as if historical authenticity (even reimagined history) is the peculiar domain of fiction. Neo-Victorian fiction's intertextual universe is part of "a cultural memory, to be re-membered, and imaginatively re-created, not revised or understood" (Mitchell, 2010: 7); whereas adaptation's intertextual potentialities roam across eras and genres in fantastic and dangerous liaisons yet to be emulated by the neo-Victorian novel.

NOTES

1 The UK ejournal *Neo-Victorian Studies* was established in late 2008; most of the texts which explicitly refer to neo-Victorian writing have emerged in the last five years.

2 "The writerly text is a perpetual present, upon which no consequent language (which would inevitably make it past) can be superimposed; the writerly text is ourselves writing" (Barthes, 1974: 5).

3 Not repealed until 2003.

4 Also adapted for BBC in 1981, but not seen by this author.

REFERENCES

Barthes, Roland. *S/Z: An Essay*. Trans. Richard Miller. New York: Hill and Wang, 1974. (Original published 1970.)

Byatt, A. S. *Possession: A Romance*. London: Vintage, 1991.

Colella, Silvana. "Olfactory Ghosts: Michel Faber's *The Crimson Petal and the White*." In *Haunting and Spectrality in Neo-Victorian Fiction: Possessing the Past*. Eds. Rosario Arias and Patricia Pulham. Basingstoke: Palgrave Macmillan, 2010, 85–109.

Crimson Petal and the White, The. Dir. Marc Munden. UK: BBC, 2011.

Dodson, Mary Lynn. "*The French Lieutenant's Woman*: Pinter and Reisz's adaptation of John Fowles's adaptation." *Literature/Film Quarterly*, 26:4, 1998, 296–303.

Emmens, Heather. "Taming the Velvet: Lesbian Identity in Cultural Adaptations of *Tipping the Velvet*." In *Adaptation in Contemporary Culture: Textual Infidelities*. Ed. Rachel Carroll. London: Continuum, 2009, 134–60.

Faber, Michel. *The Crimson Petal and the White*, Edinburgh: Canongate, 2002.

Faber, Michel. "*The Crimson Petal and the White*: Watching My Novel Reborn on TV." Guardian, April 6, 2011.

Fanny by Gaslight. Dir. Anthony Asquith. UK: Gainsborough Pictures, 1945.

Fowles, John. *The French Lieutenant's Woman*. London: Triad Granada, 1977. (Original published 1969.)

French Lieutenant's Woman, The. Dir. Karel Reisz. UK: Juniper Films, 1981.

Hadley, Louisa. *Neo-Victorian Fiction and Historical Narrative: The Victorians and Us*. New York: Palgrave Macmillan, 2010.

Heilmann, Ann and Mark Llewellyn. *Neo-Victorianism: The Victorians in the Twenty-first Century, 1999–2009*. Basingstoke: Palgrave Macmillan, 2010.

Hutcheon, Linda. *A Poetics of Postmodernism: History, Theory, Fiction*. London: Routledge, 1988.

Hutcheon, Linda. *A Theory of Adaptation*. London: Routledge, 2006.

Jeffers, Jennifer M. *Britain Colonized: Hollywood's Appropriation of British Literature*. Basingstoke: Palgrave Macmillan, 2006.

Johnston, Judith and Catherine Waters. "Introduction." In *Victorian Turns, NeoVictorian Returns: Essays on Fiction and Culture*. Eds. Penny Gay, Judith Johnston, and Catherine Waters. Newcastle upon Tyne: Cambridge Scholars, 2008, 1–11.

Llewellyn, Mark. "What is neo-Victorian Studies?" *Neo-Victorian Studies*, 1:1, 2008, 164–85.

Loesberg, Jonathan. "The Afterlife of Victorian Sexuality: Foucault and Neo-Victorian Historical Fiction." *Clio*, 36:3, 2007, 361–89.

McWilliam, Rohan. "Victorian Sensations, Neo-Victorian Romances: Response." *Victorian Studies*, 52:1, 2009, 106–13.

Mitchell, Kate. *History and Cultural Memory in Neo-Victorian Fiction: Victorian Afterimages*. Basingstoke: Palgrave Macmillan, 2010.

Palmer, Beth. "Are the Victorians still with us?: Victorian Sensation Fiction and its Legacies in the Twenty-First Century." *Victorian Studies*, 52:1, 2009, 86–98.

Pidduck, Julianne. *Contemporary Costume Film: Space, Place and the Past*. London: BFI Publishing, 2004.

Possession. Dir. Neil LaBute. USA: Warner Brothers, 2002.

Sadleir, Michael. *Fanny by Gaslight*. London: The Reprint Society, 1947. (Original published 1940.)

Sadoff, Diane F. *Victorian Vogue: British Novels on Screen*. Minneapolis: University of Minnesota Press, 2010.

Shiller, Dana. "The Redemptive Past in the Neo-Victorian Novel." *Studies in the Novel*, 29:4, 1997, 538–60.

Stam, Robert. "Introduction: The Theory and Practice of Adaptation." In *Literature and Film: A Guide to the Theory and Practice of Film Adaptation*. Eds. Robert Stam and Aessandra Raengo. Oxford: Blackwell, 2005, 1–52.

Sutherland, John. "Michael Sadleir and His Collection of Nineteenth-Century Fiction." *Nineteenth-Century Literature*, 56:2, 2001, 145–59.

Sweet, Matthew. *Inventing the Victorians*. London: Faber and Faber, 2001.

Tipping the Velvet. Dir. Geoffrey Sax. UK: BBC, 2002.

Voigts-Virchow, Eckart. "In-Yer-Victorian-Face: A Subcultural Hermeneutics of Neo-Victorianism." *Literature Interpretation Theory*, 20, 2009, 108–25.

Waters, Sarah. *Tipping the Velvet*. London: Virago, 1999.

Part V
Beyond Authors and Canonical Texts

16
Costume and Adaptation

Pamela Church Gibson and Tamar Jeffers McDonald

In the emerging scholarship around adaptation, there seems a significant absence: work around the importance of *costume*, both to the films themselves, and to their popularity and reception. This chapter seeks to remedy this, through examination of popular adaptations, claiming that costume is a vital part of the adaptive process of the text from page to screen since it is, and has been throughout film-making history, one of the primary methods of character revelation. Jane Gaines' famous assertion about Hollywood studio-era costume, that "dress tells the woman's story" (1990: 180) ignores the fact that male costume too is generally recruited to evoke character. Although Gaines maintains that the film heroes have narrative action, but the film heroines only costume, by which to illuminate their characters, closer examination reveals that both sexes have generally been characterized through their clothes, not only at the specific period in Hollywood history Gaines is commenting on (1930s–40s) but still: "story-telling wardrobes," as Turim calls them (1983: 8), are as common today as in Hollywood's golden age and found as often on television as on the larger screen. In considering a range of popular films, we end with close explorations of two contrasting pairs of adaptations, aiming to reveal not only how the characters are brought out but also suggesting a further important use of costume within adaptation: providing audiences with a range of visual pleasures, from the desirously acquisitive to the more contemplative joys accompanying cultural capital successfully engaged.

A Companion to Literature, Film, and Adaptation, First Edition. Edited by Deborah Cartmell.
© 2012 Blackwell Publishing Ltd. Published 2012 by Blackwell Publishing Ltd.

Pleasure in Dress

What little scholarship there is on film costume deals primarily, as noted, with the feminine (Gaines, 1990) and with classic Hollywood. But fashion scholars are equally guilty; many ignore cinema, while those who do address it could often give it more thought, time, and care. The arguments that have emerged in the past decade around the pleasure afforded by historical dress seem to depend heavily on psychoanalysis (see Bruzzi, 1997; Gaines, 1990). The link between spectatorial pleasure and consumption has not been made in relation to period film in general, whether heritage or not, and adaption studies has perhaps been similarly neglectful. A list of period films particularly linked to design and to consumption could include *The Piano* (Jane Campion, 1993, the costuming of which Bruzzi does indeed discuss in some detail. However, the consideration of costumes in cinema might move beyond the psychological and symbolical into the marketplace; this particular film was used by the Belgian designer Dries Van Noten as the specific inspiration for his next Autumn/Winter collection and was referenced in John Galliano's couture collection for Dior in the same year. At a much lower market level, it was reflected on the high street, in affordable sweeping skirts and lace-trimmed blouses.

Although *The Piano* is not an adaptation, if we consider the recent dominance of "heritage" cinema, which most film critics would agree established itself in the 1980s, and which has survived and evolved into different generic patterns (see Higson, 2003; Hill, 1999; Monk, 2011), most of it is made up of literary adaptations. This gives it part of its appeal to the educated middle-class audience (see Hill, 1999 and Higson, 2003); less attention has been paid in the academy to the way in which dress and decor have also been central to the popularity of this genre. Interestingly, the costume designs created for these films have often led to Oscar nominations and to awards, as with *A Room with a View* in 1985 and *The Age of Innocence* in 1993. This link between adaptation, audience pleasure, commercial success, and Academy Awards will run through this chapter, where we examine both Edith Head's Oscar-winning designs for *The Heiress* (1948) and Danilo Donati's acclaimed recreation of Renaissance dress for Zeffirelli's *Romeo and Juliet* (1968).

Capital, Cultural, and Other

One hypothesis advanced for the enormous popularity of heritage films during the 1980s was their nostalgic portrayal of a lost imperial past, which struck a chord in Thatcher's Britain and Reagan's America. There was less discussion of the direct links to the adoption of an aristocratic lifestyle by the new rich on both sides of the Atlantic, and the way in which the portrayals not only of dress but also particularly of decor were reflected in the marketplace, not merely the clothes on offer, but the furnishing, wallpaper and *objets* needed for the new country homes that were purchased during this economic boom. On both sides of the Atlantic, the new *nouveaux riches* acquired a country lifestyle, often faux-aristocratic in its pretensions, just as they had in the closing years of the nineteenth century (see Church Gibson, 2000). The wedding of Diana Spencer and Prince Charles in 1980 not only led to a rash of imitative pantomime weddings; it also enhanced the market for the romantic, in print and on screen.

This may seem merely another facet of the new consumption; however, it has more significance, since it suggests a desire not merely for the material wealth of the past but for certain aspects of the "past" itself. An understanding of the past, formerly predicated on literature, seemed more widely available within the cinema. Claire Monk has analyzed in detail the suggestion that these films appealed particularly to a middle-class audience and has taken issue with certain over-facile readings of their reception (2011). However, the "cultural capital" which accrues from period film in general and adaptations in particular is surely undeniable; the ability to discuss an adaption from the informed perspective of having read the book confers still more cultural capital on the viewer. Over the last two decades, cinematic adaptations have included mainstream versions of widely adapted and popular novels, as well as new art-house attempts to film the unfilmable, as with Raul Ruiz's critically successful interpretation of Proust (1999). The eminently filmable, particularly the Jane Austen adaptations which dominated film and television in the 1990s, did not so much influence dress, but affected different ways of buying into the past with The National Trust, garden centers, and the makers of "retro" furniture, wallpaper and fabrics all benefiting. In America, the designer Ralph Lauren became extremely rich through selling the clothes and the decor seen as epitomizing an "English country house lifestyle" (see Church Gibson, 2000). Adaptations also involved other forms of "cultural capital"; *The Wings of the Dove* (Iain Softley, 1997) drew heavily on Victorian narrative painting (Church Gibson, 2000) adding a further tranche of cultural capital for those fortunate enough to recognize these visual references.

"She sought to be eloquent in her garments" (James, 1880: 11)

Here we examine various uses of costuming in two film adaptations of Henry James' *Washington Square*: the William Wyler film, *The Heiress* (1949); and Agnieszka Holland's 1997 *Washington Square*. Wyler's *Heiress* owes its formulation of the heroine and the reworking of the narrative to the stage play of the same name by Ruth and Augustus Goetz, initially produced on Broadway in 1945 as *The Doctor's Daughter*. Holland's adaption, by contrast, returns to the original novel as its main source text, but nevertheless diverges from this to add elements of a back-story, and also takes some liberties with Catherine's fate at the end. While both Wyler's and Holland's versions choose to follow the standard Hollywood costuming tradition to illuminate the characters in their narratives, how they each choose to do this differs greatly in sartorial choices. Examination of the two films thus reveals some of the potential scope and limitations of using costume as character index.

In *Washington Square* the omniscient narrator employed by James only infrequently comments on what film theorists would refer to as the mise-en-scène: the specific costumes, objects, settings in and of the scenes being described. Nevertheless, there are a few moments when James does foreground *dress* to convey character, much as in the same way costume designers do. For example, James exerts effort in conjuring up Catherine through her clothes, adroitly conveying the young girl's personal lack of confidence clashing with her awareness of her father's social standing and what this requires of her, through conflict over her dress. In an extended sequence, James skewers both Catherine's unformed taste and her father's cold evaluation of his child, through describing her clothes and his attitude to them:

> When it had been sufficiently impressed upon her that she was a young lady . . . she suddenly developed a lively taste in dress: a lively taste is quite the expression to use. I feel as if I ought to write it quite small, her judgement in this matter was by no means infallible; it was liable to confusions and embarrassments. Her great indulgence of it was really the desire of a rather inarticulate nature to manifest itself: she sought to be eloquent in her garments and to make up for her diffidence of speech by a fine frankness of costume. But if she expressed herself in her clothes it is certain that people were not to blame for not thinking her a witty person.
>
> It made [Dr Sloper] fairly grimace, in private, to think that a child of his should be both ugly and overdressed . . . It simply appeared to him proper and reasonable that a well-bred young woman should not carry half her fortune on her back. Catherine's back was a broad one, and would have carried a good deal; but to the weight of parental displeasure she never ventured to expose it, and our heroine was twenty years old before she treated herself, for evening wear, to a red satin gown trimmed with gold fringe: though this was an article which, for many years, she had coveted in secret (James, 1880: 11–12).

There is much to unpack here. It is very interesting that James can be seen anticipating the costume designer's rubric of letting the clothes speak for the character, when he writes that Catherine hopes her exterior garments will hint at all that her interior character has to offer, but she herself is too shy to speak aloud. Unfortunately for Catherine it seems as if the "readers" of her costume statements are *mis*-reading her messages since, as the narrative voice adds rather unkindly, "if she expressed herself in her clothes it is certain that people were not to blame for not thinking her a witty person."

Both this narrator and Catherine's father, then, are critical of her style of dress, but intriguingly, only the omniscient voice acknowledges her attempts to choose *significant* outfits; her father, with all the justification for more kind judgment that he has as her relative, condemns her simply as tasteless. Dr. Sloper views her merely as "ugly and ill dressed," rather than as an inarticulate woman struggling to express some of her subjectivity in one of the few modes contemporaneously permitted well-bred young ladies. While both (male) voices thus condemn Catherine's lack of taste, only the more detached narrator seems to feel any squeamishness in criticizing her. Catherine's father views her incautious efforts at expressive dress as personal affronts to his dignity, rather than attempts to speak her character, illustrating that, for all his supposed care of her and his later insistence that she should marry well, these are facts linked more to his sense of personal importance than any real emotion for his child.

Both film adaptations of the novel use this incident of the red evening dress to offer illuminating insights into the characters of Dr. Sloper, Catherine, and Aunt Penniman, and indeed both go on to employ costume in a similarly symbolic and illustrative manner throughout the narrative.

Edith Head shared the Academy Award for costume in black and white for her work on the women's costumes in *The Heiress*, with Gile Steele who contributed the male attire. Head takes every opportunity to continue her usual habit of providing "story telling wardrobes," commenting in an interview in *American Film* that her aim always with costume was to ensure that, even if the sound went off in the cinema, the audience could follow the unfolding narrative simply by studying the costumes (Landis, 2007: 137).

The Heiress seems to have been a production in which all principles were completely dedicated to the idea of telling the story visually, through costume, mise-en-scène, and architectural details. Harry Horner, the production designer, detailed his meticulous methods of research in an article in *Hollywood Quarterly*, explaining how he had haunted New York for glimpses of appropriate houses, staircases, doorways, and parks. (Horner, 1955). Similarly Head notes that Olivia de Havilland took an active interest in the research for her role as Catherine Sloper, visiting museums, researching costumes and haircuts (Head and Ardmore, 1959: 89). Overall, however, the technique for outfitting Catherine to bring out her awkwardness was to cut the gowns so that they did not quite fit: "I made things purposely gap or wrinkle in the wrong place" (Landis, 2007: 137).

One of the challenges facing the design team of the film is that *The Heiress* was shot in black and white. Obvious color symbolism, like red for sexual allure, is therefore impossible. Edith Head was very experienced in working in monochrome, but nevertheless the black and white palette imposes restrictions not felt by Anna Shepherd, the costume designer on the later adaptation. Head's dresses for Catherine are consonant with mid-nineteenth-century fashions, and generally consist of a bodice over an undershirt visible at throat and wrists, over a full gathered bell-shaped skirt. Mostly Catherine seems to wear mid-range colors, not very dark, but not light either: one can imagine them as blues or browns. Only with the red evening dress noted in the novel is the outfit's color specifically mentioned. Head commented further on her strategy for dressing the heroine: because she was a rich man's daughter, her clothes could not be poor quality in design or fabric: instead the Head wardrobe takes the opposite tack, and swamps her in splendor, dwarfs her with luxury: "everything she wore was of the finest quality" (Landis, 2007: 137).

The opulent fabrics call out for attention, quite in contrast to Catherine's own self-effacing demeanor, but fully in keeping with the novel's comment that the young woman wished to dress "eloquently." Without knowing it, Catherine's clothes are eloquent of her own unhappiness, trapped as she is within the confines of the Washington Square house with its constant repetitions of mirrors, frames, doorways, shadows, all conspiring to suggest cages.

The film shows Catherine in fourteen different outfits, giving this one or that more emphasis as the narrative demands. The costume here supports the character readings fostered by the narrative, maintaining the costumer designer's tradition of offering character insights that the narrative does not spell out explicitly. As part of an adaptation, the costume works to concretize ideas thrown out by the novel but not dwelt on at length. For instance, Catherine's mature satisfaction with her life, at the point when Morris Townsend returns to visit her, is indicated through costume. Where the novel has a few sentences about her contentment with her life, house, and relations (James, 1880: 186), the film makes this visible though her clothes: finally she feels confident enough to wear a light, floaty outfit that she had originally bought on her trip to Paris. Although the cynicism brought to her character by her treatment by her father and Morris is also noticeable in her curt response to Maria's compliment, this is just one facet of her mature personality that Catherine has learnt to live with. Head ensured that this outfit – a dress of white lace and lavender chiffon – was the only one which properly fit de Havilland (Chierichetti, 2003: 100).

Both film adaptations of *Washington Square* use the scene with the red evening dress to illuminate the characters of vulnerable Catherine, her cold sarcastic father, and appeasing Aunt Penniman. The Wyler film, in fact, makes the dress the central point of the film's opening, as it is delivered in the opening moments to the house in a large dressmaker's box, and taken up the stairs, by Maria, the maid, to the excited Catherine, the camera leading the viewer into the house in pursuit of the large box.

When we first encounter Catherine she is wearing a standard day dress, high-necked, with a cameo brooch worn at the throat, long-sleeved, full, long and bell-skirted, in a seeming mid color. It is a fairly blank canvas used as contrast to the next two outfits she wears. The first of these is her underwear, when, in her bedroom, she is getting ready for the party to be held at the house of her aunt, Mrs. Almond. With her arms bare and her hair uncoiled from her usual bun, though still in a plait, Catherine looks much younger than usual, and is very excited about the opportunity to wear her new red dress. She seems vulnerable without her formidable skirts and tight-bodiced jackets, as if she has taken off chainmail. The new red evening dress, however, paradoxically makes her more vulnerable than this déshabille; it enables her father to wound her with his cold ironic comments.

The red dress, once on, reveals itself to be over-ruffled and over-trimmed (presumably with gold lace, as the novel tells us), as well as ill-proportioned and overly silky. Catherine looks like a piece of Victorian furniture, over-stuffed and upholstered, rather than a young woman. Although she beholds herself in the dress in the large stairwell mirror with delight, this soon turns to dismay when Dr. Sloper comments on her appearance. The dry sarcasm in his question, "Is it possible that this magnificent person is my daughter," instantly undermines Catherine's confidence. The novel adds that Catherine immediately wishes "that she had on another dress" (James, 1880: 21), and de Havilland makes the viewer feel in her awkward pose that she also wishes this.

As noted, most of Catherine's day dresses are in a mid color, cut to the same shape, and generally with white showing at the wrist and neck. On one occasion, however, her dress varies significantly: when Morris's sister, Mrs. Montgomery, comes to visit the doctor. Catherine's dress on this occasion is of watered silk, the sheen can definitely be seen when Catherine sits uncomfortably making stilted conversation with the older woman. The viewer becomes aware that Catherine is very ill at ease; she wants Mrs. Montgomery to approve of her, but seems unable to relax and talk to her in a way which might accomplish this. Her hand strays nervously to her throat on occasions; this is because, it is then realized, Catherine has worn with every other outfit a cameo or other brooch at her throat. Generally it is one with three droplets of pearls descending from it, and Catherine can dissipate her nervousness by fiddling with these while she listens or talks. The idea driving her to wear the over-frogged, heavy silk dress now becomes clear: since this is the day Morris is to talk to her father about marrying Catherine, she has tried to dress in her best, but been interrupted before perfectly ready. Morris is not expected for another hour, but the cunning doctor has asked his sister to step in before the interview. This revelation of Catherine's motives is borne out when she reappears after the doctor sends her to fetch some Madeira for their guest. She returns with the wine, but not until after Mrs. Montgomery's departure. We see why it is has taken her a while to return: although Catherine blames her delay on taking pains to make the serving tray look especially pretty, she has actually been back to her room. Now her dress is finished off with white lacy collar and cuffs, the white neck trimmed with black velvet bows, and at her throat now: her cameo. Catherine has sensed the importance of the meeting and gone to put on her psychological armor again.

Catherine's jewelry can indeed be seen to offer a separate strand within the narrative, one that is complementary to the main trajectory of the film and serves to support it by offering insights into the young woman's feelings. As noted, she generally wears a brooch at her throat, and most often small flowers of seed pearls for earrings. When she returns from Paris her earrings are noticeably larger and more prominent, indicating a development in her taste after exposure to elegant European luxuries. By the final scene, her jewelry is extremely prominent and should offer a warning to Morris, were he able to read its discourse, not to trifle with her affections again. The light chiffon dress that Catherine wears for the final scene has already been mentioned. It seems significant that Catherine is finally wearing one of her Parisian gowns; although she snaps that "it is the coolest dress I could find," it is entirely appropriate that she is wearing it when Morris comes back into her life. This was one of the gowns she had bought for the honeymoon his actions denied her. The play which the Wyler film used predominantly for its narrative puts the action "almost two years later" after Dr. Sloper's illness and death. The stage direction reveals the Goetz's conception of how this time should have dealt with the heroine:

> Catherine enters down the stairs. In her large placid way she is growing into a digni-fied and almost attractive woman. She is dressed in a filmy, pale dress, a little fussy perhaps, but effective and handsome (Goetz and Goetz, 1948: 76).

The chiffon dress designed for this scene by Head, as noted above, was the only one meant to fit de Havilland perfectly, to enable the actor to walk and move with more confidence as befitted her more mature character. Whether or not Head meant to fulfill the Goetz's idea that the dress was "a little fussy perhaps," it certainly is in contrast to the other outfits, heavy and dark, that she wears in the rest of the film. This dress has a hint of décolleté for the first time, though retaining the general cinched-waist, gentle bustle, and bell-shape of the other gowns. What seems espe-cially significant, however, is the use of cameos now. For the first time Catherine bears the flesh at her throat and has her cameo as a pendant on a ribbon hanging on her breast, rather than tightly fixed over the fastening at the top of her dress just under her chin, its tight closeness to her throat indicating a buttoned-up, repressed nature. In addition, now the pendant cameo is much larger than usual, and is matched and flanked by a pair of large, pendant cameo earrings, again much more eye-catching and sizeable than anything she has worn before. The woman with the confidence to wear this conspicuous jewelry is not to be trifled with or taken in by the machinations of her scheming aunt and the returned Morris, but fully has both the will and the wit to turn the tables on them and make them think she is as soft, forgiving, and ignorant as they both hope.

Significantly Catherine accompanies her masquerade of forgiveness with a costume-related gift. Although the novel is very explicit in noting that, returning from Paris, "Catherine had brought home a present to every one – to every one save Morris, to whom she had brought simply her undiverted heart" (James, 1880: 135), the Wyler film, following its play source, has Catherine bring Morris some buttons. This is first the occasion for a flash of Morris's contempt for Catherine to show itself, but secondly, when he sees what the buttons are made of, allows the man to reveal his mercenary side once more: "they are magnificent! They are rubies!"

Why does Catherine choose to give such an expensive gift to someone she knows is worthless? She has already baited the trap with her own seeming equanimity over taking up the elopement years later as if it had never been abandoned. The novel, which does not introduce the revenge strand which the Goetz bring to the play *The Heiress*, does not mention a gift at all; Morris returns, Catherine sends him away without the hope of being friends again. The play allows Catherine her revenge via the masquerade of acquiescence, enabling her to shut him *out* of the house in Washington Square as he once shut her *in*, by abandoning her to live with her unloving father. The buttons form part of the bait, but are not played up. Their significance as *ruby* buttons seems to lie in their setting off of resonances from the Biblical question, "Who can find a virtuous woman? For her price is far above rubies" (Proverbs 31: 10). Morris, grasping and mercenary, sees only their monetary value. He does not read symbols and signs; he does not realize the real value of the gift resided in it being from Catherine, given by her because she loved him. While fully encompassing the play's range of submerged meanings with the buttons, only the film uses them as a costume moment: the buttons she has bought Morris closely resemble the flower-like earrings she has worn throughout the film. The gift was meant to make them a matching couple. By the time he returns and she is now aware of his falseness and base motives, Catherine has moved away from wearing the modest seed pearl flowers to her showy cameos. Morris wearing the buttons would not match her now. Catherine has become the woman whose image she proudly displays on the cameo: still, calm, quiet, and pure, content to be seen without being touched. It is noticeable that Catherine no longer fiddles with her jewelry in the final scene. Even discomforted as she is by Morris' reappearance, her confidence has grown so far that she can not only face him but also trick him into revealing that his mercenary designs have never died.

The various costumes, and the developments in Catherine's clothes, accessories and hair-dressings, offer their own narrative which complements the dominant storyline by illustrating the heroine's inarticulacy and wish to express her individuality through dress; furthermore, they support the Goetz's strategy in adapting James' novel to permit Catherine small moments of revenge for her suffering.

In Agnieszka Holland's version, Catherine is much more sumptuously wardrobed, with twenty-three different outfits during the film's 115-minute running time. Of these, several seem to indicate that the film's costume designer, Anna Shepherd, has, like Head, created a separate storyline for the clothes which accompanies and supports the dominant narrative trajectory in tacit ways, with color, fabric, and design symbolism. We will examine the Holland film's take on the "red satin evening gown trimmed with gold lace" mentioned in the James novel, five striped or checked ensembles which appear at significant moments, and other outfits which convey the changes in character and fate of the central heroine.

Holland's film opens with some back-story not supplied by the Henry James novel: beginning with Catherine's birth and her mother's death in labor, the first few scenes of the film supply information about Catherine's lonely childhood. A plump, plain little girl with over-elaborate curls is seen staring out the window of a grand house; positioned at a window, she watches a man cross the Square and come up the steps to the front door. She runs squealing downstairs to throw herself at him. Thus the film shows Catherine already possessed of an abundance of energy and affection deemed unseemly by her society: for a young person of her gender, age and class, such outbursts of kinesis are frowned upon. Catherine is shown not only physically confined by the rules of contemporary Victorian America, however, but also by her clothes. Not only do the overly puffed sleeves, overly ruffled skirt, and overly numerous accessories draw attention to her plumpness and attempt constriction of her barely contained energy, the fabric itself is printed with large black and white stripes both laterally across her body and vertically dividing it. Catherine is caged within the confining feminine outfit, within the assumptions about appropriate behavior for upper class young ladies, and within the cold relationship with her father, just as clearly as within the bars of the striped dress.

This young Catherine is last seen staring out the window again; positioned next to a caged bird, she is overdetermined as trapped within her society in many ways. A slow dissolve takes the viewer to the adult Catherine standing at the same window, with a new caged bird: a slimmer and more elegant yellow canary, rather than the plump green parrot seen before, it visually matches the taller, slimmer young woman who has replaced the plump little child. Yet Catherine is still staring out of the window for her father's return. And she is still in fabric which confirms the cage society has made for her. This dress, as befits a young woman, is floor-length, rather than revealing around the knee the lacy white pantaloons the young Catherine wore, but otherwise the dresses are very similar in color and style, both featuring black and white stripes running horizontally and vertically over the fabric. As the camera replicates the shot of Dr. Sloper coming up the steps to his house, Catherine repeats her excited descent of the indoor stairs to meet him, again being cautioned by her Aunt Penniman not to gallop about; her energy is even more out of place in a young lady of her age. Catherine now controls herself enough to walk the last few steps but again is told off by her father when she goes to run up the stairs to dress for the dinner party at the Almonds'. These constant reminders of then-contemporary fiats against female energy being directed at anything more physical than dancing continue to enforce the sense of the societal cage Catherine is in; her dress fabric evokes this entrapment and that of her loveless home.

As noted, Henry James permitted his novel's omniscient narrator a small moment of dismay in viewing Catherine's attempt at "eloquent" dress: the red satin evening gown, supposed to display on her exterior the interior qualities she is too timid to express, carries only the message that she is a young lady with no fashion sense. Holland's film takes this further than the Wyler version, as it has color to play with: eschewing a red satin dress, costume designer Shepherd introduces a concoction of yellow, blue, and orange which is a nightmare of incoherence. Although the shape is historically fitting for a mid-nineteenth-century evening gown, with bare arms and a certain amount of décolleté, the dress itself engulfs and overwhelms the woman wearing it through the number of decorative details. There are rosettes of a piercing cornflower blue across the bodice, interspersed with giant yellow flowers; orange fabric bows and flowers are worn in the hair across a hair-band of the same blue. Although the fabric of the dress itself is quite restrained, with a pale blue and yellow floral motif, the amount of trimming and ruffles destroys any simplicity it might have had as a garment. There are huge orange bows on the ruffle of the full skirt, accompanied by smaller ruffles in the piercing blue and others in yellow. Overall Catherine looks like an overdressed orange, yellow and blue Christmas tree, with tassels and ribbons hanging off her like so much tinsel. The comparable outfit in the Wyler film version seems an essay in good taste beside this. Holland's Catherine is made to undermine herself entirely through not being able to edit out the many extraneous details of this outfit.

While the Holland version of the "red dress" scene changes the outfit's color, it preserves the sense of entrapment observable in other ensembles Catherine has worn. The bands of color crossing and re-crossing the body, along with the endless fussiness of too many decorative accessories, visually cages the young woman as successfully as if she were behind actual bars. Noticeably, once she meets Morris and begins to think that love, affection, and approval may have come into her life, Catherine is not seen in striped dresses for a while. She wears a plain but richly colored purple dress when she meets him coming back from her piano lesson: her only checked/caged accessory here is a shawl which she constantly drops once she meets him, hinting that he might be able to help set her free from the confines which hold her frustrated.

However, the stripes reappear when Dr. Sloper returns from talking to Morris to deliver the news to Catherine that he will not permit her marriage. Aflutter to hear his thoughts, Catherine draws him excitedly into the library, her movements swift and erratic; once she has heard his negative verdict she leaves the room slowly, almost as if drugged with misery, and sets off up the stairs to her bedroom. Her full skirt seems to weigh her down visibly and the weight of her unhappiness is summed up by her slow progress up the staircase. The fabric of the dress worn for this crucial scene again underlines that as a young woman in nineteenth-century America, Catherine has few rights of her own. She is her father's property and is his to do with as he wishes. Although she is of age to marry if she wishes, she has been brought up to be so dutiful that it does not occur to her — yet — to disobey. All this is conveyed in the dress worn in the scene: its fabric is of salmon pink with a darker red stripe, the color initially seeming cheerful but the darker stripe implying more unruly passions. Catherine is caught in the web of societal assumptions that bid young women be obedient, just as the bars on her dress fabric trap her inside a pretty pink cage, and the dress shape itself, dependent on a hoop for its swing and girth, confines her inside a metal or whalebone enclosure.

Once in Europe, the last piece of symbolically barred material is found in Catherine's wardrobe. As she and her father ride up a mountain pass in a carriage, Catherine can be seen in an elegant blue day dress worn with a modish brown chapeau, much higher than the previous poke-bonnets worn in America. The hat has a huge blue plume that flutters around her head once she and her father alight to climb the higher mountain peaks. She also wears a checked scarf around her throat, white with brown bars upon it. After her father has delivered the devastating pronouncement that he considers it "obscene" her mother died and she lived, the doctor departs, and Catherine stands alone at the top of the mountain. Her scarf flutters, unfurls itself, and is carried away completely on the breeze. With the loss of her scarf Catherine is never again seen with stripes or bars: she is no longer trapped in the ultimate cage she was confined by, that of believing she had her father's love to lose if she disobeyed him. Now she realizes that he has never cared for her, she is freed from this confining illusion.

Catherine has thus been freed from the tyranny of trying to please a father who has no love for her; she has yet to learn to live without Morris's love too. By the film's end, when she has undergone that ordeal and emerged calmer and more mature, the changes she has made to her life are evident in her costume, as well as in the camera work and mise-en-scène. The former repeated overhead shot of Dr. Sloper ascending the steps of his house is replaced with one of three women coming up the stairs; where one man ruled the household before, now, with Catherine's establishment of what seems to be "Manhattan's first day-care center" (Turan, cited in Raw, 2003: 76), many women are free to come and go, turning the door handle with confidence and admitting themselves, rather than waiting for a servant to answer the bell. Furthermore, no one is standing at the window watching eagerly and idly, as all the women inside the house have their own tasks and responsibilities now. Catherine is seen at the piano, her hair tidily held in a snood as befits a woman with work to do, rather than a lounging lady of leisure.

The scene is constructed around such parallels and contrasts, and furthers these by having all the children singing together to Catherine's accompaniment at the piano. Where before she stood as a child, pressurized, trying to please her father by singing a solo, now the children sit relaxed and sing together the whole song of which she could only manage a few notes. The room seems packed, with flowers, plants, children in overabundance everywhere; even a bird cage, now empty and atop the piano, has plants in it. Catherine's dress is simple in form but rich in fabric, further suggesting via its rich, luxurious, fabrics the fullness of the life she has made for herself, with her music and the children she has about her. The bodice seems to be of a very deep piled velvet in an intense tone somewhere between red/russet and purple. The satin skirt is of the same hue but appears lighter because of its lighter fabric. When Morris appears to petition her for her love again, Catherine sinks to the floor, her very full skirt spreading out around her like a stain or puddle. But she has not sunk under the weight of emotion, as sometimes before; she is picking up toys left by the children on the floor. Catherine has been winnowed by sadness and betrayal but emerged self-sufficient, confident, and the richness but practicality of her final outfit, with its watch as foremost ornament, rather than a merely decorative rosette, bears witness to the transformation in her character.

Both the Wyler–Head and Holland–Shepherd adaptations use costume for symbolic purposes, tacitly revealing details of character growth and development, in support of the main narrative. Both employ the appropriate shapes and garments for the historical setting, but also manage to wring thematic significance from this conformity to general period accuracy. In both films the layering of clothes, with lacy white undergarments peeking out at a neckline or beneath a richly embroidered over-sleeve, suggests the women wearing such garments are ruled by secrets, by hidden emotions. While the Head wardrobe employs symbolic pieces of jewelry, the Shepherd costume plot utilizes striped and checked fabrics to suggest the symbolic bars – societal, emotional – which confine the woman.

Other adaptations, while maintaining the usual emphasis on character revelation, can also dedicate themselves to the evocation of famous paintings or, by contrast, to playful reference to textual jokes. There is a reputable body of work on the adaptations of Shakespeare, but we yet feel there is more to say about dress and design. We believe that we should add a brief analysis of costume and consider what effect different modes of sartorial display might have on both audience and text. The next section therefore considers the lush period costuming of Zeffirelli's *Romeo and Juliet* (1968), setting the film against the fashionable updating, complete with designer clothes and accessories, of Baz Luhrmann's 1996 version of the play.

Deborah Cartmell has observed that Zeffirelli is, above all, "operatic" (2007: 212). This comes through in many ways; his cavalier disregard for the script does not mean the shortening of the play. Soliloquies and dialogue are replaced by visual set-pieces: the dancing of the Moresca when the lovers first brush against one another; the servant's performance of the Nino Rota song "What is a Maid?" whilst the two future lovers – children in a room full of much larger adults – seek one another out, circling the crowd while the adults listen enthralled and the camera picks out here a pearl-embellished sleeve, there a jeweled headdress.

Danilo Donati's elaborate, detailed, and historically authentic costumes seem to indicate close study of Renaissance paintings. The servants and the young men who initiate the first quarrel, with their parti-colored hose, resemble those seen in the background of Bellini's depiction of a Procession through Piazza San Marco in 1496. The Prince gallops into the square, followed by a troop of horsemen; with his red velvet hat and the gold-fringed bridles of his horse, and the armored soldiers behind him with lances and pennants, he could have cantered out of a canvas painted by Uccello. Juliet's high-waisted red gown with its slashed, beribboned, and bejeweled sleeves brings to mind the painting of Giovanna Tuornabuoni by Paolo Ghirlandaio. But it is not simply the visual splendor and the pleasure they provide that make these clothes important. Donati has taken inordinate care to make the colors of the clothes work with and echo the settings: the tiny oranges on the trees in the garden where Juliet, clad in a russet velvet gown, waits anxiously for the Nurse, or the mauve and blue clothes in which the lovers are secretly married, matching the swirls of color to be seen on the walls of the chapel behind them. A wardrobe supervisor who worked with Zeffirelli in the 1960s – when we might remember he not only staged operas at Covent Garden but also did a dry run for *Romeo and Juliet* at Stratford with a young Judi Dench – was interviewed as part of a wider, ongoing project. She described frequently finding him on the stage before dress rehearsals armed with brushes and small pots of paint; he would work on sections of the scenery to ensure that it would provide the same tonal values as the costumes which would pass in front of it in the performances (Church Gibson, 2012).

This extraordinary weaving of costume into the overall mise-en-scène reinforces the sensuousness of the film. Deborah Cartmell has told us that Zeffirelli's films of Shakespeare are "sensual rather than cerebral" (2007: 212). She stresses the fact that part of his radical adaptation is to present the young as innocent, as victims of the adult world around them. The costume and styling throughout – despite its Renaissance authenticity – reinforce Zeffirelli's desire to make a film that would be very much of its time. Although much has been made of its "flower power" potential and the fact that the year of its release was 1968, the year when peace, love, and flower-power were replaced by inter-generational strife on the streets, it seems more important to think of the *childlike* quality of his two unknown leads. Leonard Whiting and Olivia Hussey seem to have been cast not only for their youth and beauty, but also for their diminutive stature compared to those around them. We see Juliet sitting on the Nurse's knee; later she crouches on the floor behind her Nurse's skirts, sheltering from the wrath of her father. Her only ornament is a simple gold crucifix; her hair hangs down her back in a plait. She is borne towards us, and towards Romeo, as she dances at the Capulet house, almost child-like between two tall, burly men. Romeo is slender and excessively youthful, particularly when confronted with the muscular strength of Michael York as Tybalt.

The Nurse, to mourn Tybalt, dons a veil and a wimple, deliberately designed to give her the appearance of a nun. Decked in this false religious authority, she tells Juliet to forget Romeo and marry Paris; like Friar Laurence, the surrogate father to these children, she too is unreliable. Romeo's friend Benvolio is equally young, soft, and easily threatened by the adult world; but Mercutio is here decked in black. As played by John McEnery, he works against the typical delivery of the "Queen Mab" speech. He falters, postures, strides into the square – almost as if under the influence of some hallucinogenic drug. Romeo has to calm him gently. Mercutio's dark clothing is in sharp contrast to the violent reds, oranges, and yellow worn by the Capulets; he is lacking in any ornamentation, but Tybalt is fashionable, with his overly pointed toes and embellished codpiece.

Throughout, the costume reinforces Zeffirelli's version of the play, his wish to emphasize youth, innocence, and beauty. Interestingly, it has survived. And possibly a whole generation of high-school students really believe that had Friar John ridden a *horse*, like Balthazar, the final catastrophe might have been averted. The Friar's enforced detention in a house of pestilence is just one of the many things Zeffirelli decides to discard. The heightened emotion he substitutes for textual fidelity is emphasized by the lush textures and colors, the extravagant costuming, the carefully chosen locations, and the careful attention to the tonal values of mise-en-scène during particularly significant scenes.

When we move to more recent adaptations we find Baz Luhrmann's *Romeo + Juliet* (1996), a take on the play which was very popular on its release, but now seems overburdened by its anxiety to make visual joke after visual joke for the benefit of those who know their Shakespeare. The Out Damned Spot dry cleaner, the Agincourt cigarettes, Rosencrantzy's deli, and *TIMELY* magazine, which has "Dave

Paris" on its cover as "bachelor of the year," all suggest, through their quotes-become-brands, the very commercialization of culture which the film then itself perpetuates.

The clothes are created by Kim Barrett who also dressed the blockbuster *The Matrix*, but in addition to presenting designed costumes, the film shows off its sourced finds from luxury brands. The credits thank Dolce e Gabbana for dressing the "Capulet boys" and the house of Prada for the simple navy suit in which Romeo is married. Patrick Cox is thanked for the loafers and Reebok for the trainers seen throughout.

Luhrmann's film possesses a visual style which is relentlessly inventive, beginning with a series of aerial zooms across the cityscape. The director and costumier have settled on a schema in which the "two households" instead of being "both alike in dignity" are here alike in their gangster status. The costume design seems to cast an eye backwards to Technicolor musicals of the past: the feud between Montagues and Capulets is here figured visually as reminiscent of the WASP Jets versus the Hispanic Sharks, setting up a dizzying mise-en-abyme as *West Side Story* (1961) was itself based on *Romeo and Juliet*.

The Montagues wear bright Hawaiian shirts and drive a cheerful yellow beach buggy. The Capulets, imagined more like a Mafia family, have sleeker vehicles. Tybalt wears Cuban boots with solid silver heels. His shirt has a religious icon – catholic kitsch is everywhere from Juliet's bedroom to each clock face we see. Gregory has a tattooed head, Samson a pink quiff, but the Capulet boys have still more aggressive tattoos.

As with the costume design for the later *Titanic* (1997) which kept teen idol Leonardo di Caprio in timeless costumes that would not mar his boyish attraction by burdening it with historical detail, Romeo's clothes are less stylized. He appears more simply dressed, at first in a disheveled jacket and shirt, the seeming aftermath of a formal dinner, later in a bright blue vintage Hawaii shirt. For the feast, Barrett tells us that she took Shakespeare literally, dressing Juliet as a "bright angel" and Romeo as a "true knight," supplying the former with wings and the latter with armor. While the costume works here to enhance the text, at other times it is distracting.

It undermines, for example, the extraordinary beauty of the closing sequence, when Romeo lies beside Juliet in the church and Wagner wells up on the sound-track. The overall effect cannot but be moving, with the two young leads and the music from *Tristan und Isolde*. But the scene is marred for the keen-eyed since we cannot but notice Romeo's smart black loafers as the camera pulls away.

Put side by side, the two adaptations viewed here differ in effect and pacing. The more recent film seems overly busy, frantic. Zeffirelli is operatic, but Luhrmann is too relentless to be truly "cinematic."

Yet the film survives; partly because of the power and popularity of its story, arguably partly also due to the lasting influence of the earlier Zeffirelli film in the classroom context. Star power is also responsible: the film succeeds when it does due to the casting of di Caprio. Not only does he bring in the teen audience with his boyish good looks, but he can speak the lines as if they were his own. He almost transcends the Prada suit, the Patrick Cox loafers, the screeching sirens, and circling choppers.

Examination of this pair of popular cinematic adaptations illuminates a fundamental fact: film costume does much more than merely indicate historical setting or period. The two film versions of James' *Washington Square* illustrate how carefully costume can be utilized to provide a schematic framework of personality; not only do the outfits, accessories and hairstyles each reveal character traits of the heroine, but also, viewed across the timeframe of the narrative, they show, in their development, how Catherine changes and matures. Although the Wyler and Hollander endorse different views of Catherine, and adapt the James novella in different ways, they both employ recurrent costume motifs to demonstrate her personality's development over time. Costume is thus one of the most significant parts of the adaptive process and merits a much more frequent and respectful analysis than it usually receives. The comparison of the *Romeo and Juliet* adaptations by Zeffirelli and Luhrmann brings out the other major role of costume: to create audience pleasure. It may be overly simplifying to suggest that the older film provides the sensual pleasure of seeing Shakespeare's poetry imaginatively rendered on the screen, through the costume, decor, settings, and *objets d'art*, while the more recent one delivers the thrill of acquisitive longing for this or that luxury brand item. Both films, however, attest to the role that visual pleasure plays in lavish cinematic adaptations; taken together, all four case studies demonstrate that careful analysis of the art of adaptation cannot afford to overlook the importance of costume any longer.

REFERENCES

Bruzzi, Stella. *Undressing Cinema: Clothing and Identity in the Movies*. London: Routledge, 1997.

Cartmell, Deborah. "Franco Zeffirelli and Shakespeare." In *The Cambridge Companion to Literature on Screen*. Ed. Russell Jackson. Cambridge: Cambridge University Press, 2007, 216–25.

Chierichetti, David. *Edith Head: The Life and Times of Hollywood's Celebrated Costume Designer*. New York: HarperCollins, 2003.

Church Gibson, Pamela. *Fashion and Celebrity Culture*. Oxford: Berg, 2011.

Church Gibson, Pamela. "Theory and the Practitioner – Contested Costuming." *Film, Fashion & Consumption*, 1:4, 2012.

Gaines, Jane. "Costume and Narrative: How Dress Tells the Woman's Story." In *Fabrications: Costume and the Female Body*. Eds. Jane Gaines

and Charlotte Herzog. London: Routledge, 1990, 192–6.

Goetz, Ruth and Augustus Goetz. *The Heiress*. 1948. London: Samuel French. Film.

Head, Edith and Jane Kesner Ardmore. *The Dress Doctor*. Boston: Little, Brown, 1959.

Higson, Andrew. *English Heritage, English Cinema: Costume Drama since 1980*. Oxford: Oxford University Press, 2003.

Hill, John. *British Cinema of the 1980s*. London: BFI, 1999.

Horner, Harry. "Designing 'The Heiress'." *Hollywood Quarterly*, 5:1, 1950, 1–7.

James, Henry. *Washington Square*. Oxford: Oxford University Press, 1982.

Landis, Deborah Nadoolman. *Dressed: A Century of Hollywood Costume Design*. New York: HarperCollins, 2007. Citing interview in *American*

Film: Dialogue on Film: Edith Head, May 1978, 38.

Monk, Claire. *Heritage Film Audiences: Period Film and Contemporary Audiences in the UK*. Edinburgh: Edinburgh University Press, 2011.

Turan, Kenneth. "*Washington Square*: A New Approach to an Old Address." *latimes.com*, October 10, 1997. Cited in Laurence Raw. "Rethinking Costume Drama: Agnieszka Holland's *Washington Square* (1997)." *The Henry James Review*, 24:1, 2003, 69–81.

Turim, Maureen. "Designing Women: The Emergence of the New Sweetheart Line." *Wide Angle*, 6:2, 1983, 4–11.

17

Music into Movies

The Film of the Song

Ian Inglis

Discussions within adaptation studies have consistently noted the persistence of a cultural bias which has elevated the literary above other forms:

> The field of adaptations in the past has been dominated by scholars working primarily from an "English Lit" perspective who may be inclined to privilege the original literary text above its adaptations, thus favouring the slow individualized process of reading/interpretation above the "immediate" short-term and often shared pleasures of visual spectatorship (Whelehan, 1999: 17).

However, the transformation of music into movies actively challenges such assumptions, for here the processes are reversed: listening to music is the "short-term" activity, and watching the film becomes the "slow" process. For decades, popular music has suffered from an elitist opposition which defines it as transient, ephemeral, and ultimately lacking in value. Rupa Huq is among those who have pointed to "an inherent anti-intellectual bent . . . academic work on pop is frequently viewed with lofty contempt by educational traditionalists" (Huq, 2006: 43). And while pop and rock (and their study) may no longer face the overt disapproval of previous decades, it remains true that they are still regarded with suspicion by those who seek to maintain a rigid distinction between "high" and "low" cultural forms. In this sense, the song-as-source could not be more different from the novel-as-source: whereas the contents of the novel are invariably reduced in size to satisfy the demands of the screenplay, those of the song are invariably expanded. Yet both practices pose similar questions about authorship, intent, and faithfulness, and an

A Companion to Literature, Film, and Adaptation, First Edition. Edited by Deborah Cartmell.
© 2012 Blackwell Publishing Ltd. Published 2012 by Blackwell Publishing Ltd.

analysis of the adaptation of songs into films will suggest that the issues raised by the augmentation or elaboration of an original text are at least as important as those raised by its contraction or abbreviation.

In the decades since the emergence of rock'n'roll in the mid-1950s and the subsequent growth of a globally oriented popular music industry, cinema has found a variety of ways in which to utilize pop and rock as agents that repeatedly demonstrate the aesthetic and commercial links between music and film.[1] The earliest and most obvious strategy involved the recasting of pop stars as movie stars, which essentially followed the route established by pre- and postwar entertainers such as Gracie Fields, George Formby, Bing Crosby, and Frank Sinatra: Elvis Presley appeared in more than thirty Hollywood films, from *Love Me Tender* (Robert D. Webb, 1956) to *Change of Habit* (William A. Graham, 1969); Cliff Richard's ten movies included *Expresso Bongo* (Val Guest, 1959), *The Young Ones* (Sidney J. Furie, 1961), and *Summer Holiday* (Peter Yates, 1963); and, in a slight variation, the Beatles starred as themselves in *A Hard Day's Night* (Richard Lester, 1964) and *Help!* (Richard Lester, 1965). From the 1970s onwards, a major shift in this practice saw an increase in the number of performers seeking to avoid the limitations of the screen musical and attempting instead to define themselves as "serious" actors in nonmusical films. The extensive list includes Mick Jagger in *Ned Kelly* (Tony Richardson, 1970) and *Freejack* (Geoff Murphy, 1992); Cher in *Mask* (Peter Bogdanovich, 1985) and *Tea With Mussolini* (Franco Zeffirelli, 1999); David Bowie in *The Man Who Fell To Earth* (Nicolas Roeg, 1976) and *Merry Christmas Mr Lawrence* (Nagisa Oshima, 1983); Sting in *Plenty* (Fred Schepisi, 1985) and *Stormy Monday* (Mike Figgis, 1988); Roger Daltrey in *McVicar* (Tom Clegg, 1980) and *Buddy's Song* (Claude Whatham, 1991); and Madonna in *Body of Evidence* (Uli Edel, 1993) and *Swept Away* (Guy Ritchie, 2002).

Other approaches have included performance-based documentaries, such as *Woodstock* (Michael Wadleigh, 1970), *The Last Waltz* (Martin Scorsese, 1978), *Stop Making Sense* (Jonathan Demme, 1984), *Heart of Gold* (Jonathan Demme, 2006), and *U2 3D* (Catherine Owens and Mark Pellington, 2007); narrative films in which popular music provides the dramatic or comedic context, including *This is Spinal Tap* (Rob Reiner, 1983), *Grace of My Heart* (Alison Anders, 1996), *Still Crazy* (Brian Gibson, 1998), and *Almost Famous* (Cameron Crowe, 2000); and biopics, such as *Coal Miner's Daughter* (Michael Apted, 1980), *Sid and Nancy* (Alex Cox, 1993), *Control* (Anton Corbijn, 2007), and *Sex & Drugs & Rock'n'Roll* (Mat Whitecross, 2010). And the replacement of a newly composed film score by a (commercially attractive) soundtrack of pre-existing tracks has become a staple feature of contemporary cinema, following the early examples provided by *The Graduate* (Mike Nichols, 1967), *Easy Rider* (Dennis Hopper, 1969), and *The Big Chill* (Lawrence Kasdan, 1983).

However, there is an additional practice which, while it may have received less attention, has nonetheless made a significant contribution to the relationship between music and film. The adaptation of music itself into movies – the transformation from vinyl to celluloid – has proceeded along several trajectories. First, and at the most mundane level, there has been (particularly through the 1980s and 1990s) a spectacular growth in the routine use of song titles as film titles – even though there is often little acknowledgment of the song's presence other than its use as incidental background music and/or its reprise over the end credits. *Blue Velvet* (David Lynch, 1986) took its name from Bobby Vinton's 1963 hit single; *Stand By Me* (Rob Reiner, 1986) followed the song originally released by Ben E. King in 1961; *Peggy Sue Got Married* (Francis Ford Coppola, 1986) was titled after the 1959 Buddy Holly track; *Pretty Woman* (Garry Marshall, 1990) referenced Roy Orbison's 1964 song; *The Crying Game* (Neil Jordan, 1992) reproduced the title of Dave Berry's 1964 single; and *Boogie Nights* (Paul Thomas Anderson, 1997) used the title of the track released by Heatwave in 1976. It is noteworthy that few of these films were derived from current, or even recent, songs; but by referring to tracks twenty or thirty years old, the filmmakers actively sought to ensure that a nostalgic generation of "baby-boomers" would be alerted to their presence.[2] Secondly, in a more contrived manner, the ability to collect unrelated tracks drawn from an individual career and locate them, at opportune moments, into a fictional musical narrative has been exploited in movies such as *Across the Universe* (Julie Taymor, 2007), which was based around the compositions of the Beatles, and *Mamma Mia!* (Phyllida Lloyd, 2008), which featured the songs of Abba. In both these approaches, there is little actual correspondence between the lyrics and the screenplay. While the films may seek to use relevant songs at convenient moments, what associations there are tend to be general, and are often inferred through the audience's prior knowledge of the music: the tracks supply broad emotional triggers rather than specific references.

Thirdly, the adaptation of pre-existing albums into full-length screenplays has been a recurrent, if occasional, practice in film production. The impetus came with the development of the concept album:

> Concept albums are unified by a theme, which can be instrumental, compositional, narrative, or lyrical. In this form, the album changed from a collection of heterogeneous songs into a narrative work with a single theme, in which individual songs segue into one another. Concept albums first emerged in the 1960s as rock music aspired to the status of art, and some were accordingly termed "rock operas" (Shuker, 1998: 5).

Among the first (in 1968) were the Pretty Things' *S. F. Sorrow* and the Kinks' *Village Green Preservation Society*. These remained as purely musical texts, but as the popularity and visibility of the concept album grew in the 1970s, with releases such as David Bowie's *The Rise and Fall of Ziggy Stardust & The Spiders From Mars* (1972), the Eagles' *Desperado* (1973), and Genesis's *The Lamb Lies Down On Broadway* (1974), the commercial potential of screen adaptations (and other spin-off projects) became increasingly attractive. Thus, *Tommy* (Ken Russell, 1975), *Sgt Pepper's Lonely Hearts Club Band* (Michael Schultz, 1978), *Quadrophenia* (Franc Roddam, 1979), and *The Wall* (Alan Parker, 1982) took the "stories" presented in the corresponding albums by The Who, the Beatles and Pink Floyd as the narrative engines for their screen adaptations, and offered audiences an additional way in which to consume the original text.

Each of the albums contained a sufficient number of tracks (twenty-four in *Tommy*, seventeen in *Quadrophenia*, twenty-six in *The Wall*) to provide the variety of viewpoints, events, and personalities around which a full-length screenplay might conceivably be developed. Pete Townshend's original songs for *Tommy* told the story of an abused and traumatized boy who retreats into a deaf, dumb and blind world, only to discover that his skill on the pinball machine brings him celebrity and adulation. Townshend's expanded screenplay (co-written with director Ken Russell) not only gave roles to several leading rock musicians (Eric Clapton, Tina Turner, Elton John) but also recruited a distinguished cast of actors, including Jack Nicholson, Oliver Reed, Ann-Margret and Robert Powell. Its two Oscar and three Golden Globe nominations (Ann-Margret won the Golden Globe award for Best Actress in a Musical or Comedy) reflected its critical, as well as commercial, success. *Quadrophenia* employed a combination of musicians-as-actors (Sting, Toyah Wilcox) and actors (Ray Winstone, Leslie Ash, Michael Elphick, Timothy Spall) to tell of London teenager Jimmy's life as a mod in the mid-1960s; again, the narratives outlined in Townshend's original music were supplemented by a script written by Dave Humphries, Martin Stellman, and director Franc Roddam. Unusually, the screenplay for *The Wall* was written by the album's composer Roger Waters, after a tentative approach to Roald Dahl had been rejected; incorporating animation by Gerald Scarfe, it related the story of rock musician Pink's troubled childhood and eventual mental breakdown. Scarfe's account of the film's evolution suggests that he and Waters were co-workers rather than collaborators: "Roger and I had separate jobs – he the music and words, and I the pictures: it was my job to visualise Roger's words and music. We didn't tread on one another's toes" (Scarfe, 2010: 136). The film won two BAFTA awards – for Best Original Song ("Another Brick in the Wall") and Best Sound.

In the case of *Sgt Pepper's Lonely Hearts Club Band*, the absence of any clear narrative cues from the album's twelve tracks obliged screenwriter Henry Edwards to fashion a rather meandering plot in which the members of a successful pop group attempt to come to terms with their fame, and save their home town from impending disaster. The policy of placing rock performers (the Bee Gees, Peter Frampton, Alice Cooper, Aerosmith and Earth, Wind & Fire) alongside actors (Donald Pleasence, Steve Martin, Frankie Howerd) was repeated although, unlike the previous three examples, there was no input from the Beatles themselves. Indeed, in comparison with those movies, the film is less of an adaptation and has far more in common with the "compilation" policy displayed in *Across the Universe* and *Mamma Mia!* Its failure to provide a coherent "story" also begs the question of whether the Beatles' album should be considered a concept album at all: apart from the central conceit that the songs are performed not by the Beatles but by a "lonely hearts club band" and the diffuse sense of nostalgia that permeates every song, it is difficult to discern a consistent theme or trajectory that unifies the tracks.[3] However, the adopted (musical and visual) images of the Beatles as the celebrated members of the fictional band have become so familiar that they routinely serve as a collective conceptual justification for the album's status, and have cemented its reputation – deserved or not – as "rock's first concept album . . . conceived as an integral whole, to be heard straight through in the manner of a variety show or light opera" (Assayas and Meunier, 1996: 46–7). To preserve a sense of continuity between the album and the movie, the Beatles' producer George Martin was employed as the film's musical director, although his comments after its release indicated that he was well aware of the creative difficulty in imposing a narrative where none existed:

> The film has not been a huge success . . . I think perhaps its very title was a disad-
> vantage. It certainly was not a film of the record . . . I do not think anyone could ever
> make a film of *Sgt Pepper's Lonely Hearts Club Band* (Martin, 1979: 219).

Significantly, his disappointment with the film does not focus, as might have been expected, on issues of fidelity to the source text and the intentions of its authors, but on the ability of the material itself to undergo "the complex, conscious process of implementing changes necessary to re-present [it] under new conditions in a new medium" (Cardwell, 2002: 21). Moreover, it demonstrates that despite the undoubted commercial power of anything bearing the Beatles' brand, successful adaptation from one medium into another can never be guaranteed.

The final way (and the one I wish to discuss in detail) through which musical texts have inspired subsequent cinematic treatment can be seen in a number of instances where the lyrics of individual songs have been adapted into full-length movie screenplays. The ease with which novels, plays, and radio serials have, at different times, been adapted into films rests in part on their relative length: a 3-hour play, a 600-page novel, or a 15-part radio series would, under normal cir-cumstances, be expected to contain ample raw material for manipulation. In com-parison, a single song – often no more than a couple of verses and two or three minutes in length – might seem unpromising stuff. And yet, when movie screen-plays have emerged from such unexpected sources as theme park rides, TV com-mercials, and board games – *Pirates of the Caribbean* (Gore Verbinski, 2003), *The Haunted Mansion* (Rob Minkoff, 2003), *Johnny English* (Peter Howitt, 2003), *Clue* (Jonathan Lynn, 1985) – the pop/rock song does not appear so unlikely.

Two early examples in the post rock'n'roll era were *The Legend of Tom Dooley* (Ted Post, 1959), which was prompted by the hit versions in 1958 (by the Kingston Trio in the United States, and Lonnie Donegan in the UK) of the traditional nineteenth-century North Carolina folk song; and *Frankie and Johnny* (Frederick De Cordova, 1966), which loosely followed the events related in the turn-of-the-century ballad performed in and around St. Louis, and widely reputed to be based on one or more actual murders.[4] However, the first movie adapted from the lyrics of a contemporary pop song was *Yellow Submarine* (George Dunning, 1968). It was followed by *Alice's Restaurant* (Arthur Penn, 1969); *Ode to Billy Joe* (Max Baer Jr., 1976); *Convoy* (Sam Peckinpah, 1978); *Harper Valley PTA* (Richard C. Bennett, 1978); and *Big Bad John* (Burt Kennedy, 1990). In each case, the movies adopted and adapted the themes introduced in the original songs (performed by the Beatles, Arlo Guthrie, Bobbie Gentry, C. W. McCall, Jeannie C. Riley, and Jimmy Dean, respectively).[5]

Of course, the practice is not entirely new. Among the fifteen Irving Berlin songs that featured in the soundtrack of *Holiday Inn* (Mark Sandrich, 1942) were two that themselves became the source for subsequent movies – *Easter Parade* (Charles Walters, 1948) and *White Christmas* (Michael Curtiz, 1954). *Singin' in the Rain* (Stanley Donen and Gene Kelly, 1952) was suggested by the song written by Arthur Freed and Nacio Herb Brown for the soundtrack of *The Hollywood Revue of 1929* (Charles Reisner, 1929). In these cases, however, the songs contributed little to the narratives, apart from the provision of an indicative setting but, at the same time, the broadly romantic sentiments embodied in their lyrics (and titles) worked to introduce audiences to the films' overarching themes, as did the presence of *Holiday Inn*'s stars – Fred Astaire and Bing Crosby, respectively – in *Easter Parade* and *White Christmas*. What is new about the pop/rock-derived films listed above is that they endeavor to use music not only for its traditional functions – to establish mood, to reflect emotional and mental states, to locate time and place, to sustain structural unity – but also for its explicit provision of formal narrative content.

Yellow Submarine

In fact, *Yellow Submarine* is distinguished by the absence of an explicit narrative in its original (i.e. musical) form. Lennon and McCartney's lyrics do little more than tell of "a man who sailed to sea," whose stories inspire the Beatles themselves to follow his example and live "beneath the waves" in their own yellow submarine. Surrounded by nautical sound effects, the singalong chorus repeats itself in the manner of a nursery rhyme. The track (sung by Ringo Starr) was included on the group's seventh album *Revolver* in 1966 and was also released as the B-side to "Eleanor Rigby." However, it quickly gained in popularity, particularly with the group's younger fans, and it became a perennial item on radio request shows such as BBC's Saturday morning *Children's Favourites* (later re-named *Junior Choice*).

The decision to use the song as the basis for a movie dated back to an agreement made in 1963, when United Artists negotiated a three-picture deal with the group's manager Brian Epstein. *A Hard Day's Night* and *Help!* had been hugely profitable, but by 1967 the Beatles – tired of the demands of movie-making and largely unimpressed by the scripts they had been offered – were unwilling to cooperate with the studio's demands for the contracted final film. When it was suggested to Epstein by Al Brodax of King Features (who had produced the thirty-nine-part *The Beatles* ABC-TV cartoon series in the United States) that a full-length animated feature might satisfy his contractual obligations and require only minimal input from the group, he reluctantly agreed and the film went into production in 1967. The writers charged with turning the three-minute song into a ninety-minute movie were Brodax, Lee Minoff, TV scriptwriter Jack Mendelsohn, and Erich Segal whose subsequent screenwriting credits would include *Love Story* (Arthur Hiller, 1970), *A Change of Seasons* (Richard Lang, 1980) and *Man, Woman and Child* (Dick Richards, 1983). It soon became apparent that the song alone was not a sufficiently strong basis for an adaptation. Four previously discarded studio tracks were donated by the Beatles, but many of the eventual ideas, images and songs were imported from the group's *Sgt Pepper* album. As a result, the final screenplay was a wide-ranging, eclectic, and collaborative enterprise. The film's art director, Heinz Edelmann, has explained that "there was never one script: we had about twenty. Roger McGough of The Scaffold was responsible for much of it . . . there were no strong opponents for the Beatles, so I had to invent the Blue Meanies" (Harry, 1984: 37).

Indeed, very little of the plot has its origins in the song. The film opens in the magical-mythical world of Pepperland whose tranquil and peaceful existence is suddenly disrupted by the invasion of the Blue Meanies. One of the residents (Young Fred) escapes and journeys to Liverpool in his yellow submarine to seek the help of the Beatles. After traveling through the Seas of Time, Science, Monsters, Heads, Holes and Green, they arrive in Pepperland where they use the power of their music to restore peace and harmony. Although *Yellow Submarine* received (and has continued to receive) critical acclaim, this has largely derived from its innovative assembly of visual styles (op art, pop art, art nouveau, surrealism, comic-book art, photomontage, Dadaism) and synthesis of performative musical genres (vaudeville, pantomime, pop, rock, psychedelia, electronic, dance, brass band) rather than its narrative strength:

> The film is a masterpiece and it has opened up new and undreamed of horizons for animation. It bears seeing several times for its content to be fully appreciated . . . it has given such an impetus to full-length animation cinema that it is already a classic (Edera, 1977: 87).
>
> *Yellow Submarine* is unique. There have been pretenders and copiers who have failed miserably because they don't understand the philosophy of the design, the graphic qualities and that superb sense of colour. And the genius of it is that the Beatles' music was both a catalyst for what happened but also linked the whole film together (Pritchard and Lysaght, 1998: 262).

The Beatles' dialogue was voiced by actors (including Paul Angelis and Lance Percival) and the group's only participation was to appear as themselves in a brief sequence at the end of the movie in which they urged the audience to "go out singing."

Alice's Restaurant

Arlo Guthrie premiered his eighteen-minute, monologue-in-song "Alice's Restaurant Massacre" at the 1967 Newport Folk Festival; in the same year, it filled the first side of his debut album, *Alice's Restaurant.* As the son of folk singer Woody Guthrie, Arlo was known to many on the folk scene, but the million-plus sales of the album gave him immediate access to a much wider audience. The track opens and closes with a chorus that guarantees "You can get anything you want at Alice's restaurant," but its conversational, idiosyncratic tone is established in the spoken introduction:

> This song is called "Alice's Restaurant," and it's about Alice, and the restaurant, but "Alice's Restaurant" is not the name of the restaurant, that's just the name of the song, and that's why I called the song "Alice's Restaurant."

The lyrics are based on Guthrie's own experiences and recall, in minute detail, his unsuccessful attempts to dispose of the restaurant's garbage on Thanksgiving Day, which eventually led to his arrest, court appearance, conviction, and $50 fine; some time later, his newly acquired criminal record allows him to escape being drafted into the U.S. army. At the induction center, he expresses his mock indignation in a manner that illustrates the humorous and satirical veins running through the song:

> I went over to the sergeant and said, "Sergeant . . . you want to know if I'm moral enough to join the army, burn women, kids, houses and villages, after being a litterbug?" He looked at me and said, "Kid, we don't like your kind."

The film (in which Guthrie played himself) was released in 1969 and coincided with a string of movies that expressed a growing resentment against the perceived intolerance and aggressive authoritarianism of Richard Nixon's presidency; they included *MASH* (Robert Altman, 1970), *Catch-22* (Mike Nichols, 1970), *Zabriskie Point* (Michelangelo Antonioni, 1970), and *The Strawberry Statement* (Stuart Hagmann, 1970). In terms of its media consumption, this "counterculture" was not just ideologically, but commercially, significant: "a youthful amalgam of radical politics, oriental (or occult) mysticism, liberated sexuality, hallucinogenic drugs, communal life-styles, and rock'n'roll . . . from the onset, the counterculture was a powerful force in the marketplace" (Hoberman and Rosenbaum, 2008: 285).

As Guthrie's lengthy monologue was unusually detailed, the adaptation (supplemented by director Arthur Penn and Venable Herndon) rarely strayed from the original narrative, although in an interview at the time of filming, Penn did admit that there would be additional material, some of which would center around Arlo's family background (especially his relationship with his father) and the cultural community to which he belonged, and which would represent the socio-political climate of the late 1960s:

> The film really spans a broader period of time than the record. And I'm hoping that in the course of the film, we will go through with [Arlo] those experiences which are not dissimilar from all of ours – the kind of personal identity crisis of dying parents, and surrogate choices in parents, and love affairs. But, on the other hand, we are witnessing something in which rebellion is not the essential characteristic. These kids are on to something much more genuine . . . and so I'm hoping that the film will be able to elucidate that part of their subculture in a way that I haven't seen done elsewhere yet (Gelmis, 1970: 261).

The film's release, in August 1969, coincided with Guthrie's appearance at Woodstock, which further added to his visibility and provided invaluable advance publicity. The following year, Penn (as director) was nominated for an Oscar, and Guthrie's music for a BAFTA.

Ode to Billy Joe

The Mississippi-born singer-songwriter Bobbie Gentry released her self-composed debut single "Ode to Billie Joe" on Capitol Records in August 1967. In its first week, it sold 750,000 copies in the United States alone. It replaced the Beatles' "All You Need Is Love" at the top of the single charts, stayed there for a month, and sold more than three million copies around the world. The album of the same name topped the LP charts, and Gentry received three Grammy awards, for Best New Artist, Best Female Vocal Performance, and Best Contemporary Female Solo Vocal Performance; she was also named Best New Female Vocalist by the Academy of Country & Western Music.

> Its four minutes and fifteen seconds tell the compelling story of a pair of Delta teenagers who share a deep dark secret that ultimately leads to the boy's suicide and the girl's lifelong bereavement. Rich details of rural farm life render [it] more a short story than a pop song (George-Warren, 2007: 122).

Surrounded by a sultry studio arrangement of violins and cellos, the un-named girl remembers, over five concentrated verses, "a sleepy, dusty, Delta day," when the family's dinner-time conversation includes Mama's news that local boy Billie Joe McAllister has apparently committed suicide by leaping off the nearby Tallahatchie Bridge. The information is delivered casually, amid discussions about jobs to be completed on the farm and comments about the biscuits, black-eyed peas, and apple pie. Although Mama describes it as a "shame," Papa's response that "Billie Joe never had a lick of sense" illustrates the general indifference to his death. Mama notices that her daughter has suddenly lost her appetite, tells the family that "that nice young preacher, Brother Taylor" is coming to dinner on Sunday and then, almost as an afterthought, delivers the song's most mysterious lines: "Oh, by the way, he said he saw a girl that looked a lot like you up on Choctaw Ridge, and she and Billie Joe was throwin' somethin' off the Talla-hatchie Bridge." The final verse moves forward one year: the narrator mentions various illnesses, marriages and deaths that have taken place within the family, and concludes by revealing that much of her time is now spent gathering flowers around Choctaw Ridge and dropping them over the bridge. The steadfast refusal of Gentry (who retired from the public eye in the early 1980s after her second divorce) to reveal what it was that the girl and Billie Joe threw off the bridge helped to create an ongoing debate about the mystery at the heart of the song. Some of the more common suggestions include an aborted or miscarried fetus, a shotgun, a bundle of clothing, the body of a stillborn or unwanted baby, a suitcase, and a wreath.

When, in 1976, the film version of *Ode to Billy Joe* (its title changed from Billie to Billy) was released, the promotional posters confidently announced:

On June 3 1953, Billy Joe McAllister jumped off the Tallahatchie Bridge. Now the muddy Tallahatchie River gives up its secrets – the secrets within the haunting ballad that swept America. What the song didn't tell you, the movie will.

Robby Benson and Glynnis O'Connor were cast in the two main roles and the task of adapting Gentry's lyrics into a screenplay was given to Herman Raucher, who had previously scripted *Watermelon Man* (Melvin Van Peebles, 1970) and *Summer of '42* (Robert Mulligan, 1971). The film names the narrator as Bobbie Lee Hartley (Gentry's real name is Roberta Lee Streeter), and locates it in the early 1950s. Rather than preserve the unanswered questions in the song – what was thrown off the bridge? why did Billy Joe take his own life? – Raucher supplies an unexpected explanation. Bobbie Lee and Billy Joe's tentative ado-lescent romance is opposed by her family because of her youth; however, a more serious obstacle is Billy Joe's emergent homosexuality. When, at a barn dance, he succumbs to a sexual encounter with another man, he is overwhelmed by shame and runs away. Confused and unhappy, he commits suicide. The object thrown over the bridge is revealed as Bobbie Lee's rag doll, and her decision to discard it is symbolic of her transition from childhood towards adulthood. But while the specific version of events depicted in the screenplay may have been surprising, the creation of the film itself was not: on the first occasion he heard Bobbie Gentry's acoustic performance of "Ode to Billie Joe" its producer Jimmie Haskell noted, "the song sounded to me like a movie" (George-Warren, 2007: 123).

Convoy

In 1975, C. W. McCall's "Convoy," from his album *Black Bear Road*, was a chart-topping single in the US and UK. Written by Bill Fries (who recorded the song under the pseudonym of McCall) and Chip Davis (who co-produced the track), it intersperses a CB conversation between truckers "Rubber Duck," "Pig Pen" and "Sodbuster," with Rubber Duck's spoken account of their convoy's progress from Los Angeles to New Jersey (via Tulsa and Chicago) as "a thousand screamin' trucks" are pursued across the country by the police. For a song which had international popularity, the vocabulary is unusually specific. Parts of the dialogue are rooted in the language of the CB radio community, as shown in the opening exchange: "Breaker One-Nine, this here's the Rubber Duck. You got a copy on me, Pig Pen? Yeah, Ten-Four, Pig Pen;" other sections refer to truckers' practices and problems: "We was headin' for bear on I-One-O, 'bout a mile outta Shaky Town . . . we tore up all of our swindle sheets and left 'em settin' on the scales." Although its ideological roots are very different from those expressed in "Alice's Restaurant," part of the song's appeal may be explained by the similar oppositional stance taken by the truckers, and their defiant response to the petty restrictions imposed on their working conditions:

> The song does point up a phenomenon that began to surface in the mid-1970s. Before that time, it was expected that people who violated the law or committed anti-social acts would be caught and punished. The large number of prison songs certainly are filled with this theme, but in "Convoy" a number of people commit several illegal acts and are not caught or punished (Rogers, 1989: 199).

The song ends with the victorious truckers evading the massed ranks of police and National Guard, and smashing through the New Jersey tollgate: "So we crashed the gate, doing 98! I said, let them truckers roll, Ten-Four!"

B. L. Norton, who had written the country rock-based screenplays for *Cisco Pike* (which he also directed, in 1972) and *Outlaw Blues* (Richard T. Heffron, 1977) was asked to adapt the song's lyrics for the subsequent movie. Director Sam Peckinpah's previous films had included re-mythologized Westerns such as *The Wild Bunch* (1969), *The Ballad of Cable Hogue* (1970), *Junior Bonner* (1972), and *Pat Garrett and Billy The Kid* (1973). Given these credentials, and the song's origins, it was unsurprising that *Convoy*'s expanded narrative reproduced many of the conventions of the classic Western – the independent hero, a corrupt sheriff, the girl of dubious morals, a bar-room brawl, dramatic locations, a thrilling chase, and a happy reunion. Rubber Duck (Kris Kristofferson) remains the central protagonist, but the most significant development involves the introduction of two entirely new characters: Melissa (Ali MacGraw) as the smart and sexy girl who wins Rubber Duck's heart, and Sheriff Lyle "Cottonmouth" Wallace (Ernest Borgnine) as his vengeful pursuer. The pursuit no longer spans the country, but is confined to the photogenic desert landscapes of

Arizona and New Mexico; the climactic showdown, in which Robber Duck's truck plunges from a bridge into the river below, takes place near the US–Mexico border. Presumed dead, a disguised Rubber Duck reveals himself to Melissa at his funeral with the words, "You ever seen a duck that couldn't swim?" before taking to the road in the newly reformed convoy.

Convoy was one of a number of movies in the decade that re-imagined the traditional stagecoach chase as a high-speed road race, in which radio and/or telephone communications often replaced the shotguns and bows and arrows of previous films. *Duel* (Steven Spielberg, 1971), *Vanishing Point* (Richard C. Sarafian, 1971), *Dirty Mary Crazy Larry* (John Hough, 1974), *The Sugarland Express* (Steven Spielberg, 1974), and *Smokey and the Bandit* (Hal Needham, 1977) all, in different ways, adapted and updated the romantic Western visions of John Ford and Howard Hawks. It was also Peckinpah's penultimate film; although *Convoy* was a major financial success (grossing more than $15 million in the US alone) his only film thereafter was *The Osterman Weekend* (1983).

Harper Valley PTA

Known within the country music community as "The Storyteller," Tom T. Hall's compositions have been recorded by such performers as Johnny Cash, Loretta Lynn, Waylon Jennings, and Bobby Bare. However, his most celebrated song was recorded in 1968 by the unknown Jeannie C. Riley: "Harper Valley PTA" describes the widowed Mrs. Thompson's furious response to a note from her teenage daughter's school in which she is chastised for "wearing your dresses way too high . . . drinking, running round with men, and going wild." Accompanied by her daughter, she goes to the PTA's weekly meeting and angrily berates its members. One by one, she accuses them: Mr. Harper, Shirley Thompson, and Mrs. Taylor are drunks; Bobby Taylor is a womanizer; Mr. Baker impregnated his secretary; and Widow Jones should "keep her window shades all pulled completely down." Before leaving, she demands to know how they dare to criticize her: "This is just a little Peyton Place, and you're all Harper Valley hypocrites." Within a few weeks, it had sold a million copies in the US and went on to sell more than six million copies around the world. Riley was awarded the Grammy for Best Female Country Vocal Performance, and the record was named as Single of the Year by the Country Music Association. In the 1970s, she found it difficult to maintain her career and formally distanced herself from the song. "Harper Valley PTA" remains Hall's most successful composition and the one with which he is most readily associated: "Inspired by Ernest Hemingway, Hall brought a laconic storyteller's touch to country songwriting and singing" (Kingsbury and Axelrod, 1988: 279).

In contrast with the development of *Convoy*, the creative team behind *Harper Valley PTA* had no obvious associations with the song or its principal themes.

Director Richard C. Bennett had directed occasional episodes of US TV series such as *The Girl from Uncle, Barnaby Jones,* and *Harry O*; scriptwriter George Edwards had written the screenplays for horror movies *The Killing Kind* (Curtis Harrington, 1973) and *Ruby* (Curtis Harrington, 1977). The choice of television comedy actress Barbara Eden (familiar to sitcom audiences as Jeannie in NBC-TV's long-running *I Dream Of Jeannie*) to play the part of Stella Johnson signaled their intention to move away from a song that illustrated "the irony and hypocrisy often embedded in our behavior and attitudes . . . and the fight of a little person against the powers in the social system" (Rogers, 1989: 186–7) to present an adaptation that was overtly comedic and which employed the song (and its knowing reference to Peyton Place) as a distant starting-point rather than a central theme.

After reproducing the initial events described in Hall's lyrics, the screenplay rapidly becomes ever more fanciful. When Stella's house is bombarded with toilet paper by members of the PTA, she and her close friend Alice (Nannette Fabray) take their revenge through a series of grotesque and farcical pranks designed to humiliate the board members: these range from setting up the arrest of a naked board member outside a motel, to stampeding stolen elephants (painted pink!) through another member's house. In addition, she announces her intention to run for the position of PTA president, thus incurring the wrath of the current president Flora Simpson Reilly (Audrey Christie). Another friend, Skeeter (Bob Hastings) is kidnapped by two hired villains, imprisoned in a monastery, and rescued by Stella and Alice disguised as nuns. Stella wins the election and marries Will (Ronnie Cox) who is one of the few PTA members who supported her. A subplot involves the burgeoning romance between Stella's daughter Dee (Susan Swift) and fellow student Carlyle (Brian Cook). The movie was generally dismissed as puerile and repetitive, but the favorable reception given to other contemporaneous comedies that sought to tackle similar gender issues in more thoughtful terms – including *Nine to Five* (Colin Higgins, 1980) and *How to Beat the High Cost of Living* (Robert Scheerer, 1980) – resulted in Barbara Eden reprising her role in the television series of the same name in 1981–82.

Big Bad John

Jimmy Dean had been performing since the early 1950s, but it was not until the release of "Big Bad John" in 1961 that he rose to national, and international, prominence. The song (recited largely in monologue) which was Dean's first composition, tells the story of a pit disaster in which the trapped miners are saved by the strength and bravery of the eponymous hero. John is presented as a "gentle giant" who "stood six foot six and weighted two forty five" but was "kinda quiet and shy." His origins are shrouded in mystery, although there are rumors that in New Orleans he killed a man. When a pit shaft caves in, trapping a team of miners underground, it is John who strides through "the dust and the smoke of this man-made hell," holds aloft the broken beams, and allows his twenty companions to escape. Before he can be brought up to safety, the shaft finally collapses and he is entombed. The pit never re-opens, but a plaque commemorates his sacrifice: "At the bottom of this mine lies a big, big man – Big John." The record sold more than two million copies and won Dean a Grammy for Best Country & Western recording. In 1962, he scored another hit record with "P.T. 109," a patriotic celebration of President John F. Kennedy's spell as a torpedo boat commander in the Second World War. Thereafter, Dean continued the transition to family singer and entertainer: from 1963 to 1966 he hosted his own networked ABC-TV variety series, and appeared as reclusive millionaire Willard Whyte in the James Bond movie *Diamonds Are Forever* (Guy Hamilton, 1971).

Surprisingly, there was a three-decade gap between the song and the movie. In the 1960s and 1970s, Burt Kennedy had directed numerous Westerns, such as *Return of the Seven* (1966), *The War Wagon* (1967), *Hannie Caulder* (1971), and *The Train Robbers* (1973). Through the 1980s, he had worked mainly in television, and *Big Bad John* was only his second full-length feature film in twelve years.[6] He also co-wrote the screenplay, with Joseph Berry and C. B. Wismar. While the film does retain the accident in which John gives his life, much more is added. After shooting a man in self-defense, John (Doug English) and sweetheart Marie (Romy Windsor) are forced to flee from Louisiana. Marie's abusive stepfather (Ned Beatty) claims John has kidnapped Marie and persuades ex-lawman Cletus Morgan (played by Dean) and his friend Jake Calhoun (Jack Elam) to hunt them down. Managing to stay one step ahead of those on his trail, John eventually finds work in a Colorado mine, but the temporary safety the couple enjoy is threatened by the arrival of his various pursuers, before the climax in the mine. Although the attendant publicity promised that "from one hell of a legend comes one hell of a movie," the film is as much about the easy-going relationship between "good ole boys" Cletus and Jake as it is about the legend of John himself. The movie did confirm a partial return to filmmaking by Kennedy, who went on to direct *Suburban Commando* (1991) and *Comanche* (2000).

Five of the movies (*Yellow Submarine* is the exception) are firmly rooted in the narrative tradition of country music. The contemporary popular music industry was created – via rock'n'roll – from the synthesis of five existing musical antecedents, each of which possessed specific characteristics that would be incorporated into the structures and cultures of the songs that followed. From gospel came the call-and-response technique, in which backing vocalists answer the lead singer; from jazz came a penchant for improvisation and instrumental solo breaks; from ballads came a pre-occupation with romantic love; from the blues came a perennial emphasis on loneliness and melancholic self-reflection; and from folksong (which includes country) came the concept of story-telling:

> Country music began to take shape in the nineteenth century. From travelling entertainer to townsfolk, friend to neighbour, parent to child, scraps of ancient British airs,

blues, minstrel songs, hymns, contemporary popular songs, and, later, jazz and ragtime passed back and forth, and mingled (Kingsbury and Axelrod, 1988: 8).

Historically, country music has been a way in which the newly arrived and disparate communities of North America were able to retain some association with their native cultures; the tales embedded in those songs represented one way in which traditional stories, events, and characters that might have been forgotten in the New World were protected and preserved. And although country music (or "old-time" music as it was initially called) would later branch off into specific sub-genres (hillbilly, cowboy, honky-tonk, bluegrass and, more recently, country rock) each retained elements of the story-telling function.

Of course, the narrative component of song is not confined to country – but it is there that it finds its fullest and most persistent expression. In his discussion of country music's enduring popularity, Jimmie N. Rogers asserts from the outset that "the lyrics are the key to country music . . . a country song is a special form of communication – communication that more closely resembles interpersonal or face-to-face interaction between two people" (Rogers, 1989: ix–x). Through the density of detail and the conversational tone in which those details are delivered, the lyrical component of the country song is thus rendered as a story passed from one person/generation to another. Such songs have been classified as "ballads" or "epics:" "the ballad tells a story involving one main event. In contrast, the epic songs are long, complex, and involve several events tied together by a common theme" (Nettl, 1965: 47). In either case, however, they exemplify the oral tradition through which myths, tales and legends were transmitted in pre-literate societies, and which was maintained despite the spread of literacy in the nineteenth and twentieth centuries.

There is thus a certain irony in the fact that as we now approach a post-literate society, the ability of non-literary texts to serve as source material for interpretation and presentation in other forms is becoming increasingly evident. In addition to the previously mentioned theme park rides, television commercials and board games, screenplays have been routinely adapted from such sites as card games, comic strips, role-playing games and, most emphatically, video games.[7] It would therefore be remarkable if songs – especially songs that are well known, feature clear protagonists, and contain possibilities for narrative exploration – were exempt from these developments. Charles Jaret's attempt to determine those lyrical elements that help to make a successful country song identifies a number of recurring themes.[8] The most common are sexual (making love, kissing, flirting, cheating) "honky-tonking" (bar-room activities including drinking, picking up a partner, having a good time), rambling (being corrupted, working, driving, traveling), and sad love (crying, breaking up) – all of which feature centrally in the songs and movie adaptations discussed above. It should further be noted that it is not just the content of their songs, but general public perceptions of the lives of country performers themselves that reproduce these emotional and dramatic contours. Nowhere is this better illustrated than in the (stereo)typical concerns of the country music biopic: "its typical focus on rural poverty, its authenticity derived from suffering, its presentation of heterosexual relations as central but often difficult and violent . . . [and] . . . a propensity for early deaths" (Babington, 2006: 86).[9]

But the mere presence of such themes in country songs does not, in itself, guarantee a plausible screenplay. For that to happen, it has been suggested that certain conventions in the process of adaptation need to be observed. They are:

> the playful use of familiar elements from the original source whose recognition in a new context will evoke pleasure; the activation of narrative potentialities already implicit in the source text; the filling out of circumstantial detail by evoking resonant historical settings or piggybacking on established narrative texts or genres; a generally and often incongruously lightsome tone suggesting that this sort of adaptation is fundamentally more whimsical than the serious adaptation of novels or plays or stories (Leitch, 2007: 262).

In varying degrees, *Alice's Restaurant*, *Ode to Billy Joe*, *Convoy*, *Harper Valley PTA* and *Big Bad John* meet all these requirements.

Although *Yellow Submarine* may also appear to fulfill the same conditions, it is perhaps best understood as a promotional device for new objects rather than a reflection of an existing object. Almost uniquely at the time, the film's release incorporated the launch of a wide range of associated memorabilia – toys, games, jigsaws, souvenir books, watches, costumes, bedclothes, greetings cards, lampshades, lunchboxes, crockery, and dolls were among the dozens of products that bore little or no relationship to the themes of the original song, but which significantly increased the income generated by the project. In this sense, *Yellow Submarine* is not an adaptation but an appropriation: "An adaptation signals a relationship with an informing source text or original . . . appropriation frequently affects a more decisive growing away from the informing source into a wholly new cultural product or domain" (Sanders, 2006: 26).

NOTES

1 See, for example, Romney and Wootton (1995); Mundy (1999); Dickinson (2003, 2008); Inglis (2003); Donnelly (2005); Lannin and Caley (2005); Conrich and Tincknell (2006).

2 There are occasional exceptions to this general rule. See, for example *Take This Job and Shove It* (Gus Trikonis, 1981); the song, originally written and recorded by David Allan Coe, was a major hit in 1977 for Johnny Paycheck, and the movie followed four years later. See also

Girls Just Want To Have Fun (Alan Metter, 1985), which came just two years after Cyndi Lauper's song in 1983.

3 See Moore (2008).

4 Two earlier versions of the same story were presented in *Her Man* (Tay Garnett, 1930) and *Frankie and Johnnie* (John H. Auer and Chester Erskine, 1936).

5 The same process has also been repeated in a number of made-for-TV movies, such as *The Gambler* (Dick Lowry, 1980) and *Coward of*

the County (Dick Lowry, 1981), both of which drew from songs originally performed by Kenny Rogers, who also starred in both productions.

6   The first was *The Trouble With Spies* (also known as *Two Female Spies With Flowered Panties*) in 1987.

7   See Leitch (2007).

8   See Jaret (1982).

9   Among the country music performers whose lives have been retold in full-length biopics are Hank Williams, Woody Guthrie, Loretta Lynn, Patsy Cline, Jerry Lee Lewis, and Johnny Cash. Others, including Tammy Wynette, Naomi and Wynona Judd, Dottie West, LeAnn Rimes, and John Denver have been featured in made-for-TV movies. See Inglis (2007).

References

Assayas, Michka and Claude Meunier. *The Beatles and the Sixties*. New York: Henry Holt, 1996.

Babington, Bruce. "Star Personae and Authenticity in the Country Music Biopic." In *Film's Musical Moments*. Eds. Ian Conrich and Estella Tincknell. Edinburgh: Edinburgh University Press, 2006, 84–98.

Cardwell, Sarah. *Adaptation Revisited*. Manchester: Manchester University Press, 2002.

Conrich, Ian and Estella Tincknell. Eds. *Film's Musical Moments*. Edinburgh: Edinburgh University Press, 2006.

Dickinson, Kay. Ed. *Movie Music: The Film Reader*. London: Routledge, 2003.

Dickinson, Kay. *Off Key: When Film and Music Won't Work Together*. Oxford: Oxford University Press, 2008.

Donnelly, K. J. *The Spectre of Sound*. London: BFI, 2005.

Edera, Bruno. *Full Length Animated Feature Films*. London: Focal, 1977.

Gelmis, Joseph. *The Film Director as Superstar*. London: Secker & Warburg, 1970.

George-Warren, Holly. "Mystery Girl: The Forgotten Artistry of Bobbie Gentry." In *Listen Again: A Momentary History Of Pop Music*. Ed. Eric Weisbard. Durham NC: Duke University Press, 2007, 120–36.

Harry, Bill. *Beatlemania: The History of the Beatles on Film*. London: Virgin, 1984.

Hoberman, J. and Jonathan Rosenbaum. "*El Topo*: Through the Wasteland of the Counterculture." In *The Cult Film Reader*. Eds. Ernest Mathijs and Xavier Mendik. New York: McGraw-Hill, 2008, 284–93.

Huq, Rupa. *Beyond Subculture: Pop, Youth and Identity in a Postcolonial World*. London: Routledge, 2006.

Inglis, Ian. Ed. *Popular Music and Film*. London: Wallflower, 2003.

Inglis, Ian. "Popular Music History on Screen." *Popular Music History*, 2:1, 2007, 77–93.

Jaret, Charles. "Characteristics of Successful and Unsuccessful Country Music Songs." *Popular Music and Society*, 8:2, 1982, 113–24.

Kingsbury, Paul and Alan Axelrod. Eds. *Country: The Music and the Musicians*. New York: Abbeville, 1988.

Lannin, Steve and Matthew Caley. Eds. *Pop Fiction: The Song in Cinema*. Bristol: Intellect, 2005.

Leitch, Thomas. *Film Adaptation and its Discontents*. Baltimore, MD: Johns Hopkins University Press, 2007.

Martin, George. *All You Need is Ears*. New York: St Martin's Press, 1979.

Moore, Allan. "The Act You've Known for all these Years: A Re-encounter with *Sgt Pepper*." In *Sgt Pepper and the Beatles*. Ed. Olivier Julien. Aldershot: Ashgate, 2008, 139–46.

Mundy, John. *Popular Music on Screen*. Manchester: Manchester University Press, 1999.

Nettl, Bruno. *Folk and Traditional Music of the Western Continents*. Eaglewood Cliffs, NJ: Prentice-Hall, 1965.

Pritchard, David and Alan Lysaght. *The Beatles: An Oral History*. Toronto: Stoddart, 1998.

Rogers, Jimmie N. *The Country Music Message Revisited*. Fayetteville: University of Arkansas Press, 1989.

Romney, Jonathan and Adrian Wootton. Eds. *Celluloid Jukebox*. London: BFI, 1995.

Sanders, Julie. *Adaptation and Appropriation*. London: Routledge, 2006.

Scarfe, Gerald. *The Making of Pink Floyd The Wall*. London: Orion, 2010.

Shuker, Roy. *Key Concepts in Popular Music*. London: Routledge, 1998.

Whelehan, Imelda. "Adaptations: The Contemporary Dilemmas." In *Adaptations: From Text to Screen, Screen to Text*. Eds. Deborah Cartmell and Imelda Whelehan. London: Routledge, 1999, 3–19.

18

Rambo on Page and Screen

Jeremy Strong

There is a scene near the end of the second installment of *Rambo: First Blood Part II* (George Cosmatos, 1985) where, after a battle of extraordinary bloodiness, the hero returns with a helicopter-full of U.S. servicemen kept illegally as prisoners in Vietnam long after the end of the war. One of the freed soldiers is eager to know how the United States has changed in the intervening years. Initially reluctant to be drawn, to disappoint men who have been through so much, Rambo eventually tenders this as an answer when pressed that something "must" have altered:

> "Sure. In a way. I guess. Ronald Reagan's president."
> To which his interlocutor replies; "Ronald . . . ? Wait a minute. You don't mean the movie actor." Rambo chuckles; "Yep. 'Death Valley Days' himself."
> "Well, holy fuck."
> "Yeah, I said that many times" (Morrell, 1985: 235).

For anyone familiar with the movie, this account may have started broadly in accordance with their recollections of the film, one of the most popular, lucrative, and influential movies of the time. Yet the continuing exchange seems wholly out of synch with the ideological tenor of the film. Wasn't it, surely, a ridiculously gung-ho, right-wing piece of racist cold war ultra-violence which the then President actually commended? Wasn't the muscle-bound actor feted at the Whitehouse by the Reagans? Didn't the MIA (Missing In Action) flag actually fly over 1600 Pennsylvania Avenue, espousing a cause subsequently revealed to be a piece of propaganda that excused the administration ceasing its agreed reparations to the

A Companion to Literature, Film, and Adaptation, First Edition. Edited by Deborah Cartmell.
© 2012 Blackwell Publishing Ltd. Published 2012 by Blackwell Publishing Ltd.

Vietnamese? Yes. For this is not dialogue from the film. Rather it is taken from the novelization by David Morrell. Morrell was also the author of the original novel *First Blood*, published to some critical acclaim in 1972, and which had been a potential movie project in Hollywood for a decade before taking shape as the movie directed by Ted Kotcheff and starring Sylvester Stallone. This chapter follows the variety of ways in which Morrell, through the novelization, endeavors to retrieve a measure of authorial control over a character, and over narrative(s) that have slipped from his grasp. Through analysis of the movies, novels, and Morrell's writing about his work and that of others, I chart an ultimately fruitless attempt to reassert meanings and ideas from the initiatory novel which are altered in the first adaptation, transformed in the sequel, and finally swept away by the popular reception of and responses to that second film. As Susan Faludi observes, "conventional perceptions and cliches about the *Rambo* series are drawn almost entirely from the second of the three[1] films, which scored by far the highest returns at the box office" (1999: 365). Table 18.1 provides a timeline of *Rambo* adaptations, novelizations, and sequels.

Table 18.1 *Rambo* novels and films[2]

Year	Book	Film
1972	*First Blood*	
1982		*First Blood*
1985	*Rambo: First Blood Part II.* (novelization)	*Rambo: First Blood Part II*
1988	*Rambo III* (novelization)	*Rambo III*
2008		*Rambo*

In his essay on novelizations Jan Baetens describes the prevailing view of the "contemporary Hollywood novelization" (2007: 230); a model in which shooting scripts are followed in a plodding fashion by novelizers who are not "'real' authors, but ghost-writers hired to execute one of the side-products of the multimedia production line that the making of a Hollywood movie has become since the generalization of the Spielberg–Lucas cinema" (230). Baetens immediately and properly draws attention to the fact that such a view elides more interesting "creative forms" of what he terms "continuative" novelizations in which the screen text provides the starting point, rather than the boundary for the subsequent written works (231). But that first, rather depressing account does ring true for a great many novelizations of recent popular films. Certainly, the cover of the 1985 paperback which shows a shirtless, heavily muscled, and scarred Stallone armed with a rocket launcher and the tagline "The most violent man in the world is unleashed . . ." does not ostensibly promise anything in the dialogic, re-purposed, or subversively intertextual line. Rather, here, it promises purchasers, is the book-of-the-film.

Yet Morrell's position as writer of the novelization does not exactly accord with the more negative perspective of the business. On the one hand he is the figure charged with turning the screenplay into a novel; in this instance on a three-week schedule to meet the studio's timetable for a book to promote their release. But on the other he is the originator of the text that set the series of films, sequels, adaptations, merchandizing and books in train, a role that affords him a greater claim to "author" status than would ordinarily be the case. Something of this convoluted ancestry is evident in the credits on the front cover of the novelization (a form of words suggestive of a carefully crafted compromise); "The novel by DAVID MORRELL, Bestselling author of FIRST BLOOD, from the screenplay by Sylvester Stallone and James Cameron, *Rambo: First Blood, Part II*." In his book *Lessons From a Lifetime of Writing* – a guidebook to would-be writers – Morrell argues that the success and controversy of the movie *Rambo II* proved detrimental to his career, and his status as a novelist (Morrell, 2002: 213). His original novel had been on school and university reading lists through the 1970s and early 1980s, and had been recommended by the *English Journal* as a text to instigate discussion about "the nature of civil disobedience." But when the second film became strongly associated with U.S. foreign policy, right-wing politics and Reagan, Morrell's work was similarly tainted and his books disappeared from curricula. In particular, he describes with some vehemence how independent booksellers ceased to stock his wares.

> [They] grouped the book with the movie (without having read the book) and assumed that I was an ultra right-wing violence-crazed nutcase who wandered his home wearing combat boots and fondling a machine gun, when in fact I'm a registered Democrat and so *un*violent that I carry spiders and other insects out of my house rather than kill them because I don't want to invite bad karma (214).

To understand aspects of the relationship between the film – that is, the sequel – and its novelization it is necessary to examine some of the major changes that took place between the first novel and its subsequent adaptation. In her book *Stiffed: The Betrayal of the Modern Man* Susan Faludi devotes a long section to the winding process of this adaptation, mapping the story changes onto her broader thesis concerning the representation of, and impossible expectations placed upon, contemporary American men. In this first novel Rambo is a far less sympathetic figure than he becomes on screen. He is more prepared to initiate, escalate, and continue violence than the Stallone character who responds only reluctantly, in a limited way, and after great provocation. Alternating chapters are seen from the perspective of Rambo and of the police chief, Teasle, who pursues him. As Faludi observes, contemporary reviews of the novel "were divided in identifying the hero as either Rambo or Teasle" (1999: 383). A generation apart, they are both decorated veterans, of Vietnam and Korea respectively. Both are fatherless, and the book repeatedly describes a bond or connection that links them even though they have become adversaries. In adaptation Teasle becomes one-dimensional, a hostile redneck whose unwarranted and unrelenting pressure on Rambo provides the film's excuse for its protagonist to display his survival and military skills. The book emphatically figures Rambo as damaged by Vietnam, damaged by what he's seen and done, and represents the violence he inflicts on a small community as metonymic of the Vietnam experience. Yet the adaptation seems more interested in celebrating the talents the U.S. military and its operations have inculcated.

Although the book's surrogate father theme is resuscitated in adaptation, it is done in a fashion that reverses the novel's anti-war, "nobody wins" theme. On screen, it is now the Special Forces Colonel Trautman[3] who serves in a paternal capacity. In the first novel Trautman and Rambo have never met. Rambo only knows his voice from the loudspeakers during his training. This original Trautman is an unlikeable military manager, summoned to limit the damage his derailed graduate has wrought, and who in the final pages kills the injured Rambo by shooting him in the head. Yet on screen he becomes not only proud of Rambo, but loyal, positively doting, intervening in the final scene to take his distraught charge, his "Johnny," away – alive – from the unwelcoming town. In adaptation, the betrayal of ordinary soldiers by a politico-military elite who regard them as expendable emanates from far higher up the chain of command than the man who reminds Rambo that he "was there with you (in Vietnam) knee deep in all that blood and guts."

For the first film, Kirk Douglas had accepted the part of Trautman but, upon arrival on location discovered that the script change he had requested had not been written, namely that he shoot Rambo in a near-restoration of the book's conclusion. Says Douglas, "I thought it would have been better, dramatically, if my character realizes what a Frankenstein monster, amoral killer, and menace to society he has created, and KILLS STALLONE" (Faludi, 1999: 402). However much Stallone may have wanted Douglas in the role, neither would budge from their respective positions, and Richard Crenna was substituted in the Trautman role, providing a benevolent father in accordance with Stallone's vision of the story. Recounting his first impression of the film – a view he aired many years after his payments for the rights, for the sequel, and for the novelization – Morrell recalls "I was in a daze . . . I didn't know what I'd seen. It was a different animal" (368).

Clearly, the simple fact of the Rambo character surviving the first film is the major adaptive change that facilitates the development of the *Rambo* franchise and Morrell's relationship with subsequent *Rambo* texts. An ending to the first movie in which Rambo commits suicide was filmed and was intended to serve as the definitive finale. However, test audiences responded very badly and an alternative ending was appended,[4] making this most significant of alterations, arguably authored by its audience. Hence, even before commencing work on the novelization Morrell is already obliged to work from the foundation of a first story that has been radically rebalanced in adaptation, including a lead character who has been brought back from the dead. He cannot "pick up" where *he* left off, but must do so from the first film's version. The predominance of the films, the demand that they cohere internally and from one to the next, clearly outstrips any possibility that the novels follow each other meaningfully. (Logically, were its version of events the uncontested account, the first novel could not be followed by another.) As a novelizer, Morrell is doubly trammeled, both by the script of the second film, and by the tenor and events of the first which are, for the purposes of his task, definitive. The novelization in fact begins with an Author's note that explains "In my novel *First Blood*, Rambo died. In the films, he lives." No more substantial explanation is tendered, and of course no promotional adjunct to the movie could really sanction any discussion of how the first book had been traduced. Rather, the Author's note continues with a wealth of detail about the knife, bow, and arrows used in book and film; including the manufacturers' addresses and postcodes, coupled with the assertion that they are "works of art."

A surfeit of such information, plus a great deal of back-story, forms the principal materials with which the novelization bulks out the incidents of the script. Indeed Morrell is sufficiently interested in technical detail about military hardware that he devotes a four-page section to archery and the particularities of Rambo's bow and arrows, including – in the strangest echo of *Tristram Shandy* – a simple black and white illustration (1985: 98) in a text otherwise devoid of images. The presence of copious technical information connected to the army, espionage, or other dangerous occupations is, of course, a recurring property of many modern male-oriented thrillers. In the case of a novelization it also sits well, commercially speaking, with the imperative to produce a text that chimes with and augments its dominant sibling; offering additional pleasures that do not imperil the status of the screen experience as the main event.

In *Lessons From a Lifetime of Writing* Morrell advises authors dealing with movie producers to "make sure you retain print control of the characters in your novel" so that, in the event of a sequel, they "can't hire someone else to trash your characters in a novelization" (2002: 212). Having followed his own advice, Morrell was in the position that, despite his initial reluctance, contractually, only he could pen such a text and the producers, Carolco, were desperate for the book version. A pyrotechnic five-minute action clip from the finale convinced him that it was "going to be a big movie" (Faludi, 1999: 405), and presumably a lucrative one, and he agreed to write the novelization. Whilst he is candid about the purpose of novelizations – that they are "used primarily to promote the film" (Morrell, 2002: 212) – his rationale for participating seems over-optimistic about the effect of his intervention. "I thought I owed it to Rambo to put some of my ideas about him into the novelizations, even if those ideas would never be in the films (his antipolitician, anti-Vietnam War attitudes, for example)" (213).

Although Morrell is now stuck with the made-over Trautman as a surrogate father for Rambo, his novelization adds two more father-figures as part of his expanded characterization. As a boy, a Navajo elder – "the oldest wisest man in the village" (Morrell, 1985: 95) – teaches Rambo archery and in particular the importance of concentration. And, on his first mission in Vietnam, Rambo is rescued and tutored by a "mountain tribesman" (62) with whom he forms a "spiritual bond" that leads to his becoming a follower of Zen Buddhism. Read in the context of the movie – and it is difficult to conceive of the novelization being read in any other – a number of these additions seem profoundly unlikely; patches of prose intended to function as a contemplative corrective to the hulking screen-text, the pleasures of which are wholly vested in visceral action and wordless immediacy. Consider, for example, this section on Zen and Rambo's fearlessness:

> Rambo had learned how he himself could not show fear. Because he didn't feel it. Zen. The ultimate weapon. What reason would he have to be afraid of death once he understood that death did not exist? That nothing existed. That life itself – this tree, this rock, this butterfly – was but an illusion. A veil. A magical trick that the Holy One played on us (63).

Given that most readers will have bought the novelization to "reexperience" (Faludi 1999: 405) the film, and since the first movie had already substituted the Rambo character's interior monologue for a stoic, largely silent, performance from Stallone, these thoughts-as-prose sit uneasily with the film and the screen character to which they relate. Are readers/viewers really expected to believe that this is how Rambo (or at least the Stallone Rambo) passes his time thinking between – or even during – the action sequences? Or does Morrell imagine a segment of his readership that reads beyond, or excludes, the screen experience, perhaps indifferent to or even ignorant of the film(s)? Could there be readers that separate the literary incarnation from the actor's performance, that ignore the cues from the book's cover art and opening pages to associate what follows with the film of the same name? It is worth noting that, in his interview with Susan Faludi, Morrell says "I saw my book as an anti-war novel" but concludes "Maybe I delude myself" (quoted in Faludi, 1999: 405).

The studio's expectations that Morrell produce, on schedule, a text that would serve the interests of its big brother evidently trump the author's desire to recuperate the Rambo of his own making. Yes, the novelization has sections and references that jar with the movie's triumphal tone and its representation of an indestructible character who can win single-handedly on the big screen the war that had been lost on the ground and had been seen to be lost on countless American television sets. Morrell proffers Rambo – the student of Zen, Rambo the occasional masturbator (1985: 69), and Rambo the reader of *Catch-22* – as though to import some literary anti-war credentials at second-hand. But overwhelmingly the book does serve its commercial function, mostly adhering to the template of the Rambo make-over. Just as *Rambo II* outperformed its predecessor at the box office, so its novelization outsold Morrell's first novel, selling a million copies and remaining on *The New York Times'* best-seller list for six weeks, a measure of the film's popularity and of the intended cross-media synergy.

A key consideration here is the enormous influence of Sylvester Stallone in determining the nature of the *Rambo* films. In his *auteur*-structuralist study *Signs and*

Meaning in the Cinema Peter Wollen describes how an author-centered analysis of films "involves a kind of decipherment, decryptment" because movies may also be laden with what he terms "noise," features, which owe their presence in the texts to "the producer, the cameraman, or even the actors" (1998: 71). Of course, Wollen's argument presumes that authorship, or at least *auteur* status, will only ever be constituted in the recurring preoccupations of a director as evidenced through their evolution across a corpus of (his) films. As an interpretive approach, endeavoring to "read" *First Blood* in terms of the oeuvre of Ted Kotcheff, or *Rambo: First Blood Part Two* as it relates to the other films of its director George P. Cosmatos, is transparently unproductive. Both directors are better understood as participants in a range of projects, across a variety of genres, to films upon which they exercised varying degrees of directorial control. Yet a similar "longitudinal" analysis of the motifs and narrative tropes that are so consistently revisited across the films of Sylvester Stallone yields results more akin to those associated with *auteurist* analysis.

Although Stallone is primarily regarded as an actor (and, certainly during his period of peak celebrity, was not infrequently derided as a poor actor) it is evident that the leverage he brought to bear upon most of the films in which he appears was not confined to the particulars of his performance. From the success of *Rocky*, which he had also written, Stallone would consistently also figure as a writer and/or director of those films in which he played the lead role. In instances where he is not credited with directing, this determining influence included working with, or indeed hiring, directors who would craft the films in line with the star's wishes. By the time *First Blood* was made, Stallone had scripted three *Rocky* pictures and directed *Rocky II* and *III*. Hence he was in a strong position to insist upon an adaptation of Morrell's novel that accorded with his view of a suitable Stallone screen-persona.

"After I got involved," the film's director, Ted Kotcheff, told Faludi, "we worked on several scripts for months, but I'll tell you, the person who made the biggest difference was Sylvester Stallone." Kotcheff cited three fundamental changes Stallone made. "Stallone said to me, 'This guy shoots like he's in a shooting gallery, and it's going to alienate the audience. What if he puts 'em out of action instead of killing 'em?'" The second change was to transform Rambo from a foul-mouthed ranter into a stoical silent type. The last, and most important, was the ending (Faludi, 1999: 401).

In making the screen Rambo more sympathetic and especially in paring away dialogue and interior monologue to be replaced with an emphasis on the body and physical endeavors of a stoic lead character – whom he would portray – Stallone re-oriented *First Blood* towards a template in which he was confident and which, with *Rocky* and its sequels, had proven successful with audiences. Of course, in focusing the film so insistently upon the physique, impossible deeds, and few words of the lead, Stallone also ensured that his actor-presence would become the fulcrum of the movie. The success of this strategy is evident in the shift in titles from original film to sequel to third installment: *First Blood* being succeeded by *Rambo: First Blood*

Part Two being succeeded in turn by *Rambo III*. The title *First Blood* is relegated, then dropped altogether. Rather than being a subsequent version of a David Morrell story, the sequel is framed principally (and its successor wholly) as another outing for a character as conceived of, and indelibly associated with, Sylvester Stallone.

It is ironic that Morrell's credited contribution to successive *Rambo* screen sequels should be in terms of character when those very characters, and especially the titular lead, should be so radically changed from his original novel. The opening titles of *Rambo: First Blood Part II* state that the movie is "Based on characters created by David Morrell" with a "Story by Kevin Jarre" and "Screenplay by Sylvester Stallone and James Cameron." The titles of *Rambo III* repeat the "Characters by . . ." credit, followed by "Written by Sylvester Stallone and Sheldon Lettich." In both movies the only characters from Morrell's *First Blood*, howsoever reconceived, are Rambo and Trautman. By the 2008 release of *Rambo* Morrell's credited contribution relates solely to the distant genesis of its lead character – "Based on the character created by David Morrell." The film is "Written by Art Monterastelli and Sylvester Stallone" and "Directed by Sylvester Stallone." Both literally and figuratively *Rambo* has Sylvester Stallone written all over it.

In one respect Morrell's novelization largely refuses to reflect or engage with a significant aspect of the movie. The sustained attention to Stallone's body that forms such a defining aspect of the film is virtually absent from the book-of-the-film, despite the promise of the bare torso upon its cover. Again, it is necessary to understand the movie sequel and the novelization in the context of the first novel and its adaptation. In Morrell's novel *First Blood* Rambo is remarkable for his toughness and endurance, but the pumped-up body-builder's physique that Stallone brought to the movie and which is comprehensively examined in sustained episodes of shirtlessness is not to be found on the page. Where Morrell's opening describes "some nothing kid" (1992: 3), bearded and scruffy, the film offers a much cleaner, tidily coiffed, and evidently gym-going Rambo whose footloose existence does not appear to render him as squalid as his literary predecessor. In the novel, when Rambo is strip-searched and hosed down by the sheriff's deputies (40–1) his body is notable principally for its many scars. In the same scene on screen, Rambo/Stallone's body becomes something to be admired. Not simply for the evidence of the torments it has borne (though the suggestion of Christ-like suffering is clear enough), but mostly for its sheer size and development.

By the time of the October 1982 release of *First Blood* Stallone was already firmly associated with movies which foreground his muscularity. *Rocky* (1976), *Rocky II* (1979), and *Rocky III* (released in May 1982) had cemented the actor's association with another role that combined physical training and muscular development, the endurance of pain, and monosyllabic communication. From the mid-1970s through the 1980s Stallone's body followed a growth trajectory commensurate with his increasing box-office returns. Body-building training and supplements produced a physique that was visibly more massive, leaner, and with greater muscular definition than had been the case for *Rocky*. In *First Blood* the emphasis on his physique that had developed through the *Rocky* pictures is continued, the close attention of the camera signaling to audiences that this is a body to be considered in terms of its prodigious determining power, as well as its aesthetic and erotic possibilities: a body to be envied and longed for. For the next decade and beyond, pumped-up bodies for male leads would be *de rigueur* in what came to be called the "action" film (Neale, 2000: 52). As Steve Neale observes, the two book-length studies of these films and that era – Jeffords' *Hard Bodies: Hollywood Masculinity in the Reagan Era* and Tasker's *Spectacular Bodies: Gender, Genre and the Action Cinema* – both examine how physiques came to embody ideology (52–3).

Chuck Kleinhans notes that "in the Reagan era, many critics identified the action genre as especially ideologically reactionary when militant presidential posturing was associated with the filmic heroism of Rambo" (1996: 243). As Kleinhans acknowledges, the analysis of Tasker and others reveals that the action genre as a whole "is not so simple and obvious," that it may contain a variety of competing and different meanings. Nonetheless, it is evident that *Rambo: First Blood Part II* was seen to embody a particular complex of values; valorizing strength and violence (in the service of an ostensibly just cause), celebrating the idea of a resurgent United States exercising its will overseas, and exorcizing the memory of an era when it could not.

In respect of Stallone's body, a set of relatively consistent meanings may be said to run through his films and especially the two franchises with which he is most strongly associated. Notwithstanding the remarkable physique he developed, his characters are frequently figured as the underdogs. This theme is far more pronounced in the *Rocky* pictures where his opponents are portrayed as having superior natural gifts which he must overcome by virtue of his arduous training and perseverance. *Rocky IV* merges this motif with a United States versus Soviet Russia plotline in which Stallone's opponent is a far taller, bulkier, younger (and steroid-using) embodiment of Cold War evil. In the *Rambo* films – where his startling torso is the only such physique on display – he is the underdog principally because of the overwhelming numbers of opponents he must defeat. In *Rambo: First Blood Part II* those enemies who comprised the movie's infamous "body-count" would be (North) Vietnamese and Russian, with the clear implication that one exceptional American was superior to virtually limitless numbers of anyone else.[5]

Repeatedly, his films' narratives would figure the remarkable bodies and deeds of Stallone characters not as the results of effortless supremacy but of his capacity to "not quit," to "take a beating," to not "stay down." They are blue-collar toilers, never members of a social elite. The *Rocky* pictures in particular borrow elements of a Horatio Alger narrative template; namely a "rags to riches" story and – as with *Rambo* – an older mentor. Where films show Stallone training – that is, where he ostensibly develops the physical form upon which those narratives place such significance – they consistently figure the activities as grueling labor and the settings as either down-at-heel or natural wilderness. The type of modern, well-equipped body-building gymnasia where Stallone's body was actually transformed is invariably eschewed on screen. *Rocky* pounds the grimy streets of Philadelphia and punches beef carcasses, while *Rambo* smashes rocks with a sledgehammer and beats glowing metal in the forge. The films do not want us to understand these characters' bodies in the context of high-tech training machines, mirrored walls, water coolers, and protein 'shakes.

Whilst Morrell's novelization was not based upon viewings of the second film, but upon the script and a short action sequence, the evidence of the first film and Stallone's presence might have been enough for the writer to expect a movie in which the actor's body would loom large. Yet, while countless other filmic elements are described in loving – positively tedious – detail in the novelization, Rambo's body achieves no such sustained exploration beyond the curt, endlessly reiterated, fact that it is "muscular." On screen Rambo's military equipment and his body are presented in an identically objectifying visual idiom, and in other respects Morrell's technical descriptions form an equivalent to the film's languorous panning shots, for example; "The blade was ten inches long, made from 440C stainless steel, virtually unbreakable, its cutting edge razor sharp. It had the shape of a Bowie knife. Two inches wide, one quarter of an inch thick, it weighed one and three quarter pounds. . . . *Continues for a page*" (1985: 43). Yet the novelization has no paragraphs about pecs, no hymns to Rambo's biceps.

When describing the character of Co, a young Vietnamese woman who assists Rambo, Morrell appears comfortable using a well-worn idiom to characterize the attractions of the Oriental "other." She has "long, lush, sheeny black hair" and a "smooth curved throat," is "Small. Deceptively delicate. Gorgeous as almost every young Vietnamese woman was. With the elegance of an Oriental vase. Her eyes were wide open, expressive. Her mouth was strong, sensuous, parted in sudden fear" (65). Yet, although the film is patently more interested in the look of Rambo than in the appearance of his helpmate, Morrell does not try to find an equivalent to the many minutes of screen-time in which Stallone's gleaming torso is studied. Perhaps this was an alteration to his original vision that Morrell was happy to downplay. Perhaps, in a text clearly targeted at a male readership enamored of the film's reactionary stance, there was a concern that such description might have seemed dangerously gay. For whatever reason, the film's simultaneous fetishization of Rambo and his equipment becomes in prose a pornographic fantasy focused exclusively onto the weapons that form extensions of that body.

A modest shift in this respect can be observed in Morrell's subsequent 1988 novelization of *Rambo III*, in which the title character works with the Mujahedeen to rescue his mentor Colonel Trautman from Soviet captivity in Afghanistan.[6] In this (second) novelization there seems to exist a fuller acknowledgment of the centrality of Stallone's physique to the *Rambo* experience, and perhaps an awareness that a focus on the male form has increasingly moved into a cultural mainstream. There are some references to Rambo's muscles "rippling" (1988: 3, 6), to his "extraordinary physique" (6), and even a mildly sensual description of "Rambo's thick long hair, his bulging arm and chest muscles" (46). These elements are still, however, largely eclipsed by Morrell's evocations of Rambo's knife – which merits a couple of hundred words, plus an illustration (44–5) – and his updated bow and arrows – worth two pages and an illustration (55–7).

The metaphor of the Frankenstein monster proves oddly apt for Rambo: assembled from the contributions of many individuals, brought back from the dead, an unnatural body capable of astonishing feats and great violence, an angry creation who escapes his creator, and a character best known from texts *other* than the original. Morrell describes Rambo as "a son who grew up and out of his father's control" (1992: xi). Having lost Rambo to the movies, and to the intersection of popular culture and politics, what remained for Morrell was the attempt to steer him in print. The novelizations, as an extension of the movies, offered only a vain hope in this respect, albeit coupled with a rewarding payday. In an introduction to the original novel, an introduction written years *after* the first two movies and the arrival of Rambo as a household name and as a byword for a political worldview, Morrell now assumes that readers will be familiar with that other Rambo not of his making.

> Rambo. Complicated, troubled, indeed haunted, too often misunderstood. If you've heard about him but haven't met him before, he's about to surprise you (xii).

"Heard about?" "Met?" It is as though he cannot bring himself to say "seen," to finally accept that the literary Rambo can now only be a figure at the margin, at the margin of the screen.

NOTES

1 Faludi writes in 1999, prior to the fourth film, *Rambo*, in 2008.

2 Table 18.1 does not include other iterations that may also claim to be *Rambo* texts, for example: screenplays, an animated series, and countless popular forms that parody, copy, or other borrow recognizably *Rambo* elements.

3 In the novel he is a captain.

4 Different accounts of this prevail. Morrell (2002: 211) describes the crew returning to Canada to shoot the new finale following the test screenings. Kotcheff's account has the alternate (eventual) ending being shot during the original location shoot – at Stallone's sug-

gestion – and stored in the event of negative test screenings.

5 A meaning that was especially welcome to elements of an American audience because it reversed – in fiction – the outcome of the equivalent proposition which had failed in the real Vietnam, even with increasing numbers of U.S. service personnel.

6 Released near the end of the Cold War and shortly before the Soviet withdrawal from Afghanistan, *Rambo III* failed to achieve the box-office success and popular cultural impact of its predecessor. Post 9/11 and the U.S. invasion of Afghanistan, *Rambo III* makes (even more) awkward viewing.

REFERENCES

Baetens, J. "From Screen to Text: Novelization, the Hidden Continent." In *The Cambridge Companion to Literature on Screen*. Eds. Deborah Cartmell and Imelda Whelehan. Cambridge: Cambridge University Press, 2007, 226–38.

Faludi, S. *Stiffed: The Betrayal of the Modern Man*. London: Chatto and Windus, 1999.

Heller, J. *Catch-22*. New York: Simon & Schuster, 1961.

Jeffords, S. *Hard Bodies: Hollywood Masculinity in the Reagan Era*. New Brunswick: Rutgers University Press, 1994.

Kleinhans, C. "Class in Action." In *The Hidden Foundation: Cinema and the Question of Class*. Eds. David E. James and Rick Berg. Minneapolis: University of Minnesota Press, 1996, 240–63.

Morrell, D. *Rambo: First Blood, Part II*. London: Arrow, 1985.

Morrell, D. *Rambo III*. New York: Jove, 1988.

Morrell, D. *Lessons From a Lifetime of Writing: A Novelist Looks at His Craft*. Cincinnati: Writer's Digest, 2002.

Morrell, D. *First Blood*. London: Headline, 2006.

Neale, S. *Genre and Hollywood*. London: Routledge, 2000.

Tasker, Y. *Spectacular Bodies: Gender, Genre and the Action Cinema*. London: Routledge, 1993.

Wollen, P. *Signs and Meanings in the Cinema*. London: BFI, 1998.

Part VI

Case Studies: Adaptable and Unadaptable Texts

19

Writing for the Movies

Writing and Screening *Atonement* (2007)

Yvonne Griggs

Despite the collaborative nature of the film industry and the importance of screen-plays as commodities of vital importance to the successful realization of marketable film products, the role of the screenwriter is both historically and contemporane-ously superseded by that of the director. The pseudo authorship of films is generally accredited to directors, especially in the field of literary adaptation to screen, where there seems to be a conscious desire to replace one kind of legitimized "authorship" with another. However, Universal's 2007 film, *Atonement*, offers a working model of screenwriting and directorial synergy of the kind that results in collaborative cin-ematic adaptation of the highest order. Using Christopher Hampton's screenplay as a structural narrative template, director Joe Wright reconfigures Ian McEwan's novel to screen ensuring, through the visual and aural signs of cinema, a filmic realization of the thematic preoccupations of McEwan's prose.

Given the moral complexities of a novel like *Atonement* (2001) it is easy to catego-rize it as either a text which falls into the realms of the so-called unfilmable book, or one that requires radical reworking in order to "fit" the narrative expectations of mainstream cinema. But like the novel from which it is adapted, *Atonement* (2007) attains a postmodern playfulness that invests the cinematic narrative with ambigu-ity, reiterating in a cinematic context the novel's debates about "authorship," aes-thetics, and audience reception.

Initially, Oscar-winning screenwriter Christopher Hampton's[1] response was to take a traditional approach to story design when adapting McEwan's novel for cin-ematic consumption: it became a story of classical design, following a linear trajec-tory and employing the traditional conventions of cinematic narration. In the

A Companion to Literature, Film, and Adaptation, First Edition. Edited by Deborah Cartmell.
© 2012 Blackwell Publishing Ltd. Published 2012 by Blackwell Publishing Ltd.

process, it inevitably sacrificed the all-important "reveal" so crucial to both reader and viewer; moreover, it sacrificed the moral complexities foregrounded in the closing moments of the narrative, excising the text's exploration of the boundaries of fact and fiction, and our relationship to them. However, following the exit of the production's original director, Richard Eyre, and as a result of scripting collaboration between newly appointed director Joe Wright and Hampton, the screenplay was radically revised, the intriguing ambiguities of Ian McEwan's novel restored, and its seemingly unfilmable qualities harnessed to telling effect. Through Wright's use of visual allusions to an array of cinematic intertexts and Hampton's structurally proactive positioning of the viewer, the film becomes a challenging exercise in visual, postmodern pastiche, mirroring the kind of postmodern preoccupations of the novel, and imbibing the film text with its own questions about authorship and audience. In an interview with Rob Carnevale, Wright dismisses claims that McEwan's *Atonement* is a novel that should be regarded as "un-adaptable," arguing that those who take this stance are "underestimating the power of film." Instead, he and screenwriter Hampton remain forthright about their intention to be faithful to the so-called "spirit" of the source text they are adapting. Wright states:

> The book works, so we tried to be faithful to it. [We] kind of had faith that the film would work too if we stuck to the truth of the novel . . . We kept the book by our side throughout the whole process.

This open declaration of a desire for fidelity to the source text, despite the novel's narrative ambiguity and thematic complexity, negates the kind of tired debates usually engendered by studies of screen adaptations of literary classics, leaving us to explore instead the ways in which Hampton and Wright enter into a conscious and purposeful attempt to render the postmodern subtleties of the novel within the very different parameters of cinema. A series of drafts for Hampton's adaptation of *Atonement* (2007) were generated, three of which were written for direction by Richard Eyre; a further five drafts were completed with Joe Wright at the director's helm, and as with Hampton's initial drafts, all were read and approved by Ian McEwan as executive producer attached to the film. Hampton's first three drafts strived to retain the novel's storyline, adopting a classical and predominantly linear cinematic story design, and employing a framing device that begins where McEwan's novel ends, with an elderly Briony's return to a hotel that is the former Tallis House. However, for Wright, the nonlinear structure of the novel is paramount to its effective translation to screen since, without the mystery engendered by its arbitrary structural time-shifts and revelations, the final moments of the plot – and thus to a great extent its required narrative momentum – become redundant. Wright's desire to retain narrative complexity whilst removing the conventional cinematic signposts of explanatory voiceover or dissolves to delineate time-shifts resulted in structural changes to Hampton's initial drafts. The final draft of the screenplay is an exercise in collaborative production; it emulates the novel's meaningful defiance of classical logic, and presents us instead with a narrative that foregrounds the paradoxical nature of reality. Both novel and film negate totalizing gestures of the kind more readily associated with mainstream literature or mainstream cinema, and seek instead a story design that fosters a postmodernist preoccupation with fragmentation and uncertainty. Like the novel, the final script challenges traditional notions of narrative causality; it introduces elements of narrative intransitivity through shifting narrative perspectives which remind us at strategic moments that what we are watching is a constructed "reality," despite the film's dalliance with the classically designed mainstream genres of romance and melodrama. In a classical cinematic story design, narrational shifts of the kind built into McEwan's storyline may be deemed difficult to replicate, but in this postmodern age cinema is more than capable of mirroring the novel's postmodern twists and ironies; in the realms of New Hollywood, with its increasingly film-literate audience, there are successful cinematic forerunners. Hampton's revised script works within the same kind of postmodern cinematic context as films like *Fight Club* (1999) or *Memento* (2000), playing with the audience through fragmentation of the narrative; similarly, the cinematic reveal is an accepted structural device in mainstream cinema – films like *The Sixth Sense* (1999) and *The Others* (2001) push the boundaries of its application in recent times – while Tarentino-esque narrative-bending has become *de rigeur* since the 1990s.

This refusal to work within a coherent, explanatory mode, either at the level of narrative event or narrational discourse, invites suspension of logic at strategic moments during the course of our viewing experience. Rather than beginning with an elderly Briony who, going back in time with a conventional dissolve, recounts a linear narrative, the revamped script's opening act emulates the novel's Part One, and each subsequent part of the novel is afforded similar cinematic replication, the film's narration shifting between the tale's various protagonists. To begin with an ageing Briony and a dissolve, as Hampton's first draft envisages, places this unreliable narrator at the center of viewing experience, yet the tale itself does not revolve solely around her, even though her quest for "atonement" provides the ultimate narrative rationale behind its telling. What emerges in the final shooting script is, instead, an acknowledgment that whilst Briony remains "the backbone of the whole book" the narrative's shifting focus dictates that screen time must also be devoted solely to Cecilia and Robbie whose relationship, according to Hampton, "[is] the centre of the film" (Rich, n.d.). Hampton notes that whilst the middle sections of his initial drafts segued the narrative of Nurse Briony with that of Robbie and Cecilia during their wartime estrangement, his final script goes back to the structure of the novel where these two parts of the narrative are dealt with as separate entities, even though they take place within the same time frame (Stewart, 2007). The early intention of editing between the two narratives was felt by both Hampton and Wright to detract from what needs to be an undiluted focus on the lovers. Though the novel's central character is Briony, it is the romance narrative of Cecilia and Robbie that is foregrounded in the film's marketing: the star bodies of James McAvoy and Keira Knightley feature in the marketing posters and promotional materials, and the film's tagline ("Torn apart by betrayal. Separated by war. Bound by love.") places them at the center of the film's narrative. It could be argued that such attention to the novel's romance plot and to the film's star casting is a cynical attempt to attract a larger audience; however, as Hampton notes, the novel is also at pains to devote its narrative energies to the telling of Robbie and Cecilia's tale.

The metatextual influence of the populist works of romance writer Lucilla Andrews, whose autobiography, *No Time For Romance*, is acknowledged as one of a number of sources consulted in the creation of McEwan's novel, is in evidence throughout: notions of romance are central to this text at the level of narratology and discourse, and there are moments when the literary tone of McEwan's prose subsides into the language of populist romance fiction, leading the seasoned reader of his work to suspect the veracity of the narration long before the final "reveal" is exposed, and adding further uncertainties about authorship. These uncertainties about "authorship" were exacerbated in 2006 (post publication of the novel and during the film's production), amidst claims that McEwan had "borrowed" too heavily from Andrews' autobiographical recollections of nursing life in London's hospitals during the Second World War. The literary furor surrounding the *Mail on Sunday* article (Langdon, 2006) that suggested McEwan's "borrowing" amounted to acts of plagiarism, and the defense offered by McEwan in a *Guardian* article (McEwan, 2006) add yet another layer of paratextual discourse about authorship and "truth" to our reception of the cinematic adaptation released in 2007.

Wright's star casting of romantic leads is central to the way in which the novel is realized on screen: it is a conscious choice designed to foreground the narrative's romance plot. The multiple casting of Briony signals a similarly significant and conscious choice. By casting youthful newcomer Saoirse Ronan as the pre-pubescent Briony of Act One, Wright ensures her initial wrongdoing is seen as a forgivable consequence of her youth and inexperience. When we finally move to the closure of the tale we are presented with an aged Briony (Vanessa Redgrave), whose capacity to justify and rationalize her actions is more credible. Just as the novel places these closing moments outside the parameters of the main narrative – unlike Parts One, Two, and Three it is delineated "London, 1999" – the shooting script moves us many years on, away from the drama of the prior scenes in which the narrative is all, and into a media-controlled interview environment where the real Briony is revealed as author of everything that has preceded , and where her authorial control, though still central, may be seen to be superseded by that of the new medium in which she is now performing. Wright's conscious deviation from the novel at this point becomes of crucial importance to the film text's added complexities, and ensures that, even as the film strives to emulate its "source text," it adds its own layers of ambiguity. McEwan invites his readership to question not only notions of "originality" as a source of aesthetic value but the fetishizing of authorship by presenting us with an ultimately unreliable narrator who positions herself as one who, with the "absolute power of deciding outcomes" is "also God" (2001: 371). Wright's closing moments ask us, as audience, to challenge that authorial control firstly by presenting Briony as an author who is now subject to the editorial interventions of the recording studio, and secondly by presenting us with fragmented narrative discourse via the on-screen realization of two narrative possibilities from which to create our own final story design.

McEwan's use of intertextual literary allusion in *Atonement* (2007) adds a postmodern edge to his text,[2] but Wright's visual allusions to an array of cinematic intertexts and the script's proactive positioning of the viewer ensure that the film becomes an equally challenging exercise in visual, postmodern pastiche. One of the greatest challenges faced by the screenwriter when adapting prose to screen remains that of "voice": how does one give "voice" to the text when working in the very different medium of film – a medium in which story is predominantly told through visual and aural means? The problem is exacerbated when dealing with a narrative like *Atonement* (2001). Its shifting narrative point of view, its nonlinearity, its final disclosure present difficulties; yet its difficulties also present opportunities for the adaptor. David Bordwell argues that film has narration but no "narrator," its *audience* being the active constructor of meaning through the film text's visual and aural cues (1985: 61–2); if we agree with Bordwell's contention then *Atonement* is a film that is testimony to the "truth" of Bordwell's claims since we are left to make meaning from and sense of the close from the various clues littered throughout Acts One, Two and Three. By maintaining the novel's shifting narrative perspectives on specific narrative hinge points such as the fountain scenes and the library scenes, Hampton and Wright continually invite the audience to become actively engaged in the construction of meaning. The closing moments of the film offer the ultimate in audience participation at both an intellectual and an emotive level by offering us alternative points of closure, each appealing to either our desire for romantic completion or for intellectual transparency. But narratologist Seymour Chatman seeks to qualify Bordwell's statement, arguing that the viewer engages in participatory *reconstructive* acts (1990: 127), engendered by a covert as well as an overt cinematic narrator, said cinematic narrator (through the synergy of screenplay and directorial manipulation of cinematography, editing, sound, and mise-en-scène) creating a series of visual and aural prompts throughout the film, many of which, when revisited, cast light upon the ambiguous and unreliable nature of the story we have chosen to invest in. Chatman's challenge to Bordwell's outright rejection of the concept of "cinematic implied authorship" seems more a question of logic since what the audience is presented with in order to construct meaning has to be under the control of some guiding force; just as the narrative events and discourse of the novel are ultimately controlled by McEwan as the functioning writer of the text rather than by Briony as narrator within the text; Wright, as the directing hand behind the cinematic realization of Hampton's story template controls what we see and hear, inevitably shaping our reception and our perception of events.

In *Atonement*, the tale is revealed as the product of unreliable narration during its closing moments, at which point we can reassess what we have taken as "narrative truth" and revise our understanding thereof, rethinking our viewing position in relation to the cues/clues provided throughout by the film's *cinematic* narrator. We are presented with choices: power *is* refreshingly handed over to the film's audience, however much the cinematic narrator colludes with the fictitious author's leanings toward what we may construe as a Hollywood ending by loading the final shots with sensuous, populist images of romance. Briony, as a character within the narrative, has been construed as an unreliable narrator throughout, but the level of the unreliability of the narrative itself is not revealed until the close, introducing further ironies and inviting us to engage in debates about our role as audience, our relationship with "truth," our desire for closure and for happy Hollywood endings of the kind we have been led to believe will be forthcoming in a romance of this type. The film continues to probe questions raised by the ideologies embedded in McEwan's text by constructing other instances of oscillating "truths." Images of the Dunkirk scene, first realized from the perspective of soldiers left to the chaos of the impending evacuation, are presented as part of the narrative's "truth"; later, we are presented with a very different wartime news-reel depiction of that moment, leading us to question the veracity of historical constructions of "truth" and blurring the boundaries between fact and fiction. Both film and novel feed us "misinformation," inferring that all truth is potentially a web of fictions sewn together by an outside "author" whose reliability will always be suspect as will all kinds of "truth." *Atonement* (2007) does not sidestep these intellectual debates: rather, it embraces them and extends their credibility within the very different medium of film. By inserting a telling passage from Jane Austen's *Northanger Abbey* as a prelude to his tale, McEwan signals to the literate audience (albeit in a most oblique manner and one made clear only with hindsight), the potential instability of the story that will unfold; the young Briony is immediately aligned with her fictitious counterpart, Catherine Moreland, a heroine of similarly self-dramatizing leanings, found in a text that parodies the extremes of the Gothic novel as a form. Through such literary allusions, McEwan is able to create a sense of his narrative's artifice from the outset but to introduce textual citations into the opening of the film's narrative would serve to hijack its cinematic energies. Wright wisely chooses to invest Hampton's screenplay with a parallel sense of artifice by recourse to the more visual and aural signifiers available to the filmmaker. We open to a black screen invaded by the percussive sounds of typewriter keys, mechanically realized on-screen as the title of the film is typed onto a blank page. From the outset, our entry into the world of the film is aligned with the *act* of writing, thus foregrounding the participatory nature of our engagement. The scene opens out to reveal a shot of what at first appears to be Tallis House, a country mansion of a visual grandeur far greater than that envisaged in McEwan's novel. The "ugliness of the Tallis home – barely forty

years old, bright orange brick, squat, lead-paned baronial Gothic" (2001, 19) trans-
lates on screen to the status of an imposing Victorian mansion, with a location shoot
at Stokesay Court in Shropshire providing the kind of visual splendor more readily
associated with Heritage cinema. However, the opening image of Tallis House is
soon shown to be a miniature version thereof – one controlled by the young Briony
who, during these establishing shots, is indelibly linked to the act of writing as she
sits typing the words "The End" on what we assume is the manuscript of the play
she has written for her brother's imminent return, and yet with hindsight may
construe as a reference to the film's final revelations about authorial control and acts
of "closure." Wright introduces a series of covert messages during these opening
moments: from the artifice suggested by the doll's house shot of what is to become
the setting for Act One of the film, to the close-up shot of words signaling "the
end" of a narrative (at Briony's command), and the pervasive staccato soundtrack
we come to associate with Briony the child and adult writer. Briony's role as author
is highlighted throughout the narrative – we enter the storyline through Briony
and, to the accompaniment of a score that sustains the b-flat sound of typewriter
keys, we move with her along the corridors of Tallis House in pursuit of an audience
for her story. The written word remains particularly important to the screenplay's
structural cause and effect momentum as it is through the vehicle of Robbie's sensuous if crass note to Cecilia that we are seemingly propelled towards the climactic
moment of Act One and into Act Two. Wright also ensures the continued prominence of the written word in this opening act. Screen time is devoted not only to
Briony's fictitious writerly acts but also to Robbie's reality-bound act of constructing an apology to Cecilia. When the camera moves in to a close-up shot of the word
"cunt" as it physically materializes on the page, its power to shock, even in this age
of shlock-horror cinema, is undeniable, and the film text's cinematic energies are
consciously superseded by the energy of the written word at strategic moments. The
film plays with writerly notions of literary prestige through its window-dressing:
visually, we are led into the world of prestige cinema through its preoccupation
with the visual splendor of the country mansion location and its meticulous attention to period detail, yet our preconceived notions of the genre are distorted by the
nonliterary nature of the written word foregrounded in this sequence. It both rein-
scribes and undermines the film text's status as a work of prestige cinema, destabi-
lizing our viewing position and emulating the novel's postmodern uncertainties.

However, though we are not made aware of the extent to which Briony is impli-
cated in the shaping of the narrative in both novel and film until the closing
moments, there are subtle signs of a constant intervention; in the realms of cinema,
such interventions rest with the cinematic narrator – with cinematography, editing,
sound, and construction of mise-en-scène – but in this film text, there is a self-
conscious edge to the assertive editing, the constant rewinds, the heavily loaded
sound quality of the score, suggesting the presence of a controlling hand beyond
the cinematic norm. Hampton's script replicates the narrative uncertainties of
McEwan's novel by retaining multiple narration of vital story events such as the

pivotal fountain scene in Act One, and Wright's cinematic discourse invests each cinematic rendition of this scene with a very different tonal quality. Whilst McEwan's novel begins with the moment as perceived by its protagonists, Hampton switches the order of the narrative recount, positioning us firstly with Briony as filter for our initial reception of events. We edit between the scene as experienced firstly by Briony, the onlooker, and secondly by Cecilia and Robbie. It is a structural shift that suggests Briony's centrality within the film text, yet by editing to the scene as experienced by Cecilia and Robbie *after* Briony's loaded visualization of the moment, we are invited not only to read her accusation at the end of Act One as a fundamental misjudgment but to see the pitfalls of placing our faith in the narrative certainties presented by her. Wright underscores this narrative uncertainty through his cinematic discourse. Our first introduction to the scene comes swiftly after Briony's rehearsal plans are thwarted by her cousins. We witness the altercation between Robbie and Cecilia from the distanced and somewhat distorted vantage point of the rehearsal room window, the edges of the shot framed by the window casement, presenting us with an image that resembles a stage set construction, as if what we are watching is a scene from a play; the dumb-show enacted on screen is accompanied both by the menacing diegetic drone of a wasp and the emotive tension of the non-diegetic musical score, lending the scene a fractured, disturbing edge which is heightened by a number of close-up reaction shots that place a stunned Briony center frame. As we move back in time to rewind the incident, we edit to a shot of Cecilia running through woodland; but the staccato musical score we come to associate with Briony plays over this scene, and we return momentarily to an intense close-up shot of her looking directly into the camera lens, suggesting her continued presence, despite the shift of narrative perspective. The percussive piano music ceases when Cecilia plucks a piano string and we seem to move into a recollection of the moment from her experience from this point onwards, the break with Briony being indicated through the cessation of musical score and the introduction of purely naturalistic, diegetic sound. On first viewing, the moment becomes one in which we are invited to reassess this pivotal encounter between Cecilia and Robbie as one that is under their control; the cinematic replay of the event is infused with calm and it takes up far more screen-time, affording us access to their conversation and their reactions, both of which are absent from the child Briony's rendition of the incident. We also sense here the great distance from which Briony has viewed this scene, suggesting once more the unreliability of her recollection of events. However, on further viewings, Wright's subtle implication is that Briony remains at the center of the narration, controlling its direction and our perception of it: even when the story appears to be passed on to others within that narrative there are hints within the cinematic discourse – through editing, soundtrack, positioning within the frame – that Briony's control of the narrative is sustained throughout. Narrative "truth" is constructed as the domain of Robbie and Cecilia during this vital turning point within the narration yet it is to a close up of Briony that the camera returns for closure as she slams closed the window of our viewing experience.

Similarly, when we are positioned with Robbie at the moment he composes the doom-laden note to Cecilia, we are made privy to his ponderous thoughts through use of jump cuts, and a sense that we are rewinding the action, starting again with a clearer head as we edit constantly to scenes – seamlessly joined by emotively charged and dramatically loaded music from *La Bohème* , its tale of doomed romance permeating the film's subtext and pre-empting the narrative's final tragic disclosure – conveying an equally ponderous Cecilia, her costume and performance mode dramatically aligning her with the sensuous *femme fatale* of film noir, an image discarded before she leaves the room. The heavily edited nature of such scenes leaves the audience with a sense that life can be edited, ordered, composed at will; or a posthumous confirmation that the omnipotent authorial hand of Briony – and by implication the screenwriter/director – has been at work from the outset.

The film's theatricality and artifice continues throughout Act One of Hampton's screenplay. In a literary sense it remains an opening *act* that neatly complies with the theatrical conventions of tragedy, despite its displacement to screen. It conforms to tragedy's demand for unity of time, place, and setting, and presents us with a flawed tragic hero and a tragic narrative twist: only the prerequisite bodies are missing at this stage but with hindsight the clues are there in both novel and film, and the bodies are inevitably proffered as a possible closure to the tragedy as we enter the film's final sequences. But as film rather than prose or theater, *Atonement* (2007) must find cinematic ways of translating the artifice. Peter Childs argues that McEwan's novel displays a complexity of form by "placing itself in a realist tradition of deep, rich characterisation and social breadth" whilst also "display[ing] a modernist concern with consciousness and perceptiveness" (2006: 143); Wright's film emulates this kind of stylistic schizophrenia by playing with various cinematic genres, and as a consequence alerts us subtextually to the overarching artifice of the narrative penned by McEwan and adapted by Hampton. Christine Geraghty notes that Wright's film establishes its dependence upon two sources: McEwan's novel and the films referenced throughout (2009: 91–2) – films which engage a cine-literate audience in cinematic game-playing on a par with the literary game-playing strategies of McEwan's novel. But Wright's use of cinematic intertexts is about far more than this; it is, rather, an essential facet of Hampton's overall story design. Just as we are ultimately denied the expected narrative cause and effect closure of Hollywood cinema, Wright imbibes the film text with a sense of fracture that subverts the expectations of mainstream genre cinema by purposefully mixing his genre palette. Act One utilizes the generic conventions of heritage cinema with its stylistic homage to the Merchant Ivory brand of costume drama, yet it also embraces elements of melodrama and romance, setting up narrative expectations of romantic closure as we journey through the film with Robbie who is constructed as the narrative's wronged and heroic Everyman. We move in Act Two to moments of pure melodrama: to scenes reminiscent of David Lean's *Brief Encounter* (1945) employed here as another coded reference to forbidden love and the constructed nature of romance; and to similarly doom-laden romantic scenes from *Le Quai des Brumes*

(1938), playing whilst a bewildered Robbie meanders across the screen within a screen, and thus foregrounding once more the constructed nature of the romantic "realities" presented in this film text. Stories – romantic stories of unfulfilled love – permeate the structural design of the film via its visual cinematic referencing, constantly reminding us at a subliminal level that the stories are constructed, and thus preparing us for the final reveal. Just as McEwan's novel engages in a paratextual discourse with the work of populist romance writer Lucilla Andrews and the high art of Shakespearean tragedy with its narrational allusions to *Romeo and Juliet*, Wright's film engages in a cinematic discourse with the romance genre of the 1930s and 1940s. These visual allusions to the romance genre serve to amplify the romantic elements of Wright's narrative, but as with McEwan's literary nods to the works of Andrews and to Shakespearean tragedy, the chosen references also underline the impossibility of ultimate happiness, thus anticipating the text's final disclosures. David Jays, however, notes a closing textual allusion to Powell and Pressburger's *A Matter of Life and Death* (1946) in which Death's plans to intervene unfairly to deny the lovers their anticipated time together is challenged (2007: 34); such referencing offers us a cinematic parallel to the kind of authorial possibilities posed by Briony as the close to her narrative, and again leads us into debate not only about narrative intervention, but about what constitutes closure, what kind of closure we demand as readers and viewers.

Wright also directs the cinematic audience to other genres, again imbibing conflicting cinematic styles from different genres, different eras. The opening sequences of Act Two, with their focus on the horrors of war in general and the evacuation of Dunkirk in particular, echo epic war films from the 1940s and 50s and yet are permeated by a sense of the un-romanticized horror of contemporary films like *Saving Private Ryan* (1998), to which Wright pays homage via the film's grueling steady-cam shot of the war-torn beaches. In Act Three, there are scenes reminiscent of British social realist cinema of the 1950s: Cecilia stands in her dressing gown on the steps of her flat, pigs wallowing in the muddy yard below. Such moments stand in direct contrast to the visual country house splendor of Act One. Through cinematic allusions to films that reference both romance and war, social realism and heritage cinema, Wright creates a work that is subliminally suggestive of the unreliability inherent in Hampton's screenplay adaptation, and of an unpredictability on a par with that of McEwan's novel, leading us into similar debates about the nature of truth and the relationship between fact and fiction engendered here by cinema rather than the novel. The sense of narrative unreliability and stylistic schizophrenia is also amplified by the film's constant juxtaposition of conflicting visual and aural images from the commencement of Act Two onwards. There are subtle signs of constant intervention by the cinematic narrator, many of which only become apparent once we are aware of the narrative's close. The steady-cam shot of the beaches of Dunkirk offers conflicting visuals that marry the realist nature of cinema with its surreal propensities: functioning fair rides – from a ferris wheel to a child's carousel – and a fully operational cinema; soldiers sunbathing, singing choir-like in a bandstand, galloping on horseback, or running to the sea swathed in mud. The Dunkirk scenes present further clues as to the unreliability of the narrative delivered in Act Two, from the unlikelihood of the former moments, to those envisaged as Robbie meanders through burnt out buildings, where the carcasses of freshly butchered animals hang from the ceiling. In the closing stages of the Act, we move to soft focus for Robbie's reverse montage sequence, which should signal to us that this is a moment of narrative uncertainty, but such dream sequences are not out of place as cinematic narrational devices and so it is only with hindsight that we can revisit the scene and connect it to Briony's constructed fictional interventions. The film text is littered with other oblique clues as to its narrative unreliability: for example, after the sequence depicting Robbie's meeting with Cecilia in London, we return to France to see him clutching the letters that have formed their only means of communication during these war years, but what is strikingly incongruous is the image itself: Robbie is resting against a randomly placed writing desk in the middle of a field. It is through such loaded iconography that the cinematic narration infiltrates the screenplay with clues as to the film's final "reveal," and to the constructed nature of the narrative itself; the unreliability and artifice of language and authorship are constantly foregrounded through the use of loaded visual signifiers.

In addition to the romanticism generated by cinematic nods to other romantic films, there is something almost Mills & Boonesque about Act Two: from the constant edits to shots of the talismanic picture postcard cottage by the sea to the words screenwriter Christopher Hampton places into the mouths of his protagonists in voiceover. Robbie's lines, "I will return. Find you, love you, marry you, and live without shame," are emotive, sentimental; but whilst the lines are delivered as we move from romantically loaded picture postcard imagery, the words are visually juxtaposed against the backdrop of a war-torn France, of bombed buildings and derelict vehicles, once again underlining the schizophrenic cinematic style of this film text, and providing subliminal clues as to narrative unreliability. Such visual clues, provided by the cinematic narrator throughout Acts Two and Three, replace the overt references to writerly acts found in Act One. In Acts Two and Three the prominence of the word is superseded by the narrational devices of cinema. Unlike Act One, Act Two is characterized by a predominance of voiceover as the letters written by Robbie and Cecilia become on-screen utterances, used to seamlessly join edits from war-torn France to wartime London, whilst in Act Three Briony's writerly acts become covert operations conducted in the self-imposed solitary confinement of the water tower. The hand of the author seemingly recedes, and control of the narration is passed on to the storyline's romantic protagonists, lulling us into a false sense of narrative certainty that is shockingly undermined in the film's closing sequences.

Briony's central role as author of the piece is foregrounded in the closing moments of both novel and film. Although the revelations embedded in McEwan's novel remain the mainstay of the storyline's final moments, Hampton's script reconfigures the setting and the mode of delivery to telling cinematic effect. McEwan's narrative neatly returns to its opening country house setting and the final reveal is voiced through an elderly Briony's first-person narration – a narration that draws in all of the narrative threads in a somewhat leisurely and ponderous manner, and invites the reader to engage in the novel's deliberations about the relationship between fact and fiction, author and reader. In the voice of distanced and omnipotent author, McEwan's Briony casually reveals that the happy ending we have placed our trust in is, in fact, a fabrication; a fabrication that she, as author, deems "a final act of kindness, a stand against oblivion and despair," (2001: 372) rather than an elaborate authorial con. The novel's close is preoccupied with issues related to libel; Briony tells us that she will not be able to publish her last and latest novel whilst those whose crimes she would unveil (Paul and Lola Marshall) are alive. There is no public declaration of the novel's content or of its distortion of "truth." Instead we have a very direct address to the readership and a justification for the narrative "untruths" we have engaged with throughout. We are left to consider from a distance the role of the author and the moral obligations that accompany this kind of omnipotent control; we are left to judge whether her attempts to atone have been realized by her narrative interventions, or whether they constitute a further betrayal of the reader. There is a sense of authorial distance and a disengagement with the emotive energies of the romance narrative we have embraced thus far, and for many of McEwan's readers, this proves a postmodern twist too far.

Hampton's script – and Wright's cinematic translation of that script – ensures a transition to screen that engages in similar ideological debate within the framework of this very different medium, and yet it does not disengage its audience to the same extent. In a manner reminiscent of the novel's first-person narration, an elderly Briony speaks directly to her audience through the sister medium of television. There is immediately a greater intimacy established here, between fictitious author and fictitious TV viewer/film audience; the public, almost confessional nature of the address contrasts with the distanced inertia of the address to readership in the novel's final moments. She is the famous author, granted a television tell-all style interview prior to the release of her next book. Yet her presence as a character within the film's diegesis is cleverly retained; her address to camera is legitimized by the interview process but it invites a level of audience collusion that far exceeds that of the novel, opening up other layers of debate of pertinence to *film* as a mode of storytelling. By transforming the final section of the novel, from country house setting to television studio, Hampton also ensures that Briony's authorial powers are superseded by the medium of film. From the closing moments of Act Three, we move to a frame peopled by multiple copies of Briony's face on a series of television monitors as she asks for a break from filming. What is coded into this sequence is the assertion that it is film process, through edits and rewinds (of the kind shown during the interview), that will now be in control of narrative "truth" rather than Briony the writer, whose control of language is literally receding. By inference, we may surmise that McEwan as author of the so-called "source" text is subsumed by the apparatus of cinema, adding yet another layer to debates about authorship raised by this novel.

Wright plays with notions of author/director/audience relationships via a witty piece of casting (writer/director Anthony Minghella is Briony's interviewer) and through his on-screen realization of the two "endings" presented by Briony for audience consideration. The intimacy of speaking into camera is coupled with edits to visual realizations of the two distinct narrative possibilities: the stark "reality" of the deaths of the lovers and their romanticized cottage-by-the-sea reunion. We are invited to choose. However, just as clues suggestive of the potential unreliability of the narrative are woven into the film text from the outset, the on-screen realization of Briony's dual ending is seemingly loaded, by the cinematic narrator, in favor of romantic closure. Jays argues that, like the novel, the film's ending evokes a distanced viewer response (35) and indeed, it does ask us to pause, to engage at the level of intellect rather than in the purely emotive way traditionally inscribed by mainstream cinema. But in a testament to the imagistic power of cinema, Wright's visualization of the two endings – one sold to us as "truth," the other as "fiction" – colludes with the fictitious Briony's preference: by creating sensuous, vivid scenes of romantic reunion that bring to life the promised picture postcard close, and juxtaposing them with harsh, colorless scenes depicting the death of the lovers, Wright lures us into making an intellectually informed yet emotively motivated choice. He encourages us to choose the anticipated Hollywood-style ending rather than the austere ending that befits tragedy, and in so doing asks us to acknowledge the power of genre cinema. By inference, Wright also asks us to engage in further debates beyond the scope of the novel. The image of the drowned Cecilia echoes John Millais' famous painting of Ophelia (1851–2), yet another dead heroine of Shakespearean tragedy, and through the Christ-like positioning of her inert body, Wright invites us to question Western art's morbid preoccupation with the dead female form, both in the visual field of art and the literary field of tragedy. When placed alongside images of a vivacious, energized Cecilia playing at the water's edge with her lover, the desire to invest in the emotive embrace of mainstream cinema's romance genre – as opposed to the intellectualized images of the inert female victim of Western art and literature – is overwhelming.

Whether ultimately we view Briony's deception as a "final act of kindness" or as part of an elaborate con, what is refreshingly clear is this: in the film adaptation of McEwan's novel, the power to choose is handed back to the audience, implicating us as creators of narrative rather than passive receivers thereof, and retaining our capacity to engage with the narrative at an emotive as well as an intellectual level. The novel is, as Hampton claims in an interview with Ryan Stewart, "a tribute to the power of fiction, the film a tribute to the power of storytelling;" but Hampton's screenplay adaptation of this novel and Wright's cinematic realization of that screenplay is also a tribute to the collaborative power of cinema.

Notes

1 Christopher Hampton won an Oscar for his adapted screenplay of *Dangerous Liaisons* (1988).
2 McEwan's *Atonement* alludes to the writings of a whole range of literary figures from Jane Austen, Henry James, E. M. Forster, Virginia Woolf, D. H. Lawrence, and W. H. Auden.

References

Atonement. Dir. Joe Wright. UK/France: Universal, 2007.

Bordwell, David. *Narrative in the Fiction Film*. Madison: University of Wisconsin Press, 1985.

Brief Encounter. Dir. David Lean. UK: Cineguild, 1945.

Carnevale, Rob. "Atonement – Joe Wright Interview." n.d. *Indie London*. www.indielondon.co.uk/Film-Review/atonement-joe-wright-interview. Accessed October 10, 2010.

Chatman, Seymour. *Coming to Terms: The Rhetoric of Narrative in Fiction and Film*. Ithaca: Cornell University Press, 1990.

Childs, Peter. *The Fiction of Ian McEwan*. Houndmills: Palgrave Macmillan, 2006.

Geraghty, Christine. "Foregrounding the Media: *Atonement* (2007) as an Adaptation." *Adaptation* 2:2, 2009, 91–109.

Jays, David. "First Love, Last Rites." *Sight & Sound*, 17:10, 2007, 34–5.

A Matter of Life and Death. Dir. Michael Powell and Emeric Pressburger. UK: Eagle-Lion, 1946.

Langdon, Julia. "Ian McEwan Accused of Stealing Ideas from Romance Novelist." *The Mail on Sunday*, 2006. www.dailymail.co.uk/femail/article-418598/Ian-McEwan-accused. Accessed September 9, 2010.

McEwan, Ian. *Atonement*. London: QPD, 2001.

McEwan, Ian. "An Inspiration, Yes. Did I Copy From Another Author? No." *The Guardian*, 2006. www.guardian.co.uk/uk/2006/nov/27/bookscomment.topstories3. Accessed September 9, 2010.

Le Quai des Brumes. Dir. Marcel Carne. UK/France: Franco London Films, 1938.

Rich, Katey. *Cinema Blend*. "Atonement: Christopher Hampton Interview." n.d. Cinema Blend. October 20, 2010. www.cinemablend.com/new/Interview-Christopher-Hampton-Of-Atonement-71.

Saving Private Ryan. Dir. Stephen Spielberg. USA: Dreamworks/Paramount, 1998.

Stewart, Ryan. "TIFF [Toronto International Film Festival] Interview: Christopher Hampton, Screenwriter of Atonement." *Moviefone*, 2007. www.cinematical.com/2007/09/17/tiff-interview-christopher-hampton-screenwriter. Accessed November 9, 2011.

20

Foregrounding the Media

Atonement (2007) as an Adaptation

Christine Geraghty

Atonement, the film and the novel, can be considered a dual media success.[1] The 2001 novel maintained Ian McEwan's track record as a successful novelist, winning good reviews, Whitbread and Booker prize nominations, and selling well in the United States where it won the prestigious U.S. National Book Critics Award in 2003. Success in the United States was particularly marked: *Atonement* was "greeted by most book critics as a masterpiece that unexpectedly stayed at the top of the best seller lists of the *New York Times* for many weeks. Almost all American reviewers of the book have given it the highest praise possible" (Finney, 2004: 69).[2]

Joe Wright's 2007 adaptation was critically well received, took the best picture awards at the BAFTA and Golden Globes ceremonies and had seven Oscar nominations, all of which helped it to make an impact in the United States where its initial success led to a wider release in a larger number of cinemas. The tie-in between book and film was clearly made when the paperback version with the stars of the film on the cover was issued in August 2007. Helped by bookstore promotions connected to the film's release, the paperback sales in September were record-breaking:

> But the real story this week is the phenomenal performance of *Atonement*, which sold a combined 58,903 copies across all editions last week. The 53,357 copies of the tie-in edition sold is the highest September weekly sale in the UK since BookScan records began. . . . Life sales for the title, short-listed for the 2001 Man Booker Prize, have reached more than 900,000 across all editions. It is McEwan's first, and long overdue, number one (Stone, 2007: 17).

A Companion to Literature, Film, and Adaptation, First Edition. Edited by Deborah Cartmell.
© 2012 Blackwell Publishing Ltd. Published 2012 by Blackwell Publishing Ltd.

As we shall see, the critical response to the film on its initial release was framed by a comparison with the successful book. In this chapter, I will first examine this response to see how it was shaped by the filmmakers and their PR activity. In turning to my analysis of the film, however, I move away from the specific comparison between book and film which was the starting point for many of the reviewers. In doing so, I want to discuss the film in its own right, not as "another version of Briony's novel" (Childs, 2008: 152) or indeed of McEwan's, and to analyze how *Atonement* (2007) establishes and reflects on its own status as an adaptation. This section of the chapter begins by laying out some of the general principles of adaptation studies which are pertinent here. It moves on to a discussion of the way in which *Atonement* (2007) uses media representation as a specific means of calling attention to its status as an adaptation. I hope that, through discussing this example in some detail, the chapter makes a contribution to more general discussions about the different ways in which adaptations appeal to and are understood by their audiences.

The film was premiered at the Venice Film Festival in August 2007 and it got further festival appearances and national releases throughout the autumn and winter. Film critics in the press and online made it clear that the film's handling of the process of adaptation was important to their judgments on the film. This was as true of the trade press and popular journals as it was of the broadsheet critics and these reviewers were largely picking up on the emphasis on the film's status as an adaptation which had been established in the publicity interviews given by those involved in making the film who referred respectfully to the importance and stature of McEwan's book. In particular, Joe Wright, who took over as director from Richard Eyre in 2006, emphasized that he had found answers to some of the problems of the screenplay he was offered by returning to the novel:

> So we started again, and what I was interested in doing was a very faithful adaptation to the book. We literally kept the book on one side and the script on the other and we slowly worked through it, and that's how we came up with it (Douglas, 2007).

From Venice, *Variety* reported that the film "preserves much of the tome's metaphysical depth and all of its emotional power" and noted that "*Atonement* is immensely faithful to McEwan's novel" (Elley, 2007). *Screen International* suggested that it was "a textbook example of literary adaptation" (Hunter, 2007) and *Hollywood Reporter* that "McEwan's best-selling novel . . . had been rendered so well . . . that it ranks with the best novel adaptations of recent times" (Bennett, 2007). Helen O'Hara, reviewing the film for the populist UK film magazine *Empire*, began by jokingly reminding her readers,

> you know the book. If you use public transport, you'll recognise it as the one everyone was reading circa 2004. There was the Booker shortlisting, the reams of laudatory

articles about its author Ian McEwan. And now arrives the inevitable film adaptation . . . (O'Hara, 2007).

In *Village Voice*, Ella Taylor demonstrated her credentials for reviewing the film by beginning her article with "Re-reading Ian McEwan's *Atonement* last weekend, my first thought was I hope to God that Joe Wright . . . doesn't screw up this wonderful novel" (Taylor, 2007).

In general, the reviews, in particular the favorable ones, suggest that critics were not looking for complete faithfulness in the adaptation but the retention of the book's themes and structure and a sense that the film is doing the novel justice. O'Hara concluded that the film was "an adaptation at least as good as the novel – complex, delicate and devastating" (O'Hara, 2007). Kenneth Turan in *LA Times* wrote that "this is one of the few adaptations that gives a splendid novel the film it deserves" (Turan, 2007), while Philip French commented that "Ian McEwan's novel has been brought thrillingly to the screen" (French, 2007). Peter Bradshaw began his *Guardian* review by implying that he had had his doubts which had been triumphantly overcome:

> Well, Hampton and director Joe Wright have certainly done McEwan proud with this lavish and spectacular screen version: they are really thinking big, in every sense, and the result is exhilarating (Bradshaw, 2007).

The reviews of *Atonement* (2007) thus sought to establish the relationship between book and film as important for critical assessment. But many of them also used other references which were again taken from the publicity material promoting the film. Wright had discussed his love of old films ("I was brought up on films like *Brief Encounter*" he told *The Daily Telegraph* (Gritten, 2007)) and reviewers took their cue, particularly when it came to discussing the acting. *Variety*, in its characteristic movie-speak, commented that Keira Knightley "proves every bit as magnetic as the divas of those classic mellers [melodramas] pic consciously references" and that generally the film "consciously evokes the acting conventions and romantic clichés of '30s/'40s melodramas" (Elley, 2007). *Screen International* commended James McAvoy for "a flawless upper crust English accent" and "the look and screen presence of a 1930s matinee idol like Laurence Olivier or Robert Donat" while Knightley revealed an "inner steel beneath her cut-glass accent and Celia Johnson-style gentility" (Hunter, 2007). Critics cited films from other periods including *Gosford Park* (2001) and *Saving Private Ryan* (1998 – the Dunkirk sequence). Nick Bradshaw, in the specialist British Film Institute journal, *Sight & Sound*, added a number of others including *The Go-Between* (1979), *A Passage to India* (1984), and *The Remains of the Day* (1993), and commented that "as McEwan offered a digest of his literary heritage, so the film embraces all those literary adaptations" (2007: 49).

For some, the self-consciousness of this referencing did not save the film from falling into melodrama: the generally supportive Philip French referred back to the book to suggest that "without McEwan's subtle prose and the astute authorial observations, the film at times verges on the melodramatic" while Taylor complains bitterly that Wright has turned the first part of the novel into "just enough of a bodice ripper to reel in the youth market" and the second half into "a cheap knockoff of a 1940s war movie" (French, 2007; Taylor, 2007). This sense that the film's referencing of melodrama causes problems can also be seen in Peter Childs' sympathetic review of the film in *Adaptation*. He suggests that the film shares with the novel an emphasis on different perspectives and that this draws attention to "the film's status as adaptation, a visually realized rendition of Briony's final but fateful "version" of events. Nevertheless, Childs finally finds the film to lack the novel's complexity: "the projected fantasy of Robbie and Cecilia as lovers . . . bringing Christopher Hampton's in-many-ways fine adaptation to a clichéd romantic closure." In addition, the film cannot deal with the "postmodern twist in the novel" and fails to "explain or explore" its own status as yet another version of Briony's novel (Childs, 2008: 151–2).

It is clear then that the critical context for *Atonement* (2007), created as least in part by its own publicity machine, involves the film's relationship with two kinds of source text – the original novel and the various films consciously referenced. Note though that although the critics continually refer to the book they also indicate that neither they nor the filmmakers can assume that those interested in seeing the film have read the book. Critics take their usual care not to give away too much of the plot; French, for instance, writes that "The ending has been considerably altered, but Hampton's clever solution will surprise those who haven't read the novel and is unlikely to disappoint those who have" (French, 2007). O'Hara reminds her readers about the novel not by assuming that they have read it but that they have seen someone else reading it (O'Hara, 2007). In *Sight & Sound*, David Jays begins a feature article on the film by remembering that "in the summer of 2001 I was repeatedly told I ought to read Ian McEwan's *Atonement*" and warns his readers "to look away if you'd like to experience the same jolt as either a reader of the novel or as a viewer of Joe Wright's new film" (2007: 34). *Atonement* is not therefore a classic like *Oliver Twist* or *Pride and Prejudice*, known from a number of different versions in a variety of media. Nor does it have the status of the *Harry Potter* series or *Lord of the Rings*, books which were adapted with "exceptional fidelity" (Leitch, 2007: 127) because of anxieties about taking any liberties to which their loyal and knowledgeable fans might object. For Wright and Hampton, the original source is clearly important but they cannot assume previous knowledge on the part of the audience and, indeed, their concern about the changes they made to the ending indicates again that for at least some of the audience it will be a "revelation."[3] In the critical discourse established by the film's PR and the critics, the novel is clearly established as a source text but knowledge of its contents is limited and the film needs to appeal to an audience well beyond the original readers. It is the implications of this that I want to explore in my analysis of the film.

The fidelity model, which relies heavily on notions of media specificity and which almost inevitably results in a comparison on terms dictated by the source text, has been under attack for many years in adaptation studies. Philosophically unsustainable and often sterile in terms of the readings it offers, the fidelity model has been particularly unhelpful in making judgments about popular cinema. Those making the comparison between page and screen seem consciously or unconsciously to draw on a hierarchy of values which is at odds with the practices of popular cinema. Robert Stam, among others, has drawn attention to the value structure which underpins such an approach with its problematic response to cultural products such as film and television which appear to rely on the image rather than the word, on the generation of emotion and sensation in the viewer and on mass audiences rather than the individual reader. To his list, I would add that this value structure also often relies on the contrast between (apparently) non-generic written texts and generic screen adaptations. Childs is not alone in commenting on the point when an adaptation falls into romance or melodrama and judging that to be a betrayal of the original source.

Of course, the problems of the fidelity model were supposed to be overcome by "the impact of the posts" (Stam, 2005: 8). Despite the poststructural emphasis on intertextuality, dialogism, and crosscultural referencing, it has proved remarkably difficult to escape from this automatic act of comparison. In part this may be because the poststructural desire to throw out the hierarchical values of the fidelity model runs the risk of abandoning any clear notion of an adaptation altogether. If the notion of an original source with an overdetermining author is dropped, if all texts depend on an interplay of cultural references and sources, if *collage* rather than *écriture* is the dominant mode of writing, then all texts are "caught up in an ongoing whirl of intertextual reference and transformation, of texts generating other texts in an endless process of recycling, transformation and transmutation, with no clear point of origin" (Stam, 2000: 66). Adaptation studies would then fold back into a much broader interdisciplinary approach which took inter-media possibilities for granted: "in the workings of the human imagination, adaptation is the norm, not the exception" (Hutcheon, 2006: 177).

Something similar might be said about approaches which seem to draw more fully from cultural studies and which emphasize context and a more grounded sense of identity. One feature of recent adaptation studies has been the expansion into different kinds of sources such as memoirs, biography, newspaper articles, and historical documents. This is a welcome extension of boundaries but inevitably it blurs the distinction between an analysis based on modes of adaptation and one coming out of cultural studies more generally. Alessandro Raengo's very interesting article, for instance, analyzes the body image of baseball star, Jackie Robinson. She argues that the success of various artifacts, including a film and book of his life, is dependent on Robinson as "the only individual who can embody it." Adopting the "traditional language" of adaptation studies, she suggests that "Robinson's body provides both the 'source material' and its 'adaptation'" (Raengo, 2008: 79, 80). As with

Stam's use of intertextuality, this move engages adaptation theory with a potentially more productive model of analysis but perhaps at the expense of precision.

I would want to argue that adaptation is still a worthwhile category with distinctive features that can be analyzed. An adaptation is an adaptation not just because it is based on an original source but because it draws attention to the fact of adaptation in the text itself and/or in the paratextual material which surrounds it. Rather than rejecting adaptations as almost inevitably different and therefore worse than their sources, a number of critics have set out to ask "what is the appeal of adaptations?" (Hutcheon, 2006: 172). While I do not necessarily agree with Leitch's argument that adaptation is best considered as a genre, his emphasis on the distinctive pleasures of adaptations is helpful. Arguing that all reading or viewing involves the testing of "earlier experiences of books or plays or films against a new set of norms and values" offered by the current work, he suggests that the distinctive pleasure of adaptation lies in the way it "foregrounds this possibility and makes it more active, more exigent, more indispensable" (Leitch, 2008: 117).

Leitch draws on Hutcheon's description of readers oscillating between one text and another. Hutcheon indeed suggests that "to experience [an adaptation] *as an adaptation*, . . . we need to recognise it as such and to know its adapted text, thus allowing the latter to oscillate in our memories with what we are experiencing" (Hutcheon, 2006: 120–1). This suggests once again that an adaptation is dependent on its source and Hutcheon indeed speaks of adaptors who "rely" on the audiences' ability to "fill in the gaps" through information from the adapted text. But she also indicates that there are audience members who have no "reference to and foreknowledge of the adapted text" and argues that "for an adaptation to be successful in its own right, it must be so for both knowing and unknowing audiences" (121). I would suggest that rather than depending on such variable foreknowledge, it is better to think of an adaptation as independent (to the same extent as other texts) with the fact of adaptation recognizable from its own formal qualities. This allows us to rely less on speculations about what the audience does and to look for signifiers within the text which invite the oscillation described by Leitch and Hutcheon. I would suggest that these often involve a layering of narratives, performances, and/or settings in which one way of telling a story is set against another. Such a layering is often indicated by the foregrounding of media signifiers which invite the audience to set one media experience against another, just as the process of adaptation involves shifting from one mode of media production to the other. The effect is one of shadowing that shift in production by offering recognition of a parallel shift in perception. The advantage, though, is that while the shift in production may rely on our knowledge of the fact of adaptation (and in Hutcheon's terms may be available only to the "knowing audience"), the foregrounding of a shift in perception can lie entirely within the adaptation text itself and is therefore available to knowing and unknowing audiences alike.[4]

One of the features of Leitch's proposed genre of adaptation is an "obsession with authors, books and words" (2008: 121), which, one might note, works against the traditional association of film and image made in much adaptation theory and commonsense criticism. He suggests a number of different ways in which this can be done including featuring the author's name along with the book's title in the film title; the use of the physical properties of books in the credits (the fluttering pages, the frontispiece); and the books featured in plotlines. One could also add the use of a writer as an investigator in a story and the fact of publication as the source of a happy ending. *Atonement* (2007), as we shall see, draws heavily on writing but it also references a wide variety of other media from opera to newsreels and on a number of media transmitters such as the typewriter and the gramophone. In this analysis, I will focus on the film's foregrounding of the three media – writing, film, and television – which it uses to tell its story and which it invites the audience to reflect on in establishing a somewhat unusual media hierarchy. I suggest that these different modes dominate the three sections of the film which are also marked by a change in the actress playing Briony – the events at the Tallis country home, the wartime sequences, and the coda in which the older Briony reflects on what she has done. Of course, the film deploys the mechanisms and formal devices of cinema throughout; the foregrounding of the media in different sections precisely invites us to oscillate from that base into an awareness of other modes of storytelling.

The film opens with two acts of writing which are rendered inseparable. The first occurs in the credits. We hear first birdsong and then the sounds of a typewriter being loaded, the carriage being moved across and the sound of the keys hitting the drum as against a black background, the underlined letters of the word ATONE-MENT appear in huge close-up on the screen. This typing provides us with the film's title and can be tied later to Briony's novel but it is not what we find in the first scene in which the child Briony is revealed to be typing at her desk. Shots of her back and face and eyes alternate with those which show the old-fashioned typewriter as the camera moves up the keys to the manuscript where THE END is being written. Briony takes the sheet out of the typewriter and puts it on the pile of papers which she turns to show the second title THE TRIALS OF ARABELLA. It seems that the end of one story is the beginning of another, as Briony marches off to announce her success to her mother, the rhythm of her walk matching the staccato music that incorporates the sound of typing. What is less clear is whether the typing of the title can also be ascribed to Briony later in life or whether this is the personless objectivity of the film imposing its authority.

Writing then is established as Briony's activity and will be referred to throughout the film when for example she begins to write her first version of the lovers' story while training at St Thomas's Hospital in the wartime sequences. As in many adaptations, the writer is presented in some ways as the author of what we see but also as a potentially unreliable witness. In two crucial scenes, both seen first from Briony's perspective, she gets it wrong; her view is limited and impaired, the conclusions she draws lack evidence. By contrast, the film invites us to believe the truth of the scenes as fully rendered by cinema, without the intervention of the writer.

As is sometimes the case in cinematic renderings of writing, the young author is rendered as fallible and limited. This is reinforced by the settled nature of the generic references at this point. The film's rendering of the English 1930s country house can be understood almost as a sub-genre of the period film; as in its successful precursor *Gosford Park*, the settled hierarchies and the beautiful landscapes are meticulously presented as desirable but doomed.

But, as the film progresses, it is writing which disrupts the conventions of cinematic genre to make the medium (as opposed to the author) powerful. Briony is writing a play at this point, not a novel, and in the early scenes the mise-en-scène of the film plays with setting and scale to underline the theatricality of the country house setting and the 1930s dialogue. The first shot in the house is of its doll's house replica and as the camera pulls back a line of assorted animals, the contents of a farm set and a Noah's ark, comes into view as if marching silently towards Briony. Later on we get a similar shot of the house, this time the real one, followed by a shot from above of Briony and Cecilia as tiny figures lying on the lawn. Throughout the country house section, the actors are often posed picturesquely into groups or set against a striking piece of furniture. Briony's act of writing for theater for the first time also allows her dialogue which reflects on the problems of play production; whereas a novel creates setting through word and the reader's imagination, a play, she complains, depends on other people, the actors. In this analysis of media specificities, cinema's possibilities remain evident but unspoken.

In this section of the film, words do not act simply as signifiers for some imaginative signified. The most powerful words are unspoken and appear as writing, typed on the page, and as cinema, in huge close-ups. Here the two media combine together to convey the power of the word. Robbie's letter-writing to Cecilia is introduced by Briony's voiceover as she scribbles the words into her notebook: "he was the most dangerous man in the world". The following scene alternates shots of Robbie at the typewriter with those of Cecilia getting ready for dinner, held together by the diegetic sounds of opera played on Robbie's record player. She is all image, her face and body reflected in the mirrors and blurred by feathers, cigarette smoke, and light. Robbie too is on display; his shoulders are bared and he stretches his leg out in an athletic pose between drafts. But his focus is on the words. Initially, the words are voiced; Robbie reads them aloud and then mutters them more softly as he redrafts. As the aria reaches the top notes, a huge close-up shows the black letters as they are typed onto the soft texture of the paper, ending with a forceful full stop. We are forced to follow the sentence as it is created as if the process of writing by the character and reading by the audience were becoming one process. Then, as Robbie breaks the tension by laughing, the writing process returns to the character/author. He changes to a pen and reads aloud the "more formal," "less anatomical" version of what he wants to say. But the shock of reading the writing returns when Briony reads the letter. We see her face in two shots from below as she reads so the content of the letter is hidden and we wait for her reaction. But the audience is again confronted as, in a close-up, the word "cunt" is not only read by Briony but rewritten letter by letter. A long-shot of Briony standing small and still in the hall returns us to cinema.

The letter does its powerful work, both in allowing the release of sexual feeling by Robbie and Cecilia and confirming Briony's belief that he is a dangerous man. Her misidentification of Robbie as Lola's rapist leads to his arrest. There is a clue as to the continuing source of the story in that the country house section ends with a close-up of Briony looking down at Robbie's arrest with the sound of typewriting getting louder on the soundtrack. Writing, in the form of Briony's stories and the lovers' letters, continues to be important in the telling of the story but with the shift to 1940 the emphasis on it as a medium recedes. Briony's writing is mainly discussed rather than seen on screen and the love letters are largely handled through the cinematic device of voiceovers.

The wartime sequences are dominated by the foregrounding of cinema and an emphasis on its medium specificity. The wartime section of the film can be divided into two parts: the first, taking us up to what is in fact Robbie's death at Dunkirk is dominated by his viewpoint; the second by Briony's as she begins her training as a nurse and tries to make amends for her actions. In the 1935 section of the film, we have been presented with a series of the theatrical scenes taking place in chronological order on the set of a country house but in the wartime section there is cutting between different spaces and gaps in time are indicated by dissolves, intertitles, and montage. In addition, the concentration on the triangle of Robbie, Cecilia, and Briony which dominates the first section slips a little as the film extends its range of locations and other lives are briefly seen: Robbie's soldier companions; the French men who bring them food and drink; the dying French soldier who mistakes Briony for an English girl he knew before the war; the mother and children being evacuated "to the country"; the bent, elderly woman pushing a low pram as she makes her slow way along a London street. Their stories are hinted at rather than told but they refer back to the way British cinema of the 1940s based its approach on interweaving stories from people of different communities.

The foregrounding of cinema in this section is effected in a number of ways. There are references to the cinema of the period, the so-called golden age of the 1940s when British cinema found its story and the need to tell it. There is, for example, the inclusion of documentary footage from "the epic of Dunkirk" featuring soldiers packed into trains and downing cups of tea, with the emphasis on dogged resistance rather than hope of victory; this contrasts with the false optimism of the mock newsreel which shows the Queen visiting a chocolate factory which alerts Briony to Lola's forthcoming marriage. Other references are less direct though still clear: the scene of Robbie and Cecilia meeting in the tea room before he embarks recalls *Brief Encounter* (1945), with its restrained lovers, speaking in clipped accents in public places; the ferris wheel from *The Third Man* (1949) dominates the skyline on the beach; the soundtrack uses hymns and popular songs to demonstrate public spirit in the manner of *Millions Like Us* (1943). Also familiar from the films of the period are the wartime settings: these include the crowded hospital wards in which the stories of nurses and patients are overridden by public events; the London streets with their buses, post boxes, and crowded pavements; the cramped terraces and rundown rooms occupied by the working class who attempt to continue their everyday life; the church architecture which includes the church in which Briony sees Lola marry and the rose window at Dunkirk which, like the church in *The Bells Go Down* (1943), still stands amid the ruins.

But it is not just the subject matter which foregrounds cinema but also the form. In this section the film demonstrates its cinematic virtuosity and draws attention to the way in which cinema has been used specifically to make relationships across space and time. Certain elements are clearly brought to the fore: the five-minute steadicam shot of the Dunkirk beach was commented on by the critics and the subject of technical analysis in a number of interviews.[5] There are other examples of this drawing attention to form. The steadicam shot is followed by the scene in the cinema when Robbie, in pursuit of water, gets himself behind the screen as *Le Quai des Brumes* (1938) plays, his small figure pushed to one side by the huge faces of the stars which move together into a kiss; the distortion and the glamour of the cinema is clearly figured. And Robbie's death is presaged by a swift montage of shots summing up his life which includes a reprise of his arrest in which for the first time we hear the words that Cecilia said to him as the police took him away. These major effects stand out. They ask to be looked at and admired rather than subsumed into the oft-cited emphasis on realism of British cinema in which the audience is invited to look through rather than at the screen.

In this second section, the foregrounding of cinematic devices also involves the interweaving of time and uncertainty about viewpoint. The use of voiceover, flashbacks, and "false" shots of, for example, Robbie's mother at Dunkirk, emphasizes cinema's association with memories, dreams, and visions. On the walk to Dunkirk, the sight of the dead schoolgirls laid out in the grass has the slightly surrealistic quality of a dream. And even what looks like solid realism is not necessarily to be trusted. Briony's visit to her sister takes place in a cramped room with its net curtains, boiling kettle, and milk in a bottle. It is a realist, urban scene familiar, for instance, from Ealing Studio's postwar films such as *It Always Rains on Sunday* (1947) and *Dance Hall* (1950). But the speed of Robbie's slide past Briony in the cramped room, the intensity of her gaze through the doorway at the luminous sheets on the unmade bed and Cecilia's intense plea to Robbie – "Come back, come back to me" – indicate that all is not what it seems. We will later learn that this scene never took place.

At the end of this imagined scene, Robbie tells Briony that she is to "write it all down, just the truth – no rhymes, no embellishments, no adjectives." This suggests that writing can tell the truth in a way that cinema cannot and Robbie's words are followed by a shot of Briony on the train, apparently returning from her visit. This shot, which gradually moves into a close-up of her face, rhymes with the shot of Briony which ended the country house section; again, the percussion of the typewriter is on the soundtrack but this time the flickering lights on Briony's face also refer to the specificity of cinema and the movement of film through a projector. However, as the film moves into the third section, it is clear that television is the medium through which truth will be told. The screen goes black and we hear a voice saying "I'm sorry, could we stop for a moment?". A shot of fifteen television screens in three rows reveals the source of the voice; her words and the accompanying movement are replayed as the film establishes the setting of Briony's interview in a television studio. A brief scene of the older Briony composing herself in her dressing room gives us her face in the mirror and in the following television interview the camera gradually moves from a full shot of her seated, taken from behind the interviewer, through a head and shoulders shot which is held as she recounts her commitment to truth ("I got firsthand accounts," "In fact, what happened") before coming in for a tight close-up for her explanation of why the book is not in fact the truth but "a final act of kindness. I gave them their happiness." This camera positioning is not of course typical of a standard television interview but, in its gradual homing into a close-up and its concentration on an unglamourized, elderly face in which we can see fleeting emotions, it gives us a version of television, a version in which an interview can unexpectedly get at truth.[6] As it has done with theater, writing, and cinema itself, *Atonement* (2007) alerts the audience to the characteristics of this medium and rather unexpectedly reverses the usual cultural hierarchies in which literature is deemed a more serious and hence a better medium than cinema and cinema better than television. Here, the mechanics of television are emphasized through the rewinding and repetition but television is acknowledged as a source of truth, both about Briony, Robbie and Cecilia and about Briony's book.

Although the film retains the book's emphasis on Briony's inventive powers in elaborating a happy ending, it takes on a different resonance if we pay attention to the foregrounding of the media in this adaptation. The final shots show Robbie and Cecilia on the beach and then returning to the cottage where we leave them. Childs (2008) sees this as a clichéd romantic ending but it is more accurate to see it as *Atonement*'s (2007) return to the mode of cinema. The audience is now, in Hutcheon's terms, a "knowing" one, not because it has read the book but because it has watched this film. The ending is layered over the knowledge we have gained both about the story and the mode of telling. It is shot using the clichés associated with wartime love stories. The white cliffs of Dover shine in the background, the lovers playfully wrestle in a manner which represents the sexual activity banished from the screen in the 1940s, and the house is perfectly positioned in its natural surroundings, far from the urban threat of bombed cities. In many war films, these kinds of images were used to signify what was being fought for, a particular version of England in which personal relationships and national identity came together into a desired unity. The final shot is, of course, the shot from Cecilia's photograph, now given movement and hence, in cinema's terms, life. It is literally picture-perfect and made so, this time, by the mechanisms of cinema; Robbie and Cecilia are safely inside.

Romantic endings in cinema often have this imposed quality as if the required reso-lution can only be achieved by ignoring the unresolved aspects of the trouble that melodrama uses as the basis for stories. This is a "happy ending" in which the mechanics of cinema are exposed. If television emerges from *Atonement* (2007) as the medium in which truth can be told, then the ending establishes cinema as the place where we can knowingly respond to a different kind of emotional investment, the investment in desire that mass audiences have traditionally made in cinema.

In suggesting that the ending needs to be looked at in the light of the film's layering of different media, I am not suggesting that the ending works entirely successfully but that its problems are not a question of a lapse into cliché. First of all, the ending closes on a representation of cinema which, however knowingly expressed, may be too locked into a version of cinema which is "forever sepia" (Taylor, 2007). *Atonement* (2007) potentially offers a double view of cinema as a medium. It seeks to establish itself as a modern film capable of handling the post-modern challenge of its source but the ending runs the risk of setting up the 1940s version of British cinema invoked in the wartime sequences as the dominant way of defining cinema as a medium, at least for audiences of British films, and thus making it nostalgic, old-fashioned, or irrelevant.

Secondly, and this may indicate a more general risk run by certain kinds of adap-tations, *Atonement* (2007) illustrates that the layering which encourages the oscilla-tion between different versions of the text and assists the reading practices which Hutcheon describes can distance us from the emotional identification often assumed to be necessary for cinema. Its ending, with its emphasis not only on Briony's telling of the story but also on the specificity of cinema, more generally invites us to stand back from the central relationship and to become aware of the processes of telling which we have been through. David Jays found the film "tense but chilly" (Jays, 2007: 35) and Anthony Lane associated this coldness with the exposition of its own mechanics. He suggests that the steadicam sequence at Dunkirk

> has been lauded for its skill, yet something feels wrong. You find yourself marking off the surreal details as they are ushered into view . . . Wright is sowing the frame with incident for fear that it might lie fallow, and the result is that he risks merely drawing attention to his own style. This ties in with a general suspicion that "Atone-ment," as a story about stories, may be too self-conscious for its own good. You have to admire it, when so much of the competition seems inane and slack, but you can't help wondering, with some impatience, what happened to its heart (Lane, 2007).

Lane goes on to link this emphasis on style to the way that the ending – Briony's "last, beneficent lie" – "made me look back over the expanse of the film and realize, to my dismay, that I hardly believed a word of it;" in particular, he found that he did not "believe in the force of his [Robbie's] love for Cecilia, or of hers for him" (Lane, 2007). Lane finds himself distanced from the heart of the film not just by the themes of its source but by the way it draws attention to its own processes, its emphasis on the devices of cinema or more broadly, as I have suggested, the emphasis on the medium of telling, whether it be writing, cinema, or television. Lane's review suggests that the process of foregrounding the media in *Atonement* (2007) may undermine one of the characteristics strongly associated with mainstream cinema – its traditional ability to make the audience feel what it might mean to experience enduring love.

Textual analysis cannot outline or predict all the possible responses which audience members might have to a particular adaptation and I would argue that the oscillation between source text and adaptation, so beloved by academic analysts and indeed by those who have "read the book," is only one possible source of pleasure in a screen adaptation. At the same time, adaptations which wish to be understood as adaptations cannot just rely on audiences to arrive with the knowledge they need to appreciate what being an adaptation means in any particular context. *Atonement* (2007) is, I have argued, an adaptation which draws attention to its status as an adaptation by foregrounding the use of different media. I am not suggesting that these media (writing, cinema, television) necessarily have specific and intrinsic representational practices but that the film presents them as such and associates them with different kinds of truths. In an article on postmodernism and adaptation, Peter Brooker shifted attention from the text to the audience and argued that a movement from source to adaptation (the path followed by the makers of *Atonement* (2007), for instance) cannot be assumed on the part of the audience and that there are therefore "variations in the viewer's experience" (Brooker, 2007: 118). From this, he deduced "two simple points: that the source text may not be the chronologically first text in a reader's or viewer's experience; and, secondly, that an 'adaptation' may not be experienced as this" (118–19). He then argues that "adaptations . . . wait to be realized" and that their "intertextual and transtextual meanings are inactive, manifest, or potential," dependent on the viewer's knowledge of the "before and after" of a particular work (118–19). My argument is that the process is more dynamic for adaptations which seek to be recognized as adaptations even by those who do not know the original source. The film does not wait for the unknowing viewer to go away and read the book. The possibility of comparison is not only put in the foreground, as Leitch argues (2008: 117), but is made a necessary part of engaging with the film. Following its narrative depends on an internal oscillation between different versions of the story and its telling which, crucially, are made available in the film itself. McEwan's novel offered a particularly good opportunity for this kind of reworking but it is the film's foregrounding of different media which creates the knowing audience and establishes the film's status as an adaptation.

ACKNOWLEDGMENTS

Ideas for this article were initially presented at the Literature on Screen conference at the University of Amsterdam, 2008 and I am very grateful to the other members of the panel, Laurent Mellet and Terry Kidner, and to those who attended and joined in a spirited discussion.

Notes

1   An earlier version of this chapter occurs in *Adaptation*, 2:2, 2009, 91–109, by permission of Oxford University Press.

2   Finney's account shows how the novel changed the assessment of McEwan's overall stature.

3   Christopher Hampton commented that "We spent more time on how to do that revelation at the end than on absolutely anything else. It's so delicate. And it could go so drastically wrong if you didn't pay tremendous attention to it" (Winship, 2008).

4   My discussion of *Atonement* (2007) can be helpfully set against the textual account given by Yvonne Griggs in her chapter for this volume (Chapter 19) in which she sug-

gests ways in which the director and script-writer seek to engage the audience as creators of the narrative.

5   See, for instance, interviews with Wright in Douglas (2007); Carnevale (2007); and Palmer (2007).

6   Hampton in a discussion of this scene (Winship, 2008) referred to the television interview Dennis Potter gave at the end of his life, but one could go back to John Freeman making Gilbert Harding cry in *Face to Face* (BBC, 1960) and David Frost's confessional interviews with Richard Nixon (1977) as examples which established the use of television in this way.

References

Atonement. Dir. Joe Wright. UK/France: Universal, 2007.

Bells Go Down, The. Dir. Basil Deardon. UK: Ealing, 1943.

Bennett, Ray. "*Atonement*: Splendid Treatment of a Fine Novel about Love and War, and a Devastating Lie." Hollywood Reporter, August, 30, 2007. www.rottentomatoes.com/m/atonement. Accessed August 3, 2011.

Bradshaw, Peter. "*Atonement*." *The Guardian*, September 7, 2007.

Bradshaw, Nick. "*Atonement*." *Sight & Sound*, 17:10, 2007, 49.

Brief Encounter. Dir. David Lean. UK: Cineguild, 1945.

Brooker, Peter. "Postmodern Adaptation: Pastiche, Intertextuality and Re-functioning." In *The Cambridge Companion to Literature on Screen*. Eds. Deborah Cartmell and Imelda Whelehan. Cambridge: Cambridge University Press, 2007, 107–20.

Carnevale, Rob. "*Atonement* – Joe Wright Interview." 2007. www.indielondon.co.uk/

Film-Review/atonement-joe-wright-interview. Accessed July 25, 2011.

Childs, Peter. "*Atonement* – The Surface of Things." *Adaptation*, 1:20, 2008, 151–2.

Dance Hal. Dir. Charles Crichton. UK: Ealing, 1950.

Douglas, Edward. "Joe Wright on Directing *Atonement*." November 30, 2007. www.google.co.uk/search?sourceid=navclient&hl=en-GB&ie=UTF-8&rlz=1T4ADBF_en-GBGB236GB237&q=edward+douglas+on+directing+atonement. Accessed July 28, 2011.

Elley, Derek. "*Atonement*." *Variety*, August 29, 2007. www.variety.com/review/VE1117934523?refcatid=31. Accessed July 25, 2011.

Finney, Brian. "Briony's Stand Against Oblivion: The Making of Fiction in Ian McEwan's *Atonement*." *Journal of Modern Literature*, 27:3, 2004, 68–82.

French, Philip. "Forgive me. I have sinned." *The Observer*, September 9, 2007.

Go-Between, The. Dir. Joseph Losey. UK: Metro-Goldwyn-Mayer, 1970.

Gosford Park. Dir. Robert Altman. US/UK/Ital: USA Films, 2001.

Gritten, David. "Spotlight Falls on Movie Master." *Daily Telegraph*, August 24, 2007.

Hunter, Allan. *"Atonement." Screen International*, August 30, 2007. www.screendaily.com/atonement/4034139.article.

Hutcheon, Linda. *A Theory of Adaptation*. Abingdon: Routledge, 2006.

It Always Rains on Sunday. Dir. Robert Hamer. UK: Ealing, 1947.

Jays, David. "First Love, Last Rites." *Sight & Sound*, 17:10, 2007, 34–5.

Lane, Anthony. "Conflicting Stories." *New Yorker*, December 10, 2007, 117.

Le Quai des Brumes. Dir. Marcel Carné. France: Ciné-Alliance, 1938.

Leitch, Thomas. *Film Adaptation and its Discontents*. Baltimore: Johns Hopkins University Press, 2007.

Leitch, Thomas. "Adaptation, the Genre." *Adaptation*, 1:2, 2008, 106–20.

Millions Like Us. Dir. Sidney Gilliat and Frank Launder. UK: Gainsborough Pictures, 1943.

O'Hara, Helen. *"Atonement." Empire*, September 27, 2007. www.empireonline.com/reviews/ReviewComplete.asp?FID=11344. Accessed July 28, 2011.

Palmer, Martyn. "Of Love, War and Guilt." *The Times Magazine*, September 1, 2007, 33–6.

Passage to India, A. Dir. David Lean. UK/US: EMI, 1984.

Raengo, Alessandra. "A Necessary Signifier: The Adaptation of Robinson's Body-Image in 'The Jackie Robinson Story'." *Adaptation*, 1:2, 2008, 79–105.

Remains of the Day, The. Dir. James Ivory. UK/USA: Merchant Ivory Productions, Columbia Pictures Corporation, 1993.

Saving Private Ryan. Dir. Stephen Spielberg. US: Amblin Entertainment, DreamWorks SKG, Mark Gordon Productions, 1998.

Stam, Robert. "Beyond Fidelity: The Dialogics of Adaptation." In *Film Adaptation*. Ed. James Naremore. London: Athalone, 2000, 79–105.

Stam, Robert. "Introduction: The Theory and Practice of Adaptation." In *Literature and Film: A Guide to Theory and Practice of Adaptation*. Eds. Robert Stam and Alessandra Raengo. Oxford: Blackwell, 2005, 1–52.

Stone, Philip. "McEwan's *Atonement*." The Bookseller, 5299, September, 21, 2007, 17.

Taylor, Ella. "Sorry State of Affairs Film Adaptation of Ian McEwan's *Atonement* an Unwelcome Bodice-Ripper." *Village Voice*, November 27, 2007. www.villagevoice.com/2007-11-27/film/sorry-state-of-affairs/.

Third Man, The. Dir. Carol Reed. UK, London Film Productions, British Lion Film Corporation, 1949.

Turan, Kenneth. "Romance Amid the Sweep of History in *Atonement*." *Los Angeles Times*, December 7, 2007.

Winship, Michael. "Secrets and Lies. Excerpts from the Christopher Hampton Interview about *Atonement*." January, 2008. www.wga.org/writtenby/writtenbysub.aspx?id=2702. Accessed July 25, 2011.

21
Paratextual Adaptation

Heart of Darkness as Hearts of Darkness via Apocalypse Now

Jamie Sherry

Introduction

Joseph Conrad's oft-cited statement, "My task which I am trying to achieve is, by the power of the written word, to make you hear, to make you feel – it is, above all, to make you *see*" (1923: ix–x), has been cited as evidence of the inherent cinematic qualities of his pre-Modernist writings. Since Maurice Toureur's first silent film adaptation of Conrad's *Victory* in 1919, more than seventy film versions of his work have been produced. An admirer of the emerging medium of film, Conrad also adapted his own short story "Gaspar Ruiz" (1906) for cinema as *Gaspar the Strong Man* in 1920. Conrad's novella *Heart of Darkness* (1899) described by Cedric Watts as a "mixture of oblique autobiography, traveller's yarn, adventure story, psychological odyssey, political satire, symbolic prose-poem, black comedy, spiritual melodrama, and sceptical meditation" (1996: 45) clearly stands as the author's most widely read and best-known text. Despite this, Conrad's novella is predominantly received in mainstream culture via the cinematic dissemination of the text's adaptations, because, as Gene Moore states, the "importance of film as a means of transmitting influence should not be underestimated," due to the fact that, "far more people will have seen film versions of Conrad's works than have actually read his books" (1996: 236).

The release of Francis Ford Coppola's *Apocalypse Now* (1979), followed by the expanded *Apocalypse Now Redux* (2001), have radically refocused critical approaches to *Heart of Darkness*, spawning subsidiary paratexts, and provoking debates about the nature of adaptation and the politics of fidelity. For Thomas Elsaesser and

A Companion to Literature, Film, and Adaptation, First Edition. Edited by Deborah Cartmell.

Michael Wedel, it is the demoting of literature in wider contemporary culture, as inferred by Moore, which ultimately bestows status upon *Apocalypse Now*:

> The eighty years between the publication of Conrad's novella and the release of Coppola's film have witnessed a profound reversal in the relationship between author and text as it structures the institution of literature, which has moved from a central position in culture, to the status of one media industry amongst others (1997: 151).

The inherent problems of Conrad adaptation, such as expensive set-pieces/locations, and the rendering of literary devices such as ironic narrative ambiguity, largely prevented Orson Welles from seeing his 1939 adaptation of the novella realized. However, for adaptors who may potentially look to *Heart of Darkness* as source material, the main "problems" exist outside of the text itself. The film's associated myth and canonicity, provoked by its culturally proliferated tropes, have ultimately converged to relocate the novella, and therefore our subsequent reading of it. Conrad's and Coppola's texts are indelibly linked, in part *because* of the transformative distancing employed by the director, in an act of what Derrida (1995) calls "mutual invagination." The *bricolage* landscape of culture, in which myriad texts ceaselessly adapt each other in acts of "appropriation and contamination" (Cartmell and Whelehan, 2007: 11), reflects the complexity of our reception of an adaptation. This reception is guided by the status of *Apocalypse Now*, which itself has been manufactured through its infamously troubled production, as presented in Eleanor Coppola's "making of" documentary *Hearts of Darkness: A Filmmaker's Apocalypse* (1991) and her published diaries, *Notes on the Making of Apocalypse Now* (1991). These paratexts add another complex layer of intertextual interruption – informing and amending the discourse between reader and Conrad's precursor novella.

The intention of this chapter is to focus on Coppola's adaptation of *Heart of Darkness* as a route to understanding and expanding the following issues of adaptation theory:

1 The usurping of source material through palimpsestic rewriting, in which the subsequent adaptation either gains status and cultural value over the original text, or significantly infiltrates readings of it.

2 The paratext as adaptation – in this case a subsidiary reflection on the making of an adaptation in the form of a documentary, which both becomes tethered to the adaptation, and shares dramatic themes with the source material.

3 The influence of a precursor *phantom adaptation* on a later *completed* adaptation of the same source text.

It is hoped that this study of *Heart of Darkness* adaptations can be part of a more general movement beyond the conservative "compare–contrast," case study approach of traditional adaptation studies. By refocusing the interrogation of an adaptation from the "core" film text and towards the myriad paratexts produced prior to and as a consequence of that work, it may become possible to understand the dynamics of adaptation in a less classical mode.

The Horror of Vietnam – Coppola's *Apocalypse Now Redux*

In his introduction to *Conrad on Film*, Gene Moore states that "a great many more people have seen *Apocalypse Now* than will ever read *Heart of Darkness*" (1997: 1). He goes on to cite an interesting example of the influence of Coppola's film on a modern audience, in the form of an answer given to a literature quiz in the United States, in which a student describes the plot of *Heart of Darkness* as "the haunting tale of a seaman's quest for an enigmatic WWI officer who's gone AWOL up the Congo" (1). These observations serve to act as a starting point for what can be seen as the most difficult and profound problem of Conrad adaptation – not the obstacles of filming a literary device such as the ironic framed narrative, or the complexities of adapting Conrad's controversial politics of race, colonialism and gender, but the specific problems of adaptation reception, and the intertextual confluences between texts that revolve around an adaptation and effect its reading. Or, as Jacques Derrida puts it, the text as "a differential network, a fabric of traces referring endlessly to something other than itself, to other differential traces" (1995: 84).

Coppola's *Apocalypse Now*, in its depiction of the jaded and washed-up Captain Willard (Martin Sheen playing the Marlow of Conrad's novella) picked up from his stagnating hotel room in Saigon, and sent into Cambodia to assassinate with "extreme prejudice" Special Forces Colonel Kurtz, has become arguably the most memorable film of the 1970s. Coppola's adaptation has produced a number of significantly influential images, such as the bloated but compelling Brando and the scopophilic moral conundrum that is the dramatically violent but satirically amusing invasion scene of a Vietnamese village to the strains of Wagner's *Flight of the Valkyries* (with Robert Duvall as the charismatic Lieutenant Colonel Bill Kilgore). The film radically changed not just the war film as genre, but the film industry itself. The infamous problems the production faced, including a predicted six-week shoot actually lasting sixteen months, Walter Murch taking two years to edit a film running millions of dollars over budget, the recasting of Harvey Keitel with Martin Sheen two weeks into shooting, Coppola's suicide threats, a typhoon destroying purpose-built sets, and Sheen's heart attack, have created an enduring cinematic legend. *Apocalypse Now*, alongside Michael Cimino's financially disastrous 1980 follow-up to *The Deer Hunter*, the bloated masterpiece, *Heaven's Gate*, helped to draw to a close the romance between the studios and the New Hollywood directors – the middle-class, politicized and highly cine-literate director *auteurs* – and ushered in a new system of high-return, studio-policed blockbusters.

The mythic status of *Apocalypse Now* is enhanced not just by its radical approach to its source material, but also the way that it is married to, and actively reinterprets, a confluence of precursor texts. These include Werner Herzog's psychotic, river-based exploration of insanity, *Aguirre, the Wrath of God* (1972) as well as Michael Herr's *Dispatches* (1977), a collection of testimonies from various Vietnam veterans that so impressed Coppola that he was eventually hired to write the voice-over for Willard's "Marlow" character. Herr's accounts of the war, although not used directly in the film, were influential on Coppola whose "Bosch-like vision of the war was unquestionably colored by the surreal intensity . . . of Herr's descriptions of jungle combat" (Adair, 1981: 145).

It can be argued that Coppola's film has to some extent overtaken the cultural presence of the source text. Yet despite the fact that the film contains no direct mention of the novella (it was deliberately excluded from the credits, probably based on pressure from original screenwriter John Milius), officially negating its adaptive status, the film is indelibly linked to Conrad's source text in a culturally more profound way than many adaptations that foreground their adaptive status. This serves to illustrate the critical highlighting of the precursor text when discussing transformative adaptations, and those films which deliberately play with and interrogate the processes and reception of adaptation, as seen in films such as *Naked Lunch* (1991), *Orlando* (1992), *Adaptation* (2002), and *A Cock and Bull Story* (2005).

Originally titled *The Psychedelic Soldier*, John Milius wrote the first script for *Apocalypse Now* based on the experiences of his friends returning from the early days of the Vietnam War. Milius' intention was always to marry the experience of Vietnam with *Heart of Darkness*, but very quickly came to distance the project from being an overt "adaptation" of Conrad's text. However, in contrast to the typical *distancing* that occurs during the production of an adaptation, in this case it is possible to see that an adaptive reversal process occurs, as Coppola takes control of the script and attempts to reground the story back towards the source material during filming. In his introduction to the printed screenplay of the film (which is notably a transcript of the film, rather than an original film script) Coppola notes that:

> Instead of carrying the script day-to-day, I had a little green paperback of Conrad's *Heart of Darkness* in my pocket, filled with notes and markings. I just naturally started referring to it more than the script, and step by step, the film became more surreal and reminiscent of the great Conrad novella (2000: vii).

The influence of the source text on *Apocalypse Now*, rather than becoming progressively *decayed*, actually becomes *amplified* as Coppola reverses the production back towards Conrad. As Coppola attempts to wrest the grip of Milius' script from its transformative state, and to re-appropriate the project with is source material, the relevance of Conrad's story and the debates surrounding it also become foregrounded during interpretation.

The most significant literary motif of Conrad's novella is the now much discussed embedded narrative. Conrad immediately enables this by entering us into a world of waiting and listening, a comfortable arena for storytelling in which we are given both a sense of stillness, and a profound sense of impending doom. Marlow's boat the *Nellie* is "swung to her anchor . . . and was at rest," as the characters are forced to "wait for the turn of the tide" (Conrad, 1994: 5). London, and Gravesend in particular where the *Nellie* is anchored, whilst presented as "the biggest, and the greatest, town on earth," is also canopied by dark clouds which give the location a "brooding motionless" and "mournful gloom" (5). Conrad avoids presenting the location as a cultured and brightly lit city *not* to endow the embedded narrative with a contrast to the main action of the story, but rather to function as a foreshadowing, as the dark of London becomes a theater for the telling of Conrad's tale. The sentence, "We four affectionately watched his back as he stood in the bows looking to seaward" (5), evokes both this expectancy and the feeling of nostalgic reflection. He continues announcing that "his work was not out there in the luminous estuary, but behind him, within the brooding gloom" (5). For Marlow, London "has been one of the dark places of the earth" (7). Coppola engenders the same sense of impending menace, albeit through the Willard/Marlow character, as he quietly introspects in his Saigon Hotel:

Willard (V.O.)
. . . I'm here a week now. Waiting for a mission. Getting softer. Every minute I stay in this room, I get weaker. And every minute Charlie squats in the bush . . . he gets stronger. Each time I looked around . . . the walls moved in a little tighter (Milius and Coppola, 2000: 2).

However, the omnipotent narrator of Conrad's novella is of course not Marlow, but rather an anonymous first-person narrator. The effect of this is to create an inherently questionable world for the story, enveloped in an embedded environment, with its detached narrator conveying information to a heavily compromised reader. As the narrator self-referentially points out, "The yarns of seamen have a direct simplicity, the whole meaning of which lies within the shell of a cracked nut," a metaphor extended by the narrator to include Marlow himself for whom "the meaning of an episode was not inside like a kernel but outside, enveloping the tale" (Conrad, 1994: 8). Coppola takes the step of confronting the distancing of Marlow by Conrad and instead places him center-stage, complete with a first-person voiceover, engaging us directly as viewers and conspirators. This is in marked contrast to Conrad himself, who "took greater pains than did most users of the oblique narrative convention to preserve the possibility of critical distance between the reader and the fictional narrator" (Watts, 1996: 55). Coppola goes to equal lengths to put us into the head of Willard, viewing him at his weakest, drunk and dejected in a hotel room, musing nihilistically on his ex-wife. The action of *Apocalypse Now* follows the thoughts of Willard upstream, the voiceover giving us an account of

Kurtz the character, building tension towards the inevitable climax. However, an understanding of why Martin Sheen was given the role of Marlow (after the firing of Harvey Keitel) illuminates Coppola's desire to break down this narrative distancing. Coppola felt that Keitel was too animated and emotive in his use of method acting as he bore the emotional turmoil of Willard across his expressive face. Coppola needed someone more like Sheen – a detached observer, closed off to us, and mysteriously enigmatic. As Gilbert Adair notes, "Willard, basically, is a pair of eyes. In fact, Martin Sheen's eyes, on whose dilated pupils the whole eerie slipstream of Vietnam seems to drift past, form the movie's most powerful visual motif" (Adair, 1981: 149).

Coppola's specific use of Sheen as Willard is an attempt to conform to the first-person narrative demands of cinema, whilst also creating what amounts to a "closed-book" protagonist, cut off from us, emotionally distanced, and unpredictable. However, in the final scenes of the film, at Kurtz's camp, we have a strong sense of the kind of "doubleness" that Conrad wished to convey in his story. The confusion over idolatry is inherent in the text, the figure of Marlow quickly evoked as a figure of great standing and respect as he is seen as someone who "resembled a pilot, which to a seaman is trustworthiness personified," whilst later he is seen as having "a straight back, an ascetic aspect, and, with his arms dropped, the palms of hands outwards, resembled an idol" (Conrad, 1994: 5–6). Later still, the narrator sees Marlow "with his legs folded before him" in the "pose of a Buddha preaching" (10). There is no such idolizing of Willard in Copolla's adaptation – in fact the characters, specifically the Chief, find his presence irritating and his secrecy suspicious. The difference between Willard and Marlow is one of placement. Willard's background involves war, whilst Marlow's is seafaring and trade. When the narrator describes Marlow as "a seaman, but . . . a wanderer, too, but while most seamen lead, if one may so express it, a sedentary life. Their minds are of the stay-at-home order, and their home is always with them – the ship; and so is their country – the sea" (8). For Willard the ship is a foreign country, the sea is war. He is drawn to war with a sense of revulsion but complete abandonment, stating that "when I was here, I wanted to be there. When I was there . . . all I could think of was getting back into the jungle" (Milius and Coppola, 2000: 2). The narrator of *Heart of Darkness* notes that, "One ship is very much like another, and the sea is always the same," and "for there is nothing mysterious to a seaman unless it be the sea itself, which is the mistress of his existence and as inscrutable as Destiny" (Conrad, 1994: 8). The war for Willard is destiny, but it appears he is also the mistress of the war, exploited and used and formed into an assassin by the self-interests of the U.S. military.

The cold, impenetrableness of Sheen's Willard certainly brings to mind the storytelling of Marlow to the men on the *Nellie*. He begins by telling them that "I don't want to bother you much with what happened to me personally," trying to steer the conversation towards what he witnesses, and like the audience of *Apocalypse Now* who wish to see behind the observing eyes of Willard, the narrator points out that

Marlow was "showing in his remark the weakness of many tellers of tales who seem so often unaware of what their audience would best like to hear" (10–11).

The Precursor "Phantom Adaptation" – Orson Welles' *Heart of Darkness*

It is an indication of the influence of the New Hollywood directors that Coppola was ever considered for financing to make such an epic and costly film as *Apocalypse Now*, particularly in light of Orson Welles' failed attempt to adapt Conrad's novella in 1939. The status of *Heart of Darkness* as a problematic and intrinsically resistant text to adaptation can be traced back to this unsuccessful attempt to film Conrad's novella; the RKO studios turning their back on a prohibitively expensive production. Whilst examining Welles' battle to bring the book to the big screen affords us the possibility to understand the problematic nature of Conrad's text for an adaptor, it also enables us to examine more clearly the effect this project had on Coppola's subsequent adaptation.

Both Coppola and screenwriter John Milius were fully aware of Welles' screenplay and the problems he faced adapting the book. Rather than scaring Coppola away from the project, this stalled production instead "challenged Coppola to risk everything in an act of hubris designed to wrest from Conrad's text its legendary aura of nonadaptability" (Elsaesser and Wedel, 1997: 151). The failure of both Welles' adaptation, and his subsequent adaptation, the "Mexican Melodrama" *The Smiler with the Knife*, saw him eventually go on to make *Citizen Kane* (1941) as his debut feature, a film marked with many of the techniques he had wished to pursue in his Conrad adaptation. As well as utilizing an array of production and photography techniques, *Citizen Kane* also examined the fall of a powerful and influential man who has embarked on a corrupting, self-destructive path and who, as actor Simon Callow mentions, "dies with a mysterious phrase on his lips" (quoted in French, 1998: 117).

Welles arrived in Hollywood in 1939 on the crest of publicity generated by his successful and influential radio plays for RKO, and "after refusing several prior offers" (Higham, 1970: 9) he pushed forward with a grand and expensive adaptation of *Heart of Darkness*. The production was initially helped by the work he had done on his previous radio adaptation of *Heart of Darkness* in 1938; a brooding, dramatic piece dominated by Welles' mid-Atlantic baritone monologue. For the film adaptation, it was Welles' intention to radically transform the novella, relocating the time and place of Conrad's story to South America with "Kurtz as a modern day fascist, explicitly likened to Hitler" (French, 1998: 117). Welles, like the later Coppola, was concerned with the imperialist politics of Conrad's book, and by contemporizing the narrative to highlight the "rise of fascist dictatorships" (Naremore, 1978: 29) he hoped to make a film more relevant and directly political than a straight, faithful adaptation. To that end, Welles wished the film to be "both an attack on European imperialism and on Rousseau's view of humanity" (29) in order to expose an increasingly dangerous political situation both for Europe and the USA.

Welles' highly unusual and idiosyncratic script immediately caused problems for the production. RKO Pictures estimated that the film would "cost an immense $1,057,761" whilst once again mirroring Coppola's renegade filmmaking techniques, the "preliminary report . . . received from his Hollywood office suggested that the budget for *Heart of Darkness* was so high because Orson simply was not conforming to usual studio working procedures" (Leaming, 1985: 178). Before the project was eventually rejected by RKO, Welles even shot test footage, makeup pictures, and created a number of jungle miniatures. Welles' response to the shelving of his *Heart of Darkness* adaptation was to offer "to do *The Smiler with the Knife* for free if RKO would let him proceed with the expensive Conrad film" (Naremore, 1978: 28). The "Mexican Melodrama" was clearly a less ambitious and experimental project for Welles, but also satisfied his preoccupation with themes contained in Conrad's story. The script was based around themes of "demagoguery and manipulation" forming a narrative in which we see "a perilous journey into the heart of a jungle . . . a doppelganger theme" and "a liberal protagonist . . . set off against a fascist lookalike" (28), echoing Welles to play both Marlow and Kurtz in his original adaptation. Despite the fact that *The Smiler with the Knife* "could be described as an attempt at reinterpreting Conrad in a more popular, less experimental form" (28), Welles was once again rebutted by RKO, the project rejected, forcing the director to work on *Citizen Kane* as his debut feature film.

Accentuating the "doubleness" of Conrad's story, Welles nominated himself to play the parts of both Marlow and Kurtz, foregrounding the doppelganger relationship that the characters share by the end of the novella. But the screenplay for Welles' re-imagined *Heart of Darkness* is more notable for the way the director chooses to deal with the narratological issues of the embedded narrative. Rather than using the framing technique of a first-person narrator telling his "story" to a group of people, the cinematic flashback employed to form the bulk of the story,[1] Welles instead chooses to employ an altogether more unusual and metatextual technique to distance his audience from the authenticity of the film. Welles' adaptation was set to use a technique untested in cinema, in which the action of the film was to be seen from the first-person narrative viewpoint of Marlow. This "point of view" perspective was to be achieved using "hand-held Eyemo cameras" so that they could present a "first-person technique, with smoke coming from a pipe held in front of the lens and Welles glimpsed in mirrors" (Higham, 1970: 9). The narrative problems of attempting such a technique from an audience perspective seemed to be far away from Welles' mind, although André Bazin notes that whilst it "took an Orson Welles to think of it" ultimately it was "Robert Montgomery who achieved it some years later in *The Lady in the Lake*, in the most unconvincing manner possible" (Bazin, 1978: 52). As James Naremore notes in *The Magic World of Orson Welles* (1978):[2]

Welles's idea was to substitute the eye of the camera for the "I" of Conrad's narrator; the camera would become Marlow, whose voice, that of Welles himself, would be heard onscreen. He even wrote a brief prologue to the film, hoping to "instruct and acquaint the audience as amusingly as possible with the technique" (29–30).

The screenplay prologue that Naremore mentions is a highly self-referential and bizarre interrogation of the audience's expectations of the first-person narrator; with Welles foregrounded as director, adaptor, storyteller, and dual protagonist:

FADE OUT
DARK SCREEN
WELLES'S VOICE: Ladies and Gentlemen, this is Orson Welles. Don't worry. There's just nothing to look at for a while. You can close your eyes if you want to, but – please open them when I tell you to. . . . First of all, I am going to divide this audience into two parts – you and everybody else in the theatre. Now then, open your eyes.
IRIS INTO
INTERIOR BIRD CAGE-
1. *Shooting from inside the bird cage, as it would appear to a bird inside the cage, looking out. The cage fills the entire screen. Beyond the bars can be seen the chin and mouth of Welles, tremendously magnified.*
WELLES'S VOICE: The big hole in the middle there is my mouth. You play the part of the canary. I'm asking you to sing and you refuse. That's the plot. I offer you an olive.
A couple of Gargantuan fingers appear from below cage and thrust an enormous olive towards CAMERA, through bars of cage.
WELLES'S VOICE (cont'd): You don't want an olive. This enrages me.
Welles's chin moves down and his nose and eyes are revealed. He is scowling fiercely.
WELLES'S VOICE (cont'd): Here is a bird's-eye view of me being enraged. I threaten you with a gun.
Now the muzzle of a pistol is stuck between the bars of the cage. It looks like a Big Bertha.
WELLES'S VOICE (cont'd): That's the way a gun looks to a canary. I give you to the count of three to sing (30).

Welles appears to be at pains to make the audience aware of the mechanics of his fiction, and his position as adaptor–auteur. He attempts to negotiate the notion of the embedded narrative, in which we experience an author (Conrad) presenting a fiction in the form of a story told to us by an anonymous first-person narrator, who himself is recounting a story told by Marlow. As Naremore points out, "nothing could have announced more clearly the director's potential authority over the audience" before concluding that "the whole prologue seems designed to establish the illusion of Welles's omnipotence" (30). Whilst we are pushed away as readers from any universal notion of a singular "truth" in Conrad's story, the fictions of *Heart of Darkness* are, as stated above, based on the author's personal experiences in the Congo. However, for Welles, no such semi-autobiographical experience exists with which to comfortably situate himself within his own text. This narrative distancing, and ambiguizing, is a problem for cinema, with its omnipotent camera eye, helping us experience truth. Narrative truth breaks down in cinema only when a character is shown to be insane, helping us question their credibility; or if the "truthfulness" is foregrounded with the use of multi-perspective flashbacks, as famously used in Akira Kurosawa's *Rashômon* (1950). The issue of narrative distancing is solved in a very extreme way by Welles, the author–auteur both places himself into the foreground, and once again addresses the audience directly:

> **WELLES (cont'd):** (looking straight into lens) Now, if you're doing this right, this is what you ought to look like to me.
> DISSOLVE
> INTERIOR MOTION PICTURE THEATRE (painting)
> 5. SHOT *of inside of theatre as it would appear from the stage* or rather from the center of the moving picture screen! *Beginning on the projection booth,* CAMERA PANS DOWN *taking in the orchestra floor of the theatre, dimly lit by the reflected light from the screen.* The audience is entirely made up of motion picture cameras. When this has registered.
> **WELLES (cont'd):** I hope you get the idea.
> FADE OUT
> FADE IN
> BLACK SCREEN
> 6. *A human eye appears on the left side of the screen. Then an "equal" sign appears next to it. The capital "I". Finally the eye winks and we* DISSOLVE (31).

The prologue continues, with the audience witnessing a number of disturbing set-pieces (including a trial and a man sent to the electric chair), through the eyes of the omnipotent Marlow character. For Welles this elaborate introduction to his experimental adaptation of *Heart of Darkness* was both in contrast to Hollywood norms, and offered a chance for him to critique the audience's willing susceptibility to the cinema. And by doing so, to highlight the inherent nature of man's capacity to be duped and manipulated, whether by imperialism, fascism, or the evocative stories of film. The prologue "cut against the grain of the impersonal factory style and in doing so it provoked a commentary upon the illusory, potentially authoritarian nature of the medium" (31–2).

Coppola's use of Willard's voiceover in *Apocalypse Now*, and the sense of traveling upstream with the man himself, are certainly designed to convey a growing feeling that the character is slowly becoming like Kurtz. But we experience that dialogue from a detached, spectator's point of view; the setting of the Vietnam War designed to make us look inwards, and question our own sense of humanity, and good versus evil. Conrad's desire to push his audience to reflexively appoint the same kind of self-interrogation is achieved through the use of this omnipotent author who witnesses the story of Marlow. For Welles the connecting of the audience as complicit participants in the narrative they are watching becomes more than just a desire – but the very *point* of his adaptation. Welles' screenplay "underlined the theme of manipulation and demagogic deception" whilst also highlighting "the sense of pervasive evil, the subtle link between the audience and Kurtz which Conrad himself had implied" (32). Naremore cites Jonathan Rosenbaum, who observes that the questions raised by the introduction "whereby I = eye = camera = screen = spectator" are progressed to the point where "spectator = Marlow = Kurtz = Welles = director" (32).

It would be incorrect to assume that the postmodern approach that Welles adopted in his adaptation of *Heart of Darkness* sits in direct contrast to the more earnest, less critical (although no less radical) treatment of the material by Coppola some three and a half decades later. Welles' co-opting of features of the aborted script for his subsequent debut feature also becomes a controlling presence on Coppola's project. As Elsaesser and Wedel note, *Citizen Kane* "is haunted by the text it had displaced, and the ghost of Welles's *Heart of Darkness* would also haunt Coppola and his collaborators" (1997: 151). The cultural *presence* of Welles' project on Coppola, and indeed all subsequent adaptations of Conrad's text, can be explained in terms of what Simone Murray calls "phantom adaptations" – those projects which are commenced but never come to fully formed fruition. Whilst Murray is describing the events surrounding the ill-fated, aborted production of the Australian film project *Eucalyptus* in 2005, the principal arguments she posits are relevant for all stalled adaptations, regardless of the amount of progress made in their pre-production.[3]

For Murray, the move away from a less slavish attitude to what constitutes an "adaptation" ultimately "frustrates adaptation studies' habitual recourse to comparative textual analysis" and can therefore provoke "the discipline to engage with alternate methodologies for understanding how adaptation functions or . . . fails to function" (2008: 6). The presence of a screenplay, production photos, and a variety of other paratexts related to Welles' *Heart of Darkness*, does little to render the project as a formal adaptation for many critics. The nebulous and ethereal nature of unproduced adaptations uncovers a tendency in the field for "near-exclusive focus upon 'existing' book and screen texts," highlighting the radicalism of looking at phantom adaptations which "fundamentally disrupts such deeply ingrained critical impulses" (16). Welles' idiosyncratic screenplay was written, test shots were filmed, but most importantly, the nature of the director's adaptation exists in the conscious memory of those approaching future adaptations. Welles' version of *Heart of Darkness* exists as a study-able adaptation, regardless of whether there is a completed, fully produced movie with a theatrical release. The compare–contrast nature of adaptation studies that Murray is critiquing in her essay, seems to rely on the monolithic product – a fully formed artistic object with which to apply theory, and to use as a comparative tool. As with Welles' aborted attempt to film Miguel de Cervantes' infamously "unfilmable" *Don Quixote* in 1958, a plethora of archive and anecdotal material exists with which to study the director's *Heart of Darkness* project as a formal adaptation.

An important issue for adaptation studies, when encountering a transformative text such as Coppola's *Apocalypse Now*, is to consider any controlling element that could have influenced decision making and artistic/creative whim. Welles' *Heart of Darkness* clearly had a fundamental effect on Coppola in ways that are both obvious and unquantifiable. The figure of Coppola, energized and carrying considerable influence after the critical and financial successes of *Godfather* and *Godfather II*, is mirrored in the earlier move by the much feted Welles to move from radio to film after the successes of his plays. Both embark on a project of egomaniacal folly to adapt Conrad's *Heart of Darkness* in an unconventional way, transforming the story away from a classic cinematic interpretation. They also contemporize, and in doing so *politicize*, the narrative in order to make it relevant for their respective contemporary audiences. The influence of financial/studio pressure that completely stalls Welles' adaptation, ultimately led to both a mental and emotional collapse for Coppola, as his project is green-lit thanks to a combination of his influence and the use of his own money to finance the film. Both men grapple with their own Kurtzian sense of omnipotence and desire for conquest in the goal of adapting Conrad's book.

In the pursuit of filming this tale of obsession and "horror," both men faced the problem of artistic control over their projects, and the specter of compromise induced by studio pressure. In many ways, it could be argued that it is actually the *deferred* projects that come to represent the "true" adaptation. For Welles, *Citizen Kane* becomes a conduit for his desire to adapt *Heart of Darkness* – the film infused with Conradian tropes of multiple narrative viewpoints, the quest for power, self-delusion, and the folly of man. For Coppola, it is another text entirely that can be seen as an equally relevant, and perhaps more profound, adaptation of Conrad's dark novella.

Paratext as Adaptation – Coppola's Apocalypse

The French literary critic, Gérard Genette, has stated that texts are not closed artifacts, but rather are open to influence from other sources including their own paratexts. Genette uses the term "paratext" to describe subsidiary and secondary material such as prefaces, postscripts, footnotes, epigraphs, illustrations, and commentaries, which illuminate and inform the principal text. Genette states that "more than a boundary or a sealed border, the paratext is, rather, a threshold" (1997: 1). The influence of the paratext for Genette is extra-textual, becoming a discourse in its own right. For him the paratext is "a zone between text and off-text, a zone not only of transition but also of transaction . . . an influence on the public, an influence that . . . is at the service of a better reception for the text" (1). Taking this further, Philippe Lejeune, talking specifically about literature, sees the paratext as "a fringe of the printed text which in reality controls one's whole reading of the text" (quoted in Genette, 1997: 1).

For film, the application of the paratext and multiple texts are virtually limitless – with updated versions, director's cuts, documentaries, director's commentaries on DVDs, and archived and multiple versions of the intermedial screenplay with which to expand our reception of the official film. The 1991 release of *Hearts of Darkness: A Filmmaker's Apocalypse*, a documentary that details the torturous process of filming *Apocalypse Now*, was photographed, written, and narrated by Coppola's soon to be estranged wife Eleanor Coppola. Using behind-the-scenes footage, the documentary chronicles the appalling production difficulties faced on the set of the film in graphic detail, and stands as an essential counterpart to *Apocalypse Now*, informing and shaping our reception of its fiction through the documentary's nonfictions. The film debunks the supercilious idea that film is aesthetically inferior to literature because it is easier to produce – an attitude that Stam describes as the "myth of facility" (Stam, 2005: 7). Filmmaking in this documentary is shown as being a physical and mental nightmare, in which all concerned are routinely subjected to their own horror, in their quest to bring Conrad's story to the screen. It becomes clear that it is not fidelity to the text that is causing Coppola so many problems, but rather a strong sense of fidelity to his own personal vision and creative control. In doing so, it can be argued that Coppola's disregard for his and others' personal safety, in pursuit of his artistic goal, ultimately causes him to lose a grip on reality and his sanity. If the production of a film can mirror the narrative of the fictional story being made, then *Hearts of Darkness: A Filmmaker's Apocalypse* stands as the apex of this mutuality. In doing so, it can also be seen as an adaptation of Conrad's novella in its own right, playing out much of the concepts deemed to be at the core of his story.

The documentary opens with a press conference at the 1979 Cannes film festival, in which Coppola addresses a group of journalists via a French translator. In broken sentences he states:

> My film is not a movie. My film is not *about* Vietnam. It *is* Vietnam. It's what it was really like. It was crazy. And the way we made it was very much like the Americans were in Vietnam. We were in the jungle. There were too many of us. We had access . . . to too much money, too much equipment. And little by little we went insane.

The film documents in lurid detail the problems and calamities that effect the production of the film, with sound recordings made by Eleanor Coppola of her husband without his knowledge, in which he anxiously critiques his own work, including the admission that the film "is a $20 million disaster, why won't anyone believe me? I'm thinking of shooting myself." Over the course of the documentary, both Francis and Eleanor Coppola reference the nature of the filmmaking experience as a mirror for the story they are attempting to adapt. After reflecting on the securing of access to military helicopters from the Philippine government, Coppola admits a deliberate attempt to overlap their experiences of the film and the original story:

> The real phenomenon of being in that situation and being in the middle of that jungle and dealing with all the unfriendly elements . . . was part of what the movie was about. That was the first directorial decision, to put us all in a circumstance that reflected what the movie was about.

Eleanor's experience of watching the filmmaking through her own lens becomes a slow-burning realization that, like Marlow's narrator observer on the *Nellie*, she was being lured into an altered state. She observes this change in her husband, and herself:

> He can't go back down the river because the journey has changed him. I was watching from the point of view of the observer, not realising I was on the journey too. Now I can't go back to the way it was – neither can Francis. Neither can Willard.

Eleanor's written diary, another significant paratext, describes the lavish circumstances that they enjoyed whilst filming in Manila. It describes the decadence, the colonial need to replicate the pleasures of home, like the French plantation owners in the expanded *Redux* version of the film, producing a different modern-day Kurtz in the form of Coppola. As Coppola decamps to the jungles of the Philippines, with his Zoetrope renegade unit acting outside of Hollywood boundaries, the tales of high decadence become a parallel narrative that Coppola is expressly committed to critiquing. The stories of 250 Ifuago Indians rounded up to play the part of the Montagnard Indians in Kurtz's compound, of which some are buried up to their necks all day in the stifling heat to replicate severed heads, conflate to create the image of a Faustian madman hell-bent on seeing his personal vision realized. During filming in 1977, Eleanor, now back in the USA looking after their three children, sends a public telegram to Coppola in the Philippines:

> I would tell him what no one else was willing to say that he is setting up his own Vietnam with his supply lines of wine and steaks and air conditioners. Creating the very situation he went there to expose. That with his staff of hundreds of people carrying out his every request, he was turning into Kurtz – going too far (Coppola, 1991: 159).

Transformative adaptations of a novel can actually occur for a number of reasons. For Coppola, these changes were the result of chance, dealing with problems, choosing the least unpleasant route, and adapting to difficulties. These are the "behind the camera," extra-diegetic issues that we are seldom privy to. Eleanor points out that typhoons, illness, and Brando's size all force creative improvisations that produce some of the film's most iconic images. Brando does not play the part as first intended by Milius, instead he becomes a mythical figure – larger than life, a kind of Buddha, or a fallen hero, such as Welles' washed-up Hank Quinlan in *Touch of Evil*, someone who can no longer sustain moral subjectivity in the face of rampant corruption. In this parallel adaptation of Conrad's novella, Coppola takes center-stage in his own adaptation of *Heart of Darkness*, as filmed by his wife. As Elsaesser and Wedel state "To "become Kurtz," and thus to put oneself in the center of one's own fiction, is to realize a primary fantasy . . . giving the director-as-author his own double and alter ego, whether as superstar or doomed Lucifer" (1997: 151).

Moving beyond Barthesian notions of the "death of the author," through Brando we see the possibility for the death of the literary source and the adaptation of the cultural presence and embedded tropes of a text, rather than the words themselves. In one particularly tense moment in the documentary, as costs are spiraling, Brando admits to an exasperated Coppola, that he has not actually read *Heart of Darkness* or any drafts of the intermedial screenplay. Brando is adapting the Kurtz character through cultural agencies that exclude the text, and admits that he sees Kurtz as Orson Welles' Kane, producing a complicated, nonlinear set of intertextually pollinated connections. Whilst it is obvious that Brando's failure to read Conrad's novella is more likely a grand act of egocentric laziness, rather than any poststructuralist mission on his part to reimagine a cultural notion of Kurtz, it is clear that Brando sets out to adapt the character on his own terms, separate from the source material.

Kurtz is radically adapted by Brando, through the intertextual references to *Heart of Darkness* in T. S. Eliot, and Welles' revisioning of Kurtz in *Citizen Kane*, rather than the monolithic, canonical, precursor novella itself.

Conclusion

The scope of this chapter does not allow for an expansion on the many adaptations, spoofs, borrowings, pastiches, and conscious and unconscious intertextual readings of *Heart of Darkness*. But these texts are multifarious and involve the adaptation of Conrad's novella, as well as adaptations of Coppola's subsequent film. Manuel Aragon's *Heart of the Forest* (1979), Jonathan Lawton's 1988 reverse-gender spoof *Cannibal Women in the Avocado Jungle of Death* (1988), and the Australian feature film *Apocalypse Oz* (2006), described as "a cine-clash film hybridizing the screenplays of *Apocalypse Now* and *The Wizard of Oz*," are just some of the texts drawing upon Conrad's legacy.

The problems of adapting Conrad are clear – the ironic distancing of Conrad's narrative techniques, the many financial considerations of filming Conrad that, for instance, prevented Welles' film going into production, and which eventually bedeviled Coppola's vision for the novella. Whilst Conrad famously wanted us, as readers, to "see," adaptors of his texts have not found this mission quite so simple.

The adaptation of canonical texts in which films of high cultural status are produced problematizes future adaptations of that source text and, arguably, all texts that share thematic links. However, as we move forward into the twenty-first century, it is hoped that the film industry will become more confident in re-adapting these canonical texts, regardless of the status of a precursory high-status adaptation, with its culturally embedded tropes. As the film industry continues to call upon literature as adaptable source material for cinema, it is inevitable that multiple adaptations of canonical texts will emerge from literary sources that are not currently bestowed with multiple adaptation associations. It is within these dialogues, and adapted universes of a text, that we will better understand the relationship of literature and film, and their complex intertextual relationships with culture and society as a whole.

NOTES

1   The embedded narrative is omitted from the adaptations of many texts that use a framing device (*The Turn of the Screw*, *Dracula*, *Wuthering Heights* etc.), however, the cinematic use of the introductory storyteller leading the film into a flashback is employed by Nicholas Roeg in his 1994 adaptation of Conrad's novella (see later in this chapter).

2   I am indebted to Naremore's text due to his inclusion of excerpts from Welles' *Heart of Darkness* screenplay, of which I have drawn upon directly for this chapter.

3   However, it should be noted that Murray confines her term, excluding those projects that are "speculated about or mooted within the industry," instead focusing on those that have "progressed as close to production as possible without any actual footage having been shot and archived" (6).

REFERENCES

Adair, G. *Hollywood's Vietnam: From the Green Berets to Apocalypse Now*. New York: Proteus, 1981.

Hearts of Darkness: A Filmmakers Apocalypse. Dir. F. Bahr, G. Hickenlooper, and E. Coppola. USA: Paramount, 1991.

Bazin, A. *Orson Welles: A Critical View*. Trans. J. Rosenbau. London: Elm Tree Books, 1978.

Cartmell, D. and I. Whelehan. "Introduction – Literature on Screen: A Synoptic View." In *The Cambridge Companion to Literature on Screen*. Eds. D. Cartmell and I. Whelehan. Cambridge: Cambridge University Press, 2007, 1–12.

Conrad, J. "Preface." *The Nigger of the Narcissus*. London: Dent, 1923, vii–xii.

Conrad, J. *Heart of Darkness*. London: Penguin, 1994.

Coppola, E. *Notes on the Making of Apocalypse Now*. London: Faber & Faber, 1991.

Coppola, F. F. "Introduction." In *Apocalypse Now Redux: An Original Screenplay*. J. Milius and F. F. Coppola. New York: Hyperion, 2000, v–viii.

Derrida, J. "Living on Border Lines." In *Deconstruction and Criticism*. Eds. H. Bloom et al. New York: Continuum, 1995, 75–176.

Elsaesser, T. and M. Wedel. "The Hollow Heart of Hollywood: *Apocalypse Now* and the New Sound Space." In *Conrad on Film*. Ed. G. M. Moore. Cambridge: Cambridge University Press, 1997, 151–75.

French, K. *Karl French on* Apocalypse Now. London: Bloomsbury, 1998.

Genette, G. *Paratexts: Thresholds of Interpretation*. Cambridge: Cambridge University Press, 1997.

Higham, C. *The Films of Orson Welles*. Berkeley: University of California Press, 1970.

Leaming, B. *Orson Welles – A Biography*. London: Weidenfield and Nicolson, 1985.

Milius, J. and F. F. Coppola. *Apocalypse Now Redux: An Original Screenplay*. New York: Hyperion, 2000.

Moore, G. M. "Conrad's Influence." In *The Cambridge Companion to Joseph Conrad*. Ed. J. H. Stape. Cambridge: Cambridge University Press, 1996, 223–40.

Moore, G. M. "In Praise of Infidelity: An Introduction." In *Conrad on Film*. Ed. G. M. Moore.

Cambridge: Cambridge University Press, 1997, 1–15.

Murray, S. "Phantom Adaptations: *Eucalyptus*, the Adaptation Industry and the Film That Never was." *Adaptation*, 1:1, 2008, 5–23.

Naremore, J. *The Magic World of Orson Welles*. New York: Oxford University Press, 1978.

Stam, R. "Introduction: The Theory and Practice of Adaptation." In *Literature and Film: A Guide to the Theory and Practice of Film Adaptation*. Eds. Robert Stam and Alessandra Raengo. Oxford: Blackwell, 2005, 1–52.

Watts, C. "Heart of Darkness." In *The Cambridge Companion to Joseph Conrad*. Ed. J. H. Stape. Cambridge: Cambridge University Press, 1996, 45–62.

22

Authorship, Commerce, and *Harry Potter*

James Russell

In one of the promotional documentaries featured on the DVD release of the third Harry Potter movie, *Harry Potter and the Prisoner of Azkaban* (Alfonso Cuarón, 2004), the various creative participants came together for a remarkably harmonious and good-natured interview. Producer David Heyman began by reassuring viewers that J. K. Rowling's vision lay at the center of their efforts, saying "Our vision is born very much from the book." Screenwriter Steve Kloves added, "We tried to discover the best way to convey what Jo was expressing on the page – in movie terms." The newly appointed director, Alfonso Cuarón, perhaps unsurprisingly, agreed, and even Rowling herself suggested that the films were a relatively pure reflection of her own creative intentions. She concluded by reporting that, "I said to Steve Kloves many a time, 'I wish I had written that.' But that's what you want, isn't it? It's great when I'm looking around for all these little bits that are completely consistent with the world, but I didn't write them."[1] The overall aim of the feature was to situate Rowling at the heart of the Harry Potter phenomenon, as a source and authority without measure, and to position the filmmaking team as little more than facilitators, working humbly and carefully to transform Rowling's words into a movie that absolutely correlated with her vision.

At the same time, the film itself put the lie to many of these assertions. It was the first entry in the franchise to use distinctive stylistic techniques (digital color grading; darker, low key lighting; extended long shots which reconstruct the physical space of various areas in new ways; an increased focus on suspense and horror elements; as well as notable changes in art direction and cinematography). It was also the first Potter film to remove substantial sequences from the novel, and include

A Companion to Literature, Film, and Adaptation, First Edition. Edited by Deborah Cartmell.
© 2012 Blackwell Publishing Ltd. Published 2012 by Blackwell Publishing Ltd.

new scenes in their stead. So, on the one hand, we have a film which looks starkly different from those which have preceded it, and which diverges in notable ways from the source text. On the other hand, we are reassured that this is what J. K. Rowling wanted. In fact, she occasionally even seemed to imply that the film realized her intentions more completely than her own novel, when she noted that the filmmakers had inadvertently included scenes which anticipate events in the later, then unpublished, books.

The Potter films, then, are clearly the product of a complicated creative relationship that poses interesting, and sometimes awkward, questions for scholars of adaptation. Who is responsible for a multibillion dollar, multimedia phenomenon like *Harry Potter*? Bearing in mind the sheer number of contributors, at an individual and institutional level, who has creative control? And how does this differ from legal or financial control of the franchise? How do financial pressures affect circumstances of authorship? And how do creative relationships differ across a range of texts?

In this chapter, I use the Potter films to explore the complex process of adaptation in contemporary Hollywood. It may have started out as a series of thrilling novels for children, but Harry Potter became the quintessential product of the modern American movie industry: an ultra high-budget, transmedia franchise. It is easy to identify the author of a novel. It is more difficult to single out one creative participant as the author of an entity as economically and culturally all-encompassing as Harry Potter. To best explore the relationships that have shaped the franchise, I will combine a focus on creative endeavor with a focus on the financial and corporate agenda which also play out very visibly in the films. The chapter is divided into thee sections. The first briefly outlines critical work on authorship from within the field of adaptation studies. The second focuses on the various participants in Potter, and outlines their roles. The third looks in detail at one Potter movie to reveal how differing creative agenda can play out in practice.

Adaptation, Authorship, and the Blockbuster

Adaptation scholarship is implicitly concerned with authorial relationships. The assumption made when studying novel-to-film adaptations is that one author passes on their work to another, and adaptation studies is an attempt to understand that process of transition from a textual, theoretical, or contextual perspective. To complicate matters, the disciplines of literary, film, and media scholarship have all understood authorship in different ways. Literary criticism has tended to view the author as a relatively unproblematic figure. Despite the much vaunted "Death of the Author" proposed by poststructuralism, or Michel Foucault's notion of the "author function," writers and their intentions remain central to the majority of critical and historical writing about novels.[2] In related fashion, scholars working within film studies invariably treat directors as "authors," in rough accordance with the so-called "auteur theory" popularized in the 1960s. Even though many within the field refute the auteur theory, the value of the director as a brand, and the status of the director as a central creative contributor, remains relatively unchallenged.[3] By contrast, media and communication studies has devoted more attention to the actions of cultural institutions and processes of reception, downplaying the status of creative participants, in favor of investigating the larger social and economic function of the media.

When these scholarly approaches meet, as they do in a liminal subject like adaptation studies, opportunities to revise and rethink the nature of creativity and authorship emerge. However, many writers tend to fall back on familiar assumptions. Consequently, in her excellent *A Theory of Adaptation*, Linda Hutcheon observes:

> Films are like operas in that there are many and varied artists involved in the complex process of their adaptation. Nevertheless it is evident from both studio press releases and critical response that the director is ultimately held responsible for the overall vision and therefore for the adaptation. Yet someone else usually writes the screenplay that begins the process . . . For this reason, in a film, the director and screenwriter share the primary task of adaption (2006: 85).

Broadening the margins of creative authority to include screenwriters is reasonable and well justified, although it is worth noting that being held responsible is not quite the same as being responsible. Nonetheless, identifying the director and the screenwriter alongside the original author as important creative contributors fits well within the bounds of literary and film scholarship. There are more authors here, but they still have creative authority.

In his book *Adaptation and its Discontents*, Thomas Leitch has done more to problematize our conceptions of authorship, by treating authorial identity as a commodity. In Leitch's model, what authors actually *do* is slippery and unclear, but the status of authors becomes fixed when it has some commercial value. He writes:

> Rising to the status of auteur depends on an alignment of several marketable factors: thematic consistency, association with a popular genre, an appetite for the co-ordination and control of outsized projects, sensitivity to the possibility of broad appeal in such disparate media as movies, television, books, magazines and T-shirts (2007: 256).

Scholars writing in the field of transmedia studies seem to reinforce the suggestion that the author is a constructed figure, who exists to convey a "paratextual veneer of artistry, aura and authority," in the words of Jonathan Gray (2010: 115). The key role of the author is to promote certain modes of engagement with the text, rather than to actually create it single-handedly – which is the preserve of much larger media entities.

These issues are difficult regardless of the text being adapted and the form of adaptation. They become tortuous when dealing with the exigencies of blockbuster film production, where globalized media companies provide vast sums of money (on the basis of complex copyright arrangements) to huge production teams, resulting in a range of interconnected products targeted at a global audience, which consumes them via a panoply of media. We cannot easily assign authorship to the texts that come out of this process. Instead, we might more fruitfully try to understand blockbuster adaptations on their own terms – as the product of sometimes divergent creative and commercial impulses. The *Harry Potter* films are particularly instructive in this regard.

Production, Distribution, and Ownership

Almost everyone with an interest in Harry Potter knows the story of its creation: J. K. Rowling was an unemployed single mother, who, in 1990, had the idea for Harry Potter while daydreaming on a train journey. She quickly mapped out a seven-book sequence, and began working on the first novel, *Harry Potter and the Philosopher's Stone* in cafes around Edinburgh. The novel took five years to complete, and she then sent it to numerous agents and publishers, all bar one of whom rejected it. The book was eventually picked up by Bloomsbury – then a relatively unknown player in the publishing business – and released in 1997. Within a year, it was a global publishing phenomenon. By 1999, when the fourth book was released, Rowling was a multimillionaire celebrity, and *Harry Potter* was a household name across the world (Nel, 2001: 17–24).

This story has become a kind of foundation myth for the Potter franchise, and it informs both the popular conception of what Harry Potter is, and the status of J. K. Rowling as an author. Potter's origins are closely tied to the story of J. K. Rowling. Both begin as tragic figures. At the start of the first novel, Harry Potter is trapped in a life of obscurity and neglect with the Dursleys, but when he enters the wizarding world, he learns that he is talented and important, his life has great value, and he finds love, meaning, and acceptance. Rowling's transition from a life of impoverished unemployment to global celebrity has arguably followed a similar trajectory. As the novels were being released, the widespread adoption of the internet was accelerating the possibilities for hype and promotion, and Rowling actively used the web to speak to her fans, and provide insights into the writing process.[4] Throughout the early 2000s, the Potter novels were very visibly presented to the public as something J. K. Rowling *was actively and currently doing*. Readers were participants in an ongoing creative relationship with Rowling, which was central to the promotion of the novels.[5] Rowling's authorial importance was particularly visible as the film adaptations took shape, and she has maintained an elevated creative status ever since.

The film adaptations of Rowling's work can, however, be traced back to one key figure – David Heyman, an Englishman who had worked as a producer at Fox and Warner Bros., before setting up his own company, Heyday Films, in London. Although ostensibly independent, Heyday Films had a "first look" deal with Warner Bros., which paid his staff and funded his London office in return for first refusal for the distribution rights of Heyman's projects. As a result, Warner Bros. agreed to provide the $12 million budget for Heyday's first film, *Ravenous* (Antonia Bird, 1999), a low-budget horror movie set on the American frontier in the 1840s. *Ravenous* underperformed at the box office, generating a scant $2 million on American release, but Heyman was already busy on his next, far more lucrative project, and Warner's confidence seemed to be paying off.

Heyman first encountered *Harry Potter and the Philosopher's Stone* several months after its British release in 1997.[6] At this stage, the book was gaining limited popular momentum, but it was not yet a publishing phenomenon. Heyman registered his interest with Warner Bros., and found support in the form of British executive Lionel Wigram. He was the first movie producer to approach J. K. Rowling, and after a complex process of negotiation, Heyday acquired the right to adapt the first four proposed Potter novels, with the option of extending the contract to include the remaining three. Most reports acknowledge that Rowling chose Heyman because he promised to remain faithful to the books, and Heyman later claimed that Rowling has been able to veto script ideas she did not like (Pendreigh, 2001). The contract was signed a week before the first book was released in the United States.

However, following the acquisition of the rights, Warner Bros. and Heyday considered a number of different potential approaches to the material. Before the awesome popularity of the books became clear, some executives at Warner Bros. apparently struggled to see the commercial potential of the project.[7] Consequently, the development team considered a production deal with recently formed Dream-Works SKG, and new president of production Alan Horn attempted to bring Steven Spielberg on board as director. However, Spielberg proposed a relatively radical approach to the adaptation, which Warner Bros. ultimately retreated from. In Horn's words:

> We offered it to him. But one of the notions of Dreamwork's and Steven's was, "Let's combine a couple of the books, let's make it animated," and that was because of the [visual effects and] Pixar had demonstrated that animated movies could be extremely successful. Because of the wizardry involved, they were very effects-laden. So I don't blame them. But I did not want to combine the movie and I wanted it to be live action (Eller, 2010).

Instead, scriptwriting duties were awarded to Steve Kloves, who promised to bring in a very faithful adaptation, and Christopher Columbus, of *Home Alone* (1990) fame, was brought on board as director, despite some initial misgivings on J. K. Rowling's part. Heyman then began assembling the wider resources required to actually make the film, including a massive team of creative and administrative personnel, huge production facilities in the UK, and, of course, the cast, including Harry himself, who would be played by the son of one of Heyman's friends, Daniel Radcliffe.

At this point a number of key figures emerged, all of whom would stay with the project throughout its life, and all of whom would make a significant creative contribution. Alan Horn's tenure as president at Warner Bros. coincides exactly with the release schedules of the Potter films, and his relatively sensitive approach to the material has come to inform all of Warner Bros. major franchises. Lionel Wigram has been the link between Warner Bros. and Heyday, acting as a producer on all the films. Most importantly, David Heyman has acted as supervising producer on every release, and Heyday Films has been entirely focused on the production of *Harry Potter* movies for over a decade. Steve Kloves has written seven out of the eight scripts for the movies, and his work has increasingly taken on a focus of its own, as the novels got longer and the need for significant trimming became apparent. Stuart Craig (and many members of his team) has acted as production designer on every film – a vital role, bearing in mind the centrality of art direction and design to the look, and promotional viability, of the films. Other contributors have changed more frequently. The Potter films have had four directors as well as six cinematographers and four composers.

We should be clear about the distinction of roles and responsibilities here. Warner Bros. is the distributor. It provides the funding for production in return for the rights to distribute and merchandise the films in all international theatrical and ancillary markets. For this, it charges a significant fee that is drawn from the film's revenues. In fact, that fee is so massive that even a film like *Harry Potter and the Order of the Phoenix* (David Yates, 2007), which generated almost $1 billion on global release, appeared, at least according to the official accounts, to have made a significant loss (Anders, 2011). As numerous commentators have shown, this kind of "creative accounting" helps to conceal actual profitability in such a way as to maximize the distributors' income.[8] Nonetheless, Warner Bros. is able to fund extreme high budget projects such as Potter because it operates in the global media distribution market, and because it carefully defends and exploits the copyright relating to the Potter films. While J. K. Rowling has defended the rights to her books with equal alacrity, Warner Bros. translates its deal with Rowling into a series of movies, but also theme parks, video-games, apparel, toys, and other licensed products. Rowling benefits financially from these deals, but Warner Bros. ensures that most licensed products are adapted from the films rather than the books. The Potter brand has been overseen at Warner Bros. by executive vice president for global brand management, Diane Nelson, described in the *Los Angeles Times* as "the midwife to the Potter success story" (Eller, 2010). Along with Horn and Wigram, Nelson has acted as a vital creative contributor at the highest commercial level because she has finessed and promulgated a popular sense of what the Potter franchise *is* through her branding efforts.

In the early years, the team at Warner Bros. seemed to keep relatively close control of the production process. In addition to the machinations regarding the first adaptation, the first two films include some obvious "Hollywood" elements that diminish in later films. Chris Columbus has been the only American director associated with the adaptations, and his films featured a relatively bright, accessible aesthetic: they are upbeat in tone, there is less emphasis on the weather and the seasons, and they are structured according to a familiar children's film template.[9] They owe as much to the films of Lucas and Spielberg, and, indeed, to *Home Alone*, as they do to Rowling's original novels. These first films look and feel like carefully managed big studio releases, because they contain relatively little in the way of artistry or experimentation. Throughout these early years, it seems reasonable to assume that Warner Bros. used its status as the major financial contributor to directly influence all manner of creative decisions, from who to hire, through to the actual look of the film. The executive team at Warner Bros., from Horn and Nelson down to Lionel Wigram, has enjoyed significant creative oversight of the Potter films, and the company's creative contribution cannot be underestimated.

However, the practical business of production has always been carried out in the UK, and over time greater and greater control appears to have been ceded to Heyman and his team. In effect, as the distributor has grown more confident in Heyday Films, it has stepped back from the most direct involvement with the production process. In 2008, David Heyman described Warner Bros. hands-off approach in the following terms:

> Warners has been really good to us. They've given us lots of money and lots of independence. It defies belief how much independence we have on these films. They give us the money, they read a draft of the script. I choose the director, we make the film, they come and visit. We show them a cut of the film, they say they like it, they give us some notes, we make the changes that we want to make. We test screen it once and show it to them, and then the movie is released (Douglas, 2008).

This was one of Warner Bros. wisest decisions, and it has subsequently been a central strategy for dealing with its other franchise properties (Thompson, 2007). Although some commentators tend to perceive the commercial intentions of major distributors as antithetical to creative invention, the reality is that even the biggest franchises require a certain level of quality control and creative invention to retain viewer interest. In effect, lasting success is best realized by smaller production teams with a clear creative vision for their work, and the studio knows this. As a result, directors and producers with a proven track record can attain considerable creative freedom, even for relatively experimental approaches, as long as they make money. By contrast, excessive interference from higher levels of management (which aims to emphasize marketable elements over individual creative vision) can alienate fans, and result in a poorer quality product. A good example is *Spiderman 3* (Sam Raimi, 2007), which is generally regarded as an artistic and critical failure, despite its high grosses, due to apparent interference from executives at Sony, who pushed the production team to include certain characters and design elements that were thought to be "sellable."[10] That film's poor critical reception, and the increasingly fraught negotiations between director and producers, ultimately resulted in the distributor "rebooting" the franchise.

By stepping back, Warner Bros. elevated David Heyman's creative status, just as it did with Peter Jackson on the *Lord of the Rings* films and Christopher Nolan with *Batman* and *Superman*. Although not a well-known figure, Heyman has arguably had the greatest control over the production of the Harry Potter films. Everyone working on the franchise, from casting agents and costume designers through to directors and stars, reports to Heyman, who has logistical and creative oversight through his control of the production budget. When the films won the Michael Balcon award for Outstanding Contribution to British Cinema at the 2011 BAFTAs, Heyman gave the acceptance speech. In a subsequent interview he told *Empire* magazine "I see myself as something of a guardian because I'm the longest-serving member of the Harry Potter film family" (O'Hara, 2011). Heyman also noted that he preferred the "melancholic moments, the nice, quiet moments," in the franchise. It is, presumably, no accident that these elements of the movies have become more prevalent as Heyman's creative control has increased. Although Heyman has claimed that he has allowed the various directors total creative latitude, his decisions regarding which directors to employ have shaped the overall texture of the movies, as has his close working relationship with Steve Kloves and others.

Several clear examples of Heyman's logistical control appeared during the production of the seventh film, *Harry Potter and the Deathly Hallows Part 1* (David Yates, 2010). Executives at Warner Bros. had wanted to adapt the film into 3D during post production, but relatively late in the process, Heyman seems to have insisted that the rushed conversion be aborted, despite publicity material promising that viewers could "Complete the Journey in 3D." Heyman also seems to have agonized over where in the narrative to break the final film into two parts.[11] In each case, these operational decisions had a profound affect on the style and structure of the films.

Another key participant is Steve Kloves, the screenwriter for all but one of the films. Kloves was brought on board at the start of the process, and has remained central to the film franchise ever since. He has worked closely with Rowling, Heyman, and the various directors, but Kloves' approach to the scripts has shifted from almost total faithfulness to a more nuanced, distinctive adaptation. In particular, Kloves has removed much of the back-story from the films, emphasizing Harry's journey over and above incidental events. In addition to cutting, this has meant introducing a number of new sequences. In the seventh film, Kloves provides a pre-credit sequence which differs dramatically from the books – when Hermione is shown erasing her parents' memories, and walking out of her middle-class suburban milieu into an uncertain future. The scene, which plays wordlessly, emphasizes the sacrifice made by Hermione, and introduces a level of melancholy lacking in the original novel. Later in the film, Kloves includes another new scene where Harry and Hermione, finding themselves exhausted and abandoned in the woods, briefly dance to a song on the radio. The sequence performs a basic narrative function, in that it represents a small moment of catharsis from the ongoing troubles faced by the two leads, but it also works as a culmination of the pair's chaste but intimate friendship. Kloves told the *Los Angeles Times* that the scene came to him out of the blue:

> When I wrote it down, I thought, *"Well this is strange,"* Kloves said. But it stuck with me and I thought there were good reasons for it. I was surprised when I took it to the group that it was *very* well-received. It was real stroke of courage, just in terms of pushing the envelope in the "Potter" universe (Boucher, 2010).

In these moments, Kloves has crafted his own version of the central characters, arguably giving them a more nuanced and mature relationship than that featured in the novels.

It stands to reason that the various directors associated with the franchise have also had a significant impact on the form and style of the adaptations. Chris Columbus, the American director of the first two films, was replaced by the Mexican art-house director Alfonso Cuarón for the third, who was succeeded by Mike Newell, and then directing duties passed to David Yates for the final three films. Each director has brought a distinctive look to their entries in the franchise. Columbus, as noted above, sought to produce movies which fitted into the established vernacular of the family blockbuster. Cuarón produced a visually darker, more experimental movie. Newell seems to have adopted the iconographic approach established by Cuarón and emphasized it in *Harry Potter and the Goblet of Fire* (2005). Yates has continued to reduce the color palette, but he has also adopted a slower, more contemplative pace, focused on character over plot, and has used various devices to emphasize realism over fantasy – using more handheld footage, tighter editing, and incidental display of CGI work.

For the most part, these directors have worked within a tightly managed system – they have overseen a large and established creative team, and worked under the control of a driven and directed producer. If anything, the firm control of the franchise at all other levels means that the creative input of the director is easiest to assess. Each has supervised the work of smaller teams, to produce a complete and artistically unified product. Where Heyman has retained logistical control, the team of directors has taken control of the films' stylistic and structural elements – from shot construction and pacing, through to performance styles and editing.

Although it developed into an artistic call to arms, the "auteur theory" postulated by the critics of *Cahiers du Cinéma* in the 1950s began by making a more basic claim. André Bazin and François Truffaut justified their assertions about the artistic primacy of directors by identifying a series of U.S. directors working in the tightly controlled environment of studio production in the 1930s and 1940s, who they felt had established distinctive visual methods and thematic concerns which marked them out as artists, despite the prosaic and formulaic nature of their movies (Crofts, 1998: 313). In effect, the close controls of studio production allowed the artistry of the director to shine through. Something similar seems to occur in the case of the Harry Potter films, where the influence of the director is all the more visible for the tight control at other levels.

However, those other levels remain enormously significant. For instance, the production designer Stuart Craig has clearly had to meet the requirements of Heyman and the directors, but he has also constructed a remarkably well-realized world on the screen. As head of the design team, Craig has constructed the physical spaces of Harry Potter's world and his importance should not be underestimated. His work is all the more remarkable because it has had to serve a range of competing yet simultaneous functions. For instance, the cluttered, homely design of, say, the Burrow is, in itself, a masterly piece of design; at the same time, it serves a thematic function by neatly illustrating the shambolic yet loving character of the Weasleys (and is directly opposed, in iconographic terms, to the Dursleys' sterile suburban semi); it tells us a lot about the Weasley's social and economic status in the wizarding world; it is organized in such a way as to facilitate a series of important narrative developments, and, crucially, it can also be translated into commercial products, such as an area of the wizarding world theme park, a training level in a video-game, and a LEGO playset that currently retails at over £60. These various goals, which indicate the complexity of the production process, appear to be pursued simultaneously within the texture of the movies. The design of Hogwarts and the Ministry of Magic, as well as the tiny details such as the brooms, wands, and carefully selected costumes, are, if anything, even more accomplished in this regard.

Ultimately, then, the *Harry Potter* films are formed by different layers of creative agency. Some contributors have been motivated primarily by the need to produce a commercially viable product, others by the desire to produce artistically interesting or accomplished work. In particular, David Heyman's production decisions, Craig's control of the films' spaces, Steve Kloves' shifting sense of character, and the burgeoning visual experimentation of the various directing teams have all profoundly affected the adaptation of J. K. Rowling's original novels. We can see the interplay between these various, sometimes competing, layers of creative enterprise most clearly through a close investigation of one film.

Harry Potter and the Half-Blood Prince

Harry Potter and the Half-Blood Prince was published in July 2005, by which point interest in the novels had reached fever pitch. This sixth entry sold over eleven million copies in the UK and USA within twenty-four hours of release.[12] The film adaptation came four years later, in the summer of 2009 and it went on to become the second highest grossing entry in the franchise in the US (after the very first

release) with a $301 million domestic box office take, and the second highest gross-
ing release of the year in the global market after *Avatar*, with a $933 million
worldwide gross.[13] In commercial terms, this marked it out as a healthy addition
to the franchise which performed much as the distributor seems to have expected.

However, in other ways, *Harry Potter and the Half-Blood Prince* offers a particularly
telling illustration of the different creative agenda at play in its production. As
usual, production was supervised by Heyman in the UK, with David Yates directing
for the second time. Kloves returned as scriptwriter (after passing over duties on
the previous film), and the majority of the cast, crew, and larger production team
remained in place. Warner Bros. continued to provide funding and distribution,
although in this case the company exercised its power more overtly than usual.
Principal photography had been completed, and post-production work on the film
was being finalized in time for a November 2008 release, when in August 2008,
Warner Bros. decided to delay release by a further eight months – pushing the film
back to July 2009.

Potter fans were dismayed at the news, and executives at Warner Bros. seem to
have been motivated primarily by a desire to spread potential large revenues across
two separate financial years in order to mitigate the effect of the 2008 Writers Guild
of America strike, which impacted upon the production schedules of many films.
Alan Horn told the *Los Angeles Times* that "There is no production delay or production consideration. . . . It feels like we have an opportunity in the summer" (Boucher,
2008). He later made a press release seeking to reassure fans that:

> We share your love for *Harry Potter* and would certainly never do anything to hurt
> any of the films . . . The decision to move *Harry Potter and the Half-Blood Prince* was
> not taken lightly, and was never intended to upset our *Harry Potter* fans. We know
> you have built this series into what it is, and we thank you for your ongoing enthu-
> siasm and support.[14]

Horn offered no direct explanation of the reasoning behind the move for fans, but
the motivation seems to have been primarily commercial. The distributor had generated unexpectedly high returns from Christopher Nolan's *The Dark Knight* earlier
in 2008, but its schedule of blockbusters for 2009 was made up of fewer reliable
commercial prospects – the studio's tentpole productions for 2009 were Zack Snyder's *Watchmen* and McG's *Terminator Salvation*, neither of which performed as hoped.
Moving the more reliable Harry Potter release into a summer slot increased that
film's earning capability, but also provided greater stability in a potentially uncertain year.

The decision paid off, and in its 2009 annual report to shareholders, parent
company Time Warner noted that revenues from theatrical film releases had unexpectedly risen and that "The increase was due primarily to the success of certain
key releases in 2009, which compared favorably to 2008."[15] *Harry Potter and the
Half-Blood Prince* was identified as the foremost of these releases, making up nearly

half of the company's overall revenues in the sector. Moving the film may not seem like a creative decision, but it is a good example of Warner Bros.' ability to set the agenda for the film's production and release in accordance with its larger commercial objectives.

The film achieved success despite being one of the more visually and structurally experimental entries in the franchise. In particular, the adaptation took significant liberties with the source text that upset some fans.[16] From the very beginning Kloves' script radically alters the relationship between the central characters, and the broader on-screen universe they inhabit. Rowling's novel begins with a long sequence of exposition featuring the Minister for Magic explaining the current state of affairs in the wizarding world to the British prime minister. It then moves to an enigmatic chapter where Professor Snape promises to aid Draco Malfoy in realizing some dark and unspecified plot at Hogwarts. Finally Harry is introduced at the Dursleys' house, where he encounters Dumbledore and is taken to meet a new teacher.

The film begins, much like previous entries, with the Warner Bros. logo and the title appearing against stormy clouds. John Williams' familiar musical cue "Hedwig's Theme," plays, but is almost immediately stifled by a mournful and discordant choral composition. The scene cuts to a monochromic extreme close up of a human eye. A series of blinding flashes reveal this to be Harry, clutched in the arms of Dumbledore, at the end of the previous film. With every cut, snatches of dialogue briefly intrude over the score. The camera then slowly shifts to focus on Dumbledore's hand as it presses against Harry's shoulder. The film then suddenly cuts again to a sequence showing a trio of dark wizards attacking Diagon Alley and the Millennium Bridge in central London. The next scene finally brings us to Harry, who sits reading a newspaper in a tube station cafe late at night. All of these scenes come directly from Kloves' script, but all are also remarkably experimental in stylistic terms. They visually stress Harry's close relationship with Dumbledore, the growing danger represented by the Death Eaters, and Harry's isolation, where Rowling's novel focuses more on plot.

Similar experimentation occurs throughout the film. At one point, a fight between Potter and Malfoy descends into a blur of disjointed, monochromatic imagery. An invented scene, where the Burrow is attacked by Death Eaters, uses an identical impressionistic style. The visual techniques deployed in these moments seem to have been affected by the decision to shift release dates. Given substantially more time to work on the movie, director David Yates told the *Los Angeles Times* "You find yourself fiddling with it much more in post-production, naturally. There's a good and bad to that. You could keep adjusting things for the rest of your life" (Boucher, 2009). This release spent more time in post-production than any previous Potter movie, and as a result, many sequences have an overwrought quality that previous entries in the franchise lacked. Some of the visual qualities are the product of Yates' working relationship with cinematographer Bruno Delbonnel, who received an Academy Award nomination for his work on the film. Delbonnel described his input by saying "I wanted to do something different than the other 'Potter' films. This one is a bit more real and dark. So I went for a very gray palette, with muted colors except in a couple of scenes" (Chagollan and Egan, 2010).

Yates and Kloves also included a number of sequences which take the fairly prosaic relationships of the novel and attempt to convey greater emotional depth upon them through more reflective dialogue, understated performance and closely controlled staging and cinematography. For instance, at one point Hermione becomes jealous when Ron, failing to recognize her romantic interest in him, hooks up with another student at a party. In the book, Harry consoles Hermione, and Rowling suggests that Hermione is upset, but she emphasizes Harry's discomfort over the intensity of Hermione's feelings. In the film, Harry finds Hermione alone in tears in abandoned stairwell. She asks him "How does it feel, Harry? When you see Dean with Ginny?" When Harry appears nonplussed, she continues, "I know, Harry. You're my best friend. I see how you look at her." Ron then briefly interrupts, and Hermione dismisses him before crying all the more intensely. Harry eventually replies, "It feels like this." Throughout the scene, Nicholas Hooper's slow minimalistic score intensifies the mournful, reflective atmosphere.

These scenes are conveyed with considerable intensity, and are far more central to the narrative than they appear in the original novel. They are clearly designed to express the maudlin anguish of unrequited love, but they also emphasize Harry's love for Ginny, adding yet another level of melancholy to the character. Furthermore, Harry and Hermione are given a closer, more powerful friendship, based on their shared feelings of rejection, that asks viewers to reconsider Harry's relationship with Ron, and that pays off in later films. In this manner, the sixth movie consistently emphasizes relationships and romance over the core events of Rowling's plot. Harry's first kiss with Ginny Weasley is, again, played out more reflectively and romantically than in Rowling's novel, and at times, the corridors of Hogwarts seem full of shadowy teenage couples, kissing in the dark.

In interviews, David Yates identified romance as one of his principal concerns in the film:

> It's actually about sex, potions and rock 'n' roll. . . . It's a wonderfully fun, slightly rebellious, quite naughty stage of teenage life. In the previous film, it was about the first kiss. This film is a bit more sexualized than that. . . . The relationships are a bit more complicated and romantic and convoluted. We're pushing into new emotional and physical territory for Harry Potter (Anon, 2009).

Emphasizing the romantic preoccupations of the central characters was a decision that also meant directing attention away from key narrative events. The importance and identity of the eponymous "Half-Blood Prince" is barely mentioned in the film, despite forming the central mystery of the novel. Furthermore, numerous flashbacks involving Snape and Lord Voldemort have been excised.

Nevertheless, mainstream reviews were broadly positive, and for many reviewers the changes resulted in a more accomplished film. *Variety*'s effusive review reserved particular praise for the film's visual tone:

> Dazzlingly well made and perhaps deliberately less fanciful than the previous entries, this one is played in a mode closer to palpable life-or-death drama than any of the others and is quite effective as such . . . Director David Yates, after a prosaic series debut on the prior film, displays noticeably increased confidence here, injecting more real-world grit into what began eight years ago as purest child's fantasy . . . The sets have been stripped down to reduce Hogwarts' fairy-book aspects and emphasize its gray medieval character, and even the obligatory Quidditch match is staged with greater attention to spatial comprehensibility than ever before (McCarthy, 2009).

In the *Chicago Sun-Times* Roger Ebert made similar claims:

> I admired this Harry Potter. It opens and closes well, and has wondrous art design and cinematography as always, only more so. Hogwarts seems darker, emptier and more ominous than ever before. "I'm just beginning to realize how beautiful this place is," Harry sighs from a high turret (Ebert, 2009).

The handful of more negative reviews either echoed the complaints of fans who felt that key scenes had been excised at the expense of coherence, or saw the focus on teen romance and solemn pace infuriating. Thus, Peter Bradshaw in the *Guardian* described it as "Darker, more hormonal, more teenage-angsty and sadly more boring," while Cosmo Landesman wrote in the *Times* that "the story lines that never add up to a satisfying whole . . . (and) this love stuff is meant to give the film heart and humour, but it provides neither."[17] Even those reviewers who disliked the film tend to recognize that they disliked it because of the choices outlined above.

Ultimately, the film stuck relatively closely to the structure of Rowling's novel, but it adopted a more measured pace, consistently downplaying larger plot developments in favor of a focus on characters and their romantic concerns. The interests of all the major creative players seem to have shaped this approach. Rowling provided the characters and the details of the plot. Heyman's preference for quieter, maudlin moments seems to have shaped the overarching creative approach. Yates' preference for realism and stylistic experimentation, aided by Bruno Delbonnel's work, resulted in a more downbeat, expressive vision of Rowling's world, while his interest in romance over plot shaped the film's form. Steve Kloves' concern with character development, and his relatively serious depiction of the bonds of love and friendship between the three leads, further shaped the relationships at the film's core. As usual, Stuart Craig's design team created more minimalistic spaces and objects that rendered the world immediate and engaging. Finally, Warner Bros.' need to meet commercial *and* cultural expectations determined the management of the production team, and the ways that audiences ultimately experienced the finished film.

I entered the auditorium to watch *Harry Potter and the Half-Blood Prince* in August 2009 as a fairly uncommitted fan. I had read the books and I liked the previous films, but had never felt particularly passionate about them. I found the film a revelation – beautiful, maudlin, and, for me, deeply affecting. More than anything, I was left with a sense that it was far *better*, in terms of style and structure, than it needed to be in order to attract a general audience. The level of visual artistry on display and the sober commitment to the characters' interpersonal dilemmas could easily have been downplayed, or played more broadly, and the film would no doubt have attracted colossal audiences regardless. It would be easy to say that the film was accomplished (if one found it so), in spite of the commercial agenda surrounding it, but in truth, it cannot and should not be understood as the product of a singular vision, or of an artist working outside the system.

The implicit assumption of almost all writing on authorship is that texts need individual authors in order to be culturally valid. I disagree. The strength of the Harry Potter films is not the primacy of J. K. Rowling's original vision (although that is important), nor is it the visionary agenda of any other single contributor. Instead, the interplay between creative personnel and commercial agenda has had the most valuable and lasting impact on the cultural significance of the franchise. The film is a product of such relationships, and it is a testament to the system that produced it. A mode of production shaped *Harry Potter and the Half-Blood Prince*, and a panoply of authors brought it to the screen. Whether they rubbed along easily, as suggested in the interviews cited at the start of this chapter, or whether they were subject to bitter disputes, such relationships are the *sine qua non* of Hollywood's production ethos, and they cannot be reduced or ignored.

NOTES

1 See the featurette entitled "Creating the Vision," *Harry Potter and the Prisoner of Azkaban* Ultimate DVD release (2010): Transcript available at www.mugglenet.com/mediasp/2004/november/jkrcuarondvd.shtml (accessed May 24, 2012).

2 Although it sets out to debunk structuralist criticism, a neat summary of the authorship debate in literary studies can be found in Burke (2008: 8–19). For a discussion of the author as interpreted by Barthes and Foucault, see Kamilla Elliott (Chapter 10 this volume).

3 See, for instance, Jenkins (1995: 113–17).

4 Rowling's website is www.jkrowling.com (accessed May 24, 2012).

5 Rowling's online activities are discussed through the prism of marketing tactics in Gunelius (2008: 32–7).

6 Information in this paragraph is derived from a 2001 interview with Heyman (Pendreigh, 2001).

7 Information in this section is derived from Eller (2010).

8 See Drake (2008: 78–80).

9 For further details of this generic template see Krämer (2002).

10 A good deconstruction of the problems associated with *Spider-Man 3* can be found in Jenkins (2007).

11 See David Heyman in O'Hara (2009: 101).

12 For full details of the sales see Anon (2006).
13 Box office data is from *Box Office Mojo*, November 9, 2011. www.boxofficemojo.com/movies/?id=harrypotter6.htm.
14 Horn's press release was duplicated in full in Anon (2008).
15 These details and further discussion can be found in the 2009 *Time Warner*

Annual Report to Shareholders (Anon, 2009: 33).
16 See, for example, the forums devoted to the movie on Mugglenet.com, which mix praise with extensive criticism. www.cosforums.com/index.php (accessed May 24, 2012).
17 See Bradshaw (2009) and Landesman (2009).

References

Anon. "Potter is US Best-seller of 2005." *BBC Online*, January 7, 2006. http://news.bbc.co.uk/1/hi/entertainment/4590140.stm. Accessed May 9, 2011.

Anon. "Harry Potter Shocker." *Los Angeles Times*, August 14, 2008. http://herocomplex.latimes.com/2008/08/14/harry-potter-sh/. Accessed November 9, 2011.

Anon. Time Warner Annual Report to Shareholders 2009. 33.

Anon. "*Harry Potter and the Half-Blood Prince* Director David Yates Speaks With Us On Set." *Blastr.com*, April 23, 2009. http://blastr.com/2009/04/harry-potter-and-the-half-1.php. Accessed May 9, 2011.

Anders, Charlie Jane. "How Much Money Does a Movie Need to Make to be Profitable?" *io9*, January 31, 2011. http://io9.com/#!5747305/how-much-money-does-a-movie-need-to-make-to-be-profitable. Accessed May 9, 2011.

Bradshaw, Peter. "Review of *Harry Potter and the Half-Blood Prince*." *Guardian*, July 17, 2009. www.guardian.co.uk/film/2009/jul/17/harry-potter-half-blood-prince. Accessed November 9, 2011.

Boucher, Geoff. "Potter Film Pulls a Vanishing Act." *Los Angeles Times*, August 15, 2008. http://articles.latimes.com/2008/aug/15/business/fi-potter15. Accessed November 9, 2011.

Boucher, Geoff. "Harry Potter Countdown: A Late-Night Call from David Yates Reveals Magical Secrets." *Los Angeles Times*, June 20. 2009. http://herocomplex.latimes.com/2009/06/20/harry-potter-countdown-david-yates/. Accessed November 9, 2011.

Boucher, Geoff. "The Story Behind the Most Controversial Scene in 'Hallows'." *Los Angeles Times*, November 14, 2010. http://herocomplex.latimes.com/2010/11/14/harry-potter-countdown-the-story-behind-the-most-controversial-scene-in-hallows. Accessed November 9, 2011.

Burke, Sean. *The Death and Return of the Author: Criticism and Subjectivity in Barthes, Foucault and Derrida*. Edinburgh: Edinburgh University Press, 2008.

Chagollan, Steve and Jack Egan. "Five Cinematographers Vie for Oscar." *Variety*, February 10, 2010. www.variety.com/article/VR1118015007. Accessed November 9, 2011.

Crofts, Stephen. "Authorship and Hollywood." In *The Oxford Guide to Film Studies*. Eds. John Hill and Pamela Church Gibson. Oxford: Oxford University Press, 1998, 310–26.

Douglas, Edward. "David Heyman on the Half-Blood Prince Delay." *ComingSoon.net*, October 30, 2008. www.comingsoon.net/news/movienews.php?id=50111#ixzz1EaWz4Eoa. Accessed May 9, 2011.

Drake, Philip. "Distribution and Marketing in Contemporary Hollywood." In *The Contemporary Hollywood Film Industry*. Eds. Paul McDonald and Janet Wasko. Oxford: Blackwell, 2008, 63–82.

Ebert, Roger. "Review of *Harry Potter and the Half-Blood Prince*." *Chicago Sun-Times*, July 12, 2009. http://rogerebert.suntimes.com/apps/pbcs.dll/article?AID=/20090712/REVIEWS/907129996. Accessed November 9, 2011.

Eller, Claudia. "'Harry Potter' Countdown: Hollywood Will Look Back on Franchise as Magic Moment." *Los Angeles Times*, November 7, 2010. http://herocomplex.latimes.com/2010/11/07/harry-potter-countdown-hollywood-will-look-back-on-franchise-as-magic-moment. Accessed November 9, 2011.

Gray, Jonathan. *Show Sold Separately: Promos, Spoilers and other Media Paratexts*. New York: New York University Press, 2010.

Gunelius, Susan. *Harry Potter: The Story of a Global Business Phenomenon*. New York: Palgrave, 2008.

Harry Potter and the Deathly Hallows Part 1. Dir. D. Yates. UK/USA: Warner Bros., 2010.

Harry Potter and the Deathly Hallows Part 2. Dir. D. Yates. UK/USA: Warner Bros., 2011.

Harry Potter and the Half-Blood Prince. Dir. D. Yates. UK/USA: Warner Bros., 2009.

Hutcheon, Linda. *A Theory of Adaptation*. New York: Routledge, 2006.

Jenkins, Henry. "Historical Poetics". In *Approaches to Popular Film*. Eds. Joanne Hollows and Mark Jancovich. Manchester: Manchester University Press, 1995, 99–122.

Jenkins, Henry. "The Pleasure of Pirates and What It Tells Us About World Building in Branded Entertainment." *Confessions of an Aca/Fan: The Official Weblog of Henry Jenkins*, June 13, 2007. www.henryjenkins.org/2007/06/forced_simplicity_and_the_crit.html. Accessed May 9, 2011.

Krämer, Peter. "The Best Disney Film Disney Never Made: Children's Films and the Family Audience in American Cinema since the 1960s." In *Genre and Contemporary Hollywood*. Ed. Steve Neale. London: BFI, 2002, 185–200.

Landesman, Cosmo. "Review of *Harry Potter and the Half-Blood Prince*." *The Times*, July 19, 2009. http://entertainment.timesonline.co.uk/tol/arts_and_entertainment/film/film_reviews/article6716685.ece. Accessed November 25, 2011.

Leitch, Thomas. *Adaptation and its Discontents*. Baltimore: Johns Hopkins University Press, 2007.

McCarthy, Todd. "Review of *Harry Potter and the Half Blood Prince*." *Variety*, July 5, 2009. www.variety.com/review/VE1117940610. Accessed November 9, 2011.

Nel, Philip. *J. K. Rowling's Harry Potter Novels*. New York: Continuum, 2001.

O'Hara, Helen. "Hallowed Ground." *Empire*, June 2009, 101.

O'Hara, Helen. "Harry Potter Producer talks BAFTAs." *Empire Online*, February 21, 2011. www.empireonline.com/interviews/interview.asp?IID=1195. Accessed May 9, 2011.

Pendreigh, Brian. "Hogwarts 'n' Al." *IO Film Online*, November 9, 2001. www.iofilm.co.uk/feats/filmmaking/harry_potter.shtml. Accessed May 9, 2011.

Thompson, Kristen. *The Frodo Franchise: The Lord of the Rings and Modern Hollywood*. Berkeley: University of California Press, 2007.

23
Adapting the Unadaptable –
The Screenwriter's Perspective

Diane Lake

When I was asked to write on "unfilmable" books – books that simply were too complex to be adapted to film – I was reluctant. I mean, I'm sorry – unfilmable? There's actually no such word in the dictionary. And there's *really* no such word in the lexicon of Hollywood. And, I would claim, there's no such animal.

If a book is released that's popular, if there's enough name recognition for the book, Hollywood will find a way to film it. In fact, the techniques available to the filmmaker are so varied that telling stories visually may be quite an effective way to bring a complicated story to life and make it *more* accessible for the average person than it would be if they were to read the book.

One might say, "But what if the story is all internal – a series of internal mono-logues if you will – how can film do that justice?" But my response is a question: *Who said the job of film is to do justice to the book?* To even ask if the film can do justice to the book is to fail to understand that the book is its own entity and, even though the film may be based on the book, the film is its own entity as well. The book cannot be a film on its own. Even if I put someone on screen reading the book word for word, the very act of having someone read the book *to* the viewer would change the nature of the book.

Reading is internal. When one reads the words on the page, one reads his or her own book. When I read *War and Peace*, my experience and understanding of the book is different than yours. Just as when I look at the Mona Lisa, my interpreta-tion of the painting is not the same as yours. A book is not a vase, a static object to be photographed, to be represented in such a manner that everyone sees the same thing. A book is fluid, it is open to interpretation and every reader interprets it just

A Companion to Literature, Film, and Adaptation, First Edition. Edited by Deborah Cartmell.
© 2012 Blackwell Publishing Ltd. Published 2012 by Blackwell Publishing Ltd.

a bit differently. As Thomas Leitch says, "texts remain alive only to the extent that they can be rewritten and that to experience a text in all its power requires each reader to rewrite it" (2007: 12–13).

So it's important to understand that the most literal screen interpretation of a book that one could imagine still wouldn't be the book itself. The book tells a story, the film based on that book tells a story. Yes, it's the job of the screenwriter to bring the book to life on the screen, but the very act of telling the story of the book on film will change the book. If an adaptor were to worry about being absolutely faithful to the book, scene for scene, the resulting film would – I assure you – be a bomb. As George Bluestone says, "It is as fruitless to say that film A is better or worse than novel B as it is to pronounce Wright's Johnson's Wax Building better or worse than Tchaikovsky's *Swan Lake*" (1957: 5–6).

So if the job of a screenwriter isn't to do the book justice, what is the job of the screenwriter when adapting a book?

The fundamental job of the screenwriter is to reach inside the story to its essence and to find a *new* way to tell it filmicly. The writer knows going in that the book is a complex entity unto itself and the film may never represent it fully, may never "do it justice." But that assumes the job of an adaptor is to be faithful to the book, and I can assure, as an adaptor, I've never thought that to be my job. My job is one of a detective, to some extent. I delve into the story and try to uncover its center, its spine. I ask myself what story is being told and what part of it would make a good film. For let's be honest, if I'm adapting a 500-page novel into a 110-page screenplay I know going in that I can't tell the whole story. Give me a miniseries and I might be able to do that. But since filmgoers aren't going to sit still for a twelve-hour film, I have to make choices.

The first step to making those choices is a careful reading of the text in question. The adaptor reads with an eye not to represent what is already in the book, not to translate it scene for scene, but to uncover the soul, if you will, of the book and to think about how to bring that "soul" to life through visual storytelling.

My method of reading a book is simple. As I read the book, I mark moments/ scenes that do two things: (1) make for good visual representation in a film and (2) are crucial to the spine of the story. For example, if there's a scene where a husband slaps his wife and she pushes him down the stairs – neither of them realizing that their four-year-old daughter was peeking out her door and witnessed the whole thing – well, that's an important moment in the story for all three characters and it's visually interesting. So I put one vertical line in the margin of the book to mark that scene. If there's a scene in the book later where the wife shoots her husband, I put two vertical lines in the margin of the book to mark that scene. Two vertical lines means I *must* include it in the screenplay – that it's such a strong story point, is so integral to the telling of the story in question, that to leave it out is simply not an option. For example, in writing *Frida*, I put those two vertical lines next to the point in Hayden Herrera's biography where Frida Kahlo has her bus accident. It's simply a fact – any adaptation of Frida's life needs to include that scene. That moment was so integral to her life that to leave it out of a film about her life would be an unthinkable choice. How one might choose to include it, to dramatize it, is up to the screenwriter, of course – but dramatize it you must.

After reading the book once and marking those scenes, I go back and reread only those scenes – to try and get the feel for whether or not I've got a movie using the scenes in question.

Does this mean I then weave together those scenes to write the screenplay? I wish it was that easy. Although I've just finished the most difficult part of the process of telling the story – deciding what to leave out – writing the screenplay is much more difficult than simply weaving the most film-worthy story moments together. The writing process is also going to require me to invent.

"Invent?" – you might ask. "Isn't there enough in the book already? After all, you've already admitted that you're leaving out the majority of the book itself, why in the world would you need to invent anything new to tell the story?"

The answer to that harkens back to something I said earlier – it's not my job to regurgitate the book. My job is to find its center and find visual ways of bringing the story I've uncovered to life.

So, while in the book, the husband who was pushed down the stairs may disappear for a couple of days before coming back home and begging his wife for her forgiveness, I may decide that for the screenplay I want to follow him out the door and see where he goes. For the film I want to write, it may be quite important to understand where he goes and what he does at this crucial point in the story. The novelist may have chosen to leave that a mystery, to let the reader imagine where he might have gone. But for the story I want to tell, I might think it important that the audience know what he did and why.

It's also interesting to think about how a screenwriter can sometimes *save* time in the telling of the story on film. A book might take three chapters to play out that scene of the wife pushing the husband down the stairs while their daughter watches – the novelist might want a chapter devoted to the scene from the point of view of each of the three characters. But on film, I can do it in a very short amount of time because one close-up of that little girl's face can show the audience what is going on inside her. In film, we don't tell, we show. And showing saves time.

So how do some of these thoughts manifest themselves in the films we see? Let's take a look at a film like *The Diving Bell and the Butterfly* (2007). The film is the story of Jean Dominique Bauby, a Frenchman in the prime of life who was struck down by locked-in syndrome – which paralyzed him completely. The only part of his body he could move was his eyelid. The film was based on a book but there was also a documentary made of Bauby's struggles with his affliction. I was up to write this book as a screenplay and was given the book and the documentary by the production company. I was beat out by the English writer Ronald Harwood – seems to me that Ron gets to write all the good stuff. Anyway, putting my envy aside, it's very interesting to read the book and watch the documentary and then see the film. The film is fantastic, it's artistically stunning and it gets to the heart of the story that was told in the book and the documentary. But it's dramatically different. Harwood reached into that story and invented a visual way to tell the story that absolutely blows my mind. If Harwood had tried to be faithful to the book or the documentary, we would not be talking about this film because it either would never have been made or it would have been made and disappeared because people wouldn't have gone to see it. Harwood's invention made the film live and breathe and made Bauby's true story come to dramatic life. I mean think about it: was there ever a more "unfilmable" book than one about a man lying in a bed who can't move?

And let me tell you a couple of stories from the Lake chronicles about the process of adaptation in the real world and you'll see what I'm talking about when it comes to what the job of the screenwriter is in the process of adaptation for film. I'll tell you about two biopics I wrote – one of which was made and one of which is still in development hell.

Let's talk first about the one that has not yet been made: *Nancy*, a film I wrote for Paramount. *Nancy* is a biopic of Nancy Cunard. Cunard's father ran the famous shipping line and she was basically English aristocracy. But she rebelled against her family, went to Paris, and proceeded to live a bit of a wild and crazy life in the 1920s and 30s – the jazz age – including having a twenty-five-year-long love affair with a black jazz musician from Alabama named Henry Crowder. She was high-toned, sophisticated, fashionable, and connected while he had never gone to school and was a very simple man who loved jazz. A very famous director, whom we'll call "Charlie," was attached to this project – attached in the world of Hollywood means he promises to direct it if the studio puts up the money to make it. And the first step in that process is getting a screenwriter to write the script. So I pitched for the project and was hired by Paramount to write it for Charlie and a producer whom we'll call "Sam," who was also attached to the project. The studio sent me every book and magazine article that had ever been written about Cunard and sent me to Europe to do my research. I visited her ancestral home in rural England, the family home on Cavendish Square in London, tracked down her apartment in Paris, went to Venice and Barcelona to trace her steps, and even tracked down a farm in rural France where she had set up a printing press to publish new writers. I began actually writing the screenplay on the roof of the Hotel du Lac in Bellagio – where, across Lake Como, I could see the very expensive Villa d'Este where Cunard had stayed. I had planned to stay in Bellagio for a couple of days. I ended up staying for three weeks. I mapped out a great deal of the screenplay right there.

And the screenplay told the story of a Cunard who was pushed and pulled by the passions in her life: a Cunard who was troubled and unsure and, despite all her gay partying, often deeply unhappy, an alcoholic Cunard who died destitute and alone in Venice.

I turned the screenplay into the producer and the director and was confident I had written the best screenplay of my career. I still remember going to the first "notes" meeting. The notes meeting for a screenwriter is when you get the notes from the producer, director, and/or studio on what they would like you to change in the next draft.

I remember vividly walking into the room where the director, producer, and several assistants were waiting for me – expecting to be told I was brilliant and had written the next Academy Award winning screenplay. Everyone was pleasant, we exchanged greetings, and then something odd happened. Neither the director nor the producer spoke. Neither of them wanted, I would later realize, to be the bearer of bad tidings. No, it was the producer's head of development who said it – softly, almost apologetically – I can still hear her voice: "Well, I have to say, this just isn't what we were looking for."

Huh? What? What could they possibly mean? I remember listening, truly shocked, to what they had to say. And what did they have to say?

Well, bottom line, "Cunard's story is just too depressing. Who wants to watch a tragedy? It's such a downer."

But . . . but . . . I wanted to protest, I wanted to talk about how not every story has a happy ending. And then it hit me – wait a minute. An even more relevant question is why were they surprised? After all, they're the ones who had decided to make a film of her life, they're the ones who sent me all the books and articles about her. What were they expecting?

And – you're not going to believe this – but guess what? *No one* on the production team – not the studio, the producer, or the director – had read any of those books or articles they had sent me about her life. Not one of them knew what her life story *was*.

Well how, then, you might ask, did this project even come to be? Why was Paramount interested?

I'll tell you why. Head of the studio at the time, whom we'll call "Ashley," had had a party. At the party was the director, Charlie, who was then directing a big Bruce Willis blockbuster for Paramount. With Charlie was his wife, whom we'll call "Margo," who was in the fashion world. Margo was a big fan of Cunard's because Cunard had been a very fashionable young woman – appearing as a model on the cover of *Vogue*, starting fashion trends because of her uniqueness, etc. Studio head Ashley mentioned, at a party, always wanting to do an interracial love story but in these times of political correctness not being able to do so – you just had to be very careful. Then Margo chimed in that they should do Nancy Cunard's story – the jazz age in Paris and Venice, the fashion world, *plus* she had this long love affair with a black jazz musician from Alabama. Ashley liked that – it was easier to tell an interracial love story that happened seventy-five years ago, after all. So Ashley told Margo, "Get Charlie to sign on to direct and I'll put it in development."

And that's how it happened. Everyone thought they were going to get a story about the kicky jazz age in Europe and the black and white love story of Nancy and her lover.

Oy.

But what they got was her whole story – and it was, indeed, sad. So I had two choices. I could walk away from the project and let them hire another writer to write another version of Nancy Cunard's story, or I could find a way to do it myself.

This is always a difficult choice for the screenwriter. On the one hand, you have principles that you want to stick to – especially in the story of a real person, you feel compelled to do that person justice, to really tell their story as it actually unfolded. But on the other hand, if another writer comes onboard, who's to say that he/she will *see* the story, will *understand* this person as you do? Maybe someone will come onboard who will exploit the story and make up bizarre happenings just to increase the audience appeal or something. If you truly love the story you're writing, there's this tremendous desire to protect it. So, in general, you want to stay with the project – you want to guard it from someone who might do it harm.

I liked Cunard. I felt for her. I understood her struggle. And even if they wanted to cut out some of the sadness of her life, I still wanted to write about her.

So my second draft wasn't a rewrite at all. I simply threw out the first draft and wrote a completely new script that focused on the more positive aspects of her life. I didn't play the story out to her later years when she became more depressed and the alcoholism overtook her – I stopped at a bittersweet moment in her love story with Henry rather than a devastating one. Even in Hollywood, bittersweet love stories are still OK from time to time. Thank heaven.

Thus, I wrote a script I'm quite happy with. Everyone was quite happy with it. But at the end of the day, Paramount just didn't think audiences would care enough about Cunard for her to bring people into the theaters. So unless an actress comes along who's important and bankable and insists on playing the part, I would be surprised if Paramount ever made it.

My film that did get made was *Frida*, released in 2002, directed by Julie Taymor and starring Salma Hyack. *Frida* was nominated for six Academy Awards in 2003 and was on many top 10 lists for the year. It was based on the wonderful biography by Hayden Herrera.

How did *Frida* come to be? In the early 1990s there were three competing Frida projects – one driven by Madonna, who collected Frida's art and wanted to play her in a film; a second driven by Jennifer Lopez, who also coveted the role; and then there was the project I would become involved in that was eventually produced by Miramax.

What would become the Miramax film began in 1991. And for the next five years they kept throwing writers at the project. I came on board in 1996 and worked on it through 1997. I got the project because I had just written a script on Berthe Morisot, the French Impressionist, that Columbia studios had optioned. And Hollywood being what it is, the *Frida* producers said "Oh, she writes films about women painters. We've got a woman painter." As if, of course, all women painters were alike. I mean, these two women lived in different times, on different continents and painted radically different kinds of art . . . not to mention the obvious, that they were in absolutely no way alike.

But, in any case, I got the job.

Upon being hired, I asked to see the previous drafts that the other seven or eight writers had done. I wanted to see why they had all been fired – what had those writers done that didn't please the studio/producers? I didn't want to make the same mistakes.

But the studio refused. They didn't want my vision skewed by what others had written. They wanted me to start fresh. So they gave me Herrera's book and sent me to Mexico to do my research and be inspired.

They did, however, after I pressed them, give me one note, one word of caution: "Don't make her a whiney victim."

Aha, I thought! That's it. That's why all the other writers failed – they made Frida a whiney victim.

But guess what, as I did my research I discovered that she was – shock – a bit of a whiney victim. Certainly being in the bus accident that crippled her shaped her life, she had back surgeries, she was in casts . . . it changed her. But there was more to the story. Frida actually had unnecessary surgeries to get Diego to stay with her. They were often separating – they ended up marrying twice – but he wouldn't leave her when she was going through surgery . . . hence her playing the victim to keep him closer to her.

So when I wrote my screenplay, I simply left that out. I focused on their relationship, on the infidelities, etc., but I tried very hard not to have her come across as a victim.

Salma Hyack, who didn't sign on to the project after reading the first five years of drafts, signed on after reading my draft. But after a second draft, I left the project because I was contractually obligated to write *Picasso* for Dustin Hoffman and John Davis Productions, so Miramax subsequently got several writers to fine-tune my *Frida* screenplay. But it remained pretty much intact, save for the third act. Being afraid of how Americans might react to the fact that Frida and Diego were communists, the studio took all the politics out of the third act. So when Frida climbs a pyramid with Trotsky and all of a sudden they're in love, you're going, "I'm sorry – how did that happen?" Well, in real life it happened as much because of the political and intellectual connection between them as it did the physical . . . but that's missing from the story, so there's a kind of hole there.

In any case, the film got made and I'm happy for that. More people – throughout time – will learn of Frida and her work and her life than ever would have known about her without the film. And, like any writer, the screenwriter who does adaptations wants to bring lives and worlds to life. And the nice thing about film is that it *is* accessible and will live forever.

In many ways, Frida's life *was* unfilmable – because no one could conceive filming those scripts of her as a whiney victim, and even if we were to film her actual whiney-victimy-life, my guess is that nobody would come. To make her life filmable meant making the choice to focus only on a *part* of that life. But, at the very least, we can all now see that part. And a little of Frida is better than no Frida at all.

As a screenwriter, I want to find stories to tell that are important. If my hands are tied so that I can't tell the complete story, I'm not going to flounce off in a huff that the industry doesn't understand what art is, I'm going to do my best to tell the essence of that story in whatever way I can that will please the powers that be as well as allow the script to be written. After all, writers and artists throughout history have worked at the pleasure of the king . . . now just replace "king" with "studio" and you get an idea of what today's screenwriter goes through. But, in the end, it's worth it. I get to work in what, to my mind, is the art form of our time. Do I always agree with the studio? Not by a long shot. But I fight for what I can, and sometimes I even win a battle or two and convince the studios to take a bit of a chance — and that, too, is what adaptation is all about.

So if there's an "unfilmable" book/story out there, I've yet to see it. The particular talent of the screenwriter needs to be to dig inside *any* story and find the movie — and with every book/story I'm sent, the adrenaline starts flowing as I read, ponder, reread . . . and then imagine the film that might be.

REFERENCES

Bluestone, George. *Novels into Film: The Metamorphoses of Fiction into Cinema*. Baltimore: Johns Hopkins University Press, 1957.

Leitch, Thomas. *Film Adaptation and its Discontents: From* Gone with the Wind *to* The Passion of the Christ. Baltimore: Johns Hopkins University Press, 2007.

Frida. Dir. Julie Taymor. US: Miramax, 2002.

Index

A Companion to Literature, Film, and Adaptation, First Edition. Edited by Deborah Cartmell.
© 2012 Blackwell Publishing Ltd. Published 2012 by Blackwell Publishing Ltd.